Psychology

John M. Darley

Sam Glucksberg

Leon J. Kamin

Ronald A. Kinchla

Princeton University

PRENTICE-HALL, INC.
Englewood Cliffs, New Jersey

Library of Congress Cataloging in Publication Data
Main entry under title:

Psychology.

     Includes bibliographies and index.
      1. Psychology.   I. Darley, John M.
II. Glucksberg, Sam, joint author.   III. Kamin, Leon J., joint author.
IV. Kinchla, Ronald A., joint author.
BF121.P78   150   80-26224
ISBN 0-13-733154-1

The art on the cover, *Generations,* is a collagraph by Trudy Glucksberg, based on her graphic for *Women: A Portfolio,* Queenston Press, 1978. A personal statement, it projects the notion of continuity: "I look backward, I see my mother. I look forward, I see my daughter. In them, I see myself."

Printed in the United States of America

10 9 8 7 6 5 4 3 2 1

Prentice-Hall International, Inc., *London*
Prentice-Hall of Australia Pty. Limited, *Sydney*
Prentice-Hall of Canada, Ltd., *Toronto*
Prentice-Hall of India Private Limited, *New Delhi*
Prentice-Hall of Japan, Inc., *Tokyo*
Prentice-Hall of Southeast Asia Pte. Ltd., *Singapore*
Whitehall Books Limited, Wellington, *New Zealand*

Part opening art © 1979 by Joan Greenfield
Interior design: Joan Greenfield
Photo research: Anita Duncan
Manufacturing buyer: Edmund W. Leone

Color Portfolio: Plate 4 Photo courtesy of Inmont Corporation Plate 5 (left and right) Fritz Goro, Life Magazine, © Time Inc. Plate 6 (top, left) Scientific Publishing Company, Baltimore, Maryland (top, right; and bottom) Tom Kelley Associates, Inc./The Image Bank

(Acknowledgments are continued on p. 634, which constitutes a continuation of the copyright page.)

Overview

Contents

Part Four: Motivation and Emotion

Part Five: Development

Part Six: Personality and Clinical Psychology

Preface

Psychology as an objective natural science is now just over 100 years old. In those first 100 years we have learned a great deal about human nature, building on the work of the philosophers and scientists who, during all of recorded history, have asked the same questions that we ask today: What sorts of creatures are humans? How are we different from other animals, and how are we the same? How are we different from one another, and how are we basically the same? Psychology may well be the most complex of sciences, because it must deal with the biological aspects of the human species while still giving full recognition to our social nature. The simplest organism is more complex than our most powerful computers, and humans are undoubtedly the most complex of organisms that we know about. To understand humanity is the task of psychology. To tell students what we already understand, and to make clear what we do not understand, is the task we undertook in writing this book.

Our intention from the outset was to provide a clear description of the bodies of knowledge in the core areas of psychology. All four of us have had extensive experience in teaching psychology to introductory students, and we each have had our special points of view about what was important and how to organize the material. We soon learned that our points of view, or at least the way we each taught in the classroom, were rather personal and idiosyncratic. We found that we could not simply translate our lecture notes into clear, descriptive prose. We needed to organize our material in fresh ways if we were to approach our goal of being clear and at the same time comprehensive. Most important, we did not want to oversimplify either the basic technical material in each of psychology's core areas or the sophisticated and complex theoretical, social, and human issues that arise when basic beliefs about human nature are involved. To that end we have each concentrated on those areas of psychology that we know best, drawing freely upon the wisdom of colleagues, and especially of our students.

We deliberately did not avoid complexity. Each chapter is focused on the important philosophical and social as well as scientific issues of the area, with alternative points of view clearly represented. We deliberately did not seek out novelty for novelty's sake, shaping the text to reflect the fads and fashions of the moment. At the same time, we did try to include the most recent significant advances in each field, as well as material on topics that are just beginning to receive serious attention, such as consciousness, life-span development, and the important recent discoveries on the neurochemical bases of behavior.

The book is divided into seven parts, with an appendix on statistical measurement. This division is relatively standard, and accurately reflects how the field is generally organized. Part One provides an historical introduction to psychology and also provides the basic facts about our biological make-up. Part 2 deals with how we experience the world—our sensory systems of sight, hearing, touch, taste, smell, etc.; our perceptual system, which makes sense of our sensations; and our consciousness and states of awareness. Part 3 deals with issues of the mind—how we learn, remember, and think. Part 4 turns to the wellsprings of behavior, motivation and emotion. How we grow, develop, and change with age and experience are treated in Part 5. Part 6, Personality and Clinical Psychology, deals with some of the most intriguing and complex problems in psychology, and the last chapter in this section deals in detail with current beliefs and practices in psychotherapy. Finally, Part 7 provides an in-depth description and analysis of human interaction, the area of social psychology.

Acknowledgments

In writing this text we have drawn on many sources of advice and assistance. Drafts of the chapters have been reviewed at several stages by instructors experienced at teaching the introductory psychology course and faculty members who are experts in the various fields that we present. We gratefully acknowledge their advice:

James R. Averill, University of Massachusetts, Amherst

Robert C. Beck, Wake Forest University

David Berger, State University of New York, Cortland

Dean Berman, Wright State University

Douglas Bernstein, University of Illinois, Urbana

Michael R. Best, Southern Methodist University

Charles Brewer, Furman University

David Brodzinsky, Rutgers University

Anthony R. Caggiula, University of Pittsburgh

James C. Coyne, University of California, Berkeley

William Crain, City College of New York

Robert G. Crowder, Yale University

Stephen F. Davis, Emporia State University

Patricia D. Ebert, Niagara University

David Edwards, Iowa State University

Joseph Fitzgerald, Wayne State University

Irene Frieze, University of Pittsburgh

Alan L. Gilchrist, State University of New York, Stony Brook

Jerald Greenberg, The Ohio State University

Leonard W. Hamilton, Rutgers University

Michael Hirt, Kent State University

James E. Hoffman, University of Delaware

Robert Hogan, The Johns Hopkins University

Keith Holyoak, University of Michigan

David Hothersall, The Ohio State University

Sam L. Hutchison, Radford University

James Kalat, North Carolina State University

Alan E. Kazdin, University of Pittsburgh

John F. Kihlstrom, University of Wisconsin

Charles Levinthal, Hofstra University

Richard A. Lippa, California State University, Fullerton

Donald H. McBurney, University of Pittsburgh

Lawrence Melamed, Kent State University

Susan Mineka, University of Wisconsin

Steven Penrod, University of Wisconsin

Dan Perlman, University of
Manitoba

John B. Pittenger, University of
Arkansas, Little Rock

Oakley Ray, Vanderbilt University
and Veterans Administration
Medical Center

Sidney Rosenblum, University of
New Mexico

Wayne Shebilske, University of
Virginia

Robert S. Siegler, University of
Chicago

Michael D. Spiegler, Providence
College

David E. Weldon, Washington
University

John E. Wenrick, Palomar College

Cliff W. Wing, Duke University

Diana S. Woodruff, Temple
University

In preparing chapters, many individuals gave us assistance, ranging from assembling relevant and up-to-date reference material to suggesting area outlines, identifying new or controversial developments, or cross-checking citations for completeness and accuracy. Again, we gratefully acknowledge their help: Robin Akert, Dan Axsom, Kay Ferdinandsen, Paget Gross, Fred Rhodewalt, and Margaret Ruddy.

Various colleagues helped us by drafting major sections of material. They include Ron Comer (who contributed material to Chapters 14–17), Richard Dolinsky (Chapter 5), Nancy Eisenberg-Berg and Cathy Locke (Chapter 13), Judith R. Harris (Chapters 2, 10, and 11), Thane Pittman (Chapters 11, 18, and 19), Fred Rhodewalt (Chapter 14), and Marilyn Shaw (Chapter 10 and the Appendix).

We are also pleased to acknowledge the help of various colleagues who, by answering our spur-of-the-moment questions, removed difficulties that were blocking us at the time—Nancy Cantor, Joel Cooper, and Ned Jones gave us this kind of help.

Finally, we want to thank our development editor at Prentice-Hall, Susanna Lesan, for both her considerable editorial talent and her organizational skills. We owe much to her energies, her good judgment, and, not the least, her good humor.

J.M.D.
S.G.
L.J.K.
R.A.K.

Psychology

Part One Introduction

1 Introduction to Psychology

There are very many people who are called psychologists, and what they have in common may not be immediately obvious. Psychologist A, for example, is a clinical psychologist. He works with people who have "psychological problems." A student comes to the college's counseling center, complaining that she is unable to study, that she feels depressed and lethargic. Perhaps also she has had some difficulty sleeping, and some loss of appetite. Another student is suffering from a far more pervasive psychological disturbance. Perhaps he has recently begun to act very queer. He is often silent and withdrawn, but occasionally bursts into almost incoherent speech. He believes that there is a widespread plot against him: His professors are spying on him and reporting slanderous information to the college authorities and the police. Recently he has noticed that the food served to him in the college cafeteria tastes peculiar, and he believes that "they" are trying to poison him. He has been referred to the psychologist after creating a disturbance in the cafeteria. The clinical psychologist is an expert—as expert as the present state of knowledge will allow—in the understanding and treatment of all the problems we have described. He works with patients in such places as mental health clinics, state hospitals, prisons, and school systems.

Psychologist B seems to be a very different kind of psychologist. She is a physiological psychologist, and she has never counseled a patient in her life. She spends most of her working hours in a laboratory, surrounded by complex (and expensive) pieces of apparatus. She wants to understand more about how the brain controls and influences human behavior and feelings. To acquire such understanding, she has had to learn neuroanatomy (the physical structure of the nervous system and brain) and biochemistry. She is studying rats—she can perform many experiments on them that, for obvious reasons, cannot be performed on human subjects. Psychologist B probably holds a university professorship and is thus teaching as well as performing research. Or she may be working full-time at research, perhaps in a government laboratory devoted to health problems, or in the laboratories of a private drug manufacturer.

Psychologist C also seems to be quite unlike Psychologist A, but you may detect some similarities to Psychologist B. For several years now he has spent most of his days working with a single chimpanzee—whom, by now, he has gotten to know quite well. He is engaged in what may seem a strange endeavor; he is trying to teach the chimpanzee to communicate with humans. What may seem even stranger, he appears to be succeeding! The chimpanzee not only communicates a fair number of its basic needs and wants to Psychologist C, it also occasionally comments spontaneously on matters in which it appears to be interested.

3

The three specimen psychologists we have described give some indication of the scope of modern psychology. There are some psychologists whose interests seem very close to those of biologists or biochemists. There are others whose interests seem close to those of sociologists, anthropologists, and social philosophers. The reason for this wide scope should be obvious. Psychology is concerned with human behavior, and humans are both biological and social creatures. To ignore either our biological or social nature is to guarantee defeat in any effort truly to understand ourselves. To understand, on the other hand, how our biological and social natures interact and unite would be the crowning achievement of human thought. The task set out for modern psychology—to become nothing less than the integrator of the biological and social sciences—is neither an easy nor a boring one. Psychologists specialize in interests and knowledge at some point in their careers, but they must remain sensitive to, and informed about, the many different areas of psychology. Despite their inevitable specialization, psychologists do talk to one another, and they tend to share a common point of view. This chapter is concerned with that common point of view—how it developed, what it includes, and what it excludes.

The History of Psychology

Wilhelm Wundt, German physiologist and psychologist, one of the first to focus attention on the introspective description of experience.

There is, today, little if any disagreement among psychologists about what it is that they ought to be studying. This was not always true. The first group of people who regarded themselves as scientific psychologists flourished in Germany in the second half of the nineteenth century, around the pioneer figure of Wilhelm Wundt (1832–1920). Their interests and activities seem, from today's perspective, surprisingly narrow. They were chiefly concerned with the problem of how the mind constructs sensations and perceptions out of the raw nerve messages delivered to the brain by the sense organs. They had been trained in the physiology of the sense organs and the nervous system. Their unique contribution was to be an analysis of the contents of the mind itself, in an effort to understand the relations between physiological events and conscious mental experience.

To undertake such studies, the appropriate experimental method was that of *introspection.* The first experimental psychologists proceeded in the following way. They sat in a quiet laboratory and exposed themselves to controlled sensory stimulation of various sorts—perhaps a particular complex sound or a film of color on a textured surface. The task of the introspecting subject was to analyze carefully the conscious experience produced by exposure to such stimuli, and to report what "elementary sensations" were combined to produce the complex experience, or perception, evoked by the stimulus. This method assumed a kind of "mental chemistry." The basic notion appears to have been that, through the sense organs, the mind was endowed with a fixed number of basic sensations. Complex conscious mental experience might ultimately be understood as the result of various recombinations of these basic mental elements. It was quite in keeping with such a viewpoint to ask a conscientious and patient introspecting subject to report what sensations were involved in the complex experience of being tickled—perhaps some pressure, a little pain, and just a touch of warmth. Clearly, these early psychologists regarded their subject matter as the mind itself, and felt that the life of the mind could be revealed by the technique of careful introspection. In emphasizing "direct access" to the mind, however, they paid a price. First, the minds of animals, young children, and mentally disturbed people were simply inaccessible. Second, even in the well-trained, normal, adult human subject some mental operations might simply not be reflected in consciousness. It is noteworthy that these early workers seem not to have been much concerned with the actual behavior of their subjects. What do people *do* with the sensations and perceptions that are forever cluttering up their minds? How do perceptions and experience influence behavior? How are they used to help the individual adjust to the vicissitudes of living on this earth?

In the United States a kind of revolution took place in experimental psychology in the early twentieth century. The major figure, at least in terms of popular impact, was John B. Watson (1878–1958). To Watson it seemed transparently clear that early psychologists had gone down a blind alley. Their problem, he argued, was that they had attempted to study something that was too vague and subjective—perhaps even too "unreal"—to be a proper subject for scientific study. What is this thing called "mind"? How can we rely on the reports of introspectors about what is going on in their (to us) unobservable mind? What do we do when different introspectors give contradictory reports about the same stimulus? For psychology to become a genuine science, Watson argued, it had better concentrate on a definite subject matter that could be directly observed by all interested investigators. The proper study of psychology is, then, *behavior.* We can all observe the behavior of a subject, and agree that it occurred in a particular way at a definite time and place. We ought to discover what the determiners of behavior are. What stimuli produce what observable responses? How do the relations between stimuli and responses change with experience? This kind of program, as Watson noted, could profoundly extend the scope of experimental psychology. The *behavior* of animals, infants, and the "insane"—unlike their "minds"—could be directly studied.

John B. Watson, American psychologist and exponent of behaviorism.

For a period, at least, Watson's arguments appeared to have enormous force, not so much because of their logic, perhaps, as because of the vast expansion of psychological research the behaviorist program made possible. Then, too, there was disillusionment with the meager results of early introspectionism. Whatever the reason, it seems correct to say that at least until 1950 the vast majority of American psychologists agreed that psychology is the science of *behavior.* The mind, consciousness, and mental processes tended to be—so far as possible—ignored in psychological research. The behaviorists made no attempt to argue that the mind did not exist or that it was of no interest. They simply stressed the methodological simplicity of studying observable behavior.

But to some experimental psychologists, even during the salad days of behaviorism, it always seemed obvious that the facts of behavior demanded interpretation in terms of mental processes. The program of behaviorism stressed simple and straightforward connections between stimuli and responses (it was often called S-R psychology). Some stimuli and responses were simply and reliably related in this reflexlike way. With many stimuli, and with some kinds of subjects, however, it seemed obvious that the stimulus input was operated upon, transformed, processed, or mulled over before it was responded to. That kind of internal processing—events taking place within the organism between the stimulus input and the response output—is what we mean when we talk about thinking or about mental processes. The existence of those internal events made it necessary to replace a simple S-R psychology with a more complex S-O-R psychology, where O stands for the organism that interposes its internal processes between observable stimuli and responses. Those internal events, of course, are not directly observable. They must be *inferred*—and they are inferred from the relations that we observe between stimuli and responses. Psychology in this respect is like any other science. To understand the phenomena that we directly observe, we have to construct "models" of *un*observable structures and processes that make sense out of our observations. Models and inferences constructed to explain one set of observations may have to be revised (or even abandoned) in the face of later and different observations. The goal is to collect those kinds of observations that seem to demand interpretation in terms of a particular model of mental processes. Psychologists, as later chapters will indicate, have been reasonably successful in devising experimental procedures that seem to reveal some of the properties of internal mental processes. The structure of the mind, and mental processes, are thus very much a part of the subject matter of scientific psychology, along with the analysis of behavior.

We should note that mental processes inferred in this way do not necessarily correspond to the results of introspection, for these mental processes may be entirely unobservable even to the organism in which they are occurring. This was, in fact, a central belief of the extremely influential (and nonexperimental) branch of psychology founded by Sigmund Freud (1856–1939). Psychoanalytic theory was developed by Freud to account for the often bizarre behaviors exhibited by neurotic patients who came to him seeking relief from their problems and symptoms. The behaviors and symptoms could be understood, Freud believed, in terms of the operation of powerful mental forces of which patients themselves were entirely unaware. According to the Freudian model, *unconscious* impulses, wishes, and symbolisms profoundly affect the behavior of all of us. The techniques Freud used to infer and argue for such unconscious mental processes were, if not entirely convincing, at least stunningly original and ingenious. We shall examine Freud's model in some detail in Chapter 14, "Personality." For the present it is enough to say that modern experimental psychologists often proceed in basically the same way. For example, we might wish to know what mental processes are engaged when we instruct a subject to search through a printed page trying to locate each example of the letter "e." There is little sense in asking the subject to tell us; even after considerable experience with the task, the subject cannot do so. But there are experimental procedures that make possible highly plausible inferences about the mental processes involved in such a task.

Psychology thus seems to have come to a comfortable and sensible resolution of a problem that disturbed the first century of its development. What

Sigmund Freud, the founder of psychoanalytic theory, with its focus on the effects of unconscious mental processes on behavior.

do we study? We study the observable behavior of people and of animals. From that observable behavior we construct logical inferences about the kinds of internal mental processes that underlie the observed behavior.

Shown here are an experimental psychologist working with a pigeon in a Skinner box, and two developmental psychologists observing a child through a one-way glass panel. There are many other ways to observe behavior, which we will discuss as we come to them in later chapters.

The Methods of Psychology

Perhaps the least you might expect from psychologists is that they should agree among themselves about what the subject matter of their science is. They tend to agree, happily, on much more than just that. They have a strong predilection for the *experimental method* in acquiring reliable knowledge, and there are good and sufficient reasons to prefer the experimental method to all others. It is not always possible to use this method, however, so students of psychology should be aware not only of the virtues of the experimental method but also of the virtues—and the pitfalls—of nonexperimental methods.

The starting point for all knowledge about the world is the observation of some regularity in the flow of events. Thus long ago men observed the movements of the planets and calculated their orbits. They were regular, and this made possible the development of a powerful science of astronomy. We came to understand the movements of the planets long before it was possible to perform experiments on the orbits of bodies in space. Within the domain of psychology we can and do make systematic observations about events with which we cannot interfere experimentally. Suppose, for example, you were interested in discovering what factors produce successful and happy marriages. Perhaps like should marry like, or perhaps not. You cannot force people to marry one another for your experimental convenience, but you can measure the personality characteristics of people who are already married. Then, if you can devise a good measure of the "success" and "happiness" of a marriage, you can observe whether couples with very similar personalities tend to have more or less happy marriages than average. This kind of *survey method* is often used in psychological research.

APPLICATION
The Practice of Psychology

While all psychologists have in common years of training at the graduate level, the specific area of psychology as well as the techniques and methodology studied differ greatly.

The major subfields of psychology (and this is by no means an exhaustive list) are:

1. Experimental psychology. The term *experimental psychology* is both a general label that covers many areas of psychology and also a specific designation for a particular group of psychologists. First, any psychologist who uses the experimental method to conduct research is an experimental psychologist. The second meaning of the term has historically been applied to those psychologists who study: sensation and perception; human performance; learning; motivation and emotion; language; thinking, judging, and problem solving; and physiological processes. More than two-thirds of the experimental psychologists work in an academic setting, where they teach as well as conduct research. Some work for government agencies, research foundations, or private research centers such as Bell Telephone Laboratories.

2. Clinical and counseling psychology. The clinician diagnoses and treats individuals who suffer from emotional or adjustment problems. The clinician may conduct psychotherapy in private practice; in a state or private institution, such as a Veterans Administration Hospital; or in a number of varied settings such as juvenile courts, probation offices, prisons, or institutions for the mentally retarded. The clinician may also be a member of the psychology faculty of a university, teaching undergraduate courses, training clinical graduate students, and perhaps also conducting therapy.

The counseling psychologist is very similar to the clinician in both academic background and function. The counseling psychologist is employed in an educational setting, offering both vocational and emotional guidance to high school and college students.

3. Industrial psychology. Industrial psychology is an applied field. Psychologists in this area are primarily practitioners who apply psychological principles to the work setting, though some industrial psychologists also conduct research to solve on-the-job problems. Industrial psychologists are concerned with the "human factor" in the technological setting—how satisfied workers are with their jobs, how to increase morale and productivity, how to increase the quality of the industry's services, and how to develop better training and placement procedures. Industrial psychologists must have a special set of skills. They must be able to translate psychological knowledge and skills to practical settings, as well as be able to communicate psychological principles to an audience with little or no background in the field.

4. Engineering psychology. The majority of engineering psychologists are employed in industry, where they design equipment

The major drawback of psychological surveys is that the facts and regularities observed are often open to many different interpretations. Suppose you discovered that couples with very similar personalities did enjoy happier and more successful marriages. Would you then feel confident in advising young people to select mates with similar personalities? That would be rash counsel. Perhaps people who are happily married tend *as a result of that fact* to become like each other in personality. The mere observation that two things (similar personalities and happy marriages) occur together does not tell us which causes which, or even if one causes the other at all.

The facts revealed by a survey are basically *correlational:* We merely observe that some things tend to occur together in the real world. Correlation is usually open to many different interpretations. The true interpretation cannot, of course, violate any of the facts observed; but it may not be suggested by those facts alone. We can, of course, conduct more and more elaborate surveys,

and training devices that are appropriate to human capacities. They also design and implement training programs to ensure the efficient functioning of human-machine systems. Other engineering psychologists work in governmental agencies or in private consulting firms.

5. *School and educational psychology.* School psychologists are concerned with the problems of adjustment, mental health, and academic achievement in elementary school children. They may also administer intelligence and proficiency tests to the students, assess problem behaviors and refer these children to counseling agencies, and design and evaluate special education projects.

Educational psychologists are primarily concerned with the application of psychological principles and techniques to problems in education. They analyze educational needs, develop curriculum and teaching materials, and evaluate instructional programs.

6. *Psychometric psychology.* Psychometric psychologists develop testing instruments that evaluate intellectual, personality, educational, or social characteristics, and adapt or develop statistical techniques for the analysis of the test data gathered. They also evaluate testing instruments to determine if they are consistent and valid indicators of the concepts measured. The field of psychometrics overlaps with many of the other areas of psychology; for example, a psychometrician may construct measuring techniques in clinical, personality, or developmental psychology.

7. *Developmental psychology.* The developmental psychologist focuses on the human life-span: infancy, childhood, adolescence, adulthood, and old age. Specific issues that the developmental psychologist may study include the acquisition of language and reasoning skills; the development of altruistic behavior and moral reasoning; the development of social skills and perceptions of self and others; and issues of adjustment in adulthood.

8. *Social psychology.* Social psychologists study the interactions between people, their perceptions of one another, and the effects that groups have on the behavior of the individual.

A sample of the topics studied by social psychologists are: social perception and impression formation; aggression and violence; the formation and change of attitudes; sex roles; and conformity and social influence.

Most social psychologists hold positions in colleges and universities; some hold research positions at private foundations and governmental agencies; still others are employed in more applied settings such as public opinion and market research consulting firms.

9. *Personality psychology.* The field of personality psychology overlaps with both social and developmental psychology, and is the field in which many psychometricians work. Personality psychology is both a research area and an area of concentration in educational and clinical psychology. Personality psychology is the study of individual differences—how people differ in terms of given characteristics such as authoritarianism or emotional stability.

More than half of the positions held by personality psychologists are in universities, where both teaching and research is conducted. In addition, personality psychologists are employed by the government and private foundations.

collecting more and more different facts. Perhaps a convincing interpretation will finally emerge from the data, but it is also possible that we will miss the answer in a sea of true but uninterpretable facts.

Many surveys have demonstrated that college graduates earn considerably larger incomes than other people. This has often been interpreted to mean that college equips you with the skills and habits of mind that are necessary to earn a good income. Perhaps, consciously or not, knowledge of this fact had something to do with your deciding to attend college. But the truth is that nobody knows how, if at all, what you learn in college affects your ultimate income level. The people who attend college tend to come from certain types of background and to possess certain abilities and personality characteristics. Thus it is entirely possible that those same people, if turned loose in the real world at age 18, might earn the same relatively high incomes without ever attending college. Further, it is also possible that a college degree is an irrelevant "credential" that serves as a

In the case study method only one subject may be involved or studied, but the amount of information gathered about that subject is much more than can be gathered through the survey method.

passport to better job opportunities. That is, what one *learns* in college might be irrelevant to the economic benefits that flow from merely possessing a college degree.

Within some areas of psychology, the case study method has been an invaluable technique for gaining important information and drawing hypotheses. The case study may be regarded as a special form of the survey method: The number of subjects surveyed (one) is, of course, very much smaller than in the usual survey, but the number of possibly relevant facts collected about that individual is very large. The case study involves very detailed knowledge about a single individual. Thus if you observed some striking behavior in a person, you can sift through your knowledge of that person's history and make guesses about the causes of that behavior. Your guesses may be wrong, but they can be tested by studying new and additional cases. For example, if you knew the detailed life history of a certain person with a severe stuttering problem, you might be struck by the fact that he had an unusually domineering father who often punished him severely. Perhaps your intuition would suggest that people with domineering fathers have trouble expressing themselves and may thus become severe stutterers. This is just the sort of hunch or tentative hypothesis that psychologists derive from a case study. In this case, though, the hunch is wrong; there is no indication that stutterers have more domineering parents than do nonstutterers. The danger of the case study method is that it may confuse a striking coincidence with a true relationship.

Controlled Experimental Intervention

To illustrate the advantages of the experimental method, we shall first describe an experiment that, although it cannot ever be performed, could answer an important question. Then we shall describe a few actual examples of how a straightforward experimental approach has helped to clarify interesting psychological problems. Finally, we shall introduce a few useful technical terms that help you understand the basic structure of psychological experiments.

The available survey data establish beyond all doubt that cigarette smokers tend to die young—from lung cancer, heart disease, and many other illnesses. The data are so clear and overwhelming that no one can seriously question the fact that cigarette smoking is hazardous to health. There is not, however, any *experimental* evidence that smoking causes cancer, heart disease, or anything else in man. What other interpretation of the survey data is possible?

There is an apparent psychological component in many diseases, as is discussed in Chapter 15. There is good reason to suppose that smokers and nonsmokers differ in their psychological makeup. The heavy smoker is often a tense and "nervous" individual. Possibly, then, tense and nervous individuals tend to die young from various diseases that are the result of their psychological traits. The correlation between cigarette smoking and early death might be nothing more than that—a correlation, and not a cause-and-effect relationship.

This line of reasoning seems more clever than wise, but it is hard to find fault with the logic. What about the fact, established by surveys, that heavy smokers who give up the habit improve their chances of living a long life? That can easily be explained away. We can ask, who *are* the heavy smokers who give up the habit? Possibly, they are tense and nervous people who at last have learned to live more comfortable and relaxed lives, and thus have improved their health. The point by now may seem repetitious, but it is an important one: Without an *experimental* analysis, survey and correlational data are open to many different interpretations. Theoretically, we could provide an unambiguous answer to the connection between cigarette smoking and early death by performing a simple experiment. Take 1,000 10-year-olds. Force, at random, half of them to smoke three packs a day for as long as they live. Forbid the other half from ever smoking. Then observe how long each subject in this experiment lives, and also observe the cause of death of each subject. Presuming that the smokers die younger (it seems a safe bet), we would *know* that it is smoking—and not psychological traits correlated with smoking—that causes early death. We could also safely conclude that those causes of death that occur excessively in the smokers are the result of their smoking. Theoretically, it is possible that *some* of the causes of death now associated with heavy smoking might not occur excessively among the subjects who had been experimentally forced to smoke.

The ethical sense of anyone seriously proposing such an experiment would be grossly defective, but the experimental analysis outlined does have the simplicity and definiteness to which science aspires. We want clear and certain answers to our questions. We are much more likely to obtain such answers if, rather than passively observing what happens to occur in nature, we actively arrange an experiment.

Experimenters intervene, arrange, prepare, manipulate, and plan. Thus in a sense they are in control of what is about to occur, and they are especially prepared to record accurately both what has happened and the circumstances that were in effect when it happened. They can—within ethical and practical limits—vary those circumstances at will and observe how, if at all, the phenomenon in which they are interested is affected. That, in essence, is what the

Psychometricians develop testing instruments that evaluate intellectual, personality, educational, or social characteristics. These tests may then be administered by any one of several different types of psychologists: school and educational, clinical and counseling, developmental, or personality.

celebrated experimental method is all about. Wherever it can be applied, it provides a certainty of knowledge that cannot be duplicated by any other technique. Experimenters can repeat their experiment and obtain the same result. Thus they come to feel that they can produce the phenomenon in which they are interested at will; they can turn it on or off by arranging the conditions of their experiment appropriately. Theories of psychology should, when possible, be grounded in experimental results of this sort.

Examples of Experimental Analysis

We turn now to some actual examples of experimental analysis applied to psychological problems. The experiments described here are not especially complex, but they illustrate the kinds of questions which can be meaningfully answered by an experimental approach to psychology.

DO FISH GET JEALOUS?   We will first use the experimental method to investigate the emotional life of a fish. The fish is the three-spined stickleback, a fish richly endowed with numerous "instinctive" or "species-specific" behaviors, as we will discuss in Chapter 10. The work of Tinbergen (1951) with this fish serves as a brilliant example of how a patient and straightforward experimental analysis can help to clarify what might otherwise appear to be a mysterious problem.

The male stickleback tends to stake out a patch of water as his own territory. Within that territory, during the mating season, he courts the female. The courtship behavior is quite complicated, and it follows a stereotyped and highly predictable pattern. When another male stickleback intrudes during the mating season, the owner of the territory will attack and fight with the intruder. The attack and fighting behavior, like the courtship behavior, is stereotyped and predictable. The question is: What makes the male stickleback attack other males at this time? Those of us who have felt savage passions stir in our own breasts might be tempted to believe that the fish is in a jealous rage. To saddle a stickleback with an Othello complex, however, seems a bit extreme. Tinbergen's careful analysis of the problem followed more prosaic lines.

To answer the question, Tinbergen isolated the male stickleback in a special laboratory tank. The experimenter had provided himself with a number of wooden models of sticklebacks, and he proceeded to drop these into the tank one at a time. The models differed in various ways, as shown in Figure 1-1. Some were lifelike representations of male sticklebacks, while others were chunks of wood with no obvious resemblance to a fish. The point was to discover what properties a model must have in order to elicit attack from the live fish. The result was clear: Any model with red paint on its bottom side tended to be attacked, but even very lifelike models without red paint on the underside were not attacked. The stickleback is so constructed that during the mating season it attacks things with a red underside that drift into its territory. That is, red-on-the-underside is a "releasing stimulus" for stereotyped and instinctive attack behavior. This may seem strange, but perhaps not so strange when you learn another fact about sticklebacks: Glandular changes that take place in the male at the beginning of the mating season turn his belly red. To design the fish so that it attacks red-on-the-underside means that in its natural environment it will be attacking other males during the mating season.

Figure 1-1

The three models shown with red on the underside elicited an attack from the male stickleback even though they bore little resemblance to a stickleback. On the other hand, the lifelike model at the top was not attacked, because it did not have red on the underside. (After Tinbergen, 1951)

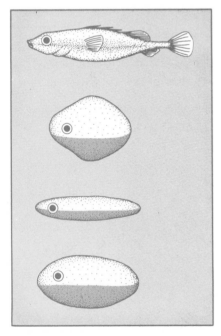

The experiment, of course, does not answer all questions about this striking behavioral adjustment. We have no idea how the visual system of the fish is hooked up to its brain and its motor system in such a way as to produce this result. Physiologists, biochemists, psychologists, and others will be working for a very long time before we can begin to provide answers to such questions. This kind of experiment has in the meantime provided real clarification and has helped to "demystify" instinctive behavior. We may wonder how widely the implications of such studies can be generalized. In many other species the releasing stimuli for various instinctive behaviors have been discovered in a similar manner. We might wonder—and investigate—whether humans too are so constructed that certain stimuli tend automatically to trigger emotional reactions.

The experimental method can be used to analyze the behavior and mental processes of more complex organisms than fish. Since so many experimental psychologists work in a university setting, college students—who are easily accessible, and often cooperative—have served as subjects in many fundamental psychological studies. We shall briefly describe one more experiment. It deals with a distinctively human problem. We include it to illustrate that the experimental method is fruitfully employed in all the various branches of psychology, including social psychology.

ARE CITY DWELLERS HEARTLESS?   We pass on now to an experimental analysis of a very complicated human social behavior. The interest of social psychologists in "bystander intervention" was spurred by a brutal incident that occurred in New York City in 1964 and was very widely reported in the press. The gradual stabbing to death of a young woman took place on the street of a residential neighborhood during the early morning hours. The young woman screamed for help, and the loud and protracted disturbance awakened many people in the neighborhood. Police investigation later established that at least 38 people had observed part or all of the murderous attack, many watching from their windows. However, not one person went to the aid of the victim. Perhaps even more remarkable, not one even telephoned the police!

This apparently heartless and inhumane behavior provoked much editorializing and philosophizing. The incident was said to reveal the dehumanizing effect of modern urban living and our callous lack of concern for our fellow beings. Some observers thought that episodes of this sort signaled the breakdown of modern civilization. Two social psychologists, however, decided to subject "bystander intervention" (or lack of it) to experimental test. To do so, it was necessary to simulate an apparently lifelike emergency that would call for intervention by a bystander. The simulation devised by Darley and Latané (1968) seems to pass muster.

The college students who served as subjects in their study were temporarily misled, and it might be well to comment now on the ethical considerations involved in studies that use human subjects. The experiment must cause no harm to the subject. Further, when the study is completed, a careful "debriefing" session should be held in which the purpose of the experiment is explained in full to the subject, as well as the reason for any necessary deception by the experimenter. In institutions that regularly conduct research with human subjects, special review panels assess the procedures and purposes of a study before it is begun to ensure that appropriate ethical standards are maintained.

The subjects in the Darley and Latané study were at first led to believe that the experiment concerned how groups of human subjects went about solving certain problems under conditions of controlled communication. Thus, each member of the group was assigned to his or her own "isolation booth." The booths were interconnected so that verbal messages could be passed from one booth to another, but each subject was otherwise isolated from all the others.

Each subject was told this "cover story" after arriving at the laboratory. The detailed rules of the "problem-solving" experiment were also explained. Some subjects were led to believe that they were part of a two-person group, while others were told that they were in three-, four-, or all the way up to 10-person groups. Each subject was escorted to an isolation booth and at no point saw the other members of the "group." The only communication allowed was through the push-button and signal-light network that linked all the booths.

The subject was never in fact a member of any group. The other students supposed to be in other booths did not exist. The "messages" the subject believed came from other booths as they all worked on a collective task were sham messages generated by the experimenters. The critical point of the experiment came when, as the subject sat alone in the booth, a dramatic message from a "fellow student" suddenly passed through an audio channel into the booth. The fellow student explained that he was not feeling well, that he really felt quite badly, that he was an epileptic, that he sometimes had severe seizures, that one seemed to be coming on, wouldn't someone please go get help? Then, through sound effects, it became clear that the student who had transmitted this appeal for help was having a convulsion. The dramatic message, however, was not genuine; it was an acted tape recording. The question of interest in this experiment is whether the real subject would do anything about the counterfeit appeal for help. The most obvious thing to do, evidently, would be to leave the booth and search for the victim's booth. The measurement recorded by the experimenter was a simple one: How many subjects emerged from the booth and how long did it take them to act after hearing the simulated emergency?

The results of this part of the study are indicated in Table 1-1. The variable manipulated by the experimenter was the number of people whom the subject believed to be in the group. The table shows that the subject was most likely to

Table 1–1: Effect of Group Size on Likelihood and Speed of Response.

Size of Group	Number of Subjects	% Response	Mean Time (sec)
2 (Subject and victim)	13	85	52
3 (Subject, victim, and 1 other)	26	12	93
6 (Subject, victim, and 4 others)	13	31	166

Adapted from Darley and Latané (1968).

act and act quickly if told that he or she was the only other member of the group. In general, the larger the number of "bystanders" when an emergency takes place, the less likely is a given subject to intervene. The theoretical analysis of bystander intervention has been advanced well beyond this first study, as we will discuss in Chapter 19. For the moment the point is how an ingenious application of the experimental method to even very complex human social behaviors can produce orderly and theoretically significant results.

The Nature of Psychological Experiments

INDEPENDENT AND DEPENDENT VARIABLES.   We stated earlier that psychologists tend to share a preference for the experimental method. It should be obvious by now that they agree that this method can be usefully applied to the vast range of phenomena with which they are concerned. The basic features of the experimental method are identical, regardless of the subject matter to which it is applied. Two terms that are very useful in understanding the structure of any experiment are independent variable and dependent variable.

The *independent variable* is something that there is reason to suppose might affect the dependent variable and that can be manipulated by the experimenter. Thus the makeup of the models dropped into the fish tank and the number of "bystanders" in the experimental group are both independent variables. In each of these experiments two or more values of each independent variable were subjected to deliberate study by the experimenter. The goal in each case was to observe whether different values of the independent variable produced different effects on the behavior of subjects.

The *dependent variable* is always some measurable aspect of the behavior of a subject, be it fish or human. Thus, whether the stickleback attacks a model and whether the subject emerges from the booth to get help are dependent variables. The dependent variable cannot be manipulated by the experimenter in the same direct fashion as the independent variable can. The value of the dependent variable, however, may be determined by the value of the independent variable that the experimenter has arbitrarily chosen for a given subject. The purpose of the experiment is in fact to discover whether such relations between the independent and dependent variables exist. In the two experiments we discussed, the dependent variable was clearly related to the independent variable.

There is often—thank goodness—a clear *functional relationship* between the values of the independent and dependent variables studied in a psychological experiment. For example, in the study of bystander intervention the likelihood that subjects would emerge from their booth was smoothly related to the number of other subjects whom they believed to be present. The data showing this relationship are clear and orderly. The probability of an individual bystander's intervening *is a function of* the number of other bystanders who are present. We would like, obviously, to discover many such functional relationships. Whenever such functional relationships are established, we accumulate information to guide us in the construction of models and theories about the underlying processes that account for the relationships. If the theories are good ones they will not only account for the data already obtained, they will also suggest the existence of functional relationships that have not yet been established. Thus theory and experiment depend very much on each other. Without experimental

HIGHLIGHT
Basic and Applied Research

All sciences have in common two research traditions: an emphasis on basic or "pure" research and an emphasis on applied or "practical" research. Basic research follows the dictum that discovering knowledge for knowledge's sake is an appropriate and justifiable enterprise, while applied research is governed by concerns with the immediate practicality and usefulness of experimental results. Examples of these two research approaches within a science are botany and agriculture, mathematics and statistics, and chemistry and pharmacology.

The various subfields of psychology can also be described as following either basic or applied research concerns, though this division is somewhat artificial. Many psychologists who conduct pure research are aware of its potential applications to real-world problems. While they may not always be the ones to implement their research findings in the social sphere, other psychologists with more applied interests may draw upon this body of work to solve social problems. In general, the distinction between basic and applied research is a matter of degree. Although examples can be found that fall neatly into one or the other category, some research bridges the two orientations.

The basic/applied research distinction has always created some tension in the field. Basic research has been criticized, particularly by the layperson, as producing a body of literature that is only of interest to other psychologists. Basic research has also been criticized (especially when federal funds are used) for expending a great deal of time and money to answer questions that are at worst esoteric and at best not directly linked to pressing social problems.

On the other hand, the applied research tradition has been criticized as being atheoretical.

---

facts we have precious little to theorize about. Without theories we would have no clear idea of how or where to find important experimental facts, what they mean when we find them, or how to relate them to other facts (see "Highlight: Basic and Applied Research").

THE NECESSITY FOR, AND LOGIC OF, CONTROL GROUPS.   The bare-bones description of the structure of an experiment suggests that the carrying out of a meaningful experimental study is as simple as child's play. Unfortunately that is not the case. Psychologists must often cudgel their brains in order to include in their studies appropriate *control groups*. We can best illustrate the logic of, and the necessity for, control groups by describing a hypothetical example—which is, by the way, not at all farfetched.

Psychologist X wondered whether a particular drug really made people feel cheerful. To test this possibility, he recruited a large number of volunteer subjects. The subjects were asked to rate how cheerful they felt on a scale ranging from 1 ("abysmally depressed") to 7 ("ecstatically delighted"). The average self-rating of the subjects was 4.3—just a trifle more toward the cheerful end of the scale than the neutral scale value of 4. Then the subjects were each given a standard dose of the drug being treated. Psychologist X waited a long enough time to be certain that the drug had been absorbed into the subjects' bloodstream, then asked them to rate their cheerfulness once again. The subjects now reported an average rating of 6.1—a little short of ecstasy, but evidently much more cheerful than they had been. With appropriate statistical formulas, Psychologist X demonstrated that so large a change in average self-rating could not reasonably be attributed to mere chance. Thus he concluded that, just as the drug manufacturer had asserted, the drug really does make people feel cheerful. Psychologist X is either in the pay of the drug manufacturer or he knows very little about how to design a psychological experiment.

Kurt Lewin, one of the first social psychologists to address the basic/applied distinction in his own field, noted that without a proper theory, applied research must follow the "costly, inefficient, and limited method of trial and error" (1951, p. 169).

Lewin's conception of psychology involved an amalgamation of both theoretical and applied interests. Lewin believed that this dual contribution to science and society was the proper and important function of psychology. The field of psychology should not only further the scientific understanding of man, but also advance the quality of social life. In the late 1960s, the subfield of social psychology debated whether Lewin's conception of the twin goals of psychology had been upheld or ignored in current research. The solution advanced was that theory-oriented research should be conducted in natural, real-world settings. There was a general call to take psychology "out of the laboratory" and into its natural environment—the social world.

A few examples of "social action" research, which combines the scholarly and applied interests discussed by Lewin, are:

1. McClelland and Cook (1980), who studied energy conservation in an apartment building by employing financial incentives. They found that the degree of group interaction and peer pressure influenced the effectiveness of the conservation programs.

2. Kassin and Wrightsman (1980), who constructed "mock" juries to test the Supreme Court's assumption that jurors discount a coerced confession and do not allow it to influence their decisions.

3. Maniscalco, Doherty, and Ullman (1980), who conducted a study to ascertain whether applicants to graduate school were discriminated against because of a physical handicap.

Lewin noted that close cooperation between the two forms of psychology could be accomplished "if the theorist does not look toward applied problems with highbrow aversion or with a fear of social problems, and if the applied psychologist realizes that there is nothing so practical as a good theory" (Lewin, 1951, p. 169).

The same experiment was performed in a different way by Psychologist Y. The subjects studied were randomly divided into two different groups—one an experimental group, the other a control group. The experimental group was treated exactly the same as Psychologist X had treated all his subjects. First they rated their moods, then they took the same drug dosage, then they rated their moods once again. The results were virtually identical to those obtained by Psychologist X. The cheerfulness ratings increased from about 4.3 to about 6.1. The subjects in Psychologist Y's control group were also treated in the same way, with one very important difference. They were given the same instructions and made the same mood ratings before and after receiving a pill. However, the pill did not contain the drug being tested—it contained only inactive ingredients. The cheerfulness ratings of the control group *also* increased from about 4.3 to about 6.1. Thus Psychologist Y properly concluded that the drug does *not* affect cheerfulness. The addition of a control group demonstrated a truism known to psychologists and physicians: People often respond to drugs and treatments in the way they think they "should." The bitter taste of a worthless patent medicine may convince some people that it is good for them, and they may then report that their symptoms are much improved.

The necessity for appropriate control groups, as the following chapters will repeatedly demonstrate, applies to all areas of psychology. The point of a control group should be clear. We are often unaware of the effects that we, or unsuspected features of the experimental treatment, may exert upon our subjects. We are conscious of manipulating one thing deliberately, but we may well be manipulating other things at the same time. Thus, in our example, the important aspect of the experimental treatment was not the contents of the pill but the suggestion to subjects that the thing they swallowed might make them feel better. To guard against such possibilities, it is essential that a control group and an experimental group be treated identically in *every respect but one*. Then, if the behavior of the two groups differs significantly, we can logically attribute the difference to the one respect (the independent variable) in which they differed.

We might note that the purposes of a control group are sometimes accomplished in an experiment without designating any particular group of subjects as the control group. Suppose the drug experiment had been carried out with subjects randomly divided into four experimental groups, all of which received the same-sized pill and the same instructions. The pills contained, for different groups, either 1, 2, 3, or 4 grams of the drug substance. If there were significant differences in the mood ratings of the four groups, we could conclude that the drug did affect cheerfulness. However, the inclusion of a *placebo control*—a group that receives a zero dosage of the real drug—would obviously provide a clearer picture of the drug's effect.

Experimental psychologists must also be extraordinarily rigorous in the use of a variety of *procedural controls*. With a drug study of the sort described, it would not be gilding the lily to insist that the experimenter, no less than the subject, not know which subjects receive the real drug and which the placebo. There are several nasty possibilities here. The experimenter, without realizing it, might use a different tone of voice when instructing those subjects who are to receive the drug. This could easily influence those subjects' behavior. The experimenter might also mishear, misread, or miscalculate the responses of the subjects in such a way as to bias the results systematically. To guard against this kind of thing, many studies are now conducted with a *double-blind procedure*. That is, the experimenter who actually deals with the subject (like the subject himself) is unaware of the experimental group to which the subject has been assigned.

The Assumption of Orderliness

The use of experimental methods in psychology must obviously be based on the belief that behavior subjected to such an analysis will turn out to be orderly, regular, and lawful. There are, as the following chapters will indicate, good grounds for such a belief. Psychological experiments have made sense out of a very large number of puzzling behavioral phenomena. Time and again psychologists have been able to show that many different behaviors are regular and lawful functions of many different independent variables. There will be at least some instances, as you read this book, when the addition of a new control group to an experimental procedure will suddenly cast a flood of light on a previously insoluble problem. However, in a sense the very successes of experimental psychology make it difficult to achieve what we would all like—a simple and complete understanding of human behavior. Probably the most difficult challenge for psychologists is the fact that behavior is simultaneously determined by *many* variables.

To predict, to control, and to understand the behavior of a gas in a cylinder, we need concern ourselves with only a very few variables. The color of the cylinder is not one of them. The behavior of human subjects, on the other hand, may well be influenced by the color of a room's wall—not to mention a quarrel earlier that day, a missed lunch, and the fact that their father died when they were

3. To bring order to human behavior, and to predict it, is a far more complicated task than any faced by the other sciences. We can make many statements of the form, If all else is equal, then B will follow A. The problem is, of course, that in the real world all else never is equal. But that does not prevent us from coming to understand some things well, and from learning that some variables are much more important than others in determining behavior.

Resistance to Psychological Analysis

The attempt to develop a science of psychology sometimes meets with considerable skepticism, if not downright resistance. One type of objection seems largely theological. That is the argument that some aspects of human behavior and of the human spirit are outside the grasp of science. That may or may not be true, but the argument is not relevant to what psychologists are trying to do. We want to understand as much as we can as definitely as we can. We use techniques and principles that have helped man to understand the natural world. The use of those techniques and principles has helped us to make progress in understanding human behavior. We do not know how far we can progress — after all, in historical perspective, we have not been practicing the science of psychology very long. Perhaps the most we can ever achieve is very partial understanding. Even so, to replace ignorance with partial understanding seems to us worthwhile. Psychologists do, however, acknowledge that there are ways of coming to understand humanity outside of science: There is no danger that the advance of psychological science will cancel the value of Shakespeare in understanding the human condition.

Another common objection to psychology can be answered more simply. This argument is that human behavior is too "spontaneous" or unpredictable to be captured by scientific laws. This is just plain wrong. In many areas of human behavior highly accurate predictions are made by all of us every day. When the traffic light in front of you turns green, you can be reasonably certain that if you drive ahead, drivers from your left and right will not ram into you. There is little doubt that if you were now to read that on p. 118 of this book there is a vivid account of the sexual problems of college students many of you would stop reading this dreary argument and turn at once to p. 118. The odds are very high that nobody you know has engaged in incestuous sexual relations, but that most of the people you know have had incestuous dreams. There are innumerable examples of human behavior that is both predictable and controllable — the task is to understand why and how.

There is still another common objection to experimental psychology, this one not so philosophical. Some maintain that despite its high-flown promises, experimental psychology turns out to be trivial. The facts and the data may be true enough, but they are neither interesting nor important. The experiments often involve animal subjects rather than humans. The problems analyzed often

HIGHLIGHT
Will the Real Psychological Truth Please Stand Up?

To acquire knowledge about the real world it is first of all necessary to observe it. The performing of an experiment is really nothing more than a very special and sophisticated form of observation. We can derive information about the world from any form of honest and careful observation of it. There are sometimes occasions, however, when our observations are impeded by preconceptions and prejudices. This seems to be a special problem for students of psychology, since all of us carry around as part of our intellectual and cultural baggage a large number of psychological "facts" that are simply untrue. People have clearly been interested in other people, and in themselves, since people first appeared on the earth. From the myriad observations that people make of themselves and others it seems obvious and inevitable that a reasonable set of psychological facts should gradually be acquired by every socialized human being, and that these facts should be passed on as part of the cultural tradition. There are indeed all sorts of folk sayings, maxims, and proverbs that express the accumulated psychological knowledge of the human race. For example, all of us learn early in life that you can't teach an old dog new tricks. This homely saying seems to capture a number of profoundly important psychological truths. Plasticity is required for learning, plasticity lessens with age, old habits interfere with the learning of new habits. The difficulty with this analysis is that we also learn another folksaying: You're never to old to learn. Will the Real Psychological Truth please stand up?

There are many other examples of contradictory bits of psychological "knowledge" in our common heritage. Thus, "Absence makes the heart grow fonder"; but, "Out of sight, out of mind." Or, "You can't make a silk purse out of a sow's ear"; but, "Clothes make the man." We can make a reasonable guess about the history that lies behind such "popular psychology." We want to understand the behavior of ourselves and of other people. When a piece of behavior has already occurred, we can always "explain" it by dipping into the large grab-bag of popular psychology and selecting out whatever psychological "law" best fits the occasion. Thus, if Grandfather first takes flying lessons at the age of 70, we have available two contradictory "laws" that between them will "explain" any outcome. Pretty obviously, true psychological laws should not contradict one another; and just as obviously, a knowledge of psychological principles should enable us to *predict* people's behavior, rather than "explaining" it *after* it has occurred. The point should be clear. We cannot rely on the practical, everyday psychology that has been passed on to all of us in the process of growing up. To the degree that it is possible to do so, it seems wise for students of psychology to discard preconceptions, or at least to be suspicious about the psychology which they think they already know.

seem small-scale and unrelated to the real problems of human life. Why perform experiments that you know cannot provide answers to the truly significant questions?

There is a very good reason for performing "simple" experiments that seem artificial and contrived. To discover the laws that govern falling bodies we do not stand passively at the foot of the Empire State Building waiting for whatever happens to drop down. We instead set up a quiet corner of a laboratory and deliberately roll balls down inclined planes. The advantages are obvious. We are prepared to make particular observations at a particular time, with as many disturbing influences as possible eliminated. We deliberately isolate, and then manipulate, a *simple system.* There is too much going on in the real world all at once for us to grasp the relations between events. We are thus better off observing a simple system, with only a few variables at work, so that we can systematically make one thing happen after another. The history of science indicates that the *general principles* unearthed by the observation of artificially simple systems also operate in the wider world. The same principles that account for the motions of billiard balls in the laboratory also explain the grander movements of the planets in heaven. The "simple" experiments described throughout this text are attempts to isolate principles that can be applied to the understanding of many phenomena. We shall point to as many such applications as we can. We should repeat, however, that even the "simple" systems studied by psychologists are almost frighteningly complex. To understand the movements of a white rat through a maze is doubtless easier than to understand the movements of a person through life, but it is not easy. And the complexity in a slab of nervous tissue removed from a human brain makes balls and planes look like a child's playthings.

Despite the resistance to psychological analysis and the difficulty of the tasks, it is certain that the work of psychologists will continue for at least two obvious reasons. First, the subject matter of psychology is enormously interesting. There is little likelihood that people will ever lose interest in trying to understand "what makes them tick," and that is what psychology is about. Second, the results of psychological inquiry and speculation are relevant both to public policy and to the more private concerns of our personal lives. We *need* to know more than we now do about psychology if we are to live better.

The impact of psychological fact (and fancy) on our lives has obviously been significant. There are some signs that it may be even stronger in the future. We hope that after reading this book you will be better able to distinguish between psychological fact and fancy. There are many facts that you should know, because this knowledge will guard you against the effects of wishful thinking and bias. There are also many psychological theories that you should know. Some are closely related to facts, some are broad and reasonable generalizations from a few known facts, and some are scarcely related to facts at all. The popular impact of a psychological theory, and of some psychological practices, often has little to do with the firmness of its factual basis. This book is designed to acquaint you with influential psychological theories and practices; but most of all it is designed to illustrate the relation between theory and practice and what is really known, by experimental means or otherwise.

Even the "simple" systems studied by psychologists are almost frighteningly complex. To understand the movements of a white rat through a maze is doubtless easier than to understand the movements of a person through life, but it is not easy.

Summary

1. Early psychologists were concerned with elementary sensations and consciousness; their chief method was introspection. Wilhelm Wundt was a pioneer in this field. *[handwritten: looking in on one's feelings & attempting to report on what one observes & experiences]*

2. In the United States, Watson revolutionized experimental psychology and claimed that psychology is the study of behavior.

3. At approximately the same time, Freud developed his theories of psychoanalysis in which the unconscious mind was a prominent idea.

4.   Methods of psychology vary, just as the various disciplines within psychology vary. Among the various methods are: *experimental method, survey method,* and *case studies.*

5.   The experimental method involves beginning with a theory and then testing that theory. Experiments must be carefully planned and repeated so that coincidence and random phenomena will not be misinterpreted as proof of the hypothesis.

6.   The *independent variable* of an experiment is something under the direct control of the experimenter; the *dependent variable* is some measurable aspect of a subject's behavior that may be affected by the independent variable.

7.   The purpose of an experiment is to discover whether such relations between the independent and dependent variables exist.

8.   Control groups are necessary in an experiment so that data may be interpreted properly: If the control group and experimental group are treated identically in every way except for the independent variable, then it is logical to conclude that any differences in behavior are a result of the independent variable.

9.   Types of experimental controls are: placebo control, procedural control, and the double-blind procedure.

Suggested Readings

BORING, E. E. *A history of experimental psychology.* New York: Appleton-Century-Crofts, 1950. This is considered the classic overview of experimental psychology. The book begins with the rise of scientific psychology in the early nineteenth century and continues through to the modern period with a discussion of such areas as behavioral and Gestalt psychology.

CRAIG, J. R., and METZE, L. P. *Methods of psychological research.* Philadelphia: Saunders, 1979. This book is also an introduction to research methods. It discusses the scientific approach to problem solving, how to use research literature, and how to define variables and design research. Several research designs are discussed. In addition, the authors discuss ethical issues in research. The final section of the book instructs the reader in how to write a research report.

EVANS, R. I. *The making of psychology: Discussions with creative contributors.* New York: Knopf, 1976. This book consists of dialogues with prominent psychologists representing the major areas of psychology. The interviews introduce the reader to the contributor's major ideas and the historical antecedents of his or her field. The psychologists interviewed include B. F. Skinner, Jean Piaget, Gordon Allport, Konrad Lorenz, Carl Rogers, Leon Festinger, C. G. Jung, and Erik Erikson.

GRAHAM, K. R. *Psychological research: Controlled interpersonal interaction.* Monterey, Cal.: Brooks/Cole, 1977. This book is an introduction to research methods. It is primarily concerned with the study of human behavior but does include some discussion of research with nonhuman subjects. It presents the logic of research design and lays the foundation for statistical analyses, but no background in statistics is required. Suggestions for research projects are given throughout the book.

GUTHRIE, R. V. *Even the rat was white: A historical view of psychology.* New York: Harper & Row, 1976. The first half of this book explores the social antecedents of psychology by outlining the relationship between psychology and anthropology. The author reviews early research approaches to black/white differences. The second half of the book discusses the impact of psychology on the education of black people and the contributions of black American psychologists.

ROBINSON, D. N. *An intellectual history of psychology.* New York: Macmillan, 1976. A particularly literate and enjoyable exploration of the history of ideas that has culminated in the subject matter termed "psychology." The book discusses in detail the philosophical tradition and the emergence of scientific psychology. Students who are interested in intellectual history will particularly enjoy this book.

SHERMAN, R. *A career in psychology.* Washington, D.C.: American Psychological Association, 1965; WOODS, P. J. (Ed.) *Career opportunities for psychologists.* Washington, D.C.: American Psychological Association, 1976; WOODS, P. J. *The psychology major: Training and employment strategies.* Washington, D.C.: American Psychological Association, 1979. These three books discuss career opportunities and educational requirements in all areas of psychology. In addition, the American Psychological Association has several pamphlets on careers in psychology, which can be obtained by writing the APA, 1200 17th St., N.W., Washington, D.C. 20036.

WATSON, R. I. *The great psychologists.* Philadelphia: Lippincott, 1978. An examination of the historical unfolding of psychology through the works of its chief proponents. Drawing heavily on original sources, the book discusses the writings of Plato and Aristotle, Déscartes, Kant, Wundt, Binet, James, Cattell, Watson, French, and contemporary American and European psychologists.

WERTHEIMER, M. *A brief history of psychology.* New York: Holt, Rinehart and Winston, 1979. A very readable little book that traces the emergence of psychology from the writings of the ancient Greeks and other philosophical traditions to the development of psychology as a separate field through the nineteenth and twentieth centuries. This is a good source to launch the reader on a historical exploration of psychology.

2

The Biological Framework

Psychology is primarily concerned with what organisms (people and animals) *do*—that is, how they behave. But there are many different types of psychologists, and they ask many different kinds of questions and take different approaches to answering these questions. One major difference is in the attitude adopted toward studying what is *inside* an organism—in particular, the anatomy (structure) and physiology (functioning) of its nervous system. The two most extreme points of view are held by the behaviorists on the one hand and the physiological psychologists on the other.

The behaviorists, led by B. F. Skinner, maintain that what goes on inside an organism is none of their concern. They believe that a psychologist should try to predict an organism's response in a given situation on the basis of its past experiences, and never mind what goes on underneath its skin. This is called the *black box* approach because the organism is regarded as a black box—you can expose it to stimuli and record its response, but you can't open it and look inside. Physiological psychologists adopt the opposite strategy: They are primarily interested in what's inside the black box. The assumption is that an organism's behavior will become predictable when enough is known about its anatomy and physiology.

The two extreme positions have often been likened to the two ways of learning about a machine such as a car. The first method is to see what happens when you press the various buttons and pedals, and when you put (or fail to put) gasoline into the gas tank. The second method is to look under the hood and see which wire is connected to what, and which gear turns what other gear. Obviously, both methods are valid and would lead, in time, to a fairly good understanding of the behavior of the car. But neither method alone can give us the complete picture—for that, we need *both* methods. Thus in this book we shall combine the two approaches. First we shall look at the organism's behavior, and then we shall try to make connections with what is found "under the hood." This chapter will introduce you to the body mechanisms that are of chief concern to psychologists.

Heredity

All the instructions for building a car—including the recipes for the steel of the axles, the plastic of the dashboard, and the glass of the headlights—would fill several thick volumes. Yet the instructions for making the infinitely more complex human body—including the recipes for the hard surface of the teeth, the flexible fibers of the muscles, and the transparent surface of the eye—can be fit into the microscopic area of a single cell. These instructions are contained in the *genes.*

Not only do genes determine whether you have blue eyes or brown, curly hair or straight; they also provide the directions for the construction of the nervous system, the endocrine system, the sense organs, the muscles. We sometimes think of genes as being primarily involved in producing *differences* among people; it is important to remember that they are also responsible for the many things that all humans have in common.

Genes and Chromosomes

Located within the nucleus of every cell in the body of an organism, genes are composed of DNA (deoxyribonucleic acid). This complex molecule, shaped like a spiral staircase, has the remarkable ability to break in half lengthwise and form two new molecules identical to the first. The information in each gene is coded within the structure of the long helical DNA molecule by the precise ordering of its four organic bases (adenine, guanine, cytosine, and thymine). This code determines which of the 20 amino acids will be used, and in what order, in forming the protein that is synthesized by the cell. The kinds of protein that are consequently produced determine, in turn, the course of development. In other words, the information coded within the gene determines whether development results in a grasshopper, a sea anemone, a cow, or a human.

A large number (a thousand or more) genes grouped together in a specific order form a *chromosome.* Chromosomes occur in pairs in the nuclei of the cells of the body. The number of chromosomes varies from species to species—fruit flies have 8, frogs 26, rats 42, chimpanzees 48, and chickens, oddly enough, have 78. Humans have a relatively modest number: 46 (23 pairs). In each of these pairs one chromosome is inherited from the father and one from the mother.

When a human ovum (egg cell) is formed, it receives just one chromosome from each pair, so the ovum contains only 23 chromosomes instead of 46. Sperm cells also contain only 23 chromosomes—one randomly selected from each pair. When a sperm cell unites with an ovum at the moment of conception, the chromosomes from the mother join with those from the father, giving the fertilized ovum the full complement of 46. Since the chances are equal of getting either member of the mother's 23 pairs of chromosomes and either member of the father's 23 pairs, a given couple could theoretically produce 2^{23} times 2^{23} different combinations of chromosomes. Thus, genetically speaking, each of us had only one chance in about 70 trillion of being conceived! Despite this genetic diversity, a child still tends to resemble its parents, for the simple reason that half of its genes are shared with its mother and half with its father.

Figure 2-1 shows the 46 chromosomes of the normal human male (left) and female (right). Genetic sex is determined by the so-called *sex chromosomes.* There are two sorts of sex chromosome, X chromosomes and Y chromosomes. Every fertilized egg contains one X chromosome that is contributed by the mother. The second member of the pair, contributed by the father, may be either another X chromosome—in which case a female is formed—or a Y chromosome—which produces a male. Since only males have the Y chromosome, the genetic sex of a

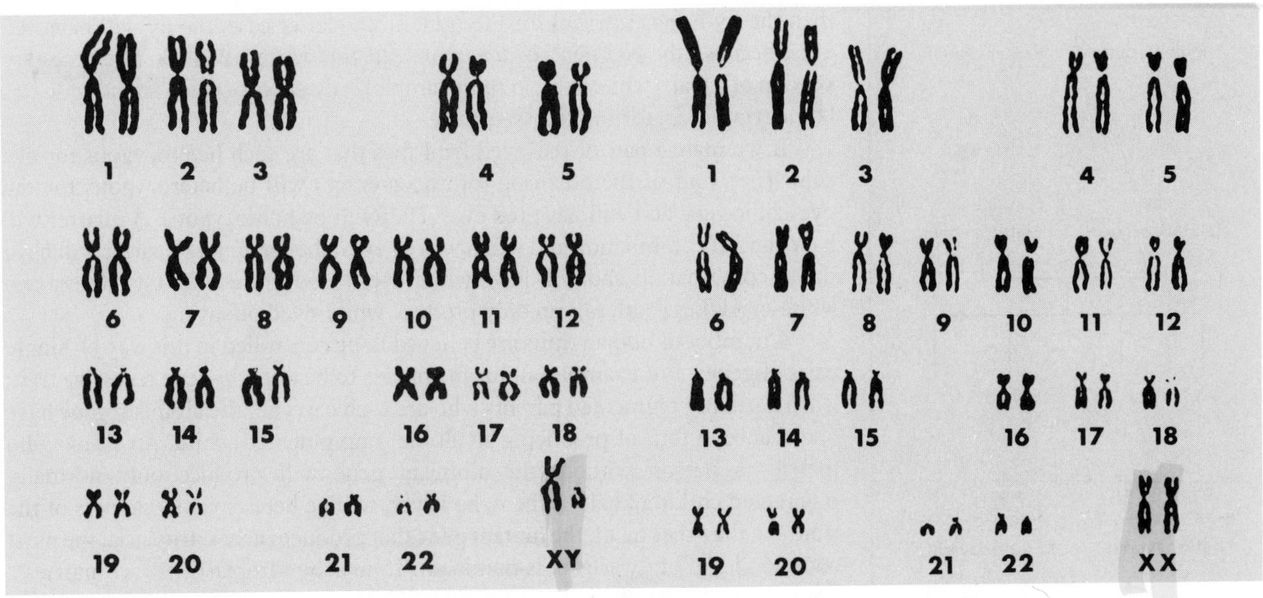

Figure 2-1

On the left are the 23 pairs of chromosomes of a normal male, and on the right the 23 pairs of chromosomes of a normal female. These photos show the result of a process known as karyotyping, in which a dividing cell is flattened and stained, and a magnified photograph is taken of the chromosomes. The picture of each individual chromosome is then cut out, and they are arranged according to size and shape.

child is entirely determined by which one of the father's two sex chromosomes the child inherits. Occasionally something goes wrong with this process and a child is produced with only one X chromosome, or two Xs and a Y, or two Ys and an X. At other times hormonal abnormalities may cause a child whose genetic sex is male to appear female and be reared as a girl, or vice versa. (Such cases are discussed in Chapter 10, Biological Bases of Motivation.)

The 44 other chromosomes normally occur in matched pairs, although here again there are occasional genetic errors. In the most common of these there are 3 chromosomes instead of 2 in the 21st set; the result is a child born with *Down's syndrome* (formerly called "mongolism"), which consists of mental deficiency combined with various physical abnormalities.

Although chromosomes are large enough to be visible through a good microscope, this is not the case with genes. No one knows exactly how many genes there are in a human cell (the total number has been estimated to be somewhere between 20,000 and 125,000) or in exactly what order they are arranged on the chromosomes. Most of what is known about genetic action is derived by inference from breeding experiments, such as those that Gregor Mendel performed on pea plants more than a century ago. Modern geneticists generally use fruit flies for their experiments, partly because it is possible to produce three or four generations of fruit flies in the time it takes for one pea plant to mature.

SINGLE-GENE TRAITS.   The genes for any particular trait are believed to be located at the same place on each of the two chromosomes that make up a normal pair. At a given location, a gene might occur in any one of several different forms, called *alleles*. Consider, for example, a trait that is controlled by a single gene, such as eye color in the fruit fly. We'll assume that two alleles are possible: one for red eyes (which we'll call *E*) and one for white eyes (*e*). If a fly has two of the same kind of allele, either *EE* or *ee*, it is *homozygous* for the trait. If allele *E* appears at the eye-color locus on one chromosome and *e* on the other,

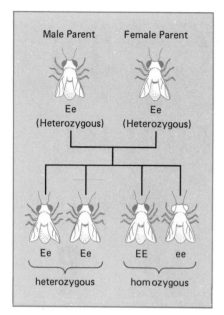

Figure 2-2

Eye color in the fruit fly is a single-gene trait. The gene for red eyes (E) is dominant over the gene for white eyes (e). Each off-spring fly represents one-quarter of the off-spring. Of course, since genes pair ran-domly, the offspring of any given pair of flies may deviate considerably from the ex-pected proportions.

then the fly is *heterozygous* for the trait. In the latter case, the fly will have red eyes, because the red gene is *dominant* and the white *recessive*. The recessive version of a trait (white eyes, in this example) only appears when an individual is homozygous (*ee*) for the recessive gene.

If we mate a pair of red-eyed fruit flies that are each heterozygous for eye color (*Ee*), half of the offspring (on the average) will be heterozygous for the eye-color gene and will have red eyes. Half will be homozygous: A quarter will have the *EE* combination and will have red eyes, the remaining quarter will have the *ee* combination and will have white eyes (see Figure 2-2). Of course, two white-eyed flies (both *ee*) can only produce white-eyed offspring.

A number of human traits are believed to be controlled in this way by single pairs of genes. For example, albinism appears to be a single-gene recessive trait: Two normally pigmented parents who are each carrying the albinism gene have one chance in four of producing an albino (unpigmented) child. An albino who marries a person without the albinism gene will produce only normally pigmented children; half of them, however, will be heterozygous carriers of the trait. On the other hand, the mutant gene that produces achondroplasia, the most common form of dwarfism, is dominant. If an achondroplastic dwarf marries a normal-sized individual, half of their children will be dwarfs; two dwarfs have only one chance in four of having a normal-sized child.

SEX-LINKED TRAITS.   The situation becomes more complicated when the gene for a trait is located on the sex chromosomes. In that case, it is known as a *sex-linked trait*, and the chances of having it generally depend on whether you're male or female. The two best-known examples of sex-linked traits are color blindness and hemophilia (the condition in which the blood does not clot normally). The genes for these abnormalities are located on the X chromosome. A female has *two* X chromosomes, and if either one contains a normal gene for these traits, the abnormalities are not expressed—they are recessive. A female can only be color blind or hemophiliac in the unlikely event that she inherits the gene from both parents. But a male lacks a second X chromosome, so if the single X chromosome contains a gene for hemophilia, say, there is nothing to oppose it and the child is born with the condition. This condition can be inherited only from the *mother*, since a male always receives his X chromosome from his female parent.

POLYGENIC TRAITS.   Very few human traits are fully controlled by a single pair of genes; most of a person's characteristics, such as height, skin color, and artistic ability, are *polygenic*—determined by the action of more than one gene pair. Even human eye color, although following fairly well the pattern of a single-gene trait (brown dominant, blue recessive) is probably a polygenic trait. Two blue-eyed parents *can*, on rare occasion, have a brown-eyed child.

The Study of Heredity

Breeding experiments have been used to study polygenic traits in animals. One technique is called *selective breeding*. Tryon (1942) performed such an experiment with a group of rats that differed in their ability to negotiate a complex maze. The rats were separated into two groups, a "bright" group and a "dull" group, on the basis of their maze-running ability. Then bright females were mated with bright males, dull females with dull males. In the second generation this procedure was repeated, and so on for several generations. Tryon found that by the eighth generation he had two distinct groups of rats, a bright group and a dull group, with hardly any overlap between the two. Just about every member of the group that was bred for brightness was better at maze running than an average rat of the first generation; just about every member of the group bred for dullness was worse. The conclusions were that differences in rats' "intelligence" are genetically determined, and that selective breeding of the brightest (or the dullest) rats increases the probability that a rat will inherit the brightness-producing (or dullness-producing) genes. Similar experiments have been performed—with similar results—using active versus inactive rats, emotional versus phlegmatic rats, and even alcoholic versus sober rats! These results come as no surprise to animal breeders, whose efforts have produced such diverse specimens as the Chihuahua, the bulldog, and the Great Dane.

HEREDITY AND ENVIRONMENT.   Tryon's rats were presumably treated alike—they all lived in the same kinds of cages, ate the same type of food, and had the same amount of maze-running experience. Thus any systematic differences in the scores made by the two groups of rats can be confidently attributed to differences in heredity. More commonly, experimenters use rats or mice that have been interbred (by breeding sisters to brothers for a number of generations) until genetic variations among them are minimized and the individual members of the strain are practically carbon copies of one another. Then differences in environment are introduced—for example, one subgroup is raised in bare cages, the other in an "enriched" environment. Any nonrandom differences that are found between the two subgroups can therefore be safely attributed to differences in environment.

Such techniques cannot, of course, be used with human beings. A perennial question asked of psychologists is: How much of human behavior is inherited and how much is due to the effects of environment? Often it is impossible to answer this question because there is generally no way to hold environment constant and vary only heredity (as Tryon did), or to hold heredity constant and vary only environment (as experimenters with inbred rats do).

TWIN STUDIES.   Nature, however, occasionally provides us with the perfect opportunity to view heredity held constant. In the United States 1 out of every 86 births results in twins. Of these, the major proportion—about three-quarters—are *fraternal twins.* Fraternal twins are conceived when a woman's ovaries release two ova instead of one and each ovum is fertilized separately by a different sperm. Thus fraternal twins are no more closely related than ordinary siblings—on the average, they share 50 percent of their genes with each other (the same proportion that they share with each of their parents). Fraternal twins do not even have to have the same father: There are several authenticated cases of twins fathered by two different men.

The other quarter of twins are *identical.* Sometimes a fertilized egg, for unknown reasons, splits in two and forms two embryos instead of one. The genetic material in these two twins is identical—they have 100 percent of their genes in common—so any differences between them must be due to environment. Bear in mind, though, that "environment" includes what happens *before* birth as well as after. One member of a pair of twins is often more favorably situated in the uterus than the other; birth weights of twins often differ considerably. There is also an advantage to the baby born first—the second-born is more likely to suffer the ill effects of having been deprived of oxygen for a longer period of time.

WHAT WE HAVE LEARNED FROM TWIN STUDIES.   Many human characteristics have been studied with the goal of determining the relative contributions of heredity and environment. Consider the data that have emerged from the many surveys of the mental illness called *schizophrenia*. The incidence of this disease in the population as a whole is about 1 percent, but the chances of having schizophrenia are much higher—between 10 and 15 percent—for a person who has a schizophrenic parent or a schizophrenic brother or sister. These data suggest that schizophrenia runs in families. However, they do not make it clear whether the disease is caused by the genetic similarity of close relatives or the fact that their environments are similar.

The results of twin studies show that *both* heredity and environment play a role. Several surveys made over the past 30 years show that the agreement between fraternal twins (who have approximately the same environment but different heredity) is about the same as that between other siblings—10 or 15 percent; but for identical twins (who have approximately the same environment *plus* the same heredity) the agreement is much higher—about 50 percent. If schizophrenia were *entirely* determined by the genes, the agreement between identical twins would be 100 percent: If one twin had it, the other would have to have it too. Since this is not the case, environmental factors must also be important. And even identical twins do not have exactly the same environment.

Twin studies have focused on a number of other physical and mental traits. The results of these studies will be reported wherever they are relevant throughout this book.

It should be remembered that genes do not *directly* produce mental illness or any other psychological trait: Genes simply provide the directions for building a body. When a psychological trait is shown to be hereditary it means that it's the product of some inherited characteristic of the body—probably some anatomical, physiological, or chemical variation in the nervous system or the endocrine system. These two important body systems will be the focus of the remainder of this chapter.

The Nervous System

In everyday language, "nervous" means "anxious" or "excitable," and "nerves" are what you're a bundle of when you're particularly anxious (not to be confused with "nerve," which is what you have a lot of when you're not anxious *enough*). Here, however, "nervous" simply means "having to do with nerves," the parts of the body that specialize in transmitting information. Like all other body tissue, the nervous system is composed of cells, most of which are too minute to be seen with the naked eye. The long pale nerves you see when you dissect a frog or a cat in a biology lab actually contain a large number of individual nerve cells or *neurons*. A diagram of a typical neuron is shown in Figure 2-3.

The nervous system is divided into the *central nervous system,* consisting of all the neurons that are entirely within the brain and the spinal cord; and the *peripheral nervous system,* consisting of all the neurons that are partly or completely outside the brain and the spinal cord. The peripheral nervous system can be further divided into *sensory neurons,* which carry information toward the central nervous system; and *motor neurons,* which carry signals from the central nervous system toward the muscles. Everything you know about the world outside yourself, everything you know about what goes on inside your body, has traveled to your central nervous system by sensory neurons. And every effect you have had on the world was carried out, in one way or another, through the action of motor neurons.

Neurons arose quite early in the course of evolution; animals as primitive as jellyfish have sensory and motor neurons. Neurons haven't even changed very much: A squid or a leech has basically the same kind of neurons a human has. In fact, much of our knowledge of neural functioning has come from studies of the nervous system of the squid.

In simple animals like the jellyfish, sensory neurons transmit their signals directly to motor neurons. But only a little higher on the evolutionary ladder— for example, in *Ascaris,* a parasitic roundworm—a third class of neurons intervenes between the sensory and the motor neurons. These intermediate neurons, called *interneurons,* process the signals sent to them by sensory neurons and by other interneurons. Then, on the basis of all the information they receive, they may or may not send a signal to the motor neurons for transmission to the muscles. Clearly, this three-stage system is capable of producing more complex forms of behavior than a two-stage system.

In *Ascaris* and other invertebrates, bunches of interneurons form clumps called *ganglia.* In general, both the proportion of neurons in the interneuron class and the total number of cells in the nervous system are greater in the more highly developed species.

By the time we get to the vertebrates (fish, amphibians, reptiles, birds, and mammals), the ganglion has become a full-fledged brain. We like to believe that the brain has reached its highest state of development in the human species—and perhaps it has, judging by some of our achievements. But it is well to remember that humans have neither the largest brains in the animal kingdom (elephants and porpoises have larger brains) nor even the highest brain-weight-to-total-weight ratio (it is about 1:50 in humans, but 1:20 in certain monkeys). There is no need, though, to feel overly humble. The human brain has somewhere between 10^{10} and 10^{11} neurons, or between 10 billion and 100 billion—as many as there are stars in our galaxy!

Development of the Nervous System

Even more remarkable, just about all these neurons are present in the human brain at birth—and all grown from the single cell that is the fertilized ovum. That means that brain-cell formation during the 9 months of fetal life must proceed at an average rate of 250,000 per minute! Of course, the rate of cell formation is not the same throughout development, because cells increase in number geometrically rather than arithmetically—one cell becomes two, two become four, and so on. Looking at it this way, it only takes about 36 generations of neurons to complete the human brain, or one division every 7 or 8 days.

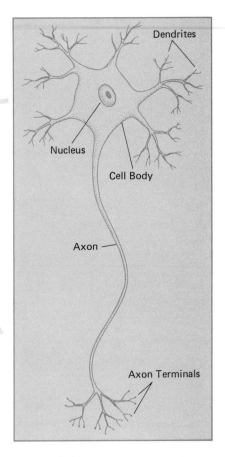

Figure 2-3

This is an idealized diagram of a typical neuron—actual neurons vary tremendously in shape and size. Neurons receive stimulation through their dendrites or the cell body; the message is transmitted by way of the axon, which may be as much as a meter in length.

GROWTH OF THE BRAIN.   Approximately 9 months after conception neurons in the human nervous system lose their ability to divide. Unlike most other cells in the body, neurons that die are not replaced. (Outside the central nervous system, however, an axon that is severed may be regenerated if the cell body remains intact.) Despite the fact that no new neurons are formed after birth, the brain continues to grow, from about 350 grams in a newborn infant to about 1,400 grams at puberty. This quadrupling in weight is partly due to an increase in the size of individual cells. In addition, the axons of many cells gradually grow a multilayered jacket of insulation made up of a fatty substance called *myelin*. Since the transmission of neural impulses is as much as 20 times faster in myelinated fibers, the process of myelination is essential to the maturation of the nervous system. About half the cells in the nervous system eventually acquire a myelin sheath.

Probably the most important factor in the brain's growth in size during childhood is the proliferation of a second kind of brain cell, the *glial* cell. Unlike neurons, glial cells continue to divide; by adulthood they are 10 times as numerous as neurons. When a neuron dies, a glial cell grows to fill the gap.

Glial cells were once thought to serve primarily to hold the neurons together ("glial" comes from the Greek word for "glue"). Now it is known that they have several other functions. They are responsible for the myelination of axons in the brain, they direct the growth of neuronal pathways or interconnections, and they play a general role in nervous system metabolism.

We have said that no new neurons are formed after fetal development; yet it has been estimated that only 3 percent of the brain's neurons die during the course of an average lifetime. Neurons are able to live so long for the same reason that people are: Parts of them are continuously being replaced as they wear out or are used up. In a neuron, all replacement parts are manufactured in the cell body, and must be transported from there to wherever they are needed. A slow-moving system known as *axonal transport* carries the new cellular components down the axon to their destination. Cells in the brain are no more than a few centimeters in length, but in the peripheral nervous system—where an axon may extend more than a meter from its cell body—it may take weeks for the replacement parts to reach their intended site.

CONNECTIONS AMONG NEURONS.   Nervous system development does not consist merely of the production of cells. It is necessary for these cells to be properly "hooked up" with one another so that neural signals can be transmitted along pathways of interconnecting fibers. The transfer of information between two neurons takes place at a junction called a *synapse*. Nerves do not actually touch each other at a synapse; instead, the neural impulse is chemically transmitted across a tiny gap two millionths of a centimeter in width. This mechanism will be discussed in greater detail in the next section of this chapter.

How Neurons Work

Although neurons vary tremendously in shape and in size (from microscopic to over a meter in length) they all have the same job: to transmit signals. They all do this in exactly the same way, by means of a traveling pulse of electrical energy that moves down the axon to the terminals of the axon tips. The pulse, called the *action potential*, is always the same. A neuron either fires or it doesn't; once it

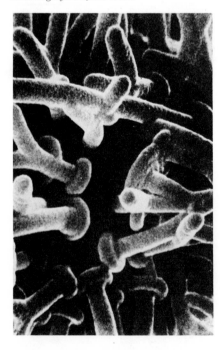

A photograph of axons and axon terminals taken with a scanning electron microscope and magnified 5,000 times.

fires, the impulse is always of the same magnitude. This is known as the *all-or-none law* of neural action.

Since a neuron cannot respond to a more intense stimulus with a more intense signal, how does it "code" such information? By its rate of firing. After a neuron is fired, there is a very brief period, about a thousandth of a second long, during which it cannot fire again. This is called the *absolute refractory period*. Then there is a considerably longer time, called the *relative refractory period*, when a normal stimulus will not trigger the neural impulse but an intense one will. Thus intense stimulation will cause the neuron to fire at a faster rate—up to several hundred times a second.

ELECTROCHEMICAL EFFECTS. A neuron, like other cells, is enclosed by a semipermeable membrane. The concentrations of various substances in the fluids within this membrane generally differ from the concentrations outside the cell. In particular, in a resting (nonfiring) neuron the concentration of potassium ions is 10 times higher than in the fluids outside the cell; sodium ions are only a tenth as concentrated inside the cell as outside. The resting neuron must expend energy in order to maintain these concentrations. It does this by pumping sodium ions out of the cell and receiving potassium ions in exchange (see Figure 2-4). The differential ionic concentrations create a polarization, or potential difference, across the cell membrane. That is, the interior of the cell has a negative electrical charge with respect to the exterior. This difference, usually about − 70 millivolts, is called the cell's *resting potential*.

Any incoming signals that bring the neuron's resting potential closer to zero bring the neuron nearer to the point at which a neural impulse is triggered, a point called the *threshold*. The threshold of most neurons is around − 50 millivolts. When part of a neuron reaches the threshold level, an action potential is triggered at that place (see Figure 2-5). What happens is that sodium ions are suddenly allowed to rush in, and they do so with such rapidity that the polarity of the cell at that place changes almost instantaneously from negative to positive. This change brings the adjacent part of the cell below threshold, and the same

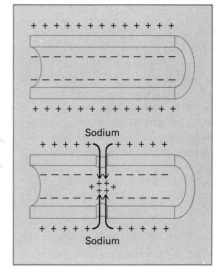

Figure 2-4

(Top) This is a schematic diagram of a section of a neuron, sliced lengthwise. The outside of the neuron has a negative charge relative to the inside, due to the higher concentration of sodium ions outside the cell and potassium ions inside it.
(Bottom) An action potential is triggered, and sodium ions flow into the cell at that place. The action potential moves along the cell to the end of the axon. Immediately after the action potential occurs, the cell begins to restore its resting potential by pumping the sodium ions out again.

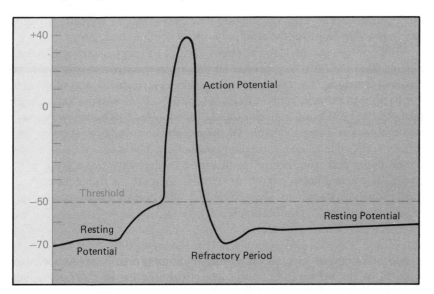

Figure 2-5

Voltage readings are shown at a given place on the neuron, over a period of 20 or 30 milliseconds (thousandths of a second). At first (left) the cell is resting; it then reaches threshold and an action potential is triggered (middle). After a brief refractory period, the cell returns to its resting potential (right).

APPLICATION
Neurotransmitters—
Chemicals with a Message

Because synaptic transmission takes place outside the cell walls, it appears to be especially vulnerable to disruption. Many drugs or poisons exert their effects by interfering in some way with chemical neurotransmission. For example, at the junction between a neuron and the cell membrane of a skeletal muscle, the excitatory neurotransmitter is always ACh. Thus a substance that interferes with the action of ACh can produce paralysis. The results can be fatal if the paralysis involves the muscles used in breathing. Botulinus toxin works in this way, by blocking the release of ACh. (Botulinus toxin is sometimes present in improperly canned foods; it can be destroyed if the food is boiled for 5 minutes before eating.)

Other poisons block the uptake of ACh by the postsynaptic membrane; these include curare and cobra venom. Still others, such as the venom of the black widow spider and certain nerve gases developed for chemical warfare, cause *too much* ACh to build up in the synaptic space, so that eventually the neuron can no longer respond to it.

Another class of substances works by interfering with *inhibitory* neurotransmitters, leading to convulsions and often death. The poison strychnine operates in this way, as does the toxin produced in the body by the tetanus bacterium.

NEUROTRANSMITTERS IN THE BRAIN
When it comes to synaptic transmission in the brain, the neurotransmitter situation is incredibly complicated. Dozens of substances are involved, with different transmitters used in different brain areas and for different functions.

The psychological effects of many *psychoactive drugs* result from their action on neurotransmission. Hallucinogenic drugs such as mescaline and psilocybin are structurally similar to dopamine and norepinephrine, and may mimic the effects of these neurotransmitters at certain sites in the brain. The lysergic acid diethylamide (LSD) molecule resembles the neurotransmitter serotonin, which is believed to be involved in sensory perception. The stimulant caffeine affects neurotransmission in a more complex way, by increasing the amount of a substance (cyclic adenosine monophosphate, or cyclic AMP) that initiates the action of neurotransmitters such as norepinephrine and dopamine. An-

---

thing happens there. Thus the impulse is carried—with no decrease in magnitude—down the length of the cell, like a row of dominos falling over.

If the process sounds slow and clumsy, it isn't—the impulse travels at speeds ranging from 1 to 120 meters per second. The faster speeds occur in cells that are sheathed in myelin. The reason is that the fatty covering over most of the axon insulates the membrane from the fluids outside the cell. Transfer of ions can only take place at breaks in the myelin sheath, called *nodes,* that occur every one or two millimeters along the axon. In these fibers the electrical impulse leaps rapidly from node to node, speeding conduction. The neural impulse cannot travel unimpeded from neuron to neuron like electricity flowing through a circuit. The neural impulse must stop when it comes to the end of an axon. To cross the gap between it and the next neuron—the *synaptic space*—another type of signal is required: a chemical signal.

The Synapse

A synapse can occur anyplace on a neuron, but most often it involves an axon terminal of the transmitting neuron and a dendrite or the cell body of the receiving neuron. The parts of these two cells that are nearly (but not quite)

other stimulant, cocaine, acts by interfering with the mechanism that normally inactivates the neurotransmitters. This slows the reuptake of these substances, so that more transmitter remains in the synapse. Several antidepressant drugs, such as imipramine (Tofranil), work in a similar way—by slowing the reuptake of norepinephrine and serotonin.

In order for the brain to work properly, the proper neurotransmitter must be produced in the proper synapse at just the right time; this substance must be received by the postsynaptic cell, and then be inactivated soon enough so that it does not interfere with the next transmission, but not *too* soon. Given the complexity of the process, it is not surprising that things sometimes go wrong. Two neurological disorders that have been traced to malfunctions of neurotransmission are Parkinson's disease and Huntington's chorea. Parkinson's disease is characterized by tremors and muscular rigidity (especially of the face), and difficulty in making voluntary movements. This disorder has been traced to a deficiency of dopamine in certain parts of the brain. Huntington's chorea is a hereditary disease that first appears in middle age. It is characterized by jerky, uncoordinated motions of the face and body and by progressive mental deterioration. A deficiency of the neurotransmitter GABA is believed to be responsible. Huntington's chorea is carried by a dominant gene, so each child of an affected individual has a 50 percent chance of developing the disease.

You might think that such disorders can be treated simply by supplying the missing substances. That is not always possible, however, because of the *blood-brain barrier*. Nature has evolved a system for protecting the brain from toxic substances that might reach it through its rich supply of blood vessels. Blood vessels in the brain are less permeable than in other parts of the body; in addition, they are closely surrounded by glial cells. Only certain substances, such as oxygen, carbon dioxide, and glucose (blood sugar), can pass through this mesh. Large molecules are generally not accepted, unless they are soluble in the fatty membranes of the glial cells. Thus neither dopamine nor GABA can enter the brain from the bloodstream. For dopamine, there is an alternative: L-DOPA, which does pass through the blood-brain barrier and is metabolized into dopamine in the brain. L-DOPA has been used successfully in the treatment of Parkinson's disease. Unfortunately, no metabolic precursor of GABA has yet been found that will penetrate the brain; thus there is still no effective treatment for Huntington's chorea.

Finally, neurotransmitters are now believed to be involved in several types of mental disorder. The most common of these, schizophrenia, has been tentatively linked with an abnormally high level of dopamine in the brain. Antipsychotic drugs such as chlorpromazine (Thorazine) seem to work by interfering with the uptake of dopamine by the postsynaptic membrane. The causes and treatments of mental disorders will be covered more fully in Chapters 16 and 17.

touching each other are called, respectively, the *presynaptic membrane* and the *postsynaptic membrane* (see Figure 2-6). When a neural impulse arrives at an axon terminal it causes small saclike *vesicles* to release their chemical contents through the presynaptic membrane and into the synaptic space. The released substance, called a *neurotransmitter,* reacts with the postsynaptic membrane and changes the resting potential of the receiving cell.

At some synapses this change is *excitatory*—the resting potential gets closer to the threshold at which a neural impulse is triggered. (If it's already close, release of the neurotransmitter might cause the cell to fire.) Other synapses have an *inhibitory* effect—the neurotransmitter causes an increase in polarization, so that the resting potential of the receiving cell gets further away from the threshold point. Since a cell usually has many, many synapses impinging on it, whether or not it fires at a given moment depends on the results of a kind of vote—if the positives outweigh the negatives, it fires; otherwise it doesn't.

The first neurotransmitter to be identified was acetylcholine (ACh), and for a time neurophysiologists thought that ACh was *the* neurotransmitter. The picture soon became a lot more complicated, and at this point more than 30 substances have been identified as neurotransmitters—for example, amines such

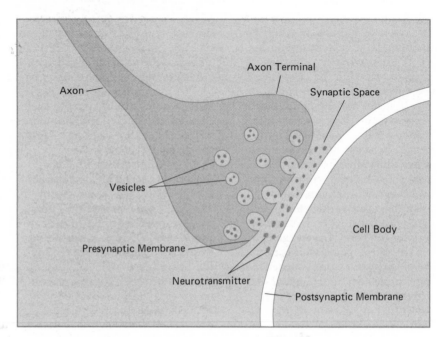

Figure 2-6

Synaptic transmission occurs when the neurotransmitter is released into the synaptic space. Almost immediately, the neurotransmitter is broken down and reabsorbed by the presynaptic membrane in order to clear the way for other transmissions.

as epinephrine, norepinephrine, dopamine, and serotonin; and amino acids such as gamma-aminobutyric acid (GABA) and glutamic acid. Recent research has shown that neurotransmission is involved, in one way or another, in many neurological disorders and in the actions of many drugs and poisons.

The Peripheral Nervous System

The nervous system is organized in a hierarchy of divisions. The first division is between the central nervous system (the brain and the spinal cord) and the peripheral nervous system (the neurons that are located, entirely or in part, outside of the central nervous system). The peripheral nervous system, in turn, can be divided into two classes of neurons: sensory and motor. Sensory neurons are connected to receptor cells located in the skin, in muscles and joints, in internal organs, and in the sense organs. They carry information from these receptors toward the spinal cord or the brain. Motor neurons carry information away from the spinal cord or brain; they form synapses with muscle cells at places called *neuromuscular junctions.*

Psychologists sometimes use the terms *afferent* and *efferent* instead of sensory and motor. Afferent fibers carry impulses *toward* the central nervous system; efferent fibers carry impulses *away* from it. These terms are lamentably difficult to keep straight, but it might help to think of their Latin roots: afferent comes from the root *ad* (toward), as in "admit"; efferent comes from the root *ex* (out), as in "expel."

Motor neurons can be divided into two classes: *somatic* and *autonomic.* The somatic motor system is in charge of the skeletal or *striated* muscles. The autonomic motor system controls the *smooth* muscles (located in the digestive system, other internal organs and glands, and the walls of the blood vessels) and the *cardiac* muscles in the heart. Sometimes striated muscles are described as "voluntary" and smooth muscles as "involuntary," but this distinction is at best a rough approximation. The smooth muscles of the bladder are readily brought under voluntary control, whereas many involuntary movements—called *re-flexes*—are performed by skeletal muscles.

Neurons in the body are generally collected into nerves, which are bundles of parallel fibers covered by membrane. Nerves from the head and neck enter the central nervous system directly into the brain; these are the 12 pairs of *cranial nerves*. Those from below the neck enter the spinal cord as *spinal nerves*. Perhaps the best known nerve is the one that rudely announces its presence when you hit your so-called funny bone: It is the ulnar nerve, which passes close to the surface at the outside of the elbow.

Most nerves contain a mixture of sensory and motor fibers. However, spinal nerves sort themselves out before entering the spinal cord. Sensory fibers enter from the back or dorsal side, forming the *dorsal root;* motor fibers enter from the front or ventral side, forming the *ventral root.*

Peripheral nerves are composed primarily of axons. A somatic motor neuron, for example, has its cell body within the spinal cord and sends out one extremely long axon that may reach all the way to the toe. In the autonomic motor system, on the other hand, the (generally shorter) journey is made in two or three stages: One axon leaves the spinal cord and forms a synapse with another cell, which goes the rest of the way or synapses with a third cell. The many neurons that make up an autonomic nerve all have their synapses and cell bodies in the same place—within a *ganglion,* visible as a bulge on the nerve. Peripheral sensory nerves also have their cell bodies clustered in ganglia; these are located just outside the spinal cord, on the dorsal root.

The Spinal Cord

This column of neural tissue, only about 2 centimeters in diameter, runs downward from the brain through the hollow bones of the spine like a thread through a string of beads. A cross section of the spinal cord (see Figure 2-7) shows two areas that differ somewhat in appearance: a butterfly-shaped area of "gray matter" in the middle, surrounded by "white matter." The grayish area consists mostly of cell bodies, the whitish area of myelinated axons that carry neural impulses upward, downward, or across the cord.

The spinal cord has two major jobs: to carry information back and forth between the body and the brain, and to provide the necessary connections between the sensory and motor neurons involved in reflexes.

REFLEXES.   In a physical examination the doctor usually asks you to cross your legs and then strikes with a rubber hammer just below your kneecap. Unless you inhibit it by tensing your muscles, your leg swings up in the familiar *knee-jerk reflex.* This is a good example of the simplest kind of reflex: the monosynaptic reflex arc. The doctor's hammer strikes a tendon that pulls a muscle and causes it to stretch. The movement fires sensory neurons that go from the muscle all the way to the spinal cord. In the spinal cord the sensory neurons synapse directly onto motor neurons, which lead back to the knee. Thus the impulses received in the spinal cord are "reflected" right back to the muscle, causing it to contract. Figure 2-8 shows the neural pathway of the knee-jerk reflex.

Figure 2-7

The diagram shows a cross-section of the spinal cord, with the dorsal and ventral roots and gray and white matter.

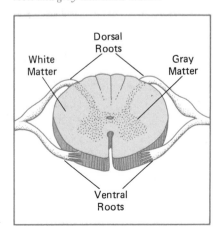

HIGHLIGHT
How We Have Learned What We Know about the Nervous System

It seems strange now to think that the *neuron doctrine*—the idea that the nervous system is not a continuous network but is composed of many separate cells—was generally accepted only in the past 50 or 60 years. The microscope was invented around 1600; yet it was not until the very end of the 19th century that the neuron doctrine was proposed by Ramón y Cajal. There were two reasons for this lag: Neurons are not usually found in isolation but in densely packed groups, and cells do not show up well under a microscope unless they are stained. Early techniques stained entire packs of neurons at once, producing solid blobs of color.

The breakthrough came around 1880, with the invention of the *Golgi stain* by the Spanish physician Camillo Golgi. For rea-

sons that are still obscure, this technique stains only one or two cells out of every hundred. The cells that are stained show up in entirety, from the axon terminals to the thinnest dendrite branches. The stained cells are, in effect, miraculously "dissected out" from their fellows.

Many neurologists, including Golgi himself, at first rejected the neuron doctrine. Opposition to the doctrine gradually dwindled as evidence in its favor accumulated. The matter was definitively settled in the 1950s, when another major technological breakthrough—the electron microscope—finally produced indisputable evidence of the synaptic space.

STUDYING INDIVIDUAL CELLS
Another technological improvement was responsible for most of

our detailed knowledge of how neurons work. This is the *microelectrode*, an electrode made of metallic wire so thin that its tip can actually be pushed inside a living axon without damaging it. With one microelectrode inside the cell and another outside, it is possible to measure the electrical potentials of functioning neurons.

Electrodes can be used to stimulate as well as to record. A stimulating electrode is similar in construction to the recording electrode just described, but it is used to administer a tiny electric shock to one or more neurons. The results may be used to trace neural pathways, or to provide information about the role of some area of the nervous system.

BRAIN AREAS
When it comes to studying areas

Figure 2-8

The neural pathway of the knee-jerk reflex, a monosynaptic reflex arc.

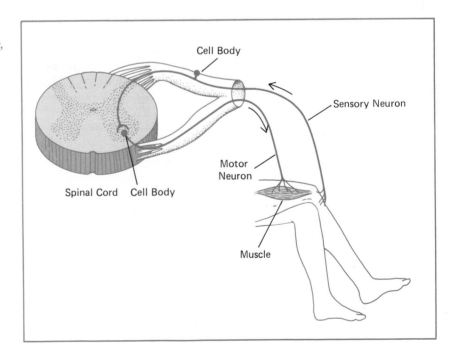

of the brain—whole populations of neurons instead of single cells—a number of techniques have been used. Perhaps the most common of these is the *lesioning method.* Some part of an animal's brain is removed or destroyed, producing an injury known as a *lesion,* and the resulting changes in the animal's behavior (when it has recuperated from the surgery) are noted. The animal most often used in such studies is the laboratory rat, which offers the experimenter the advantages of a brain that has already been extensively mapped and that does not vary much in size or shape. Areas on the surface of the rat's brain can be removed by cutting. Lesions in deeper areas, however, are usually made with electrodes. The rat is anesthetized and put in a *stereotaxic device,* which holds its head stationary. The device also controls the precise placement of electrodes in the rat's brain. An electrode, insulated except at the tip, is inserted stereotaxically to a given depth, and an electric current (strong enough to

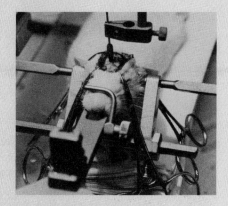

destroy the surrounding tissue) is sent through it.

The stereotaxic device is also used in experiments that use electrical stimulation, rather than destruction, of brain tissue. In this method electrodes are inserted stereotaxically and then used to deliver mild electrical stimulation to the region in question. It is possible to leave the electrode permanently in place, attaching it to the skull with a small plastic carrier.

THE HUMAN BRAIN
Practically everything we know

about the human brain was learned from the brains of people who had something wrong with them. For example, people with some neurological or psychological defect are sometimes autopsied after their death, and their brains are examined. Occasionally an abnormality is found that can be linked with the defect—an injury, a tumor, or even a microscopic irregularity of the cellular architecture.

You may wonder whether data collected from human patients with brain diseases or injuries, or from animals whose brains have been intentionally damaged, can tell us anything about the functioning of a normal brain. The answer is a qualified "yes." Although each individual observation must be considered with caution, in the long run a coherent picture emerges. Scientific knowledge is seldom attained in a single leap: It is gained when results acquired from a number of different sources, using a variety of different techniques, all lead to the same conclusion.

Although this reflex appears to serve no useful purpose other than pleasing your doctor, it is one of a large number of reflexes that make it possible to stand and walk erect. Such reflexes enable you to keep your balance when, for example, someone pushes down unexpectedly on your shoulders or knocks you sideward.

Few reflexes, however, are as simple as the knee jerk. Most involve at least one additional neuron, an interneuron. For instance, when you touch something that is hot and your hand withdraws automatically, the sensory neurons from the finger carry the message to the spinal cord. The message to the arm to withdraw the hand comes out of a *different* level of the spinal cord. To transmit the signal from the sensory neuron at one level to the motor neuron on another, at least one more neuron—and two more synapses—are required. Interneurons are also needed whenever the reflex crosses the spinal cord to the opposite side of the body. If you're barefoot and you step on something sharp, not only does the hurt foot withdraw, but the *other* leg stiffens so you won't fall down.

The signals from the burnt hand or the hurt foot do not stop at the spinal cord. They continue upward to the brain. Only when the message gets to the brain do you become aware of the sensation of pain—by which time your hand or foot has already jerked back. A person whose spinal cord is severed in an accident cannot feel any sensations from the areas of the body innervated (supplied with nerves) by the part of the spinal cord below the break. Yet many reflexes remain intact.

The Brain

Although it makes up only 2 or 2.5 percent of the weight of an adult human body, the brain's rich supply of blood vessels furnish it with about a fifth of the body's circulating blood. It uses a fifth of the body's supply of glucose (blood sugar), and a fifth of the oxygen. If the supply of oxygen is cut off for only 7 or 8 seconds, unconsciousness results; after 1 minute neurons start to degenerate. The same results follow if the supply of glucose is cut off—for example, by an overdose of insulin.

The interior portions of the brain have an additional circulatory system. This is the series of interconnected hollows (ventricles) that are filled with *cerebrospinal fluid,* a plasmalike liquid that aids in the nourishment of brain tissue and the disposal of wastes.

Removed from its protective bony case and deprived of its blood supply, the surface of the brain is grayish in color. This is the "gray matter" or *cortex,* which forms a coating 2 or 3 millimeters thick over most of the outside of the human brain. It is composed chiefly of-cell bodies. Underneath is the "white matter," composed primarily of axon fibers. It gets its whitish coloring from the coating of myelin that covers the axons.

Almost everything that is visible in the intact brain is *cerebrum* (see Figure 2-9). The two hemispheres of the cerebrum, with their wrinkled wrapping of cerebral cortex, resemble the two connected halves of a walnut (without the shell). Poking out from beneath the rear of the cerebrum is the *cerebellum,* with an even more heavily convoluted surface.

Extending downward from between the cerebral hemispheres is the lower

Figure 2-9

A photograph of the human brain.

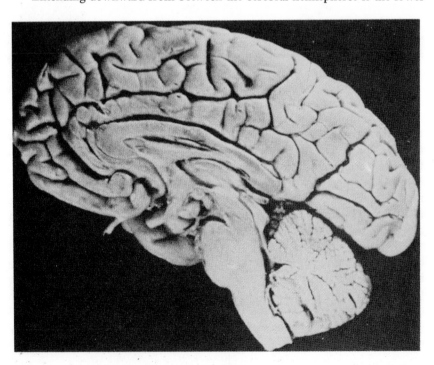

portion of the *brain stem,* which continues through a hole in the base of the skull and becomes the spinal cord. There is no clear-cut separation between the top of the spinal cord and the bottom of the brain; as in many other brain areas, the transition is gradual. But something very important is happening during that transition. Most of the fibers coming from the left side of the spinal cord are crossing over to the right, and vice versa. The left side of the spinal cord serves the left side of the body, but in the brain there is a reversal of this pattern. For reasons that may always remain a mystery, the left side of the brain controls the *right* side of the body, and the right side controls the left side of the body. Thus when a person suffers a stroke and develops paralysis in the left hand or the left side of the face, physicians know that the damage (usually caused by a blocked blood vessel) occurred on the right side of the brain. Fortunately some recovery of function is usually possible, since unaffected brain areas are often able to take over the functions of the dead neurons.

The Organization of the Brain

Neuroanatomists generally divide the brain into three parts: hindbrain, midbrain, and forebrain. In the adult human being, however, this division makes little sense because almost everything is forebrain, and most of the rest is hindbrain. These three divisions arose from structures that serve separate functions in the most primitive vertebrates: the hindbrain for balance and coordination of movement, the midbrain for vision, and the forebrain for smell. Although the organization of the human brain is considerably different and markedly more complicated, the three divisions can still be seen in the human embryo, arising as three separate lumps at the head end of the developing nervous system. Figure 2-10 shows the location of some of the major areas of the human brain.

The Hindbrain
The hindbrain consists of the *medulla,* the *pons,* and the *cerebellum.* The medulla and the pons are two adjacent swellings of the brain stem, just above the spinal cord. The medulla controls some very important involuntary functions such as breathing, heartbeat, and digestion. In addition, several of the cranial nerves enter the brain at this point. Other cranial nerves enter at the pons, which serves mainly as a way station for neural pathways going to other brain areas.

The cerebellum (the name means "little cerebrum") is in charge of body equilibrium, muscle tone, and particularly the regulation of smoothly coordinated movements. Disorders of this brain area, sometimes seen in elderly people, lead to a characteristic kind of tremor that is most noticeable when the hand is making (or attempting to make) a purposeful movement.

The Midbrain
In the submammalian vertebrates the midbrain is the primary area for processing sensory information from the eyes and ears. In mammals that function is

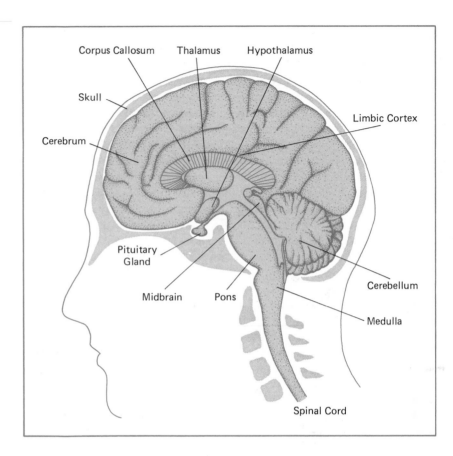

Figure 2-10

A diagram of the human brain, sectioned down the middle.

largely taken over by the cerebral cortex, and the midbrain shrinks in relative size and importance. Some visual and auditory fibers still travel to the midbrain, however. In primates the midbrain's role in vision involves the control of eye movements; it sends out three pairs of cranial nerves to the eye muscles.

The midbrain possesses one other characteristic worthy of note. Many of the neurons that use the neurotransmitter dopamine originate in this area and send their projections upward to the forebrain. These pathways have been implicated in the regulation of complex movements and of emotional responses.

The hindbrain and the midbrain together make up the *brain stem.*

The Reticular Formation

Scattered through the brain stem is an intricate network of cells known collectively as the *reticular formation.* These cells receive inputs from several sensory systems; they send outputs upward to the forebrain. The reticular formation plays an important role in sleep and arousal. When the reticular formation of a sleepy animal is given a small electric shock through an electrode implanted in its brain, the animal immediately becomes alert and attentive.

The Forebrain

The forebrain is composed of two parts: the *diencephalon* and the *cerebrum* (*telencephalon*). The diencephalon contains the *thalamus,* a fairly large bilobed

HIGHLIGHT
"Pleasure Centers" in the Brain

The discovery was made in 1953, at McGill University in Canada. James Olds, who was then a post-doctoral student, and Peter Milner, a graduate student, were testing the effects of electrical stimulation of the reticular formation, using electrodes permanently implanted in the brains of rats. One day an electrode aimed for the reticular formation went astray and ended up—as it was later discovered—in a nerve pathway near the hypothalamus. The rat recovered from the surgery and became a subject in Olds and Milner's experiment: A series of tiny electric shocks, each three or four volts in magnitude, were administered to its brain through the implanted electrode.

The results were surprising. The rat was free to run around in a large cage, and if it happened to be in a certain corner of the cage when the shock went on, it would tend to return to that corner. Olds and Milner soon discovered that they could induce the rat to remain in any part of the cage they chose, simply by administering the shocks only when the rat was in that location. It was clear that the rat was actively seeking electrical stimulation of the brain (ESB), and that it must have found the stimulation in some way pleasurable or rewarding (Olds and Milner, 1954).

Later, a lever was put in the rat's cage. Each time the rat pushed the lever it received an ESB lasting about a second. The animal quickly learned to press the lever, and was soon administering ESBs to itself at a rate of one every 5 seconds. Olds and his associates went on to test many other brain sites, and found that some electrode placements produced even higher rates of responding, up to 5,000 an hour. Rats with electrodes in these sites preferred to stimulate their brains rather than eat or sleep. One rat pressed the lever continuously for 26 hours straight before collapsing in exhaustion.

The brain locations involved include the limbic system and parts of the hypothalamus and the midbrain, all closely linked by extensive neural interconnections. In a rat's brain, that covers a lot of territory: Olds has estimated that almost a third of a rat's brain produces positive ESB results. A much smaller number of brain areas produce negative reactions—the rat will press the lever once by chance, but will thereafter avoid it. These aversive brain sites are often located quite close to the positive sites.

Olds coined the term "pleasure centers" to describe the parts of the brain that produce a positive response to ESB. Rats are not the only species with pleasure centers: The original findings have since been extended to many other animal species, including goldfish, chickens, guinea pigs, rabbits, cats, dogs, dolphins, and monkeys.

There has been considerable speculation about the nature of the rewarding effects of ESB. It was noticed quite soon that some male rats had ejaculations with ESB, and for a while it was thought that the stimulation produced its effects through sexual gratification—that these rats were treating themselves to as many as thousands of orgasms an hour! Clearly, though, sex is not the only motivation involved in ESB. Some positive brain areas are associated with the hunger drive, others with thirst. A leading theory (Deutsch, 1960) of positive ESB effects is that the brain stimulation creates or increases the drive, and at the same time relieves it. However, some brain areas that yield positive ESB results do not seem to be tied to a single drive.

Naturally, one is interested in knowing what effects this kind of ESB would have on a human being. Could one turn a person into a lever-pressing zombie by implanting electrodes in a human brain? Probably not, judging from the small amount of data that is presently available. There are some indications of pleasurable sensations (Sem-Jacobsen and Torkildsen, 1960), but these appear to be fairly mild compared with what animal experiments have led us to expect.

area at the midline of the brain. In mammals, whose cerebral cortex is the main locus for sensory processing, the thalamus is an important way station for receiving information from the various sense organs and relaying it—in an orderly fashion—to the cortex. For example, 80 percent of the axons of the optic nerve go directly to the *lateral geniculate nucleus* in the thalamus. (A nucleus is a ganglion located in the brain.) There these optic fibers synapse with other

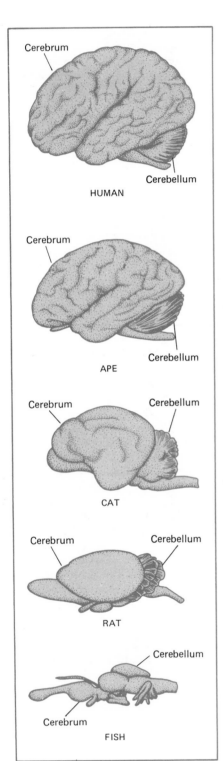

Figure 2-11 *The brains of some repre-*
sentative vertebrates.

neurons that project to the visual area of the cortex. Other nuclei in the thalamus receive information from the ears and from the sensory fibers that come up the spinal cord. This area also receives inputs from the reticular formation and from feedback fibers coming down from the cortex. Clearly, this is a major center for collecting and integrating sensory information.

The other part of the diencephalon is the *hypothalamus,* located (as its name implies) below the thalamus. This is an extremely important part of the brain because of its role in maintaining balance in many of the body's systems. For example, damage to the hypothalamus can disrupt temperature regulation, resulting in death from fever. Another important function of the hypothalamus is the regulation of motivated behavior (such as eating, drinking, and sexual activity) and of emotional responses. The hypothalamus has been somewhat irreverently described as being in charge of the four Fs: fleeing, fighting, feeding, and mating.

Hanging from the hypothalamus like an apple from a tree is the *pituitary gland.* Although this organ is an endocrine gland and not really part of the nervous system, it receives neural inputs from the hypothalamus. Thus there is a connection between neural and hormonal mechanisms in the brain.

The Cerebrum

As Figure 2-11 shows, it is the cerebrum that has undergone the most dramatic increase in size going up the evolutionary ladder from fish to humans. The human cerebrum is composed of two heavily wrinkled hemispheres, which are (in appearance) almost perfect mirror images of each other. The gray carpet of cortex—a layer of cells roughly 2 millimeters thick—extends into the fissures and down the two flat facing sides of the hemispheres, until it is stopped by the *corpus callosum,* a wide band of white matter that connects the two halves.

Under the cortex are several brain areas, known collectively as the *basal ganglia,* that are primarily concerned with the regulation of movement. One of these areas, the *corpus striatum,* receives dopamine-containing fibers from the midbrain. A deficiency of dopamine affects the cells of the corpus striatum, producing Parkinson's disease.

The remainder of the cerebrum can be subdivided into the *limbic system* and the *neocortex.* The limbic system is an oddly assorted set of structures (including the hippocampus, the amygdala, and the septum) that are grouped together on the basis of function rather than anatomy. These structures are responsible for the production and control of emotional responses.

The limbic system receives dopamine-containing fibers from the midbrain; abnormally high levels of dopamine have been found in this area in the brains of deceased schizophrenics (Iverson, 1979). There are also close neural ties between the limbic system and the hypothalamus. In fact, on a strictly functional basis, parts of the hypothalamus can be considered part of the limbic system.

The role of the limbic system in emotionality has been shown by recent experiments performed with animals. Such experiments have shown that electrical stimulation of the amygdala or of certain parts of the hypothalamus (by electrodes permanently implanted in an animal's brain) produces all the signs of rage in laboratory animals. A cat, for example, hisses and bares its teeth and claws. Destruction of the amygdala has a taming effect in most species, resulting in an animal that is totally lacking in aggressiveness. Lesions in the septal area, on the other hand, tend to produce an increase in fear and anger reactions. Sexual disturbances, either hypersexuality or reduced sexuality, are also associated with damage to various parts of the limbic system. Perhaps the most interesting result is the finding of so-called pleasure centers in the limbic system and the related areas of the hypothalamus.

The Neocortex

At last we come to the part of the brain that is responsible for all the things that distinguish humans from animals. The neocortex (often called simply the "cortex") is the outer layer of the cerebrum. This part of the brain began as a thin layer of cells in rodents, developed a few wrinkles in carnivores such as cats, expanded dramatically in the primates, and then suddenly swelled to tremendous proportions—pushing out the walls of the skull in the process—in the human race. The human neocortex has been estimated to contain "no fewer than 70 percent of all the neurons in the central nervous system" (Nauta and Feirtag, 1979). Neuroanatomists divide the neocortex of each hemisphere into four regions or *lobes* (see Figure 2-12); these lobes are separated from one another by landmarks such as the *central fissure* (which goes over the top of the head, cutting across both hemispheres) and the *lateral fissure* (on the side of each hemisphere).

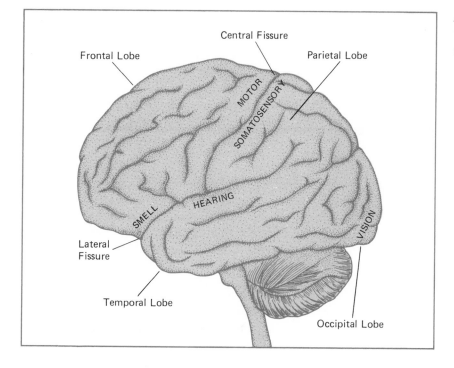

Figure 2-12

The four lobes of the neocortex and several important cortical areas are shown.

Our knowledge of the functions of the neocortex has been greatly expanded by modern techniques of brain surgery. The Canadian neurosurgeon Wilder Penfield perfected a technique in which the patient remains conscious during the operation. The surgeon can then "map" areas of the cortex by applying a small electric current and noting what the patient reports or what movements occur.

Sensory and Motor Areas of the Neocortex

The human neocortex, like that of other mammals, is partly taken up by sensory and motor functions. Two areas that have been extensively mapped are the *somatosensory* and the *motor* areas. These lie in a band that goes over the top of the brain, just behind and just in front of the central fissure.

THE MOTOR CORTEX.   Mild electrical stimulation of a specific point on the motor cortex causes a movement of a specific part of the body. If a point on the right hemisphere is stimulated, a body part on the left side will respond, and vice versa. Moving the electrode to a different spot produces movement of another part of the body. Penfield found that some regions of the body—for instance, the fingers and the face—are represented by relatively large areas of the motor cortex, whereas other parts—the trunk and the legs—are allotted relatively small areas. The right side of Figure 2-13 is a graphic depiction of the resulting map of the motor cortex. In this picture, called a *motor homunculus,* each part of the body is shown larger or smaller, according to how much motor cortex is devoted to it. This is an approximate index of how many neurons serve that body part, which reflects the precision with which it can be controlled.

Figure 2-13

(Left) A cross-section of the somatosensory cortex, and a somatosensory homunculus. The sizes of the body parts are drawn in proportion to the amount of cortex devoted to them.
(Right) A cross-section of the motor cortex of the human cerebrum and a motor homunculus. (After Penfield and Rasmussen, 1950)

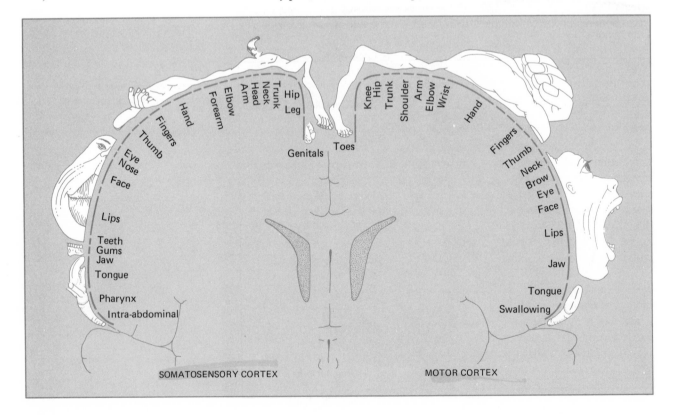

THE SOMATOSENSORY CORTEX.   A similar mapping procedure on the posterior side of the central fissure produces a *somatosensory homunculus,* shown on the left side of Figure 2-13. In this case, the result of the electrical stimulation is a sensation somewhere in the body (again, on the opposite side). The two homunculi are quite similar—the parts of the body, such as the face and hands, that take up a lot of motor cortex also take up a lot of somatosensory cortex. Note that *all* somatosensory information is represented in this brain area: warmth, cold, pressure, pain, and awareness of location and motion of body parts. This information comes from the somatosensory neurons of the spinal cord and of the cranial nerves, and assembles in the thalamus before reaching the cortex. The neural pathways that serve the sense of taste also end up on the somatosensory cortex.

THE AUDITORY CORTEX.   Auditory information from the ears is projected to the auditory cortex, which is just below the lateral fissure. The auditory cortex on each hemisphere receives inputs from *both* ears; however, each hemisphere gets more of its information from the ear on the opposite side of the head. Most neurons in the auditory cortex are "tuned" to sounds of a particular frequency or pitch. That is, a given neuron fires rapidly when sounds of a certain frequency are heard; it fires at slower rates to higher or lower frequencies. Different neurons are tuned to different frequencies.

THE VISUAL CORTEX.   Information from the eyes is carried to the brain by the two optic nerves and ultimately reaches the occipital lobe, in the very back of the head. Information from both eyes reaches both hemispheres, but it is divided up in a rather peculiar way: Neural signals from the right side of each eye reach the right side of the brain, those from the left go to the left side of the brain. This means that the visual field is divided in two. If you stare at the crease between the left- and right-hand pages of this book, the left-hand page is represented on your *right* occipital lobe, the right-hand page on your *left!* In order to accomplish this partition, each optic nerve has to split in half, with the two halves nearest the nose crossing over to go to the opposite side of the brain. The point where they cross is known as the *optic chiasm.*

Association Areas of the Neocortex

If we subtract all sensory and motor areas from the neocortex, the parts that remain are called *association areas.* It is to these areas that we owe our ability to speak, to read, to think, and (no doubt) to laugh. The association areas receive no direct inputs from the outside world; nor do they produce any outputs that result directly in motor responses. As the British brain biochemist Steven Rose (1975) has put it, "Neurons of the association areas talk only to one another and to other cortical neurons."

SPEECH AREAS.   The first part of the neocortex to be correctly assigned a specific function was a region known as *Broca's area,* located near the part of the motor cortex that controls movements of the mouth and jaws (see Figure 2-14). The discovery that this area plays an important role in the production of speech was made in 1861 by the French neurologist Paul Broca. One of Broca's patients was a man called "Tan," who totally lacked meaningful speech although he was able to communicate with gestures. After Tan's death Broca examined his brain and found a lesion just above the lateral fissure, on the left hemisphere.

Figure 2-14

The usual locations of the brain areas that serve language functions are shown on the left cerebral hemisphere. The locations of these language centers vary somewhat from person to person; in some individuals they are on the right hemisphere.

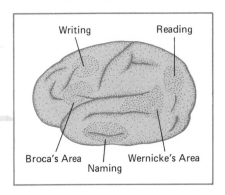

The disorder that Tan had suffered from is called *aphasia*. People with Broca's aphasia are able to understand speech and to use their vocal apparatus in other ways (they can sing, for instance); but they speak—if at all—only with great difficulty. Words are wrested out one by one, and they do not form complete sentences.

A second kind of aphasia was described by Carl Wernicke in 1874. It is associated with a brain area called *Wernicke's area,* located on the lower side of the lateral fissure near the auditory cortex. Damage to Wernicke's area produces a type of language difficulty in which both comprehension and speech are affected. People with Wernicke's aphasia speak fluently and in recognizable sentences, but the content of their speech is often bizarre or nonsensical.

The kind of brain damage that produces Broca's or Wernicke's aphasia usually involves only one hemisphere—the left, in most cases. Injuries to the same areas on the right side generally do not affect language ability. This fact, noted by Broca himself, was the first indication that the two hemispheres are not identical in function. We will now take a closer look at the differences between the two sides of the brain.

Right and Left Brain

When a person suffers a massive injury to the left hemisphere of the brain (most often because of a stroke), there are usually two results: paralysis of all or part of the right side of the body, and a loss of the use of language. Perhaps a double-edged tragedy of this kind served as the inspiration for the Psalmist who wrote: "If I forget thee, O Jerusalem, let my right hand forget her cunning. If I do not remember thee, let my tongue cleave to the roof of my mouth" (Psalm 137).

The connection between speech and handedness has been known for over a century—it was too obvious to miss. Most people use the left side of the brain to process language, and the right hand—which is controlled by the left side of the brain—to perform tasks that require skill. A little more than 90 percent of humans are right-handed, and this preponderance has prevailed for at least 5,000 years (Coren and Porac, 1977) and probably goes back to the earliest hominids (Dart, 1949). Apes, however, like subprimate vertebrates, do not tend to right-dominance. In most animal species individual members may favor one paw over the other, but the favored side is as likely to be the left as the right (Corballis and Beale, 1976).

The fact that the left side of the brain generally controls both the dominant hand and the ability to speak led some psychologists to dub it the "dominant hemisphere," and to wonder whether the right side might be just another one of those useless parts that we have inherited from our animal ancestors. There are two reasons why this view is no longer popularly held. First, there is the problem of left-handers. Second, there is the fact, recognized only in recent years, that the right side of the brain has its uses, too.

LEFT-HANDED PEOPLE.   If right-hand, left-brain dominance is charac-teristically human, how do we account for left-handers? One possibility is that they were simply formed backward, like the supposed "mirror-image twin." There *are* sets of twins whose hair and fingerprints whorl in opposite directions, but the overwhelming majority of twins—and of left-handed people—have their

*Table 2–1: The Location of the Brain Area Devoted to Speech, and
Its Relationship to Handedness.*

	Right-Handed People	Left-Handed and Ambidextrous People
Speech on left hemisphere	92%	69%
Speech on right hemisphere	7%	18%
Speech on both hemispheres	1%	13%

From Milner, Branch, and Rasmussen (1966).

insides formed just like everybody else's: The asymmetrical locations of the heart, the stomach, and the intestines are normal. There are very, very few truly "backward" people, and they are not necessarily left-handed.

Another puzzle is that although the speech centers of right-handers are almost invariably in the left hemisphere, these centers are not always in the right hemisphere in left-handers. As Table 2-1 shows, most left-handers process language with the hemisphere associated with their *non*dominant hand. Still more perplexing, a considerable proportion have speech centers on *both* sides of the brain.

Some psychologists have proposed that these atypical cases are the results of early brain injuries: If the left side of the brain is injured (at birth, say), the right takes over some of its duties. That this can happen is unquestionable. Stroke victims often regain many of their abilities, as cells surrounding the damaged tissue, or in the same location on the opposite hemisphere, take over some of the functions of the dead neurons. If an injury to the left hemisphere occurs early enough—in the first year or two of life—there is often no language deficit. However, there is no evidence that brain damage is responsible for left-handedness. Quite the contrary. Left-handers are known to recover their language abilities after a stroke more rapidly than right-handers, and this would not be likely if part of the brain had already been damaged. People who are right-handed but have close relatives who are left-handers also have a more favorable prognosis for recovery of speech after a stroke.

Clearly, there is a hereditary component to handedness. If both your parents are right-handed, the probability of your being left-handed is only 8 percent; if one parent is left-handed, it is 20 percent; if both are left-handed, it is 55 percent (Rife, 1940). Note that if left-handedness were a simple one-gene recessive trait, the children of two left-handers should all be left-handed.

A theory to account for all of these findings was first proposed by Annett (1972) and later elaborated by Corballis and Beale (1976). According to this theory, two factors are involved in the lateralization (sidedness) of the hand and brain: an inherited component and a random component. You inherit either a tendency toward lateralization or a tendency toward symmetry. In the former case, you are right-handed and have your speech centers on the left hemisphere. In the latter case, you have no innate tendency toward lateralization, and the random component takes over: Both handedness and lateralization of the brain are determined by chance.

WHAT THE OTHER HEMISPHERE DOES.   An ordinary right-handed person with speech centers in the normal place on the left hemisphere *does* suffer deficits if damage occurs to the right side of the brain. For example, there is an impairment of the ability to perceive the emotional responses of other people (Geshwind, 1979). An ordinary person with a lesion on the language side of the brain may not understand the meaning of what someone else is saying, but will understand that the speaker is angry, or is joking. In contrast, a person with a lesion on the right hemisphere will understand the words, but may be unable to recognize the emotional tone. This person may show further signs of emotional impairment, such as unconcern about any other disabilities that resulted from the brain injury.

Many other specialized functions are believed to be represented primarily on the right hemisphere: for example, perception of melody, of nonverbal patterns, and of spatial relationships. However, the two sides of the brain normally work together, and there are usually no signs of their differing roles. Information is carried freely back and forth between the two hemispheres by the wide band of tissue known as the corpus callosum, or the "great cerebral commissure." What happens, though, if the corpus callosum is severed?

Split-Brain People and Animals

In addition to providing for routine communication between the two sides of the brain, the corpus callosum allows the abnormal electrical discharges that cause epileptic seizures to spread from one hemisphere to another. In an attempt to control this disability and confine the seizures to one hemisphere, a daring surgical procedure was carried out in 1961 by P. J. Vogel and J. E. Bogen of the California College of Medicine. They severed the corpus callosum and one or two other smaller commissures that link the two sides of the cerebrum together.

The "split-brain" operation served the purpose it was designed for — in fact, it eliminated almost all epileptic attacks, even those confined to one hemisphere. More remarkably, the small group of people who underwent this surgery appeared to the casual observer to be completely normal. They showed no noticeable changes either in intelligence or in personality. One patient awoke after the operation and, still drowsy from the anesthetic, joked that he had a "splitting headache" (Gazzaniga, 1967).

It took some fairly subtle psychological testing to reveal the strange kinds of deficits that the surgery produced. A series of experiments reported by Gazzaniga demonstrated these deficits. When an object such as a pencil was placed in the right (dominant) hand of one of the split-brain subjects, he easily identified it by touch and said "pencil." But if the pencil was placed in his left hand and the subject couldn't see it, he could not say what the object was. Yet there was nothing wrong with the hand itself: The subject could identify the object by pointing (with his left hand) to a card on which the word "pencil" was printed, or he could use the left hand to pick out a pencil from among a group of objects hidden from view behind a screen. It was simply that information from the left hand was delivered to the right hemisphere, and the right hemisphere could not speak. Because the corpus callosum had been severed, the information never reached the speech centers on the left hemisphere. The left hemisphere didn't have the slightest idea what the left hand was holding!

Similar results were found if words or pictures were shown to only one hemisphere. This experiment made use of the fact that the visual field is split down the middle, with half going to the left hemisphere, half to the right. If a normal person looks at a point on a screen and a picture is flashed on the screen too briefly to allow eye movements, the part of the picture to the right of the point goes to the left hemisphere; the part to the left goes to the right hemisphere. This technique was used with the split-brain subjects. In one experiment the word "heart" was flashed on the screen with "he" on one side of the point and "art" on the other. If the subject was asked what he saw, he said "art"—the part of the word transmitted to the left (speaking) side of his brain. But if he was asked instead to point with his left hand to the word he had seen, he pointed to a card that said "he." Notice that neither hemisphere knew that the word had been "heart." Notice also that although the right hemisphere was unable to speak, it was able to read and to understand spoken commands.

The split-brain patient is in the curious position of having two separate minds in a single body. The left mind has language and can readily communicate its experiences. The right mind, though not as verbal, can perform many acts independently. It can actually do some things *better* than the left mind. For instance, it is better at arranging blocks to match a given pattern, and at drawing pictures of figures such as cubes. The drawings made with the left hand are clumsy but fairly accurate; the drawings made with the right hand are neater, but wrong.

The two minds of a split-brain patient are each capable of learning and remembering, but the memories of each are not accessible to the other side. Experiments with split-brain animals have made this apparent. When the corpus callosum of an animal is severed, the result is two approximately equal hemispheres. If the right hemisphere of such an animal is taught to discriminate (with its left paw) between two different shapes, it turns out that the left hemisphere has learned nothing. It takes the left hemisphere just as long to learn the discrimination as it took the right hemisphere (Sperry, 1964).

The fact that split-brain animals and people have two independent minds should not be taken to mean that everybody has. In the intact brain there is complete, immediate, and constant communication between the two hemispheres. Learning and memories are shared. Each side has full access to the special talents and abilities of the other half. That is why consciousness in a person with a complete corpus callosum is unitary. The Russian poet Osip Mandelstam has written, "A leap—and my mind is whole."

The Autonomic Nervous System and the Endocrine Glands

Earlier we said that the motor division of the peripheral nervous system has two parts: somatic and autonomic. So far we have concentrated primarily on the somatic motor system, which innervates striated (skeletal) muscles. Now we return to the autonomic motor system, which innervates two kinds of muscles: the smooth muscles of the glands and internal organs, and the specialized cardiac muscles of the heart. It is because these muscles generally function without voluntary control (although voluntary control can often be imposed upon them) that we call this system *autonomic* ("self-governed").

The autonomic system itself has two divisions: *sympathetic* and *parasympathetic*. Most organs and glands are innervated by both the sympathetic and the parasympathetic systems, which have opposing effects on them. The sympathetic system is concerned, to a large extent, with emergency situations and stress, whereas the parasympathetic system maintains the routine "vegetative" functions such as digestion. Another way of putting it is that the sympathetic system is associated with activation and expenditure of energy, while the parasympathetic system tends to conserve energy.

Inputs to the autonomic nervous system come from a number of areas of the central nervous system. In general, such inputs do not come directly but make many connections along the way. One important pathway starts in the sensory areas of the neocortex and filters downward through the association areas, the limbic system, the hypothalamus, the reticular formation, and the spinal cord. This pathway would be used when, for example, you see or hear something frightening. The physiological responses that accompany the feeling of fear—accelerated heart rate and breathing, increase in blood pressure, inhibition of digestion, and so on—are produced by the action of the sympathetic nervous system. These physiological responses are counteracted by the opposing effects of the parasympathetic nervous system, which tends to return the activity of the organs to their normal levels.

Anatomy of the Autonomic Nervous System

SYMPATHETIC.   As shown in Figure 2-15, neurons of the sympathetic system exit from the central portion of the spinal cord, below the neck and above the small of the back. Each of these neurons synapses immediately within one of the ganglia of the *sympathetic chains*. There are two of these long chains of ganglia, one lying along each side of the spinal cord.

Some of the axons that leave the sympathetic chain go directly to the organs they innervate. Others travel to secondary ganglia and synapse with another set of neurons that go the rest of the way. A secondary sympathetic ganglion is known as a *plexus;* the best known of these is the solar plexus, located behind the stomach.

Because all the neurons of the sympathetic system come together in the sympathetic chain, they tend to work in unison. The effects produced by this system and by the parasympathetic system are shown in Figure 2-15.

PARASYMPATHETIC.   Parasympathetic motor fibers leave the central nervous system from one of two locations: from the very bottom of the spinal cord, or directly from the brain in a cranial nerve. One of the cranial nerves, the *vagus* nerve, is the only exception to the rule that cranial nerves serve the head and neck. Some of the axons in this nerve provide the parasympathetic innervation of the heart, the lungs, and the digestive system.

Parasympathetic neurons also form ganglia, but these are generally located near the organs they help control. Because the parasympathetic system has no

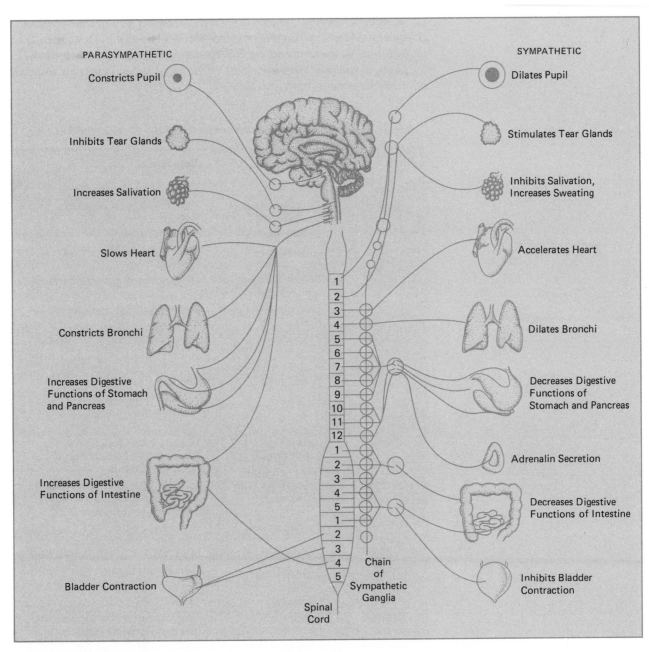

PARASYMPATHETIC

Constricts Pupil

Inhibits Tear Glands

Increases Salivation

Slows Heart

Constricts Bronchi

Increases Digestive
Functions of Stomach
and Pancreas

Increases Digestive
Functions of Intestine

Bladder Contraction

SYMPATHETIC

Dilates Pupil

Stimulates Tear Glands

Inhibits Salivation,
Increases Sweating

Accelerates Heart

Dilates Bronchi

Decreases Digestive
Functions of
Stomach and Pancreas

Adrenalin Secretion

Decreases Digestive
Functions of Intestine

Inhibits Bladder
Contraction

Chain
of
Sympathetic
Ganglia

Spinal
Cord

unifying structure like the sympathetic chain, the parasympathetic ganglia are more independent of one another than the sympathetic ganglia, and do not necessarily act in concert. Moreover, some parts of the body receive sympathetic innervation but not parasympathetic—the sweat glands, the hair follicles, and the smaller blood vessels.

The Endocrine System
The glands of the endocrine system interact closely with one another and with

Figure 2-15

The parasympathetic (left) and sympathetic (right) nervous systems. Parasympathetic nerves arise from the brain and from the base of the spinal cord, sympathetic nerves from the remainder of the spinal cord. Nevertheless, the two sets of nerves serve the same organs.

the autonomic nervous system to regulate a number of vital metabolic and physiological functions. Endocrine glands are *ductless*—that is, they secrete their hormones or "chemical messengers" directly into the bloodstream, which carries the hormones all over the body. A list of the major endocrine glands and their principal hormones is given in Table 2-2.

Table 2–2: Major Glands and Hormones of the Endocrine System.

Gland	Hormone	Main Effect
Pituitary		
Anterior lobe	Adrenocorticotropic hormone (ACTH)	Stimulates adrenal cortex to produce steroids
	Growth hormone	Stimulates growth
	Thyrotropin	Stimulates thyroid to produce thyroxin
	Follicle-stimulating hormone (FSH)	Development of ova and sperm
	Luteinizing hormone (LH)	Maturation of ova and sperm; ovulation
	Prolactin	Production of milk in nursing female
Posterior lobe	Antidiuretic hormone (Vasopressin)	Prevents excess loss of fluids through urination
	Oxytocin	Uterine contractions, release of milk during nursing
Adrenal		
Cortex	Steroids (e.g., Cortisol)	Increase of blood glucose. Maintenance of metabolism and level of minerals in body
Medulla	Epinephrine (Adrenalin)	Increases blood pressure, heart rate, blood glucose, and perspiration. Stimulates production of ACTH
	Norepinephrine	Increases blood pressure, slows heart rate. Stimulates production of ACTH
Thyroid	Thyroxin	Increases metabolism
Pancreas		
Alpha cells	Glucagon	Increases blood glucose
Beta cells	Insulin	Enables body cells to use glucose (thereby decreasing blood glucose)
Parathyroid	Parathormone	Maintains level of calcium in blood
Ovaries (in female)	Estrogens	Development of female reproductive organs, secondary sex characteristics, and sexual behavior
	Progesterone	Thickening of lining of uterus and maintenance of pregnancy
Testes (in male)	Androgens (e.g., Testosterone)	Development of male reproductive organs, secondary sex characteristics, and sexual behavior

Each hormone exerts its effects on a target organ somewhere in the body. In some cases, the target organs themselves are other endocrine glands. Hormones that control the secretion of other hormones are described as *tropic.*

The primary secretor of tropic hormones is the *pituitary gland,* located at the base of the brain and attached by a stalk to the hypothalamus. Because of its influence on many of the other endocrine glands, this tiny organ is often called the "master gland."

The pituitary consists of two parts, the *anterior* and the *posterior.* The anterior pituitary puts out several tropic hormones that regulate the functions of other glands. It, in turn, is regulated by the hypothalamus. For example, if the blood level of the hormone *thyroxin* becomes too low, the hypothalamus reacts by stimulating the anterior pituitary to secrete the hormone *thyrotropin.* Thyrotropin, released into the bloodstream, reaches the thyroid gland (located in the neck) and causes it to secrete more thyroxin. Thyroxin is important in the maintenance of the body's rate of metabolism. Too little thyroxin produces a condition known as *hypothyroidism,* which is associated with depression and fatigue. Hypothyroidism is particularly dangerous in childhood, when it causes a serious retardation of growth and mental development. Too much thyroxin also has ill effects: It produces *hyperthyroidism,* which leads to irritability, restlessness, and weight loss.

The anterior pituitary puts out several other important hormones. One of these is the *growth hormone,* too much of which results in a giant, too little in a dwarf. The *gonadotropic hormones* stimulate the ovaries to secrete the female sex hormones, the testes to secrete the male sex hormones.

STRESS HORMONES.   Two endocrine glands act with the autonomic nervous system to generate the body's reaction to fear and other forms of stress. The hormonal response to stress begins when the hypothalamus triggers the anterior pituitary to release *adrenocorticotropic hormone* (ACTH). The target of this hormone is the outer surface (cortex) of the adrenal glands, located on top of the kidneys. In response to stimulation by ACTH, the adrenal cortex secretes hormones called *steroids,* which regulate the blood levels of glucose and of certain minerals (sodium, potassium, and chloride). In addition, the hypothalamus acts through the sympathetic nervous system to stimulate the inner part of the adrenal gland—the adrenal medulla—to secrete *epinephrine* (also called "adrenalin") and *norepinephrine.* These hormones complement the action of the sympathetic nervous system. For example, they increase glucose levels and raise blood pressure. Their effects will be examined in more detail in Chapter 11, Human Motivation and Emotion, in the section on emotion.

We have already discussed norepinephrine in its role as a neurotransmitter in the brain. The same substance, secreted by the adrenal medulla instead of by the presynaptic membrane, acts as a hormone. The two functions of norepinephrine are kept separate by the blood-brain barrier, which prevents most of the circulating norepinephrine from entering the brain.

We are only beginning to understand the complex relationships between hormones and neurotransmitters, between chemistry and behavior. Research in this field is currently very active, and likely to produce exciting results.

Summary

1.   A person's heredity is determined by the *genes,* located on the *chromosomes* in the nuclei of body cells.

2.   The nervous system has two divisions: the *central nervous system,* consisting of the brain and spinal cord, and the *peripheral nervous system,* consisting of all the neurons outside the brain and spinal cord. Peripheral neurons are either *sensory* or *motor.*

3.   A *neuron* is a cell that transmits information; the message is transmitted by means of a pulse of electrical energy that travels down the neuron's axon to the axon terminals at the axon tip; this pulse is the *action potential.*

4.   The transfer of information between two neurons takes place at a junction called the *synapse;* for a message to cross the synaptic space a substance called a *neurotransmitter* is released, sending a chemical signal from one neuron to another.

5.   The spinal cord carries information between the brain and the body and also provides the connections between the sensory and motor neurons involved in spinal reflexes.

6.   The hindbrain consists of the *medulla,* the *pons,* and the *cerebellum;* the cerebellum is in charge of equilibrium, muscle tone, and coordination. The hindbrain and the midbrain comprise the *brain stem.*

7.   Scattered throughout the brain stem is an intricate network of cells known as the *reticular formation;* this system has a role in sleep and arousal.

8.   The forebrain consists of the *thalamus,* the *hypothalamus,* and the *cerebrum.* The thalamus is an important collection and integration center for sensory information; the hypothalamus regulates motivated behavior and maintains a balance in many body systems.

9.   The cerebrum includes the *limbic system,* which plays a major role in emotional behavior, and the *neocortex,* which contains about 70 percent of all neurons in the central nervous system.

10.   Some areas of the neocortex have specialized functions; these areas include the *motor cortex,* the *visual cortex,* the *auditory cortex,* and the *somatosensory cortex* (which receives sensory information from the skin, joints and muscles, and internal organs). Such abilities as thinking, speaking, and reading are localized in the *association areas* of the cortex.

11.   The cerebrum consists of a right hemisphere and a left hemisphere; the left hemisphere controls the right side of the body. Language abilities are generally localized in the left hemisphere; the right hemisphere may function in abilities such as spatial relationships and perception of nonverbal patterns.

12.   The peripheral motor system has two divisions: *somatic* and *autonomic.* The somatic motor system innervates skeletal muscles. The autonomic system is

composed of two subdivisions, the *sympathetic* and the *parasympathetic*. The sympathetic system is associated with activation and expenditure of energy (especially in stress situations), and the parasympathetic system is associated with the maintenance of routine functions such as digestion.

13. The *endocrine system* consists of glands which secrete hormones that regulate a number of vital metabolic and physiologic functions; the endocrine system interacts closely with the autonomic nervous system.

Suggested Readings

The Brain (A Scientific American Book). San Francisco: Freeman, 1979. This is a paperback edition of the September, 1979, issue of *Scientific American*, containing 11 articles by eminent brain researchers. Superbly illustrated.

CORBALLIS, M. C., and BEALE, I. L. *The Psychology of Left and Right.* Hillsdale, NJ: Erlbaum, 1976. Left-right confusions, mirror images, and the psychology and biology of handedness and brain lateralization.

GAZZANIGA, M. S. *The Bisected Brain.* New York: Appleton, 1970. A leading investigator describes in detail the effects of split-brain surgery.

KAPLAN, A. R. (Ed.). *Human Behavior Genetics.* Springfield, Ill.: Thomas, 1976. Discusses genetic aspects of behavior, twin studies, schizophrenia, personality, and intelligence.

LEVINTHAL, C. F. *The Physiological Approach in Psychology.* Englewood Cliffs, NJ: Prentice-Hall, 1979. Lucid coverage of a wide range of topics in physiological psychology. Particularly informative on hormones, neurotransmitters, and nervous system chemistry.

ROSE, S. *The Conscious Brain.* New York: Knopf, 1975. A personal account of brain research by a British scientist. Written in a clear and interesting manner, but with a strong anti-American bias.

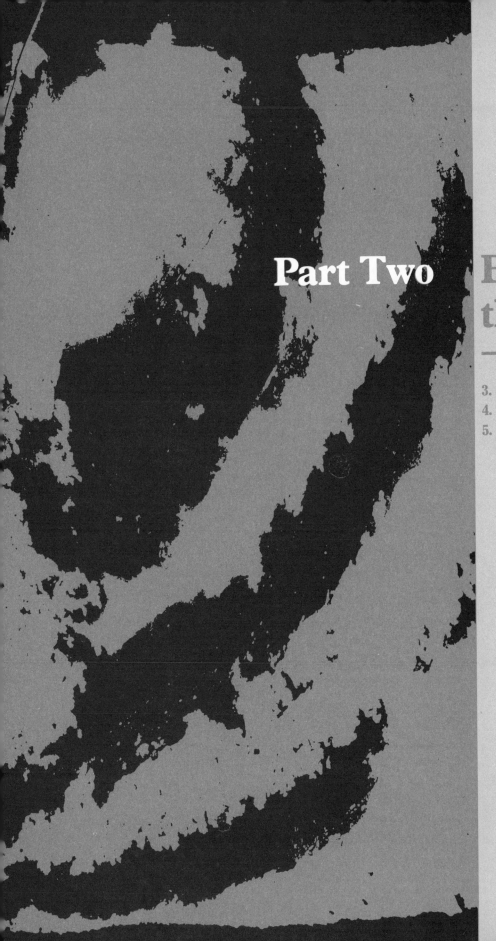

Part Two

Experiencing the World

3

Sensation

All our lives our brains remain in total darkness, insulated from the outside world by layers of flesh and bone. All knowledge of that world is carried into the brain through the sensory systems. These systems respond to certain aspects of the environment to produce subjective sensations such as light, sound, and taste. This chapter considers exactly how each sensory system does this.

It should be understood at the outset that sensations are private or subjective events. You may describe your sensations to others, but no one else can directly experience them. Nevertheless, if a particular change in the physical environment evokes similar reports from many different people, it seems reasonable to assume that they experienced similar sensations. For example, turning up the volume control on a phonograph causes most listeners to describe the sound as growing louder. This shows a consistent relationship between a physical stimulus (the amount of energy coming from the loudspeaker) and the listeners' sensations (or at least their descriptions of what they hear). Relations of this sort are often referred to as *psychophysical relations,* since they seem to relate physical and psychological variables (stimuli and sensations).

We must be very careful in making inferences about sensations on the basis of verbal reports. Such reports not only are limited by a subject's verbal skills, but they are also easily influenced by what subjects expect to experience. Magicians often make use of spectators' expectations to trick them into believing they saw or heard or felt things that didn't actually occur. If you hold an open paper bag at arm's length and covertly snap a finger against the bag while passing the other hand above the bag, your audience will usually report seeing you drop something into the bag. The sound of something striking the bag influences their visual perception, because the sequence of sound and arm movement is so highly correlated with the event they thought they had seen.

Such judgmental biases and expectancies not only play a role in magicians' illusions, they also color almost all of your everyday experience, most often in ways that aid perception. The underlying reason for this is that activity in your various sensory systems is highly correlated, or *redundant.* For example, when people speak to you, the movement of their lips is highly correlated with the sound of their voice. We use this correlation or redundancy between the visual and auditory sensations so automatically that ventriloquists can trick us into attributing the source of their voice to their dummy, simply because it is the dummy's mouth that moves. In many circumstances this automatic connection of sight and sound is very useful; it allows us, for example, to visually keep track of a person's conversation at a crowded party when voice sounds are sometimes partially obscured. In fact, many deaf people learn to understand speech through lip reading alone.

The redundancy that operates in all normal perceptual processes makes it difficult to judge just what was involved in any one sensory event. Only by carefully controlling stimulus redundancy and by asking subjects very simple questions about their sensations is it possible to reveal consistent psychophysical relationships that shed light on the nature of our sensory systems. Thus, before describing the individual sensory systems, we shall consider some generally useful techniques for establishing psychophysical relationships.

Measuring Sensory Capacities

Sensory Limits

Each sensory system is sensitive to some form of physical energy. Our auditory system responds to certain rapid variations in air pressure (sound), while our visual system responds to specific forms of electromagnetic energy (light). But we aren't sensitive to every aspect of our environment; there are limits to our sensitivity. First, we can sense only forms of energy for which we have "receivers" or *receptor organs* (eyes, ears, etc.). For example, we are surrounded by electromagnetic energy coming from many radio and television stations, yet unless we have the radio or television turned on we see and hear none of it. Secondly, energy must be intense enough to produce a noticeable sensation: A source of light must be strong enough for us to see it; a source of sound must be intense enough for us to hear it.

Some of the earliest work in experimental psychology (by Fechner in 1860) was aimed at assessing our sensory limits. Psychologists found that by varying the strength or intensity of a stimulus, they could determine the minimum level capable of evoking a sensation. This level, called the *absolute threshold* for the stimulus, marks the boundary between energy levels strong enough to evoke a noticeable sensation and those too weak to do so. Another kind of sensory limit was defined by our ability to notice a *change* in sensation. For example, a source of light has to be changed (increased or decreased) a minimum amount for someone to notice that change. Again, early experimental psychologists tried to measure exactly how small a difference in a physical stimulus would be noticed. They referred to this as the *difference threshold.*

The methods developed to measure absolute and difference thresholds were the earliest attempts at precise measurement in psychology. They are still of interest, not only on historical grounds, but also because they are simple and adequate for most purposes.

Measuring Absolute and Difference Thresholds

You can obtain a rough measure of an absolute threshold simply by asking a subject to adjust a stimulus intensity until it just begins to evoke a sensation; for example, "Slowly increase the energy level of this light source by turning this knob until you just begin to see the light." For many purposes, the method of adjustment is a perfectly good procedure and leads to a reasonably consistent measure of the absolute threshold. Yet certain problems emerge when you attempt to be more precise. First of all, subjects won't be entirely consistent if asked to repeat this procedure; they will set the threshold intensity at a slightly different value each time. Nor will they indicate exactly the same threshold intensity if asked to reverse the procedure—that is, to begin with a high intensity and slowly reduce it until the sensation disappears.

In an attempt to obtain more consistent threshold measures, the *method of constant stimuli* was developed. A fixed set of stimulus intensities was repeatedly presented in a randomly determined sequence over a series of test trials. On each trial one intensity was presented and subjects reported whether or not they experienced any sensation; for example, "Yes, I saw the light that time," or "No, I didn't see anything that time." Ideally this method would reveal an intensity level above which subjects always reported a sensation, and below which they never did. Unfortunately, things are not quite that simple. The nature of the problem is illustrated in Figure 3-1. Between the high intensities, which almost always evoked a yes report, and the very low intensities, which almost never did, there was a middle range where the proportion of reported sensations gradually increased with the intensity. Stimuli in this range sometimes evoked a sensation and at other times did not. What, then, should be called the absolute threshold? It was decided that the most reasonable answer was to call the absolute threshold the intensity that had a 50 percent chance of evoking a sensation. Figure 3-1 shows how this threshold was calculated.

In measuring difference thresholds, instead of varying the absolute level of the stimulus, a series of stimulus *differences* was presented to a subject, who reported whether or not they evoked different sensations. ("Did the light seem to change its appearance?" "Is this sound louder than that sound?") The same general pattern of results emerged: There was a range of stimulus differences so small they almost never evoked a reported change in sensation, a range of large differences that almost always did, and a middle range in which the proportion of noticeable differences increased slowly with the size of the stimulus difference.

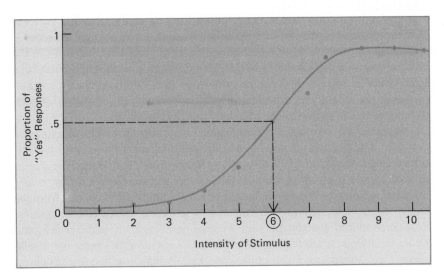

Figure 3-1

The absolute threshold of a stimulus is the intensity that has a 50 percent chance of evoking a sensation. As shown in the graph here, when the intensity reaches the point at which subjects respond "yes" 50 percent of the time, this intensity is called the absolute threshold of the stimulus.

Table 3–1: Some Typical Values of Weber's Constant for Various Types of Stimuli.

Type of Stimulus	Weber's Constant
Electric Shock	.01
Heaviness	.02
Length	.03
Vibration	.04
Loudness	.05
Brightness	.08

After Teghtsonian (1971).

Thus the graph in Figure 3-1 is also characteristic of difference threshold data, only here the units would refer to the size of the stimulus difference. Again, the best measure of the difference threshold seems to be the physical difference that is noticed 50 percent of the time. This difference threshold has often been referred to as the *just noticeable difference (JND)*.

A very general feature of difference thresholds was apparent long before formal measurement techniques were developed: People are usually more sensitive to changes in weak stimuli than they are to similar changes in stronger or more intense stimuli. For example, if you were listening to a voice in an otherwise quiet room, you would readily notice the addition of a second voice. Yet the addition of one voice to the chatter of many voices at a large cocktail party would probably go unnoticed. Similarly, you would probably notice a difference in weight between an empty paper cup and one containing a penny, yet you wouldn't notice a difference between a cup containing 100 pennies and one holding 101, even though the difference in weight (one penny) is exactly the same in both cases.

In 1834 a German psychophysicist named Ernst Weber suggested that the difference threshold (JND) for each type of stimulus is a constant fraction or proportion (K) of the stimulus being changed; that is, that the JND equals K times the intensity of the stimulus. This is often referred to as *Weber's law,* and the constant of proportionality (K) is called *Weber's constant.* For example, Weber's constant for lifted weights, or heaviness, is about .02. This means that the JND for a 50-gram weight is .02 times 50 grams, or 1 gram, while the JND for a 500-gram weight is .02 times 500 grams, or 10 grams. Table 3-1 indicates some typical values of Weber's constant for other types of stimuli.

More recent research indicates that Weber's law should be viewed as only a rough characterization of our sensitivity to changes in stimulation. It fails in the case of very weak or very intense stimuli, and is only approximately true for the middle range of stimuli. Nevertheless, it is a useful, general approximation of human sensitivity to stimulus differences.

Psychophysical Scaling

Sensory limits are only one aspect of our sensory capacities. Another aspect is how the strength or quality of a sensation changes as the physical stimulus is changed. For example, how rapidly does loudness grow with increases in the physical intensity of a sound? How does brightness grow as the energy level of a light source is increased? Attempts to answer such questions have produced measurement techniques called *psychophysical scaling.* The function of such techniques can be shown by the following practical problem.

Suppose you were asked to design a volume control for a phonograph that produced a subjectively constant increase in loudness as the control knob is turned clockwise for one full revolution (360 degrees); that is, each degree of rotation should seem to increase the loudness by the same amount. You might consider building the control so that the physical sound energy coming from the loudspeakers increased at a constant rate as the knob turned (each degree of rotation produced exactly the same increase in energy). If you did this, you would be disappointed, for the same amount of rotation (the same increase in energy) would produce much larger changes in loudness at the lower volume settings than at the higher ones. A more satisfactory system—and the one actually used in most volume controls—is indicated in Figure 3-2. Only if a given rotation produces progressively larger increases in sound energy as the knob is turned will listeners hear a constant growth in loudness (broken line).

You might agree, as did Gustav Fechner in 1860, that the relation between sound energy and loudness could be predicted from Weber's study of difference thresholds. The argument goes something like this. If the JND is the smallest noticeable difference in sensation, then larger differences could be considered the sum of many JNDs. Since Weber's law states that the size of a JND increases as stimulus intensity increases, progressively larger increases in intensity should be required to produce the same difference in sensation. Fechner showed that this argument implies that the relation between physical stimulus intensity and the strength of sensation is a logarithmic one in which a constant *ratio* of stimulus intensity produces a constant *difference* in sensation. This logarithmic relation, often referred to as *Fechner's law,* implies that an increase in weight from 50 to 100 grams, for example, should produce the same increase in the sensation of heaviness as an increase from 25 to 50 grams, or from 100 to 200.

Fechner's law has proven to be less generally applicable than he had hoped. This is partly because Weber's law itself is only a rough approximation (it tends to fail at extreme intensity levels), and partly because there are more direct ways of measuring the relations between physical stimulus variables and sensation.

In 1956 S. S. Stevens showed that you could ask subjects to specify the strength of a sensation simply by assigning it a number. He called this method *magnitude estimation.* For example, you could present a stimulus of a certain light intensity and tell subjects that it has a brightness of 10, then present another light intensity and ask them to assign it a number indicating its relative brightness. If subjects believe the second light is twice as bright as the first, they should assign it the number 20; if they think it is only half as bright, they should give it the number 5, and so on. You could repeat this procedure with many different light intensities until you had a clear picture of the average number assigned to each. The black line in Figure 3-3 shows the type of relation defined in this way. Increases in light intensity produce progressively smaller changes in perceived brightness—the same general conclusion Fechner drew from Weber's law. However, Stevens argued that this is only true for certain types of stimulation. For example, magnitude estimation of the sensation evoked by electrical shock grows slowly at first, and then more rapidly as the shock is increased (the color line in Figure 3-3)—the opposite of the result predicted by Fechner's law.

Stevens proposed a more general way of characterizing such relations. This is referred to as *Stevens's power law,* since it asserts that sensation (S) is proportional to stimulus intensity (I) raised to some power (b): $S = kI^b$, where k is a constant that varies with the unit of measurement being used. The three curves in Figure 3-3 follow this rule, with b equal to .33 for brightness, 1 for apparent length, and 3.5 for electrical shock. When b is less than 1, as it is for brightness, sensation grows progressively more slowly as intensity increases, but when b is greater than 1, as it is for shock, sensation grows progressively more rapidly as intensity increases. When b equals 1, as it does for apparent length, sensation is directly proportional to intensity.

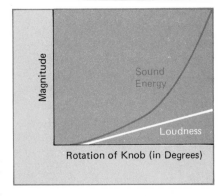

Figure 3-2

In order for loudness to increase equally for each degree of rotation, energy must increase progressively more and more.

Figure 3-3

The graph shows the average estimated magnitudes of sensation (S) for various intensities (I) of light, line length, and electrical shock. These curves can be described by Stevens's power law, $S = kI^b$, with the exponent b equal to .33 for brightness, 1 for apparent length, and 3.5 for shock. (Stevens, 1961)

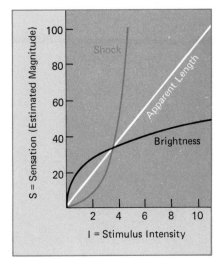

Figure 3-4

Performance of a detection task can be summarized by the proportion of times the subject reports signals when they are presented, "hits" (p_H), and the proportion of times a signal is erroneously reported when none was presented, "false alarms" (p_{FA}). Any performance can be represented as a point on the type of graph shown here. For example, point A indicates a performance in which p_H equals .75 and p_{FA} equals .5. It has been found that instructing a subject to be more or less conservative in reporting signals shifts the performance point along a curve called a receiver operating characteristic (ROC). *Thus, giving subjects "conservative instructions" might shift their performance from point A to point C along the same ROC curve, labeled* $d' = 1$. *In contrast, increasing signal intensity slightly might shift performance from point A to point B, which lies on another ROC curve, labeled* $d' = 2$. *Notice that the higher the value of d', the closer the subject can come to perfect discrimination (the upper left corner of the graph where p_H equals 1 and p_{FA} equals 0). Thus d' is a measure of sensitivity or discriminability. It is independent of the subject's tendency to be "liberal" or "conservative," since this only shifts performance along a particular ROC curve, indicating the same value of* d'.

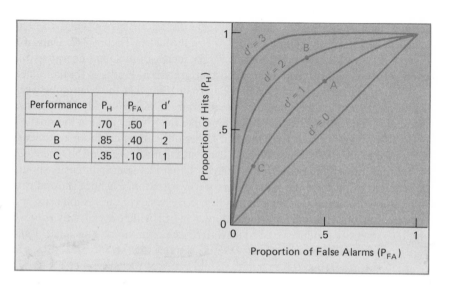

Performance	P_H	P_{FA}	d'
A	.70	.50	1
B	.85	.40	2
C	.35	.10	1

Signal Detection Theory

While the traditional techniques for measuring sensory thresholds and sensitivity to changes in sensation are adequate for most purposes, there are some problems. Underlying the concept of a "threshold" or a "JND" is the idea that people either simply do or do not detect a test stimulus each time it is presented. Yet subjects often say they are uncertain whether they detected anything; for example, "I thought I might have heard something that time, but I'm really not sure." If subjects are instructed to report a detection even when they are uncertain ("liberal instructions"), they tend to report more detections, and this liberal reporting *lowers* the measured threshold. On the other hand, if subjects are discouraged from reporting a detection when they are uncertain ("conservative instructions"), they tend to report fewer detections, and this *raises* the measured threshold. Thus these two different types of instruction produce results that reflect shifts in subjects' judgmental standards rather than any real change in their sensitivity to the test stimuli. It would be useful to have a measure of sensitivity that isn't influenced by instructional effects. Such a measure, termed *d'*, is provided by the *signal detection theory* (Green and Swets, 1966). The way in which this measure is obtained is illustrated in Figure 3-4. The central idea is that the sensations evoked by very weak test stimuli may also occur in their absence, due to random firing of nerves or random motions of air molecules. Thus subjects' interpretation of such sensations is a sort of statistical decision or inference. They must decide whether the sensations were really evoked by a test stimulus, or were simply a product of irrelevant background "noise" in their own sensory system.

To understand the sorts of things that can influence a statistical decision, suppose you are spending the night in an old house. Such houses spontaneously generate a variety of sounds as they expand or contract with the temperature, old pipes rattle in their fittings, or loose shingles and shutters are tossed by the wind. Lying in bed, you hear a sound. Is it a prowler or simply part of the normal background noise? Your decision will be influenced by at least two factors: how unusual the sound is compared to the usual noises of the house, and how worried you are about prowlers. Certainly a rash of recent burglaries or a warning from the sheriff would increase your tendency to suspect a prowler. In other words, you would be influenced by your estimate of how likely it is that a prowler would be there. This is often referred to as your *expectancy*. And if you know there has been a recent series of homicides in the neighborhood, you would be far more likely to investigate the noise than if you knew there had been incidents of simple prowling. Thus the cost or consequence of an erroneous decision is also an important consideration. While such judgmental factors also influence your interpretation of weak stimuli, they do *not* affect the d' measure of sensitivity shown in Figure 3-4.

Hearing

Auditory Stimuli

The type of environmental stimulus that normally produces the sensation of sound is a rapid variation in air pressure next to your ears. This is usually caused by a similar variation introduced into the air some distance away and slightly earlier in time. If you were high in the stands watching the half-time show at a football game, you would see the bass drum being struck a few moments before you heard the sound. The rapid variations in air pressure produced by the vibrating surface of the drum spread through the air at about 1,100 feet per second, so that a similar, but weaker, pattern of variation is eventually produced next to your ears. If the drummer were 1,100 feet away, the sound would take 1 second to reach your ear. You would see the drum being hit before this, since light travels much faster than sound (186,000 miles per second). Other sources of sound (horns, cheering fans, a plane overhead) produce additional patterns of pressure variation that could reach your ears at the same time as those from the drum, mixing with and adding to them to produce an even more complex pattern of variation. Even a single human voice is a very complex pattern of pressure variations. Figure 3-5 shows the variations made during a 1-second interval by a speaker making the sound "ah."

PURE TONES.   It is possible to consider complex patterns of the sort shown in Figure 3-5 as being made up of much simpler patterns called *pure tones*. Figure 3-6 illustrates particular pure tones. They consist of a rapid increase and decrease of air pressure over time in a regular pattern called a *sine wave*. All pure tones have this general form, although they differ in frequency and in amplitude. The *frequency* of a pure tone is defined as the number of complete cycles of pressure variation occurring in 1 second. (A complete cycle is the sequence of change from the highest pressure down to the lowest pressure and back to the highest pressure again.) Frequency is usually expressed in cycles per second or *hertz (Hz)*. The *amplitude* of a pure tone is the greatest change from normal air pressure level produced during the cyclic variation in pressure. Figure 3-6 shows pure tones that differ in frequency and amplitude. Roughly speaking, the sensation of *pitch* is determined by the frequency of a tone, and its loudness by

Figure 3-5

This is a typical waveform of the speech sound "ah." Even as simple a speech sound as this one involves a complex variation in sound pressure amplitude over time. (Denes and Pinson, 1963)

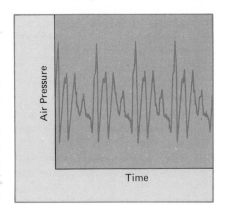

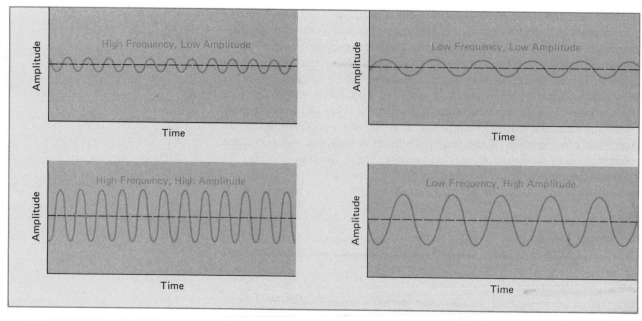

Figure 3-6

The graph shows four pure tones that differ in how rapidly the cycles of air pressure variation occur (frequency) and in the magnitude of that variation (amplitude).

Figure 3-7

The graph below shows the range of pure tones we normally hear.

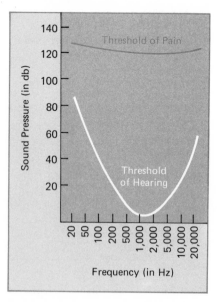

the amplitude. For example, the higher-pitched notes on a piano are produced by shorter strings that vibrate more frequently, while the lower-pitched tones are produced by longer strings that vibrate more slowly. The harder a particular key is struck, the more the string vibrates back and forth, producing a higher-amplitude tone, which sounds louder.

Most people can only hear tones whose frequencies are between 20 and 20,000 Hz, and people vary in their sensitivity to tones within this range. Figure 3-7 illustrates the range of pure tones we normally hear. The lower curve shows the lowest audible (threshold) energy for each frequency, and the upper curve shows the highest tolerable energy (anything higher causes pain and damage to the ear). Notice that sound energy is expressed in bels. The *bel*, or *decibel, scale* (1 bel equals 10 decibels) is named in honor of Alexander Graham Bell. One bel represents a tenfold (10^1) increase in energy, two bels a hundredfold (10^2) increase, and three bels a thousandfold increase (10^3). Zero on the bel scale corresponds to the normal threshold energy for a 1,000 Hz tone. The threshold energy of a 20 Hz tone is over 80 db (8 bels); thus the threshold energy for a 20 Hz tone is more than 10^8 times as great as that for a 1,000 Hz tone.

The average energy level of the sound frequencies we hear in normal conversation is about 60 db or 6 bels. This means it is 10^6 or 1,000,000 times the energy level of a 1,000 Hz tone. Prolonged exposure to sounds above 80 or 90 db can produce permanent hearing loss. For example, a subway train 20 feet away represents about 10 db, while the sounds at a rock music concert may be as high as 150 db for those standing near the speakers.

COMBINATIONS OF PURE TONES.   We rarely hear a single pure tone under normal circumstances, although the sound of a single note played on a flute comes close to it. Pure tones can be produced electronically for such purposes as tests of hearing or the composition of "electronic music." (If you have ever heard electronic music, you probably noticed the unnatural purity of the individual notes.) A single note played on most other musical instruments is really a mixture of pure tones. This can be seen in Figure 3-8, which shows the same note (C) produced by an *oscillator* (an electronic device capable of producing a pure tone) and a piano. The piano produces several tones at once—the fundamental tone (128 Hz for C) and several overtones. The *fundamental tone* is the basic frequency of the note and sounds the loudest. The *overtones* are multiples of the fundamental and sound softer than the fundamental. On the piano you can hear as many as 15 overtones besides the fundamental tone. These overtones (also called *harmonics*) blend with the fundamental tone to give the note its characteristic quality or *timbre*. The *timbre*, or pattern of overtones, varies with each instrument. It is determined by the material the instrument is made of, its design, and the way it is played. It is the timbre that makes the same note sound different when it comes from a tuba, a piano, or a human voice.

Most of the sounds we hear contain a wide range of frequencies. In fact, the sound of a shower running in an empty bathtub includes approximately equal amounts of all the audible frequencies. Such a sound is often called *white noise*. Other sounds, such as speech, may contain constantly shifting mixtures of energy at various frequencies. Since we are not equally sensitive to all frequencies, the loudness of a sound made up of many frequencies depends on the specific amount of energy at each frequency.

The Ear

The ear is made up of three major structural components: the outer ear, the middle ear, and the cochlea. The outer ear, or *pinna*, is essentially a funnel that

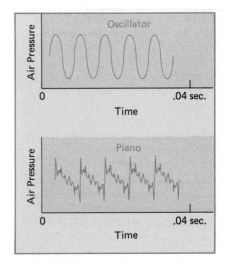

Figure 3-8

(Top) A pure tone of 128 Hz produced by an oscillator contains only that frequency. (Bottom) The note C_3 on a piano has the same fundamental frequency (128 Hz) but also contains other overtones.

Figure 3-9

A diagram of the ear, showing the outer ear, the middle ear, and the cochlea.

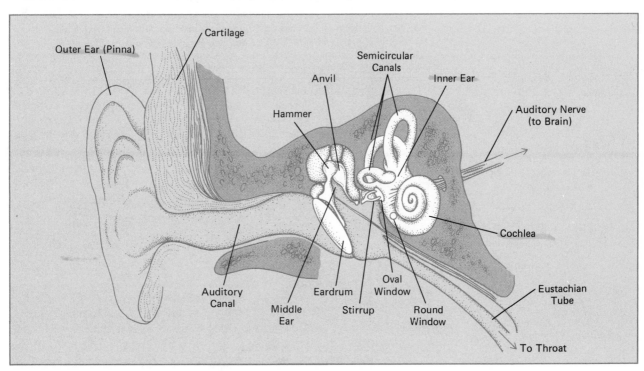

APPLICATION
Hearing Loss and Treatment

There are a number of ways in which the hearing mechanism can break down, starting with the eardrum and working inward. Damage to the eardrum itself can occur in many ways, the most common being the effect of external pressure (a blow to the ears, a nearby explosion, or extreme water pressure during a scuba dive). Ordinarily the pressure within the middle ear is matched to the external air pressure by means of the air entering the *Eustachian tube,* a small channel that runs from the rear of your mouth to the middle ear. However, a difference in external air pressure may puncture the eardrum when changes in pressure occur too rapidly, or if the Eusta-

chian tube is blocked because of a heavy cold or a failure to swallow frequently enough (which opens the tubes) during changes in pressure (during a scuba dive or when an airplane takes off or lands). If the puncture isn't too severe, this damage may be repaired through ear surgery, but the scar tissue in the repaired eardrum may produce permanent changes in the ear's response to various frequencies.

In another common form of deafness, the tiny bones in the middle ear fuse because of calcium deposits, and this fusion effectively blocks the mechanical transmission of sound to the cochlea. Delicate surgical techniques can break the calcium deposits

and restore the flexibility of the bones. This surgery produces a dramatic and almost complete return of normal hearing.

The basilar membrane is susceptible to damage in a number of ways. First of all, there is the progressive deterioration due to age, which seems to affect the high-frequency regions of the membrane first. This produces heightened thresholds for the higher frequencies. A *hearing aid,* which selectively amplifies the higher frequencies, can restore normal hearing to many elderly people.

A very similar pattern of hearing loss occurs if a patient is given extensive doses of mycine, which seems to cause progressive

Figure 3-10
A. The cochlea, or inner ear, is a coiled, snail-shaped canal; it is the part of the ear that contains the organ of hearing, called the organ of Corti.
B. An "uncoiled" drawing of the normally coiled structure of the cochlea. It is easier to see here how the pressure vibrations enter through the oval window, pass through a liquid-filled channel to the end of the cochlea, and pass back through another channel to the round window.

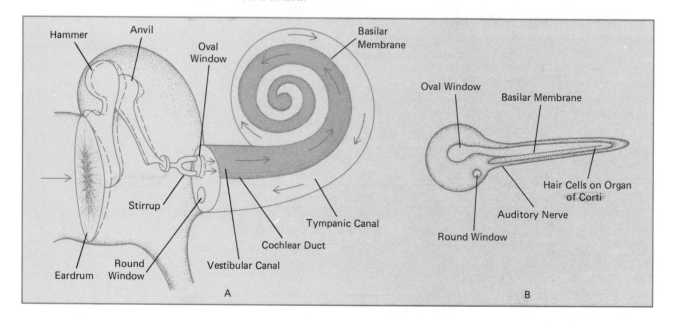

damage to the hair cells in the basilar membrane similar to the degeneration caused by age. Again, a hearing aid may restore normal hearing if the damage is not too extensive.

Exposure to very intense sounds can also cause damage to the basilar membrane. If the sound is primarily of one frequency, there may be damage to only one region, producing a *tonal gap;* that is, a loss of sensitivity to a narrow range of tones (as shown in the accompanying graph). Again, if damage is not too great, a special hearing aid that amplifies only those frequencies to which sensitivity is reduced may restore normal hearing. Fortunately, there is tremendous redundancy in most sounds, which means that the ability to hear only a small part of the total frequency range may be all that is necessary for comprehension.

People with tonal gaps are often unaware of any problem, since their brain automatically compensates for the loss.

Finally, there are various forms of nerve damage in the acoustic pathways or in the auditory projection areas in the cortex. These may be caused by a variety of factors, including birth defects, disease, blows to the head, and tumors. It is hard to make up for the loss of hearing caused by nerve damage. One way is to use another sensory system that provides the same information in a different form. For example, deaf people become quite adept at interpreting speech from lip movements (lip reading). While normal people also rely on lip movements to some extent, it is only when hearing is lost that most people fully use the redundant visual information to interpret speech.

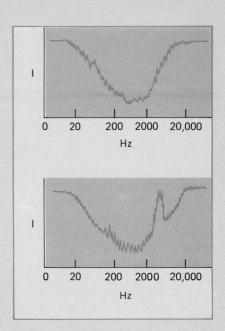

Audiograms showing threshold intensity for various frequencies from (top) a normal subject and (bottom) a subject with a tonal gap around 5,000 Hz.

channels the air pressure variations into the head, where they are concentrated against the surface of a flexible membrane called the *eardrum,* causing it to vibrate (see Figure 3-9). These movements of the eardrum are then transmitted through the *middle ear* by a series of three small bones called the *hammer,* the *anvil,* and the *stirrup.* The hammer connects the eardrum to the anvil, which, in turn, is connected by the stirrup to another flexible membrane covering a small opening in the *cochlea.* This membrane, called the *oval window,* is much smaller than the eardrum. The bones connecting the two cause movements of the eardrum to produce smaller but more powerful variations in pressure against the oval window.

It is in the cochlea that the movements begun by pressure variations against the eardrum are changed into patterns of neural activity that produce the sensation of hearing. The amplified pressure variations on the oval window are transmitted through liquid-filled channels within the cochlea. When the liquid or fluid in the channel moves, it twists the basilar membrane, which is the wall of one channel. Hair cells in the basilar membrane are attached to neurons that fire (transmit a neural impulse) when the hair cell is twisted by the movement of the membrane. Figure 3-10A shows the snail-shaped cochlea; a better view of the liquid-filled channels within the cochlea is shown in Figure 3-10B, which is an "uncoiled" drawing of the normally coiled structure. Notice how the pressure vibrations enter by the oval window, pass through a liquid-filled channel to the end of the cochlea, and pass back through another channel to the *round window,* where they are absorbed.

Chapter 3:
Sensation

71

Theories of Hearing

Neural impulses are transmitted from neurons in the hair cells of the basilar membrane. The main question about hearing is how these neural impulses are coded to give different kinds of information—for instance, how do we know that a tone is a certain pitch (how do we tell middle C from a note an octave below that)?

One theory of pitch perception, called the *place theory,* is based on the idea that different sound frequencies (different pitches) actually trigger different neurons. It has been found that the frequency of vibrations determines which portion of the basilar membrane is moved or twisted most (Békésy, 1955). Thus the pitch information could be conveyed according to which neurons on which part of the membrane are stimulated.

One problem with this theory is that not all frequencies seem to cause the basilar membrane to twist more in one place than another. In fact, only high and (to some extent) middle frequencies seem to do this; pitch information about low frequencies must be transmitted in another way.

An alternative way in which pitch information could be coded into neural activity is in terms of the rate (rather than the place) at which neurons are triggered. This is called the *frequency theory* of pitch perception (Wever and Bray, 1937). In fact, it can be shown that the rate or frequency of pulses traveling up the auditory nerve to the brain matches that of a tone over a wide range of frequencies. This is not too surprising for low frequencies, since individual nerves can respond over and over at these low rates. Yet it is impossible for a single fiber to fire, recover, and fire again as fast as would be necessary to follow a high-frequency tone. However, such high firing rates could be the product of several different sets of fibers, each firing in turn at a lower rate, but combining to produce the higher overall rate (just as when you listen to ten carpenters hammering, you hear many more hammer blows per minute than any one carpenter could make). This is often referred to as the *volley principle,* named for the way in which rows of soldiers in the Revolutionary War could load, fire, and reload one after another to produce more frequent volleys than could one row alone.

It seems clear that some combination of place theory and frequency theory is required to give a complete account of the coding of sound into neural patterns.

Seeing

Visual Stimuli

Our eyes are sensitive to a narrow range of electromagnetic energy, wavelengths between 400 and 760 nanometers. This range is referred to as the *visual spectrum,* or, more simply, *light.* Particular sources of light vary in their brightness and color, depending on (among other things) the amount of energy present from each part of the spectrum—the light's spectral composition. Furthermore, most of our visual experience involves complex patterns of

HIGHLIGHT
Sinusoidal Gratings: The Pure Tones of Vision

In recent years interest has developed in a type of visual stimulus that may be as useful in the study of vision as pure tones have been in the study of audition. In fact, the two types of stimuli have much in common. Where a pure tone is a regular cyclical variation in air pressure over time, the visual stimulus is a regular cyclical variation in brightness across space. Because the formal mathematical name for such cyclical variation is a *sine wave*, the patterns are often referred to as *sinusoidal gratings*. An example of one is shown in Figure A. Just as a pure tone can be described or specified in terms of its frequency and amplitude, a grating has two corresponding properties called spatial frequency and contrast. *Spatial frequency* refers to how rapidly the brightness variations occur across space, and *contrast* refers to the difference in brightness between the lightest and darkest parts of the grating.

We can see certain spatial frequencies better than others, just as we can hear certain frequencies of tones better than others. We require less amplitude in order to hear some tones, and we require less contrast in order to see some spatial frequencies. This aspect of vision is immediately apparent when you look at the pattern of brightness variations shown in Figure B. This pattern consists of sinusoidal gratings whose frequency increases as you go from left to right and whose contrast increases as you go from top to bottom. Thus, the higher up on the pattern you can see each frequency of grating, the less contrast you need in order to see it; i.e., the more sensitive you are to that spatial frequency. For most people, the boundary between those gratings they can see and those they can't is shaped like the curve shown in Figure B (if you view the page at normal reading distance). Notice that this is a sort

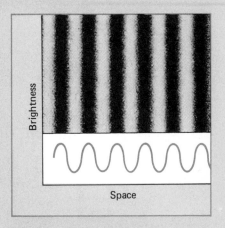

Figure A.

A sinusoidal grating is shown above with a curve below showing how brightness varies in a regular, cyclical (sinusoidal) fashion across space. Other gratings can differ in how rapidly the cycles occur (frequency) and the difference in brightness between the lightest and darkest parts of the pattern (contrast).

of threshold curve much like the audiometric function shown earlier in Figure 3-7, only here it indicates your sensitivity to various spatial frequencies. Traditional measures of acuity, such as the Snellen chart, only indicate our limited ability to see fine detail (high spatial frequencies). The curve shown in Figure B also indicates our limited ability to see brightness variations that occur too slowly (low spatial frequencies).

Just as complex sounds can be interpreted as combinations of many pure tones, complex spatial patterns of brightness variation can be interpreted as combinations of many sinusoidal gratings. Thus, further specification of our ability to see various gratings may prove as useful in the study of vision as pure tones have in the study of audition.

Figure B.

The stimulus pattern (below, left) contains sinusoidal gratings that increase in frequency from left to right and in contrast from top to bottom. For most people the boundary between the gratings they can see and those they can't is shaped like the curve shown on the graph (below, right). This indicates sensitivity to each spatial frequency: the less contrast required to make it visible, the greater the sensitivity.

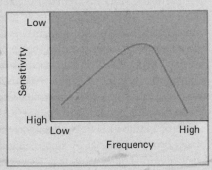

Figure 3-11

A Snellen chart, shown above, is a standard set of letters of various sizes. It is used to measure visual acuity. If the smallest row of letters a subject can read at 20 feet corresponds to the smallest row of letters a normal (average) person can read at 20 feet, the person is said to have normal acuity, or "20/20 vision." However, if the smallest row of letters the subject can read at 20 feet corresponds to the smallest row at an even greater distance, say 50 feet, the person would be said to have below-normal acuity, or "20/50 vision."

An example of better than normal acuity would be someone with "20/10 vision," since this would mean they could see the letters as clearly at 20 feet as a normal person at only 10 feet.

light — spatial patterns defined by variations in light across our field of view, and temporal patterns defined by variations in light over time. There are limits to our ability to discern both sorts of patterns. You've probably taken an eye test (called a *Snellen test*) that determined your ability to read progressively smaller rows of letters (see Figure 3-11.) Such tests measure *visual acuity,* the ability to discern fine details in spatial patterns of light. Your acuity is best in the very center of your field of view, and much poorer everywhere else. You normally don't notice this, since you can easily shift your eyes to gaze directly at any detail of interest (as you do when you read). Your ability to discern rapid variations in light in temporal patterns is also limited. For example, an ordinary fluorescent bulb isn't really on all the time, its brightness is actually flickering off and on 60 times a second. Yet you see it as being on continuously. The light projected onto a motion picture screen is actually flickered off and on about 64 times a second, yet the picture seems to be illuminated continuously. This phenomenon is called *flicker fusion.*

What light in your visual environment reaches your eyes? If you stood in the center of a large circle, the combined field of view from both eyes — your *visual field* — would include over 200 degrees of the circle's 360-degree circumference. The size of an object as it appears in this visual field depends both on its physical size and its distance from you. This is why it is often useful to describe the size of an object by how much of your visual field it occupies; that is, by how many degrees of the imaginary surrounding circle's circumference it would cover. This is referred to as an object's size in *degrees visual angle.* A convenient reference is that your fingernail seen at arm's length has a width of about 1 degree visual angle (whereas the moon is only $\frac{1}{2}$ a degree).

The Eye

In 1637 the philosopher-scientist René Descartes removed the eye from a dead bull, carefully scraped away the covering from the rear of the eyeball, and replaced it with a thin paper film. He then held the front of the eye facing toward a lighted candle. Clearly visible through the paper at the rear of the eye was an upside down image of the candle. Since then, scientists have learned considerably more about the eye, but its basic property was clear to Descartes: It projects an image of the scene in front of the eye onto the rear wall of the eye. On this rear wall is a complicated tapestry of tissue called the *retina.* It is in the retina that light-sensitive cells convert the projected pattern of light into patterns of neural activity.

Figure 3-12 is a schematic cross section of the eye, showing some of its major parts. The optical system at the front of the eye that projects the image onto the retina consists of a slightly protruding, clear outer cap called the *cornea* and an inner component called the *lens.* Fine adjustment in the shape of the lens is required to focus either near or far objects onto the retina. These fine adjustments are termed *accommodation* and are produced by changes in the tension of small muscles, the *ciliary muscles,* connected to the lens. Between the cornea and the lens is a richly pigmented structure called the *iris* (from the Greek word for rainbow). The pigments in the iris determine whether the eye is blue, black, brown, or hazel. A small, ringlike opening in the iris forms the round, black *pupil.* The size of this circular opening controls the amount of light

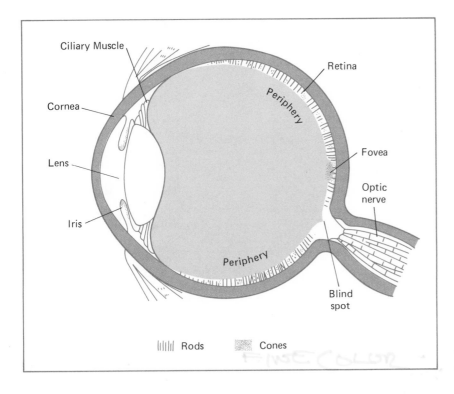

IIIIII Rods   Cones

Figure 3-12
A cross section of the eye.

entering the eye and varies as a function of the level of illumination. The diameter of the pupil is greatest in a dimly illuminated environment and smallest in a brightly lighted environment. Inside the pupil the light passes through the lens, which focuses it onto the retina, the inner lining of the back of the eyeball.

There are two major landmarks on the retina: the fovea and the blind spot. The *fovea* is a tiny spot on the retina positioned behind the lens. It corresponds to the center of your field of view, where your visual acuity is highest. The *blind spot,* the center of a radiating web of blood vessels, is the point where blood vessels and neurons pass out through the wall of the eye. The blind spot is totally insensitive to light. (You aren't normally aware of this because the blind spot is at a different point in the visual field of each eye, so that what one eye misses, the other eye sees.)

Figure 3-13 presents a cross-sectional drawing of the retina. Note that light has to pass through a network of nerve cells and blood vessels before reaching the actual photoreceptors of the eye, the rods and cones (named for their shapes. Indeed, it has been said that rods and cones have their backs turned to the light.

Rods and Cones

There are approximately 120 million rods and 6 to 8 million cones on the retina. Most of the cones are on the fovea, which is the center of the field of vision, where acuity is highest. Cones are primarily responsible for the ability to see fine detail; they function best in daylight or bright light and are also responsible for the ability to see color.

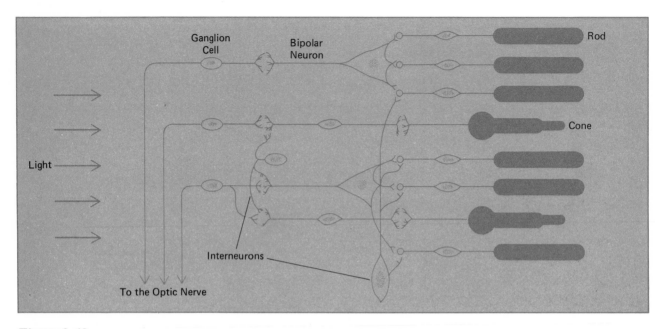

Figure 3-13

A cross section of the retina. Note that light has to pass through blood vessels and nerve cells before reaching the rods and cones.

Rods are distributed on the retina outside of the fovea. We depend on the rods for our ability to see at night or in dim light. Rods do not distinguish colors—this is why at night you do not see colors, only black and white and gray. You may have also noticed that at night you see things better out of the corners or sides of your eye—this is because you are depending on your rods for night vision, and they are located off the center of the retina.

It is in the rods and cones that light energy triggers a complex photochemical process that results in neural activity that we experience as sight. The critical step in this process seems to be the breaking down or bleaching of photosensitive pigment in these cells by light. This chemical activity stimulates the neurons attached to the rods or cones, and this firing of the neurons is signalled to the brain. Then the chemicals recombine to form new pigment.

VISUAL ADAPTATION.   Rods and cones differ in their sensitivity to light and in the rate at which the bleaching and recombination of pigment takes place. This difference is important in *visual adaptation,* the adjustment in visual sensitivity in response to changes in the level of illumination. On a clear dark night we can see a single candle flame over 50 kilometers away. We can also see quite well on a sunny, snow-covered ski slope where the levels of light energy affecting our eyes may be over one trillion times greater than that of the candle flame. However, to function effectively in either situation, our visual system must have time to adjust its sensitivity to the level of illumination. This process of adjustment is called adaptation. *Dark adaptation* begins when you leave a brightly lighted environment and enter a darkened one; for example, when you leave a sunny street to enter a darkened movie theater. *Light adaptation* begins when this sequence is reversed; for example, when you leave the theater and step back into the sunlight. Both types of adaptation take time. Your sensitivity to

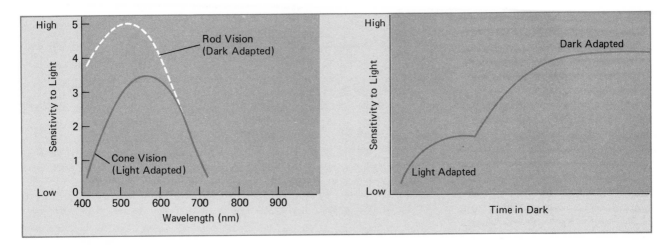

light is often so low on entering a darkened theater that you find it difficult to locate a seat. Yet gradually, over a period of minutes, your sensitivity increases, until even the faces of the audience are clearly visible. When you eventually emerge from the theater, your eyes are so sensitive to the previously comfortable sunlight that you may squint or shade them for a few moments until you adapt to the light.

How does this take place? As we discussed earlier, the basic process of vision is a photochemical one—the breaking down or bleaching of chemical pigments in rods and cones. It seems possible to account for much (but not all) of light and dark adaptation in terms of the balance between the breaking down (bleaching) and reconstitution of pigments in the rods and cones.

Pigment in the rods is much more sensitive to light than pigment in the cones. This means that it takes a less intense light stimulus to start the breaking down of the pigment in rods than it does in cones (see Figure 3-14). In fact, when you are light adapted you are relying primarily on the less-sensitive cones for vision, because most of the highly sensitive pigment in the rods is depleted. Only when you remain in a dimly illuminated environment long enough to dark adapt completely does the highly sensitive pigment in the rods reach its highest concentration. This allows you to see very dim stimuli that are too weak to affect the less-sensitive cones.

Exposing parts of your retina to different amounts of light for even a few seconds produces differences in their level of light adaptation. If you then look at an evenly illuminated screen, that part of your retina made less sensitive to light causes you to see an illusionary darker region on the screen, called a *negative afterimage*. You can experience this for yourself by turning to Plate 3 of the color insert.

Adaptation makes a big difference in the visual threshold—to be detected in a light-adapted versus a dark-adapted state, a stimulus must be 100,000 times as intense.

NEURAL ACTIVITY IN THE RETINA. The firing of a single rod or cone is not communicated to the brain in a simple one-retinal-cell-to-one-brain-cell

Figure 3-14

Two things happen as your eyes adapt to the dark. They gradually become more sensitive to light (the threshold becomes lower) and their sensitivity to various wavelengths of light (spectral sensitivity) shifts from the pattern typical of cones to that typical of rods. The process shown above takes approximately 40 minutes, with the break in the curve occurring after approximately 13 minutes.

HIGHLIGHT
Receptive Fields

A valuable technique for studying the relation between visual stimuli and neural activity at various points in the visual system is the analysis of *receptive fields*. This is done by inserting a tiny microelectrode into a neuron and seeing how variations in the visual field influence neural activity. Usually the neuron responds when certain types of stimuli are presented in specific regions of the visual field. The type of evoking stimuli and the specific region of the visual field define a "receptive field" for that neuron.

The accompanying figure shows an experimental setup used by Hubel and Wiesel (1959) to study the receptive fields of neurons in a cat's visual cortex. The cat was first anesthetized and made completely motionless through the injection of certain drugs. A microelectrode was then slowly inserted into the cat's visual cortex until the pattern of electrical activity showed it was positioned within a single cell. The cat's eye was held open and focused on a screen. Various stimulus patterns were then projected onto the screen until one elicited a change in the activity of the neuron. By slowly varying the stimulus, it was possible to map exactly which region of the cat's visual field (i.e., region of its retina) responded to the stimulus.

Similar procedures have been used to map receptive fields for neurons at various other points in the visual system. The most important finding of this type of research is that as one works back from the retina toward the visual cortex, the receptive fields become larger and the type of evoking stimulus pattern more complex—that is, as visual information is passed on from the retina to the brain, it seems to be progressively processed or coded. Individual cells in the cortex respond primarily to specific types of stimuli in certain regions of the visual field.

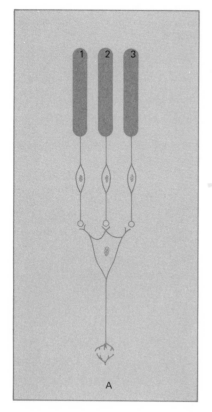

fashion. Considerable interaction in neural activity occurs in the network of cells lying just above the rods and cones in the retina. Rods and cones connect to *bipolar cells,* which in turn connect to *ganglion cells* whose axons exit the eye through the optic nerve. There are also horizontal interconnections between each of these cells, as shown in Figure 3-13. This network of cells is really a sort of peripheral brain that carries out the first steps in the analysis of the visual image. Two important types of neural interaction that take place in the retina are convergence and lateral inhibition. *Convergence* is the flowing together of neural activity into common paths, much as automobiles leave their driveways to go into a common street. An example of this would be several rods or cones all influencing the same ganglion cell (see Figure 3-15). The firing of any one or more of these receptor elements could trigger activity in the same ganglion cell, so that the ganglion cell would respond to stimulation over a wider region of the retina than could a single rod or cone, and in that sense be more sensitive. However, this increase in area of sensitivity would be accompanied by a loss in spatial information, since firing of the ganglion cell wouldn't identify which of the converging rods or cones had been stimulated. Thus, neural convergence involves a loss of the type of spatial information most important for acuity. It is

Figure 3-15

Cells 1, 2, and 3 converge on a single cell (cell A). Because of this convergence, there is no way of knowing whether activity at cell A was initiated by cell 1, 2, or 3—or any combination of the three.

COLOR PERCEPTION

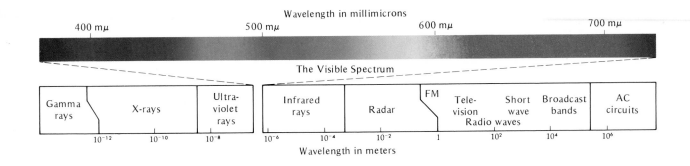

Wavelength in millimicrons

400 mμ   500 mμ   600 mμ   700 mμ

The Visible Spectrum

Gamma rays	X-rays	Ultra-violet rays		Infrared rays	Radar	FM	Tele-vision	Short wave	Broadcast bands	AC circuits
	10^{-12}	10^{-10}	10^{-8}	10^{-6}	10^{-4}	10^{-2}	1	10^{2}	10^{4}	10^{6}

Radio waves

Wavelength in meters

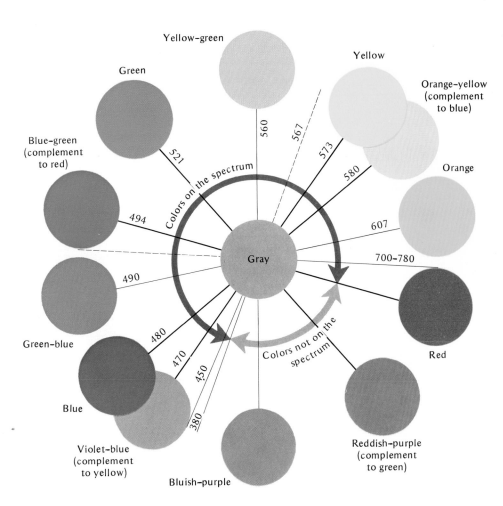

Yellow-green

Green

Yellow

Orange-yellow
(complement
to blue)

Blue-green
(complement
to red)

560   567   573   580

521   Orange

Colors on the spectrum

494   607

490   Gray   700–780

Colors not on the spectrum

Green-blue   480

470   Red

450

Blue   380

Violet-blue
(complement
to yellow)

Reddish-purple
(complement
to green)

Bluish-purple

PLATE 1

The Color Spectrum. The color spectrum can be produced by passing white light through a prism. The fact that different wavelengths bend at different angles as they pass through glass causes the white light to be broken up into its component colors as shown at left. The rainbow appears in the sky when sunlight passes through droplets of water falling from rain clouds, producing the same prismatic effect.

PLATE 2

The Color Circle. The colors on this circle are laid out in identical order in which they appear in the spectrum, and a few nonspectral colors are added. The distance (along the circumference) between each of the colors is such that colors opposite one another are complementaries. A mixture of two complements will produce a neutral gray. Mixing noncomplementary hues will produce a hue midway between the two along the circumference of the circle.

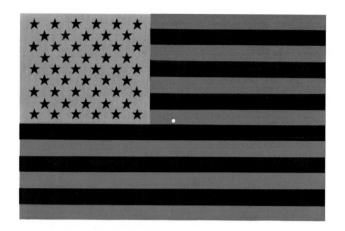

PLATE 3

Color Afterimage. Stare at the white dot in the center for about 60 seconds and then quickly shift your gaze to a white surface. Since the colors of this flag are the complements of the traditional red, white, and blue, the negative afterimage of it will look like the flag we are used to seeing. If you look around, the afterimage will appear to be wherever you are looking.

PLATE 4

The Color Solid. The color solid contains all of the distinguishable sensations of color. Hue varies as one travels around the circumference of the solid. The horizontal dimension depicts brightness and the vertical dimension depicts saturation. A complete solid would contain 350,000 patches of discriminable colors.

PLATE 5

Color Mixing. The area of overlap of the red, green, and blue lights shows what happens when the three primaries are additively mixed: all three lights together yield white. But, since paint pigments absorb most wavelengths and reflect only a few, a mixture of the three primaries of paint is subtractive and all wavelengths are absorbed, producing black.

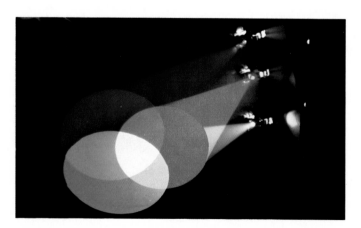

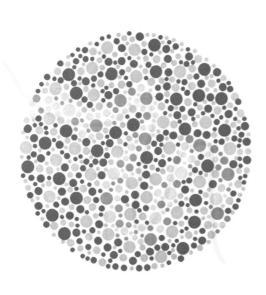

PLATE 6

Color Blindness. Color blindness, the insensitivity to one or more of the three primary colors of light, is a sex-linked genetic defect which appears almost exclusively in males. The extreme example of color blindness is the monochromat who perceives all colors as shades of gray. More common, however, is the dichromat who is sensitive to only two of the three primary colors and is therefore partially color blind. The photograph on the bottom has been altered in the darkroom to show how it might appear to an individual with red-green color blindness. A plate from the Dvorine Pseudo-Isochromatic Series of color-blindness tests is also shown. Certain observers with blue-yellow color confusion will not be able to see the figure embedded in the mosaic.

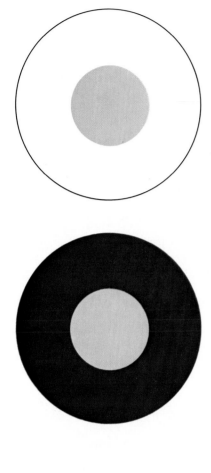

PLATE 7

Simultaneous Color Contrast. The two figures on the left depict brightness contrast and the two below depict hue contrast. The important point about each is that sensations related to the inner or target circles are affected by the type of surround. In the case of brightness contrast, lateral inhibition causes the target with the dark surround to appear lighter than the target with the light surround. In the hue contrast figures, the blue surround produces a complementary (yellow) tinge in the gray target, while the reverse is true for the yellow surround. Placing a piece of tissue paper over the hue contrast figures will enhance this effect. The mechanism of lateral inhibition, extended to refer to like-cell inhibition only, accounts for hue contrast effects.

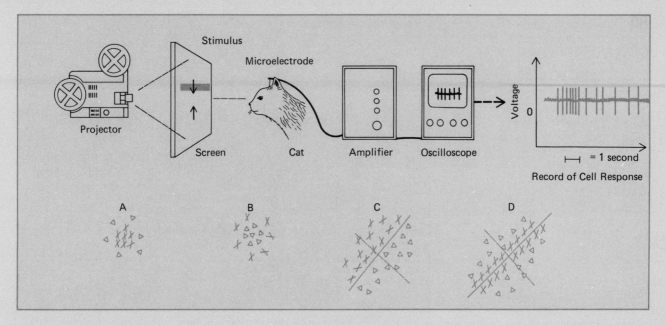

A through D are maps of several receptive fields showing where a light stimulus increases cell firing (X) or inhibits it (△). (Hubel and Wiesel, 1959; redrawn from Thompson, 1971)

clear that there is considerable convergence of retina elements; although there are about 120 million rods and 6 to 8 million cones, only 1 million neurons leave the eye in the optic nerve. Convergence occurs primarily in the periphery of the retina and mostly in the rods; there is hardly any convergence of the cones on the fovea. This is consistent with the high degree of acuity in the center of our visual field, and the lower acuity on the periphery.

Another basic form of neural interaction on the retina is *lateral inhibition*. Here the firing of one neuron causes an inhibition (reduction) of activity in nearby cells. In a sense, the image represented in the firing of rods and cones is similar to a line drawing, since lateral inhibition makes the contours of the image sharper. This actually aids acuity, so it is not surprising that lateral inhibition is most characteristic of the interactions of the cones in the fovea, where acuity is highest.

Optic Pathways to the Brain

Figure 3-16 shows the pathways between the retina and the brain. A major feature of this system is that signals from the left half of each retina are transmitted to the left hemisphere of the brain, while signals from the right half of each retina project to the right hemisphere of the brain. Half of the neurons in each optic nerve cross over at a point called the *optic chiasm* and come together with neurons carrying information from the corresponding half of the retina in the other eye. There they join with new nerve bundles to carry the information to the visual cortex. However, this does *not* mean that each cortical hemisphere receives information from only one half of the visual field. The two hemispheres

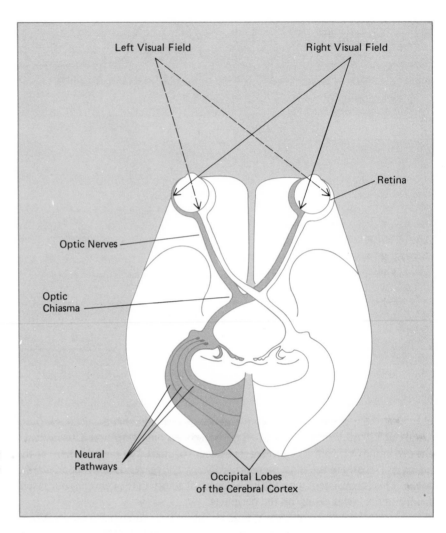

Left Visual Field   *Right Visual Field*

Retina

Optic Nerves

Optic Chiasma

Neural Pathways

Occipital Lobes of the Cerebral Cortex

Figure 3-16

This diagram shows how information from the eyes is transmitted to the brain. The left side of the visual field falls on the right side of the retina of each eye. The nerves from the right side of each retina project to the right hemisphere of the brain.

have many interconnections through which information can be transferred from one side of the brain to the other, as we discussed in Chapter 2.

Color Vision

There are three dimensions used to describe our sensation of color: brightness, hue, and saturation. *Brightness* refers to the amount of energy present in the light rays. As the amount of energy or intensity increases, the stimulus appears brighter. Brightness also depends on the context in which we see the stimulus, the general level of illumination, and other elements, which we will discuss in Chapter 4, "Perception."

Hue corresponds to our names for colors—when we differentiate between brown and blue, for example, we are talking about two different hues. As the wavelength varies on the visual spectrum we see different hues. But hue and wavelength are not interchangeable—any hue can be produced either by a single wavelength or by a mixture of quite different wavelengths. "Light rays of different wavelength can be mixed together in infinite variations without affecting each other—when 'red light' and 'green light' add together to form 'yellow,' the yellow is in us, not in the light, which remains unchanged by the mixing" (Hochberg, 1978, p. 30).

The third dimension is *saturation* or purity of color. This quality is based on how much one wavelength predominates in the stimulus. If all energy is concentrated at a single wavelength, the hue seems very pure; as other wavelengths are added, the hue becomes grayer, more diluted.

These three dimensions are shown in Plate 4 of the color insert.

MIXTURES OF WAVELENGTHS.   Most of what we see is a mixture of many wavelengths. The particular mixture, or *energy spectrum,* is determined first of all by the original source of light, since each source emits a particular amount of energy at each wavelength. The particular mixture of light can be further modified by *filtering* or *reflection* of some light source (see Figure 3-17). Only the wavelengths we see as green are transmitted through the green part of a stained glass window; the rest are filtered out. Green grass reflects only those wavelengths we see as green; the rest are absorbed (converted to heat energy).

There are basically two different ways to produce a particular mixture of wavelengths. You can add different sources of light to produce an *additive*

see menu)
add all - wt light

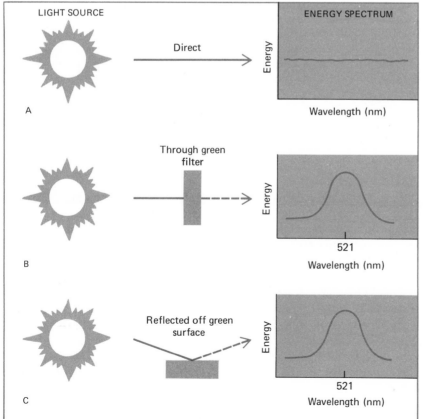

Figure 3-17

If the original source of light is the sun, as shown here, then its color, as determined by its energy spectrum, is white (or desaturated) because it contains a wide range or mixture of wavelengths.

But if the sun is seen through a green filter (such as a stained glass window) or reflected off a green surface (such as grass), then its color is green—the rest of the wavelengths are either filtered out or absorbed (converted to heat energy).

APPLICATION
Visual Impairment and Treatment

One way of reviewing how the eye normally works is to consider how things can go wrong and the ways such problems can be treated. For example, the cornea, which accomplishes about 70 percent of the focusing in the eye, is normally very clear. However, various injuries and diseases (such as cataracts) can leave it so scarred or clouded that vision is lost or seriously impaired. Fortunately, surgeons are able to replace a damaged cornea with a clear one taken from the eye of a donor. While antibodies in our blood normally attack foreign tissue, the cornea is protected from such rejection because it contains no blood vessels, getting its nourishment instead from the watery aqueous humor behind it and the tears with which it is constantly bathed. A more common defect of the cornea is an irregular shape that makes it impossible to bring all parts of an image into focus at the same time. This condition, called *astigmatism,* can be corrected by eyeglasses ground to make up for the irregular shape of the cornea.

The colorfully pigmented tissue of the iris normally limits the light entering the eye through its small round opening, the pupil. However, albinos suffer from a lack of pigmentation and their pale, unpigmented iris is incapable of effectively blocking light. In bright environments they must wear darkened contact lenses or heavily tinted glasses to reduce the glare.

The lenses of the eyes often stiffen with age, until the ciliary muscles can no longer adjust their shape to focus on near or far objects. Benjamin Franklin invented a solution to this problem: the bifocal lens, the upper half of which provides a sharp image of distant objects, and the lower half of near objects. Even if the lens in your eye is naturally flexible, it can't alter its shape enough to make up for an eyeball that is too long or too short. The figure here illustrates the problem of focusing on distant objects when the retina is too long (a condition called *myopia* or *nearsightedness*) and the problem of focusing on near objects when the retina is too short (a condition called *hyperopia* or *farsightedness*). Each of these conditions can be corrected by contact lenses or eyeglasses that give the eye more focusing power.

A disease called *glaucoma* causes a progressive increase in the internal pressure of the eye that eventually destroys the retina. An early symptom of this disease is a loss of flexibility in the eyeball caused by the building internal pressure. (Surprisingly, one of the most successful drugs for controlling this pressure increase is marijuana. In 1976 someone suffering from glaucoma became the first person in the United States to use marijuana legally on a prescription basis.)

There can be problems with the retina itself. Sometimes a

mixture or you can reflect light off various pigments that subtract or absorb specific wavelengths to produce a *subtractive mixture.* For example, an additive mixture occurs if you project two colored light sources onto the same area of a screen; a subtractive mixture occurs when you mix paints together. The general laws of color mixing are shown on Plate 5 of the color insert.

THEORIES OF COLOR VISION. How is the sensation of color produced in the brain? One clue to this puzzle is that we see colors quite well in very bright light when only the cones are responding, whereas we don't distinguish colors under very weak illumination, when only the rods are sensitive enough to respond. For example, a dark-adapted person could recognize forms in a color photograph by the light of the moon, but they would appear in shades of gray. This suggests that the cones are primarily responsible for translating spectral (wavelength) information into the neural patterns (codes) that signal colors to the brain.

It has been known since at least the time of Isaac Newton that it is possible

blow to the head tears or detaches a small part of the retina from the rear surface of the eyeball (the *sclera*). This can often be repaired using a recently developed surgical technique. A tiny, high-intensity laser beam is briefly focused on the retina, causing a tiny burn. The resulting spot of scar tissue reconnects the retina to the rear surface of the eye, much like a tiny thumbtack.

Of course, not all visual problems are correctable, and many people have to adjust to a life without vision. Blind people often show an amazing increase in their ability to use information from other sensory systems. They can identify people by the sound of their step or the odor of their perfume, and can sense obstacles or the shape of a room by the way sounds echo.

The accompanying photo shows the alphabet of raised dots developed by the Frenchman Louis Braille. The Braille alphabet allows blind people to read more than 50 words a minute with the tips of their fingers. Recent advances in technology have made it possible for blind people to use hand-held optical scanning devices that automatically translate print into patterns of pressure stimulation, or even computer-generated speech sounds.

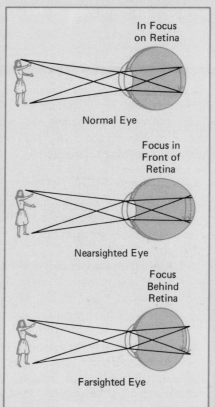

In Focus on Retina

Normal Eye

Focus in Front of Retina

Nearsighted Eye

Focus Behind Retina

Farsighted Eye

The figure on the left shows the problem of focusing on distant objects when the retina is too long (nearsightedness), and the problem of focusing on near objects when the retina is too short (farsightedness).

The photograph below shows a book printed in the Braille alphabet. In this alphabet the letters are coded as a pattern of raised dots, which are read by running one's fingers over them. In this way information from another sensory system (the sense of touch) supplies the information that most of us get through vision, an example of sensory redundancy.

to create virtually all colors by mixing blue, green, and red light. The British scientist Sir Thomas Young speculated in 1802 that only three types of color receptors are required to see all colors: one primarily sensitive to blue, one to green, and one to red. According to this theory, the stronger each of the three colors is in the visual stimulus, the stronger each type of receptor reacts. Thus, if the visual stimulus contains a lot of blue light the blue receptors will respond strongly; if it contains mostly red or green light the red or green receptors will react. The resulting pattern of neural responses is interpreted by the brain as color. If the stimulus contains energy from all parts of the spectrum, all three types of receptors respond and the sensation of white is evoked. If only the green and red receptors are stimulated, the sensation is yellow. Any visual stimulus that produces the same *pattern* of activity in the three types of receptors is seen as the same color.

Young's three-receptor theory was elaborated some 50 years later by the German physiologist Hermann von Helmholtz and became known as the

Chapter 3: Sensation

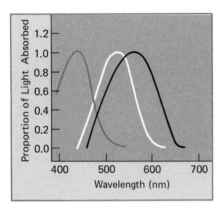

Figure 3-18

The Young-Helmholtz theory of color vision is based on the existence of three types of cones, each type primarily sensitive to wavelengths on a different part of the spectrum, as shown here.

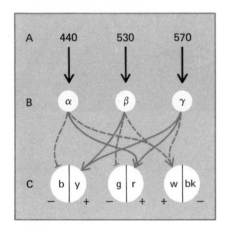

Figure 3-19

Hering's opponent-process theory of color vision is based on the existence of three separate color systems: green-red, blue-yellow, and white-black. Since the effect of the two components in each system is opposite, each system's signal to the brain shows how much of each component is in the visual stimulus. (Hurvich and Jameson, 1957, 1974).

Young-Helmholtz theory. To this day, it is one of the two most influential theories of color vision. In fact, modern measuring techniques have shown that there are three types of cones, each primarily sensitive to a different part of the spectrum (see Figure 3-18). However, while the Young-Helmholtz theory provides a reasonable interpretation of many aspects of color vision, it is not as successful in explaining others, for example, *color blindness.* By far the most common form of color blindness is an inability to discriminate red from green (about 7 percent of all males and 1 percent of all females have this problem). A less common type is the inability to distinguish blue from yellow. And there are even some people who see the world only in shades of gray, like a black and white photograph.

Ewald Hering, a German physiologist who was a contemporary of Helmholtz's, was the author of the second leading theory of color vision, the *opponent-process theory.* Hering argued that there were three separate color systems: red-green, blue-yellow, and black-white. According to his theory, the effect of the two components in each system is opposite (antagonistic), so that each system's signal to the brain indicates how much of each component is in the visual stimulus. Hering argued that *dichromats,* people who can't distinguish red from green or who can't distinguish blue from yellow, are simply missing one of the antagonistic color systems. *Monochromats,* people who can see the world only in shades of gray, are missing both color systems (only their black-white system is functional).

Elaboration of Hering's opponent-process theory over the years (Hurvich, 1978) has provided an interpretation for most of the phenomena of color vision (see Figure 3-19). Furthermore, it has become clear that it is not incompatible with the Young-Helmholtz theory. It seems likely that color vision really involves some combination of a three-cone system in the retina of the sort envisioned by Young, and the three opponent-process systems in the retina or further along the optic pathways envisioned by Hering.

Other Senses

Clearly, vision and audition are the most highly developed of our senses. However, each of our other senses also provides important information about our environment.

Taste

The physical stimuli for taste are chemical substances (sugar, wine, or pizza) that touch the surface of the tongue or, to some extent, the soft palate, the pharynx, and the larynx. Yet the sensation of taste produced by these substances is heavily influenced by other factors such as color, texture, temperature, and smell. This is why margarine is colored yellow and fruits are dyed before being put on sale. What is popularly meant by "taste" is really a complex perception involving other senses as well. Nevertheless, it is possible to study taste alone. Békésy (1966) applied various substances to very tiny areas of the tongue and found only

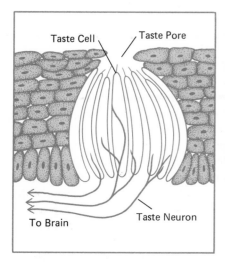

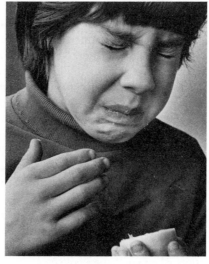

Figure 3-20

The diagram shows the construction of a taste bud, the main receptor for taste. In the photo on the right, the taste buds responding to sour substances have triggered impulses in the neurons attached to the cells, causing a strong reaction to the sour taste of the lemon.

four basic sensations: sweet, sour, salt, and bitter. That is, each small area responded to only one class of chemical substance, yielding one of the four sensations. Normally the substances we taste are spread over the whole surface of the tongue and we experience combinations or patterns of these basic tastes, which may seem quite different from any one of them. Furthermore, some tastes arise more slowly than others. For example, a wine taster might describe a sip of wine as "first fruity, followed by a huskier mellow flavor, and finally a golden aftertaste."

Taste buds are the main receptors for taste. There are about 9,000 of these tiny structures, located mostly on the tip, sides, and rear of the tongue. An example of one type of taste bud is shown in Figure 3-20. Each bud consists of about a dozen individual taste cells clustered together. Liquids, or substances dissolved in saliva, affect the individual taste cells and trigger impulses in neurons attached to each bud. By recording the electrical activity in individual cells, it is possible to show that each cell responds mainly (but not exclusively) to sweet, sour, salty, or bitter substances. Although two cells on the same taste bud may be "tuned" to respond primarily to different tastes, the cells on the tip of the tongue are mainly sensitive to sweet and salty tastes, those on the sides to sour, and those at the back to bitter. These cells are constantly dying and being replaced, so that a whole new set of cells is produced over any 7-day period. If you temporarily lose part of your taste sense by burning some of your taste buds with hot coffee, you can count on recovery within 7 days as new buds replace the injured ones. However, as we age, some of our taste buds die and aren't replaced, and there is a permanent change in our sense of taste.

Smell

The basic stimuli for the sense of smell (*olfaction*) are airborne molecules that enter our nasal cavities. While it is known that these molecules must be soluble (in either water or fat) in order to produce a sensation of odor, little more can be said regarding the relation between the physical character of the molecules and the odor they evoke. Although many people have tried to set up categories of

odor, there is no generally accepted classification scheme. One such attempt is a seven-category system—camphoraceous, pungent, ethereal, floral, pepperminty, putrid, and musty (Amoore et al., 1964). However, even these odors may be broken down into more categories. At present the variety of classification schemes serves mainly to illustrate the complexity of odors.

The olfactory receptors are located on the *olfactory epithelium.* It consists of two surfaces located deep inside our two nasal cavities. One reason so little is known about the olfactory system is that it is difficult to reach or electrically record from the receptor cells in the epithelium. Furthermore, it is difficult to control the presentation of stimuli (airborne, soluble molecules), although there have been elaborate attempts to do so. The movement of air in our nasal passages is very complicated. It is known that the act of sniffing alters the shape of the cavities so that more air passes over the olfactory epithelium, thereby exposing it to molecules of matter in the air that stimulate the odor sense. The congestion of the nasal passages when you have a cold makes it harder for the soluble molecules to reach the sense bulbs, which is why there is a reduced sensitivity to odors when you have a cold.

The basic receptor units are cells buried in and under the epithelium that project their tips (bulbs), along with small hairlike cilia, into the layer of mucus covering the epithelium. It is the reaction of the bulbs and cilia to the soluble molecules trapped in the mucus that triggers the nervous impulse. The actual coding of the smell information is not well understood.

Skin Sensations

Many different types of physical stimuli evoke sensations from the skin, such as the wind or rain against your skin or the gentle caress of a warm hand. For scientific purposes, it is useful to employ less interesting but simpler and more measurable stimuli. For example, the sensation of pressure may be evoked by pressing the tip of a tiny hair against the skin. Warmth or cold may be evoked by touching the skin with a tiny metal point of a certain temperature. Pain may be evoked by intense application of either pressure or temperature stimuli. It is possible to "map" skin sensitivity by drawing a small grid on the skin and then systematically applying each type of stimulus to each square of the grid. Figure 3-21 shows a typical distribution of sensitivity for each sensation. If enough pressure, heat, or cold is applied at one point, its effect will be distributed over a wider area, so these maps are based on low levels of stimulation. Very hot water will stimulate both cold *and* warmth receptors, producing a sensation of "hot." A curious property of these spots of sensitivity is that stimulation of a cold spot with a warm metal tip evokes the sensation of cold, while stimulation of a warm spot with a cold tip evokes the sensation of warmth (this is known as *paradoxical cold* or *warmth,* respectively). Of course, under most circumstances our skin is stimulated over large areas, so that whole populations of these spots are stimulated in unison or rapid succession.

The distribution of sensitivity spots varies considerably from one part of the body to another. For example, there are many more pressure-sensitive spots on your lips and fingertips than on your back. This can be demonstrated by measuring how far two stimulated points must be separated for you to notice that two rather than only one point is being applied to the skin. It turns out that

Figure 3-21

The diagrams below show a map of the typical distribution of skin sensitivity to pain, pressure, cold, and warmth.

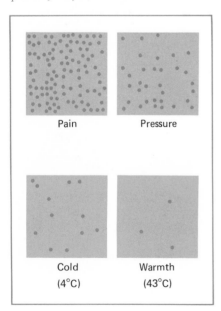

Pain   Pressure

Cold   Warmth
(4°C)   (43°C)

the smallest discernible separation on your back is over 35 times as great as on your fingertips.

Neurons in the skin have a variety of endings: Some are attached to the base of hair follicles, some have a type of enclosed or encapsulated ending, and some have free endings. At one time it was believed that specific sensitivity (warm, cold, or pain) was determined by the type of ending. But close examination of the skin tissue identified as a cold, warm, or pain spot failed to reveal any consistent association between the type of nerve ending and sensitivity. It is clear that the neurons attached to hair follicles generally respond to light pressure. However, we are also sensitive to light pressure on skin areas that have no hair, such as the lips or fingertips.

Most of the skin sensations we experience should be thought of as complex patterns of stimulation involving multiple receptor systems. For example, stimulating both hot and cold spots at the same time produces a sensation of extreme heat, while the successive stimulation of adjacent pressure spots produces the sensation of being tickled.

Sensations of Bodily Position

As you move about in the world your body is influenced by gravity and inertia. Your muscles constantly flex and relax in relation to these forces. For example, you hold your body erect against the pull of gravity, or you put an arm in motion and then brake it as your fork approaches a plate. Considering the number of cooperative muscles involved, it is truly amazing that you can bring a fork to rest precisely under several peas, let alone perform a gymnast's back somersault on a narrow balance beam. While vision is an important part of these processes, two other sensory systems cooperate in feeding your brain the information required to perform these complex acts: the *kinesthetic sense* and the *equilibratory sense*.

KINESTHESIS.   Sense organs in the joints and muscles send signals to the brain that indicate the position of the joints and the degree of tension in the muscles. These sensors are responsible for our kinesthetic sense. Ballet dancers unconsciously use these sensors to monitor the position of their limbs, just as you do when you perform the more mundane acts of walking, sitting, or lifting. A rare form of disease called *tabes dorsalis* robs its victims of the kinesthetic sense in their legs. They compensate for this by visually monitoring their position in order to walk. Their slow, oddly shuffling gait is a vivid illustration of the importance of kinesthesis. Most people become aware of the importance of kinesthesis only when temporarily robbed of it: for example, when the dentist puts your tongue to sleep by a shot of novocaine and your speech becomes slurred, or when your leg "goes to sleep" because you have sat on it too long.

EQUILIBRATORY SENSE.   Two sensory organs located next to the cochlea in the inner ear are responsible for our general sense of equilibrium or balance. They are the semicircular canals and the vestibular sacs.

The *semicircular canals* are three ringlike structures, each oriented in a different plane at right angles to the other, just like the three surfaces forming the corner of a box. They are filled with fluid that moves in the canals when they are rotated, just as the water in a glass will rotate with respect to the glass when the glass is turned. The movement of the liquid twists small hair cells, triggering neurons attached to these cells. Any bodily movement influences the three

separate semicircular canals in a specific way, and the pattern of neural activity signals the direction of motion to the brain.

The other system that aids equilibrium is the *vestibular sacs* located between the cochlea and the semicircular canals. These sacs are filled with a jellylike substance containing small bones called *otoliths*. Hair cells embedded in the jellylike substance are twisted by the gravitational pull on the otoliths, producing nerve impulses. While the semicircular canals only respond to movement of shifts in position, gravitational pull on the otoliths in the vestibular sacs continuously signals the head's position even when the head is motionless. Disease or infection of the middle ear can produce an almost constant sense of *vertigo* (dizzyness) because this signaling function is interrupted.

The emphasis in this chapter has been on the sensory systems that constantly send information about the outside world and other parts of our bodies back to the brain. It is in the brain that this information is integrated and interpreted. It is here that warmth, pressure, odor, and visual sensations become your experience of being held by your mother, and that a pattern of light and dark contours on the retina becomes the words of a novel. This is the act of perception to which we now turn.

Summary

1. All knowledge of the world is carried into the brain through the various sensory systems; activity in these systems is highly correlated, or *redundant*.

2. Before we can sense some form of energy, the stimulus must be at or above the absolute threshold.

3. A method of determining difference thresholds is *Weber's law;* other types of psychophysical scaling include *Fechner's law* and *Stevens's power law.*

4. Auditory stimuli are complex patterns of variations of air pressure; in the auditory system, stimuli are converted into patterns of neural activity that we experience as sound.

5. The sensation of pitch is determined primarily by the frequency of a tone; loudness is determined by the amplitude of the tone.

6. One theory of pitch perception, the *place theory,* is based on the idea that different sound frequencies (different pitches) actually trigger different neurons. An alternative way in which pitch information could be coded into neural activity is in terms of the rate at which neurons are triggered, the *frequency theory* of pitch perception.

7. The visible spectrum, or light, is the range of wavelengths of electromagnetic radiation between 400 and 760 nanometers.

8. The optical system at the front of the eye—consisting of the cornea and the lens—projects an image onto the retina. The eye's receptors are the rods and the cones of the retina.

9.   When the rods and cones receive light energy, this triggers a complex photochemical process resulting in neural activity that we experience as sight.

10.   The Young-Helmholtz theory of color vision assumes that there are three types of cones, each primarily sensitive to a different part of the spectrum. Hering's opponent-process theory identifies three antagonistic pairs of color systems in the retina or along the optic pathways. It seems likely that color vision involves a combination of these theories.

11.   The physical stimuli for taste are chemical substances (generally food) that touch the taste buds on the tongue.

12.   Other factors influencing the sense of taste are color, texture, temperature, and smell.

13.   The basic stimuli for smell (*olfaction*) are airborne molecules that enter the nasal cavities; the olfactory receptors are buried in and under the *olfactory epithelium,* located deep inside the nasal cavities.

14.   Many different types of physical stimuli evoke skin sensations; these sensations include pressure, warm, cold, and pain.

15.   Two sensory systems that provide the brain with information needed for the body to move properly are the *kinesthetic sense* and the *equilibratory sense.*

16.   Sense organs in the joints and muscles define the kinesthetic sense; semicircular canals and vestibular sacs in the inner ear are responsible for equilibrium (balance).

Suggested Readings

CORNSWEET, T. M. *Visual perception.* New York: Academic Press, 1971. An advanced review of the experimental methodology employed in the study of vision.

EGAN, J. P. *Signal detection theory and ROC analysis.* New York: Academic Press, 1975. A quantitative development of signal detection theory for advanced students.

GELDARD, F. *The human senses* (2nd ed.). New York: Wiley, 1972. A comprehensive development of the human sensory systems, suitable for advanced students.

LINDSAY, P. H., and NORMAN, D. A. *Human information processing* (2nd ed.). New York: Academic Press, 1977. The senses are discussed as components of an information-processing system, with analogies drawn from computer pattern recognition.

MCBURNEY, D., and COLLINGS, V. *Introduction to sensation and perception.* Englewood Cliffs, N.J.: Prentice-Hall, 1977. A clearly written and concise general introduction to sensation and perception.

SCHIFFMAN, H. R. *Sensation and perception.* New York: Wiley, 1976. A well-written introduction to a broad range of topics in sensation and perception.

Perception

Your senses are constantly affected by such aspects of the environment as electromagnetic radiation entering your eyes, rapid variations in air pressure next to your ears, and mechanical deformation of your touch receptors. Yet you aren't normally aware of isolated sensations. Instead you experience "things": see a person, a car, a printed word; hear a voice, a car's horn; feel the touch of a hand, or cool rain on your face. This interpretation of the information provided by your sensory systems is often referred to as *perception*. Ordinarily this process of interpretation is so automatic and successful that you aren't even aware of it. Only when you are in error and perceive an illusion, or when stimuli are highly ambiguous, do you think much about the interpretations that ordinarily occur so easily. A major goal of this chapter is to make you aware that almost all your perceptions are to some degree educated guesses about the world based on prior experience. To do this, we will deal primarily with visual perception, both because it is the richest source of sensory information and because it illustrates general perceptual principles that apply to other sensory modes as well. (Speech perception will be discussed in Chapter 8, "Language and Thought.") We will begin by considering some of these general principles of perception. Then we will show how they apply to a variety of important perceptual processes.

Some General Principles

Redundancy and Perception

As a newborn infant you may not understand the relation between the sound of your mother's voice, the sight of her face, and the feel of her warmth, but you rapidly learn that these are all closely related aspects of a single thing, "mother." Soon one sensation becomes a reliable *signal* or *cue* for the experience of the others: For instance, the sound of her voice often comes just before the sight of her face above your crib, or the sensation of being held. Almost every aspect of your experience involves relationships of this sort. As these relationships are learned, they begin to color every sensory experience you have. Individual sensations are interpreted as signals or cues for things in the world that can be reliably inferred from them.

Figure 4-1 shows a photograph sliced into 10 equal columns. Notice that you can infer quite a bit about the five odd-numbered columns from the five even-numbered columns (and vice versa). Why? Because you know a great deal

Figure 4-1

This is a photograph that has been cut into 10 equal columns. Note that you can infer quite a lot about the five odd-numbered columns above from the five even-numbered columns below (and vice versa). This is because you know a great deal about the structure of faces and about how one part is related to another.

about the structure of faces and how one part is related to another. Thus information about the parts of the face above could come from direct examination of it or by inference from the parts shown below. Since the same information is available in both ways (that is, repeated), it is said to be *redundant*. You know from past experience that normal faces have features such as eyes, nose, and mouth. When you hear people speak you don't have to see them to know their lips are moving; but if you are deaf, you may have to depend on reading lips to know what people are saying. In this way sensory data are redundant.

The dominant view of perception over the last 100 years or so has been that sensory redundancy, which you know through experience, allows you to draw broad inferences about the world from very limited sensory information. These inferences are usually so accurate, highly practised, and practically automatic that you are almost totally unaware of making them. This is why one of the early proponents of this view, Hermann von Helmholtz (1925), referred to them as *unconscious inferences.*

For example, our language is highly redundant—you can often finish a sentence in your mind after hearing or seeing only part of it. Read the two phrases in the triangles shown in Figure 4-2. Most people see nothing wrong with these phrases until they look at them more than once. Without realizing it, they simply ignore the extra word in each phrase. Clearly, they make rapid inferences about each phrase, based on prior reading experience, without actually reading each word. While such automatic or unconscious inferential processes may have misled you in this instance, they are normally an efficient and useful part of reading, allowing you to rapidly read a sentence without stopping to carefully examine each word.

This view of perception is not universally accepted, however. Modern proponents of this view have been challenged by adherents of a view associated with the work of James J. Gibson (1966; Gibson and Gibson, 1972). Gibson argued that traditional perceptual research failed to consider the active, information-seeking interaction between organisms and their environments. He believed that human sensory systems have evolved to extract far more complex forms of information from our environments than the stimuli used in traditional perception research. Rather than simply supplying cues from which our brain subsequently draws inferences, our sensory systems have evolved to be perceptual systems in their own right, systems sensitive to complex aspects of our environment sufficient to evoke immediate perceptual experience without any intervening inferential process. Proponents of Gibson's view such as Neisser (1967, 1976), Shaw and Bransford (1977), and Turvey and Shaw (1978) have called for more ecologically valid experiments in perception, experiments that involve the complex patterns of stimulation encountered as we move about in normal environments, rather than those used in traditional sensory research.

Attention: Selectivity in Perception

Another basic principle of perception is that we seem unable to deal with all potentially perceptible aspects of our environment at the same time. The study of how we selectively perceive one aspect or another is the study of *attention.*

HIGHLIGHT
Gibsonian Invariants

The late psychologist James J. Gibson (1966; Gibson and Gibson, 1972) argued that traditional perceptual research ignored many aspects of our natural visual environment that serve as important perceptual cues. Look at the scenes shown on the right. While the scenes differ in many respects, they share one feature—a gradual shift in the average pattern of detail as you go from top to bottom. This shift is called a *texture gradient;* it is an almost invariant feature of nature when one is looking out across a surface. The retinal size of all objects diminishes with distance; thus this gradient is a strong cue for the perception of depth. While it is tempting to think of this cue as something the mind constructs out of the constituent details, Gibson argued that the sensation of a gradient may be as primitive and fundamental a sensory experience as hue or pitch.

Another example of a Gibsonian invariant is the pattern of retinal stimulation produced when you look at something you're moving toward. As you pass objects, their contours tend to stream off to the periphery of your retina in an accelerated fashion. In fact, some may be moving so fast that they are essentially blurred lines radiating toward the periphery of your field of view. Although the details of each image are different, the peripheral streaming is an in-

variant, common feature. Again, this may provide a primitive cue for movement that is as immediate and direct as any other aspect of your visual experience.

Gibson's work has encouraged perceptual psychologists to take a fresh look at the patterns of visual stimulation encountered in natural environments. Earlier laboratory work may have been limited by a preoccupation with simple, easily manipulated, physical dimensions of light such as wavelength and intensity. Texture gradients and peripheral streaming are only two of the more complex invariants of our natural visual experience that play a major role in perception.

These three photos show how texture gradients can be a strong cue for depth.

Have you ever been at a party gazing with apparent interest into the eyes of someone speaking to you, only to realize that you're really listening to a conversation going on behind you? Both voices, your partner's and the one you're really attending to, are entering your ears and evoking patterns of sensory

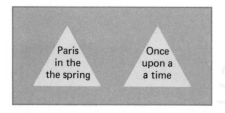

Figure 4-2

Read the phrases in the two triangles. Did you notice something wrong? Most people have to be told that there is an extra word in each phrase—they do not notice it right away. This is because we normally read rapidly, without examining every word.

activity. Yet you selectively perceive only one of them. You may not be oblivious of everything your partner is saying, but you find it difficult to listen closely to both conversations at the same time. Thus you may occasionally switch your full attention back to your partner in order to keep the conversation going. A situation of this sort, often referred to as the "cocktail party phenomenon," illustrates a major feature of perception, its *selectivity*. It seems possible to attend closely to only part of the sensory activity evoked by our environment at any one time; the rest goes virtually unnoticed. For example, you are probably sitting as you read this. Without moving, shift your attention to the sensations produced by the pressure of your body against the surfaces supporting it. Exactly where is the chair pressing against your back? Which parts of your left foot are pressing against something? As you attempt to answer questions of this sort, you selectively attend to sensory activity that was present earlier but unnoticed.

Overt selective processes involve orienting behavior, such as where you choose to orient your eyes. Just as you select which television channel you wish to watch by turning the channel selector, you select those parts of your visual environment you wish to see clearly by shifting your direction of gaze. Each new glance brings a different part of the environment onto the high-acuity foveal region of your retina. Later in this chapter we will consider the role of eye movements in the perception of pictures and in reading. Here we will simply consider certain aspects of this overt selective process that seem relevant to covert selectivity as well. First, notice that your eyes have a *limited capacity*—there is only so much room on your fovea. Looking at one thing usually means *not* looking at something else, or at least not seeing it clearly (it might fall on a lower-acuity region of the retina). One way of sharing or allocating your limited visual capacity is to shift your gaze from one place to another, an overt form of *attention switching*. We can record such eye movements with special devices. This allows us to study attentional processes of this sort, and reveals a great deal about the selective aspects of perception. There are also, however, *covert selective processes*. How can we answer questions regarding capacity limitations, allocation patterns, and attention switching when there is no overt orienting response?

The "cocktail party phenomenon" was used by a number of early experimenters to study covert selective processes. Subjects heard two voices speaking at the same time (usually one voice in the right ear and a different voice in the left). They were instructed to listen primarily to one voice or the other, or, in some instances, to try to listen to both simultaneously. Figure 4-3 shows the sort of negative relation that was generally found between a subject's comprehension of each voice. Increased comprehension of one is generally associated with reduced comprehension of the other. To ensure that subjects really attended to one of the voices, they were often instructed to repeat out loud, or *shadow*, everything that the voice said. An English psychologist named Donald Broadbent (1958) proposed that subjects have the capacity to listen to only one voice at a time. This *all-or-none switching* implies that the negative relation shown in Figure 4-3 reflects the proportion of time the subject spent listening to each voice.

This sort of tradeoff between attending to one voice or another, however, can be explained as a simultaneous sharing of attention rather than a switching

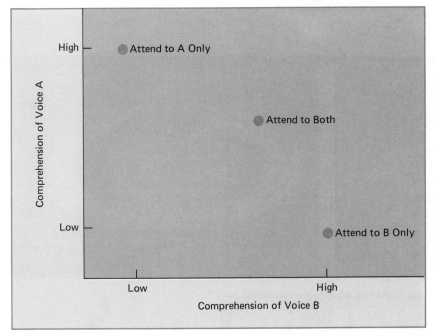

Figure 4-3

The graph shows the negative relation between a subject's comprehension of each voice—increased comprehension of one is generally associated with reduced comprehension of the other. (Broadbent, 1958)

back and forth. That is, you may attend primarily to one voice, but at the same time allocate some small portion of your attention to the other voice. This view, sometimes referred to as the *filter theory,* was advanced by Anne Triesman to account for subjects' apparent sensitivity to certain kinds of information presented to the non-attended ear. For example, they were likely to notice it if the non-attended voice said a stimulus such as their own name. They were also likely to make a mistake in shadowing if the meaning of the sentence they were speaking suddenly shifted to the non-attended ear. In fact, subjects may even shift their shadowing to follow the voice that is more consistent with the meaning of a sentence.

Another view of attention (Norman, 1976) is that selection occurs not by selectively blocking or filtering sensory information, but by selectively *processing* information already evoked or activated in memory by incoming sensory information.

It should also be noted that highly practised and familiar stimuli (such as your own name) often seem to be perceived so automatically that it is almost impossible to ignore them (Schneider and Shiffrin, 1977). A good example of such *automaticity* in perception is the so-called *Stroop effect* (Stroop, 1935). Subjects are shown words that are printed in different colors of ink. They are told to ignore the words and just name the ink colors. They have little difficulty doing this, except when the words are names of different colors. For example, if the word "red" is printed in green ink, subjects often hesitate or stumble in saying "green," as if they have difficulty ignoring the word's meaning (the Stroop effect). Normally the highly practiced and almost automatic perception of word meaning facilitates reading. However, this same automaticity makes it difficult to ignore meaning and pay attention only to certain other aspects of the stimulus. Thus, the Stroop effect is a failure of selective perception.

At present there is no one generally accepted theory of attention. In fact, it seems likely that many different processes are responsible for the selectivity of perception (Kinchla, 1980).

Figure 4-4

Organization is highly dependent on experience. Today's television generation of children would quickly recognize the planet Saturn as a sphere surrounded by a ring, as shown in the two photographs above, but an early astronomer who didn't know anything about Saturn couldn't "see" it correctly, as his drawings indicate (below, left). Without a clue (e.g., man on a horse) you may have the same problem "seeing" (organizing) a comprehensible form in the figure on the right.

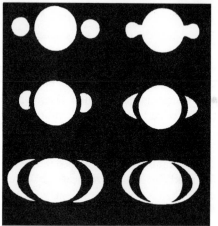

Organization

As we have already emphasized, you are rarely aware of isolated sensations. Your mind constantly organizes sensory activity to perceive *things.* Complex sequences of auditory stimulation are perceived as words, a car motor, water running. Complex patterns of visual stimulation are seen as people, cars, printed words. Much of our ability to organize or structure complex patterns of sensory activity into meaningful forms depends on experience (see Figure 4-4). However, certain kinds of perceptual organization seem so universal and natural that it has been proposed they are innate rather than the product of earlier experience.

GESTALT PRINCIPLES OF ORGANIZATION.   The Gestalt psychologists (Koffka, 1935; Kohler, 1940) believed that a number of innate organizational tendencies influence the way we see. They believed that these tendencies do not depend on experience but are the result of certain inborn brain processes. While many contemporary psychologists feel that these tendencies are the result of experience and learning, all agree that they are strong and virtually universal tendencies.

Examples of such apparently universal organizational tendencies are the *Gestalt principles of grouping.* These refer to the human tendency to organize sets

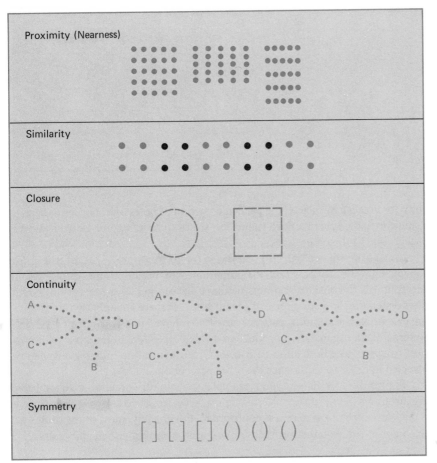

Figure 4-5

The Gestalt principles of grouping are shown here. These are the human tendency to organize isolated stimuli into groups on the basis of five characteristics: proximity, similarity, closure, continuity, and symmetry.

1. Proximity: The dots on the left can be seen as horizontal or vertical rows—neither organization dominates. But just by changing the proximity of certain dots, as in the two other examples, we experience the dots as vertical columns (middle), or horizontal rows (right).

2. Similarity: The similarity of color here makes you perceive these dots as forming black squares and color squares, rather than a row of black and colored dots.

3. Closure: even though the lines are broken, we still see these figures as a circle and a square—an example of how we tend to "close" or "fill in" missing parts from what we know of the whole.

4. Continuity: Because of continuity, we are much more likely to see the figure on the left as being made up of two lines, A to B and C to D, than we are to see it as a figure made up of lines A to D and C to B or A to C and B to D.

5. Symmetry: We are much more likely to perceive this as a row of six figures than as a row of twelve lines, because of the tendency to organize stimuli into symmetrical figures.

of isolated stimuli into groups on the basis of *proximity* (closeness), *similarity, closure, continuity,* and *symmetry.* These principles are illustrated and explained in Figure 4-5.

FIGURE-GROUND ORGANIZATION. Another basic organizational tendency that the Gestalt psychologists argued is innate is referred to as *figure-ground organization*—the tendency to perceive things (figures) standing out against a background (ground). For example, as you read this page, the words are black figures standing out against the white background of the paper. Normally this type of organization is so efficient and automatic that it occurs unnoticed. However, consider the pattern shown in Figure 4-6. Here the normal figure-ground organization suggested by the generally white background of the page encourages you to see the black regions as "figure" and the white regions as "ground." Only after some time and effort can you reverse this original organization and see the word "guess" as a white figure against a black background.

While figure-ground organization has traditionally referred to visual perception, there seem to be similar organizational processes in hearing. For example, the "cocktail party phenomenon" can be interpreted as a choice of which voice to hear as "figure" standing out against a background of another

Figure 4-6

An example is shown here of a reversible figure and ground. The black figure against a white ground will reverse to show the word "fly" in white against a black ground.

Figure 4-7

These are examples of reversible patterns. They can also be described as ambiguous figures, since it is not clear which pattern should predominate, unlike Figure 4-6, in which the pattern that revealed the word "fly" is clearly the more appropriate organization.

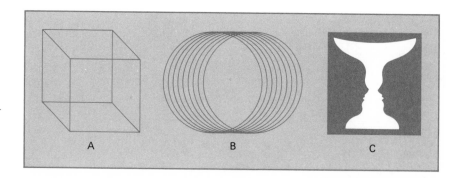

voice (or voices). Similarly, the particular stream of notes one chooses to hear as a single melodic line in a Bach fugue also seems to be a "figure" heard against a background of the other notes.

BISTABLE OR REVERSIBLE STIMULUS PATTERNS.   One of the most convincing ways to illustrate the importance of organizational processes in perception is to consider stimulus patterns that are perceived in very different ways depending on your choice of organization. If there are only two alternative organizations, the stimulus patterns are often referred to as *bistable* or *reversible* patterns. Each organization produces a stable perception, although it is impossible to experience both simultaneously. One organization must be changed or reversed in order to experience the other perception.

Figure 4-7 presents several examples of stimuli susceptible to multiple organizations. Some of the patterns could also be described as *ambiguous,* since it is unclear which organization is appropriate. Fortunately, most of the things we see occur in contexts that provide ample cues for resolving such ambiguity.

Constancies: Invariance Amidst Change

Although sensory activity may vary enormously from moment to moment, you perceive many aspects of the world as stable and invariant. For example, a person seen from different angles or distances produces different patterns of stimulation on your retina, yet you still "see" the same person. You draw similar inferences about the world from different patterns of sensory activity. Such inferences give a stability or constancy to your perceptions of the world despite great changes in sensory activity. This phenomenon is often referred to as *perceptual constancy.* We will discuss three types of constancy: size, shape, and color.

SIZE CONSTANCY.   A person walking away from you casts a smaller and smaller image onto your retina, yet you see that person's size as remaining constant. This is illustrated in Figure 4-8. One explanation of it is that your interpretation of an object's size depends on both the size of its image on your retina and how far away you perceive it to be. Two objects casting the same-size image onto your retina should be perceived as different in size if they appear to be at different distances. The object that looks farther away from you should seem to be larger. Thus *size constancy* is the almost automatic tendency to compensate for changes in the size of the retinal image caused by changes in viewing distance.

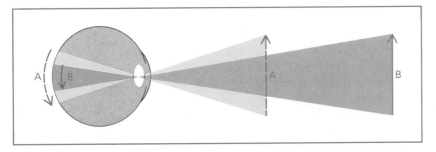

Some psychologists argue that this process of compensation is unnecessary to explain size constancy. They say that size constancy occurs because both the object and its surroundings change together as the distance of the object changes. In other words, your friend at a distance looks smaller, but so do the buildings around him, and the trees and the cars. When close up, all of these—your friend and his surroundings—look larger, but they are in the same *relationship* to one another. In other words, size remains constant because the relationship between the object and its surroundings stays the same.

SHAPE CONSTANCY. Shape constancy is the tendency to perceive objects as having the same shape in spite of variations in the shape they cast onto your retina (see Figure 4-9). As you watch a door opening, your view of it may change from a rectangle to a trapezoid. However, your past experience with doors causes you to infer or understand automatically that the door itself is not changing shape, only your particular view of it. Another example is the way plates on a table appear when viewed from above and then from off to one side—the image they cast on your retina changes from circular to elliptical, but you perceive them in both cases as circular plates.

Shape constancy depends on both familiarity with the shapes of objects and knowledge of their position in space relative to you. You may have had the experience of sitting far to one side in a movie theater and, at least at first, being keenly aware of the distortion produced by your perspective of the screen. However, you are capable of rapidly accommodating to the situation, and before long you were probably able to follow the movie without even noticing the distortion.

The Ames room uses a visual illusion to pit size constancy against shape constancy. In Figure 4-10 you seem to be looking at a normal room with one very tall, one average-sized, and one very short man in it. This is really a very distorted room. As shown in the diagram, the rear wall is tilted away from you at an extreme angle, and you are really looking at it from the side (as if you were sitting on one side of a movie theater, as in the earlier example). The man who seems to be very short is really much farther away from you and produces a much smaller image on your retina than the other two men. Instead of seeing the three men as similar in height but at different distances from you, you perceive both ends of the rear wall to be equally far away, and automatically infer that the men are of different heights. The strange shape of the room produces this misinterpretation.

The most important feature of the Ames room illusion is that you have a very strong expectancy concerning the shapes of normal rooms. And although

Figure 4-8

Object A and Object B are the same size, but because A is closer it casts a much larger image on the retina than B. However, because we are able to take into account distance cues and our experience of objects and people we do not always experience things as the size of the image they cast on the retina. If A and B were people, for instance, we would not think that person A was twice as tall as person B. This is the principle of size constancy.

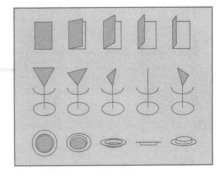

Figure 4-9

Three examples of shape constancy are shown here. The opening door is actually many different shapes, yet we still see it as basically a rectangular door. We do the same thing with a triangle and a circle—although when we look at them from different angles they cast quite different shaped images on our retina, we experience them as a triangle and a circle because of shape constancy.

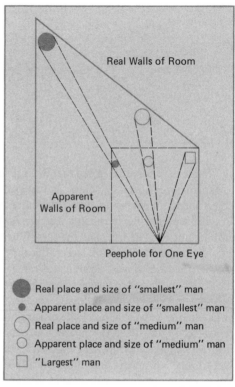

Real Walls of Room

Apparent
Walls of Room

Peephole for One Eye

● Real place and size of "smallest" man
• Apparent place and size of "smallest" man
○ Real place and size of "medium" man
○ Apparent place and size of "medium" man
□ "Largest" man

Figure 4-10

*The Ames room is really a very distorted
room, as shown in the diagram on the right.
The distortion causes a visual illusion that
pits size constancy against shape constancy.
Your expectancy of the shape of normal
rooms causes you to see these three men as
impossibly varying in size.*

you know there is something wrong about the difference in height between the
three men, shape constancy wins out over size constancy. Because you don't
perceive the true shape of the room, the size distortion occurs. In order to see the
room as normal, you must ignore distance cues.

When people have a chance to explore the Ames room, particularly if they
are allowed to touch the walls and experience for themselves the way they slant,
the illusion is gradually destroyed. But just explaining it to someone, even
showing a diagram, does not seem to destroy the illusion. Look at the
photograph again. Can you see the room differently now that you know the
trick? Intellectual knowledge seems to have little effect on perception—that's
how magicians stay in business.

COLOR CONSTANCY.   The light reflected into your eyes from a person's
skin varies a lot with the type of illumination in the room (firelight, sunlight,
moonlight, fluorescent light), yet the color of the skin does not seem to change.
This is called *color constancy,* another perceptual process that gives stability to
our perceptions.

Learning and expectation have a lot to do with color constancy. If you are
shown an orange or a banana under hidden colored lights that distort its natural
color, you still tend to perceive the orange as orange or the banana as yellow. If
you are shown colored pieces of paper under the same conditions, even if you are
told what colors they are "supposed" to be, your perceptions will probably be
more highly influenced by the colored lights.

Depth Perception

How does your mind make inferences about a three-dimensional world on the basis of the two-dimensional patterns of light projected onto each retina? In considering this it is useful to distinguish between cues that are available from the retina of a single eye, *monocular cues,* and those that depend on combining information from both your eyes, *binocular cues.*

Monocular Cues for Depth

Cover one of your eyes with your hand and look about you with the other eye. You still have a clear sense of seeing things at different distances, although not quite so vivid perhaps. Hold one finger out in front of the uncovered eye. Notice that when you focus on the finger, the background is out of focus and blurred, and when you focus on the background, the reverse is true. Thus focusing, or *accommodation,* produces a strong monocular depth cue: differences in the sharpness of objects at different distances. Notice that although an artist could paint what you saw given a particular accommodation, the blurred and un-blurred parts of the painting wouldn't change as you refocused your eye. This is probably why few artists have used this as a major cue for depth. Monocular cues that *are* often used to represent depth in paintings are *interposition, elevation, shadowing, linear perspective,* and *texture gradient.* These are illustrated in Figure 4-11.

Binocular Cues for Depth

A slightly different view of the world is sent to the brain from each of your eyes. These two monocular views are automatically combined into a single subjective view, sometimes called the *cyclopean view* after the mythical one-eyed Cyclops. Since your eyes are separated by a few centimeters, the view from one is almost never exactly the same as the view from the other. The left eye sees more of the left side of an object, and the right eye sees more of the right side (see Figure 4-12). Differences in these two views are called *binocular disparity* and play a major role in the perception of depth or distance.

   If a contour is projected onto the same part of the retina in each eye, there is no disparity in the representation of that contour in each monocular view, and the contour is perceived as flat. Such a contour will be seen clearly and vividly in the combined cyclopean view, a process termed *binocular fusion.* However, if a specific contour is projected onto *different* parts of the two retinas, there will be a disparity or difference in its representation in each monocular view. If the disparity is small, the contour will be seen as three-dimensional. But if the

Figure 4-11

1. Interposition: If one object seems to be covering another, it will be perceived as being closer. 2. Elevation: The higher the object in the horizontal plane, the farther away it seems to be. 3. Shadowing: Shadows or shading tend to give an impression of depth. 4. Linear perspective: Parallel lines seem to converge at a point in the distance, which is what gives the illusion of depth to this drawing. 5. Texture gradient: As distance increases, the texture of objects becomes finer until details merge into an overall perception. This variance in texture is a strong clue to depth.

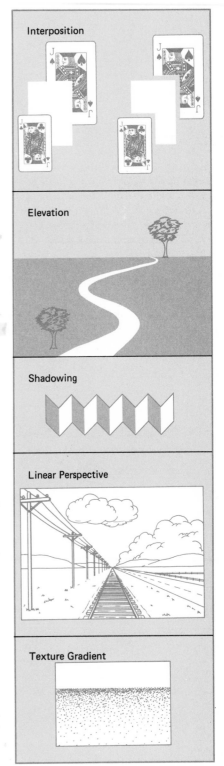

Interposition

Elevation

Shadowing

Linear Perspective

Texture Gradient

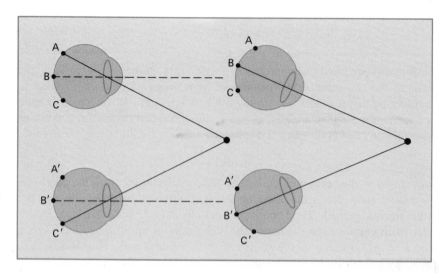

Figure 4-12

When your eyes are pointing straight ahead, as at left, the image of a single point close to your eyes will fall on different places on each retina. When your eyes converge, as shown on the right, the image will fall on identical spots on each retina.

disparity is large, the contour will not appear clear and vivid in the cyclopean view. It may appear as a double image or fade and fluctuate at times.

If there is a well-defined contour in one monocular view and homogeneous region (no details or contours) in the corresponding part of the other monocular view, the contour will tend to dominate and be seen in the cyclopean view. However, suppose there are inconsistent contours in corresponding regions of the two monocular views (different contours are projected onto a particular part of the retina in each eye). You will alternately see one or the other, but usually not both, in the cyclopean view. This fluctuation usually occurs every second or so and is referred to as *binocular rivalry*, since the inconsistent contours in the two monocular views seem to compete for inclusion in the cyclopean view.

Why aren't we more aware of binocular disparity and rivalry? The principal reason is that when you attend to some detail, you rotate your eyes to minimize binocular disparity for that detail, thereby producing fusion. You do this by aiming your eyes so that the detail of current interest is projected onto each fovea. If this detail is some distance away, the two eyes may be pointing virtually straight ahead. However, when you attend to something closer, it's necessary to turn each eye slightly inward to point directly at the same detail. This inward rotation is called *convergence.* The nearer the detail is to you, the greater the convergence required to produce fusion. You can illustrate this for yourself by looking at your finger at arm's length and then slowly bringing it close to your nose. You can feel the inward rotation (convergence) of your eyes that is required to see it as it moves closer. Since different amounts of convergence are required to fuse details at different distances, fusion of details at one distance usually produces binocular disparity for details at other distances. (Look at your finger up close and notice the double images behind it.) As you successively attend to details at different distances, you shift convergence, successively producing fusion and disparity for things at each distance. The brain automatically interprets the shifts in convergence, fusion, and disparity as cues indicating relative distance. This whole process, termed *binocular perception* or *stereopsis,* is a major part of our sense of a third dimension (depth) in vision.

HIGHLIGHT
Experience and Perception: Size Constancy

The photograph below shows the kind of densely foliated tropical rain forest inhabited by the pygmies of the Congo. Anthropologist Colin Turnbull has described these people and their way of life in the rain forest, where they were probably driven centuries before by other tribes. Many pygmies never leave this world. Turnbull describes what happened when a pygmy named Kenge took his very first trip out of the dense mountain forest into the valley below:

Then he saw the buffalo, still grazing lazily several miles away, far down below. He turned to me and said, "What insects are those?" At first I hardly understood; then I realized that in the forest the range of vision is so limited that there is no great need to make an automatic allowance for distance when judging size. Out here in the plains, however, Kenge was looking for the first time over apparently unending miles of unfamiliar grasslands, with not a tree worth the name to give him any basis for comparison.

When I told Kenge that the insects were buffalo, he roared with laughter and told me not to tell such stupid lies. Kenge still did not believe, but he strained his eyes to see more clearly and asked what kind of buffalo were so small. I told him they were sometimes nearly twice the size of a forest buffalo, and he shrugged his shoulders and said we would not be standing out there in the open if they were. I tried telling him they were possibly as far away as from Epulu to the village of Kopu, beyond Eboyo. He began scraping the mud off his arms and legs, no longer interested in such fantasies. . . . The road led on down to within about half a mile of where the herd was grazing, and as we got closer the "insects" must have seemed to get bigger and bigger. Kenge, who was now sitting on the outside, kept his face glued to the window, which nothing would make him lower. I even had to raise mine to keep him happy. I was never able to discover just what he thought was happening—whether he thought that the insects were changing into buffalo, or that they were miniature buffalo growing rapidly as we approached. His only comment was that they were not real buffalo, and he was not going to get out of the car again until we left the park.

How unsophisticated the pygmy seems—he was apparently so used to the densely foliated underbrush of the tropical rain forest that he couldn't maintain size constancy when viewing objects at the unfamiliar distances he encountered in the valley. But are we really that much more sophisticated? Or are our perceptions limited in much the same way?

Almost everyone has seen a full moon close to the horizon and marveled at how much larger it seemed than when viewed directly overhead. In fact, there isn't any real difference in the size of the moon—it always subtends a visual angle of about one-half degree. Rather, this *moon illusion* seems to be a failure of size constancy. We seem to judge its size as if it were closer to us when seen overhead than when

near the horizon (as shown above). One explanation for this (Gregory, 1973) is that the outlines of objects near the horizon are powerful depth cues indicating that the moon is even farther away than the horizon. These depth cues are missing when the moon is overhead, so it seems closer (and therefore smaller, since its visual angle is the same). This interpretation is consistent with the fact that viewing the moon through a rolled-up magazine or other tube eliminates these depth cues, and the moon illusion.

The size illusions experienced in the Ames room shown earlier in Figure 4-10 also show how experience affects our perception. Even after you are told the true shape of the room, the illusion tends to persist. However, if you are allowed to move about in the room, to explore its shape actively, to reach into one corner after another with a long stick, the illusion gradually disappears. No doubt Kenge's problem of size constancy would also slowly disappear as he gained more experience outside the rain forest. Who knows, perhaps even the moon illusion will gradually disappear as humans become more experienced with extraterrestrial space.

Many modern ideas about human perception have come from efforts to program computers to recognize patterns. One of the most important of these ideas is the concept of *image structure.* The accompanying figure shows how an image can be "parsed" into a hierarchy of forms. This procedure is called *syntactic scene analysis;* it reveals the structure of an image (a scene) in the same way that the parsing of a sentence reveals its grammatical (syntactical) structure. By programming computers to use knowledge of image structure, it's possible to take advantage of structural redundancy in most images—the correlation between a form and its parts.

It has been proposed that human perceptual processes use knowledge of such structural redundancy in much the same way. Early theories (Selfridge, 1959) emphasized a bottom-up perceptual sequence: Lower-order (smaller) features such as lines, points, and intersections are perceived first and then synthesized into higher-order (larger) forms. For example, recognition of an eye would be a strong cue for perception of a head. This view was encouraged by the work on receptive fields, as we discussed in Chapter 3: Simple *feature detectors* in the retina seem to feed into progressively more complex receptive fields as one progresses to higher visual centers. Other theories have emphasized a top-down sequence of perception in which higher-order (larger) forms are recognized first, then analyzed into lower-order (smaller) forms (Navon, 1977; Broadbent, 1977). Thus recognition of a head is a strong cue for perception of two small circular components as eyes. This top-down sequence seems to occur when you look at the impossible figure shown in Figure 4-14. Only after a while do you realize that the lower-order components (each separate angle) are inconsistent with the higher-order form (a triangle) you first see.

There are also theories that propose the occurrence of both sequences of processing. In one

Perception of Pictures

Most of the important characteristics of perception that we have discussed can be demonstrated in terms of how we look at pictures (paintings, drawings, or photographs). As with all perception, we draw as much from our earlier experiences (what we expect to see) as we do from the actual signals our eyes send to our brain. This process of interpretation is so automatic that we're usually unaware of what is happening. In this section we shall try to slow down the process to try to show exactly what is going on when you look at a picture.

Eye Movements

When you look at a photograph or a painting you may think that you take in the whole image at once, but actually you slowly build up a perception of the whole picture based on a series of separate looks. These are produced by successively moving your eye (such movement is called a *saccade*) and briefly (for about 150 msec) holding it still (this is called a *fixation*). Almost the whole image of the picture is cast onto some part of the retina during each fixation. As we discussed in Chapter 3, the ability to see detail lies in the fovea—acuity falls off very rapidly on the periphery of the eye. Thus, you move your eyes over the picture so that the fovea can pick up the details. This process of making a number of fixations is like making a picture from a series of snapshots, each of which shows most of the image but only a small part in sharp focus.

such theory, analysis by synthesis (Neisser, 1967), analysis of some lower-order form is aided by a tentative synthesis of a higher-order form.

Recently, even more sophisticated programs for computer pattern recognition have been developed that not only utilize structural knowledge but are capable of learning it as well (Raphael, 1976). Winston (1975) developed a program that can learn such abstract structural concepts as the class of forms called "arches" or "tables." It learns by being shown numerous examples of these classes, much as a child learns the alphabet in school. It then abstracts a general structural description to use in classifying new forms.

It seems clear that this sort of work should influence theories of human perceptual development and learning, as well as more general theories of human cognition.

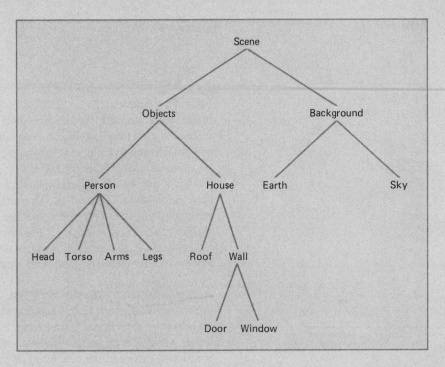

The diagram above shows a top-down sequence of perception as it might occur when examining a photograph or painting of a person standing in front of a house.

 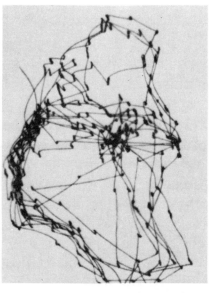

Figure 4-13

The network of lines on the right is a pattern of eye movements made by someone looking at a photograph of a piece of sculpture (Egyptian Queen Nefertiti) on the left. The pattern was recorded by bouncing a beam of light off the white of the eye as the person looked at the photograph for 2 minutes. (Yarbus, 1967)

The locations of these fixations are not random. They seem to concentrate on parts of the picture that are particularly informative and only rarely on highly redundant parts that can easily be inferred from the rest of the image. For example, in Figure 4-13 most of a subject's fixations were on details of the face;

Chapter 4: Perception

105

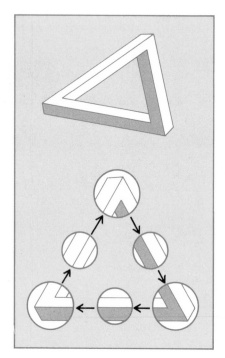

Figure 4-14

If you made the series of fixations on the triangle that is indicated here, each of your high-acuity foveal views (as shown in the circles below) would be entirely acceptable alone, but it would be impossible to put them together to form an acceptable perception of the whole object. (After Lindsay and Norman, 1972, p. 25.)

parts of the head and the neck, which could easily be guessed from the rest of the image, were sampled infrequently. This is an example of the sort of dynamic information-seeking interaction between the person and the environment that was emphasized by Gibson (1966), as we discussed earlier.

The fact that it takes time to see a picture, even though you feel you took it all in in a single look, is clearly shown in the way you "see" impossible figures, such as the one in Figure 4-14. The various parts of such figures seem to make sense until you try to put them together. Note how reasonable each part of the picture appears at first. Each separate fixation by your eyes takes in a seemingly logical detail of the figure; it is only when you put them all together, or try to, that you realize there are impossible contradictions in the separate parts.

Three Dimensions from Two

When you think about it, it is amazing that a pattern of light and dark pigments on a flat two-dimensional surface can evoke the perception of a three-dimensional world. To create this illusion, painters use a number of the depth cues mentioned earlier in the chapter. The problem, however, puzzled painters for centuries. It is only fairly recently that artists have been completely successful in creating this illusion.

M. C. Escher, a Dutch engraver, wanted to portray different levels of psychological space that could be evoked by two-dimensional images. In Figure 4-15 you first perceive the representation of a three-dimensional world containing some objects on a table top: a bottle, a drawing pad, and a book on which

Figure 4-15

Reptiles, by M. C. Escher.

Figure 4-16
Rippled Surface, by M. C. Escher.

some lizards appear to be crawling. Follow the path of the lizards as they climb a geometrically shaped object and down over a cup onto the drawing tablet. There they appear to merge into the drawing page, becoming simply flat figures drawn onto the page of the book. As you scan the drawing, one of the "flat" drawings suddenly becomes a three-dimensional lizard, climbing up onto the book to join his other companions. The point of the illustration is that the lizards exist in three distinct levels of psychological space. First, although you don't pay too much attention to it, you're obviously aware that Figure 4-15 is a "flat" figure in your own book. In looking at this flat figure you imagine another three-dimensional world containing the table top on which are located the drawing pad, the book, and the lizards. Finally, there is still another world represented by the drawings in the pad. By having the lizards move in and out of the normally isolated worlds, Escher provokes the viewer into an appreciation of their separate psychological existence.

Figure 4-17
Three Worlds, by M. C. Escher.

In one sense, Escher was both a master artist and a major perceptual psychologist, although he received credit for neither until very late in his life. Now his work is valued for his insights about psychological spaces. Figure 4-16 shows one of his representations of a complex space consisting of the rippling surface of a pond on which are reflected trees stretching up into a sky containing a distant full moon—all this by the clever juxtaposition of black, white, and gray on the flat surface of his engraving. In Figure 4-17 the surface of the water is indicated not by distorted reflections, as in the previous picture, but by a pattern of leaves floating on the surface of the water (an example of a texture gradient). The leaves define the water "surface" by their orientation and by the fact that they diminish in size as the surface seems to recede from us. Furthermore, there

Figure 4-18

The converging straight lines in this figure give a strong sensation of depth, an example of the use of linear perspective. This in turn produces the illusion that the figure on the right is larger than the figures on the left.

Figure 4-19

The kind of linear perspective shown here in real life in a photograph is what creates the Ponzo illusion in the drawing beneath it. Thus the cues given by this linear perspective make it seem that one band is longer than the other, whereas both are exactly the same size.

is another space beneath the water, a carp's world from which the carp watches us through the leaves. Finally, reflections of trees stretch off into still another space above the water. These etchings of Escher show the mastery of the modern artist in representing complex three-dimensional worlds on the flat surfaces of a painting. Very little is required for the mind to "see" a flat drawing as three-dimensional space.

Illusions Induced by Two-Dimensional Depth Cues

The mind's ability to use these two-dimensional cues for three-dimensional space is so automatic and deeply engrained that it can produce strong illusionary effects. For example, the converging straight lines in Figure 4-18 evoke such a strong perception of depth that it is hard not to "see" the figure on the right as being larger than the figures on the left. All three figures project exactly the same-size image on your retina. However, when you perceive the representation

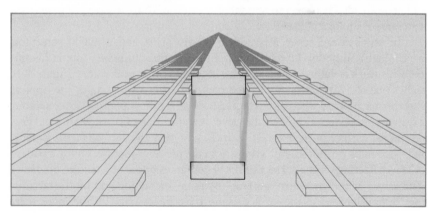

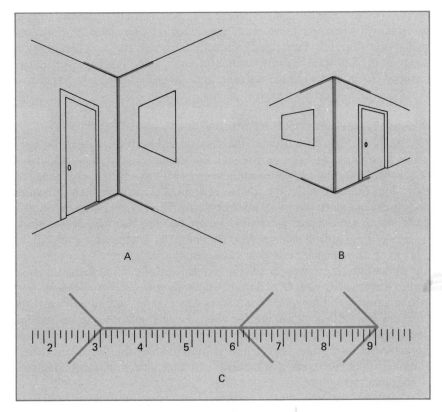

Figure 4-20

The Müller-Lyer illusion is shown in two different ways here. In both cases the line between the arrows is exactly the same length, although in each case one seems visibly longer than the other. Notice that in C, even though the figures appear against a ruler, quite clearly showing that the two lines are the same length, the illusion persists.

as a three-dimensional space (a perception strongly suggested by the linear perspective), the figure on the right will be seen as farthest away. Thus, according to the "automatic" rules of size constancy, the figure on the right must be much larger than those on the left, since it projects the same-size retinal image.

Two other illusions that have been explained in a similar fashion (Gregory, 1973) are shown here. The *Ponzo illusion* (Figure 4-19) seems to involve linear perspective cues much like those in Figure 4-18. The *Müller-Lyer illusion* (Figure 4-20) may also be interpreted as involving linear perspective cues—in one case those seen in the corner of a room, and in the other those seen on the outside corner of a building. In each case, these two-dimensional cues may automatically evoke an unconscious perception of a three-dimensional space. The illusionary appearance of differing lengths would then be consistent with the rules of size constancy.

Movement Perception

As you shift your direction of gaze or move about in the world, the images cast onto your retina constantly shift and change. Yet your brain is remarkably good at maintaining a sort of *location constancy*. A room doesn't seem to move just because you move or look about. There is an invariance or constancy in your perception of where things are, even though their representation on your retina changes considerably. Your mind constantly takes into account changes in the direction of your gaze and the position of your body. Only when these two factors seem insufficient to account for changes in the location of objects in your visual field do you perceive them as moving.

Absolute and Relative Retinal Movement

It is useful to distinguish between the absolute and relative position of objects within your visual field (on your retina). For example, as you read this line of text, a word's absolute position within your visual field changes each time you move your eyes. However, the relative position of (separation between) words doesn't change, since the words all shift across the field (retina) together. You don't perceive the words as moving simply because their absolute position within your visual field changes. You automatically interpret these changes as due to eye movements. Since your brain initiates the efferent commands that move your eyes, it can compare that movement with the absolute movement of objects across your retina. Only if the two differ do you perceive movement. You can demonstrate this for yourself as follows. Close one eye and slightly move the other one by pressing it from the side with your finger. Since your brain didn't send out any efferent command to move your eye, the absolute movement of the image across your retina is perceived as movement of the scene "out there," almost as if you were seeing movements of a huge photograph that filled your whole visual field.

Another situation in which a misperception of absolute movement occurs is when you watch a small, *stationary* point of light in an otherwise totally dark room. After a while you tend to see the light as slowly moving about even though it really remains stationary. This is the so-called *autokinetic effect.* It can be shown that the primary cause of this illusion is your inability to keep track of exactly where your eyes are pointing. You believe your eyes are stationary, but they really have shifted position slightly. This produces absolute movement of the light across your retina, which is erroneously interpreted as movement of the light rather than of your eyes. Why isn't this inability to perfectly control the position of your eyes a problem in other situations—for instance, in a well-lighted room? Probably because interpreting absolute movement of the image on your retina as movements of the room is so implausible (in the absence of sounds and other sensations suggesting something like an earthquake) that you automatically attribute the image motion to small eye movements (Kinchla and Allen, 1970).

There is still another situation in which you may misperceive (misinterpret) absolute retinal movement. Sitting next to the window on a train, you may perceive another adjacent train slowly begin to move. Then suddenly you realize that it is really your own train beginning to move. You erroneously attributed the absolute movement of the adjacent train's image across your retina to that train's movement rather than your own. Ordinarily you don't make mistakes like this since other cues clearly indicate your own body motion (kinesthetic, tactile, auditory). However, whan a train begins to move very slowly and smoothly, these cues may not be available.

Fortunately, you rarely if ever have to rely solely on absolute retinal motion. Objects are ordinarily seen to move in well-illuminated visual fields against complex backgrounds. Thus the relative motion of object and background within your visual field is a strong cue for motion. The advantage of such cues is evident if you have ever tried to discern the movement of a small cloud high overhead in an otherwise clear blue sky. If the cloud is moving slowly, its movement may be hard to see. However, if you can view the cloud in reference to some stationary point, such as the edge of a roof, its motion may be easily discerned. In addition to changes in the separation between cloud and roof (relative movement), the cloud may actually slowly pass behind the edge of the roof. This progressive covering up of one object by another is another strong cue for motion that arises whenever objects move against clearly visible backgrounds.

People often misperceive relative retinal movement when a small spot of light is projected onto a large screen. If the screen is suddenly moved slightly, people often perceive the spot as moving. This is called *induced motion.* In most environments we have little difficulty discerning stationary reference points when interpreting relative retinal movement.

Stroboscopic Motion

An important aspect of visual motion perception is that a succession of still (static) images can produce the perception of smooth continuous motion. This is called the *phi illusion* or *stroboscopic motion* (Figure 4-21). It is what makes a string of successively illuminated lights on a theater marquee appear to move. It also causes us to perceive smooth motion when watching a movie, though we are looking at a series of still photographs shown one after another on the screen.

The succession of images must be sufficiently fast to produce the phi illusion. You probably have seen early Charlie Chaplin movies in which the movement is jerky. This is because only 16 pictures a second were taken in these early movies. Modern films show up to 24 separate pictures a second to produce the illusion of smooth motion. Television presents up to 30 separate images a second.

Reading

Reading is clearly one of our most important, efficient, and highly practiced information-processing skills. Just as with most forms of perception, you are unconscious of the many components of this skill because the process has become so automatic. In this section we will try to make you aware of these components. To do this, it will be useful to present an earlier view of the reading process. This view grew out of early research on eye movements during reading, and is currently advanced by many companies selling speed-reading courses. We shall first show how this view developed, then raise some questions about it, and finally present an alternative view that seems more consistent with modern research on reading and perception.

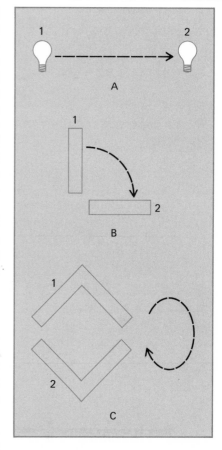

Figure 4-21

If after just the right delay (50 to 100 msec) form 1 is replaced by form 2 in A, B, or C, stroboscopic motion will be perceived, as indicated by the dotted line. In A this will be a smooth horizontal motion of the point from left to right. In B it will be a smooth "tipping" of the bar from vertical to horizontal. In C the angular form will appear to flip over. These effects suggest that there is a cognitive or interpretive aspect to stroboscopic motion: You perceive the most "reasonable" pattern of movement.

Early Ideas about Reading

One of the first people to study eye movements was G. T. Buswell (1922). He recorded these movements by bouncing a light from a tiny mirror on the edge of a subject's contact lens onto a photographic film. As discussed earlier, the eye successively makes a quick (1 or 2 msec) move (a saccade), then briefly (150 to 200 msec) holds still (a fixation). Figure 4-22 shows the typical pattern of eye movements during silent reading by both slow and fast readers. Slow readers make many fixations per line of text and often go back over parts of the line they have already passed. Such right-to-left shifts in fixation are called *recursions.*

In contrast, fast readers usually make only three or four fixations per line in an orderly left-to-right sequence without going back over the line. This suggested to early investigators that fast readers have learned to move their eyes in a more efficient manner, taking in more information during each fixation than poor or slow readers. They also discovered that when fast silent readers read out loud, their pattern of eye movements become more similar to those of slow silent readers; that is, there are many more fixations per line and more recursions. Maybe, investigators thought, slow readers simply haven't learned to read silently and are still trying to voice each word as they read. In fact, many slow silent readers could be seen to move their lips as they read, just as beginning readers often do. If this were the problem, then slow readers might be helped by teaching them not to vocalize during silent reading and to move their eyes in the

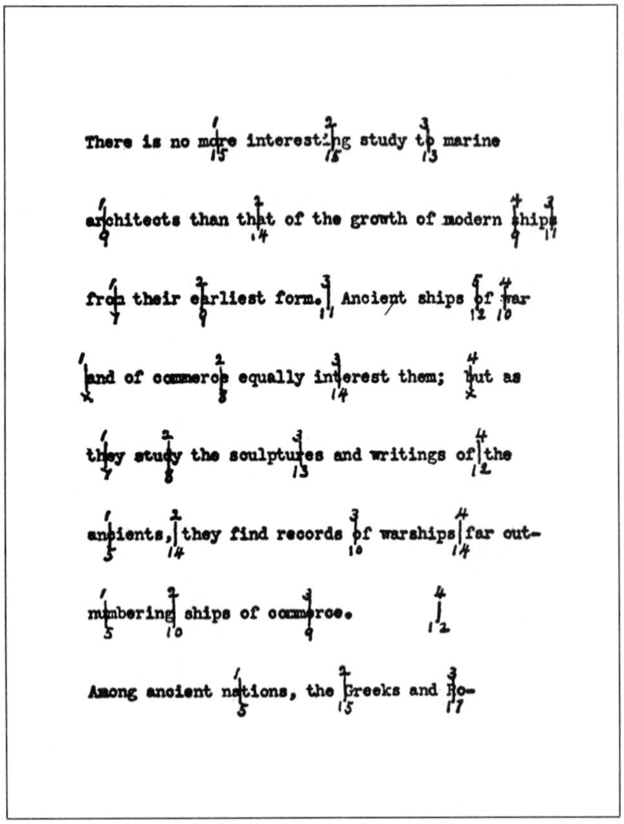

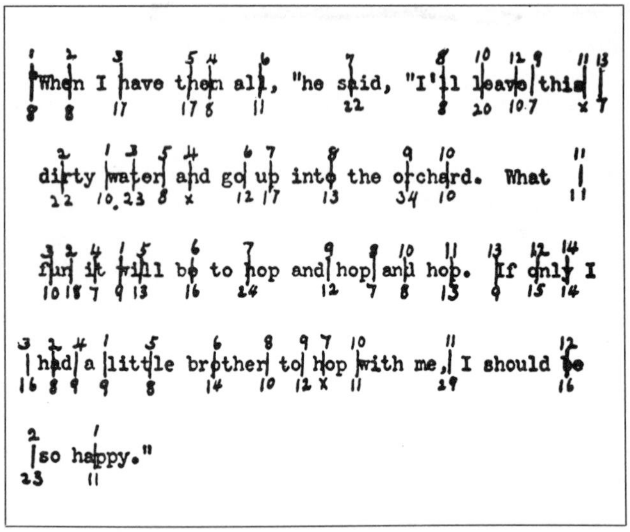

Figure 4-22

Eye movements by a fast reader (left) and a slow or beginning reader (above) during silent reading. The center of each fixation is shown by a vertical slash, the number above which shows the order in which the fixations occurred (the number below it shows the duration of fixations in quarters of a second). The slow reader takes many more fixations per line and often moves back over the line. The fast reader makes only four or five fixations per line and few recursions. (Buswell, 1922)

more efficient pattern adopted by fast readers, taking in more information during each fixation.

But how much information does a good reader take in during a single fixation? To answer this question, early investigators used a device called a *tachistoscope,* which flashes printing onto a screen for precise periods of time. For example, a test subject could be asked to fixate on a particular part of the screen and then a sentence could be projected onto the screen for perhaps 100 msec. This was sufficiently fast to ensure that the subject held only a single fixation while the sentence was on the screen. The experimenters were amazed to find that with practice subjects seemed able to read almost a whole sentence during a single presentation. Perhaps, then, subjects could be trained to read whole lines of text with a single 100-msec fixation. Since the rapid eye movement between fixations only takes 2 or 3 msec, subjects might be trained to read up to 10 lines a second. This is the basic strategy behind many speed-reading courses. Students are encouraged to break old reading habits and absorb a whole line of text in a single fixation. This is done first by tachistoscopic presentation and then by training students to fix their gaze briefly on the center of each line of text during regular reading. To make this easier, students are often told to slowly run the tip of their finger down the center of each page, fixating briefly on each line as the tip of the finger passes that line. In addition, they are encouraged to pick out key words and main ideas. To assess the effectiveness of such training, students are given comprehension tests to determine how well they understood the material they read. In fact, prospective customers of speed-reading courses are often asked to read something at their normal reading speed and then given a comprehension test. For example, they might read eight pages in 10 minutes and correctly answer 80 percent of the questions on the comprehension test. They are then given an initial speed-reading lesson. After it they are asked to "speed-read" the same number of pages in a comparable text. They may read eight pages in 5 minutes and then correctly answer 75 percent of the questions on a subsequent comprehension test. This usually convinces prospective students they have "doubled their reading speed" (eight pages in 5 minutes instead of 10 minutes) with "virtually no loss of comprehension" (75 percent correct instead of 80 percent).

Some Questions

The view of speed reading just outlined seems based on rather convincing evidence. However, let's examine this evidence in light of modern research on reading (Carver, 1972; Carpenter and Just, 1980; Smith, 1970). First of all, can we really read a whole line of text during a single 100-msec fixation? There are really two parts to this question: *When* do we actually read the material? *How much* of it do we really read?

It would seem that we read it during the 100 msec it appears on the screen. However, it can easily be demonstrated that this is not so (e.g., Sperling, 1960). If a second line of text is presented immediately after the first and in the same position on the screen, this second line will normally prevent us from reading the first line by obscuring or *masking* it. Therefore we don't fully read the first line during the 100 msec it is on the screen; we complete our reading after it disappears. If the second line of text is presented up to 1 second after the first, it may interfere with our reading of the first line. It's almost as if a picture of the first line persists briefly in our visual system after the 100-msec presentation, and it is this picture that we actually read. The idea that we can read a new line of text every 100 msec seems untenable in light of these poststimulus masking effects.

The second question about speed reading is how much we actually read in a single look. What do we mean by this? Suppose you were reading a story about farmers. Consider the following sentence, in which some letters have been replaced by a capital letter X:

XXX XARMER PLOWED THE FIXXX.

Could you guess the missing parts of the sentence from the parts you can see? Most people would quickly guess that the complete sentence is: The farmer plowed the field. How about the following sentence?

XXX XRACTOR WAS IN THE BXXX.

Again, given the context, you would quickly read it as: The tractor was in the barn. Because language is *redundant,* you can infer a great deal about the missing parts of the sentence from the parts you can see. Your ability to make inferences of this sort depends on your knowledge of the structure of language. The more you know, the less you need of a sentence to guess the rest. This suggests that the number of fixations a reader makes along a line depends on how easy it is to infer one part of the sentence from another part; that is, the degree of redundancy in the sentence. The more redundancy, the fewer fixations. In fact, even fast readers make many more fixations per line when the material is less redundant. Figure

Figure 4-23

This figure shows a fast English reader learning to read Latin. As you can see, a normally fast reader reverts to a beginner's pattern of eye movements when learning to read another language. This indicates that eye movements reflect familiarity with the material being read rather than simply good (or bad) reading habits. (Buswell, 1922)

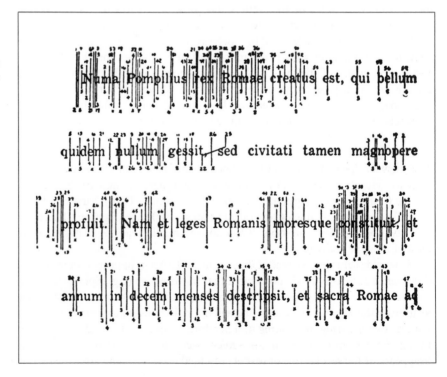

4-23 is a dramatic example of this. It shows the pattern of eye movements a fast reader displays when reading unfamiliar Latin text.

The high degree of redundancy in most written material also makes it difficult to design accurate measures of comprehension. For example, a comprehension test to assess your understanding of the story about farmers might contain the following question:

The farmer wore _____ when he worked.

(a) a suit
(b) overalls
(c) a dress
(d) shorts

While the correct answer might have been stated explicitly in the story, you could make an educated guess based on other knowledge you had gained from the story (or from just the word "farmer" in the question). It is very difficult to devise comprehension questions whose answers could *not* be deduced from only partial knowledge of the material. Even if you guess on all of the questions of a multiple-choice test with four alternatives for each question, you should get about 25 percent correct. If you had any knowledge at all of the material, you could do appreciably better. Notice that the poorer the comprehension test, the easier it would be to impress prospective customers with a speed-reading course. Since such courses are a lucrative business, we would expect the salespeople to encourage prospective students.

To read eight pages in 5 minutes instead of 10 with a drop in comprehension of only five percent (from 80 percent to 75 percent) seems impressive. However, suppose someone who hadn't even read the material took the comprehension test and got 70 percent of the answers correct. That would change the interpretation of the earlier evidence completely. In fact, many of the comprehension tests used in speed-reading courses are not well designed, and people who haven't even read the material could do as well as 70 percent correct answers.

An Alternate View

Thus it would seem that good readers are fast because they need only a few samples of each line to draw accurate inferences about the rest of the line. This is what allows them to read with only a few fixations per line. They aren't good readers because of the way they move their eyes; they can move their eyes the way they do because they are good readers.

Does this mean that speed-reading courses are a sham and don't really teach you anything? No—simply that these courses might better be described as *speed-skimming courses* (Carver, 1972). They train you to skim rapidly and remember the major features of the text, key ideas, terms, and concepts. This is a very useful skill. Many people don't realize how much they can get out of many books and articles merely by skimming them. This level of reading is adequate and even desirable for much material, and slower, more careful reading would be a waste of time. Many students do not vary their speed of reading to fit material and the goals they have in mind, and for them a course that shows how to skim material rapidly could be very helpful.

Summary

1.   One sensation can be a cue for the experience of other sensations; because sensory data are *redundant,* we can make inferences from limited sensory input.

2.   *Selectivity* is the process that allow us to attend to certain sensory stimuli at a given time while screening out other stimuli.

3.   According to Gestalt principles of organization, we tend to organize visual stimuli into groups on the basis of *proximity, similarity, symmetry, closure,* and *continuity.*

4.   Another Gestalt organizational principle is figure-ground organization, the tendency to perceive things (figures) standing out against a background (ground).

5.   *Bistable* or *reversible figures* are stimulus patterns that have two alternative organizations. *Ambiguous figures* are those open to multiple organizations.

6.   Although sensory activity may vary enormously from moment to moment, we perceive many aspects of the world as stable and invariant, because of *perceptual constancy,* which includes *size constancy, shape constancy,* and *color constancy.*

7.   Monocular cues for depth perception include *accommodation, interposition, elevation, shadowing, relative size,* and *texture gradients.*

8.   The left eye and the right eye see slightly different versions of the same object, because each sees it from a slightly different angle. These differences are called *binocular disparity. Convergence* of the eyes is required to produce fusion of the two views.

9. *Binocular perception* or *stereopsis* is the process by which the brain automatically interprets the shifts in convergence, fusion, and disparity as cues indicating relative distance.

10.   Perception of pictures involves eye movements (*saccades*) and *fixations;* the eyes move over the picture so that the fovea can pick up the details. These eye movements are concentrated on the most informative parts of the picture.

11.   The *autokinetic effect* and *induced motion* are two examples of misperception of retinal movement. In the *phi illusion* a succession of static images produces the perception of continuous motion.

Suggested Readings

GIBSON, J. J. *The senses considered as perceptual systems.* Boston: Houghton Mifflin, 1966.
  Gibson's influential and controversial refutation of traditional perception research.

GREGORY, R. L. *The intelligent eye.* New York: McGraw-Hill, 1970. A lively introduction to some fascinating aspects of visual perception, including a number of stereographic illustrations.

GREGORY, R. L. *Eye and brain: The psychology of seeing.* New York: McGraw-Hill, 1973. A beautifully illustrated and highly readable introduction to visual perception.

HABER, R. N., and HERSHENSON, M. *The psychology of visual perception.* New York: Holt, Rinehart and Winston, 1973. An advanced text covering a wide range of experimental work on visual perception.

LINDSAY, P. H., and NORMAN, D. A. *Human information processing* (2nd ed.). New York: Academic Press, 1977. Discusses perception from the point of view of computer science and biology.

HOCHBERG, J. *Perception* (2nd ed.). Englewood Cliffs, N.J.: Prentice-Hall, 1978. A detailed discussion of past and current theories of perception; includes a chapter on social perception and communication.

LACHMAN, R., MISTLER-LACHMAN, J., and BUTTERFIELD, E. C. *Cognitive psychology and information processing: An introduction.* Hillsdale, N.J.: Erlbaum, 1979. An advanced and comprehensive review of the modern information processing approach to human perception.

5 Altered States of Awareness

I was sitting in front of a piano . . . I remember I wasn't playing the piano, I was just sort of putting my fingers on the keys and moving them around . . . . I was at an amusement park. I got in line, they were having pizzas . . . There was another scene, there was a band . . . A drum major tossed a baton as high as he could . . . it landed on top of some chair and it started bouncing toward me. I grabbed it and threw it back at him . . . It sort of changed real quick; I was walking up these steps . . . there was going to be a robbery . . . Then there were all these rocks in the water, big, there was a big slab of marble . . . I don't know how a 20-pound rock floats, but some of them were. We were just filling this hole up with marble slabs" (McCarley, 1978, p. 65).

As an account of real events, this selection is outlandish; it doesn't make sense, nothing follows logically, and some of the observations are truly impossible. But as a report of a dream, it is typical. Most of us have had dreams of this form at one time or another. We can accept their bizarreness, though the whole recollection still remains incomprehensible. What do we know about this other part of our lives?

A dream is only one of a number of altered states of awareness, in which we somehow experience reality differently from the way we do in our normal, waking, conscious state. In this chapter we will look at some of these altered states, presenting what is currently known about sleep, dreaming, hypnosis, meditation, and the effects of certain drugs.

Sleep and Dreaming

People spend one-third of their lives asleep. For most of us that means about 25 years will be spent in an unconscious state—a lot of time to spend doing nothing! Truly this would be an inefficient way to behave if we were really inactive, but recent research indicates that this is not the case. It would seem obvious that all this activity has a major purpose in our life cycle, but it is not clear what this purpose is.

Though people probably have been fascinated by the topic of sleep since they first thought about it, only in the last 25 years has scientific investigation begun its rapid development. Most of this work is conducted in "sleep laboratories," where volunteers agree to spend the night (or nights) hooked up to various electronic recording devices: the EEG (electroencephalogram), which records the patterns of brain waves; the EOG (electrooculogram), which measures eye movements; and the EMG (electromyogram), which measures muscle tension or electrical activity in the muscles.

The actual moment of sleep onset is not best measured by any of these methods, but by optical reactions to light. In a typical study, subjects participating in the experiment have their eyelids taped open, and this is followed by a bright light that is flashed into the subjects' eyes. They are instructed to press a button whenever they see the light, and at some point the pressing stops; that is the point at which sleep begins. (What is really amazing in this demonstration is that sleep has the power to overcome what seem to be overwhelming odds. Could you fall asleep with someone flashing a light in your taped-open eyes?)

Figure 5-1

(Top) This person is participating in an experiment in a sleep laboratory. The wires attached to his head produce an EEG pattern similar to the one shown below. (Bottom) The EEG here shows brain wave patterns of the four stages of sleep and Stage 1 REM sleep. Note the appearance of spikes in Stages 2–4 as sleep becomes deeper and the brain wave pattern becomes more irregular. (Luce and Segal, 1966)

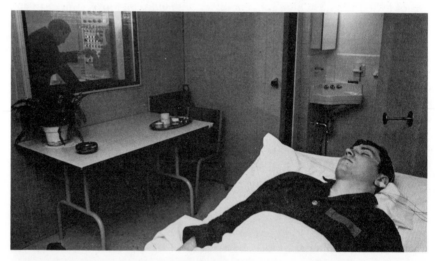

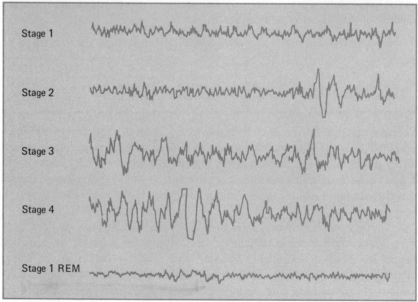

Stage 1

Stage 2

Stage 3

Stage 4

Stage 1 REM

Stages of Sleep

There are four stages of sleep that we go through in a fairly continuous cycle through the night. These four stages can be identified by different EEG patterns of brain waves.

The EEG changes that mark the differences between the four stages of sleep show an increasing irregularity as sleep becomes deeper and as the person moves from Stage 1 to Stage 4 of sleep. This is shown in Figure 5-1. The brain waves of wakefulness (alpha rhythms) are quite regular. When sleep begins and the person enters Stage 1, the brain wave pattern remains regular, but the amplitude or height of the waves decreases. A few minutes later sleep becomes deeper and the sleeper enters Stage 2, in which the EEG pattern starts to become irregular and other brain wave types, called *spikes,* appear (see Figure 5-1). Several minutes later, the sleeper experiences Stage 3, with its ever-greater EEG irregularity. After about 10 minutes the deepest period of sleep is reached, Stage 4, with its high, spiked brain waves. Sleepers in Stage 4 are difficult to waken; in children this is the stage in which sleep walking, night terrors, and bed-wetting may occur (Dement, 1974).

This progression from Stage 1 to Stage 4 and back again to Stage 1 can take anywhere from 40 to 80 minutes. At this point there is a change—the EEG shows a pattern of brain waves similar to Stage 1 sleep, but there is something new added, the presence of *rapid eye movements,* or *REMs.* The existence of this different type of sleep was discovered in 1953 by Aserinsky and Kleitman. It is called *REM sleep* because of the rapid eye movements that distinguish it from the four stages of non-REM or *NREM sleep.*

REM Sleep

Almost 25 percent of our sleep each night (1½ to 2 hours) is REM sleep. The REM periods occur with considerable regularity, about every 90 minutes, with different stages of NREM sleep occurring in the intervals between (see Figure 5-2). As the night goes on, Stages 3 and 4 of NREM tend to occur less frequently; the sleeper alternates mainly between longer REM periods and Stage 2. Near the end of the sleep cycle there are also short periods of wakefulness.

During REM sleep the muscles become relaxed to the point of paralysis, as

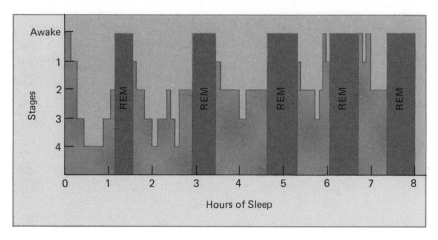

Figure 5-2

The chart shows the typical progression through the night of Stages 1–4 and Stage 1 REM sleep. Stages 1–4 are indicated on the x axis, and REM stages are represented by darker bars on the graph. As noted in the text, the REM periods occur about every 90 minutes throughout the night. (Dement, 1974)

measured by an electromyogram (EMG). This is why REM sleep is sometimes referred to as "paradoxical sleep," because the brain wave pattern is similar to that of a waking person, but the person is deep in sleep with no tension in the muscles and no response to outside stimuli.

The amount of normal sleep and the percent of it that is REM sleep changes throughout our lives. Figure 5-3 shows this—a 1-week-old baby sleeps about 16 hours a day, with 50 percent of that being REM sleep. By age 5 the amount of REM sleep is about the same as an adult, 20 percent, but the total sleep time continues to decline throughout life.

Soon after the discovery of two different types of sleep, it was proposed by Dement and Kleitman (1957) that rapid eye movements indicate that the sleeper is dreaming, whereas dreaming does not take place during NREM sleep. To prove this they tried waking subjects each time the EOG indicated a pattern of rapid eye movements; about 85 percent of the subjects were able to recall a dream when they were awakened during a REM period. However, not all REM sleep is associated with dreams—and some dreams occur during NREM periods.

There have been several explanations of what rapid eye movements mean—one theory was that rapid eye movements are actually attempts by the sleeper to visually follow the course of the dream, much like watching a movie; now, however, it seems more likely that rapid eye movements are simply indications of the intense brain activity occurring during these periods of sleep. What is not known is what function REM sleep serves in humans. It is clear, however, that it is very important. If people are deprived of REM sleep, by being awakened as soon as they enter the REM period, they become irritated and uncomfortable. Sleepers will tend to compensate for REM deprivation in one night by increasing the number of REM periods on the next night or nights (a

Figure 5-3

The average amount of sleep and the percent of it that is REM sleep changes throughout our lives. For example, in the first few weeks of life babies sleep about 16 hours a day, and half of that is REM sleep. By middle age, adults sleep about 6 hours a night, with about 25 percent of it being REM sleep. (Roffwarg et al., 1966)

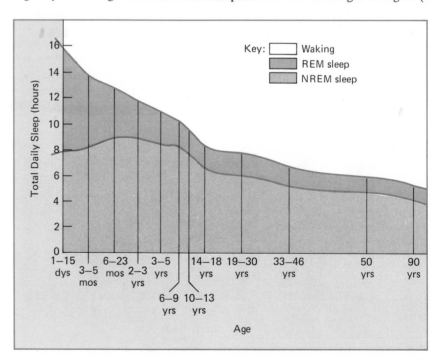

phenomenon called "REM rebound"). A similar effect does not occur with NREM sleep. In one experiment, a volunteer was awakened four successive nights each time he entered a REM period. On the fifth night, his sleep pattern showed 30 REM periods, over four times what the normal amount would be (Dement, 1974).

Why We Dream

To Sigmund Freud (1935/1969), dreams were the "royal road to the unconscious." During sleep, the conscious mind is, for the most part, not active. As a result, many of those disturbing ideas, feelings, and recollections that we try to avoid thinking about when we are awake spill over when we are asleep, because the conscious mind is not an effective monitor during sleep. Nevertheless, even during sleep we defend against threatening thoughts by disguising them, often in fantastic images. These images make up our dreams, and an interpretation of dreams can provide insight into the hidden, repressed corners of the mind. (Freud's theories are discussed in greater detail in Chapter 14.)

Sleep and dream researchers who are not receptive to Freud's view explain the issue differently. McCarley suggests that dreams do not indicate "a process of disguise or concealment, but a process of activation" (1978, p. 72). He feels that this might explain why so many dream reports mention strenuous activity such as running, climbing, and so on. Also, the bizarre quality of dreams, with their sudden shifts in space and time, might be due to the activation of more than one brain system at the same time.

There is also a theory proposing that the dream is a way of processing daytime memories (Palumbo, 1978). So many events, big and small, impinge on us in the course of our daily existence that if we were to stop and consider each one we would become confused and overwhelmed. Nevertheless, much of this information is important to our adequate functioning and should be examined. What, then, is the role of the dream in this process? As these waking events come crowding in on us, they are held, many unevaluated, in a limited memory system. These experiences remain in the system until we fall asleep at night. Then they are released and the dream acts to process, evaluate, and organize our experiences for whatever use we may later find for them (Palumbo, 1978). Thus we need to dream in order to sort out the events and solve some of the problems that might have arisen during the day.

Consistent with this idea is the finding that dreams show a pattern of alternating buildups of emotional tension followed by a release of tension; the number of buildup-release cycles appears to depend on the amount of tension present during the waking period (Cartwright, 1978).

Dream Content

Whatever the function of the dream, its content can be dazzling. Yet even as vivid and strange as the content may be, it still contains glimpses of the commonplace. The setting might be your home or somewhere near it, and the characters might be friends, relatives, and your pet dog, even though in the dream the dog might be dancing to the latest disco tune. The point is that we draw on everyday material to stock the content of our dreams. But what about other events? Suppose there is a quite audible sound, though one not loud enough to awaken the sleeper—will that sound be fed into the dream? Certainly, this sometimes happens. For example, most people have had the experience of integrating the sound of the alarm clock into an ongoing dream. There is some research from the sleep laboratory that is directed to this issue.

In one experiment, 4-year-old children had various common stimuli presented to them during a REM sleep period. The stimuli might be a few drops of water, a puff of air, or the like. They were then awakened and asked what they had been dreaming. One girl reported that when the air puff was administered, she dreamt of sailing in a boat with the wind blowing in her face. The drops of water resulted in a dream about being sprayed with a hose; and when a ball of cotton was rubbed lightly on her skin, she dreamt of her sister playing with a cuddly toy lion (Foulkes and Pivik, 1969). In a similar demonstration, 5 to 10 minutes after REM sleep onset adults were presented with the first name of a person. Though the names were not always integrated into a dream, there were a substantial number of cases where it had influence. "Robert" resulted in a dream about a rabbit, for example.

In a more recent experiment, which attempted to assess the role of visual factors in dream content, individuals wore red goggles on several days during their entire waking activity. The goggles, obviously, gave their whole visual environment a reddish hue. On the nights following the days in which the red goggles were worn, these subjects experienced four times as many dreams with a tint near the red end of the color spectrum (red, orange, or yellow) as they did when they did not wear the goggles (Roffwarg et al., 1978). Aside from showing the influence of one's waking, visual experience on dreaming, this experiment also suggests that color has an important role in dreaming.

Remembering Dreams

One of the most striking observations about dreams is that they are usually quite difficult to remember after only a short period of wakefulness. Results from the sleep laboratory indicate that about 80 to 85 percent of dreams are recalled from REM sleep, fewer from NREM sleep. But this high proportion occurs only if the individual reports the dream immediately upon awakening and only if he or she is awakened while in the midst of the dream or directly after it has ended. With delays, the memory for dreams deteriorates rapidly (Goodenough, 1978). This also helps explain why, when dreams are recalled, it is usually the last dream of the night that is remembered best. Of course, as Cartwright points out (1978), the last dream of the night is also the longest, strangest, and most exciting—other factors that probably have strong effects on memory.

Hypnosis

Sleep and dreaming are natural daily events, but to many people there seems to be some relation between them and hypnosis, which is not so natural a phenomenon. In fact, sleep and hypnosis differ in several basic ways—for

This is a painting of an early class in hypnosis given by Charcot, a French doctor who was a teacher of Sigmund Freud and a clinician in his own right. It was due to Charcot that the French Academy of Sciences accepted hypnotism as a legitimate form of treatment.

instance, a hypnotized person does not show the same brain wave pattern as a sleeping person—the pattern in hypnosis is similar to that of a waking person. There are some similarities, however; in the hypnotic trance state people are thinking, perceiving, and often acting out their perceptions—but, as in sleep, they appear to be unaware of the world around them.

The following section will discuss our increasing understanding of hypnosis, which is, like the progress in sleep research, quite recent.

What Is Hypnosis?

The term *hypnosis* comes from the Greek word *hypnos,* which means sleep. It can be defined as ". . . that state or condition in which subjects are able to respond to appropriate suggestions with distortions of perception and memory" (Orne, 1977, p. 19). The psychological characteristics of someone under hypnosis include an increase in suggestibility, the limiting of attention to a very small stimulus field, a decrease in reality testing, and the acceptance of logically irrational perceptions.

Early researchers in the field of hypnosis believed that once a hypnotic trance was induced, subjects would be able to perform tasks that they would normally find impossible—the greater the depth of the trance, the more profound the difference in performance would be. Actually, what many people assume to be one of the most dramatic components of the phenomenon, the hypnotic trance, is not that dramatic at all. It is unnecessary to use swinging pendants and whirling disks; all that is needed is a responsive person and some simple suggestions from the hypnotist—your arm is getting heavy, your eyes are closing, you are finding it difficult to move your hands, and so on. One performing hypnotist has commented on the simplicity of inducing the trance state: "Hypnotism is easy once you get the knack of it. The knack comes to most people easily; I hypnotized my first subject on the first trial" (Wolff, no date, p. 3).

One of the common questions about hypnosis is whether hypnotized people will do things that they wouldn't ordinarily do without hypnosis—jumping out of windows, shooting themselves in the foot, or whatever. The answer is no (Orne, 1977). A hypnotized person is neither unperceptive nor out of control, even though the nature of the control might change somewhat—some voluntary acts, such as brushing one's hair when a certain word is heard, might become less voluntary. But the person is still in contact with reality and is still able to make judgments. If people under hypnosis are told to look at a blank wall and it is suggested that there is a picture of a ship there, they will be able to see and describe the picture. But they will know that the picture they are "seeing" is not real, that it is a hallucination. It might float around or it might be possible to see through it as if it were an apparition. Similarly, people are unlikely to dive out of a 20-story window under the mistaken impression that they are taking a dip in the back-yard swimming pool. They know that the window is not a ground-level diving board.

Hypnotic Responsiveness

About 15 percent of the population can be greatly affected by hypnotic suggestion, while about 5 to 10 percent show no effect at all (they seem unable to be hypnotized); the rest of the population falls somewhere between these two extremes. These individual differences in responsiveness are the subject of much of hypnosis research.

The fact that there are large individual differences in hypnotic responsiveness (that is, that people vary greatly in the degree to which they respond to hypnosis) is one of the most important discoveries in this field. In general, hypnotic susceptibility rises in childhood to a maximum in the pre-teenage years, then declines slowly thereafter (see Figure 5-4). But the variation in scores in this cycle is quite low—essentially susceptibility to hypnosis is stable over time. An individual who is highly responsive to hypnosis today will be highly responsive 10 years from now. And, further, a person who has low hypnotic responsivity is not likely to develop high responsivity in the future. This suggests a genetic component; in support of this view, it is found that monozygotic twins are more likely to have the same level of hypnotic responsiveness than dizygotic twins (Hilgard, 1975).

High responsivity to hypnosis is not a general personality trait, however—the person who is responsive to hypnosis is not likely to be more suggestible than other people in nonhypnotic situations, and easily hypnotized people are not more compliant than others in a nonhypnotic condition (Orne, 1977).

In recent research, Evans (1977) has found that people who are highly susceptible to hypnosis are more likely to be people who can voluntarily control sleep. That is, they can fall asleep easily and in different locations like a plane or train, they take daytime naps, and so on. These individuals may have a general ability to control their level of consciousness, an ability that is useful both in hypnosis and in falling asleep easily. And people who are highly susceptible to hypnosis also learn meditation techniques rapidly.

The importance of individual differences in hypnotic responsiveness has outweighed the role of the trance state itself. In reviewing the research findings, Hilgard (1975) has concluded that the responsiveness is due more to the subject's characteristics than to the hypnotically induced state. In fact, some investigators feel that equal, or even stronger, effects can be produced by having subjects simulate the hypnotic condition rather than by actually inducing a trance.

What does it mean to simulate or make believe one is hypnotized? Barber and Wilson (1977) asked subjects "to feel as if you're looking at a TV program. . . ." They asked them to let their thinking and imagination move with the suggestion by recalling a TV program they liked and letting themselves "see" it again in their mind's eye. "I'd like you to respond in the way in which you'll benefit most . . . and that is to focus your thinking and to imagine to the best of your ability. Just let your thinking and your creative imagination go along with the instructions so you can fully experience the many interesting things your mind can do" (Barber and Wilson, 1977, pp. 36–37). Notice that no attempt is made to induce a hypnotic trance—in fact, the instructions emphasize just the opposite.

Following this procedure, the subjects were given tests suggesting that their finger was anesthetized, that time was slowing down, or that they were reexperiencing the feelings they had when they attended elementary school as a child. When comparing these people who were simulating hypnosis with other people in a trance state, the evidence showed that the simulators were more responsive to suggestion; their finger felt more anesthetized or they were more

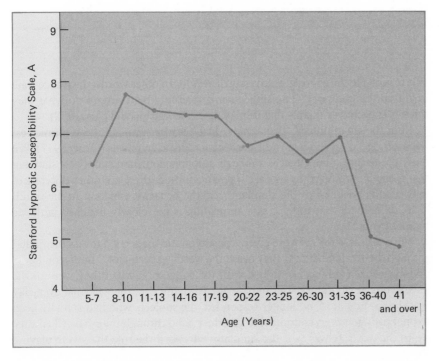

Figure 5-4

Hypnotic responsiveness or susceptibility rises in childhood to a height at about 8 to 10 years of age, then gradually diminishes until, at about age 30, there is a dramatic decrease, which continues on through the adult years. (Morgan and Hilgard, 1972)

HIGHLIGHT
Hypnosis: Its Checkered Past

The history of hypnosis is a checkered past filled with intrigue, dramatic personalities, and a murky stew of garbled thinking occasionally clarified by a legitimate scientific insight. It was this kind of past that threw hypnosis into disrepute and delayed the development of our current knowledge.

The story centers on a Viennese named Friedrich Anton Mesmer (1734–1815), who took the view that magnets could influence the functioning of the human body. He applied these notions in his medical practice to relieve his patients of long-term paralyses and other symptoms. Through a mixture of medical prowess, sheer egotism, and the showmanship of a performing magician, Mesmer accidentally stumbled onto a process for inducing hypnosis. Mesmer believed quite sincerely that he possessed an above-normal

Mesmer (left) and his patients seated around a tub filled with iron fragments.

able to recreate the age-regressed state of a child. In other words, the trance state might not be necessary. The subjects might simply be trying to do what they think is expected of them—that is, playing a role (Sarbin and Cos, 1972).

But the situation isn't that simple. Just because simulation can mimic real hypnosis doesn't mean that there is no such thing as hypnosis (Orne, 1977). We don't prove that some effect is a fake or a nonphenomenon simply by showing that it can be produced in another way. In addition, there are other differences between the behavior of the simulator and the behavior apparent in the trance state, differences that suggest that simulation is not closely matched with the hypnotic trance.

In one case, subjects were given a posthypnotic suggestion to run their hand through their hair whenever they heard the word "experiment." Both simulators and hypnotized subjects complied with the suggestion when they were in the psychological laboratory. But outside the laboratory, in their normal everyday world, the simulators no longer responded; the subjects who had actually been hypnotized, however, continued to run their hand through their hair when they heard the word. It was as if the simulators dropped the role they were playing

amount of magnetic fluid and that his influence could be channelled toward his patients. Seating his patients—up to 30 of them at a time—around a tub filled with iron fragments, Mesmer, wearing a coat of lilac silk, walked up and down carrying a long iron wand, with which he touched the bodies of the patients, and especially those parts that were diseased. Often laying aside the wand, he magnetized them with his eyes, fixing his gaze on theirs. . . . (Binet and Frere, 1901, in Sarbin, 1962, pp. 753–54)

In light of our present knowledge of mental disorders, it seems likely that Mesmer's patients were suffering from hysterical conversion reactions—that is, their disorders had a predominantly psychological cause. Thus, the power of suggestion was very strong; indeed, the patients' belief that he could cure them was an important element in his success. The trappings of the chamber that housed the tub, and the flamboyant manner and dress of a man who probably looked like a medieval wizard, all helped to enhance the strong effects of suggestion.

Mesmer's results were undeniably impressive, and it took only a short time before word of them reached the established scientific community. In 1784, a royal commission was convened in Paris, the city where Mesmer conducted most of his healing sessions. The American Ambassador, Benjamin Franklin, presided. The investigators found no evidence of actual magnetic powers, and therefore supposed the cause to be a secret of Mesmer's, for how could he possibly produce these effects without knowing how he did it?

The French government is said to have offered him 20,000 francs to disclose the secret and Mesmer to have refused—refused, of course, to tell what he never knew, for he had no secret to disclose. As a result he gradually fell into disrepute, and finally, denounced as an imposter, he withdrew from Paris to Switzerland, where he died in 1815 (Boring, 1929, p. 118).

The confusion and reputation that surrounded hypnotic phenomena were the result, then, of the way the matter first was described and the questionable behavior of its early practitioners. When investigators dealt with hypnosis more soberly, the real advances in the field began. Braid, in the mid-nineteenth century, proposed two basic ideas about hypnosis that proved to be correct. One was that concentration on a particular idea could occur with such intensity that memories would not carry over from the hypnotic to the normal state. The other was that suggestion was basic to hypnosis (Sarbin, 1962).

Later, Charcot, a teacher of Sigmund Freud and an expert clinician in his own right, saw the relationship between hypnosis and instances of paralysis and amnesia (conversion reactions) brought on by psychological stresses. Thus, the study of hypnosis was well along on its march to respectability and, largely due to Charcot, the French Academy of Sciences finally accepted the phenomenon as legitimate.

when they thought it was no longer relevant. The hypnotized subjects, on the other hand, went on responding to some special effect of the posthypnotic suggestion. Orne, who with his colleagues conducted this last demonstration (Orne, Sheenan, and Evans, 1968), later added: "regardless of how we describe hypnosis, it is real in the sense that the subject believes in his experience and is not merely acting as if he did" (Orne, 1977). This is not to say that simulators don't play their role quite well, some even reporting visual or auditory hallucinations. But when later questioned about their experiences and cautioned to answer honestly, many denied that the hallucinations were ever experienced, while others described events that were hardly as moving as those earlier reported (Bowers, 1967).

Pain Reduction Through Hypnosis

From the standpoint of the practical application of hypnotic phenomena, there seems to be no better example than its use in reducing chronic pain. Hypnosis has proven to be a remarkably effective anesthetic—indeed, the widespread use of hypnosis as a medical anesthetic in surgery in the nineteenth century was halted only by the introduction of ether and chloroform as more acceptable anesthetics.

In the typical laboratory investigations of pain reduction, two types of pain have been studied most extensively—ischemic pain and cold-pressor pain. In *ischemic pain* a blood pressure cuff or tourniquet is attached to the person's arm and tightened; this is followed by exercising the hand and fingers. There is almost no pain at first, then very severe pain starts, becoming almost intolerable by 10 to 20 minutes from the time the tourniquet is applied. Ischemic pain shares many of the same characteristics as postoperative pain in a hospital (Hilgard, 1971). In *cold-pressor pain,* the person's hand and arm are placed in ice water. The pain is severe and increases very rapidly; 30–45 seconds are as much as most people can tolerate.

Under hypnosis it is suggested to subjects that they will feel no pain from either of these two procedures. With the cold-pressor test, subjects who are highly responsive to hypnosis show substantial pain reduction through hypnosis in 67 percent of the cases. With subjects who are of medium or low responsiveness the results are less dramatic, with reductions through hypnosis in 17 and 13 percent of the cases (Hilgard, 1975). There is a positive effect through hypnosis in all cases, however, no matter how much or how little the person responds to hypnosis.

Tests with ischemic pain have yielded comparable results. In the cases of ischemic pain, moreover, when the pain disappears the corresponding blood pressure rise is also eliminated (Hilgard, 1971).

Of course, there are other agents that can be administered for the relief of pain, such as aspirin or morphine. How does hypnosis compare to these drugs? In a recently completed investigation, Stern and his colleagues (1977) compared the effects of hypnosis, acupuncture, morphine, diazepam (the main ingredient in the tranquilizer Valium), aspirin, and a placebo. The results, in terms of the subject's pain intensity ratings, are illustrated in Figure 5-5 (Stern, Brown, Ulett, and Sletten, 1977).

The outcome is clear: In both the cold-pressor and ischemic tests the greatest reduction of pain occurred in the hypnotic condition; morphine was second, and acupuncture was a close third. Diazepam, aspirin, and the placebo were ineffective in reducing the type of pain produced in these experiments. Once again, the superiority of hypnosis in pain reduction was more prominent among those individuals who were highly responsive to hypnosis.

While the hypnotic suggestion that pain will be reduced or eliminated seems to be quite effective, hypnosis is also helpful in treating the *fear* of pain, with its resulting hypersensitivity. That is, if we think something is going to hurt, it often hurts all the more; anxiety is often our worst enemy. Actually, some situations such as major surgery are much less painful than most people suppose, because there are not many pain receptors below the level of the skin. Anesthesia is often administered not so much to prevent pain (except in the first incision of the knife) as to reduce anxiety and tenseness and prevent shock (Barber, Spanos, and Chaves, 1974). Psychological factors are important, and we have all witnessed at one time or another how powerful and unpleasant they can be.

In one case a man with an intense neurotic fear of dental pain consulted a psychotherapist for help. Hypnotic suggestions that his mouth would be anesthetized and that he would feel no pain seemed to do no good, so the therapist tried a different approach. Placing the patient in a hypnotic trance, the therapist suggested that it would be the patient's left hand that would be "excruciatingly hypersensitive." In fact, no mention was made of mouth pain at all. The patient was assured that the dentist would be extremely careful not to touch his left hand. It worked: The overwhelming fear of dental pain was shifted to the hand, and the dentist was able to complete "extensive dental work . . . *without* any direct suggestions of anesthesia or use of chemical agents" (Beahrs, 1971, pp. 83–84).

Why is it that hypnosis works so well in reducing pain? A theory to account for the effects has been proposed by Ernest Hilgard, one of the most active researchers in the field. The theory has two components. The first simply involves waking suggestion—we just try to tell ourselves that the pain will be reduced, or we try not to think about it, depending on a "diversion of attention, relaxation, and reduced anxiety" (Hilgard, 1977). This path is open to anyone, whether of high, medium, or low responsiveness to hypnosis. Actually, the technique can be used by people who are not hypnotically responsive at all. At most, however, this waking suggestion will reduce the perception of pain by about 20 percent. The second component accounts for the remaining 80 percent reduction, and it seems to be available only to those individuals who have high hypnotic responsivity. Hilgard describes it as an "amnesic-like" process in which hypnosis prevents the perception of pain from entering the person's awareness (Hilgard, 1977).

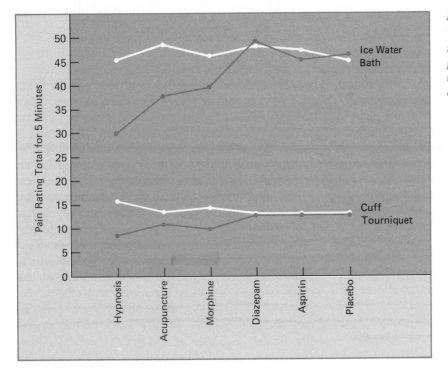

Figure 5-5

The graph shows the result of an investigation comparing hypnosis in the relief of pain to other agents, such as acupuncture, morphine, diazepam, aspirin, and a placebo. (Stern et al., 1977)

Posthypnotic Effects

In posthypnotic suggestion, a person is given a suggestion during hypnosis that is to be acted on only when the person is no longer hypnotized. For example, one might be told that an ear will itch whenever the hypnotist says "dog." The idea is that the effects of the suggestion will carry over from the hypnotic to the normal state. Since this is often an undesired outcome, most hypnotists make it a point to prevent it by telling the subjects that they will not remember suggestions made in the trance state when they come out of it. After all, the stage hypnotist does not want the subject to leave the theater still hallucinating that there is a hippopotamus standing next to him, nor would the psychotherapist in the case mentioned earlier want the patient to leave the dentist's office continuing to believe that his left hand is hypersensitive. It is felt that the signal to cancel the prior suggestion does work to prevent this from happening, and, when it doesn't, there is usually some simple explanation, as in the following example:

> Evans likewise suggested amnesia to the number 6 to a group of subjects. He intended this amnesia to last for the duration of the session, but one subject misunderstood the instruction to mean that the amnesia for the number 6 was to last until a later scheduled session. The subject was a high school mathematics teacher, who proceeded to experience great teaching difficulty in the classroom during the interim. (Perry, 1977, p. 264)

Suppose the hypnotist forgets to cancel the suggestion or the subject misinterprets the instruction—will the subject continue to respond to it for days, years, a lifetime? It all seems very risky. Actually, there seems to be little or no risk that these dire outcomes will occur, and in most cases, unless a specific posthypnotic suggestion is given, the trance effects simply disappear by themselves. It is as if subjects give themselves a signal to cancel the suggestion. In some cases, subjects actually instruct themselves to remove the suggestion.

Meditation

In one sense, meditation means reflection, consideration of a problem, or focusing on an issue. In its presently popular sense, derived mainly from the mysticism of Eastern philosophies, it means almost the opposite. Here the intent is not to concentrate on anything, but to block out all thoughts from consciousness. It seems impossible to avoid all thought, but this is just what is thought to be necessary for successful meditation.

The technique involves concentrating on a particular word or sound—in Transcendental Meditation it is called a *mantra*—and to use this to block out other thoughts. In Transcendental Meditation the mantra is a secret sound, which differs with each person and is told to the meditator by his or her instructor. Other practitioners suggest that any sound will do—the word "one," for example. Still others suggest concentrating on one's own breathing, or on a visual stimulus.

Can some form of meditation, practiced daily, actually improve an individual's health and reverse stress-related illness? Many claims about the health benefits of meditation have been made, including the following:

1. increasing blood lactate, which would produce muscle relaxation

2. increasing airway conductance in breathing passages, which would help to treat asthma

3. improving body rhythms, which would allow insomniacs to naturally correct sleep imbalance.

In terms of the actual, measurable, physiological effects of meditation, there is consistent evidence to indicate that during meditative states the individual consumes less oxygen (10 to 20 percent lower than during wakefulness), breathes more slowly, and has a slower heart rate. The galvanic skin response (GSR) rises and shows less spontaneous fluctuations, indicative of a calm bodily state. Brain wave patterns of meditators indicate a preponderance of alpha waves typical of presleep or relaxed, drowsy states. To summarize, we can say that the physiological effect of meditation seems to be a general lowering of body metabolism.

While some of the research in this area is promising, many of the studies were conducted on samples of subjects that differed widely in general characteristics, and on individuals who were highly specialized in their meditative techniques. Thus the generalizability of the results is still in question, and more extensive, systematic research is needed.

To give an example: While no consistent changes in blood pressure have been identified during meditation, a few long-term studies have shown that some hypertensive patients have been able to reduce their blood pressure over time. However, the changes were small and occurred only if the subjects meditated regularly (Benson, 1975). Further, some of these people were taking medication to treat the hypertension at the same time, which makes the results even more difficult to judge.

If incessant stimulation of the sympathetic nervous system is largely responsible for the incidence of stress-related illness, then the quiessence of the nervous system found during meditation may indeed be a step toward improved health. We will discuss the topic of stress-related illness in depth in Chapter 15.

The important aspect of the technique is to try to restrict attention to one thing and by doing this to block out sensations from the outside world and your own internal thoughts. In theory, the result of this is a state of pure awareness in which one experiences the world (truth) directly, without the screen of one's own illusory perceptions to distort it. A nonmystical result is a physical relaxation, a release of tension, which accompanies meditation. It is this aspect of meditation that may have important implications in the treatment of stress-related diseases, although there is still much research to be done in this area before we can be certain that meditation is indeed an effective treatment for such diseases (see above, "Application: Meditation and Stress").

There are some striking similarities in meditation and hypnosis. In a recent investigation, meditators were compared with people who were highly responsive to hypnosis, using a number of psychological measures (Barmark and Caunitz, 1979). The only difference that emerged was that the highly responsive people experienced more vivid visual imagery—the events they visualized in their mind's eye were more striking. When questioned about the feelings

experienced when they are just sitting quietly, both the meditative and the responsive hypnotic groups were more relaxed, less attentive to their body posture, and less able to distinguish between themselves and other objects than were other people. Additionally, the meditative group experienced their bodies as lighter and warmer, and time passed more quickly. The responsive hypnotic people were less attentive to their environment and were able to concentrate more, but this would make sense, since an aim of meditation is to *avoid* excessive concentration.

One important difference between hypnosis and meditation, on the other hand, is that hypnotized subjects are responsive to suggestions for alterations in perception and memory, as discussed earlier, while this is not the case with people who are meditating. In the next section we will look at the way drugs produce altered states of consciousness by affecting perception and memory, as well as other aspects of the personality.

Drugs

The National Institute on Drug Abuse defines a drug as "any chemical substance that affects a person in such a way as to bring about physiological, emotional, or behavioral change." The effects of drugs on the nervous system and behavior will be the subject of our discussion in this section. Topics such as drug addiction and the use of drugs in therapy will be presented in the chapters on abnormal psychology and therapy.

To understand the effects of drugs on behavior, it is important to be acquainted with the many types of drugs in existence, as well as the various kinds of actions these drugs can have. We can loosely group all drugs affecting behavior or consciousness under the heading *psychoactive drugs,* which include stimulants, depressants, hypnotics, anesthetics, hallucinogens, alcohol, and tobacco, among others.

The actions of drugs can be described in a number of ways. For example, two drugs can have an additive effect when the effect on the nervous system is the *sum* of the effects of both drugs. Or drugs can have a potentiating interaction; this means that one drug multiplies the effects of the other. Still another type of interaction is antagonistic: In this case, the action of one drug blocks the effects of another.

Stimulants

Stimulants act to energize the central nervous system. Some, like the nicotine in cigarettes or the caffeine in coffee, are so common and relatively mild in action that we hardly think of them as stimulants at all. Others, such as amphetamines and cocaine, produce a high psychological dependence and are more likely to be seriously abused.

In moderate amounts, stimulants increase alertness and reduce fatigue. In higher doses they can produce anxiety and irritability. People who take stimulants often experience a feeling of inexhaustible energy, and become excited and euphoric; in physiological terms, the pupils dilate, the pulse rate and blood pressure increase, and appetite is suppressed because the blood sugar level is raised.

AMPHETAMINES. Amphetamines act on the central nervous system by increasing the release of norepinephrine and related substances. Since the affected substances are closely linked with the sympathetic division of the autonomic nervous system, the use of amphetamines produces results similar to the "emergency arousal" actions of the sympathetic division. The result is a feeling of heightened activity and alertness.

Since amphetamines suppress the appetite, one of the first major medical uses of these drugs was as diet aids. At one time, 85 percent of prescriptions for amphetamines were for weight control. In the late 1960s, the federal government placed more restrictions on dispensing amphetamines, and their use has since declined. Nevertheless, they are probably the most often abused of the stimulants.

COCAINE. Like amphetamines, cocaine acts on the nervous system by affecting the action of substances such as norepinephrine. However, cocaine affects these substances in a different way. Whereas amphetamines increase the release of norepinephrine, cocaine interferes with the mechanism for inactivating these substances, as we discussed in Chapter 2, "The Biological Framework." Thus, cocaine increases the amount of neurotransmitter left in the synapse and available at the receptors. This results in the same feeling of heightened energy that comes from amphetamines.

Cocaine has been around for a very long time and is believed to be the strongest natural stimulant known. It is produced from the coca plant, which grows in the Andes Mountains. Inhabitants of that region chew on the leaves of the plant in order to increase their energy. Although it is occasionally injected, the most common form of cocaine use is sniffing, or "snorting." Though it produces a feeling of euphoria, extra alertness, and immense power, these effects are quite short acting.

Cocaine also has some limited medical use as a local anesthetic and is used most commonly in ear, nose, and throat surgery. It first numbs the nerve endings of the affected tissues and then, through the bloodstream, arrives at the cortex of the brain.

Depressants

Depressants make up a large class of drugs that affect the central nervous system. Although there is a broad range of depressants, for our purposes we will group these drugs into just three categories: narcotics, sedatives, and alcohol.

NARCOTICS.   The broad definition of narcotics includes all drugs that are used medically as *analgesics* (pain relievers). However, the term *narcotics* is used more commonly today to refer only to opium and its derivatives. Opium itself,

used at least since 300 B.C., is produced from the dried, milk-like fluid that comes from the seed pods of poppies. Morphine and heroin are made from opium; in addition, a large number of synthetic opiates are now on the market.

Narcotics act to relieve pain by depressing the central nervous system and hence producing mental haziness, drowsiness, a slowing of digestive processes, and a reduction of muscular coordination.

SEDATIVES. Sedatives depress the central nervous system and relax the muscles. The resulting effects are a reduction of anxiety and tension, and the onset of a mildly euphoric state. However, in excessive amounts, they impair judgment, lead to disorientation, and produce a kind of intoxication with slurred speech and a loss of motor coordination.

ALCOHOL. Alcohol is a central nervous system depressant. Because it affects brain regions that control inhibition, alcohol is often thought of as a stimulant. After all, the person using alcohol at first feels in an open and expansive mood, highly sociable, and easygoing. However, despite the fact that alcohol numbs the inhibitor centers of the brain and produces gregarious behavior initially, the subsequent effects of alcohol are clearly those of a depressant: Coordination is lost; perception of sensations such as temperature or pain is dulled; speech is slurred; thought processes are impaired; and vision becomes hazy. Larger doses of alcohol can lead to dullness of sensation, then general sedation, sleep, coma, and ultimately death.

Interestingly, alcohol is not digested—it is absorbed. About 20 percent is absorbed first by the stomach, which gives the initial reaction; the rest is absorbed by the small intestine. The degree of the effect alcohol has on the body and behavior is dependent on the rate of absorption and on the rate at which alcohol is metabolized.

Alcohol cannot be chemically broken down by digestion; the body must rely on other processes to break it down. Alcohol is absorbed directly into the bloodstream through stomach and intestine walls, though the entire process can be slowed down if the alcohol must fight its way through a stomach lined with protein-rich foods such as milk, meat, and eggs. Eventually the alcohol reaches the liver, where it can be metabolized—that is, chemically broken down into water and carbon dioxide. However, this process takes time; the liver is able to deal only with one-third to one-half ounce of alcohol in an hour. This amount is the equivalent of 2 oz. of liquor, 6 oz. of wine, or 12 oz. of beer. If the liver is required to handle more than this amount per hour, some chemical compromises are necessary, the job doesn't get done as well, and the liver is abused.

Alcohol's effect on emotional behavior is inconsistent, varying from one person to another. Some become friendly or silly; others become sad or uncommunicative. Apparently these large individual differences involve a complex interaction of factors—the basic personality of the drinker, the social setting, the reason for drinking, and so on. For example, it has been noted that alcohol tends to remove inhibitions. But one individual might be more inhibited than another before drinking, and therefore the behavior while drinking will vary. It's also possible that a person might try to prevent the lack of motor control by monitoring his or her behavior more closely.

The amount of alcohol a person can drink before becoming drunk depends on many factors: how much tolerance has developed, how long it has been since the person has eaten, and the person's body weight. Tolerance does develop in experienced drinkers, and they are able to consume more alcohol than others before becoming drunk. As we mentioned before, drinking has less of an effect on a full stomach, since the absorption rate is slowed down; the heavier the person, the more alcohol that can be consumed without intoxication, also because the absorption rate is retarded.

Alcohol is in widespread use all over the world; in many societies, including our own, it is a major health and social problem. Alcohol abuse and the treatment of alcoholism will be discussed in more detail in Chapters 16 and 17.

Hallucinogens

The National Institute of Drug Abuse defines hallucinogens as drugs that "affect sensation, thinking, self-awareness, and emotion. Changes in time and space perception, delusions (false beliefs), and hallucinations (experiencing nonexisting sensations) may be mild or overwhelming, depending on the dose and quality of the drug. Effects vary; the same person may have different reactions on different occasions."

It is clear from this definition that the effects of hallucinogens are unpredictable. It is probably this unpredictability that limits the use of hallucinogens; people rarely take them on a daily basis. While the way these drugs act on the brain is not well understood, it has been noted that certain psychological variables seem to affect what sensations the hallucinogen will produce. These variables include the subject's expectation of what the drug will do, the subject's mood and attitude, and the subject's motivations.

Among the hallucinogens are: LSD, peyote, mescaline, psilocybin, and PCP (angel dust). Marijuana will also be included in this section, although for the most part its effects are milder than the other drugs described here.

LSD. Lysergic acid diethylamide, or LSD, is probably the most typical of the hallucinogens. Aside from altering the perception of shapes and colors, and the inducement of a feeling of dreaming, LSD also can produce anxiety, dizziness, and nausea.

Little is actually known about the way LSD works. One peculiarity of LSD is its tendency to produce *flashbacks*. A flashback is a recurrence of hallucinations, days or possibly months after LSD was taken. While these flashbacks may occur spontaneously, they can also result from stress, medication, or marijuana use.

MARIJUANA.   The latest national survey in 1977 showed that 16 million people currently use marijuana. Current users include 4 percent of 12-year-olds, 15 percent of 14-year-olds, and 31 percent of 18- to 21-year-olds. More than 4 million people aged 12 to 17 were using marijuana in 1977, and one in nine high school seniors used it daily. The proportion of people who had begun using marijuana before the ninth grade has nearly doubled since 1972.

Marijuana is produced from Cannabis, a plant that is grown throughout the world. It is used commercially for hemp fiber and as an oil in the production of some paints. Cannabis contains THC, tetrahydrocannabinol, which is the major psychoactive ingredient in marijuana. Drug experts are disturbed about the rapidly increasing potency of marijuana available in this country. In 1975 the average sample contained 0.4 percent THC. By last year the average was 4 percent THC, a tenfold increase in strength. The reason that this concerns researchers is that unlike alcohol, which is soluble in water and thus rapidly washed out of the body, THC is fat-soluble and can remain and accumulate in the body for a week or more after the marijuana is smoked (Brady, 1980).

While the effects of marijuana vary widely from one person to another, low doses usually produce a feeling of well-being, relaxation, and an increased sense of touch, taste, and sound. Some users find marijuana a stimulant, some a depressant. One of the explanations for the variability in effects of the drug is that marijuana is primarily a mood enhancer; whatever mood the person is in when taking the drug is heightened. This obviously can have very different effects, depending on what mood one is in.

Like alcohol, marijuana interferes with psychomotor functions such as reaction time, coordination, visual perception, and other skills important for driving and operating machinery safely. Actual tests of marijuana-intoxicated drivers have clearly shown that their driving is impaired, yet they tend to think they are driving better than usual (Brady, 1980).

Other short-term and long-term effects of marijuana are still being argued and researched. One of the problems with accurately defining the effects of marijuana is that the way in which it is used by Americans has not yet been the

subject of long-term study; it may be 20 years or more before the necessary studies can be completed. At the moment, effects such as a "motivational syndrome" among young users, and physical damage to lungs, heart, and reproductive organs have not been proven conclusively and are the subject of much contradictory research.

Summary

1.   NREM sleep has four stages, which differ in terms of brain wave patterns and muscular changes. REM sleep, characterized by rapid eye movements and dreaming, occurs at 90-minute intervals throughout the sleep cycle.

2.   There are a number of theories about why people dream. Freud believed that a dream is the expression of unconscious impulses and thoughts when a person's conscious defenses are lowered during sleep. Other theorists believe that dreams are a way of processing daytime memories.

3.   *Hypnosis* can be defined as a condition in which subjects are able to respond to appropriate suggestions with distortions of perception and memory.

4.   Individual differences exist in responsiveness to hypnosis; about 15 percent of the population can be greatly affected by hypnotic suggestion, while about 5 to 10 percent show no effect at all; the rest fall somewhere between these two extremes.

5.   Pain reduction through hypnosis has been tested with both *ischemic* and *cold-pressor pain;* those who are highly responsive to hypnosis show substantial pain reduction, while the results are less dramatic with those who are of medium or low responsiveness to hypnosis.

6.   *Meditation* is concentration on one thought or word (in Transcendental Meditation the word is called a *mantra*) in order to block out all other sensations and thoughts.

7.   Drugs affecting behavior or consciousness are called *psychoactive drugs;* they include stimulants, depressants, hypnotics, anesthetics, hallucinogens, and alcohol, among others.

Suggested Readings

BOWERS, K. *Hypnosis for the seriously curious.* Monterey, Calif.: Brooks/Cole, 1976. An extensive review of experimental studies of hypnosis.

DEMENT, W. *Some must watch while some must sleep.* New York: Norton, 1978. A more advanced treatment of modern experimental methods of studying sleep.

GOLEMAN, D., and DAVIDSON, R. J. (Eds.) *Consciousness: Brain, states of awareness, and mysticism.* New York: Harper & Row, 1979. A collection of articles about consciousness, ranging from neuroscience to mysticism in approach.

GRINSPOON, L., and HEDBLOM, P. *The speed culture: Amphetamine use and abuse in America.* Cambridge, Mass: Harvard University Press, 1975. An extensive and technical review of the use of stimulants.

HILGARD, E. R. *Divided consciousness.* New York: Wiley, 1977. An excellent introduction to hypnosis and altered states of consciousness by one of the foremost investigators in the field.

JAYNES, J. *The origin of consciousness in the breakdown of the bicameral mind.* Boston: Houghton Mifflin, 1977. A fascinating, if controversial, view of consciousness as a relatively recent evolutionary development in human history.

NARANJO, C., and ORNSTEIN, R. E. *On the psychology of meditation.* New York: Penguin, 1977. An introduction to meditation, its history and current practice.

ORNSTEIN, R. E. *The psychology of consciousness* (2nd ed.). New York: Harcourt Brace Jovanovich, 1977. An introductory level review of a wide range of work on human consciousness from a humanistic point of view.

WOLMAN, B. *Handbook of dreams: Research, theories, and applications.* New York: Van Nostrand, 1979. A broad collection of articles on dreaming.

Part Three

Learning and Cognitive Processes

6 Conditioning and Learning

The behavior of people, and of animals, is continually changed by the experiences that they have in the world. To be once bitten is to be twice shy; and the burnt child avoids the flame. Practice, we are told, makes perfect—and experience is the great teacher. We can define *learning* as the relatively permanent changes in behavior that are a result of past experience. Those changes, for the most part, serve to adjust us to the world in which we live. We can and do learn some maladjustive behaviors, but most of us profit from experience most of the time. The obvious function of learning is to make us able to go about the business of living in an effective way. The newborn mammal knows nothing about the world, and depends for its survival on parental care. Through learning—as well as through growth—it is transformed into a knowledgeable and effective adult creature.

The experimental analysis of learning has occupied the attention of very many psychologists. The search for basic principles of learning, with wide applicability, has often involved the use of animals as experimental subjects. The emphasis in this chapter will be on those relatively simple forms of learning that can be most effectively manipulated and studied in animal subjects. Though such learning may be relatively simple, it is of fundamental importance, and, as we shall see, it occurs in humans in much the same way as in humbler creatures. The effects of humans' more complex learning processes, made possible by their enormous cerebral cortex and by their unique capacity for language, will be evident in later chapters. This "higher" learning does not take the place of the more primitive processes that we share with other animals. To understand some areas of human behavior—and especially behavior involving strong emotions—a thorough knowledge of *conditioning* is needed.

Pavlov's Basic Discoveries

The name of Ivan Pavlov (1849–1936) is known to almost everybody, and with good reason. The phenomena of conditioning were first discovered and analyzed in great detail in his laboratory. Pavlov's research, carried out over a period of many years, represented a genuine intellectual revolution. The work was a brilliant application of the methods of natural science to problems of learning and behavior that had previously been untouched. The long-lasting significance of Pavlov's contribution can be seen in the fact that, even today, the technical vocabulary used by psychologists when they discuss learning is largely Pavlovian. This is all the more remarkable when you consider that Pavlov was not a psychologist—and, indeed, had little respect for, or sympathy with, his psychological contemporaries.

To understand what Pavlov accomplished, and how it came about, it is important to know that, before his work on conditioned reflexes, Pavlov had won a Nobel Prize (1904) for his research on the physiology of the digestive system. Pavlov's interest in conditioning—and his whole approach to it—was a logical outgrowth of his interest as a physiologist in the digestive glands. In his work on the digestive system Pavlov used dogs as experimental subjects. The salivary gland plays an important role in the digestive process, and Pavlov developed a special fistula operation to study its functioning in intact dogs. This made it possible for him to collect, and to measure precisely, the salivary secretions of his subjects. In this way he could examine the amount of salivary secretion that occurred when chemicals of various sorts were placed on the dog's tongue or when the dog ate. The saliva that flowed when food was placed in the dog's mouth was the sort of thing with which an experimental physiologist could deal routinely.

Pavlov noted, however, a disturbing phenomenon. There were times when a dog salivated a great deal, even though no food had been placed in its mouth. There was no good "physiological" reason for such salivation, but, on the other hand, it did not seem to occur at random. The "non-physiological" salivary flow was very likely to occur if the dog smelled food, or heard the food bowls clattering in the laboratory kitchen, or caught sight of the attendant who usually fed it. This sort of salivary flow had been called "psychic secretion," to distinguish it from the more "respectable" and orderly physiological salivary flow, which could be studied by physiologists. This kind of distinction made no sense to Pavlov. The salivary gland secreted only one kind of saliva, and "psychic secretion" meant merely that the activity of the salivary gland was influenced by the brain. Thus, if one wished really to understand the functioning of the digestive system, the physiology of still another organ—the brain—had also to be studied. Pavlov decided to begin an experimental analysis of the elusive phenomena of "psychic secretion." This was *not* conceived as a study of learning and behavior. To Pavlov, his studies of conditioned reflexes were a way of investigating the physiological functioning of the brain. Throughout his life Pavlov was less interested in the behavioral phenomena he so brilliantly analyzed than in the hypothetical brain processes which, he inferred, must be causing the behaviors. The final irony is that, based as it was on an inadequate knowledge of neuroanatomy and neurophysiology, Pavlov's "brain physiology" has been discarded. The permanent contribution made by Pavlov's work on conditioned reflexes belongs not to physiology, but to behavioral psychology.

The Basic Experiment

To show the various phenomena of conditioning, Pavlov thought up a simple and effective experimental procedure, illustrated in Figure 6-1. The subject was a dog, surgically prepared so that careful measurements of salivary flow could be obtained. The dog was held in a stock and isolated in a sound-proofed chamber. Through various mechanical devices, meat powder could

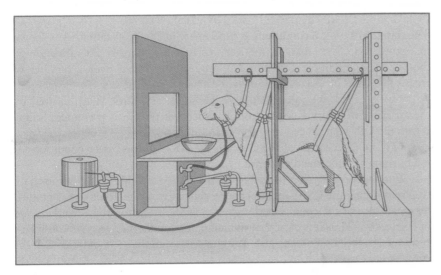

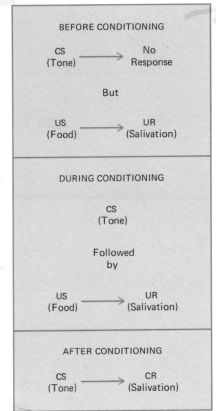

Figure 6-1

Pavlovian dog, surgically prepared for measurement of salivary flow, restrained in a conditioning chamber.

Figure 6-2

The relations between stimuli and responses during three phases of the establishment of a conditioned response.

either be placed directly on the dog's tongue or put in a food dish set before the dog. The experimenter could present, as desired, any of several controlled stimuli, such as the sound of a metronome or the flashing of a light.

The starting point for Pavlov's demonstration was the *unconditioned reflex* of salivation. The unconditioned reflex is an innate, built-in reaction or response to a stimulus. The normal dog is so built that, whenever meat powder is placed upon its tongue, the response of salivation will occur. The nerve pathways that underlie this reflexive response are, so to speak, prewired. The sound of a metronome, on the other hand, will not cause a normal dog to salivate. The sound will probably elicit some response from the dog—its ears may prick up, or it may turn to look at the source of the sound. We can be quite certain, however, that it will not salivate. What Pavlov now went on to do, put very simply, was to teach the dog to salivate in response to the sound of the metronome. The trick is very simple: we merely sound the metronome, and shortly after we present the dog with meat powder. This sequence—metronome followed by meat powder—is repeated for a number of trials. The dog, on the first couple of trials, salivates only when the meat powder (the *unconditioned stimulus,* or US) is presented. After a few trials, however, it begins to salivate when the metronome (the *conditioned stimulus,* or CS) is presented. The salivation now occurs before meat powder is presented. The metronome, which before had no relation to salivation, now reliably elicits a salivary response. When salivation occurs to a previously neutral CS, such as the metronome, we refer to it as a conditioned reflex, or a *conditioned response* (CR). The basic procedure for establishing a conditioned response is outlined in Figure 6-2.

Pavlov's basic experiment is a clear example of what has come to be known as the law of "classical" conditioning: Whenever a previously neutral stimulus (CS) is presented *in close temporal contiguity* (close in time) with an unconditioned stimulus (US), the response made to the US will come to be made to the CS. This is, of course, a law about learning. The experience of the regular sequence, metronome followed by food, has adaptively modified the dog's behavior.

Acquisition, Extinction, and Reinforcement

The course of a typical conditioning experiment in Pavlov's laboratory is shown in Figure 6-3. Note that on the very early trials there is no salivation to the CS. The conditioned response is gradually acquired over a number of trials. The bank of trials during which the animal is learning the conditioned response is called, logically enough, *acquisition*. The basic rule followed by the experimenter during acquisition is: Whenever the CS is presented, follow it with the US. That procedure—the CS followed by the US—is called *reinforcement*. The reinforcement of the CS with the US is the necessary condition for establishing a conditioned response.

What happens if, after the subject has acquired a conditioned response, we stop reinforcing the CS? That procedure, called *extinction*, leads to the gradual disappearance of the conditioned response, as shown in the right-hand section of Figure 6-3. Thus it is clear that to maintain a conditioned response one must continue reinforcing the response. Withholding reinforcement extinguishes the conditioned response.

The extinction of a response, however, does not mean that the response has been "forgotten." That was shown clearly by something Pavlov called *spontaneous recovery*. When a dog has been subjected to acquisition and then extinction of a conditioned response, it is returned to its home cage until the next day. Then it is placed into the conditioning chamber once again, and the metronome is sounded. The dog will now salivate to the metronome for a couple of trials, without being reinforced, even though the response had seemed to be completely extinguished the day before. This spontaneous recovery of the response shows that extinction has not "erased" the conditioned response; as one might expect, after a cycle of acquisition and extinction, *reacquisition* of the response will occur much more rapidly than did the original acquisition. The extinction procedure evidently teaches the dog that—at least for the time being—the CS is *no longer* followed by the US. The fact that it once was, however, is not forgotten.

Figure 6-3

The acquisition, extinction, spontaneous recovery, and reacquisition of a conditioned salivary response. Typically, the measure of conditioning is the number of drops of saliva elicited by the CS on each trial. Note that on the day following extinction, the first presentation of the CS elicits quite a large response.

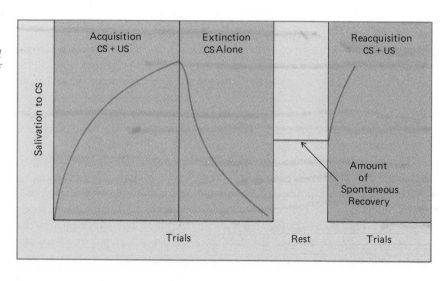

Generalization

When a conditioned response has been established to a particular CS, stimuli similar to that CS will also tend to elicit the response, a process that is called *generalization*. The strength of the response will be greater the more similar the new stimulus is to the original CS. The nature of generalization was illustrated clearly in a simple example by Pavlov. The CS was a mechanical scratching of the dog's skin, which had been paired with meat powder (the US). When the conditioned response (salivation) had been firmly established, the dog was tested with scratches on different parts of its body. The closer the scratch was to the point at which the original CS had been applied, the more salivation.

Generalization can easily be shown in man. The galvanic skin response (GSR), a change in the electrical resistance of the skin related to sweating, is an unconditioned emotional reaction (see Chapter 11). When college students receive an electric shock, *one* of their emotional reactions is a marked GSR. The GSR is easily conditioned: If a pure tone is sounded shortly before the students receive a shock, after only one or two trials they show a pronounced GSR to the tone. When students were conditioned to a particular tone, higher and lower tones also elicited a GSR. The magnitude of the GSR was greater when the test tone was close to the tone used as a CS during conditioning (Hovland, 1937). The typical form of a generalization gradient is shown in Figure 6-4.

With people, the similarity of one stimulus to another may depend critically on language and symbolization. Thus Diven (1936) conditioned college students to make a GSR in response to the word "barn" embedded in a list of recited words. This was easily accomplished by following the word "barn" with an electric shock. When conditioning had been established, the subjects also displayed GSRs to such rural words as "cow" or "hay"—but not to such neutral words as "table" or "chair." The generalization in this case has nothing to do with the physical similarity of one word to another, but obviously depends on the meanings of the words.

The fact that conditioned responses generalize to stimuli similar to the CS has obvious adaptive value. The precise measurement and control over CSs that is possible in the laboratory is not much like what happens in real life, where stimuli are always changing from one occasion to the next. When a tiger has clawed you once, you are very likely to display a GSR and other conditioned emotional reactions the next time you see a tiger. The conditioning would not be very useful, however, if as a result of your first experience you responded only to the sight of a tiger approaching from your right with a distinctive wart on its nose.

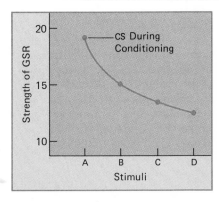

Figure 6-4

An example of generalization. The subjects had been conditioned originally to a CS (A) of a given frequency. When tested with the original tone, and with tones B, C, and D of differing frequencies, a clear generalization gradient appeared. The closer the frequency of the test tone to the frequency of tone A, the greater was the magnitude of the response to the tone. (Hovland, 1937)

Discrimination

Discrimination, also studied by Pavlov, is a logical supplement to generalization. Though conditioning generalizes to stimuli similar to the CS, it is possible to learn *not* to respond to similar stimuli, while continuing to respond to the CS itself. The procedure used by Pavlov to demonstrate discrimination is, in retrospect, perfectly obvious. We can condition a dog to respond to a tone of, let us say, 1,000 Hz. When conditioning is established, we now see that

The technique for bringing reflex responses under the control of previously ineffective stimuli can have some unusual and interesting applications. The basic logic of the classical conditioning procedure led Mowrer (1938) to develop a simple treatment for enuresis (bed-wetting) in children. Mowrer reasoned that in many cases of enuresis the child has simply failed to learn to wake up in response to the stimuli arising from a full bladder. This necessary bit of learning could be brought about by an imaginative use of conditioning.

The ringing of a loud bell can be thought of as an unconditioned stimulus, which reliably awakens a sleeping child. What will happen if we follow the stimulation from a full bladder with the sound of a loud bell? The principle of classical conditioning tells us that after a few such paired presentations, the response of waking up—at first made only to the bell—should begin to occur in response to the stimulation from a full bladder. Then, of course, the child can go to the bathroom instead of wetting the bed while asleep.

There is no great trick in arranging for a bell to ring shortly after the child's bladder is full. The child sleeps on a special fine mesh sheet so constructed that the first drop of urine closes a circuit that sets off the alarm bell. This arrangement guarantees that shortly after the sleeping child is stimulated by a full bladder, he or she will be awakened by the bell. With a few nights of this treatment, most children begin to wake up in response to the stimulation from a full bladder—before wetting the bed.

The treatment of enuresis

the dog also salivates—though not as much—to tones of 900 or 1,100 Hz. To establish a discrimination, we now present in a scrambled order tones of 900, 1,000, and 1,100 Hz. Whenever the 1,000 Hz tone is presented it is reinforced. When the 900 and 1,100 Hz tones are presented they are *not* reinforced. The result is that, after a fair number of trials, the dog will salivate to the 1,000 Hz tone while no longer salivating to the other tones.

This procedure, as Pavlov noted, seems ideally suited to the study of the sensory capacities of animals. Whenever the animal learns to discriminate between two similar stimuli, that tells us that it can tell the two stimuli apart. With a procedure of this sort, Pavlov was able to show that his dogs could discriminate between tones of 1,000 and 1,012 Hz. The usefulness of discrimination should be obvious. Without some check on the generalization process, you might find yourself making terrified emotional responses to the sight of a caged tiger, or even to an alley cat.

Higher-Order Conditioning

The fact that conditioning always involves, at the outset, an unconditioned reflex might seem to set limits on what this says about human behavior. While we do learn conditioned responses having to do with food, pain, and other biologically important events, much of human learning at least is far removed from such primitive considerations. That did not stop Pavlov from speculating that *all* learning might involve nothing more than long chains of conditioned responses. To support this idea, Pavlov pointed to the phenomenon of higher-order conditioning.

To establish a higher-order conditioned response, Pavlov began as usual by pairing a neutral CS with meat powder (the US). The CS might be the sound of a metronome, and we shall refer to it as CS_1. When CS_1 had been firmly

may seem a homely and unimportant matter, but Siegel's (1976) application of a classical conditioning model to some of the phenomena of drug tolerance appears to have profound and obvious medical significance. When a person uses a drug such as morphine or heroin, he or she rapidly develops a tolerance for the drug. That is, larger and larger drug doses are required to produce the same (or any) effect on behavior and feeling. The physiological basis for such tolerance effects is not clearly understood, but Siegel's studies suggest that classical conditioning may play a large role.

When a neutral CS precedes injection of a drug, the response conditioned to the CS is often a "compensatory" response, the opposite of the immediate effect of the drug itself. For example, morphine lessens sensitivity to pain. Thus, when a rat is injected for the first time with morphine, it will not pull its paw away from the surface of an experimental "hot-plate" as quickly as it normally would. With repeated injections of the drug, however, the increased pain tolerance slowly diminishes. When the drug-tolerant rat is now given a placebo injection of saline, it shows *supersensitivity* to pain. This indicates that the stimuli associated with the injection must elicit a conditioned response *opposite* to the pain-reducing effect of the drug itself. This conditioned compensatory effect, Siegel argues, is responsible for the development of drug tolerance.

The remarkable observation made by Siegel is that such conditioned effects are very sensitive to the precise environmental cues associated with the injection. Thus, a rat that has been repeatedly injected with morphine in a particular room will show drug tolerance as long as the injections are given in the same room. When an injection is given in a distinctively different room, however, the full effect of the drug is restored. This indicates that drug tolerance effects are not an inevitable consequence of repeated drug usage. The tolerance effect, like all conditioned responses, is sensitive to changes in the conditioned stimuli.

conditioned, Pavlov moved on to a new neutral CS, such as a flashing light, which we shall call CS_2. CS_2, however, was never paired with meat powder. Instead, CS_2 was presented just before CS_1, and the pairing of CS_2 with CS_1 was *not* followed by meat powder. The earlier conditioning of CS_1, however, guaranteed that the animal would salivate when CS_1 was presented. In most cases, after a number of CS_2/CS_1 pairings the animal was conditioned to salivate to CS_2. The important point to note is that CS_2 has never been paired with meat powder; rather, it has been paired with CS_1, which earlier had been paired with meat powder. This is why this process is called higher-order conditioning, because a well-conditioned CS, such as CS_1, can itself serve as a US. The role played by CS_1 in establishing conditioning to CS_2 is very much like the role normally played by the US, the meat powder.

To drive the point home, Pavlov went on to still another new CS, called CS_3. The CS_3 (perhaps the smell of camphor) was paired with CS_2, which, as a result of higher-order conditioning, now caused salivation. With some dogs, at least, Pavlov was able to establish a "third-order" conditioned response. This kind of outcome encouraged his belief that much human learning depended on higher-order conditioning, with nonbiological stimuli (especially words) serving in effect as USs. Thus, in humans, a verbal threat may be as effective a reinforcer in making one afraid of the threatener as a physical attack would have been. Presumably, during one's childhood, threatening gestures and words have in fact been paired with actual physical attack and pain. There is no doubt that higher-order conditioning does occur, and that fact clearly extends the boundaries of conditioning well beyond meat powder and other biological reinforcers. To speculate that all learning is nothing but a chain of conditioned responses, however, goes wildly beyond any observable facts. Pavlov's excessive enthusiasm was that of a pioneer, dazzled by sights never before observed.

Conditioned Inhibition

There were many other conditioning phenomena first discovered by Pavlov, and they are still of major concern to students and theorists of the learning process. We shall conclude, however, with one more example. To show conditioned inhibition, Pavlov used several neutral stimuli while working with the same dog. The dog was first conditioned to salivate to each of two stimuli, CS_1 and CS_2. This was of course done in the usual way, by pairing each of these CSs with meat powder. Then, on some trials, Pavlov presented a new stimulus, CS_3, at the same time as CS_1. Whenever the combination CS_3 plus CS_1 was presented, there was no reinforcement. There were trials when CS_1 was presented by itself, without CS_3. Whenever that occurred, CS_1 was reinforced. This is a kind of discrimination training. When CS_1 occurs alone, food always follows; but when CS_1 occurs together with CS_3, food never follows. There is nothing surprising in the fact that, after a number of trials, the dog comes to respond reliably to CS_1, while not responding to the combination of CS_1 and CS_3.

While this discrimination was being learned, Pavlov continued on some trials to present CS_2, which was always reinforced. Then, after the discrimination had been learned, Pavlov presented the dog with a new combination of stimuli, CS_2 and CS_3. The dog did *not* salivate to that combination—in spite of the fact that a conditioned response would surely have occurred if CS_2 had been presented alone. That meant, Pavlov reasoned, that CS_3 had been made into a *conditioned inhibitor* of responding. Though CS_3 had signalled nonreinforcement only when presented with CS_1, the conditioning had obviously given CS_3 a more general property. The dog now behaved as if CS_3 were a generalized signal for nonreinforcement of all conditioned responses. When CS_3 is presented together with any normally effective CS, it inhibits the conditioned response that would otherwise occur.

Variables That Affect Classical Conditioning

There are many variables that affect the strength of conditioned responses and the rate at which they are acquired. The more intense the US (for example, intensity of shock or amount of meat powder), the more rapid the conditioning and the stronger the response. The same thing can be seen if the intensity of the CS is varied (that is, if a metronome CS is made louder, or a light CS is made brighter, the conditioned response is more rapidly acquired, more strongly performed, etc.).

Perhaps the most critical variable of all is the time relation between the CS and the US. The CS can be presented a little before the US, it can be presented at the same time as the US, or it can be presented a little after the US. The outcomes of these three basic arrangements differ very widely, as can be seen in Figure 6-5. The figure shows the results of a study with human subjects, using a conditioned finger–withdrawal response. The procedure involves the pairing of a tone (CS) with a shock (US) given to the subject's finger. The unconditioned response to shock on the finger is to jerk the finger away. When conditioning occurs, the finger is withdrawn in response to the tone.

The backward conditioning procedure—in which the CS is presented *after* the US—results in virtually no conditioning. With simultaneous conditioning procedures—when CS and US occur at the same time—there is also very little,

Figure 6-5

The strength of conditioned finger withdrawal in humans as a function of the time interval between CS and US. Note that negative time intervals refer to a procedure in which the US is presented before the CS. (Spooner and Kellogg, 1947)

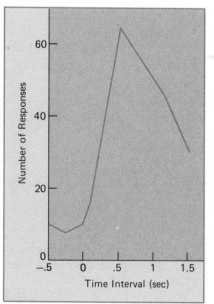

if any, conditioning. The forward conditioning procedure (CS presented before US) is effective, but how effective it is depends on the time interval between the CS and US. The strongest conditioning takes place when the CS is presented about 500 milliseconds before the US. When the time between the two stimuli is either more or less than that, the amount of conditioning drops off quite quickly. With conditioned finger-withdrawal in humans, an interval of only a couple of seconds between CS and US is long enough to eliminate almost all traces of conditioning. This pattern of results is characteristic of many human conditioning studies, and of some animal studies as well. There are many animal studies, however, in which effective conditioning has been observed with much longer time intervals—on the order of minutes—between CS and US (Kamin, 1965). In such studies, however, it is still the case that backward and simultaneous conditioning procedures are quite ineffective. Further, as might be expected, conditioning weakens as the time interval between CS and US is increased.

Perhaps you have been wondering how conditioning can be assessed when the CS and US are presented either simultaneously or close together in time. When this is done, how can one know whether a response is an unconditioned reaction to the US or a conditioned reaction to the CS? The solution is to randomly insert "catch" or test trials along with the reinforced acquisition trials. The CS is presented alone, without the US, on such test trials, so that any response occurring on a test trial is obviously a conditioned response.

The effects of varying the time relations between CS and US are consistent with the idea that conditioning basically serves a signalling function. We are so built that we learn to respond in an appropriate preparatory way to signals that tell us that something important is *about* to happen. From this point of view, the failure to obtain simultaneous or backward conditioning makes good sense. There is no reason to "prepare" for events that have already taken place. We should note, however, that the failure to observe a conditioned response does not necessarily mean that the subject has not learned that the CS and US regularly occur in sequence. There is no doubt that human subjects, who fail to show conditioned finger-withdrawal when two seconds or more elapse between CS and US, become quite aware of the fact that the CS means that shock will soon occur. Perhaps the failure to obtain conditioning with longer times between CS and US in humans reflects the fact that, with a couple of seconds to think matters over, there is time enough for more complicated cognitive processes to override the basic conditioning process. We do know that, in humans, instructions to try to enhance or to inhibit conditioned responding have a considerable effect.

Classical Conditioning in Overview

Pavlov's analysis of salivary conditioning in dogs laid bare the structure of a fundamental learning process that has very wide applicability. There have been successful studies of conditioning performed on a wide variety of animal species. The unconditioned stimuli (and thus the conditioned responses) that have been used are many, and almost all forms of stimulation for which animals have senses have served as conditioned stimuli.

The core concept of conditioning is an ancient one, well appreciated by Aristotle and by the English empiricist philosophers. Pavlovian conditioning obviously involves a process of *association*. Put very loosely, one might say that the dog has learned to associate the sound of a metronome with the delivery of food because the two things repeatedly occur close together in time. Therefore, it salivates when it hears the metronome. To put matters so loosely, however, would be to ignore Pavlov's main message. To Pavlov, conditioning was an automatic, blind, "stamping-in" kind of process. There had to be definite, quantitative laws that determined the rate at which conditioning occurred and that could be discovered by experimental analysis. To talk glibly about the "association of ideas" or about the metronome's making the dog "think about" or "expect" food had nothing to do with science. There was no need, Pavlov stressed, to talk about the animal's "mind" at all. We could observe the CSs and the USs, the conditioned and unconditioned responses, and we could isolate variables that systematically affected conditioning. To Pavlov, of course, the aim of it all was to discover what physical processes in the brain were involved in conditioned associations. The unconditioned reflex obviously depended on the existence of a definite pathway within the nervous system, connecting stimulus and response. The conditioned reflex, in Pavlov's view, had to depend on no less definite a pathway—but new, conditioned pathways must be gradually stamped in in the course of conditioning. This remains an entirely logical inference. We are not, however, much closer to actual observation of such pathways—or to detailed knowledge of how they might be made—than Pavlov was.

Operant Conditioning

Pavlovian conditioning provides a mechanism through which previously ineffective or neutral stimuli come to elicit responses that were formerly elicted only by an unconditioned stimulus. That is, Pavlovian conditioning vastly extends the range of stimuli to which an organism responds. Taken by itself, however, Pavlovian conditioning does not directly affect responses. The animal that came into the world with nothing but a Pavlovian learning mechanism might learn to salivate and to jerk its paw in response to a great many previously neutral stimuli, but it would not be capable of doing much else. There must, one might speculate, be a learning mechanism that works in a more direct way to change and to shape responses. There is; today this process is usually called *operant conditioning*.

Thorndike's Pioneer Studies

The first studies of what has come to be known as operant conditioning were done in the United States by Edward L. Thorndike, at about the same time that Pavlov began his experiments on conditioned reflexes. Though Thorndike and Pavlov shared a basically mechanistic approach toward their studies, Thorndike, as a psychologist, was much less interested in hypothetical brain processes than Pavlov. Thorndike, influenced by the great success of Darwin's evolutionary theory, set about to study the way in which "animal intelligence" served to adjust the animal to the world in which it must live. The cat was Thorndike's preferred subject, and to present it with the kind of problem it might have to

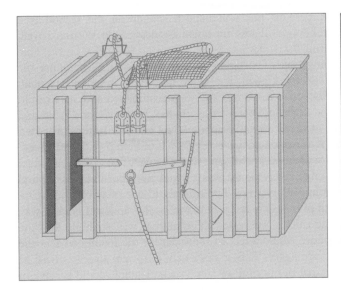
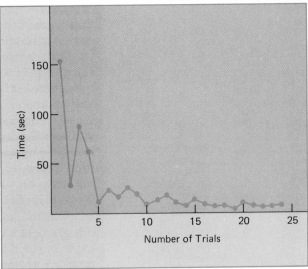

Figure 6-6

(Left) The original "puzzle box" used by Thorndike in his pioneering studies of animal learning.
(Right) This is one of the earliest "learning curves" in the history of the experimental study of conditioning. The time required by one of Thorndike's cats to escape from the puzzle box gradually decreased with trials, but with obvious reversals.

learn to adjust to in the world outside the laboratory he used what he called a puzzle box, shown in Figure 6-6. Before being put in the box the cat had been given no food for some time. There was a bit of fish or liver on a dish outside the box, easily visible (and smellable) to the cat. The problem for the hungry cat is obvious enough: how to get out of the box and get the food. The box had been built so that if the cat brushed against a loop of string inside the box a latch would open, permitting the cat to step outside the box and get the food.

To measure learning in this situation, Thorndike recorded the time it took the cat, on consecutive trials, to escape from the box. This *latency* measure is simply the amount of time between the moment the cat is put inside the box and the moment it gets out. Presumably, if the cat learns to solve this problem, the time it takes to get out of the box will become less as trials progress. The results for a typical cat are given in Figure 6-6. The language in which Thorndike described this learning curve has had a profound influence on theories of conditioning and learning.

Quite a lot of time is required to escape from the box during the early trials, but—with some reversals—it gradually becomes less until, after a number of trials, getting out of the box is accomplished very promptly. The gradual nature of the learning curve caused Thorndike to talk about "trial-and-error" learning. The reason why so much time is needed during the early trials is because the cat is making or emitting, more or less at random, one response after another. The cat might run to the front of the box, then hurl itself against the side, then jump up and down, then yowl. These trial-and-error responses, however, don't work. They don't change anything much, and they certainly don't solve the problem. The *first* solution of the problem seems to occur quite by accident; eventually, in the course of prowling around the box, the cat brushes against the string, gets out of the box, and eats the food. When put in the box for the next trial, the cat does *not* promptly brush against the string. The same kinds of responses made on the first trial, and perhaps some new ones, will tend to occur. The cat will eventually hit the string, however, and perhaps this will happen sooner on the second trial than on the first. Probably still less time will be needed on the third trial, and less again on the fourth.

What is happening, said Thorndike, is that the response (brushing the string) that is followed by a good and satisfying effect is being gradually strengthened. The ineffective responses are not strengthened and, as a result, tend to drop out. The final outcome of this gradual process is the rapid and smooth performance of the "correct" response. The law of effect, as proposed by Thorndike, states that responses that are followed in time by a "good effect" tend to be repeated when the animal is next in the same situation. The gradual strengthening of an effective response was viewed by Thorndike as a blind and automatic "stamping-in" process. The animal did not "size-up" the situation in a blinding flash of insight—that was shown by the slow and gradual way in which the learning curve progressed. The animal was so built that the *consequence* of a response would affect to some degree the likelihood that the response would be made again. This is obviously adaptive, and it is hard to imagine how animals that did not follow some such principle could survive in the world. However, it is important to note that the law of effect does not refer to the *logical* consequences of a response—it refers only to whatever actually does happen right after a response is made. The fact that, in Thorndike's experiment, there was a connection between brushing the string and opening the latch is an unnecessary coincidence as far as the cat's learning is concerned. The law of effect says that, if Thorndike had opened up the puzzle box every time the cat scratched its left ear, the cat would have learned to scratch its left ear in much the same way that it learned to brush against the string.

Skinner's Experiments

Thorndike's law of effect remains very much alive, although both his dated language and his primitive apparatus have been replaced. We no longer talk about "good" or "satisfying" effects. The Pavlovian term *reinforcement* is now applied to operant as well as classical conditioning. In operant conditioning, a *positive reinforcer* is some event (such as food) that, if presented just after a response, increases the likelihood that the response will be repeated. There are also *negative reinforcers*. They are events (such as electric shock) that, if stopped when a response is made, also increase the likelihood that the response will be repeated.

The most productive and influential analyst of operant conditioning and reinforcement—indeed, the man who gave it its name—has been B. F. Skinner. To study operant conditioning in fine detail, Skinner created the operant conditioning chamber, now universally known as the "Skinner box." Though the size and the precise contents of a Skinner box vary for different species, the basic idea remains the same. The animal is put in a light- and sound-proofed chamber, within which not much can go on. There is always, however, a device of some sort within the box, which the animal can use to make a response. With the rat, for example, a small lever is usually placed on one wall of the box (see Figure 6-7). The rat can push the lever with its paws; for that matter, it can also push the lever with its nose, or in any other way it sees fit. A pigeon can peck at a small illuminated disk placed on one wall. In

Figure 6-7

The rat in a Skinner box. Normally, of course, the Skinner box is placed into a sound- and light-proofed chamber. The visible equipment is used to program events (reinforcers, lights, tones, shocks) taking place inside the box.

the box there must also be something to deliver reinforcers. In the box shown in Figure 6-7 an automatic feeder can put a small pellet of food in a cup near the lever. There are other boxes built so that a small dipper of water can be given to the rat when it responds correctly. The typical reinforcer for the pigeon is brief access to a hopper full of grain. Whatever species, response device, or reinforcer may be used, the basic principle remains the same. When a response is made on the device, it is promptly followed by a reinforcer. The first response is often made as an accidental by-product of exploring the box, although, as we shall see later, "shaping" procedures are often used to encourage that first response. In any event, when the first response is made it is followed right away by a reinforcer. The effect of the reinforcer is predictable: the animal tends to repeat the response, and thus to get more reinforcers. This increased likelihood of responding does not occur, of course, unless responses are reinforced.

The basic measure of learning used in operant conditioning of this kind is the *rate* of occurrence of the response over time. The outcome of an operant conditioning study is shown on a *cumulative recorder* (Figure 6-8). The recorder is hooked up to the lever (or other device) in such a way that each time the animal responds a pen is moved one step upwards on a roll of paper moving under it at a constant speed. As the animal makes more responses over time, the pen continues to move up one step with each response. Thus the animal's rate of response is reflected in the slope of the *cumulative record* drawn by the pen. When the animal is responding rapidly, the slope of the cumulative record is steep. When the animal is not responding at all, the cumulative record has no slope—the pen merely traces a horizontal line on the moving paper. Figure 6-9 is the cumulative record of a rat placed in a Skinner box and rewarded with a food pellet each time it responded.

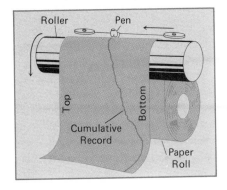

Figure 6-8

The working parts of a cumulative recorder, keeping track of the responses made by an animal in a Skinner box.

Figure 6-9

The cumulative record made by a rat reinforced with a small food pellet for each lever press made in a Skinner box.

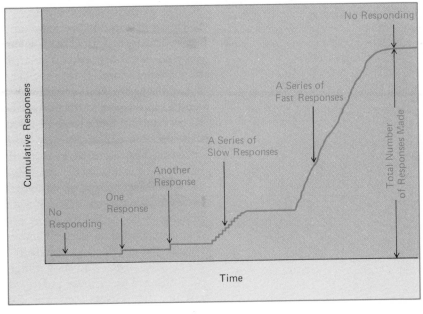

The technique of shaping was used by animal trainers long before psychologists studied it. Whoever trained these chimpanzees could not afford to wait until they spontaneously began balancing as we see them now. This balancing act was achieved instead through gradual reinforcement of successive approximations.

Shaping

We have already referred to the procedure of *shaping*. This technique was known to, and widely practiced by, animal trainers long before Skinner studied it. To illustrate shaping, try to imagine what you would do in order to train a dog to roll over. The basic principle of operant conditioning tells you that, if you reward a hungry dog with food every time it rolls over, it should learn to roll over. The problem is that, even though you are armed and ready with food as a reinforcer, the dog is not very likely to roll over out of the blue. There is thus no way to reinforce the desired behavior. This, it should be noted, is the difference between operant and Pavlovian conditioning. There is a real sense in which you can force a dog to salivate, and thus condition the dog to salivate to a chosen CS—you simply put food powder in its mouth to cause salivation. To get a dog to roll over—and to condition rolling over by reinforcing the response—is much more complicated.

The trick is to reinforce *successive approximations* of the desired behavior (sitting down, lying down, lying on its side, and, finally, rolling over). When the dog sits, perhaps helped along by a shove in that direction, the trainer, early in the game, reinforces sitting. This increases the likelihood that the dog will sit. The next approximation is lying down. Then, when the dog has made progress, the required response is made tougher. To get reinforcement the dog must now lie on its side. The art of shaping means gradually extending the required response, sometimes dropping back and reinforcing earlier, simpler responses, until at length the judicious dispensing of reinforcers has shaped the animal's behavior all the way along to the final goal. The amazing feats of circus animals have been built up by gradual reinforcement of successive approximations. This is a clear and powerful demonstration of operant conditioning acting to modify (shape) responses.

Partial Reinforcement and Reinforcement Schedules

So far our examples of operant conditioning have involved *continuous reinforcement*. That is, each time the response occurs, it is reinforced. That, however, is by no means necessary. The experimenter can choose to reinforce a given response only some of the time. There is a very predictable outcome to such a *partial reinforcement* procedure: When a response is acquired through partial reinforcement, and extinction is then undertaken (when the response is no longer reinforced), the response persists much more strongly than it would have if it had been reinforced every time it occurred. (This partial reinforcement effect has also occurred in classical conditioning, though it has more often been studied in operant conditioning.)

The effect of partial reinforcement in producing extreme *resistance to extinction* is not as strange as it might seem at first. When, during acquisition, the response is reinforced only part of the time, the animal is being trained to continue responding even though many responses are not reinforced. Persistence "pays off," and eventually the response will be reinforced (Amsel, 1967). Thus, when extinction training begins, the conditions are not dramatically changed from those prevailing during acquisition. Think of a vending machine that delivers candy bars for coins 50 percent of the time. When you

are used to the sporadic pay-offs of such a machine (many seem to be located in public places), you are not likely to notice right away if the machine breaks down entirely. There is a good likelihood that you will put in several coins—show resistance to extinction—before concluding that the response is no longer rewarded. That will not happen if, in the past, the machine has always delivered each time you put in a coin; in such a case, once the machine stops paying off, you will probably quickly stop putting in coins.

If in the past a vending machine has always delivered each time you put in a coin, once the machine stops paying off, one of your reactions will probably be to quickly stop putting in coins.

The partial reinforcement effect is both powerful and widespread, but there are many practical training situations in which it seems to be totally ignored. For example, suppose that you wish to train a child to perform a socially desirable behavior. While common sense suggests that this could best be done by rewarding the behavior each time it occurs, the partial reinforcement effect suggests otherwise. We usually want to "build in" desirable behaviors in our children; the behavior should persist even when it is no longer followed by the direct rewards that seem right for children. To build in such persistence and resistance to extinction, partial reinforcement seems a better bet than continuous reinforcement.

The attempt to break an undesirable habit very often runs afoul of the partial reinforcement effect. Thus, imagine a little girl who cries each night when put to bed. The parents come to realize that they have unknowingly reinforced this behavior by picking up and comforting her. To break her now bothersome habit, her parents adopt a psychologically sound principle: The habit will no longer be reinforced. When she cries on future nights, they will no longer comfort her. This withholding of reinforcement should gradually eliminate the habit. The difficulty is that after a few nights of listening to the child cry herself to sleep, her parents relent and—just this once—pick her up and comfort her. The child has now experienced partial reinforcement of her bed-time crying. The habit will now be harder than ever to extinguish.

There are many different arrangements between responses and the occasional use of reinforcement, all of which are partial reinforcement procedures. The relation set up between a response and its reinforcer is called a *schedule of reinforcement.* The outcomes of many different reinforcement schedules have been described in detail by Ferster and Skinner (1957). The most interesting fact is that the same schedule has very much the same effect, no matter what response, what reinforcer, and what species are involved. The cumulative record produced by a pigeon pecking a key for grain under a certain kind of schedule cannot be distinguished from the cumulative record produced by a person pulling a plunger for cigarette rewards under the same schedule.

The wide variety of different reinforcement schedules can be conveniently broken down along two different dimensions. First, reinforcement can depend upon either the passage of a certain amount of *time* since the last reinforcement, or upon the animal's having performed a certain *number of responses* since the last reinforcement. Second, the amount of time (or number of responses) required since the last reinforcement can be either *fixed* or *variable.* This simplified classification gives rise to four basic reinforcement schedules. The outcomes of the four basic schedules are indicated in the cumulative records shown in Figure 6-10. The results are what you might expect.

With a *fixed-interval schedule,* the rule is that a certain amount of time (say, three minutes) must pass between two reinforcements. Thus, when a response has been rewarded, nothing the animal does during the next three minutes can produce another reward. The first response to be made *after* the passage of three minutes is the next one to be reinforced. The animal's behavior, after some experience with this schedule, seems quite sensible. There is no responding for some time after receipt of a reinforcer. Then, as the three-

An example of a fixed-interval schedule is the 9-to-5 working day, sometimes recorded on a time clock to note the exact interval worked. The reinforcer arrives once a week or once every two weeks in the form of a paycheck.

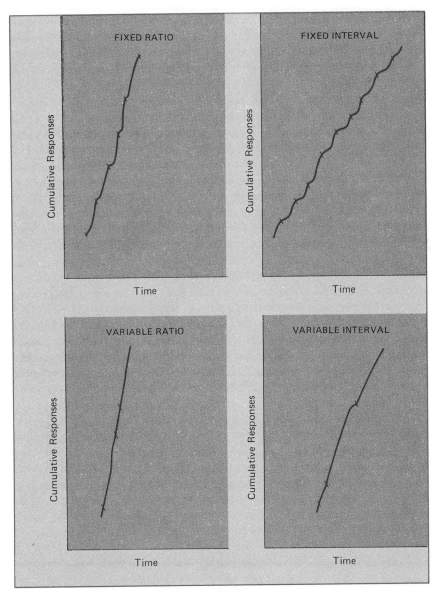

Figure 6-10

The typical outcomes of four partial reinforcement schedules, in the form of cumulative records. Slash mark indicates delivery of a reinforcement. The pause after each reinforcement is very characteristic of fixed-ratio schedules, while the "scalloped" shape of the record is typical of fixed-interval schedules.

minute mark begins to approach, the animal starts to respond at a growing rate until it receives its reinforcer. The cycle then begins again. The animal is obviously engaging in a form of timing behavior, though its timing is not entirely accurate. In somewhat the same way, in school many people stop studying right after a test and then gradually start up again as the date of the next test approaches.

The results produced by a *variable-interval schedule* are very different. With a three-minute variable-interval schedule, the *average* time between two reinforcers is three minutes, but the actual times between pairs of reinforcers differ widely and unpredictably. Thus, very occasionally, two reinforcers may be delivered only a few seconds apart; on other occasions, ten minutes may pass before the next reinforcer is made available. There is no way for the animal to know whether its *next* reinforcer will be made available in a matter of seconds, or only after many minutes. The result is a very steady rate of response over time: the cumulative record closely approximates a straight line with moderate slope. This means that the animal will receive almost all the reinforcers made available to it by the schedule, almost as soon as they are made available. (The reinforcers are "set up" by an automatic timing device and then released by the next response to occur.) To refer back to the earlier example of stopping studying right after a test, one way teachers could discourage this kind of study pattern would be to give unannounced spot quizzes. Since students would not know when they were to be tested, they wouldn't be as likely to stop studying for any great length of time.

The *fixed-ratio schedule* is one in which, after a response is reinforced, a definite number of responses (say, 50) must be made before the next reinforcement occurs. The faster the 50 responses are made, the sooner the animal receives its next reward. The animal can increase the frequency and thus the amount of reward by working at a rapid rate. (This may remind you of payment by "piecework" in factories.) The animal subjected to a fixed-ratio schedule works hard; it makes a great many responses very rapidly, and thus earns many reinforcers. There is often a pause or "break" right after a reinforcer has been received, but the animal soon sets to work again with a vengeance. Probably the most rapid rates of response, however, are produced by a *variable-ratio schedule.* With such a schedule, the number of responses required for the next reinforcement vary unpredictably. There may be one or two occasions when the next response is reinforced, while on other occasions several hundreds, or even thousands, of responses may be required. With this kind of schedule, the animal can again get the most rewards by working rapidly, and it does so. When the animal has had some experience with variable-ratio reinforcement, it can be induced to make literally thousands of responses between reinforcers. The hold of gambling over many people is notorious. The chronic gambler, who is exposed to a variable-ratio reinforcement schedule, literally cannot quit. The occasional and unpredictable reinforcement is—to the delight and profit of the casinos—enough to keep the gambler going through very long stretches without any reinforcement.

Variables That Affect Operant Conditioning

There are many phenomena observed in operant conditioning that seem very similar to those already noted in Pavlovian conditioning. Thus, at the simplest level, acquisition, extinction, and spontaneous recovery occur in the same way; acquisition depends on reinforcing a response, and extinction occurs when reinforcement is withheld. Further, generalization and discrimination are easily shown in operant conditioning studies. When, for example, a pigeon has been reinforced for pecking at a key illuminated by light of a given wavelength, it will also peck—but at lower rates—at lights of different wavelengths. There is no great trick to teaching the pigeon to discriminate between two different wavelengths—you simply reinforce responding to one wavelength, while not reinforcing responses to the other wavelength.

The acquisition of operant conditioning is affected, in the obvious way, by the magnitude of reinforcement—just as Pavlovian conditioning is a function of the strength of the US. There is also a critical time interval that profoundly affects operant conditioning. To maximize operant conditioning, the reinforcer must be delivered just after the response occurs. The time (if any) between a response and the subsequent reinforcement is referred to as the *delay of reinforcement*. With animals, at least, even quite short delays of reinforcement—on the order of 5 or 10 seconds—are often enough to prevent operant conditioning from taking place at all; and any delay, no matter how short, slows down the rate of acquisition (see Figure 6-11). Though delay of reinforcement is also an important variable in human studies, language and symbolic thought make it possible for humans to bridge very long time spans between responses and their reinforcement.

Reward and Punishment

The facts of operant conditioning indicate that whether or not a response will be repeated depends on events that follow it. Most studies of operant conditioning have examined the effects of positive reinforcers, or rewards. There are also studies in which a response has the effect of *stopping* or removing a negative reinforcer. Thus, if a rat is dropped onto an electrified grid floor and can stop the shock by pressing a lever, it will learn to do so. With successive trials the rat will press the lever more and more rapidly. The termination of shock is reinforcing in much the same way that the presentation of food or water is.

To everyday speech, however, the opposite of reward is *punishment*. We speak of punishment when we follow a response by the *presentation* of a negative reinforcer such as shock. Perhaps it seems obvious that the effect of punishment should be the exact opposite to that of reward. Where reward "stamps in" preceding responses, punishment might be expected to stamp them out. The effect of punishment, however, has been a matter of great dispute, in part because of the views of B. F. Skinner.

The effect of punishing a formerly rewarded response, Skinner argued, was to *suppress* performance of the response temporarily. The punishment would not permanently eliminate the animal's tendency to make the response. When punishment ended, the animal would once again perform the forbidden response. The effective way to eliminate an unwanted response is to make sure that it is no longer positively reinforced (to extinguish it)—or to reinforce positively those responses that are incompatible with it. Punishment is a notoriously ineffective way of changing our behavior, said Skinner—look at the results of our penal system! Perhaps the reason why we continue to use ineffective punishment procedures is because the delivery of punishment is positively reinforcing to those who dish it out!

Though Skinner's moral arguments against the use of punishment may be justified, there is no doubt that punishment, if strong enough, does "work." That is, in experiments, previously reinforced responses that are immediately followed by punishment no longer occur; and, as is the case with reward, a delay between a response and its punishment weakens the effect considerably. The "suppression" of a punished response can, for all practical purposes, be made permanent. Thus, in practice, despite Skinner's talk about "temporary suppression," intense punishment can eliminate an unwanted response at least as effec-

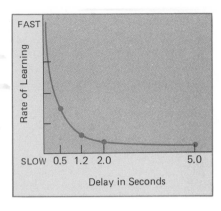

Figure 6-11

A delay-of-reward gradient observed in operant conditioning in rats. Note that even a very small delay between responding and the subsequent reinforcement can drastically slow down the rate of learning. (After Grice, 1948)

tively as ordinary extinction can. There are nevertheless some serious drawbacks to the use of punishment. Punishment affects much more than the particular response that it follows; that is, the punished animal seems *generally* suppressed and inhibited. The punished animal becomes generally fearful of the situation in which punishment occurs, and will tend to avoid whomever (or whatever) is handing out punishment. Further, quite unlike reward, punishment does not tell the punished individual what to do; it merely says what *not* to do, without providing satisfactory alternatives. Therefore, when using punishment, one way to make it more effective is to give the person (or animal) rewarded alternatives to the undesired, to-be-punished response.

Secondary Reinforcement

The phenomenon of secondary reinforcement in operant conditioning is very similar to Pavlovian higher-order conditioning. The majority of reinforcers that have been used in experimental studies have (like Pavlovian USs) obvious biological bases. We can, however, transform a previously neutral stimulus into a reasonably effective reinforcer of operant responses. The sound of a buzzer is not normally reinforcing to a rat. When the only consequence of pressing a Skinner box lever is the sound of a buzzer, very little lever-pressing occurs. The results are quite different if, before being placed in the Skinner box, the animal is exposed to a number of paired presentations of the buzzer and food. The animal, during these buzzer-food pairings, does not need to perform any response to get the food. Then, if lever-pressing produces the buzzer, the animal will make a fair number of presses in the Skinner box—even though the presses are *not* followed by food or by any other primary reinforcer. The buzzer has become—as a result of its pairing with a primary reinforcer, food—a *secondary reinforcer*. The secondary reinforcer can be used in operant conditioning in the same way as a primary reinforcer, but its capacity to reinforce operant responses is a product of learning. The principle involved in establishing a secondary reinforcer is very similar to Pavlovian conditioning: Present the stimulus close together in time with a primary reinforcer.

Once established, the power of a secondary reinforcer seems to be quite general. Thus, a buzzer previously paired with food will reinforce lever presses made when the animal is no longer hungry, but merely thirsty (Estes, 1949). In most studies, however, the effectiveness of a secondary reinforcer is rather short-lived. The secondary reinforcer will indeed work for a while, but the animal will not continue to perform indefinitely for secondary reinforcement alone. To extend the "useful life" of a secondary reinforcer, one obvious technique is to use partial reinforcement procedures. Thus, when the buzzer-food association is being established, the buzzer is only sometimes followed by food. Then, in the Skinner box, lever-pressing is only sometimes followed by the buzzer. This partial-reinforcement procedure can result in a rat's making many thousands of lever presses with no reward other than secondary reinforcement (Zimmerman, 1957). There have been many learning theorists who, like Pavlov, have thought that much human behavior might be understood as the result of a long chain of secondary reinforcements. Thus, you might think of money as a once neutral stimulus that, in your past, has been paired with a number of different primary reinforcers. The effectiveness of money as a reinforcer of human

Eric Heiden's five gold medals, which he won at the 1980 Winter Olympics, are a good example of a secondary reinforcer.

behavior is obvious, and it seems clear that people continue to work for money in and of itself, and no longer to satisfy needs. The smiling approval of fellow humans might also be thought of as a secondary reinforcer. When we are growing up, smiling human faces (often parental) are paired with the delivery of basic primary reinforcers.

Avoidance Learning

This rather special form of operant conditioning has been at the center of a number of interesting disagreements among theorists of animal learning. In an avoidance learning procedure, the animal is presented with a warning signal (CS) that occurs a few seconds before delivery of a noxious US, often electric shock. The animal, however, can avoid the shock by performing some specified response to the CS, *before* the shock is scheduled to occur. Thus, if it performs the required response quickly enough, the animal can avoid the shocks entirely. It can be shown that animals can learn such avoidance responses with great efficiency. Further, once they are learned, they can persist for thousands of trials during which the animal continues to avoid all shock (Solomon et al., 1953).

What reinforces avoidance responding? To a *cognitive* theory of learning, such as those described in the final section of this chapter, avoidance learning poses no special problems. The pairing of the warning signal with shock has taught the animal to expect shock when the signal occurs. When shock is expected, the animal sensibly performs the response required in order to avoid shock. Within the more mechanistic framework of operant and Pavlovian conditioning theories, one cannot talk about animals "expecting" shocks or about animals acting "purposefully" to avoid some future event. What, therefore, is in the here-and-now that can possibly be "stamping in" the avoidance response?

The typical avoidance learning experiment has been performed in such a way that, when the avoidance response is made, the animal not only causes shock to be omitted on that trial. The response is also followed by the immediate termination of the warning signal itself. This, as reflection should suggest, might very well be a reinforcing event. The warning signal is at first a neutral stimulus; but, once it has been paired a few times with shock, it should become a secondary negative reinforcer. That is, any response that is followed by stopping the warning signal is in theory being reinforced. The "avoidance" response might be learned not because it serves to avoid a threatened shock, but because it is followed by the prompt turning off of the warning signal!

These speculations, if correct, suggest that an animal should learn to perform a response that has no effect at all on whether the shock occurs, but that does serve to terminate the warning signal preceding shock. This has been shown to be the case. When an animal's response is followed by termination of a warning buzzer—and is then followed on each trial by an unavoidable shock—the response is acquired (Kamin, 1956). When the response is followed by a slightly *delayed* termination of the buzzer, it is less effectively learned than when termination promptly follows the response. When termination of the buzzer is delayed as little as five seconds following the response, rats fail to learn an avoidance response at all. This failure to learn occurs even when, on trials when the response is made, shock is entirely avoided. Thus, delayed termination

APPLICATION
The Use of Operant Conditioning Techniques

With just a little planning, and without any apparatus at all, it should be possible for you to demonstrate some of the basic phenomena of operant conditioning—while apparently engaging in casual conversation with a friend. The following experiment was reported by Verplanck (1955), and can easily be repeated by anyone.

The basic rule of operant conditioning, of course, is to follow a particular response with the delivery of a reinforcer. The response selected for reinforcement was any statement of opinion made in the course of conversation. That is, whenever the subject uttered a sentence beginning with "It seems to me" or "I think" or "I believe," the experimenter reinforced the statement. The reinforcer was verbal agreement, perhaps given with a nod of smiling approval. Thus, whenever the subject expressed an opinion, the experimenter responded with some such remark as "That's true," or "I agree," or "How right you are!" The delivery of such verbal reinforcement had a marked effect on the subject's behavior. There was a clear increase in the frequency with

which the subject made statements of opinion. To clinch matters, the experimenter went on to demonstrate that extinction could be brought about simply by withholding further reinforcement. When this happened, the statements of opinion decreased markedly.

Two notes of caution must be sounded for readers who wish to repeat this experiment. First, you may have to wait some time before your subject utters a first statement of opinion (recall that in operant conditioning a response must occur before it can be reinforced). Second, it is possible that your subject may "catch on" to what you are doing.

The following case study, taken from Ayllon (1963), illustrates an ingenious and systematic use of basic operant conditioning concepts in a mental hospital setting. The patient was a schizophrenic woman who, among other symptoms, wore enormous amounts of clothing —many sweaters, shawls, dresses, underclothes, and even sheets and towels wrapped around her body. The total weight of her clothing was 25 pounds.

To get the patient to give up this odd symptom, Ayllon made effective use of shaping technique, with food as a reinforcer. To get into the hospital dining room, the patient had to step on a scale, and to weigh less than a target weight selected by the experimenter. Thus, at first, the patient had to reduce the weight of her clothing to 23 (rather than 25) pounds. When this limit was met, a stricter limit was used, and so on. Though the patient missed a few meals during this shaping process, in a few months she was wearing only 3 pounds of clothing. The systematic use of food as a reinforcer had gradually eliminated a bizarre psychiatric symptom.

The conditioning treatment, of course, in no way "cured" the patient of her schizophrenia. However, as Ayllon pointed out, once the odd symptom was eliminated, other patients in the hospital were more likely to talk to and interact with the woman. Her family, in fact, took her home for a visit for the first time in 9 years, pointing out that the patient no longer looked like a "circus freak."

of the warning signal in an avoidance learning experiment acts like any other delay-of-reward in operant conditioning (Kamin, 1957; see Figure 6-11). These and similar results suggest that much animal learning with all the earmarks of "foresight" may be understood more simply in terms of the "blind" and mechanical processes of conditioning.

Though the fine details of operant conditioning can be studied most effectively with animal subjects, there is every reason to suppose that the same processes also apply in human learning. To show the power of operant conditioning techniques in humans, you might try to repeat for yourself the verbal conditioning procedure described in the accompanying box. The box also describes a fascinating case study of the use of operant conditioning procedures in a mental hospital. This kind of practical application of operant conditioning ideas is the basis of a growing technology of *behavior modification*. When such techniques are applied to changing abnormal behavior, the term *behavior therapy* is used. The ethical problems and some of the philosophical considerations involved in controlling people's behavior through the use of reinforcement have been discussed at length by Skinner, in such works as *Beyond Freedom and Dignity*. Perhaps the major point made by Skinner is that, long before we could talk about it very intelligibly, we were already controlling one another's behavior by giving and withholding reinforcement. The rational use of reinforcement in designing human cultures and societies may result in increased efficiency, but it introduces nothing fundamentally new.

Pavlovian and Operant Conditioning Compared

We have now looked in some detail at two different forms of conditioning. There are some obvious differences between the two types of conditioning, but there are also some important similarities. We shall now, in addition to comparing one form of conditioning with the other, try to understand how, in practice, the two conditioning processes tend always to be occurring at the same time. We shall also try to see whether, armed with no other concepts than those provided by the study of conditioning, we can account adequately for *all* animal learning.

The *differences* between Pavlovian and operant conditioning seem fairly obvious. The Pavlovian kind of experiment is performed on a basically passive animal, generally kept under rather severe restraints. The sequence of CS followed by US is continually repeated, and the animal begins to make a reflex-like response to the CS. In operant conditioning, on the other hand, the animal quite literally operates actively on its environment. The animal must itself push the lever, or peck the key, before its response can be followed by reinforcement. Without activity on the animal's part—often motivated by a strong drive state such as hunger—there could be no operant conditioning. The basic principle of shaping, moreover, allows for progressive (and sometimes quite startling) changes in the response itself. The control over a fixed response is not merely "switched" from one stimulus to another; the response itself changes.

With all these apparent differences in mind, it is also the case that both kinds of conditioning clearly involve very basic processes of association. The association between a response and a subsequent reinforcing stimulus does not seem fundamentally different in kind from the association between a conditioned and an unconditioned stimulus. The kind of "stamping in" process envisioned by both Pavlov and Thorndike could easily include both of these (as well as other) associations. In short, there may be a single basic associative learning process that underlies both types of conditioning. This seems even more likely when one recognizes that, in fact, it is extraordinarily difficult to design an experimental situation in which one or the other kind of conditioning takes place in "pure" form. Thus, even in Pavlovian salivary conditioning, responses occur (salivation is one of them) that are promptly followed in time by the delivery of an operant reinforcer (food)! How do we know that the food powder dropped on the dog's tongue is not *operantly* reinforcing the response of salivating to the CS?

There have been some attempts to argue that two types of conditioning may apply to two different types of *responses*. Thus, the suggestion has often been made that Pavlovian conditioning might only affect responses controlled by the autonomic nervous system, while operant conditioning might apply only to responses controlled by the skeletal nervous system. The same basic distinction has been made more loosely, by contrasting "involuntary" with "voluntary" responses.

Theories of learning aside, it is a matter of considerable practical importance to discover whether *operant* reinforcement can condition responses controlled by the autonomic nervous system. Consider the rate at which the heart beats. This is controlled by the autonomic nervous system. There are people with medical conditions that require them to develop a slower heart rate. What, if anything, can we do to teach such people to slow down their heart rates?

The animal research of Miller and DiCara (1967) was directed toward problems of this sort. The experiments are of necessity quite complex. For example, one must rule out reflexive changes of heart rate brought about by skeletal responses rather than by operant reinforcement. For example, a man told that he would receive a large reward for speeding up his heart rate could easily do so; all he needs to do is run up a few flights of stairs. This kind of reflexive change in heart rate is obviously not a direct effect of an operant reinforcer acting on the heart itself. To rule out this kind of response, the animals' muscles were paralyzed by a drug, which in turn made artificial respiration necessary. There are not many operant reinforcements that can be given to paralyzed and artificially respirated subjects, but stimulation of a "pleasure center" in the brain, through a depth electrode, is one (see Chapter 2). The procedure adopted was, in some animals, whenever a spontaneous small increase in heart rate occurred, it was followed by a reinforcing brain stimulation. With other animals, small *decreases* in heart rate were promptly followed by the same brain stimulation. This kind of shaping procedure was effective; animals rewarded for increased heart rates sped up their heart rates quite a lot during a session, while animals reinforced for decreased heart rates did the opposite.

These and other impressive results were at one time routinely reported from Miller's laboratory (Miller, 1969). Theoretically, the data showed that autonomic nervous system responses, like all others, are influenced by operant reinforcers that follow them in time. Practically, the results held out considerable promise for the development of *behavioral medicine* in humans. There is in principle no reason why conditioning techniques cannot be used—together with drugs and surgery—to affect the functioning of the internal organs. The first flush of enthusiasm, however, may have been excessive. The impressive early successes first reported by Miller and DiCara have not been routinely repeated (Miller and Dworkin, 1974). There is, on the other hand, an accumulating number of successful—and sometimes spectacular—therapeutic results reported by practitioners of behavioral medicine.

The use of autonomic conditioning techniques in a medical setting is well illustrated in a case study described by Kremer and his associates. The patient, a 56-year-old man, had suffered severe nerve damage after hurting his neck in a fall. He was left with severe pain in his hands, and had become overly dependent on pain-killing drugs, which provided only slight relief. He had noted, however, that the pain lessened when the skin temperature of his hands increased—for example, when soaking in a hot tub.

The psychologist and the physicians working with this patient asked him to practice trying to increase his hand temperature by simply thinking about the memory of past occasions when his hands had been warm. To aid this learning, the patient was given a number of training sessions with *biofeedback.* That is, the patient was hooked up to a sensitive recording apparatus that gave him immediate information about very small changes in his hand temperature. Practicing with the aid of this device, within a few days the patient was able to increase his hand temperature by as much as 3°C by simply imagining that his hands were warm. This provided great relief of his pain, and he was able to transfer this conditioning to real-life situations. His use of pain-killing drugs dropped dramatically. Similar medically relevant uses of conditioning procedures and biofeedback have been described by other researchers as well (Blizard et al., 1975; Lynch et al., 1976).

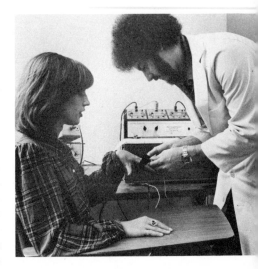

Experiments have shown that when subjects are given feedback of their present bodily states in the form of audible tones, moving graphs, or dials, they can in turn learn to control such bodily reactions as brain wave pattern, blood pressure, and muscle tension. The biofeedback technique has been most successfully applied as an adjunct to treatment for chronic headaches.

When the basic phenomena of Pavlovian and operant conditioning were being discovered, there was a tendency for many workers in the field to believe that—whether or not they were basically one process—the two forms of conditioning would between them provide an entirely adequate account of at least animal learning. Perhaps, it was even suggested, with the right modifications to account for the conditioning of language, even all of human learning could be understood in this way. That early enthusiasm has now faded. There is no question but that conditioning plays an important part in the learning of animals, and in humans. There are more *cognitive* learning processes, however, which not only play the major role in human learning but also seem quite evident in animal experimentation. We shall, in the next section of this chapter, describe some studies of "cognitive" learning in animals. For the moment, we can point out that the main way conditioning applies in humans may be precisely in that area where cognition and reason seem so ineffective—in the conditioning of emotional responses. This is discussed in Chapter 11.

The pioneers who began the systematic study of animal learning often assumed that the general laws of learning would be very much the same in all animal species. Thus, it made no real difference if one studied rats, pigeons, goldfish, or flatworms. The effects of delay of reinforcement, or of partial reinforcement, might equally well be studied in any of these species. Further, the particular stimuli chosen for use in an experiment were not thought to matter; that is, any neutral CS might be paired with any US, and the course of conditioning would be much the same. In recent years these views have changed considerably, in large measure due to the remarkable work on "bait shyness" reported by Garcia and his associates (Garcia and Koelling, 1966; Garcia, McGowan, and Green, 1972). The bait-shyness phenomenon is clearly demonstrated in the behavior of the rat. When a rat eats poisoned food, it will not—assuming it survives—eat the poisoned bait a second time. This learning to avoid a normally favored food takes place in only one trial. This happens even though the illness produced by poison may not occur until several hours after the rat has eaten the poisoned food. How does the rat know that the food—eaten long ago—caused its illness?

It must be, Garcia has argued, that evolution has given the rat a tendency to associate internal bodily states, such as illness, with the smell and taste of food—even when long time periods pass between eating and the subsequent illness. This kind of learning would obviously be adaptive in the rat's natural environment. The rat, needless to say, will not learn to associate the sound of a buzzer with an illness that occurs six hours later; but it *will* associate a particular food with an illness occurring hours later. These and similar results indicate that, by studying animals in lab experiments rather than "in the wild," we are likely to overlook some special capacities possessed by individual species. That in no way denies, however, the fact that the basic findings discussed in this chapter have been observed repeatedly across a wide range of species. The bait-shyness phenomenon itself can be viewed as a remarkable modification of the normal effects of the time between CS and US, rather than as an utterly new phenomenon. In experimental studies of bait-shyness it is clearly the case that the tendency to avoid the distinctive food is less, the longer the interval between eating the food and the following illness. This seems quite in accord with basic Pavlovian principles.

Cognitive Learning in Animals

Though most studies of animal learning have been performed in a conditioning framework, critics have been quick to point out that—real though the phenomena of conditioning may be—such studies do not tap the more "mental" or "cognitive" forms of learning. The most vigorous criticism of early conditioning studies came from the Gestalt psychologists (see Chapter 4). They argued that the learning observed by Pavlov and by Thorndike seemed blind, robot-like, and automatic exactly because the experimental situations into which the animals had been placed did not allow for truly intelligent or insightful behavior. There is not much chance for a beast to display its cleverness when it is caged in a virtually empty Skinner box or locked into a conditioning stock. To study *insight*—a form of learning and problem solving depending on complex cognitive activity—it is necessary to observe animals in a freer experimental situation. The experimenter must take pains to make available all the various elements which, when appropriately related to each other by the animal, yield an insightful solution.

Insight Learning

The classical studies of insight learning were reported in 1925 by Wolfgang Köhler. The subjects of his studies were chimpanzees. That is not surprising: The cognitive processes involved in insightful learning are characteristic of higher animals with a well-developed cortex. The chicken or the snail, though

HIGHLIGHT
Conditioning, Attention, and Surprise

The kinds of data that have encouraged cognitive analyses of conditioning are well illustrated by the phenomenon of *blocking* (Kamin, 1968). When the CS in a conditioning study is made up of two different stimuli (say, a light and a noise presented at the same time), animals normally condition to each of the two stimuli. When tested alone, the light and the noise will each elicit a conditioned response. That seems obvious enough—each of the stimuli has been paired close together in time with the US (say, a shock). The results are very different, however, if the animal is first conditioned to either the light alone paired with the US or the noise alone paired with the US. Then, despite continued reinforcement of the compound with the US, the animal fails to condition to the new, added CS element. The previous conditioning of Stimulus A in some way *blocks* conditioning to Stimulus B when the AB compound is later reinforced.

Possibly the blocking of conditioning occurs because the previously conditioned element (Stimulus A) engages so much of the animal's attention that it simply does not notice the newly added Stimulus B, and thus fails

to condition to it. There are many indications, however, that this is not the case. Thus if, when Stimulus B is first added on to the previously conditioned Stimulus A, reinforcement is withheld, the animal rapidly learns that Stimulus B is a conditioned inhibitor, a signal of nonreinforcement. To have learned this, the animal must have been paying attention to Stimulus B. Possibly, then, the animal stops paying attention to Stimulus B only when, as in the usual blocking experiment, Stimulus B provides no new information. When Stimulus B is added to Stimulus A, and the compound is followed by the very same US that A alone has previously signalled, B is a *redundant* (noninformative) stimulus. Perhaps animals learn to ignore, or "tune out," CSs that prove to be redundant, and thus do not condition to them. This kind of theory of the blocking phenomenon has been advanced by Mackintosh (1975).

In a similar vein, Kamin (1969) has suggested that the kinds of associations normally formed during conditioning are made when, and only when, the US *surprises* the animal. With a normal conditioning procedure, using only one CS, the US is—at

least on early trials—a surprising and important event. The surprise makes the animal "look back," or scan, its memory of very recent events. When the animal "locates" the CS, it forms an association between CS and US—but only as a consequence of having been surprised by the US. The dog, so to speak, having been surprised by the sudden appearance of meat powder, wonders what on earth could have produced the meat. Thinking back over what has recently happened, the dog remembers the metronome and thus associates metronome with meat.

This kind of cognitive account obviously fits the data of blocking experiments. When Stimulus A has earlier become conditioned, its occurrence informs the animal that the US is about to follow. The addition of Stimulus B to Stimulus A at this point will not be followed by any surprising event—only by the same old US. Thus, the animal will *not* form an association between B and the US, even though they have occurred close together in time. When the addition of B to A is followed by a changed US, or the withholding of the US, the animal is surprised—and learns what Stimulus B signals.

---

easily conditioned, would not be a good bet for experiments on insight.

The kind of procedure used by Köhler can best be seen in the two-stick problem. The chimp is in its cage, and easily visible on the floor outside the cage is a tempting banana. There is a short stick on the floor of the cage, and a longer stick on the floor just outside the cage. When presented with this problem the chimp is most likely, first of all, to reach between the cage bars in a futile effort to obtain the banana. When this fails, the chimp may fly into a temper tantrum. When calm returns, the eye of the chimp may suddenly fall on the stick inside its cage. Then, very quickly, the chimp picks up the short stick, runs to the front

Chapter 6:
Conditioning and Learning

171

of the cage, and tries to rake the banana in with the stick. The stick, however, is not long enough. This failure may produce a *real* temper tantrum. To shorten the story, a bright chimp will eventually notice the long stick just outside the cage. Then, quick as a flash—we talk of the "flash of insight"—the chimp will rake in the long stick with the short stick, and immediately use the long stick to rake in the banana. (The same kind of insightful solutions occurred when the banana was suspended from the cage ceiling, out of reach, and three boxes were scattered about the cage floor. The chimps, after sizing up the situation, would stack the three boxes into a kind of tower, climb the tower, and obtain the banana.)

These problem solutions, in Köhler's view, depended on the chimp's ability to restructure cognitive elements into new and purposeful wholes. The chimp clearly seems to be thinking, much as you and I do. The insight, Köhler stressed, was not the result of blind, Thorndikeian, trial-and-error, random responses. When the chimp got the point, the insight came very suddenly—and irreversibly. When an animal (or person) learns something insightfully, rather than by rote (repetitive drill), it is less likely to forget the solution, Köhler maintained. There is a basically arbitrary nature to the associations which, in conditioning studies, experimenters impress upon their subjects. With insight studies, the elements the animal is allowed to relate to one another form a meaningful whole and a sensible cognitive structure.

Learning Sets

The gap between gradual conditioning and sudden insight may not be quite as fundamental as Köhler maintained. Though Köhler did not stress the fact, the chimps with which he worked had lived free in the wild before serving as experimental subjects. They doubtless had had previous experience with the use of sticks, and with the climbing of structures. The insightful solutions did not really come out of the blue. Presumably, the chimps' accumulation of past experiences had played some role in the appearance of an insightful problem solution.

The way in which previous problem solutions transfer to aid the prompt solution of a new problem has been studied in detail by Harlow (1949). The subjects of Harlow's experiments were monkeys, tested in the kind of apparatus shown in Figure 6-12. The problem put to the monkey is a two-choice discrimination. There is a small food reward, which, on each trial, is consistently placed under one of two objects. For example, in the first problem the monkey may be presented with a square box and a round box. The food is always under the square box, which is sometimes presented to the monkey's right and other times to the monkey's left. To get the food reward on any trial, the monkey must reach out and lift the square box; there is no reward on trials when the monkey lifts the round box. When first presented with such a problem, the animal will operate on a chance basis and will tend to select the correct box on about 50 percent of the trials. With later trials, however, the monkey's performance will improve until, finally, it is correct on 100 percent of the trials. Then the animal is presented with a *new* two-choice discrimination. This time, for example, a black triangular box and a white triangular box might be used, with food always under the black box. The monkey will gradually solve this problem,

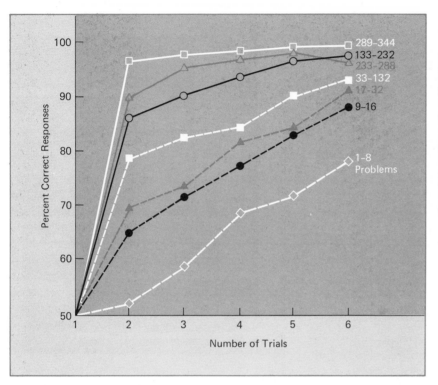

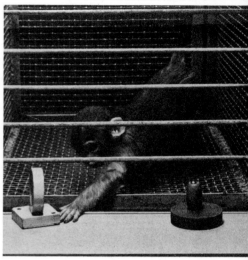

Figure 6-12

(Left) These curves summarize the results of Harlow's learning set studies. Note that during the first eight problems the monkey performs little better than chance (50 percent correct) for the first six trials. By the time 289 problems have been solved, the monkey is almost always correct on the second trial of any new problem. (Harlow, 1949)

(Right) The monkey in a Harlow learning set experiment reaching for the one of two objects under which the food reward has been placed.

too—and it will probably need fewer trials to master the second discrimination than were taken to learn the first. The monkey is given a whole series of new two-choice discriminations to learn, with the results shown in Figure 6-12.

The monkey eventually arrives at a state in which any new two-choice discrimination is solved immediately. When first presented with two new objects, the monkey reaches at random for one or the other. When its first choice happens to be correct, the monkey stays with it on all following trials, never bothering to pick up the other object. When its first choice happens to be incorrect, the monkey immediately switches to the other object and selects it on all following trials. This "insightful" behavior provides impressively rapid solutions to new problems; but note that the insight is itself the product of a gradual trial-and-error learning process. The improvement in the rate of solution of new problems, as a consequence of experience with past problems, is referred to as the acquisition of a *learning set.* The animal, while gradually solving a particular problem, is learning more than particular responses; it is also *learning how to learn.* That is, it may also learn general techniques and approaches that will be useful in the solution of new problems. The monkey, needless to say, is more likely to acquire learning sets than is the rat.

Latent Learning

The importance of cognitive factors in animal learning was clearly shown by the maze studies done by Edward C. Tolman and his followers. The kind of multiple-entry maze used in such studies can be seen in Figure 6-13. The hungry rat must work its way from the start box to the end box, in which there is

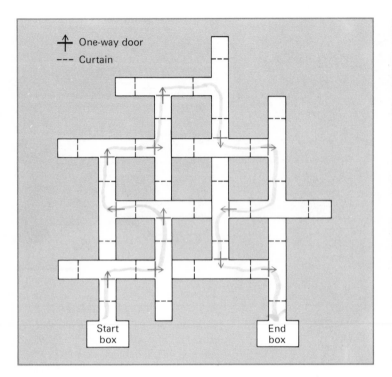

Figure 6-13

Floor plan and photo of the type of maze used in the study of latent learning in rats. (Tolman and Honzik, 1930)

a food reward. There are many possible blind alleys on the way. When the rat is first put in the maze it will enter many blind alleys (make many errors) as it goes from the start box to the goal box. With more trials, learning is shown by a steady decrease in the number of errors.

Though it is possible to theorize that reward in the goal box stamps in a particular sequence of right-turning and left-turning responses, Tolman argued that this was not the case. What the rat learns, according to Tolman, is a kind of "cognitive map," or mental picture, of the maze. That kind of learning—the storing of information about the world—takes place even when there is no reinforcement. To make these points, Tolman did experiments on *latent learning*. The outcome of a classic study by Tolman and Honzik (1930) is shown in Figure 6-14. Three different groups of rats were run through the same maze. The first group received a food reward in the goal box on each trial. These animals gradually reduced their number of errors to a near-zero level, and there is nothing surprising about that. The second group of rats received no reinforcement in the goal box. Though their errors declined slightly over time, they continued to make many more errors than did the reinforced group. There is again nothing surprising in this. The most interesting result is that for the third group. They received no reinforcement during the first 10 days. Then, on the eleventh day, for the first time food was given in the goal box. When placed into the maze on the next (twelfth) day, these animals made almost no errors. The single reinforcement brought about a dramatic improvement in their performance, so that they ran the maze about as well as the group that had been rewarded on all the earlier days. The rats had shown, in Tolman's term, *latent learning.* The early days of wandering through the maze without reinforcement had led to the build-

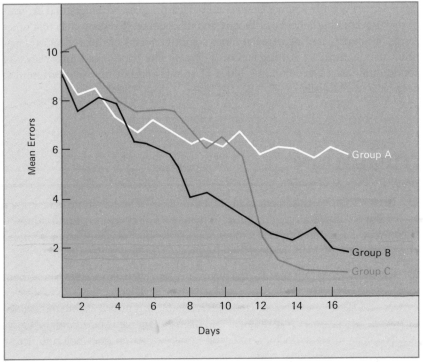

Figure 6-14

The results of the classic study of latent learning. Group A never received a food reward in the maze, while Group B was rewarded on each day. The reward was given to Group C for the first time on Day 11. Note the immediate change in their behavior on Day 12. (Tolman and Honzik, 1930)

ing up of a mental picture of the maze. Then, when the animals were shown on the eleventh day that the goal box now contained reinforcement, they used this latent cognitive learning to run through the maze without errors.

The latent learning studies, in addition to pointing toward the operation of cognitive factors in animal learning, force us to make a clear distinction between *learning* and *performance*. The performance of an animal may not change much from trial to trial, but that does not necessarily mean that the animal is not learning. The learning may involve cognitive restructuring that remains latent until some event—such as the sudden introduction of reinforcement—prompts the animal to use what it has learned. The distinction between learning and performance is often made by students who do poorly on an exam. Though the exam performance was very poor, the student may argue, it did not really reflect what the student insists he or she has learned from the course. The grading systems of schools, however, are geared to performance, not to latent learning.

There are, as we have seen, many forms of animal learning that seem to demand interpretation in terms of cognitive factors. There is also the possibility that even such simple forms of learning as conditioning may involve cognition. As mentioned earlier, we can think of the CS as causing the animal to "expect" the US, and we can think of the animal as "expecting" that a particular response will be followed by reinforcement. Though most theorists have argued that such language only serves to complicate simple processes, in recent years "cognitive-type" language and concepts have been worked into theoretical accounts of elementary conditioning.

With the steady accumulation of knowledge over the years, many of the controversies that once dominated the study of animal learning have pretty well disappeared. We now know that *some* animal learning can be understood in terms of the "stamping in" theory of Pavlov and Thorndike. We know also that other forms of animal learning demand more cognitive forms of theoretical explanation, such as those of Köhler and of Tolman. The widespread importance of conditioning as a basic building block of animal—and of human—learning has been clearly established.

Summary

1.   Pavlov's basic experiment is a clear example of what has come to be known as the law of classical conditioning: Whenever a previously neutral stimulus (CS) is presented in close temporal contiguity with an unconditioned stimulus (US), the response made to the US will come to be made to the CS.

2.   The basic rule followed by the experimenter during acquisition is: Whenever the CS is presented, follow it with the US. That procedure—CS followed by US—is called *reinforcement.* If the CS is no longer reinforced, the conditioned response disappears—this is known as *extinction. Spontaneous recovery* of a response occurs after extinction, indicating that extinction does not completely erase the conditioned response.

3.   When a conditioned response has been established to a particular conditioned stimulus, stimuli similar to that CS will also tend to elicit the response, in a process called *generalization.* In *discrimination,* the subject learns not to respond to similar stimuli while continuing to respond to the CS itself.

4.   Pavlov noted that a CS established in one series of trials could then, on its own, act as a US in a second series of trials. This is called *higher-order conditioning.* Much human learning depends on such conditioning.

5.   In operant conditioning, the *presentation* of a positive reinforcer increases the likelihood that a response will be repeated. The *termination* of a negative reinforcer also increases the likelihood that the response will be repeated.

6.   *Shaping* is the technique used to modify or change responses. In shaping one reinforces the successive approximations of a particular response until the desired behavior is performed.

7.   In general, reinforcing every correct response is less effective than some type of partial reinforcement, which leads to learning that is more resistant to extinction. Schedules of reinforcement can be based on either the number of responses (ratio) or the time elapsed between responses (interval), and can be either variable or fixed. The four basic schedules are thus *fixed interval, variable interval, fixed ratio,* and *variable ratio.*

8.   *Punishment* is the opposite of reward or reinforcement. There are a number of serious drawbacks to punishment: It tends to generally suppress and inhibit responding; it causes the person or animal to become fearful of the situation in which it occurred and of the person who administered it; and it does not tell a person or animal what to do, it merely says what *not* to do, without presenting satisfactory alternatives.

9. A *primary reinforcer* is one that is rewarding by itself, without any association with other reinforcers. The value of a *secondary reinforcer* must be learned by associating it with primary reinforcers.

10. *Insight,* a form of learning and problem solving that depends on cognitive activity, was studied by Köhler, who described it as the ability to restructure cognitive elements into new and purposeful wholes.

11. Trial-and-error learning and insightful learning can be combined in learning how to learn or acquiring a *learning set,* which was studied by Harlow.

12. Latent learning shows a clear distinction between learning and performance. If some event such as the use of reinforcement prompts the animal to use what it has learned, its performance may change immediately, showing that such learning has in fact taken place.

Suggested Readings

FLAHERTY, C. F., HAMILTON, L. W., GANDELMAN, R. J., and SPEAR, N. E. *Learning and memory.* Chicago: Rand McNally, 1977. A wide-ranging, clearly spelled out text on animal learning, with much material on human learning and memory as well.

HILGARD, E. R., and BOWER, G. H. *Theories of learning,* 4th ed. Englewood Cliffs, N. J.: Prentice-Hall, 1975. As implied by the title, the emphasis is on theory, not data. Much material of historical interest.

HONIG, W. K., and STADDON, J. E. R. (Eds.) *The handbook of operant behavior.* Englewood Cliffs, N.J.: Prentice-Hall, 1977. Individual chapters by different authorities, covering a wide range of subject matters, each in considerable detail.

MACKINTOSH, N. J. *The psychology of animal learning.* New York: Academic Press, 1974. *The* comprehensive text on animal learning, but difficult going for the beginner.

RACHLIN, H. *Introduction to modern behaviorism,* 2nd ed. San Francisco: Freeman, 1976. This brief volume reviews most of the facts and concepts of both classical and operant conditioning, placing them in an historical context.

REYNOLDS, G. S. *A primer of operant conditioning,* rev. ed. Glenview, Ill.: Scott, Foresman, 1975. Despite the title, this clear and elementary text also includes material on classical conditioning.

SCHWARTZ, B. *Psychology of learning and behavior.* New York: Norton, 1978. An up-to-date and thorough text, especially strong on recent developments.

SKINNER, B. F. *Beyond freedom and dignity.* New York: Knopf, 1971. The inventor of the Skinner box as cultural guru and philosopher.

7 Memory

After you make an appointment with someone, you may simply hope you will remember it, or you may jot it down in your calendar. In other words, you can either rely on your own internal memory or use some sort of external memory. Fortunately, given the enormous amount of information we wish to retain and the limits of our internal memory, there are many forms of external memory systems—ranging from a string tied to a finger to huge computer memories. *Memory system* simply means something that allows you to retain information over time. Thus a book, a tape recording, and a photograph are all external memory systems. Each preserves information in a particular form, and each is best suited to preserving certain types of information.

Our central interest in this chapter is internal human memory, but because psychological ideas about internal memory are often expressed as analogies with external forms of memory, it is useful to begin by considering some external memory systems.

Some Useful Terminology for Describing Memory Systems

The terms "encoding," "retention," and "retrieval" are often used to describe three basic aspects of memory systems. *Encoding* refers to the way information is first stored or represented in a system. *Retention* refers to the way the information is preserved in a system over time. And *retrieval* refers to the way the information is finally recovered from a system. The three aspects can be illustrated in terms of that most familiar external memory system, a book. Information is first *encoded* into patterns of ink in the form of words when the book is printed. It is *retained* over time by the persistence of this pattern, although information can be lost if the ink or paper is of a poor quality, or if the book is physically damaged (by water or fire, etc.). Finally, the information in the book is *retrieved* or recovered when it is read.

The same distinctions can also be made in terms of another external memory system, a tape recording. Here information—for example, a lecturer's voice—is encoded in the form of magnetic patterns laid down on the tape as it moves past the recording head. Retention of the information depends on the persistence of this pattern over time. Again, information can be lost if the tape is

Table 7–1: Examples of Codes.

English:	C O D E
Morse Code:	· · ·, – – –, – · ·, ·
Binary Code:	00011, 01111, 00100, 00101

One way of storing information is by recording it on tape. It is easy to record a person's voice in this way, but information loss is possible through erasing the tape.

physically damaged, exposed to strong magnetic fields, or if another recording is made over the first. Finally, information is retrieved from the tape by playing it back.

We will use the phrase *information loss* in a very general way to refer to what happens when anything interferes with the accurate retrieval of information. Thus information loss can occur during encoding, retention, or retrieval. For example, a tape recorder could lose information because of improper recording (encoding), accidental erasure during retention, or a broken playback system that prevents retrieval. Note that if the defective playback system were repaired, it would then be possible to recover the information, as long as it was still on the tape. The point is that although failure to recover information from a memory system is an instance of information loss, the information is not necessarily permanently beyond retrieval. This point can be illustrated in another way. Suppose you consulted a card catalogue in a library and then went to the place where the book should be shelved. If it wasn't there, and hadn't been checked out, you couldn't retrieve the information in that book. However, you wouldn't know whether the book had been permanently lost or was simply misplaced. You might make an exhaustive search of the stacks for the missing book—another retrieval process. But even if this failed, you couldn't rule out the possibility that the book might eventually turn up, so you couldn't consider the loss permanent. Later we shall consider similar issues in human memory, when it is difficult to decide whether information is permanently lost or only temporarily irretrievable.

Notice that information is represented in different ways in each of the memory systems we have considered (printed letters, magnetic patterns, etc.). Each of these representations or *codes* has its special properties, such as the ease and speed with which you can encode various forms of information and the sorts of things that will *interfere* with retention. For example, the nature of a person's voice is normally easier to store on magnetic tape than on the printed page, although a good writer may describe a voice quite accurately. Also, the retention of printed words is uninfluenced by magnetic fields, but a tape recording can be completely erased by such fields.

A number of different codes may also be used in the same memory system. For example, a novel can be printed in different languages. This is an encoding of the same information in the same form of memory system (a book) using a different code (French or English). In another example, Table 7-1 illustrates a variety of codes for representing English words.

Information held in a memory system may also be *recoded*, either by retrieving the information from that system and coding it into another system, or by recoding it into the same system. Suppose you had a friend make a tape recording of a lecture you had to miss. You might listen to the tape that evening and then either write a summary of the main ideas into another memory system, your notebook, or simply make another tape recording of your summary. In either case, there are two important aspects of this recoding process: the information loss or reduction involved, and the reorganization of the information. *Information reduction* occurs because there is less information about the lecture in the recoded summary than there was on the original tape. Even if the lecture were typed out verbatim, some reduction would be inevitable because the

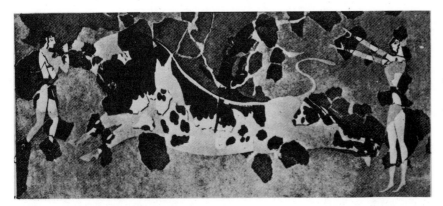

Figure 7-1

This ancient wall painting from Crete is a kind of memory system, since it retains information about how things looked centuries ago. The ravages of time have interfered with retention, producing some loss of information. It was possible in this case to restore or reconstruct much of what was lost, based on what was left and the restorer's knowledge of the normal relationship (redundancy) between different parts of an image.

typed pages wouldn't contain the sounds of the lecturer's voice. In any case, many details of the lecture (jokes, illustrations, etc.) are purposely left out of a summary. *Organization* of information can also be changed during the recoding process. The information on the tape is in the exact sequence in which the lecturer presented it. You might choose to summarize the principal points in a very different sequence if such a *reorganization* seems simpler.

It should be emphasized that recoding doesn't always involve information reduction. In fact, some recoding processes involve *reconstructive* or *redintegrative* processes that may actually add to, or elaborate upon, the retrieved information (see Figure 7-1). Such reconstructive or redintegrative processes would allow you to fill in text in an old manuscript that had been partly destroyed, or to bridge gaps caused by static on a tape recording of a human voice. In each case you reconstruct the missing information through educated guessing based on the information that wasn't lost and your knowledge of linguistic redundancy. This is the same sort of inferential process that occurs so automatically in perception, as we discussed in Chapter 4. For example, you often infer parts of a scene or printed sentence that you don't gaze at directly from those you do.

One last way of characterizing memory systems is in terms of their *capacity.* For example, a salesman might use a small pocket notebook to record appointments during the day, then at the end of the day transfer these appointments to a larger notebook in his office. The pocket notebook has a lower capacity for storing information than the large office notebook. However, the pocket notebook has compensating advantages, such as its physical size and transportability, that make it easier and faster to use during the day. The office notebook has a greater capacity, but in order to retrieve information from it during the day, the salesman must return to, or at least phone, his office. Thus the two memory systems differ in speed of encoding and retrieval as well as capacity.

The Analogy with Computer Memory Systems

A rich technical language for describing computer memory systems has been developed in recent years. Psychologists have found this language useful in describing the way our mind stores, retains, and retrieves information. While human memory is undoubtedly far more complex than the most sophisticated computer memory, there are some useful similarities. Computers use a variety of

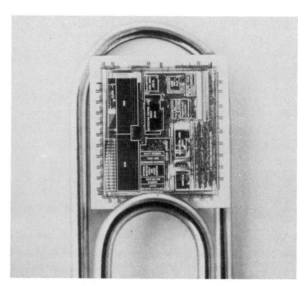

Shown here is a computer used to store Social Security information. The memory chip on the right (shown against a paperclip to indicate size) is what enables the computer to store massive amounts of information in a small space.

systems to store information, and each has its own special characteristics. Large amounts of information can be stored on magnetic tapes, but retrieval of this information requires winding and unwinding a large spool of tape. Other memory systems allow more rapid recovery of information, but have less capacity than magnetic tapes.

Computers also represent (code), transform (recode), and organize information in a variety of ways. For example, a computer might contain information about the employees of some company. This information could be represented or coded on magnetic tape as a list of social security numbers, names, or job titles, or all three. The choice of method for organizing or ordering information on the tape will depend on what the computer will do with that information. For example, if the computer is to print out a telephone directory, it might be best to store the names alphabetically on the tape, since the tape could then be read in sequence as the names are printed without extensive winding and rewinding. Humans also seem to represent or code information in a variety of ways, transforming and reorganizing it so that it is easier to retrieve or use.

Developing Theories about Memory Systems

As we have seen, it is possible to describe external memory systems in terms of such properties as their capacity, codes, speed of encoding and retrieval, susceptibility to interference, and so on. Many psychologists have found it useful to describe human memory in similar terms. How is this possible? External memory systems can be examined directly, whereas the covert or internal memory systems involved in human memory usually can't (although some of the physiological studies we discuss later might be interpreted as direct examinations). Fortunately, you can often infer quite a bit about a memory system from the way it functions or behaves, even if you can't examine it directly. Careful observation of how humans perform various memory tasks has suggested a variety of theoretical conjectures about the nature of human memory. Before considering these theoretical ideas, let us look at some of the experimental tasks used to study human memory.

Types of Memory Tasks

Psychologists study human memory by observing people perform memory tasks. Three important types of memory tasks are recall, recognition, and relearning.

Recall

One of the earliest ways developed to test human memory (Ebbinghaus, 1885) is to allow subjects to study a list of items (words or nonsense syllables) and then ask them to *recall* as many as possible, either by naming them or writing them down. Take a minute to study the following list of words:

> house
> tree
> car
> grass
> coin
> candle
> barn
> bus
> gun
> soup

Figure 7-2

The colored line shows the relation between how long subjects studied a list of words and how many terms they could recall in the 1-minute recall period. The white line shows how many terms were recalled with a longer recall period of 3 minutes.

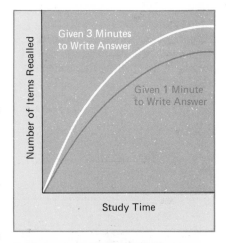

Now cover the list and write out as many of the items as you can remember. The color curve in Figure 7-2 shows the relation between how long subjects study lists of this sort and how many items they can successfully recall during a 1-minute recall period. Not surprisingly, the longer they study, the more items they can recall. However, the longer they study, the more study time is required to add one additional word to those they can recall. Another important feature of recall tasks is indicated by the white line in Figure 7-2. This shows how many items were recalled after various periods of study given a longer recall period (the time allowed to write out the items)—3 minutes rather than 1 minute. Items that aren't available in 1 minute may be recalled if subjects are given more time.

A recall task is like trying to name each state in the United States, or answering such questions as "What is her name?" or "What is your phone number?" The more you use or study such information, the more likely you are to recall it. However, an interesting aspect of recall is that it may take some time for it to occur, even though you're immediately quite confident it will. You may feel the correct answer is on the tip of your tongue, and yet be unable to produce it for some time. This *tip-of-the-tongue (TOT) phenomenon* suggests that recall is an active process that takes both time and concentration. Still, you may have the TOT experience and yet finally have to give up trying to recall some fact. Then, after a few moments, you may find the fact pops into your mind without any conscious effort on your part.

In order to control more precisely how long each word in a recall list is available for study, experimenters often present the words serially (one after another), with each word seen for the same amount of time. With this kind of presentation, words at the beginning and end of the list are more likely to be

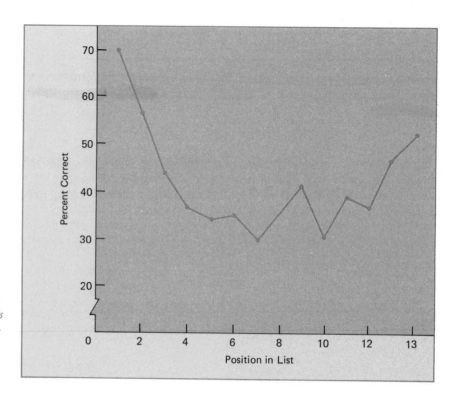

Figure 7-3

This graph shows the serial position effect: The position of the words in the list, which determines the order in which they are presented, affects recall. Higher recall of words at the beginning of the list is called the primacy effect, and higher recall of words at the end of the list (the most recently presented words) is called the recency effect.

recalled than those in the middle. This is called the *serial position effect* and is illustrated in graph form in Figure 7-3. The higher recall of the words at the beginning of the list is referred to as a *primacy effect;* the higher recall of words at the end of the list (the most recently presented words) is called a *recency effect.*

It is important to note that your ability to recall something can be strongly influenced by other stimuli presented at the time of recall. Such stimuli are often referred to as *recall cues.* For example, your ability to recall someone's name might be aided by such recall cues as hearing his or her voice or seeing a picture of the person. In fact, simply asking someone to recall something can be considered a recall cue. There is no doubt that such stimuli as "What is your address?" or "What items were on the list you just read?" tend to influence what you remember.

The fact that contiguity or repeated pairing of stimuli makes one a good recall cue for the other explains a phenomenon called *state-dependent learning.* Things learned in a particular environment (indoors, outdoors, a noisy dormitory, a quiet library) or in particular physiological state (fatigued, intoxicated, cold, warm) are often recalled better in the same environment or state. For instance, if you studied for an exam in a cold, small room, you might not recall the information as well in a warm, large room as you would in a cold, small one. Similarly, the bodily sensations associated with mild intoxication could serve as recall cues for things learned in that state.

To sum up, both external and internal stimuli present at the time you learn something are likely to be good recall cues, a phenomenon Tulving (1978) called *encoding specificity.*

Recognition

Another way to test memory is to use a recognition task. Consider the following list. Some of these terms were in the list you saw earlier; others are new or *distractor* items. Check those items you remember seeing in the earlier list.

grass   heart   gun
bike   car   bus
phone   soup   bridge
coin   tree   cliff
house   door   barn
boat   bat   rifle

Notice that in this case a word is presented and you must decide whether or not you recognize it from a previous list. This is similar to asking someone "Is that Mary?" or "Is your phone number 621-7753?" rather than "Who is that?" or "What is your phone number?" as in the recall task. Here the answer to the recall question is actually there, and you must say whether or not you recognize it.

In general, people are more likely to recognize an item than to recall it. This may be simply because presentation of the item is a good recall cue. This idea was explored by Tulving and Watkins (1973), whose results are shown in Figure 7-4. They varied how much of an item was present at the time of recall by varying how many of its letters were shown to the subject. When no letters were shown, as in a simple recall task, recall was low. The more letters shown, the better the recall, indicating that presenting even part of an item serves as a recall cue. Finally, when the whole item was presented, as in a conventional recognition task, the subject was most likely to recall seeing the item earlier. So recognition may be thought of as a special case of recall, in which the item itself serves as a recall cue.

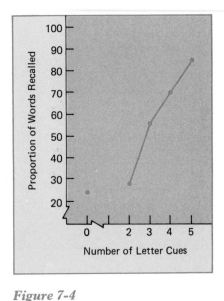

Figure 7-4

In this experiment Tulving and Watkins varied how much of an item (a 5-letter word) was presented to subjects to see how it would affect recall of the item. Their results are shown in the graph above: When no letters were shown, as in a simple recall task, recall is low; the more letters shown, the better the recall; and when the whole item is presented, as in a recognition task, recall is highest. (Tulving and Watkins, 1973)

Relearning

Even when people seem to have totally forgotten something they learned earlier, they may be able to *relearn* it faster than they did originally. This reduction in time to learn, or *savings*, suggests that they actually had some memory of the material before they began to relearn it. Suppose subjects study a list of 20 items for successive 1-minute periods with a recall test following each study period. Proceeding in this way, it might take 15 study periods (minutes) before all 20 items can be recalled on the following test. Several weeks later the subjects might claim they can't recall any of the words.

Now suppose you have them relearn the words, using exactly the same procedure as before. You might find that a perfect performance on the recall test occurs after only 10 study periods, a *savings score* of 5 minutes (time for the original learning minus time for relearning). This savings score may also be expressed as a percentage of the original time:

$$100 \times {}^5/_{15} = 33 \text{ percent.}$$

This savings suggests that the subjects actually did remember something from the original learning, even though they couldn't recall any of the items before the relearning session.

Forgetting: Information Loss in Human Memory

As illustrated earlier, information is lost in external memory systems in ways that are characteristic of each system. Information loss or forgetting also occurs in human memory. The ways in which this occurs, and the factors that influence it, have led to a variety of theoretical conjectures concerning the nature of human memory. Before considering these theoretical ideas, let's look at some of the factors involved in information loss or forgetting.

The Effect of Retention Time

The most obvious factor in forgetting is the passage of time. In general, the longer the interval between learning and recall (the retention interval), the less likely it is that we will remember something (see Figure 7-5). Yet there are many exceptions to this general rule. You often remember events that occurred during a time of crisis, such as the death of a friend or a moment of personal peril, even though they took place many years ago. It is, in fact, remarkable how clearly most people can remember things of this sort. On the other hand, you may forget the name of someone just introduced to you before you finish shaking hands. Thus the passage of time alone is not a reliable indicator of whether something will be remembered. More important, it seems, is how well the information was learned or encoded originally, what happens to the person during the retention period, and the situation in which retrieval is attempted.

Distraction and Attentional Problems

You are unlikely to remember people's names if you don't pay attention when they are introduced. Nor will you find it easy to remember the details of your last

Figure 7-5

The most obvious factor in forgetting is the passage of time, as shown in this graph. Note that retention decreases very rapidly at first, then much more slowly after the first 9 hours.

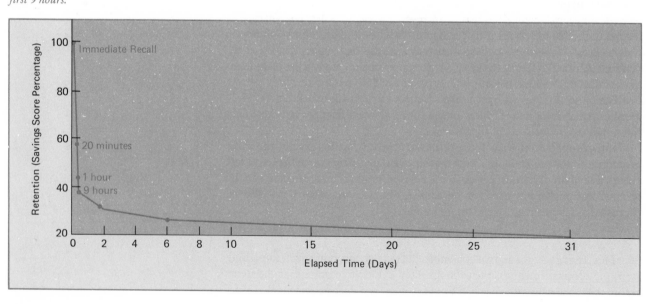

psychology lecture while driving at high speed through heavy traffic. There is a difference between these two examples. Distractions that occur while you are trying to retrieve information usually affect your memory only temporarily (you probably will remember the lecture once you are safely home). But if your attention is distracted when information is first presented, the information may not even be encoded. In Chapter 4 we considered a number of attentional problems, such as being able to attend closely to only one person's voice at a time. If someone else is speaking at the same time, you neither perceive nor remember much of what that person says. Thus an important determinant of what you remember is what you attend to.

Even if you do attend to information as it is presented, distraction immediately afterward may also produce information loss. You may, for instance, have noticed you're more likely to forget someone's name if you are distracted right after being introduced, even though you did pay attention to the introduction. An experiment by Peterson and Peterson (1959) illustrates an effect of this sort. Their subjects heard three-consonant trigrams, such as P, T, K or L, C, J, which they were then asked to recall after retention intervals ranging from 3 to 18 seconds. If allowed to attend solely to this task, the subjects could perform it perfectly. However, they couldn't if they had to perform a distracting task during the retention interval (counting backwards by 3's from a number seen right after hearing the trigram). Figure 7-6 shows how this distracting task caused the letters to be rapidly forgotten, with almost no recall after 18 seconds. Thus it is clear that more than simply attending to information as it is presented is required to avoid forgetting it.

Interference from Other Memories

Your ability to remember something may be impaired, or interfered with, by memories of other things, particularly if those things are quite similar or conceptually related. Suppose you have been shown through several homes by a real estate salesman. Thinking back, you might have difficulty deciding exactly which homes had specific features, sometimes erroneously remembering a feature of one house as belonging to another, or sometimes being unsure whether you really saw a particular feature at all, since you saw so many. The more similar the houses and the more of them you saw, the more likely you would be to experience confusions of this sort.

Phenomena very much like this have been studied experimentally. Subjects are shown a series of word lists and then asked to recall items from a particular list. The more lists they are shown, and the more similar the words in the lists, the more poorly the subjects perform (see Figure 7-7). The simplest form of this experiment requires three groups of subjects, and two lists of words, List A and List B. Two groups of subjects learn only one list, either A or B. The third group learns both lists, first A and then B. The two-list group is typically poorer at recalling either list than the corresponding one-list group. This indicates both that learning List A interferes with recall of B, and that learning List B interferes with recall of A. The interference of A with recall of B is termed *proactive interference*, since A was learned before B. The interference of B with recall of A is called *retroactive interference*. Both types of interference depend on the similarity of the words on each list. For example, there will be more interference

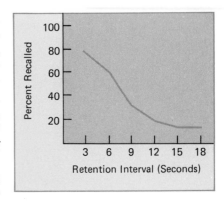

Figure 7-6

In this experiment, subjects heard three-consonant trigrams (such as P, T, K) and were asked to recall them after retention intervals ranging from 3 to 18 seconds. If subjects performed a distracting task during the retention interval, it caused the letters to be rapidly forgotten, with almost no recall after 18 seconds. (Peterson and Peterson, 1959)

Figure 7-7

When subjects are shown a series of word lists and then asked to recall items from a particular list, the more lists they are shown, and the more similar the words in the lists, the more poorly they perform.

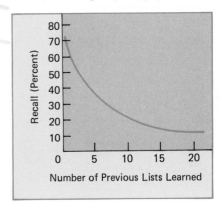

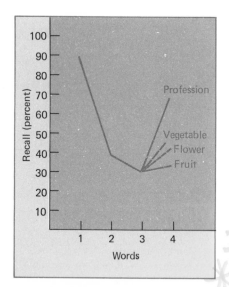

Figure 7-8

The graph shows evidence of a release from interference if there is a distinct category shift in the fourth word presented in the list. That is, there is less proactive interference if the item is unrelated to the words already retained in memory. (Wickens, 1973)

if both lists are vegetable names than if one is vegetables and the other is fruit.

These effects can be demonstrated in even simpler form. Wickens (1972) presented subjects with a series of words and then tested their recall. While the list was much longer, only recall of the first four words is of interest here. The first three words on each subject's list were names of fruits; the fourth word varied for different groups of subjects—it was the name of a fruit, a vegetable, a flower, or a profession. The rest of the list was identical for all subjects. Figure 7-8 shows how recall gradually falls off for the first three words as proactive interference increases the primacy effect shown earlier (in Figure 7-3). However, the amount of proactive interference indicated on the fourth item clearly depends on its similarity to the first three. It is as if there is a *release from interference* when there is a distinct *category shift*.

It seems, then, that the likelihood of forgetting something because of interference from other information in memory depends on the item's relation to that information.

Emotional Factors

Often you seem to remember something better if you have had a strong emotional response to it. You probably vividly recall details of some moment when you felt great elation or excitement. You probably have equally vivid memories about certain moments of grief or sorrow. Of course, both sorts of events are ones you may discuss often. Each time you describe the event to someone or someone mentions it to you is another opportunity to encode information about it. This is surely one reason you remember such events better than others. Another reason is that things you feel strongly about usually command your attention and make you less likely to be distracted by other things. For example, anxiety about an upcoming exam can make you attend closely to your reading rather than periodically shifting your attention to television or your roommates' conversation.

Emotional factors can also interfere with memory through their effect on your attention. For example, too much anxiety can distract you from listening to a lecture. You may spend your time looking nervously about the classroom at your fellow students, or looking out the window thinking about your problems. Similarly, when taking an exam, you may spend more time thinking about the consequences of failure than retrieving information relevant to the questions.

Sigmund Freud (1938) argued that many of the seemingly innocent failures of memory that occur in everyday life are the product of subconscious motives and emotions. Forgetting your car keys may be caused by a subconscious desire to stay home from work. Forgetting someone's name or an appointment may be an expression of subconscious anger. Freud called such subconsciously purposeful forgetting *repression* and made the gradual uncovering of such repressed memories, particularly those associated with early traumatic experiences, a central goal of psychoanalysis. He argued that when patients finally remember such events, they are freed from feelings of anxiety and maladaptive behavior caused by such repressed memories, a process he called *catharsis.*

The experimental evidence for repression is very slim. Glucksberg and King (1967) developed a way to test for repression in the laboratory (see Figure 7-9). They had subjects learn a list of paired associates. Each pair consisted of a

List 1		Inferred Chained Word	List 2
A	B	C	D
CEF	stem	flower	smell*
DAX	memory	mind	brain*
YOV	soldier	army	navy
VUX	trouble	bad	good*
WUB	wish	want	need
GEX	justice	peace	war*
JID	thief	steal	take*
ZIL	ocean	water	drink
LAJ	command	order	disorder
MYV	fruit	apple	tree*

*These words were paired with a shock in the second stage of the experiment.

Figure 7-9

In this experiment by Glucksberg and King, subjects first learned the nonsense syllables and their paired associates in columns A and B. Next they learned the remote associates shown in Column D; some of these were accompanied by a mild electric shock. (The words in Column C show the implied link between columns B and D.) The idea was that the remote associates that were followed by shock would take on aversive associations, which would spread to the related word in the paired associates list and produce repression of the nonsense syllable in such pairs. (Glucksberg and King, 1968)

nonsense syllable ("vig") and an associated word ("train"). They then presented the subjects with a list of words that were remote associates of the words in the paired associate list. For example, the word "track" would be a remote associate of the word "train," because asking a subject to list words related to train usually produces the response "track," but only after several less remote associates are reported. As the list of remote associates was presented, the experimenter gave the subjects an electric shock after certain words. The idea was that these words would take on aversive or unpleasant associations, which would spread to the related word in the paired associate list and would produce "repression" of the nonsense syllable in such pairs. Glucksberg and King found that there was indeed lower recall of such nonsense syllables. Unfortunately, their results are also subject to other interpretations, such as the possibility that the higher emotional arousal produced by the words associated with shock hindered recall.

Emotional problems can produce almost total failure of memory for even recent events that are too painful for a person to deal with. A mother may be unable to remember anything that happened on the day her child drowned. A man may leave his home for work one day, then find himself in a distant city months later with no memory of what has happened to him since he left home. Such *fugue states* seem to satisfy some psychological or emotional need, and are discussed in more detail in Chapter 16.

Organic Causes of Forgetting

Many causes of forgetting have a clear organic basis. These *organic amnesias* are usually caused by some sort of damage to the brain resulting from disease, injury to the head, or brain surgery. For example, in *senile brain disease,* which affects some older people, gradual reduction in the brain's oxygen supply and general atrophy of the brain produce an overall reduction in cognitive function, including memory.

More specific effects on memory may be produced by other types of brain damage. If the damage causes loss of memory only for events occurring *after* it, it is termed *anterograde amnesia.* If it affects events occurring *before* it, it is termed *retrograde amnesia.*

Korsakoff's syndrome is a disease associated with chronic alcoholism and poor diet; it causes permanent brain damage. While victims of this disease have some retrograde amnesia, they can remember most of their earlier life. However, they don't remember new information for more than a few minutes. People who have this chronic anterograde amnesia can meet someone, or read a magazine, and a few minutes later fail to recognize the person, or read the magazine as if it were new. Each day they start afresh with memories only of their early life. Similar chronic patterns of anterograde amnesia can also be produced by damage to the hippocampus. Milner (1970) studied a patient, H. M., whose hippocampus was surgically lesioned to reduce epileptic seizures. The patient had a normal IQ but couldn't remember new information for more than a few minutes.

Retrograde amnesias, usually of a temporary nature, are often caused by a blow to the head. (They can also be caused by electroconvulsive shock, which is sometimes used to treat severely depressed mental patients.) These amnesias may extend back a few moments, days, or even weeks, depending on the severity of the blow to the head. As time passes, the older events are usually recalled first,

Retrograde amnesia is often caused by a blow to the head. Depending on the severity of the blow, the amnesia may extend back a few moments or a few weeks. The motorcyclist in this accident may not later remember any of the events leading up to it.

until finally there is no amnesia. Sometimes, however, memory of events that occurred during the last few minutes before the injury (or electroconvulsive shock) seems to be permanently lost. It is almost as if these events were never completely encoded.

Human Memory Systems

Some Early Ideas

Early ideas about memory were closely related to ideas about learning. Plato likened human memory to soft wax on which experiences produce imprints—forgetting occurs as successive imprints gradually obliterate earlier ones. Plato's conception of memories as impressions or *traces* was elaborated by Aristotle to include *associations* of these traces—retrieving one memory could lead you to others through an organized network of associations. The conception of learning as the formation of associations has been central to many theories of learning up to the present day. Formation of these associations was often attributed to simple *temporal contiguity:* Things that happen at the same time tend to become associated. Memory of one will then evoke a memory of the other. This was the view of Ebbinghaus (1885), who initiated many of the methods for studying human memory considered earlier in this chapter. He argued that repeated pairing of *nonsense syllables,* such as DAX with VAP, gradually strengthened associations until the presentation of DAX would consistently evoke a memory of VAP.

Many early theorists thought of the associations between memory traces as "neural paths." These paths, much like paths between jungle villages, were supposed to become clearer through repeated use; if not used they would gradually fade away or decay. Notice the difference between the idea of forgetting as simple decay through disuse and Plato's conception of new impressions overlying and obscuring old ones. Arguments as to whether forgetting occurs because of decay or simply the interfering effects of new memories have continued to this day.

The concept of associated neural traces was elaborated in *consolidation theory* (Muller and Pilzecker, 1900). According to this theory, the neural paths "reverberate" or remain active for some time after they are formed, and this continued activity is necessary for them to "consolidate" or become permanent. Proponents of consolidation theory pointed to the retrograde amnesia sometimes produced by a blow to the head or electroconvulsive shock (ECS) as evidence for their view: These traumatic events prevent consolidation of the traces laid down by immediately preceding events, causing a loss of memory for such events. Similar effects were shown in lower animals given ECS immediately after learning.

Multiprocess Theories of Human Memory

Early learning theorists hoped to account for all learning, by both humans and lower organisms, in terms of a few basic models; for example, by association

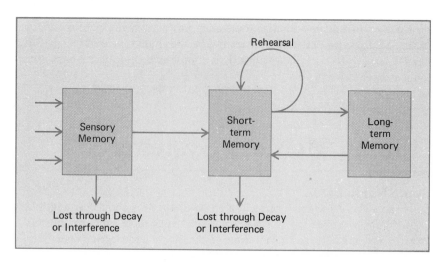

Figure 7-10

Atkinson and Shiffrin's multiprocess view of human memory is shown in this model. Sensory information is briefly retained in some type of sensory memory system; some of it is then recoded into short-term memory, where it may be retained through rehearsal. The longer it remains in short-term memory, the more likely it is to be transferred into long-term memory. While information can be lost from sensory and short-term memories through decay or interference, retention in long-term memory is assumed to be virtually permanent.

based on contiguity, or by reinforcement as in Pavlovian or operant conditioning. It was hoped that memory could be accounted for in the same way. However, by the 1950s many psychologists had grown pessimistic about achieving a unified theory. Influenced by work on communication theory, decision making, and computer science, they began to develop models for specific aspects of human information processing. Some concentrated on how humans retain information for intervals as brief as a few minutes or even seconds. Others were less interested in short-term memory and instead studied how people retain and retrieve information over periods of days, weeks, and even years. Still other psychologists focused on how people remember visual images or sounds, how they remember particular experiences or episodes rather than facts, and so on.

Out of this varied work emerged a picture of human memory *not* as a single memory system, but as a number of interrelated memory systems, each with its own special properties. This multiprocess view of human memory is reflected in the highly influential theory proposed by Atkinson and Shiffrin (1971, 1977). They attempted to integrate earlier work on both short-term and long-term memory systems. Their integrative theory is illustrated schematically in Figure 7-10. Sensory information is briefly retained in *sensory memory* systems; some of it is then recoded into *short-term memory,* where it may be maintained through a process called *rehearsal.* The longer the information resides in short-term memory, the more likely it is to be finally recoded or transferred into *long-term memory.* Retention in long-term memory was assumed to be virtually permanent, although effective strategies were required for successful retrieval. Let's consider the basis for this view of human memory and the types of phenomena it has been used to explain.

Sensory Memory

Earlier, in Chapter 4, we discussed phenomena that seemed to imply a brief persistence of sensory activity after a stimulus has been removed. This was discussed in the section on reading. It was discovered that when a sentence is displayed tachistoscopically for 100 msec, we do not actually read the full line during the 100 msec it is on the screen. It's almost as if a picture of the line persists briefly in our visual system after the 100-msec presentation, and it is this picture that we actually read. An even simpler example of visual persistence can be seen when a brightly glowing cigarette is moved rapidly back and forth in the dark. It seems to have a tail behind it, indicating that you continue to see light a short time after it has ceased falling on a particular part of the retina. Is this persistence in visual sensation a form of memory? Certainly information about an image is being retained over time, even though that time is very brief, so it would seem to meet the basic definition of a memory system.

This and other evidence has led to the idea of an *iconic memory system* (an *icon* is an image or pictorial representation). This system seems able to retain at least some information about visual images for periods up to 1 or 2 seconds. The information appears to be in a form or code quite similar to the original sensation. It also seems susceptible to disturbance by other visual stimulation. For example, as we pointed out in Chapter 4, while subjects can read short sentences presented tachistoscopically for only 100 milliseconds, reading can be prevented (or at least reduced) by highly contoured patterns presented up to 1 second after the sentence. This suggests that the sentence is not simply read during its 100 milliseconds exposure. Since reading can be disrupted by a subsequent "masking" pattern, it must occur at least partly *after* the exposure. It is as if the subjects continued to read from an iconic image of the sentence. The backward masking effect has been interpreted as a form of retroactive interference that produces information loss in the iconic memory system.

Certain characteristics of hearing may be evidence of an *echoic memory system* (Neisser, 1967). As with iconic memory, the information retained seems to be in a form or code quite similar to the original sensation and susceptible to disturbance by other auditory stimulation. For example, the ability to discriminate the pitch of a briefly presented tone can be reduced by the subsequent presentation of an auditory masking tone (Massaro, 1970). This backward masking effect occurs at delays of up to a quarter of a second. (It should be pointed out that this does not prove the echoic memory system retains information for only a quarter of a second; it may simply be that pitch recognition is completed in a quarter of a second, and therefore longer retention doesn't affect pitch judgments.)

Iconic and echoic memory systems represent what many theorists, including Atkinson and Shiffrin, have referred to as *sensory memory systems*. Such systems have been suggested for other senses as well as for vision and hearing. They seem to briefly retain a representation of sensory information in a code quite similar to the original sensation, and are susceptible to disturbance by subsequent stimulation of the same sort. These systems may hold sensory information until it can be selectively processed and recoded into a short-term memory system.

Short-Term Memory

The idea that information is rapidly recoded from iconic memory into a short-term memory system was proposed by Sperling (1960). He showed subjects a list of 12 letters but asked them to report only a specific group of

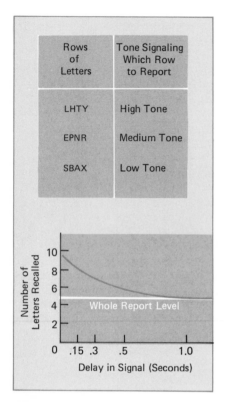

Figure 7-11

Subjects were presented with three rows of four letters each, then presented with a tone cueing the row of letters that they were to report. The number of letters recalled decreased according to how long the tone was delayed: If the tone was delayed for more than a second or so, subjects had much more difficulty reporting the letters correctly. (Sperling, 1960)

four letters. Subjects were shown three rows of four letters each, for 50 milliseconds. This was followed immediately by a signal tone that told them the particular row of letters they were to report (see Figure 7-11). In most cases subjects could report the letters no matter which row was cued. Since they could no longer see the letters when the tone was sounded they could not have reported the letters correctly unless they had all 12 letters in their memory. This information, however, was rapidly lost; if the tone was delayed for more than a second or so, subjects had much more difficulty reporting the letters correctly. Sperling interpreted this to mean that information was originally retained in an iconic memory system and then recoded into a short-term verbal memory system as a list of letter names. While this second system could retain information for longer periods than the iconic memory, it had a limited capacity of only 4 or 5 names. Only if the cue was presented before too much information was lost from iconic memory could the subject selectively encode the names of the cued letters into the verbal memory system.

The idea that our short-term memory has a capacity of only a few items goes back at least to Ebbinghaus, who reported that the longest list of nonsense syllables we can recall perfectly after only one presentation is about 6 or 7. Similarly, the number of digits (digit span) a normal adult can successfully recall immediately after hearing them spoken is about 7 or 8. A variety of evidence suggesting that the capacity of short-term memory is somewhere between 5 and 9 is discussed in a famous paper by George Miller (1956) entitled "The Magic Number Seven Plus or Minus 2." Miller pointed out that these 5 to 9 things should be thought of as "chunks" of information rather than individual letters. For example, Figure 7-12 illustrates how subjects can be taught to "chunk" sets of 3 binary digits (1's or 0's) into a single octal digit (0 through 7). Their immediate memory for the binary digits was originally about 7; after training on the chunking or recoding procedure they could remember almost 7 octal digits, which correspond to about 21 binary units. Recoding into more parsimonious "chunks," then, can effectively increase your short-term memory capacity.

Figure 7-12

Subjects can be taught to group sets of 3 binary digits into a single octal digit. Original memory for binary digits was about 7; after training on the chunking procedure, subjects could remember 7 octal digits, or 21 binary digits.

Three-Digit Binary Code		One-Digit Octal Code
000	=	0
001	=	1
010	=	2
011	=	3
100	=	4
101	=	5
110	=	6
111	=	7

Binary Number:	110	101	111	001	100	110	111
Recoded into Octal Number:	6	5	7	1	4	6	7

HIGHLIGHT
Short-Term Memory for Letters: Two Kinds of Code?

A basic question about any memory system is how information is represented or coded in that system. An elegantly simple experiment by Thorsen, Hochhaus, and Stanners (1976) illustrates how questions of this sort about human memory can be addressed experimentally.

On each of a series of trials, subjects were shown two letters, one after the other, with an interval between the letters of up to 2 seconds. On each trial, after seeing the second letter, subjects were to press one of two buttons as rapidly as possible, to indicate whether the letters were the same (e.g., an F followed by an F) or different (an X followed by a Y). On a random half of the trials the letters were the same, and on the rest of the trials they were different.

The experimenters were primarily interested in a subject's reaction times on trials when the letters were *different*. They reasoned that if the first letter were represented (coded) in a visual form—a *structural code*—subjects would have the most difficulty (take longest) distinguishing letters that looked alike (had a similar structure), such as P and R or X and Y. On the other hand,

if the first letter were represented in memory by its name or sound—an *acoustical code*—then subjects should have the most difficulty (take longest) distinguishing letters that sounded alike, such as E and P or X and S.

The most important aspects of their results are shown in Figure A. The color line shows the average time to respond "different" to two letters that look alike (but don't sound alike) for

Figure A

Average time to respond "different" at various interletter intervals for visually similar (VS) letters (P/R, X/Y, K/X) and for acoustically similar (AS) letters (E/D, P/E, X/S).

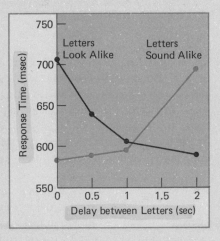

intervals between the letters of either 0, .5, 1.0, or 2 seconds. The white line shows the corresponding times for responses to letters that sound alike but don't look alike.

Notice that when the letters are presented in immediate succession, subjects take longer to distinguish those that look alike than those that sound alike, as if the comparison were based on a visual or structural code. However, as the interval between letters increases, this pattern gradually changes until it is totally reversed for intervals of 2 seconds. Then subjects take longer to distinguish letters that sound alike, as if the comparison were based on an acoustical code.

Many psychologists interpret these and other results (Posner et al., 1969) as indicating that visual information about a letter is initially represented in memory in a structural code, then rapidly recoded into an acoustical code during the first 1 or 2 seconds. Whether this is the *only* interpretation of these results is open to debate. Nevertheless, this experiment illustrates how psychologists have attempted to identify the nature of representation or coding in memory.

REHEARSAL AND TRANSFER. Atkinson and Shiffrin believed that information could be retained in short-term memory through a process of *rehearsal*, repeating it over and over. The longer the rehearsal period, the more likely that the information would be transferred to long-term memory. This theory provides an interpretation of the Peterson and Peterson experiment we described earlier. Distracting subjects immediately after they heard a trigram prevents rehearsal, so the trigram is rapidly lost and unlikely to enter long-term memory.

HIGHLIGHT:
Retrieving Information from Short-Term Memory

Sternberg (1966) devised an experimental method for studying how fast people can retrieve information from short-term memory. This method, often referred to as Sternberg's *memory-scanning procedure,* is a simple form of recognition task. On each of a series of trials, subjects are shown a small set of items, called the *memory set;* then, a few moments later, another item, called a *probe.* The subjects' task is to decide as quickly as possible whether or not the probe was one of the memory set shown on that trial. For example, in Sternberg's original experiments, each memory set consisted of from 1 to 6 digits, shown one after another. The probe was also a digit shown 2 seconds after the last digit of the memory set. Subjects were to quickly press one button if the probe was also in the memory set, a "yes" response, or another button if it wasn't, a "no" response. Both types of trials occurred equally often in a random order.

Table A gives several examples of such trials. Notice that the number of digits in the memory set ranges from 1 in Example A to 6 in Example C. Sternberg wondered how the variation in the size of the memory set would influence the speed of a subject's response. He speculated that the more items a subject had to retain

Table A: Examples of Test Trials.

Example	Memory Set	Probe	Correct Response
A	2,5	5	yes
B	8	3	no
C	6,8,5,9, 2,0	2	yes
D	9,3,6	0	no
E	2,1,9,4,7	2	yes

A similar explanation can be given for the shape of the serial position curve in recall. Rundus (1971) conducted an experiment in which subjects were slowly shown a list of words, one word at a time. They were instructed to "rehearse out loud" any words they wished as the list was presented. This allowed Rundus to count how often each word was rehearsed. The primacy effect can be explained by the more frequent rehearsal of early items, thereby (according to Atkinson and Shiffrin) allowing them more opportunity to transfer into long-term memory. The recency effect can be attributed to those items remaining in short-term memory after the list is presented.

The rehearsal theory provides an alternative to consolidation theory's interpretation of retrograde amnesia caused by trauma. It proposes that the trauma-induced loss of information from short-term memory before it could be rehearsed and transferred to long-term memory causes retrograde amnesias, rather than the failure to consolidate a memory trace.

Finally, the pattern of memory in Korsakoff's syndrome patients also seems consistent with the idea of separate short- and long-term memory systems. Perhaps these patients have normal short-term memories, but have lost the ability to transfer new information into their long-term memory.

Notice how closely related the idea of short-term memory is to the concept of consciousness. Information in short-term memory seems readily accessible. It is normally information we are currently working with, transforming, rehearsing, recoding. In fact, it is the almost immediate accessibility of information in working memory that distinguishes it from the larger store of information in longer-term memory systems, which usually involve lengthier retrieval proin short-term memory, the longer it would take to retrieve or "scan" those items, to decide if one matched the probe.

Figure A shows the approximately linear relation Sternberg found between the number of items in the memory set and average response time. Each additional item in the memory set added about 38 msec to that time. This suggested to Sternberg that subjects "scanned" or compared the items in a short-term memory one after another (serially), with each item taking about 38 msec—a *high-speed, serial-scanning process*.

A surprising feature of Sternberg's results was the fact that both "yes" and "no" responses could be described by linear functions with the same slope.

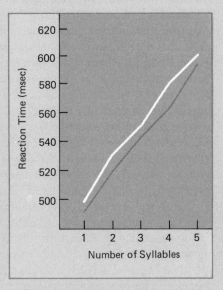

Figure A
The average time to answer "yes" (black circles) or "no" (color cirlces) for memory sets. (Sternberg, 1966)

This is not what one would expect if the serial scanning process ended as soon as an item in the memory set was found to match the probe.

A process of this sort would require you to scan all the items to decide "no," but (on the average) only half the items to decide "yes." Thus the slope of the "yes" response function in Figure A should be only half that of the "no" response function.

This led Sternberg to propose that *all* items are scanned before either a "yes" or "no" decision is made.

It is now clear that there are other ways of interpreting Sternberg's data, but his interpretation is elegantly simple and difficult to disprove. It remains a fine example of the interplay between theory and data in the study of human memory.

cesses. Consider how long it can take you to recall the name of an old acquaintance or your mother's birthday. It is as if you are using a very different sort of memory system, one that has a much larger capacity than short-term memory but involves lengthier and more complicated retrieval processes. While information can be retrieved or recoded into short-term memory, its limited capacity seems to restrict the information that is readily accessible at any one time.

Long-Term Memory and Depth-of-Processing Theory

Atkinson and Shiffrin argued that the probability of encoding information into long-term memory was directly related to the time that information remained in working memory. It seems clear, however, that one does many things to information in short-term memory beyond the simple rehearsal process suggested by Atkinson and Shiffrin. First of all, information may be combined with other information to form more complex representations or codes, a process sometimes referred to as *elaboration*. For example, on hearing the word "boat," you might encode it into short-term memory. You might then retrieve information held in long-term memory and visualize a boat you had previously sailed on. Thus you would now have a representation of a word just spoken, plus information of an earlier experience. The more you thought about boats, the more complex representations you might develop. Any of these may be encoded and available for retrieval later. The question arises: Is it simply the amount of time an item spends in short-term memory that increases its long-term retention, or is retention increased by the multiplicity and complexity of representations that the item evokes as you continue to think about it?

Craik and Lockhart (1972) proposed the latter view as an alternative to Atkinson and Shiffrin's multiple memory systems. They argued that we ignore most of the information available in our ongoing sensory experiences, so it is never elaborated into more complex representations. This is why it is unlikely to be remembered. For example, as you drive down a street many signs are projected onto your retina. Some you attend to and think about to varying degrees, others go totally unnoticed. A stop sign usually requires only a small amount of attention or thought, while a sign advertising a movie you recently read about could evoke a complex series of thoughts drawing on a large amount of associated information in memory. Thus it could be argued that the *depth of processing* we give any experience determines the number and complexity of its encodings and therefore how likely we are to recall it in the future.

Craik and Tulving (1975) conducted an experiment to evaluate depth of processing. They presented a series of words to subjects along with questions asking something about each word (Figure 7-10). Some questions, such as "Is the word in capital letters?", only required a surface analysis of the word. Other questions required deeper processing: for example, "Would the word fit in the sentence 'The boy played the ____?'" Later, when subjects were given an unexpected recognition test, their ability to recognize a word was directly related to the depth of processing required by the earlier question about that word.

A closely related aspect of depth of processing is the *organization* that occurs during elaboration. This can involve reordering material from the sequence in which it was experienced into a sequence more consistent with some logical structure. You often do this when abstracting or summarizing a lecture, particularly when the lecturer's organization of the material seems less satisfactory than your own. Note that such recoding or reorganization of information is one way in which our general world knowledge (general rules or principles, facts, etc.) may derive from our ongoing experience. Memory for particular sequences of our own experiences (*episodic memory*) and memory for general knowledge (*semantic memory*) may simply reflect different levels or forms of organization rather than different memory systems.

We mentioned earlier that stimuli present when something is originally learned (encoded) may later serve as effective recall cues, a phenomenon Tulving (1978) called encoding specificity. If as you originally learned something you organized it into categories and thought about those category names, the names might later serve as useful recall cues. For example, suppose you were asked to remember the following list of foods:

peach
potato
beef
pork
pear
beet
plum
radish
chicken

After looking at the list for a few moments you would probably notice that it contained the names of three fruits, three vegetables, and three meats. Thus you could reorganize it to reflect this structure:

fruits	peach
	pear
	plum
vegetables	potato
	beet
	radish
meats	chicken
	pork
	beef

In attempting to recall the list, it is likely that you would first retrieve a category name, which then, according to encoding specificity, would serve as a cue for the recall of items in that category.

Your understanding of a story's structure (see Figure 7-13) might aid recall in a very similar fashion. In thinking about the story structure, you could

Figure 7-13

Understanding a story's structure can aid recall. In thinking about the structure of the King Story shown here, you might develop more elaborate codes to characterize the story; these codes would serve as cues for recalling details of the story. (Pollard-Gott et al., 1979)

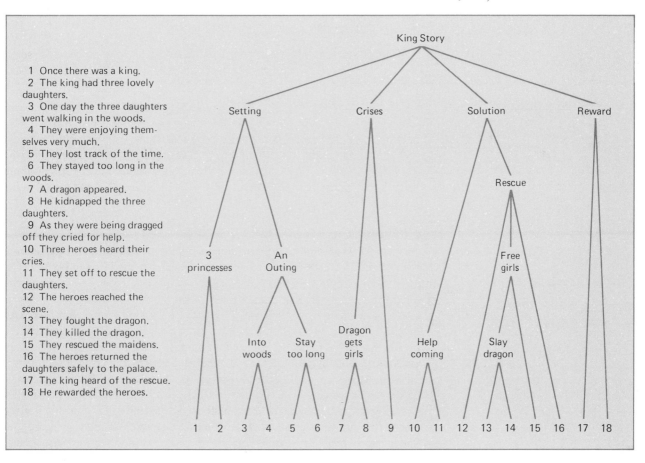

1 Once there was a king.
2 The king had three lovely daughters.
3 One day the three daughters went walking in the woods.
4 They were enjoying themselves very much.
5 They lost track of the time.
6 They stayed too long in the woods.
7 A dragon appeared.
8 He kidnapped the three daughters.
9 As they were being dragged off they cried for help.
10 Three heroes heard their cries.
11 They set off to rescue the daughters.
12 The heroes reached the scene.
13 They fought the dragon.
14 They killed the dragon.
15 They rescued the maidens.
16 The heroes returned the daughters safely to the palace.
17 The king heard of the rescue.
18 He rewarded the heroes.

Can you remember how many right turns you normally make when walking from one campus building to another? Or how many windows there are in the front of your house? Many people say they would answer such questions by taking an imaginary walk across campus and noticing how often they turned right, or creating a mental image of their house and "looking at it" to count the windows. This suggests that remembering may sometimes be like seeing. Although this is a controversial issue, there are a number of studies that seem to support this view.

Both the work on iconic memory and the study by Thorsen and Hochhaus described in an earlier box suggest very short-term vis-

ual memory systems (1 to 2 seconds). Other experiments imply that retrieval of information over much longer retention intervals may also have "visual" properties.

Pavio (1978) asked subjects to recall how clocks looked at various times and to compare the angles formed by the hour and minute hands. For example, he asked, "Is the angle larger at 4:25

Figure A

When asked to mentally compare the angles formed by the two hands of a clock at different times, the reaction time to decide which was larger decreased as angular differences increased. (Pavio, 1978)

or 9:10?" As can be seen in Figure A, the angle in this case is larger at 9:10. The graph in Figure A indicates how the average reaction

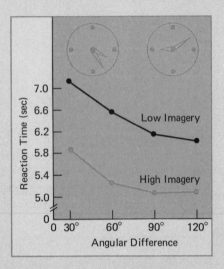

develop more elaborate codes to characterize the story—for example, "It began with a description of his early childhood." This code, which would probably be easier to recall than the details of the story, could serve as a cue for recalling these details, just as did the category names (fruits, vegetables, and meats) in the preceding examples.

Constructive Memory

In Chapter 4 we emphasized the role of stimulus redundancy in perception. Because different aspects of a stimulus are often correlated (redundant), we can infer things about one aspect from another. (Linear perspective is a strong cue for depth.) It appears that the same sort of thing happens when information is retrieved from human memory. Suppose, for example, you were asked to describe someone you met only briefly a year ago. You might first recall that the person was an automobile salesman. You might then recall that he had an outgoing personality, was quite verbal, and argued persuasively. But wait! Is this information based on your actual experience with this man or on your stereotype of car salesmen (that is, on what you believe to be the typical personality characteristics of car salesmen)? Certainly people's choice of occupation is often correlated with their personality. It would be possible, but very surprising, to find an introverted, inarticulate car salesman who couldn't argue very persua-

time (time to decide) decreased as the *difference* between the two angles increased. Thus when the angles are similar in size (for example, 12:10 and 1:05), answers are given more slowly than when they are very different (for example, 4:25 and 9:15).

The important point is that this pattern of results is similar to that obtained when the subjects are actually shown two clock faces and asked to compare the angles. Thus, when asked to compare how two times would look from memory, subjects act as if they were seeing a mental image.

Kosslyn, Ball, and Reiser (1978) had subjects memorize a map similar to the one shown in Figure B. They then asked them to "visualize" the map from memory, focusing on a particular object such as the "hut" in the lower left corner of the island. The subjects were then told to "imagine a black dot moving from that object to another point on the map"; for example, to the "marsh" in the upper left of the island. As indicated on the graph in Figure B, the time it took to visualize the dot moving from one point to another was a linear function of the actual distance on the map. Again, it was as if subjects were actually seeing a dot move across a remembered image of the map, since the further it had to move, the longer it took.

If remembering how something looked is really like seeing it again, such visualization may interfere with normal vision. Segal and Fusella (1970) asked subjects to either form a visual image (for example, the image of a horse) or an auditory image (for example, the sound of a doorbell). They found that when subjects formed visual images they were poorer at detecting visual signals than when they imagined sounds. Similar *modality-specific interference* during visualization has been demonstrated by Brooks (1968) and Byrne (1974).

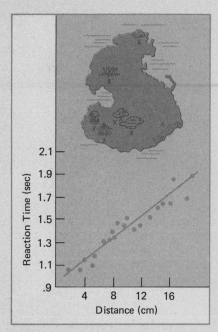

Figure B
If asked to visualize a dot moving from one point (X) to another in a previously memorized map, visualization time was a linear function of distance on the map. (Kosslyn, Ball, and Reiser, 1978)

sively. Thus remembering a person's occupation often allows us to make useful inferences about his or her personality. In fact, we make such inferences so often and so automatically that we often have difficulty deciding whether we are recalling our actual experiences with people, or making inferences about what their behavior was like on the basis of what we remember about their occupation. Inferences of this sort can sometimes distort our recollection of people so that we treat them unfairly, just as our perceptions can sometimes be biased because of inappropriate inferences. However, most such inferences aid retrieval, just as they do perception. Even if you can recall only a few major details of some past event, you can often fill in or construct details you can't recall on the basis of your knowledge of redundancy. Thus the sort of constructive process we illustrated earlier with regard to external memory systems (Figure 7-2) seems to occur in internal memory as well.

One interesting aspect of constructive processes in memory is the difficulty it produces in interpreting the *recall of dreams*. Suppose you are trying to recall a dream you had the night before. You remember dreaming you were sitting in your kitchen, and then, a short while later, driving your car. Now, in the real world it would be impossible to get from your kitchen to your car without leaving the house and walking to your car. In other words, the two events you do remember—sitting in your kitchen and driving a car—are almost perfectly *correlated* with the intermediate event of moving from the kitchen to the car. If you were recalling these events from real life instead of from a dream, you would be quite safe in assuming you had moved from the kitchen to the car. In fact, you might find it hard to tell whether you really remember walking to the car or have simply inferred it from events you do recall. You probably make such automatic inferences during your attempts to recall dreams, but in the dream world events aren't constrained by the rules of physical reality. Therefore we have no way of determining how much people really remember about their dreams and how much they automatically infer during reconstruction on the basis of inappropriate physical laws.

Improving Memory

Methods for improving memory are called *mnemonic techniques* or simply *mnemonics*. They can be as trivial as tying a string around your finger, or highly elaborate strategies that themselves take considerable time to learn. Many of these techniques were developed hundreds of years ago by actors, politicians, scholars, magicians, and priests. While the originators of these techniques weren't familiar with modern theories of human memory, most mnemonics can be understood in terms of these theories, and seem to involve only a few basic principles.

Basic Principles

It seems clear that the more you think about something, the more likely you are to remember it. However, as we have seen, this usually means more than simple repetitive rehearsal of the information. It also involves elaboration and reorganization of the information, which produce multiple encodings and useful recall cues. The importance of such cues is obvious if you consider how information is usually retrieved from long-term memory. The process can take some time and often has discernible stages. Each retrieved piece of information aids the retrieval of more information—thus the retrieval process may require several steps to recover information gradually. In other words, if you can't immediately recall a particular fact, you may find it possible to recall something that will serve as an effective recall cue for the information you want to remember. Thus a common feature of most mnemonic techniques is the use of recall cues that are easier to retrieve than the information they subsequently help you to remember.

How does one select appropriate cues and how does something come to function as a cue? First of all, a cue will serve no useful purpose unless it can be recalled. Second, it is of no use to recall the cue if it isn't an effective one. For example, a string tied around your finger is an external memory cue that may help you remember something else. It has the advantage of being easily retrieved, but it may not be an effective recall cue. You may be aware that the knot on your finger was put there to remind you of something, but be totally unable to remember what that something was.

The phenomenon of encoding specificity suggests one principle for making cues effective. The cue should be present at the time you originally encoded the information. For example, you were thinking about something when you tied the string around your finger; thus, according to the principle of encoding specificity, seeing the string may be a good cue for remembering those thoughts. This principle should apply not only to physical, contextual cues but also to cognitive cues. Visiting the house you grew up in may be an effective cue for many childhood memories, but simply visualizing the house may also serve to evoke similar memories.

Something may also serve as a cue if it is closely related to the information you want to remember. This relation may be as simple as "rhymes with" or "has the same first letter"; or more complex, such as a category name. For example, you might remember that your shopping list included "vegetables," which, in turn, would help you recall specific members of this category. Similarly, suppose you want to remember the information in a chapter or story. The title of a specific section or structural component of the material could serve as a recall cue for information in that component. For example, the structure of the king story was illustrated earlier in Figure 7-13. The terms "setting," "crises," "solution," and "reward" could serve as recall cues for various major parts of the story (e.g., "crises" for the information in sentences 7, 8, and 9). Outlining material helps you remember it because the phrases you use to characterize each section can function as recall cues.

Mnemonics

One of the oldest mnemonics was used by ancient Greek orators to help them remember the sequence of points they wanted to discuss in a speech. The technique is called the *method of loci*. The basic idea is to use some well-learned sequence of locations as a series of cues for the information you want to remember. For example, suppose you wanted to remember the following shopping list: milk, cereal, eggs, and bread. You could use the familiar sequence of locations encountered on entering your own house as an easily recalled sequence of cues. These might be in sequence: your front porch, the hallway inside the front door, the living room, and the kitchen. One of the best ways to make each of these a cue is to think about each in turn with the thing to be remembered. In particular, develop a clear visualization involving each cue and each grocery item. Thus you might visualize your front porch covered with milk, dripping over the edges of the porch and down the front steps. Next you might visualize your front hall ankle deep in cereal, crunching underfoot as you waded through it. Your living room could be completely covered with eggs—eggs splattered against the wall, breaking under your feet. Finally, you could visualize your kitchen full of loaves of bread, fluffy loaves piled one upon the other, pouring out of your oven and filling the whole kitchen. Then when you reached the store, you could take a mental walk through your house, using each location as a cue for a particular item.

A closely related type of mnemonic involves learning a series of *peg words* in order. To do this, you use an easily recalled series: the numbers 1 to 10. These numbers will be the cues for words that rhyme with each number. These words, in turn, will be cues for things you wish to remember. For example, the numbers can be used to recall the following list of rhyming words:

one	bun
two	shoe
three	tree
four	door
five	hive
six	sticks
seven	heaven
eight	date
nine	vine
ten	hen

After only a few moments of practice each number should become an effective cue word. In order to use these words as cues for the items you wish to remember, you must somehow associate them in your memory. This can be done in much the same fashion as in the method of loci: Each item to be remembered is visualized in conjunction with the cue word. For example, suppose you wanted to use this method to remember the same shopping list (milk, cereal, eggs, bread). You could first visualize a bun with milk; perhaps an overturned milk bottle with a soggy bun in a puddle of milk. Next a shoe filled with cereal. Then a green tree growing up through an enormous pile of pure white eggs, or a tree with eggs in place of fruit. And finally, a loaf of bread caught in a closing door. Then you would use the numbers as cues for the rhyming words, which would, in turn, cue a recall of the visualization and the grocery item.

Many techniques for remembering take advantage of the fact that certain stimuli are presented to you when you need to recall something, and such stimuli are particularly useful as recall or retrieval cues. Consider the *key word method* developed by Atkinson and Raugh (1975) for learning foreign languages. At first foreign words may not be good direct cues for their English equivalent. However, they can often be used as an indirect recall cue. Many foreign words are good cues for English words that rhyme with them. For example, the word "maison" in French corresponds to "house" in English. "Maison" approximately rhymes with the English word "mason," and it is easy to visualize a stone mason building a house. Thus "maison" would be a cue for mason, which would be a cue for house.

A generally useful sort of cue is an abbreviation or reductive coding of a more complex phrase. An *acronym* is a word made up from parts of the words in a more complex phrase—a type of "chunking" procedure. Comsat, for example, is an abbreviation of "communication satellite." Not only is it an abbreviation, but it is a good cue for the longer title.

How to Remember

The preceding mnemonic techniques may be useful in special instances. More importantly, however, they illustrate general strategies that may be applied whenever you want to remember something. Here are some things you can do to aid your memory:

1. Think about the information you want to remember as long, and as often, as possible.

APPLICATION
Unusual Memories

It is popularly believed that some people are born with an extraordinary ability to remember things, a sort of super-memory. Actually, there is very little hard evidence to support this belief, even though psychologists have long been interested in studying such people.

Many of those who claim to have super-memories make their living on the stage, and are referred to as *mnemonists*. Like magicians, many mnemonists are quite secretive about their methods. However, there is little reason to believe they actually have super-memories. Like magicians, many simply employ outright deception, such as a confederate in the audience or a hidden radio system. Others use mnemonic techniques that, with sufficient practice, could be used just as effectively by anyone. Of course, such mnemonists would like their audiences to believe they are using extraordinary mental powers rather than elaborations of the basic mnemonic techniques described in this chapter.

One interesting case of someone who actually seemed to combine mnemonic techniques with unusual mental abilities is presented in the book *The Mind of a Mnemonist* by the Russian neurophysiologist Luria (1920). His subject seemed to have an unusually well-developed capacity for visualization, which he used to recall information. He reported being able to associate information with visual experience quite easily. In fact, his subjective experiences could be described as synesthetic. *Synesthesia* refers to experiences in one sensory mode evoked by stimulation of another. Luria's subject had intense visual associations to nonvisual stimuli. Thus he often described auditory tones as having a vivid color. He wasn't very good at remembering certain things, particularly aspects of a stimulus that didn't lend themselves to visualization. Other interesting studies of mnemonists have been reported by Aitkin (1962), Hunt and Love (1972), and Coltheart and Glick (1974).

Another type of super-memory is *eidetic imagery* or, as it is more commonly called, *photographic memory*. This is an ability to remember how something looked in such vivid detail that it is like actually seeing it again. Strangely, considering how many people claim to know, or have heard of, or be related to someone who has this ability, there is very little evidence that such an ability exists. Early studies of eidetic imagery used such questionable methods that it is difficult to draw any clear conclusions from them.

More recently Leask, Haber, and Haber (1969) tested 500 schoolchildren and classified only about 7 percent as eidetic and even these children could have been described as simply having very good imagery rather than a photographic memory.

What appeared to be the first really convincing evidence of true eidetic imagery was reported by Stromeyer and Psotka in 1970. Their subject was shown one member of a pair of random-dot stereograms on one day, and then saw the second a day later. The two patterns were such that, when fused stereoptically, a viewer would see a digit standing out against a background. Each pattern by itself consisted of thousands of tiny black-and-white squares arranged in a totally random pattern. So it would seem impossible for subjects to identify the digit unless they had a virtually photographic memory of the first pattern, which they could then "fuse" with the pattern seen a day later. The apparent ability of one subject to do this has been cited as finally proving the existence of eidetic imagery. Unfortunately, that subject subsequently refused to demonstrate her skill, and the study has never been successfully repeated. Thus it is still questionable whether true eidetic imagery exists.

2. Don't just repeat it over and over. Try to elaborate, rephrase, and reorganize it.

3. If possible, ask questions about the material you wish to remember. This not only gives you more time to think about it, it also forces you to consider different aspects and details of the material.

4. Think of ways in which you might use recall cues. What do you associate with the material that may be easier to recall and could then act as a recall

cue? Are there key words you could learn to recall through rhyming or visualization? They would serve as good recall cues.

5.   Outline or think about the structure of the information. Is there a way of naming or describing major components of the structure so that these names might serve as recall cues?

6.   Is the information redundant? Could you recode or reduce the information to a simpler form from which it would be easy to reconstruct the rest? In other words, what are the key ideas? Can you summarize or abbreviate?

7.   Practice retrieval. Don't just study material, put it aside occasionally and practice remembering it. Can you remember things in sequence so that one thing serves as a recall cue for the next thing? Practice going through these sequences, and try to devise better ones.

Summary

1.   *Encoding* is the way information is first stored in a memory system; *retention* is the way information is preserved over time; and *retrieval* is the way information is recovered from memory

2.   Psychologists study human memory through three basic types of memory tasks: *recall, recognition,* and *relearning.*

3.   In general, people are better at recognition tasks than recall tasks; the items used in recognition tests seem to act as recall cues. People are often able to relearn a task faster than they originally learned it; the reduction in learning time is called *savings.*

4.   Factors involved in forgetting include passage of time, distraction or attentional problems, interference from other memories, emotional factors, and organic causes.

5.   Multiprocess theories of memory posit three basic types of memory systems: (a) *sensory memory,* in which sensory impressions are stored in a form or code quite similar to the original sensation; (b) *short-term memory,* in which information is recoded from sensory memory and retained through rehearsal; (c) *long-term memory,* where information is transferred as a function of the amount of time spent in rehearsal in short-term memory.

6.   A single-process theory of long-term memory states that the type of processing of information, rather than different kinds of memory systems, accounts for the difference in the way we remember things. In this view, the amount of analysis and thought given to any experience or information (in a process called *elaboration*) determines the complexity of its encodings and, therefore, the likelihood of recalling that information in the future.

7.   Related to depth of processing is organization; this can include organizing recall cues such as category names or structure of a story.

8. *Constructive memory* makes use of redundancy of information; examples are recalling childhood experiences or dreams.

9. Mnemonic techniques involve the effective use of recall clues. Some effective methods include the *method of loci, peg words,* the *key word method,* and the use of reductive coding or *acronyms.*

Suggested Readings

BOWER, G. H. (Ed.) *Human memory: Basic processes.* New York: Academic Press, 1977. A collection of articles for advanced students on theories and issues in human memory. Includes updates by the authors of the articles, commenting on their earlier research and conclusions.

KIHLSTROM, J., and EVANS, F. *Functional disorders of memory.* Hillsdale, N.J.: Erlbaum, 1979. The authors approach the study of human memory through an examination of failures of normal memory.

KLATZKY, R. *Human memory: Structures and processes* (2nd ed.). San Francisco: Freeman, 1980. An excellent and widely used undergraduate text in human memory.

LACHMAN, R., LACHMAN, J., and BUTTERFIELD, E. *Cognitive psychology and information processing: An introduction.* Hillsdale, N.J.: Erlbaum, 1979. An up-to-date review of research in memory from an information-processing point of view.

LURIA, A. R. *The mind of mnemonist.* New York: Basic Books, 1968. A fascinating and detailed account of a mnemonist by a famous Russian scientist.

NORMAN, D. *Memory and attention: An introduction to human information processing* (2nd ed.). New York: Wiley, 1976. A highly readable introduction to information-processing theories of memory and experimental methods used in studying human memory.

8 Language and Thought

High speed digital computers with vast memories and incredibly fast computing capabilities have revolutionized many areas of science, technology, and commerce. Yet these machines, with all their computing power, cannot do what a child of two or three can already do; they cannot understand and produce simple, ordinary human speech. In the late 1950s the availability of computers raised hopes for the eventual design and production of machines that could scan a printed text and convert the patterns of light and dark on a printed page into sounds, enabling the blind to "read." Much effort was also devoted to developing computer programs and devices that could automatically translate material from one language into another. Both of these efforts were dismal failures.

At the time these attempts were made, we were relatively ignorant about some of the fundamental properties of human language and about how people perceive speech sounds and understand what those sounds mean. We now know something about these matters, and thus know some of the problems and difficulties involved in designing such machines. We now realize that when such machines are to be built, they will have to be able to do the kinds of things people do when they engage in ordinary conversation, reading, and writing.

Holding ordinary conversation seems as easy and natural as breathing or walking. But when we look carefully at the nature of human language and the mental activities that must take place when we speak, listen to speech, or think, we realize the complexity of the processes involved. As we describe the activities involved in language, keep in mind the sorts of things a machine or computer program must "know" if it is to deal efficiently and appropriately with ordinary human language.

The Nature of Human Language

Language Universals

On the surface, languages such as Chinese or Turkish seem quite different from one another. They sound different, seem to have different grammatical rules, and, to a native English speaker, may not even sound like languages at all. The stream of speech coming from someone speaking a totally foreign language may not even sound as though there are separate words; it sometimes sounds like a continuous rush of gibberish.

Despite these surface differences, all human languages share certain criterial properties, or design features that enable them to be productive in two important

HIGHLIGHT
Speech Sounds and Speech Perception

A New Yorker, a Texan, an Iowan, and a Vermonter can all say the word "ball," and can be understood perfectly well by one another. Yet, the precise sound of the vowel represented by the letter *a* will be different in each case. Similarly, the sounds represented by the letter *p* in the words "pin" and "spin" are also different, yet we tend to hear those two *p* sounds as identical. In each of these two examples, a single phoneme—the vowel sound in "ball" in one case, the sound of the letter *p* in the other—is heard and recognized correctly, despite marked differences in the physical sound itself. This poses an intriguing question: When are two speech sounds functionally the same, and when are they different?

For any specific language, speech sounds are called different phonemes if substitution of one for another actually changes the meanings of words in which they appear. For example, changing the sound of *r* to the sound of *l* in the word "rip" changes the word itself. In contrast, changing the quality of the sound of *r* from the typical English pronunciation to the trilling Scots pronunciation does not change the word "rip"

into another word. Therefore, *r* and *l* are considered two separate and distinct phonemes in English, while the trilled and untrilled *r*'s are merely variants (allophones) of the same phoneme. Are the sounds of *r* and *l* inherently more "different" or more discriminable than the two variants of *r*? Not to speakers of Japanese, a language that does not treat *r* and *l* as two separate phonemes. This does not, of course, indicate defective hearing among Japanese. We who speak English also do not hear some of the differences between the phonemes of other languages. For

ways. First, the number of sentences in any human language is, theoretically, infinite and unlimited. Second, any idea or concept that can be expressed in any one language can, in principle, also be expressed in any other language, even though some languages may require fewer words than others to express the same idea. What are the criterial properties of languages that give them these capabilities?

Roger Brown (1965) has summarized the minimal design features of all human languages. First, all languages use a limited number of speech sounds, called *phonemes*. Most languages use less than 100 phonemes. English, for example, has about 45 phonemes, while Hawaiian manages with even fewer, about 13. Each of these speech sounds (like the three sounds represented by the letters *C A T*) is meaningless on its own, yet when phonemes are combined to form words they form the basis of speech. If we had a pictorial alphabet, each symbol of which had a meaning, the particular kinds of combinations that would be possible would be severely limited. But the 45 meaningless phonemes of English can be put together to form hundreds of thousands of words just because they are, like the letters of the alphabet, meaningless when they stand alone. This is the second way that all languages are alike. Third, all languages assign meanings to words arbitrarily. That is, a word does not have to sound like the thing it refers to. Therefore, we are free to coin new words, change the meanings of old words, and in general build a vocabulary to suit our communicative and symbolic needs. Finally, all languages combine words in systematic ways to form sentences. In principle the number of sentences that can be generated, starting with a finite and small set of speech sounds, is infinite. Every language spoken on earth has these characteristics, and also has the capacity to create an unlimited set of sentences that can be used to express any conceivable set of ideas.

example, the sounds represented by the letters *k* and *c* in the phrase "keep cool" sound exactly alike to us, yet they are actually different sounds and are treated as such in Arabic. (Note the placement of the tongue for the sound of *k* in "keep," where it touches the roof of the mouth toward the back, and the more forward placement for the sound of *c* in "cool.") When we learn a language, one of the first things we learn is to hear differences among those speech sounds that are specifically important in that language, and to ignore others.

We also learn to recognize certain physically different speech sounds as the same. For example, the *d* sounds in the syllables "dee" and "doo" sound exactly alike to us, even though the physical stimuli for these two sounds are quite different (as shown in the illustration below). In doing these things, people use not only the stimulus information in the sounds themselves, but the context as well. People are better able to recognize speech sounds when they form words than when

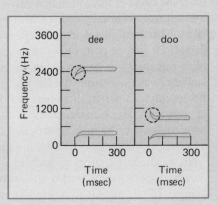

they form nonsense syllables (Stevens and House, 1972). Common words are heard more clearly than uncommon ones (Pollack et al., 1959), and grammatical and meaningful sentences are heard more clearly than nonsensical sentences (Miller and Isard, 1963). A computerized pattern recognition device—like the kind that recognizes the computer-patterned letters and numerals on bank checks—can use only the physical stimuli it gets, and must rely completely on them. People, on the other hand, can tolerate a remarkable amount of variability and distortion by using their knowledge of the language and of the world to identify accurately the speech sounds that occur in ordinary streams of conversation.

Morphemes, Words, and Meanings

The smallest unit of speech that has meaning is the *morpheme*. A morpheme may be a word, or it may be a part of a word. Common prefixes and suffixes, as in the words "*a*typical," "*non*sense," "jump*ed*," and "lesson*s*," are one type of morpheme. These morphemes must always be used with at least one other morpheme to form a word, and so they are called *bound* morphemes. *Free* morphemes correspond roughly to words: words like "man" and "page" are simultaneously single morphemes and words. Finally, many words consist of several morphemes put together, both free and bound, such as "*de* + composed," "*counter* + attacked," and so on.

Morphemes and words are made by combining phonemes according to the phonetic and morphemic rules of the language. The phonetic rules of English, for example, have been worked out in some detail. These rules describe our implicit knowledge of our language. For example, most native English speakers would agree that "spab," even though it is not a word in the language, is a possible sound sequence, while "sbab" is not. The particular rule, in this case, says that a voiced consonant may not follow the sound represented by the letter *s*. Therefore, not only "sbab," but "svab" and "sdad" are also "illegal." We know this intuitively, although few of us can state the rule explicitly.

The grammar of a language contains rules for the allowable sequences of sounds and for morpheme combinations, but, as we mentioned earlier, there are essentially no rules for assigning meanings to words. With a very few exceptions, the meanings of words are assigned arbitrarily—the words bear no physical resemblance to the things they name. Because meanings are assigned arbitrarily, we can have as many words as we need. Indeed, if word sounds had to resemble the things or concepts they symbolize, how could a language have words like "justice" or "poverty"?

Chapter 8:
Language and Thought

211

ASPECTS OF MEANING: DENOTATIVE AND CONNOTATIVE.   Aside from function words, such as "and," "or," "on," "it," "of," which specify relations among things, content words, such as nouns and verbs, symbolize at least two different kinds of meanings, denotative and connotative. The *denotative* meaning of a word is usually defined as the thing or class of things that the word can label. This meaning is like a dictionary definition of a word. But dictionary definitions are, at best, only rough guides to what a word denotes. In order for a dictionary to be useful, one must already have a good command of the language and a reasonable knowledge of one's physical and social world. For example, a partial dictionary definition of the word "chaste" is "innocent of unlawful sexual intercourse." A third grader who had been assigned this word to look up in a dictionary did so, and when asked to use the word in a sentence, wrote "The amoeba is a chaste animal." Clearly, one aspect of the word's denotative meaning had been understood, but not several other important aspects, such as that the word can only be applied to adult human beings. If we include this kind of knowledge of what words mean, then the meanings of words look more like encyclopedia entries than dictionary entries. For example, a dictionary entry for the word "dog" is "a carnivorous domesticated mammal probably descended from the common wolf" (Merriam-Webster, 1973). An encyclopedia would provide the additional information that dogs are furry, that they make excellent pets, that some dogs are used for hunting and others for herding, that they come in a variety of sizes and shapes, and so on. The denotative meaning of the word "dog," then, is really the sum total of the ideas shared by people in our culture of what a "dog" is.

When the word "dog" is used in a conversation, one or more aspects of our conception of what a dog is may be appropriate to the intended meaning of the sentence. For example, if someone says that her dog only eats prime beef, then the word "dog" clearly refers to a pet. However, if someone says that the movie he went to last week was a real dog, then the word "dog" refers to a particular property or attribute of dogs, in this case a rather negative property. These examples illustrate one of the primary characteristics of word meanings in isolation. Virtually any word, when considered out of context, can be interpreted in many ways. Clearly, when we refer to a word's meaning, we can really refer to a range or class of meanings that the word may have when used in sentences or conversational contexts.

It would be difficult enough to program a computer to interpret the denotative meanings of words because, as we have seen, virtually all words can be interpreted in more than one way. This difficulty is compounded by the *connotative,* or emotional, meanings of words. This emotional (sometimes called *affective*) meaning of a word essentially reflects how we feel about the thing that the word represents. This meaning is measured by the *semantic differential,* a technique devised by Osgood and his associates (1957). The semantic differential is a set of rating scales. Each scale has a pair of opposite adjectives, as shown in Figure 8-1. The word to be rated is put at the top of the scale, and people are asked to rate that word on each of the scales below it. "Home," for example, might be rated as more round than angular, more passive than active, good rather than bad, rather warm, and relaxed. The word "prison" might be rated as more angular than round, bad rather than good, and relatively

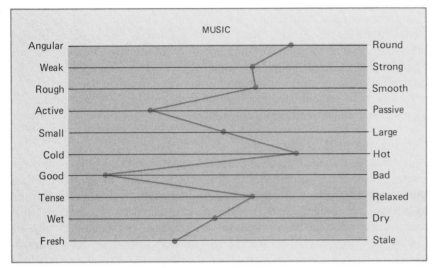

Figure 8-1

How one person rated the word "music" on the semantic differential. How would you rate "music" on these scales? (Glucksberg and Danks, 1975)

cold. If a word is rated as good, then it will probably also be rated as smooth rather than rough, and relaxed rather than tense. Because the ratings on some scales tend to go together (that is, they *correlate* with one another), the ratings of the 10 scales can be summarized in terms of three general scales, or *dimensions,* of connotative meaning. These three general summary scales are the good-bad scale, the active-passive scale, and the strong-weak scale, representing the three major dimensions of connotative meaning, respectively: *evaluation, activity,* and *potency.*

These three dimensions of connotative meaning are independent of one another. If a word is rated highly positive on any one of the three dimensions, it may still be rated highly negative, neutral, or positive on one or the other of the remaining dimensions. For example, "gnat" might be rated as bad, active, and weak; "butterfly," as good, active, and weak. For ordinary words, any combination of evaluation, activity, and potency ratings is possible.

Just as the denotative meanings of words will vary with context, so will connotative meanings. Sometimes even a small change in context will have a sizable effect. For example, the connotative meaning of the word "home" in the sentence "He went home" is rated higher on evaluation (better) than when it appears in the sentence "He is at his home." Clearly, how we feel about words will depend upon the contexts in which they appear. The evaluative and activity connotations of the word "inventive" would be quite different in the phrases "an inventive assassin" and "an inventive poet."

Are the three dimensions of connotative meaning—evaluation, activity, and potency—unique to the English language, or do they also characterize the connotative meanings of words in other languages? Obviously, the connotative meaning of any particular word may vary considerably from one language and culture to another. For example, "peasant" may be rated as bad, passive, and weak by Americans, and good, active, and strong by mainland Chinese. This is to be expected when peoples differ in culture, ideology, and experience. However, extensive cross-cultural research by Osgood and his colleagues (1957) has revealed a striking universality in the structure of connotative meaning. Using the semantic differential in many different cultures and languages, including American, British, Dutch, French, Finnish, and Japanese (among others), the same three major dimensions of connotative meaning appear again and again, even though the connotative meanings themselves may be different. People the world over seem to react emotionally in the same general ways, using the same three dimensions of evaluation, activity, and potency in judging the connotative meanings of words.

Sentences and Messages

PHRASE STRUCTURE RULES AND TRANSFORMATIONAL RULES.   In every language, words are combined into sentences according to set rules. These word-combining rules form the *syntax* of a language, and they can be used to generate all the grammatical sentences of a language. To date, no such complete grammar has been written for any language, but theoretical linguists like Noam Chomsky (1957) have argued convincingly that any such grammar would need at least two types of rules—phrase structure rules and transformational rules.

Phrase structure rules are those rules that govern the organization of the various parts of a sentence. To illustrate how phrase structure rules can be used to generate the sentences of a language, let us assume that there is a language with just four types of words: nouns, verbs, articles, and adjectives. The lexicon (vocabulary) of this language, then, can be represented as follows:

N → man, woman, horse, dog, etc. . . . (nouns)
V → saw, heard, hit, etc. . . . (verbs)
Art → a, the . . . (articles)
Adj → happy, sad, fat, timid, etc. . . . (adjectives)

The symbol → means "can be rewritten as," hence wherever the symbols [N → man] appear, it means that we can substitute the word "man" for the symbol *N*. Phrase structure rules are rewrite rules of this type, but they can refer to parts of sentences, such as noun phrases and verb phrases, as well as to single words. The sentence "A fat man hit the dog" can, under the rewrite rules of this partial grammar, be described in terms of its parts: The first three words are a noun phrase (NP), the last three words are a verb phrase (VP). These parts can be broken down even further. The noun phrase consists of an article, an adjective, and a noun. The verb phrase consists of a verb plus a noun phrase. These relationships can be summarized in two ways. One way is in terms of a tree structure diagram, as in Figure 8-2. The other way, which is equivalent to the diagram, is in the form of a set of phrase structure (rewrite) rules:

Rule 1.   S → NP + VP. This rule states that a sentence, S, consists of, or can be rewritten as, a noun phrase (NP) plus a verb phrase (VP).
Rule 2.   NP → Art + [Adj] + N. This rule states that a noun phrase (NP) consists of an article (Art) plus, optionally, an adjective (Adj), plus a noun.
Rule 3.   VP → V + NP. This rule states that a verb phrase (VP) consists of a verb (V) plus a noun phrase (NP).

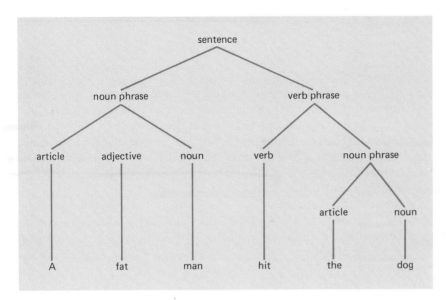

Figure 8-2

Phrase structure analysis of the sentence,
"A fat man hit the dog."

This grammar, which was devised for illustrative purposes by Victoria Fromkin (1976), can, with just the 13-word lexicon listed above, generate 4,800 sentences.

Notice, however, that these 4,800 sentences represent a tiny fraction of the kinds of sentences that could occur in English. For example, all the verbs are in the simple past tense. All the nouns are in singular form, and they refer only to animate beings. Only simple declarative sentences can be generated—this small grammar does not generate questions, commands, or any of the many other kinds of sentences we normally use. Yet, with very small additions to the rules, the number of sentences that can be generated can increase enormously. Merely by allowing each verb to appear in present as well as past tense, we double the number of verb phrases and so double the number of different sentences we can have. If we also double the number of available nouns by allowing each to appear in both singular and plural form, we could then generate 36,400 different sentences (80 different NPs multiplied by 480 different VPs). How many sentences could we generate if we now again double the number of available nouns by simply adding four new ones in both singular and plural form?*

Phrase structure rules not only tell us how sentences can be constructed, they also provide a description of those sentences. For example, the sentences

John saw Mary.
Peter heard Sally.

strike us as being quite similar to each other, even though the words are different. One way they are similar is that they have the same grammatical structure—they both have been generated by the same phrase structure rules (in this case, S → NP + VP; NP → N; VP → V + NP). However, some sentences that appear similar to one another have quite different structures.

* This would give us 160 NPs and 960 VPs, which can yield 153,600 sentences.

Consider the following two sentences:

John saw Mary.
Mary was seen by John.

Here we have two sentences with different phrase structures, yet they are obviously related; indeed, they mean roughly the same thing. In each case, John is the person who saw someone and Mary is the person who was seen. The grammatical rules that spell out the relationships *between* sentences are called *transformational* rules. These are rules that specify how one sentence can be "transformed" into another. In this way, transformational rules specify how various types of sentences are related to one another.

SURFACE STRUCTURE AND DEEP STRUCTURE.   Essentially, these types of phrase structure and transformational rules make explicit some of the intuitions we have about our language. For example, most of us feel, intuitively, that the two sentences

John is easy to please.
John is eager to please.

are similar to and yet different from one another. They share a surface similarity in that they differ by just one word—"eager" versus "easy". They have the same *surface structure*. However, they differ quite markedly in terms of their underlying organization and intent, that is, their *deep structure*. This intuition of ours, that these two sentences are really basically different, can be demonstrated by applying the same transformation to each sentence.

John is easy to please.   It is easy to please John.
John is eager to please.   It is eager to please John.

The difference between the original two sentence types is now obvious and explicit. The first can be transformed in this way and still make sense, but the second cannot. Therefore, the original two sentences have different deep structures; they are basically different sentence types.

These grammatical rules make explicit some of the intuitive and implicit knowledge we have about our native language. The full set of rules for a language would also specify the literal meanings of sentences. But would such a set of rules enable a computer to interpret the meanings of ordinary language? Unfortunately it would not, because people often disregard the *literal* meaning in order to understand the *intended* or *conveyed* meaning. For example, the literal meaning of the statement "Can you pass the salt" is, roughly, "Are you physically or otherwise capable of passing the salt?" In most ordinary contexts, such as when people are sitting around a table eating lunch, the literal meaning of that sentence makes no sense. The intended meaning—"please pass the salt"— does. Similarly, if you say to someone who is standing by a closed window "Gee, it's hot in here," it would probably be understood that you are not merely commenting on the weather but are asking that a window be opened.

These examples illustrate how people combine all the information they have about the language, about the situation they are in, and about other people, to figure out or construct the meaning of the speech they hear or read. The process of speech comprehension involves more than the interpretation of the

Figure 8-3

Which picture helps to interpret this paragraph:

If the balloon popped, the sound wouldn't be able to carry, since everything would be too far away from the correct floor. A closed window would also prevent the sound from carrying, since most of the buildings tend to be well insulated. Since the whole operation depends on a steady flow of electricity, a break in the middle of the wire would also cause problems. Of course, the fellow could shout, but the human voice is not loud enough to carry that far. An additional problem is that a string could break on the instrument. Then there would be no accompaniment to the message. It is clear that the best situation would involve less distance. Then there would be fewer potential problems. With face-to-face contact, the least number of things could go wrong.

People who were shown the picture on the left understood this paragraph and could remember it much better than people who were shown the picture on the right (Bransford and Johnson, 1972, p. 719).

language itself. What people ordinarily do has been illustrated nicely by an ingenious series of experiments by John Bransford and his colleagues (1971, 1972). Bransford asked people to read or listen to a set of sentences under one of two conditions. In one condition, a context was provided that helped people to make sense of the sentences. In another, an inappropriate or irrelevant context was provided. What typically happens is that people are able to remember much more when they have a context that helps them to interpret the material to be remembered than when they do not (see Figure 8-3).

When we interpret speech we go beyond the literal meaning in yet another way. If someone were to say to you, "Peter forgot to close the door," you would get more information than is contained in the literal interpretation of that sentence. For example, you would probably be left with the following beliefs, among others: that Peter was supposed to or intended to close the door;

that Peter was able to do so; that the door was indeed open at some time; that something undesirable might have happened or did happen because the door was left open; that the undesirable consequences of Peter's forgetfulness might have been a robbery, or rain soaking the floor, or that a canary or dog had escaped, and so on. Here too, as in the illustration experiment by Bransford, we bring the relevant knowledge of our social and physical world into play whenever we deal with speech in meaningful ways.

Learning a First Language

Most children utter their first words toward the end of their first year. By the time they are two, most children have an active vocabulary of more than 200 words, and the ability to speak in short simple sentences. Within three to four years of their birth, children have acquired the basic grammar of their language. The apparent ease and speed of first language learning has led some theorists to postulate an innate *language acquisition device,* or *LAD* (Chomsky, 1975). This LAD is roughly defined as some characteristic property of the human mind that is uniquely and specially tuned for language acquisition. As we describe the various steps children go through on their way to full language competence, we shall see that there may be many LADs, each consisting of a specific characteristic of the human organism that helps us to learn one or another aspect of language.

Is Language Learned or Innate?

Until Noam Chomsky revolutionized linguistics with his theory of transformational generative grammar, people believed that language was learned in the same ways that other skills and habits are learned. Speech sounds were learned by imitation. Word meanings were learned by associating the sound of a word with the thing that the word named. Finally, syntax—the set of rules for combining words to form sentences—was learned by making associations between words. Thus, the expression "the red ball" would be learned by associating "the" with "red," and "red" with "ball."

This simple form of learning undoubtedly does occur during language acquisition. Some aspects of word meanings can be acquired by classical (Pavlovian) conditioning. For example, if a word or nonsense syllable is repeatedly paired with an unpleasant event, then that word itself becomes unpleasant (Staats and Staats, 1957). Operant conditioning techniques have been used to teach simple word meanings to such special types of people as autistic children and mentally retarded patients. If a child is positively reinforced for making an appropriate sound (for example, the word "truck" in the presence of a toy truck), then the child could gradually learn to associate the word and its referent—the thing it names.

Chomsky's contribution to the psychology of language acquisition was to point out convincingly that the more interesting and sophisticated aspects of language could not, in principle, be learned by conditioning or by imitation.

The sounds of a language are not composed of a set of independent, discrete sounds. Instead, they form a phonemic system, obeying a set of rules. Each language has its own set of sounds, and its own sound system. We could not add an English speech sound like *th* as in "the" to the German speech sound system, because it just doesn't fit. Word meanings are not just labels for things, but instead represent concepts. Knowing the word "dog" implies that one knows what dogs are, how they differ from cats, and how they differ from everything else we know about in the world. Finally, learning the syntax of a language must involve rule-discovery procedures. The syntactic rules of a language are not transparent—they are not given explicitly in speech. Indeed, most of us cannot readily describe the rules we use to form grammatical sentences, but the fact that we can do so is an incontrovertible sign that the rules are there. If the rules are not explicitly laid out in the speech that a child hears, and if parents don't teach the rules explicitly, then how could imitation and reinforcement learning work?

The mistakes young children make illustrate that they are learning rules, not just imitating the speech they hear. When children say "Daddy runned" or "This is my bestest color," they are not imitating the speech that they have heard, they are using a rule that they have somehow discovered.

Chomsky and his followers believe that children are born with an innate knowledge of the general form of linguistic rules. Others believe that children can discover such rules during the course of their growing up in a speaking community. In either case, there is general agreement that language learning involves more complicated learning mechanisms than imitation and conditioning, even though these simpler mechanisms are involved.

From Prespeech to Speech

From the moment they are born, infants prepare for learning language by learning many of the prerequisites for language. They learn to distinguish between speech and non-speech sounds—between words and the sneezes, coughs, grunts, and all those other noises that people make. They learn how to produce the speech sounds of their native language. They learn to differentiate between self and others, and they learn concepts of objects. And, of course, they learn that things have names. Infants also learn, even if only in the crudest of terms, about communicative *intentions*—that when their mother or father makes speech sounds, some meaning or communication is intended (Bruner, 1974/75). Once this idea has been grasped, children can begin to figure out *what* meanings are being expressed (MacNamara, 1972).

INFANT PERCEPTION AND VOCALIZATIONS. Until quite recently very little was known about newborns' perceptual abilities, or about the development of their vocal abilities. Beginning in the early 1970s, scientists began to investigate these two aspects of language development, with surprising results.

It had long been believed that the newborn's auditory sensitivity is quite poor, and that the ability to distinguish among minimally different speech sounds could develop only with learning and experience. This is undoubtedly true for many speech sounds, but human infants have a head start in being able to discriminate among *some* important speech sounds virtually at birth. Eimas and his colleagues (1971) discovered that infants between one and four

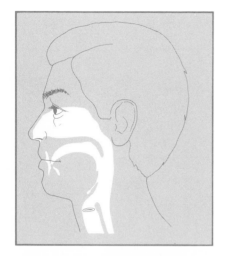

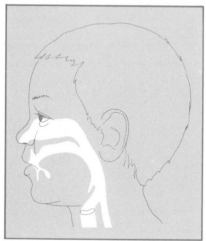

Figure 8-4

(Top) The typical vocal tract of a human adult. The oral cavity is relatively large and its shape and size can be varied rather extensively by moving the tongue around. (Bottom) The typical vocal tract of a human infant at birth. The infant's oral cavity is quite small because the tongue takes up so much space and because the larynx is high up in the throat. This vocal tract cannot be varied much at all, and so cannot produce a variety of speech sounds.

months discriminated between the syllables [*ba*] and [*pa*] exactly as adults do. This early ability to hear at least some of the important speech sounds, especially those that are common to most human languages, surely must be helpful to children as they begin to pick up the sound patterns of speech.

In contrast to the very early appearance of speech perception abilities, the human infant's ability to produce speech sounds at birth is very poor indeed. The major reason for this is the shape and structure of the baby's vocal tract (see Figure 8-4). At birth, it is more like the vocal tract of a chimpanzee than the vocal tract of an adult human. The larynx is relatively high, and the tongue takes up virtually all of the space in the oral cavity. These two factors provide a very small resonant chamber that cannot be adjusted very much to produce differences in vowel sounds. This means that the infant simply does not have the vocal machinery to produce speech sounds at birth (Oller and Warren, 1976).

While this vocal tract structure is not suited for speech, it is perfectly suited for sucking and drinking without gagging or choking. This configuration of tongue, larynx, and epiglottis virtually guarantees that the infant can breathe only through the nose, and that the epiglottis will protect the breathing passages from any liquids or solids taken by mouth. It's as if Mother Nature intended the infant to eat first, talk later.

From birth to 6 weeks, infant vocalizations seem to be purely reflexive. The baby cries, fusses, spits, sneezes, and coughs. From 6 weeks to about 4 months, the baby begins to combine these vocalizations with the speechlike sounds of cooing and gurgling. These sounds somewhat resemble consonant-vowel syllables, and are usually addressed to the mother or father. By about 4 months, the shape and structure of the baby's vocal tract have matured, and the baby begins to produce a variety of speechlike sounds.

Babies seem to practice one or two types of sounds at a time. For example, an infant might spend four weeks producing raspberries, then two days of high-pitched squealing, usually making these sounds while looking at people or at interesting objects. This vocal play appears to serve two functions. First, it obviously attracts attention and plays a role in communication between the infant and other people. Second, it enables infants to learn what they can do with their vocal apparatus, preparing for the imitation and learning that will occur between 6 months and 1 year.

By the sixth month infants can voluntarily control consonants, and they engage in a characteristic form of baby talk called *reduplicated babbling*. Typically, this consists of a front consonant and a vowel, such as "da da da da da" or "ma ma ma ma ma." It may not be coincidental that the words for father and mother in many human languages sound like this babbling—virtually all infants, regardless of the language spoken in the home, say things like this. Almost as soon as infants have mastered control over simple consonant-vowel sounds, they stop making them, and instead use *expressive jargon*. This involves a variety of syllables, with far less repetition than reduplicated babbling, and with a suprising similarity to the intonation patterns of adult speech. Indeed, it sounds very much like normal adult speech, but not a bit of it is intelligible. It is almost as if infants have learned the broad characteristics of the sounds of the language, including many of the vowels and consonants, as well as the intonation patterns, and are now practicing their new-found vocal skills.

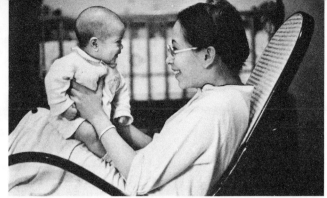

SOCIAL AND COGNITIVE DEVELOPMENT. During this first year of life other prerequisites to language learning become established. Babies begin to *imitate* adult actions. Nonverbal communication occurs in a variety of settings—play, feeding, dressing, bathing, bedtime. Baby and parent begin to understand one another's intentions, motivations, and behaviors. This interpersonal understanding is a necessary step toward learning the meanings of words. It is much like visiting a foreign country and figuring out the names of things. The most common way is to notice that someone is talking about, say, bread or cheese, and then associating the words you hear with the appropriate things. This requires that you know what a person is talking about *before* you understand the language. Similarly, young children "learn their language by first determining, independent of language, the meaning which a speaker intends to convey to them, and by then working out the relationship between the meaning and the language. To put it another way, the infant uses meaning as a clue to language, rather than language as a clue to meaning" (MacNamara, 1972, p. 1).

The behaviors of parents and infants seem designed to maximize the chances of their understanding one another without relying upon spoken language. A mother will try to capture an infant's attention when naming something. Infants, by their fourth month, will tend to look at what their mother is looking at, thus ensuring that when infant and mother interact, they are paying attention to the same thing (Bruner, 1974/5). In these as well as in other more subtle ways, infants can find out what their mother is saying and talking about and can begin to learn the meanings of the words their mother uses.

Acquiring a Vocabulary

When children utter their first words, they do so one at a time. For example, a child might say "doggie," or "milk," or "Mama." What could each of these utterances mean? During this stage of one-word utterances the child may often use a single word to express a whole message. For example, the word "milk" could mean "I want more milk" or "Where is the milk?" These one-word utterances can never be interpreted without considering the specific situation the child is in, and what he or she and others are doing at the moment. They are called *holophrastic* utterances because just one word expresses a whole message.

Single words can also be used to refer to several different things. The word "dog," for example, may often be used to refer to other furry, four-legged animals, such as cats, horses, or sheep. This kind of *overextension* of a word's meaning is quite common in young children. Sometimes such overextensions are signs that the child has not yet learned the precise meaning of a word. At other times, it is simply a child's way of talking about something whose name isn't yet known. In this latter case, the word "dog" is being used holophrastically to express the meaning "an animal that is like a dog."

Chapter 8:
Language and Thought

221

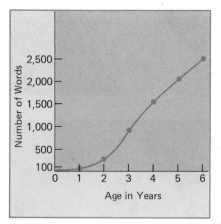

Figure 8-5

Starting with a few words at the age of 1 year, children learn, on the average, about 270 words by age 2, and by age 6 have a vocabulary of over 2,500 words. (Lenneberg, 1967; Smith, 1926)

At first, new words are learned rather slowly. Gradually, the rate of learning increases, and then accelerates quite rapidly, so that by 24 months an average working vocabulary of almost 300 words is not unusual, with many of the words having been learned toward the end of the second year (see Figure 8-5).

What do children talk about during the early part of language acquisition? Katherine Nelson, of Yale University, watched 18 children as they spoke their first 50 words. Her observations suggest that children do not learn words passively, or by merely imitating what their parents say. Instead, they tend to talk about what interests them (Nelson, 1973).

Among the first 10 words used by every child were the names for animals, food, and toys. Not once in the first 50 words did "diaper," "pants," "sweater," or "mittens" appear, even though parents must have used these words quite often. In general, young children seem to name the things that they handle or play with directly, and the things that do something, like move or make noises. They do not name things that just sit there, like furniture, or grass, or stores.

During this naming and learning period parents prepare the way for the next advance, two-word and three-word utterances. In addition to talking in short sentences themselves, parents will often expand a child's short utterances. If a child says "milk," a parent might say "Tommy want more milk?" This reply is based on the parent's best guess about the child's communicative intent. If the parent has guessed correctly, the reply can serve as a model for an expanded utterance. If the parent has guessed incorrectly, the reply tells the child that his or her one-word utterance is sometimes inadequate and ambiguous. In either case, children can get useful information about language and communication.

From Words to Sentences

Some time around the middle of the second year the one-word utterances of holophrastic speech begin to be replaced by the child's first sentences—two-word utterances. The particular words that children put together in these early and primitive sentences are carefully chosen. In many respects they resemble the kinds of word choices we make when we compose telegrams. We leave out relatively unimportant words, and include only those words we absolutely need to get our message across.

Young children who are unable to put together more than two or three words at a time tend to be *telegraphic* in this sense. They do not, of course, deliberately decide which words to use and which to omit. They do, however, use the few words and limited grammar that they have to good effect. Like the single-word utterances of holophrastic speech, two-word utterances are used to express a wide variety of meanings. Thus, the sentence "Mommy lunch" might be used to express any one of several different meanings: "That lunch belongs to Mommy," or "Mommy is eating lunch," and so on (Bloom, 1970; 1973).

Children throughout the world, in different cultures and in different language communities, behave in pretty much the same ways during this stage of language development. They all proceed from holophrastic speech to telegraphic two-word sentences, and they all talk about the same kinds of things (Slobin, 1971). All children name things and people. All children have a way of announcing that they have noticed something (for instance, "Hi doggie!"). All children have simple ways of expressing important things such as the hoped-for reappearance of something, like "More milk," or the equally important facts of disappearance, like "Allgone cookie." The kinds of semantic relations and functions of language expressed by children the world over are the same (see Table 8-1).

Once children have mastered two-word utterances, they begin to learn the syntax of the language. One of the more sensitive measures of a child's level of language development is the number of words (or morphemes) used per utterance. This measure, devised by Roger Brown and his colleagues at Harvard, is

Table 8–1: Two-Word Sentences in Child Speech from Several Languages.

Function of Utterance	Language				
	English	German	Russian	Finnish	Samoan
LOCATE, NAME	there book that car see doggie	buch da [book there] gukuk wauwau [see doggie]	Tosya tam [Tosya there]	tuossa Rina [there Rina] vettä siinä [water there]	Keith lea [Keith there]
DEMAND, DESIRE	more milk give candy want gum	mehr milch [more milk] bitte apfel [please apple]	yeshchë moloko [more milk] day chasy [give watch]	anna Rina [give Rina]	mai pepe [give doll] fia moo [want sleep]
NEGATE	no wet no wash not hungry allgone milk	nicht blasen [not blow] kaffee nein [coffee no]	vody net [water no] gus' tyu-tyu [goose gone]	ei susi [not wolf] enää pipi [anymore sore]	le 'ai [not eat] uma mea [allgone thing]
DESCRIBE EVENT OR SITUATION	Bambi go mail come hit ball block fall baby highchair	puppe kommt [doll comes] tiktak hängt [clock hangs] sofa sitzen [sofa sit] messer schneiden [cut knife]	mama prua [mama walk] papa bay-bay [papa sleep] korka upala [crust fell] nashla yaichko [found egg] baba kresio [grandma armchair]	Seppo putoo [Seppo fall] talli 'bm-bm' [garage 'car']	pa'u pepe [fall doll] tapale 'oe [hit you] tu'u lalo [put down]
SHOW POSSESSION	my shoe mama dress	mein ball [my ball] mamas hut [mama's hat]	mami chashka [mama's cup] pup moya [navel my]	täti auto [aunt car]	lole a'u [candy my] polo 'oe [ball your] paluni mama [balloon mama]
MODIFY, QUALIFY	pretty dress big boat	milch heiss [milk hot] armer wauwau [poor dog]	mama khoroshaya [mama good] papa bol'shoy [papa big]	rikki auto [broken car] torni iso [tower big]	fa'ali'i pepe [headstrong baby]
QUESTION	where ball	wo ball [where ball]	gde papa [where papa]	missä pallo [where ball]	fea Punafu [where Punafu]

From Slobin (1971).

called MLU—mean length of utterance (1973). With increasing cognitive and linguistic sophistication, children's utterances tend, on average, to get longer (see Figure 8-6). This reflects at least two kinds of developmental changes. First, it reflects the child's capacity to organize and produce longer sequences of words, irrespective of the grammatical complexity of those sequences. Second, it reflects the child's learning of more complex grammatical forms. In early speech, a child might say "Go home?" Later, the same meaning might be expressed in more adultlike form, "Can we go home now?"

Children's acquisition of the syntax of the language involves more than learning how to string more and more words together. It also involves the learning of the syntactic rules that make it possible for them to produce new sentences, as well as to make some revealing mistakes. Sometimes when children first learn to express the past tense in English, they will use the standard form, as in "walk-ed," and sporadically also use irregular forms, like "went." When they really learn the rule—adding the suffix -ed to a verb stem—they apply this rule

Figure 8-6

Mean length of utterance increases with age. This increase is shown for three children studied by Brown (1973).

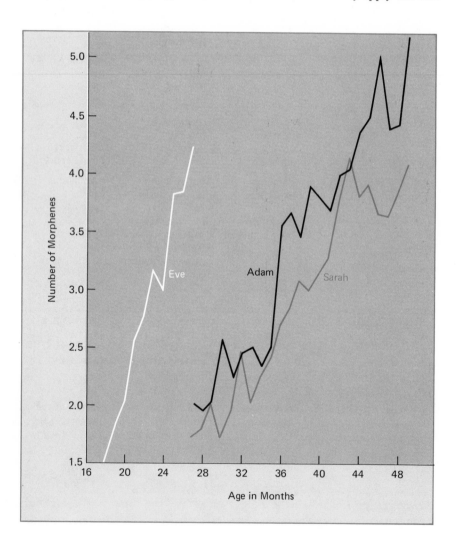

to all verbs and say things like "goed" instead of "went," "breaked" instead of "broke," and so on. It then takes several years to learn the exceptions to the rule. This pattern of rule-learning, overgeneralizing the rule, and finally learning the exceptions to the rule has been observed in every language that has these kinds of rules and exceptions.

The rules of grammar, even though they may lead to some mistakes, greatly simplify the task of language learning. Once we have a rule, we need not memorize every form of every word in the language. We can even generalize the grammar to words that don't exist. In an ingenious experiment, Jean Berko (1958) taught nonsense names to 5- and 6-year-old children. A child would be shown a drawing of an unfamiliar animal (see Figure 8-7), and told, "This is a wug." Then Berko would point to a second picture and say, "There are two of them. There are two _____." The children then completed the sentence and said "wugs," indicating that they indeed knew the rule for pluralization in English.

Of course, knowing a rule does not mean that we are conscious of that knowledge, or that we can describe the rule. Even literate adults can know rules without being aware of them. For example, what rules do we follow to produce *tag questions*, such as "John went home yesterday, didn't he?" or "John didn't go home yesterday, did he?" What are the rules that specify that the phrase "a large red Turkish truck" is correct, while the phrase "a Turkish red large truck" is incorrect? We must know these rules because we follow them when we speak, but, clearly, we don't know them consciously.

From Sentences to Communication

A telephone rings, and a 3-year-old child answers. The caller asks, "Is your mommy home?" The child immediately puts the phone down and calls for Mother to answer the phone. This child has understood the *intent* of the caller —to speak to Mother. At this age, most children use the immediate situation to help them interpret what people say. They may very often ignore the details of the speech they hear. Somewhat older children may go to the other extreme. They will rely completely on the literal meaning of a sentence and ignore the social or conversational context. Thus, a 4-year-old who is asked "Is your mommy home?" may very well answer "Yes," and wait for the conversation to continue.

From about 3 to 6 years, children learn a great deal about conversational behavior. This includes learning how to tell whether to take a statement literally or not, as in our telephone example. It also includes the development of awareness and sensitivity to other people's feelings and their needs for information. Young children tend to ask for things or tell people to do things directly. They will say "Swing me," or "I want a cookie." Older children, starting at about 4 to 5 years of age, will use adultlike, indirect requests. They will say "Do you want to swing me?" or "Can I have a cookie?" They will also provide reasons for requests, like "Gimme the hammer—I *need* it."

This gradual shift away from direct requests to indirect and rationalized statements reflects an increasing understanding of social and interpersonal factors in communication. When adults talk to one another they routinely tailor their speech to suit their listeners. For example, when two strangers are given a communication problem that involves talking about unusual geometric forms

Figure 8-7

This is the test used to assess children's knowledge of suffix rules. (Berko, 1958)

 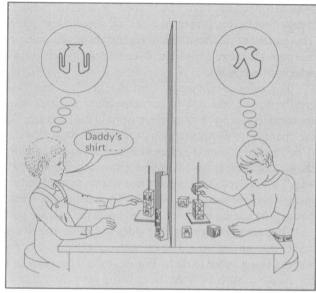

Figure 8-8 (Left)

In the adult communication task, the speaker had to describe six odd designs on a paper in front of him and give the number that went with each; a listener on the other side of an opaque barrier had to assign the correct number to copies of the same designs. Adult speakers communicated successfully by giving detailed descriptions the first time a design was used; when the same form appeared in later trials, speakers shortened their descriptions (for example, "The spaceman's helmet," and the just "Helmet"), and continued to be well understood by listeners. (Krauss and Glucksberg, 1977)

Figure 8-9 (Right)

In the children's version of the task, the speaker had to describe the design on blocks appearing at the base of a dispenser and then stack the blocks on a peg. The listener's task was to select the correct blocks from a randomly ordered collection and stack them in the same order. The youngest speakers gave noncommunicative descriptions that were usually misunderstood. (Krauss and Glucksberg, 1977)

(as in Figure 8-8), they begin by using long descriptive phrases, and then gradually shorten those phrases as they tacitly develop a two-person code (Krauss and Glucksberg, 1977). When nursery school children are given a version of this task (Figure 8-9), they behave as if a tacit code had already been developed. The descriptions they give to one another are short, idiosyncratic, and virtually uninformative to the listeners (Glucksberg et al., 1966).

With further development of their language and social skills, children learn when and how to adjust what they say and how they say it, depending upon who their listeners are. Four-year-olds appear to know how to adjust their speech in some obvious situations. For example, they will use longer sentences and more complex grammatical construction when talking to adults than when talking to 2-year-olds (Shatz and Gelman, 1973). Further elaboration and development of these social-linguistic skills will enable them to make the same subtle and fine-tuned adjustments that adults make during ordinary conversation.

Language and Thought

Can animals other than humans learn a language? Can animals who have no language reason or solve problems? Is there any connection between being able to talk and being able to think?

Nonhuman Language

Virtually all animals communicate with one another. A honey bee returning from a food source will perform a dance in the hive that informs the other

APPLICATION
Can an Ape Learn Language?

The Gardners taught the chimpanzee Washoe a crude version of American Sign Language, ASL. Other chimpanzees have been taught to communicate with people and to construct sentence-like strings of symbols in different ways. David Premack (1976) taught the chimpanzee Sarah to make symbol strings by placing magnetized plastic forms on a magnetic board (see below, left). Duane Rumbaugh (1977) taught a chimpanzee named Lana to use a computerlike keyboard with illuminated push buttons to communicate in a system he called *Yerkish* (see below, right). In each of these cases it was claimed that the chimpanzee had mastered an essential component of natural language, the ability to create a sentence.

Quite recently, Herbert Terrace reported the results of an intensive study of a chimpanzee named Nim Chimpsky (pun was intended). Over a period of several years Nim made more than 19,000 multiple-sign utterances in the version of ASL that Terrace taught her. These utterances were then carefully analyzed for evidence of syntactic regularities. According to Terrace, most of the multiple-sign utterances were either simple repetitions, like "tickle me tickle" or "hug me Nim," or they were inadvertently cued by a human teacher. Terrace analyzed the film records of other chimpanzees who had been taught ASL, including Washoe, and concluded that they, too, do not show clear evidence that the chimpanzees had mastered even an elementary form of snytax. Terrace concludes, "Apes can learn many isolated symbols (as can dogs, horses, and other non-human species), but they show no unequivocal evidence of having mastered the conversational . . . or syntactic organization of language" (Terrace et al., 1979, p. 901).

The key word in this quotation is "unequivocal." The Gardners strongly disagree with Terrace's conclusion. They argue that Washoe did use languagelike rules, and that she did show "conversational give-and-take" between herself and human companions (Gardner and Gardner, 1980). The evidence is, then, equivocal, and we will have to wait for more complete studies of chimpanzees' learning to "talk" before the final answer is in. Can an ape learn to create a sentence? Maybe.

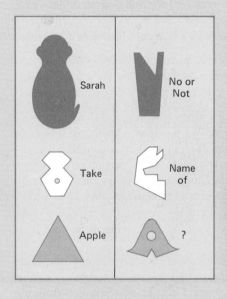

bees where the food is (von Frisch, 1967). Wolves, lions, and other pack-hunting animals communicate with one another when coordinating a hunt. Until recently, however, no animal has learned even the rudiments of a human language.

People have always wondered whether animals, and particularly chimpanzees, could be taught a language. Early attempts to teach chimpanzees to talk were complete failures (Kellogg and Kellogg, 1933; Hayes, 1951). Allen and Beatrice Gardner, of the University of Nevada, suspected that chimps could not talk because they lacked the necessary vocal apparatus, not because they weren't smart enough. Acting on this hunch, they decided to teach American Sign Language (ASL)—used by many American deaf people—to a young female chimp, Washoe. Washoe learned to sign quite easily and rapidly, and after about two years she began to combine signs into short, simple sentences—much like the early sentences of human children (Gardner and Gardner, 1969).

Washoe, like a human child, is now able to produce word combinations that can be interpreted quite readily. Her combinations seem to express the same semantic relations that are expressed universally in young children's utterances (see Table 8-1). Furthermore, Washoe used virtually all of her combinations spontaneously, without having them taught to her or having any opportunity to imitate them.

Since the Gardners' pioneering work with Washoe, several other chimpanzees—and at least one gorilla—have been taught fairly complex human-like communication systems. Some of them also have learned ASL. Others learned somewhat different nonvocal systems. In every case, the animal seemed to learn the system much the same way that human children learn their own language, and used the system much like children use their early speech. They seemed to start conversations, make requests, comment on happenings around them, and, perhaps most important, create spontaneous and untaught symbol combinations. There is, however, some disagreement as to how language-like these ape-created utterances really are.

Concepts

A concept is our knowledge about a category of objects or events. When we have a concept of, say, *chairs,* we can recognize that something is a chair even if we have never seen it or one just like it before. We would also know that it belongs to a larger category of things called *furniture.* Having such concepts is enormously useful and efficient. We do not have to learn what something is every time we encounter something new. Most of the things and events we encounter every day are examples of well-known categories, even though they may be new to us in many ways. By having a concept of what a thing or event is we can classify new examples as instances of well-learned categories, thus saving us an enormous amount of unnecessary learning.

For example, my concept of *cats* allows me to recognize any one of an infinite number of different animals as *cats,* and to classify accurately almost any animal I might see as being a cat or not. I also know where cats fit in the animal kingdom, and I can compare them with other animals such as dogs, elephants, or fish. I know pretty much what to expect from any cat I might meet, and, therefore, I would know what to do if I should meet one.

How do we acquire such concepts? One way is to learn a set of rules that defines a category. In one of the most influential studies of concept formation, Heidbreder (1947) found that people learn classification rules based on concrete ideas more easily than they learn rules based on abstract properties, like numbers (see Figure 8-10). The relative difficulty of concrete and abstract concepts can also be seen in the developing child. Children's early concepts are primarily concrete, including such things as dogs, people, toys and candy. Later, concepts like *living things* come in, as well as such concepts as *fairness, honesty,* and *truth.* At first, these abstract concepts are quite simple: *truth* may be defined as "not

Figure 8-10

The nine pictures of Series 1 were shown one at a time. The pair of stockings were called LING, the circular object was called FARD, the face was called RELK, and so on, as shown. People had to learn which concepts went with each of these nonsense names. Concrete object concepts (RELK–Faces; LETH–Build-ings; and MUL–trees) were learned most quickly. Spatial form or pattern concepts (FARD–circle; PRAN–crossed linear forms; and STOD–broken figure 8) were more difficult. Most difficult were the number concepts (LING–2, MANK–6, DILT–5). (Heidbreder, 1947)

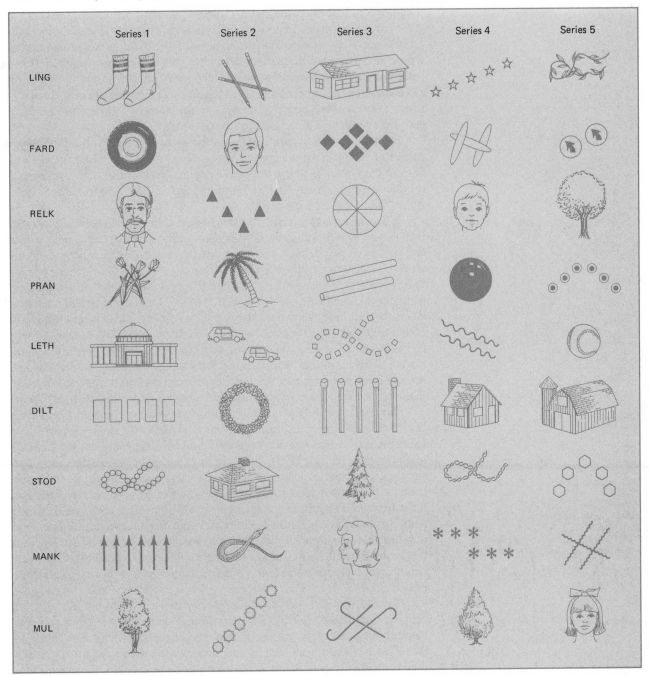

lying." In adulthood, the concept of *truth* is far more complex, and few of us would even try to define it.

Concepts can also be easy or difficult to learn depending on the types of rules that define them. When a single rule defines a concept, it is a *simple* concept. In this sense, all of the concepts shown in Figure 8-10 are *simple* concepts, whether they are abstract or concrete. When the rules become more complicated, then the concepts become more difficult to learn. Bruner and Goodnow (1956) used arbitrary concepts to see what kinds of classification rules were hardest to learn. When classification decisions had to be based on two or more rules, it took longer to learn the concept than when only one rule was required. When something must have two or more features or characteristics in order to qualify as a member of the category it is called a *conjunctive* concept. The concept of *registered voter* is a conjunctive concept. A person must be 18 years old, a citizen, and also a resident of a particular district in order to qualify.

Even more difficult are *disjunctive* concepts. These involve "either–or" rules. For example, the category *U.S. citizen* is defined as someone (a) who was born in the United States; *or* (b) whose parents were United States citizens; *or* (c) who was naturalized in a U.S. District Court. If any one of these conditions is met, then the person is a citizen.

When the rules for classifying examples of a concept can be stated explicitly, then that concept is well defined. Many everyday concepts (for example, *citizen* and *voter*) are well defined, but many others are not. For such fuzzy concepts we do not seem to use simple rules to define categories. Instead, we can classify things in terms of their similarity to the most typical examples of that category. Consider the category of things we call *birds*. All birds share certain characteristics: they all have wings, and they all have feathers. However, it would not bother us to learn that someone had discovered a wingless bird, or that someone had managed to breed a wingless and featherless bird for the domestic poultry market. This means that wings and feathers are not necessary or defining features of birds, although they are certainly characteristic of them. Other features that we associate with birds are their ability to fly, sing, build nests, and so on.

Our concept of *bird*, then, consists of what we expect birds to look and act like. On this basis, people agree that robins and sparrows are highly typical birds. Chickens and turkeys are not quite as typical, and penguins and ostriches are highly atypical (Rosch, 1977). Similarly, our concept of *fruit* enables us to classify things as fruits, and also to know that apples, pears, and oranges are typical fruits, while watermelons, papayas, and blueberries are atypical. Atypical fruits differ from typical fruits in one or more ways. Watermelons are larger than most fruits, papayas have an unusual texture and taste, and blueberries are small and, of course, blue (how many other blue fruits are there?). Notice that we do not use the technical definition of fruit in our everyday life, and so tomatoes and cucumbers are not included in the fruit category despite the fact that they are technically fruits.

How do we learn everyday concepts like these if we do not learn a set of defining rules? Rosch (1977) has suggested that after extensive experience with members of a category, such as birds, we gradually learn what most birds are like. This includes things such as their average size, their most usual coloring, their common behavior patterns, and everything else about them that is *birdlike*.

It would *not* include such things as having two eyes or warm blood, because lots of other kinds of animals have these features too. In other words, we learn what most birds have in common with one another, and what most birds have that other kinds of animals do not. This enables us to distinguish between birds and all the other animals that are not birds, and also gives us a notion of what a typical bird is like. Our concept of *bird,* then, is the sum total of what we have learned about birds and about other kinds of animals.

The Functions of Language in Thought

The chimpanzees who have learned language-like communication systems also provide striking illustrations of some of the noncommunicative uses of language. Obviously, languages and language-like signs or symbol systems are designed primarily for communicative functions. But the ability to express ideas, urges, or concepts in words or in signs can also have profound effects on other abilities. For example, people can express aggression or anger either physically (by hitting someone), or verbally. A chimpanzee trained by Herbert Terrace and his colleagues at Columbia University would sometimes threaten and bite people. After she had learned the sign for "bite," she seldom actually threatened or bit—she simply signed "bite" and that seemed enough to do two things: First, it told people that she was angry; second, it seemed to vent her anger. The chimp seldom bit people after symbolically expressing her anger!

Having a language can also help in solving conceptual problems. One problem that is difficult for chimpanzees to solve is *cross-modal matching*—telling whether or not two objects are the same or different when one of the objects can be seen but not touched, and the other object can be touched but not seen. Lana, a chimp who was taught a computer-based sign system, could solve such problems easily when the objects involved were ones that she had names for. She had much more difficulty with objects that she had no names for (Rumbaugh et al., 1979).

"The thing to bear in mind, gentlemen, is not just that Daisy has mastered a rudimentary sign language but that she can link these signs together to express meaningful abstract concepts." (Drawing by Lorenz; © 1974 The New Yorker Magazine, Inc.)

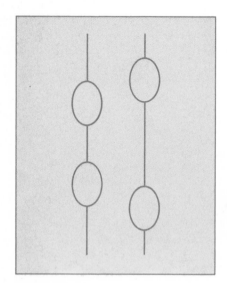

Figure 8-11

What is this a picture of? See the text for an explanation.

Children, too, display changes in their abilities to solve certain kinds of problems when they learn how to use language. One such problem is the *far transposition* test. A child is first taught that to find a toy or a piece of candy he or she must choose the smaller of two boxes. After learning this, the child is given two new boxes, both of which are quite different in size from the original training pair. Children who could not express the original learning in words—"pick the smaller one"—generally could not succeed in transferring the knowledge they gained in the first test to the second test. Most of the children who could express the answer verbally did succeed (Kuenne, 1946).

Language, then, does more than serve communicative functions. It can help us to control and guide our behavior, and it can be useful in thinking and problem solving.

Linguistic Relativity

In the late nineteenth century and early part of this century, linguists and anthropologists worked primarily with exotic cultures and languages—for example, American Indian, Samoan, tribal African, and Eskimo. The languages they studied were strikingly different from the familiar European languages, and the modes of thinking and action also seemed strikingly different. Did the culture influence the development of the language or could it be that modes of thought and conceptualization are prisoners of the language—that what and how people think depends upon the particular language they speak?

This idea—that the particular language a person speaks determines how the world is perceived and conceptualized—is known as the Whorfian hypothesis, after Benjamin Whorf (1956), one of the first proponents of *linguistic relativity*.

There is ample evidence that the way we describe things can affect how those things might be perceived, remembered, or thought about. The labels we give to ambiguous stimuli will influence how they are seen and how they are remembered. Look at Figure 8-11. It can be seen either as two strings with beads on them, or as a bear cub climbing the far side of a tree. In a classic experiment,

Figure 8-12

The drawings in the center column were shown to people together with the labels of List 1 or the labels of List 2. When asked to draw the original pictures from memory, people tended to make the pictures more like their labels than the original was. (Carmichael, Hogan, and Walter, 1932)

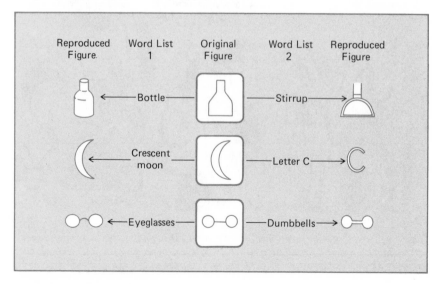

232

APPLICATION
Are Some Languages Better than Others?

Is English better than French? Is Portuguese better than Hungarian? Except for reasons of snobbery or chauvinism, the answer to both these questions is no. All known languages, from the Dani of Western New Guinea to the English of the Court of St. James, are equally complex and equally grammatical. There are no criteria that would enable us to judge whether any one language is better or worse than any other.

What about the dialects of a single language? Are some versions of English better than others? Is a Vermont or Maine accent better than a Texas or Louisiana accent? Are all of these regional accents inferior to "standard" English? If so, what is "standard" English, and who speaks it?

In England, the standard was once defined by the type of people who spoke it. In 1931, a British linguist wrote this definition of the "best" English: "Every one knows that there is a kind of English which is neither provincial nor vulgar, a type which most people would willingly speak if they could, and desire to speak if they do not . . . it is the type spoken by members of the great Public* Schools, and by those classes in society which normally frequent these . . . this is the best kind of English . . . because it is spoken by those often very

* The "public" schools of England are really the expensive and exclusive private schools.

properly called 'the best people'" (Wyld, 1931, p. 605).

What is the American equivalent to this? Perhaps the kind of radio and television broadcast English that has no trace of a regional accent. The more obvious the regional accent, the less standard the speech. Obviously, this criterion is as arbitrary as the social class criterion used by Mr. Wyld in 1931. Ultimately, our feelings about regional and ethnic accents reflect our feelings about the people themselves. If a particular group has high status, then their accents are acceptable (for example, an upper class British or sophisticated French accent). If a group has low status, then their accents are judged as unacceptable.

---

people were shown drawings that could be named in either of two ways (see Figure 8-12). The names of the drawings substantially influenced how they were later drawn from memory (Carmichael, Hogan, and Walter, 1932).

These kinds of experiments suggested a way to test the Whorfian hypothesis. If different languages provide different sets of names for, say, colors, then people who speak different languages should show differential color memory. For example, in ordinary English we have about six basic color terms—red, orange, yellow, green, blue, and violet (plus, of course, black and white). In the language of the Dani, a tribe in Western New Guinea, there are only two color words. One term refers to all the dark, cool colors, the other to all the light, warm colors. Do English speakers conceptualize colors differently from speakers of Dani?

Eleanor Rosch and Daniel Olivier (Heider and Olivier, 1972) tested Dani natives and American college students for their ability to remember and discriminate among colors. The Americans and the Danis were equal in their ability to discriminate shades of difference among colors. The Americans were slightly better at remembering which one of 40 different color chips had been shown to them 30 seconds before. However, these two groups of very different people fundamentally perceive and conceptualize color in identical ways. Both Danis and Americans link together the same colors. Colors that are only somewhat similar to Americans are also only somewhat similar to the Danis. The colors that Americans confuse in memory are the same ones that the Dani confuse in memory. In other words, the perceived degrees of similarity and difference among colors are the same in these two language groups. The color names available to these two groups of people have not influenced basic aspects of perception and knowledge of colors.

These findings as well as many others offer no support for the extreme form of the Whorfian hypothesis. The influence of language upon thought may be pervasive, but the differences among human languages do not seem to cause important differences in how people perceive and conceptualize the world (Glucksberg and Danks, 1975).

Reasoning, Problem Solving, and Creativity

Reasoning

Do kangaroos have livers? Even if you have never learned this fact directly (and it's most unlikely that you have), you can still answer the question correctly. The answer is not recalled or remembered, but *generated* by reasoning. In *deductive* reasoning, the steps are explicit and the conclusions firm. In order to answer the kangaroo question deductively, we could transform the question into a syllogism (a three-term reasoning format):

> All kangaroos are animals.
> All animals have livers.
> Conclusion: Kangaroos have livers.

We could also answer the question *inductively:*

> Many animals that I know have livers. The kangaroo resembles these animals in many ways. Therefore, it is more than likely that kangaroos have livers. But I wouldn't bet my life on it.

In both cases, information that we already have permits us to generate additional information. This is one of the more important functions of reasoning.

We also use reasoning to judge the validity of arguments. In general, college students are quite good at detecting logical flaws in syllogisms. For example, many students would agree that this argument is false:

> All Xs are Y.
> All Zs are Y.
> Therefore, all Xs are Zs.

This same logic problem, however, can be made either easier or more difficult by changing the particular terms used. For example, it is most clearly recognized as false if we already know that the conclusion is, in the real world, false:

> All Israelis are people.
> All Egyptians are people.
> Therefore, all Israelis are Egyptians.

In contrast, if we tend to agree with the conclusion, then it is more difficult to detect the logical flaw:

> Welfare is giving to the poor.
> Charity is giving to the poor.
> Therefore, welfare is charity.

These examples illustrate how our knowledge and our biases can interfere with our ability to use deductive logic (Wason and Johnson-Laird, 1972).

Problem Solving

Problems are novel situations that require novel behaviors, or situations for which no one has ever found satisfactory solutions or for which there *are* no satisfactory solutions. When we can't answer a question by using our memory, or when we can't deal with a situation by doing what we did the last time, then we are faced with a problem. Some problems are difficult to solve because, for one reason or another, they set us off on the wrong track. These kinds of problems involve *negative set*. Other kinds of problems are difficult because they require putting together information in new and original ways; they require creativity.

NEGATIVE SET.   Someone faced with a problem can go off on the wrong track for any one of several reasons. In the nine-dot problem (in Figure 8-13), the spatial characteristics of the arrangement implicitly influence people to stay within the imaginary square formed by the dots. In Luchins' water jar problems (Table 8-2), people have to figure out how to get a specified amount of water from three jars with different fluid capacities. An incorrect or negative set can easily be established. The first problem is simple enough. Problems 2 through 6 can be solved by the same method: Jar B minus Jar A, minus twice Jar C. Problems 7 and 8 can also be solved this way, but notice that they can be solved much more easily by using only two jars. Problem 9 cannot be solved at all in the usual three-jar way. People who have learned to solve problems 2 through 6 often continue to use the habitual three-jar solution for problems 7 and 8, and get stuck on

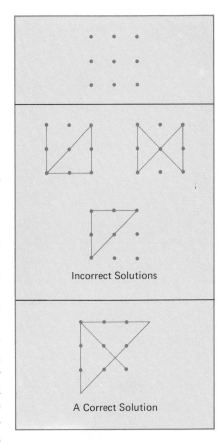

Incorrect Solutions

A Correct Solution

Figure 8-13

The nine-dot problem. Connect the dots by drawing only four straight lines. Do not retrace any lines, and do not lift your pencil from the paper.

Table 8–2: Luchins' Water Jar Problems.
How do you measure out the right amount of water using Jars A, B, and C?

Problem Number	Jars Available for Use			Required Amount
	A	B	C	
1	29	3		20
2	21	127	3	100
3	14	163	25	99
4	18	43	10	5
5	9	42	6	21
6	20	59	4	31
7	23	49	3	20
8	15	39	3	18
9	28	76	3	25

From Luchins (1942).

problem 9. People who have not had this set-inducing experience have no difficulties at all with problem 9 (Luchins, 1942).

Max Wertheimer, in his book *Productive Thinking* (1945/1959), describes a classroom example of this kind of negative set. Children who had already learned how to find the area of a rectangle applied that formula (the product of two sides) to the problem of finding the area of a parallelogram. The teacher then taught the class the correct formula: area = base × altitude (see Figure 8-14A). Wertheimer decided to find out what the children had learned by giving the class an area problem with the parallelogram shown in Figure 8-14B. Two kinds of solutions were attempted. The attempt shown in Figure 8-14C shows a complete lack of understanding and a rote and inappropriate application of the method. Figure 8-14D shows an appropriate application of the method, along with an understanding of that method.

Habitual ways of thinking about ordinary objects can also lead to a kind of negative set called *functional fixedness* (Duncker, 1945). One such problem is shown in Figure 8-15. When people are asked to mount a candle on the wall, with only tacks in a box and a book of matches, as many as 50 percent fail to

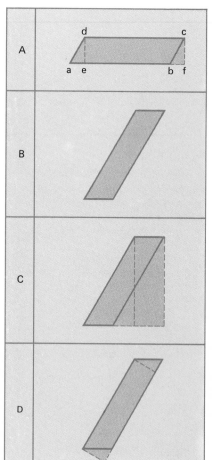

Figure 8-14 (Left)

Children were first taught to find the area of parallelograms, using the diagram shown in A. They were then given the parallelogram shown in B and asked to find the area. One kind of solution attempt, C, indicated a complete lack of understanding. The solution method illustrated in D demonstrated that the child understood the nature of the problem and the solution. (Wertheimer, 1945/1959)

Figure 8-15 (Below)

The candle problem: Using only the materials on the table, how can the candle be mounted on the wall? The solution is shown on the right. (Glucksberg and Weisberg, 1966)

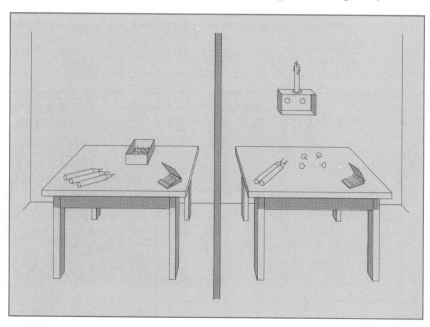

notice that the tack box can be used as a candle holder. When, however, the box is explicitly labeled as a *box,* all the people tested solved the problem in less than a minute (Glucksberg and Weisberg, 1966). In effect, telling people that a box was available short-circuited the usual response of trying to use tacks or melted wax alone to make a candle holder.

Creativity

The kinds of laboratory puzzles we have been dealing with bear little overt resemblance to the problems faced by scientists, engineers, or creative artists. They do, however, share one important property with real-world problems: the person begins either by not knowing at all what to do, or by going off on a wrong track. Both the laboratory puzzles and the real-world problems require novel behavior—a change of habitual modes of acting and thinking.

Real-world problems often are far more complex and require much more work to be solved. Many creative problem solutions and discoveries seem to occur in four stages: preparation, incubation, illumination, and verification. Gutenberg's invention of the printing press illustrates these stages. The *preparation* stage consisted of several substages. The first was his explicit goal—to reproduce the Bible economically. The second consisted of learning about and considering several ways to print letters. He considered and thought about how wood block printing is done by rubbing paper or material on the block. Because carving letters in wood is laborious and slow, he searched for alternatives. He got the idea of type-casting from coin-stampings and seals. In his own words, "Do you not see that you can repeat as many times as necessary the seal covered with signs and characters?" (Gutenberg, in Koestler, 1964, p. 123).

Many, if not all, of the elements of the printing press were now available in Gutenberg's mind. However, he was still stuck with the notion of rubbing to make an imprint—he was on the wrong track. The idea of making an imprint by pressure did not occur to him until after a period of *incubation*—a period of time during which no progress seemed to be made, and during which little conscious thought seemed to be applied to the problem. The moment of *illumination* came to Gutenberg when, as he put it, "I took part in the wine harvest. I watched the wine flowing, and going back from the effect to the cause, I studied the power of this press . . ." Suddenly, the idea occurs—put together the wine-press and the seal, and the letter-press is created! The *verification* follows. Will the idea actually work?

Many first-hand accounts of important discoveries follow this pattern. A goal is clearly set, and then potentially relevant information is gathered. This preparation done, a period of apparent inactivity follows. This can often be a period of incubation involving a great deal of unconscious activity. Sometimes, this leads to a flash of illumination or insight. Finally, if the idea is promising, it is tested and verified.

The moment of illumination itself often involves the coming together of familiar elements in new ways. The gifted mathematician, Henri Poincaré, wrote, "to create consists of making new combinations of associative elements that are useful" (1929). A psychologist who devised a test of creativity (see Table 8-3) described creative thinking as "the forming of associative elements

Table 8–3: A Test of Creativity: The Remote Associates Test (RAT).

Find a word that is associated to each of these three words:

| rat | blue | cottage |

Answer: cheese

Here are four other examples*:

1. railroad	girl	class
2. book	blood	gear
3. writer	cast	blood
4. sky	note	room

* Answers: working, worm, type, blue.

(After Mednick, 1962).

into new combinations which either meet new requirements or are in some way useful" (Mednick, 1962, p. 221).

This definition of creative behavior brings us full circle to the child learning language—putting together elements (like words) into new combinations that are useful (sentences).

Summary

1.   All languages share certain features: (a) a limited number of speech sounds, called *phonemes,* which can be combined to form countless words; (b) meanings assigned arbitrarily to words; (c) words combined in systematic ways to form a theoretically infinite number of sentences. Because they share these features, any idea or concept that can be expressed in one language can also be expressed in any other language.

2.   The morpheme is the smallest unit of speech that has meaning. The *denotative meaning* of a word is the thing or class of things the word can label. The *connotative meaning* reflects how we feel about the thing the word stands for.

3.   The *semantic differential* is a rating scale of the three major dimensions of connotative meaning: evaluation, activity, and potency.

4.   Words are combined into sentences according to rules, which form the *syntax* of a language. *Phrase structure rules* govern the organization of various parts of a sentence; *transformational rules* specify the relationships between sentences and spell out how one type of sentence can be transformed into another.

5.   Chomsky believes that children are born with an innate *language acquisition device (LAD).* Others believe that children discover basic linguistic rules as part of growing up in a speaking community.

6.   By the sixth month infants engage in *reduplicated babbling.* In the next phase, they use *expressive jargon,* a variety of syllables that sound like adult speech but are unintelligible.

7.   The one-word utterances of children are called *holophrastic* utterances because just one word expresses a whole phrase or sentence. A child's first sentences, which are two-word utterances, are *telegraphic* in the use of words—only the most important words are included.

8.   One of the non-communicative uses of language is to help solve conceptual problems; being able to label things and to express what we have learned in words helps in thinking and problem solving.

9.   Whorf's *linguistic relativity hypothesis*—that differences in languages cause important differences in the way people perceive and conceptualize the world—does not seem to be borne out in recent experiments.

10.   Our knowledge and our biases can interfere with our ability to reason—if we agree with a conclusion it is harder to detect a flaw in the logic involved.

11. Some problems are difficult to solve because they set us off on the wrong track; such problems involve *negative set.* One kind of negative set is *functional fixedness,* in which habitual ways of thinking about ordinary objects block the solution of the problem.

12. Creativity is often the result of a four-stage process involving *preparation, incubation, illumination,* and *verification.*

Suggested Readings

CLARK, H. H., and CLARK, E. V. *Psychology and Language: An Introduction to Psycholinguistics.* New York: Harcourt Brace Jovanovich, 1977. A comprehensive survey of linguistics and psychology, with particular attention to the mental processes people use to comprehend language.

FOSS, D. J., and HAKES, D. T. *Psycholinguistics: An Introduction to the Psychology of Language.* Englewood Cliffs, N.J.: Prentice-Hall, 1978: Provides an extensive coverage of language comprehension research.

GLUCKSBERG, S., and DANKS, J. H. *Experimental Psycholinguistics.* Hillsdale, N.J.: Erlbaum, 1975. A clear introduction to the concepts of speech perception, semantics, and syntax in the context of the experimental psychology of language.

BOURNE, L. E. JR., EKSTRAND, B. R., and DOMINOWSKI, R. L. *The Psychology of Thinking.* Englewood Cliffs, N.J.: Prentice-Hall, 1971. Covers the contemporary literature on thinking as this topic has been treated in psychology.

JOHNSON-LAIRD, P. N., and WASON, P. C. (Eds). *Thinking: Readings in Cognitive Science.* Cambridge: The University Press, 1977. Covers contemporary literature on thinking and includes work from computer science, linguistics, and philosophy.

LACHMAN, R., LACHMAN, J. L., and BUTTERFIELD, E. C. *Cognitive Psychology and Information Processing.* Hillsdale, N.J.: Erlbaum, 1979. History of contemporary cognitive psychology, ranging from decision making through perception to language comprehension and discourse processing — sophisticated and important treatment of the field.

ROSCH, E., and LLOYD, B. B. (Eds.). *Cognition and Categorization.* Hillsdale, N.J.: Erlbaum, 1978. Reviews the literature on categorization and concept formation, bringing together a representative set of essays from various disciplines and approaches.

WEISBERG, R. W. *Memory, Thought and Behavior.* New York: Oxford University Press, 1980. Argues convincingly that the role of memory in thinking and problem solving has been seriously overlooked, and shows how selective retrieval of relevant information from memory can play critical roles in creative thinking and problem solving.

Intelligence

There are few, if any, applications of psychology that have had as much impact on our lives as the intelligence test. The fact that you are a college student reading this book makes it almost certain that your score on a standardized intelligence test is higher than average—and the fact that you were known to have a higher than average score may be responsible for the fact that you are in college at all. The kinds of courses you were encouraged to take in high school were very likely influenced by teachers' knowledge of your intelligence test score. The college you are attending almost certainly examined your score on a "scholastic aptitude test"—a kind of intelligence test—before deciding to admit you. The results of intelligence tests have deeply affected the personal lives and careers of millions of people.

The data collected by intelligence testers have also played a prominent role in influencing our ideas about education and, for that matter, about social policy in general. We know, for example, that intelligence test scores tend to run in families. That is, parents with high test scores tend to have children with high test scores—just as parents with low test scores tend to have children with low test scores. Furthermore, there are quite large average differences in measured intelligence among social classes and ethnic and racial groups. These differences are also somehow passed on from one generation to the next. Do these facts mean, as some have suggested, that differences in intelligence are largely a matter of heredity? Do they mean, as others have argued, that intelligence test scores are largely determined by environment, which in turn is shared by members of the same family, social class, or race? Are individual differences *within* a race largely determined by heredity, while differences in the average test scores *between* races are largely determined by environment? If differences in test scores are mostly determined by the genes, would that mean that education and other environmental influences cannot increase intelligence beyond some genetically fixed level? These are obviously important and controversial questions, which we shall try to answer in this chapter.

Binet and the IQ

The Background of Binet's Test

The first useful intelligence test was devised in France by Alfred Binet and his collaborator, Theophile Simon. The first version of their test, published in 1905, marked a radical departure from earlier efforts to measure intelligence or mental ability. The first impetus toward the development of "mental tests" had been given by Charles Darwin's cousin, Francis Galton. The differences among people were in Galton's view largely caused by heredity; and mankind could improve itself, Galton argued, if gifted individuals were encouraged to mate with other gifted people, and if the ungifted were discouraged (or prevented) from mating at all. These ideas were adopted by the eugenics movement, founded by Galton. To support his arguments about the importance of heredity, Galton demonstrated that "eminence" in British life tended to run in families. The sons and grandsons of eminent jurists were more likely than the average person to themselves become eminent jurists, for example. This and other such facts suggested to Galton the importance of the genes in allowing one to become eminent. There were also, Galton noted, differences among races in the frequency of eminent people or men of genius—there were many such superior individuals to be found among the British, and virtually none in Africa or India.

Throughout his life Galton maintained an active interest in measuring and testing human "specimens," recording, cataloguing, and calculating the differences among them. The quantitative "mental tests" used by Galton and his early followers, however, were very simple. Perhaps because of his strong biological leanings, Galton concentrated on such "laboratory-like" tests as simple reaction time, and on measures of sensory thresholds and capacities. These could be measured with precision, and there were large differences among individuals on such tests. The difficulty was that performance on such tests did not seem to be related to what most people would recognize as signs of real intelligence or mental ability. For example, it was not the case that an excellent student reacted more quickly to the sound of a buzzer than did an inferior student.

The task that faced Binet was much more down to earth and practical than Galton's concern with eugenics. The school authorities in the city of Paris had asked Binet to come up with a testing procedure that could help to pick out students with low academic aptitude—that is, those students who could not profit much from the regular school curriculum, and for whom special classes should be set up. That meant, of course, that the test Binet made had to be related to— had to be able to *predict*—a child's performance in school.

The Concept of Mental Age

The point of departure for Binet was a simple but powerful idea: Normally, as children grow older, their mental powers increase. We do not expect a normal 2-year-old to learn the multiplication tables, no matter how often they are recited in his or her presence. However, if the same child has failed to learn the multiplication tables by the age of 12, we might well be concerned that the child is not very intelligent. (That assumes, of course, that the child has been exposed repeatedly to the multiplication tables, at school or elsewhere.)

The normal growth of mental power with age suggested to Binet the concept of *mental age.* That is, it is reasonable to expect the average 9-year-old to possess certain pieces of knowledge and to be able to solve certain kinds of "intellectual" problems. Whatever intellectual skills the average 9-year-old possesses define the mental age of 9. Further, children who are only 7 or 8 years of age should have difficulty coping with test material that is appropriate for 9-year-olds. Older children, of course, should find the 9-year-old material very easy.

Binet next set about interviewing and examining numbers of Paris school children, trying to find out precisely what intellectual accomplishments were characteristic of children of different ages. From his point of view, a good item for inclusion in his test was one that most (but not all) children of a given age could answer correctly. Further, the proportion of children younger than that age who could answer the item should be small, while the proportion of older children answering successfully should be large. In practice, Binet selected items that about three-fourths of children of a given age could answer. If one found, as Binet did, a number of such items for 9-year-olds, the child who could answer those items was said to have a mental age of 9. That same child usually could answer the items that Binet had placed on his 8-year-old scale; but he or she would have difficulty with items on the 10-year-old scale.

The kinds of items that Binet included in his scales dealt directly with knowledge, thinking, reasoning, and judgment—the kinds of materials involved in successful school performance. Table 9-1 lists a number of representative items that Binet's test asked children of different ages.

Table 9–1: Intelligence Test Items at Three Different Levels of the Stanford-Binet Test.

Year Two

1. Put a circle, triangle, and square in proper place in a formboard.
2. Identify by name toys representing common objects such as a cat, a button, a cup, etc.
3. Identify parts of the body: Show the hair, mouth, ears, and hands on a doll.
4. Identify pictures of objects such as a shoe, a table, a flag, etc.

Year Six

1. Define such objects as an orange, an envelope, a straw, etc.
2. Reproduce from memory a pattern of seven beads on a string.
3. Identify missing parts from a picture, such as a wheel off a wagon.
4. Give the examiner the correct number of blocks up to 10.
5. Identify the figure that is different from four other figures (four chairs and a table are shown).

Year Ten

1. Define such words as "roar," "muzzle," and "haste."
2. Read a standard paragraph and be able to recall the major ideas.
3. Name 28 words of any type in 1 minute.
4. Repeat correctly a sequence of six digits.

Adapted from Terman (1937).

The child who could answer the items on the scale for 10-year-olds was assigned a mental age of 10. To assess the child's brightness or dullness, however, the child's mental age had to be compared to his or her chronological age. For an 8-year-old to have a mental age of 10 means one thing; for a 12-year-old to have a mental age of 10 means something else. The first child seems obviously bright, while the second child seems dull.

The Concept of IQ

For Binet it was enough simply to compare the child's mental and chronological ages. His original concern was to be able to pick out, for special education classes, children who would not profit from the regular school curriculum. To Binet it seemed clear that a young child whose mental age lagged behind his or her chronological age by as much as 2 years was backward and needed special educational attention.

The concept of "intelligence quotient," or IQ, was introduced by a German psychologist, Wilhelm Stern. The IQ, as proposed by Stern, represented the *ratio* of a child's mental age to his or her chronological age. To be rid of fractions, the ratio was multiplied by 100. This meant that, for any chronological age, the average IQ was 100. Obviously, if a child's mental age was greater than the chronological age, the IQ would be above 100. If the mental age were lower than the chronological age, the IQ would be below 100. For a 10-year-old child with a mental age of 12, the formula for calculating IQ gives the following result:

$$IQ = \frac{\text{Mental Age}}{\text{Chronological Age}} \times 100 = \frac{12}{10} \times 100 = 120$$

If the same 10-year-old had a mental age of 8, the IQ would be calculated as 80.

The Stanford-Binet Test

The Stanford-Binet test, a translated and modified version of Binet's original scale, was introduced into the United States by Lewis Terman in 1916. The standardization of test items—determining what items corresponded to what mental ages—had of course to be revised, using a standardization sample of American children. A *standardization sample,* at least in theory, is representative of the entire population, and thus provides the norms, or standards of performance, to which the performance of any individual can then be compared. The Stanford-Binet test has been modified and restandardized on new samples of children in 1937, in 1960, and in 1972. Note that, with the passage of time, any intelligence test must be restandardized. When given the same test items that had been used in 1937, American children of 1972 performed at a considerably higher level than their 1937 predecessors. This might reflect changed schooling conditions, or the impact of exposure to television. Whatever the cause, it is important to understand that the IQ is a relative, not an absolute, measure. It expresses an individual's standing relative to the performance of some specific standardization sample. The same performance that was typical of 5-year-olds in 1937 is inferior to the performance of today's 5-year-olds; but the average IQ of 5-year-olds has, of course, remained at 100.

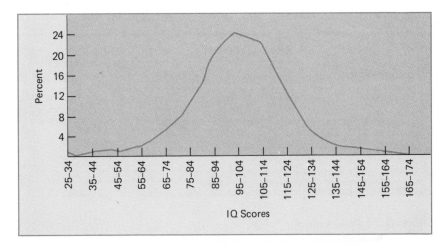

Figure 9-1

The approximate distribution of IQs in the population.

Though the Stanford-Binet test contains scales for adults, it is mostly used with children between 2 and 14 years of age. The basic Binet procedure of separate items for each mental age level has been kept, and the items are of much the same sort as those used by Binet. For each age level there is a scale consisting of six different items. To determine a child's IQ, the first step is to discover his or her *basal* mental age. That is the highest mental age level at which the child can pass all six items. When the basal age level has been discovered, the tester continues with items from the next highest mental age level. This process continues until a mental age level is reached at which the child can pass no items at all. The child's mental age is the basal age plus some credit for each item passed in scales above the basal age level. Since each mental age scale contains six items, each passed item above the basal mental age level is worth 2 more months of mental age.

With earlier versions of the Stanford-Binet test, a literal intelligence quotient was calculated, and the child's mental age was divided by the chrono-logical age. This is no longer done, however. The performance of the children in the standardization sample has now been scored in such a way that the average IQ at each age is 100, *and* the standard deviation at each age is 16. The standard deviation of 16 means that IQ scores are symmetrically distributed around an average of 100, with about 97.5 percent of all IQs falling between 68 and 132. The approximate distribution of IQs is shown in Figure 9-1.

Stability of IQ

Do children's IQs remain stable as they grow older? That is, will bright 5-year-olds (compared to other 5-year-olds) be equally bright when, seven years later, they are compared to 12-year-olds? The answer is that they are quite likely to remain relatively bright, but that there are many individual exceptions.

We would not, of course, expect individuals' measured IQs to remain exactly the same each time they are tested; if nothing else, there is some error of measurement involved in mental testing, as there is in all forms of measure-ment. The *reliability* of the Stanford-Binet is such that we should not be

Table 9–2: Correlations among IQ Scores at Different Ages.

| | Retest Age (Years) | | | | |
Test Age (Years)	5	7	10	14	18
2	.32	.46	.37	.28	.31
5		.73	.71	.61	.56
7			.77	.75	.71
10				.86	.73
14					.76

From Honzik, Macfarlane, and Allen (1948).

surprised if a child's measured IQ changes by as much as 10 points from week to week. A perfectly reliable test would be one which, when it was given to the same individuals on two separate occasions, produced exactly the same scores each time. In such a test, the agreement between the two sets of scores would be expressed as a *correlation coefficient.* In a perfectly reliable test the correlation coefficient would be 1.00; if there were no relation or agreement between the scores, the correlation coefficient would be .00. There is a clear and obvious tendency for IQs taken early in childhood to be highly correlated with IQs taken in later childhood, or in adulthood. The correlations in IQ scores of the same individuals tested at different ages are illustrated in Table 9-2. The IQ at any age is obviously correlated with the IQ at any other age; but it is also the case (sensibly enough) that the correlations are smaller when many years separate the two tests.

The fact that, for the most part, IQ remains relatively stable throughout life should not obscure the equally obvious fact that many dramatic changes in IQ—clearly involving more than measurement error—do take place. Thus, for example, Honzik and her colleagues (1948) tested a group of children repeatedly between the ages of 2 and 18, and reported that 37 percent of the subjects showed IQ differences of at least 20 points between two different testings. Figure 9-2 illustrates two examples of IQs changing progressively, and dramatically, over time. These examples should serve as a caution against premature labeling and tracking of a child with a low (or high) IQ. There are clearly individual cases in which IQ does change very markedly.

The Test Defines Intelligence

For practical purposes, what psychologists mean by the word "intelligence" has been pretty well defined by the content of the Stanford-Binet and other widely used intelligence tests. In other words, you are an intelligent person if you can do well on the sorts of questions asked by intelligence tests. This may seem to be an empty statement, but it is not entirely so. The validity of the test items was established by the fact that children who did well on the test also did well in their school subjects. *Validity* is the degree to which scores on a test correlate with some criterion independent of the test itself—in this case, school grades. To Binet, it was essential that teachers' judgments of the brightness or dullness of students should correspond to the same students'

Figure 9-2

The changes in IQ over time of two different children, who were tested repeatedly from age 2 to age 18. (Honzik, Macfarlane, and Allen, 1948)

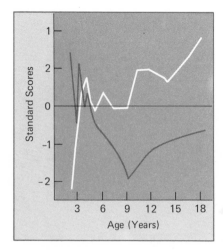

scores on his test. This was in fact found to be the case. Ever since Binet's time, revised or new tests of intelligence have been validated by their correlation with school grades—or by their correlation with Binet's test. Thus it is no accident that a child's IQ score can be used to predict his or her performance in school. The precise magnitude of the correlation varies with a number of conditions, but as a general rule IQ correlates in the neighborhood of .40 to .60 with school grades. That is a substantial, but very far from perfect, correlation. That is, other things besides IQ also determine school grades.

The fact that IQ tests have been validated against performance in school has an interesting consequence. We are defining as "intelligence" precisely those skills that are involved in the learning of academic subjects in school. If the curriculum of the Paris school system had been vastly different from what it in fact was in 1904, today's intelligence tests might contain very different kinds of items. That form of nimble-wittedness involved in "street smarts"—a smartness highly adaptive for modern urban street life—seems scarcely represented in IQ tests.

The Test as Diagnostic Instrument

Though IQ scores can be used to predict school performance, Binet had much more than that in mind. He thought of the test as a diagnostic instrument. The test was to be used to help identify those children who would do very poorly in school. The problem with those children, Binet believed, was that their intelligence had not yet been developed enough. The task of the educator, once the test had located such backward children, was to *develop and increase* their intelligence by special educational procedures. Thus Binet definitely did not think of the test as measuring some fixed or unchangeable quantity. He argued that the right instruction—a form of "mental orthopedics"—could increase the intelligence of lagging children. This optimistic attitude about test scores and the possibility of training children to become more intelligent has not been very common among testers who followed Binet. To the degree that IQ tests serve a diagnostic purpose, they are usually used to help assign children to classes thought right for their measured level of intelligence. The basic assumption is made that the IQ will remain constant, and that classroom experience will neither increase nor decrease the IQ.

Achievement, Aptitude, and Capacity

We live in a society that uses many different kinds of tests for many different purposes. It is important to understand both the purpose of a particular test and the assumptions that underlie its use. There are, at one extreme, *achievement tests*. Their purpose is to measure, as accurately as possible, how much you have learned before taking the test. Thus, when you finish a college course, you usually take an exam. The purpose of the exam is to assess how much of the course content you have learned. Though it is possible that students with high IQs may receive higher exam grades, they receive no special credit for having a high IQ. The slower, plodding student who works hard may receive a higher grade than the brilliant student who did not study. This is wholly appropriate, since the only purpose of the exam, as an achievement test, is to measure how much of the tested material has in fact been learned.

There are other occasions, however, when tests are used to *predict* some future performance. For example, the military wants to predict the likelihood that a given candidate for aircraft pilot training will successfully complete the complicated and expensive course of training. To fly a plane well requires, among other things, good physical coordination and a good sense of mechanical matters. Thus, all candidates for pilot training are normally given a battery of *aptitude tests*, including tests of mechanical aptitude and of eye-hand coordination, which will be used to predict how well they'll do in the training program. People with poor scores on such tests tend to fail pilot training.

The distinction between an achievement test and an aptitude test thus depends on the purpose to which the test is put. It is difficult, if not impossible, to distinguish between the two types of tests on other grounds. The very same item can be—and often is—included in both achievement and aptitude tests. Think back to the entrance examination you took before being accepted by your college. The college thought of that exam as an aptitude test, from which they predicted that you would do well in college. That is, your "scholastic aptitude" was found to be high. The questions you answered, however, were very similar to questions that you had earlier answered in high school course examinations. The same questions were then regarded as part of an achievement test. When you did poorly on such an achievement test in high school, you might have argued that the test did not reflect your *aptitude*—only the fact that you had not studied enough for it. Those who do poorly on a test of scholastic aptitude can just as reasonably argue that the test reflects nothing more than their failure to study enough—but in this instance, the failure to study would have occurred over a long time span. The failure to have studied, it should be obvious, does not necessarily mean that person *could* not have mastered the material on the aptitude test.

People—including psychologists—often make the mistake of thinking that an aptitude test can somehow measure a person's *capacity* to learn. The assumption is made that everyone has some fixed limit to his or her learning ability, and that that limit is at least partly determined by heredity. That may be a plausible assumption, but it is clearly wrong to believe that any test can directly measure a person's hereditary potential or capacity. The results of *all* tests necessarily depend upon a person's past experiences, present motivation, and many other factors. There is not and cannot be any direct test of "innate intelligence." These points have been made clearly by a distinguished committee of mental test specialists appointed by the American Psychological Association (Cleary et al., 1975). These authorities were clear in pointing out that the assumption that all members of our society had had an "equal opportunity" to learn the materials presented in IQ tests was not correct. Of course, it is possible to argue that *most* people have had *almost* equal opportunities, and that tests are therefore more or less *approximate* indicators of mental capacity. When language is this imprecise, however, the potential for disagreement and controversy is obvious.

Intelligence and Age

It is obvious that, throughout childhood, intellectual capability continues to increase with age. For that reason, different kinds of items must be introduced

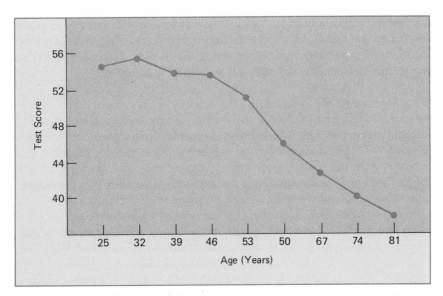

Figure 9-3

The graph shows the results of a longitu-dinal study in which the same subjects were tested from the age of 25 on. The results show a decline in mental test scores with age. (Schaie, Labouvie, and Buech, 1973)

into the scales that are used to measure the IQs of older children. The items for older children are, of course, more complex and difficult. What, however, happens to intellectual capability beyond childhood, as people pass through adulthood and old age?

To answer this question, it is necessary to compare the performances of adults of differing ages when tested with the same material. The early studies of intelligence and age (for example, Jones and Conrad, 1933) suggested that a gradual decline in intelligence began in the early twenties, and that the average decline in intellectual powers by the age of 60 was very large. We now know, however, that at least a good part of this apparent decline was an effect produced by *cross-sectional* studies of the aging process. Within a study that is cross-sectional in design, different individuals are tested at different ages. Thus, for example, we might test some 20-year-olds, some 40-year-olds, and some 60-year-olds, all on the same day. When the performances of older and younger subjects are compared, we not only observe the effects of biological age, we are also comparing groups of subjects born at different times and exposed to differing educational practices and cultural conditions. The more satisfactory way of studying the effects of age is in *longitudinal* studies. These studies continually test the *same* subjects as they grow older. The difficulty with longitudinal studies is that, for obvious reasons, they take a very long time to carry out. Figure 9-3 summarizes the results of one such study. The best data now available suggest that performance on IQ test material may increase until about the age of 25, then hold relatively steady until about 40. From about 40 on there appears to be some decline, and a sharper decline sets in at about age 60 (Schaie, Labouvie, and Buech, 1973). The relevant data from both longitudinal and cross-sectional studies have been discussed in detail by Botwinick (1977).

These trends, however, are true only of average scores. There is evidence to indicate that highly educated people, who tend to keep up intellectual interests and activities throughout life, show very little decline. There is also evidence that not all mental abilities are equally likely to decline with age. For example, vocabulary and verbal skills may even improve with age, while skills involving spatial visualization and deductive reasoning may decline. In general, tasks that require quick responding are especially vulnerable to aging.

The Mentally Retarded

The original purpose of Binet's test was to identify backward students. The test, and others based on it, is still used in an effort to diagnose the "mentally retarded." To be so diagnosed, an IQ below 70 is usually regarded as a necessary—but not sufficient—condition. That is, it is only when a low IQ is coupled with inadequate social and occupational adjustment that the label of retardation is correctly applied. There are many low-IQ children who appear definitely retarded in the classroom, but not on the playground or in their home environments. These children usually, after leaving school, are able to find productive employment and to function successfully and independently. They merge imperceptibly into the rest of the normal population.

Typically, distinctions are made among various degrees of mental retardation. Mild retardation, with IQs ranging from about 55 to 69, occurs in about 2 percent of the population; among such people, prospects for successful adaptation to independent adult life are reasonably good. Moderate retardation, with IQs between 40 and 54, occurs in about .1 percent of the population. Severe retardation—with IQs below 40—is much rarer, occurring in some .003 percent of the population. The severely retarded usually need institutional care throughout their lives. With the right training they can be taught many self-help skills, and the quality of their lives can be improved. We do not know any way of making the severely retarded become much more normal in their level of intellectual functioning.

For most mentally retarded people, no clear physical cause can be found. This type of relatively mild retardation is often called "familial-cultural." Those so diagnosed are generally born to parents with low IQs and have been reared in depressed and deprived conditions. There are other cases of retardation—often very severe—that are clearly related to catastrophic biological accidents of some kind, or to known genetic defects. For example, prenatal infection of the mother, or a lack of adequate oxygen during birth, may result in brain damage to the fetus, producing severe retardation. The usually severe retardation known as Down's syndrome (once called "mongolism") is known to be caused by the presence of an extra 47th chromosome in the cells of the affected child. The extra chromosome produces a number of characteristic physical abnormalities, as well as mental retardation. The risk of having a child with Down's syndrome is very much higher among mothers in their 40s than among younger mothers.

Phenylketonuria (PKU) is a rare form of retardation, known to depend on the inheritance of a particular recessive gene. It was first noted in 1934 that a few retarded children, some of whom were siblings, excreted phenylpyruvic acid in their urine. We now know that the mental retardation of these children was in some way produced by the overaccumulation of that amino acid in their bodies. Thus, a defect in metabolism caused by inheritance of a particular gene must ultimately injure the central nervous system in such a way as to

This child was born with Down's syndrome, which is caused by the presence of an extra, 47th chromosome in the cells. This extra chromosome produces a number of physical abnormalities, as well as mental retardation.

produce this form of mental retardation. Happily, a successful treatment for this genetic defect is available. The child must be fed a diet very low in phenylalanine. The dietary treatment, if begun early enough, prevents the accumulation of the responsible amino acid, and the child develops with a normal IQ. PKU, it must be stressed, is a rare form of retardation. There are no similarly successful treatments—nor such clearly understood causes—for most forms of retardation.

Children with High IQs

Terman, in 1925, began to study a large group of California school children with very high IQs, averaging about 150. The original children, numbering over 1,000, have been followed through life for more than 50 years. The project was often referred to by Terman as a study of "genius," but "children with high IQs" seems to be a more accurate description. These children, selected at a young age because of outstandingly high IQs, for the most part went on to live productive and "successful" lives. They earned many college and advanced degrees, and many became doctors, lawyers, professors, or novelists. They wrote many books and scientific papers. They earned good incomes. They weighed more at birth than the average infant, and they were taller and healthier than most children throughout childhood. They seemed as adults to be socially well-adjusted members of their communities, and to be content with the way they had lived their lives.

These findings clearly disprove the notion that high-IQ children are in some way unbalanced or "freakish." They also indicate that, if all we know about a school child is that he or she has a very high IQ, it is a good bet that he or she will go on to lead the kind of "successful" life described above—though, it should be said, not *all* of Terman's subjects succeeded. There is no indication, however, that these very high-IQ children produced works of genuinely creative genius. There is really no proof, either, that their successes had been *caused* by their very high IQs. Almost all of Terman's subjects had been born into professional and well-to-do families. This kind of family background might well be responsible for their good childhood health and for much of their adult success—quite apart from their high IQs. We do not know, for example, whether the lower-IQ sisters and brothers of Terman's selected subjects were any less successful than the subjects themselves. Though Terman would doubtless have expected such a difference, we do not in fact have the necessary data.

Types of Intelligence Tests

Individual vs. Group Tests

The benchmark against which more recently developed IQ tests have been measured is the Stanford-Binet test. When new tests are proposed, their validity as IQ tests is often demonstrated by showing that they are highly correlated with Stanford-Binet scores. The Stanford-Binet test does have scales that can be

The testing kit for the Wechsler Intelligence Scale for Children is shown in the photo on the left. On the right, a child is working on the Object Assembly portion of the test. She has before her pieces with part of a picture on each and must put them together to form an object (in this case, a horse).

used with adults, but it was basically designed to test children. To measure adults, a number of awkward assumptions had to be made; for instance, by assuming that mental growth stopped at age 16, and by assigning that "chronological age" to all adults, approximate "IQs"could be calculated.

The measurement of adult IQ was greatly advanced by the development of the Wechsler Adult Intelligence Scale (WAIS). First presented in 1939, this test was most recently revised in 1955 (but a new, restandardized WAIS is expected in 1981). The success of his adult scale prompted Wechsler to develop the Wechsler Intelligence Scale for Children (WISC-R), revised in 1974, and designed for children aged 6–16. Most recently, for even younger children, the Wechsler Preschool and Primary Scale of Intelligence has been presented.

The various Wechsler scales, although designed for different age groups, are very much alike in their basic form and types of content. They are all substantially correlated with the Stanford-Binet, with which they have much in common—but from which they differ in some important ways. The outstanding similarity is that both the Stanford-Binet and Wechsler tests are designed to be administered by a trained examiner to one person at a time. The examiner must use training and judgment in deciding whether or not the answer to a given item is correct. The one-on-one testing session takes about an hour in each case, and a skilled examiner can note not only the child's answers but also his or her mannerisms, emotional state, cooperativeness, and so on.

The Wechsler scales were the first to use the concept of a *deviation IQ*. The decision was made that the average test score for people of any age should be 100, and that the standard deviation of these IQs should be 15 at every age. This result is accomplished by statistical adjustment of the actual raw scores obtained in the standardization samples among people of different ages. That is, one's IQ is determined by comparing one's performance to that of people one's own age in the standardization sample for the test. To have a Wechsler IQ of 130 means that you have done better on the test than about 97.5 percent of people *your age* in the standardization sample. Thus, if you have recently taken the WAIS, you are being compared to a standardization sample studied in 1955. The deviation IQ procedure also means that if you are 18 years old, and your 65-year-old grandparent has done just a little worse than you in answering the test questions, your grandparent will have a considerably higher IQ than you. That is so because, in the standardization sample, the average 65-year-old could answer fewer questions than the average 18-year-old.

The Wechsler scales also differ from the Stanford-Binet by breaking down the total IQ into two separate components—a verbal IQ and a performance IQ. The Stanford-Binet contains many different kinds of testing material mixed together, and provides a single "global" IQ score. The WAIS, however, separates its material into 11 different subscales, which are shown in Table 9-3. The first six scales together are combined to give a verbal IQ, while the last five scales give a performance IQ. The total IQ is basically the average of the two. The verbal and performance IQs are substantially correlated with each other, and each is correlated with the Stanford-Binet IQ—the verbal IQ somewhat more so. There are individual cases, however, in which the verbal and performance IQs are very different. This can often be informative, and might indicate language difficulty, or reading or perceptual disabilities.

Group tests of intelligence sacrifice the detail and the kinds of intimate personal knowledge available from an individual testing session, but they are obviously necessary if very large groups of people are to be examined. The first impetus for group tests came at the time of World War I, when the United States

Table 9–3: Sample Questions from the Wechsler Adult Intelligence Scale.

Verbal Scale	
Information	What is steam made of? What is pepper?
Comprehension	Why is copper often used in electrical wires? Why do some people save sales receipts?
Arithmetic	It takes three people nine days to paint a house. How many people would it take to do it in three days? An automobile goes 25 miles in 45 minutes. How far would it go in 20 minutes?
Digit Repetition	Repeat the following numbers in order: 1,3,7,2,5,4 Repeat the following numbers in reverse order: 5,8,2,4,9,6
Similarities	In what way are a circle and a triangle alike? In what way are an egg and a seed alike?
Vocabulary	What is a hippopotamus? What does "resemble" mean?

Performance Scale	
Picture Arrangement	A story is told in three or more cartoon panels placed in the incorrect order; put them together to tell the story.
Picture Completion	Point out what's missing from each picture.
Block Design	After looking at a pattern or design, try to arrange small cubes in the same pattern.
Object Assembly	Given pieces with part of a picture on each, put them together to form such objects as a hand or a profile.
Digit Symbol	Learn a different symbol for each number and then fill in the blank under the number with the correct symbol. (This test is timed.)

Army decided to test draftees. Two group tests—the Alpha and the Beta—were quickly developed; sample items from each are given in Figure 9-4. Typically, group tests are administered at the same time to large numbers of people, with paper, pencil, and multiple-choice answer blanks. Though some of the items included in the Alpha test seem amusing and unfair today, the basic form of the Alpha test is very similar to that of many verbal paper-and-pencil tests in use today. The Army General Classification Test of World War II and its more recent replacements are more sophisticated than the old Alpha, as are most of the group test now used in school systems and in industry. The Beta test of World War I is rather unusual. The test was designed as a *performance* test. To

Figure 9-4

Specimen items from the Army Alpha and Beta Tests of World War I.

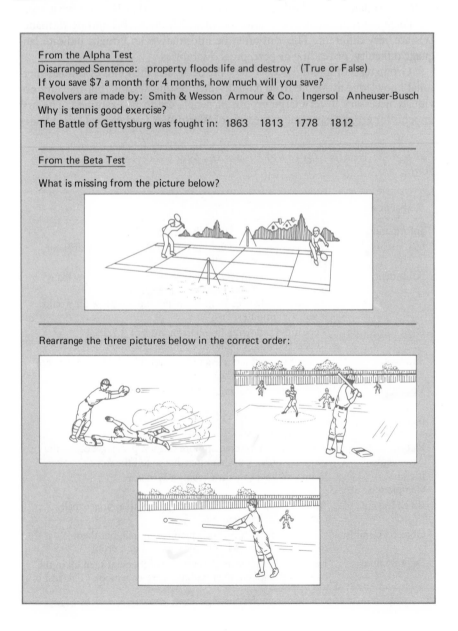

From the Alpha Test

Disarranged Sentence: property floods life and destroy   (True or False)

If you save $7 a month for 4 months, how much will you save?

Revolvers are made by: Smith & Wesson Armour & Co. Ingersol Anheuser-Busch

Why is tennis good exercise?

The Battle of Gettysburg was fought in: 1863   1813   1778   1812

From the Beta Test

What is missing from the picture below?

Rearrange the three pictures below in the correct order:

measure accurately the IQs of illiterate or foreign-born draftees, the test had to be "nonverbal"—it couldn't depend on reading skill, or familiarity with the English language. The kinds of material shown in Figure 9-4 were written with that aim in mind. The test, however, had to be given to large groups of men. The instructions were thus given in "pantomime." Readers may decide for themselves whether this performance test fairly measured the IQs of the foreign-born and the illiterate.

Performance Tests and "Culture Fairness"

To say that one has measured "intelligence," rather than what a person happens to have learned, it is necessary that the test be fair in allowing the testees to *use* their intelligence. It is obvious that much verbal material is highly specialized knowledge, not available to all people. Thus, an item such as "Wundt is to Wertheimer as Watson is to ____?" might be a fair test of the intelligence of someone who has studied psychology, but clearly not for anybody else. The item "Sunday is to Monday as January is to ____?" would probably be regarded as fair by most test-makers, at least for people who speak English. They assume that everyone has been exposed over and over to the names and sequences of the days and the months. That is, if material is "equally" familiar to everyone, it is fair game for an IQ test. The other approach to fairness, in theory, is to use material with which everybody is equally *un*familiar; for example, the testee may be asked to see relationships among groups of geometric forms.

Performance tests of IQ try to avoid some of the more obvious biases of verbal materials by concentrating on materials such as making designs from blocks, completing incomplete drawings, fitting the right peg into the right hole, seeing relations among geometric forms, etc. Cattell (1949) called his version of such a test "culture free." Perhaps the most widely used such test is Raven's Progressive Matrices (1947), which depends entirely on seeing relations among geometric figures. To call any test "culture free" is obviously an exaggeration. To begin with, the instructions must be communicated to the testee in some way. Further, members of some cultures find the very idea of being tested strange or offensive. The best that might be hoped for is that some tests might be relatively more "culture fair" than others. The differences among human cultures, however, are enormous, complex, and subtle. We cannot be sure that by reducing the verbal content of a test we are making it fair to all cultures and subcultures. The attempt to develop "culture-fair" tests seems on the whole to have been disappointing. Within the United States, at least, results obtained with them have not differed greatly from those obtained with more traditional tests. Perhaps, in view of the substantial correlation between the verbal and performance scales in Wechsler's tests, this is not at all surprising.

Factorially Designed Tests

Though Wechsler did split the total IQ into verbal and performance IQs, he agreed entirely with Binet in stressing the importance of "general intelligence." This was wholly in keeping with the views of a pioneering English psychologist, Charles Spearman. Test items, in Spearman's view, all measured a general mental capacity, labelled *g*. They did so, however, with different degrees of purity.

That was because all items also measured some *specific* ability (*s*), and different items measured different specific abilities in different amounts. When all the items were combined into a single test of general intelligence, the various specific abilities contained in the many different items tended to cancel one another out. The result, assuming the right mixture of different kinds of specific items, was a fair measure of general intelligence.

This might be clearer if you think of it in terms of athletic ability instead of intelligence. Some people seem to be good at all athletic skills, and some seem to be poor at them all, even after serious effort. That is, all sports tap some abilities in common. However, there are also some who are good at one sport but not at others. It would be hard to imagine Nadia Comenici playing center in the NBA, and it would be hard to imagine Wilt Chamberlain on the balance beam. The same holds true for intelligence.

Spearman's "two-factor" theory of test items was supported by his work with the mathematical procedure of *factor analysis*. This procedure, by examining the intercorrelations among large numbers of items and tests, attempts to "extract out" what all the items have in common. Factor analysis is discussed in more detail in Chapter 14.

Within the United States, Louis Thurstone (1938) challenged Spearman's views. Thurstone argued that a single IQ score was misleading, often covering over sharp differences—within the same individual—in several different mental abilities. For example, people skilled in the use of words might be backward in the use of numbers, and it is better to know this than to state (accurately) that they have an average IQ on a test containing many kinds of items. Thurstone, by analyzing the intercorrelations among a large number of different tests given to the same people, felt that he had discovered at least seven independent or "pure" factors of mental ability. Thus he developed, and marketed, seven separate subtests. The seven factors, each with its own test, were: verbal comprehension, word fluency, number, space, memory, perceptual speed, and reasoning.

There is nothing sacred about Thurstone's seven factors. Had he done his work in factor analysis using other kinds of items, or other subjects, he would no doubt have discovered somewhat different factors. Further, the seven factors reported by Thurstone are *not* independent of one another. That is, people high on one factor tend to be high on all other factors as well, to a significant degree. This intercorrelation among the factors, of course, brings us back to Spearman, *g*, and the idea of general intelligence. The other tack, however, has been taken by a distinguished American factor analyst, J. P. Guilford. The "structure of intellect" theory presented by Guilford (1967) states that there are no fewer than 120 factors of intelligence, each representing a different intellectual ability. The idea of sitting still while taking 120 tests will not appeal to many!

Though it seems clear that in many instances a "profile" or breakdown of different mental skills should be more informative than a single number representing IQ, the fact is that tests measuring general IQ (sometimes divided into verbal vs. performance or verbal vs. quantitative parts) are still much more commonly used. Probably that is because the general IQ tests, lumping together many different skills, do a reasonable job of predicting average school performance. There is no evidence that the factorially designed tests do any better, or even as well.

Tests of Divergent Thinking

The search by Guilford for 120 separate factors of mental ability encouraged him and his followers to develop radically different kinds of mental tests. Perhaps the most interesting of them are based on the distinction between *convergent* and *divergent* thinking. With many problems—as with most problems in IQ tests—the solution depends on logically "narrowing down" or converging on the one correct answer. With other problems, the solution depends on being able to let one's thoughts "roam" creatively along different or divergent pathways, resulting in original and surprising ideas—*not* arriving at one predetermined answer. To test divergent thinking ability—which has sometimes been identified with creativity—Guilford and Hoepfner (1971) have used such items as: "Name as many uses as you can think of for a toothpick," or "Imagine all of the things that might possibly happen if all national and local laws were suddenly abolished." To do well on such a test the subject must respond not with one correct answer but with many novel ideas.

Though a number of tests of divergent thinking have been developed, it has turned out that, at least to a considerable degree, scores on such tests are correlated with scores on "convergent" IQ tests. This seems to be mostly because people with low IQ scores tend also to have low divergent thinking or "creativity" scores. Within groups with high traditional IQs, however, there is a lot of variation in divergent thinking ability. There are many high-IQ people who are quite poor at divergent thinking.

We do not know to what degree, if any, people with high scores on divergent thinking tests are in fact creative in real life. There are no doubt many factors involved in real-life creativity that are not captured by simple divergent thinking tests. We do know that divergent thinking scores are not as correlated with school grades as IQ is. The relations between IQ, genuinely creative thinking, school grades, and accomplishment are obviously complex. Thus, for example, Albert Einstein had an indifferent school career, and James Watson, who solved the riddle of the DNA molecule, had an unspectacular IQ of 115. There are school counselors, however, who advise students not to attempt college unless they have an IQ of 120! The prediction from IQ or from school grades to actual accomplishment clearly cannot be made with anything like certainty.

Nature, Nurture, and Test Scores

The Concept of Heritability

There are some people with high IQs, many people with average IQs, and some people with low IQs. That is to say, there is much variation among people in IQ test scores. What causes these differences among people? To what extent are they produced by the different genes that people inherit? To what extent are they produced by the different environments that people experience as they grow up? These questions, having to do with the relative importance of nature and of nurture, have given rise to much controversy—and not a little passion—since the birth of IQ testing.

Everyone agrees, of course, that human genes are a necessary precondition for the development of human intelligence and of IQ. There is no environment that can raise the intellectual level of a fish, a bird, or a monkey to that of a normal human being. Everyone also agrees that exposure to human language and society is an absolute necessity for the development of those skills measured by IQ tests. Without this, having normal human genes alone cannot result in a normal IQ score. Thus it is obviously correct to state that *both* genes *and* environment are inextricably involved in the development of IQ—or, for that matter, the development of any other trait.

The controversy has to do with the differences in IQ among normal human beings, all of them possessing normal sets of human genes. There are, within normal limits, great differences in the sets of genes that all of us inherit from our parents. The question is, are these undoubted differences in our genes largely, moderately, or only slightly related to the differences among us in IQ test scores?

The concept of the *heritability ratio* is one effort to give a quantitative answer to this question. In theory, the heritability of IQ can be estimated by comparing the IQ correlations of various types of biological relatives. For example, we know that parents and children have 50 percent of their genes in common. Grandparents and grandchildren have only 25 percent of their genes in common. Put very simply, if the heritability of IQ were very high, we would expect the IQ correlation between parent and child to be about .50, and that between grandparent and grandchild to be about .25. The actual procedures used in calculating heritability are quite complex, but the basic idea is to see how closely the resemblance in IQ of relatives corresponds to their resemblance in genetic makeup (that is, the proportion of genes they have in common).

Arthur Jensen, in an influential 1969 article, summarized a number of studies of IQ correlations among relatives within the white population. The data, Jensen argued, indicated that the heritability of IQ among whites was about .80. That figure, if correct, would indicate that 80 percent of the variance in IQ among individuals is due to the fact that they have different genes. The *variance*, as a statistical measure, is simply the square of the standard deviation; the variance in IQ, thus, is 225—the square of the standard deviation of 15. Thus, as matters now stand, about 95 percent of whites have IQs between 70 and 130. To say that the heritability of IQ is .80 is to assert that if all whites were to be brought up in the *same* (average) environment, the variance in IQ would then be .80 times 225, or 180. That is, the standard deviation of IQ would be 13.4, so that 95 percent of IQ scores would fall between about 73 and 127. This large remaining variation in IQ scores would be *entirely* the product of genetic differences among people since, in our hypothetical example, all individuals had been reared in the same environment. The same kinds of calculations indicate that if the heritability of IQ were .20, rearing all individuals in the same average environment should compress the range of IQs so that 95 percent of all scores would fall between 87 and 113.

We must note, however, that there are very great difficulties involved in calculating the heritability of a human trait. The basic problem is that close biological relatives not only have many genes in common, they also tend to have highly similar environments. The more closely related people are biologically, the more similar their environments are likely to have been. This *covariance* of genes and environment, together with other difficulties, has convinced at least some authorities (Feldman and Lewontin, 1975; Layzer, 1974) that accurate or meaningful heritability estimates cannot be made for human populations. (With animals or plants, no such problem exists. The breeding of individual plants or animals can be controlled, and offspring can be assigned at random to strictly controlled environments.)

The paragraphs that follow will examine the data from which Jensen and many others have tried to calculate the heritability of IQ. We shall not be concerned, however, with attempting to estimate a precise heritability ratio. We shall ask—more modestly, but more realistically—do the available data suggest that genetic differences are responsible for a large, moderate, or small proportion of the differences in IQ among people? These terms may seem very imprecise, but—as we shall see—so are the available data. Throughout our examination of the relevant research studies, we shall try to focus on a critical question: Does this study effectively separate the effects of heredity from those of environment? To the extent that genes and environment are allowed to covary in any study, a meaningful answer about the relative importance of each cannot be obtained.

Genetic Relatedness and IQ

The simplest way—in theory, at least—of studying the genetic basis of IQ is to study identical twins who have been brought up apart from each other. Pairs of identical twins are the only individuals in the world whose genes are entirely the same. Thus it is obvious that if IQ is largely determined by inheritance, pairs of identical twins ought to resemble each other greatly in IQ scores. This should be true even if the twins have been reared in entirely different environments. Most twin pairs, of course, grow up in the same household and share very similar environments. There are, however, a few rare cases of identical twins who have been separated very early in life and brought up in different families. Those rare cases—separated identical twins—make up a kind of natural experiment on heredity and environment. The basic logic is simple. Two separated identical twins have their heredity in common, but not their environments. Thus, if their IQs are very similar, that must be due to the one factor they have in common—their heredity.

STUDIES OF SEPARATED IDENTICAL TWINS.   There have been, for obvious reasons, few studies of separated twins. Four investigators, however, have gathered large enough samples to make some statistical analysis possible. The largest and apparently most impressive study was made in England by the late Sir Cyril Burt (1966). The Burt study, said to be based on 53 pairs of separated twins, reported a very high IQ correlation between twins. Further, Burt indicated that there was no correlation at all in the socioeconomic status levels of the households in which the separated twins had been reared. Twins reared in households with vastly different socioeconomic levels resembled each other greatly in IQ—just as did twins reared in very similar households. Taken at face value, Burt's study appeared to provide very strong evidence for an overwhelming genetic effect on IQ. However, it has recently become clear that Burt's study cannot be taken at face value. There is clear evidence that much of Burt's

APPLICATION
Cyril Burt: Science, Fraud, and Policy

The late Sir Cyril Burt (1883–1971) was doubtless England's most distinguished psychologist—knighted by his monarch, and given a medal by the American Psychological Association. Burt served for many years as a school psychologist of the London County Council. He was the first person in the English-speaking world to hold such a position. Throughout his long life, Burt conducted research on the inheritance of mental ability. He reported that he had managed to locate 53 pairs of separated identical twins. With the assistance of two collaborators, J. Conway and Margaret Howard, the twins had been IQ tested. Though the twins were said to have been reared in wholly unrelated environments, they resembled one another dramatically in IQ. Burt was also the only investigator who was able to test,

in the same population, large numbers of pairs of biological relatives of every sort—grandparents and grandchildren, second cousins, uncles and nieces, etc. The IQ correlations that Burt reported for various kinds of relatives corresponded with remarkable precision to the values one would expect if IQ were almost entirely determined by the genes. Professor Arthur Jensen (1972) clearly spoke for many when he wrote that Burt's work was "the most satisfactory attempt" to estimate the heritability of IQ; and that Burt's "larger, more representative samples than any other investigator had ever assembled" would "secure Burt's place in the history of science."

Things began to unravel when it was first pointed out (Kamin, 1973) that in later published pa-

pers, as the size of Burt's twin samples gradually increased, the IQ correlations remained identical to the third decimal place! That is so unlikely an outcome as to be unbelievable. There were many other mutual contradictions and inconsistencies revealed by cross-checking of Burt's many published papers. There was also a disturbing ambiguity in Burt's research reports—no details were given about what IQ tests had been used, or when or where the testing had been carried out. By 1974, Jensen was ready to agree that Burt's data were "useless for hypothesis testing." But Jensen maintained that Burt had been merely careless, not fraudulent—and that data other than Burt's ("the most satisfactory") also supported the idea of a high heritability of IQ.

In 1976 Oliver Gillie, a re-

published work was fraudulent, and much of his data invented. Psychologists are now unanimous—regardless of their views about heredity and environment—in rejecting Burt's suspect data.

The second largest study was also done in England by Shields (1962), who managed to test 40 pairs of separated twins. The IQ correlation obtained by Shields was .77—not as high as Burt's, but still very substantial. The difficulty, however, is that in the Shields study most of the twins seem to have been reared in quite similar environments. There were some who were not separated at all until they were 7 or 8 years old, and 27 of the 40 pairs were actually brought up in related branches of the same family. The twins had usually been born into poor families, and the mother had felt unable to take on the burden of two more infants at the same time. The most common single pattern was for the mother to keep one child and to give the other to her sister (or to the father's sister) to rear. This, of course, tended to result in the "separated" twins having similar environments. Thus, Shields says of one pair: "The paternal aunts decided to take one twin each, and they have brought them up amicably, living next-door to one another in the same Midlands colliery village. . . . They are constantly in and out of each other's houses." This kind of close contact and highly similar environment also occurred even when the twins were brought up by unrelated families. Thus, Shields writes of another pair: "Brought up within a few hundred yards of one another. . . . Told they were twins after girls discovered it for

porter for the *London Sunday Times,* charged in a front-page article that Burt had perpetrated the most sensational scientific fraud of the century. Burt's "collaborators" and "coauthors"—J. Conway, Margaret Howard, and others—appeared never to have existed. Testimony was available that Burt himself had written papers using their names, and that at the least they were unknown to anybody, and clearly not in England, during the time when they were supposedly testing twins! This frank labeling of Burt as a fraud was attacked by some IQ testing authorities as "unfounded defamation" (Jensen, 1976) and "McCarthyism . . . character assassination" (Eysenck, 1977). The argument about whether Burt was careless or a fraud has now been put to rest. The authorized Burt biography by Leslie Hearnshaw has now appeared (1979). With Burt's private papers and documents available to him, Hearnshaw was reluctantly forced to conclude that at least much of Burt's data was the result of systematic fraud.

With the disappearance of Burt's "data," the *least* that can be said is that the case for substantial heritability of IQ has been weakened. The unhappy Burt story, moreover, provokes some troublesome thoughts. *Why* did Burt invent false data? Throughout his life, Burt was interested in—and had great influence upon—educational policy in England. He argued that the "eleven-plus exam"—a form of IQ test given at age 11—should be given to all school children, and that the result of that exam was a measure of the "innate intelligence" of the child. Thus, in Burt's view, it was proper to use this test result as the basis for "streaming" children, irreversibly, into one of three educational channels. There was only one track—requiring a very high test score—that led on to university training. With Burt's great influence, this policy was in fact adopted. Further, Burt argued (1943) that limited educational resources in the school system should go primarily to the "gifted." The majority were genetically too inferior to profit much from academic training. The "data" provided by Burt were used by him to support his policy recommendations.

Perhaps more disturbing than the fact that a distinguished psychologist could lie—there have been a few celebrated frauds in almost all the sciences—is the fact that so many accepted Burt's data, uncritically, at face value. This must mean that preconceived ideas about what is true prevent scientists in at least some areas from exercising their normal critical judgments. With hindsight, the embarrassing flaws and discrepancies in Burt's published work are painfully obvious. That flawed and fraudulent work, however, was communicated to a whole generation of students of psychology, education, and genetics as serious science.

themselves, having gravitated to one another at school at the age of 5 . . . they were never apart, wanted to sit at the same desk . . ."

For the 27 Shields pairs reared in related branches of the same family, the IQ correlation was .83. For the 13 pairs reared in unrelated families, the correlation was a significantly lower .51. That is clear evidence that "separated" identical twins resemble each other more if the environments in which they have been reared are similar. We cannot deduce what the IQ correlation would be if—as Burt falsely claimed—there were *no* systematic similarities in the environments of separated pairs. The correlation, if such an ideal experiment could in fact be performed, might conceivably be .00, though few psychologists would expect this outcome. There is some reason to suppose that the correlation might be lower than the .51 observed among the Shields pairs reared by unrelated families. We have seen that even among these pairs there were substantial similarities in environment.

The two remaining studies reported results basically similar to those of Shields. The 19 pairs studied in the United States by Newman, Freeman, and Holzinger (1937) correlated .67, while the 12 pairs studied in Denmark by Juel-Nielsen (1965) correlated .62. These correlations seem substantial, but they cannot be attributed entirely to heredity. The twins in these studies, like those observed by Shields, tended to be reared in quite similar environments, and often had considerable contact with each other. Further, there is reason to be-

lieve that the particular IQ tests used in these studies were not accurately standardized for age and for sex (Kamin, 1974). Since a pair of identical twins is always of the same age and same sex, any tendency for the test to favor a particular
age group or sex will tend to make the twins appear more similar in IQ than they
really are.

To sum up, the actual studies of separated identical twins have produced
results much less conclusive than might have been obtained in an ideal—but
in practice impossible to perform—experiment. The twins who have been studied do resemble each other in IQ, but—once Burt's data are rejected—they have
also experienced quite similar environments. Thus there is no way to know how
much of the observed IQ correlation might be due to identical genes, and how
much to similar environments. There is obviously much room for disagreement
in interpreting these data; if there were not, the argument about heredity, environment, and IQ would long since have ended.

STUDIES OF ADOPTED CHILDREN.   The fact of adoption makes possible
other kinds of studies that, in principle, might be able to unravel the combined
effects of heredity and environment on IQ. There are a number of interesting
and relevant questions which can be asked about the IQs of adopted children.
We might ask, first, do adopted children tend to have normal IQs? The answer
is very clear: The average IQ of adopted children is distinctly superior. This
tends to be the case even when the biological parents of the adopted children
have very low IQs. For example, 100 adoptees in Iowa had an average IQ of 117
(Skodak and Skeels, 1949). The biological mothers of the same children had an
average IQ of only 87. We can safely conclude that the source of the superior
IQs of the adopted children must have been the excellent environment that most
adoptive parents give their children. Those families that choose to adopt children—and that are selected by adoption agencies as suitable parents—tend to be
highly advantaged. They obviously provide environments that foster the development of high IQ in their children. The fact that the sort of environment
provided by adoptive parents produces children with high IQs tells us that environment clearly can have quite a large effect on IQ. By itself, however, it tells
us little about the relative importance of heredity and environment.

There have been a number of attempts to compare the IQ correlation between adopted parents and adopted children with that between ordinary, biological parents and children. Biological children, living in normal families, have
received both their genes and their environment from their parents. Adopted
children, however, have received only their environment from their adoptive
parents. Thus, to the extent that genes are important determiners of IQ, one
would expect the correlation between biological parent-child pairs to be larger
than that between adoptive parent-child pairs.

The earliest studies of adopted children showed clearly that the IQ correlation between adoptive parent and child was relatively small—and clearly smaller
than that observed between parent and child in ordinary biological families
(Burks, 1928; Leahy, 1935). This kind of comparison, however, may be misleading. We have already noted that adoptive parents, having been rigorously
selected by adoption agencies, are a very special kind of people. There is relatively little variation among them in IQ, and relatively little variation in the
excellence of the environments they provide for their adopted children. When

there is little variation in a measurement, correlations involving that measure tend to be low. The special and unique characteristics of adoptive families make it hazardous to compare them to ordinary families.

There are, however, many adoptive families that contain not only an adopted child, but also a *biological* child of the same parents. These families seem especially suited for investigating the nature–nurture problem. They are all "special" families, all having wished to adopt a child, and all having been selected as suitable by adoption agencies. Within each family, the adopted child has received only the environment from the parents, and the biological child has received both genes and environment from the very same parents. To the degree that IQ is passed on through the genes, it is obvious that within such families the correlation between parent and biological child should be larger than that between parent and adopted child.

There have been two recent adoption studies that collected the necessary data from a reasonably large number of these special families. The correlations between the *mother* and her two kinds of children, in each of the studies, are given in Table 9-4 (top). There is obviously no significant difference between the two correlations, within either study. The child's IQ resembles the mother's IQ to the same degree, whether or not the child and mother are genetically related. This result clearly does not support the idea that IQ is a very heritable trait. The study by Scarr and Weinberg (1977), it might be noted, has one rather unusual feature. The adopted children are black, and the adoptive parents—as well as the biological children of the parents—are white.

The picture seems rather different, however, when the correlations between the *father* and his two kinds of children are considered. These data, given in Table 9-4 (bottom), show that the father more closely resembles his biological than his adopted child. That is especially the case in Scarr and Weinberg's transracial adoption study. There is no obvious reason why the data for fathers and for mothers should differ in this way, although it is possible to invent plausible reasons. They would not be very convincing, however, without further and more detailed studies.

We can also look at correlations between various types of siblings in these

Table 9-4: Mother–Child and Father–Child IQ Correlations in Adoptive Families with Biological Children.

	Texas Adoption Project (Horn et al., 1979)	Transracial Adoption (Scarr & Weinberg, 1977)
Correlation of mother and biological child	.20 (N = 162)	.34 (N = 100)
Correlation of mother and adopted child	.22 (N = 151)	.29 (N = 66)
Correlation of father and biological child	.28 (N = 163)	.34 (N = 102)
Correlation of father and adopted child	.12 (N = 152)	.07 (N = 67)

Table 9-5: Sibling IQ Correlations in Adoptive Families with Biological Children.

	Texas Adoption Project (Horn et al., 1979)	Transracial Adoption (Scarr & Weinberg, 1977)
Biological-biological (related) pairs	.35 (N=46)	.37 (N=75)
Adopted-adopted (unrelated) pairs	——	.49 (N=21)
Biological-adopted (unrelated) pairs	.29 (N=197)	.30 (N=134)

two studies. The families contain some pairs of biological siblings. That is, the parents have had two or more biological children of their own. Within each of these families there are also one or more adopted children. There are therefore two kinds of biologically unrelated sibling pairs. There are some pairs of genetically unrelated adopted children reared by the same parents; and there are some genetically unrelated pairs consisting of one biological child and one adopted child of the same parents. The correlations for all three types of sibling pairs, in each study, are given in Table 9-5. The samples are in some cases relatively small, and the correlations fluctuate somewhat. What is clear, however, is that there is no tendency for the biologically related pairs to be more highly correlated than the unrelated pairs. Within the Scarr and Weinberg study, the biological pairs are all white, the adopted pairs are all black, and the biological-adopted pairs consist of one white and one black child each.

The Texas Adoption Project was able to obtain the IQ scores of the biological mothers of the adopted children. Their average IQ was lower, by about six points, than that of the adoptive mothers. Despite this, the adopted children and the biological children of the adoptive parents each had the same average IQ of 112. Thus it is clear that the adoptive parents were able to transmit high IQs equally to *all* their children—whether or not they shared genes with them. These IQ averages, according to the authors of the Texas Project, suggest "a heritability of IQ that is close to zero" (Horn et al., 1979). From a consideration of all the correlational data in their study, the same authors suggested that "moderate heritabilities" are indicated. These conclusions have some special force, since the authors had begun their study expecting to find a very high heritability of IQ, presumably in the neighborhood of .80. Perhaps the best summary we can make of modern, well-designed adoption studies is that their data are not consistent with a very high heritability of IQ. Depending on which aspects of the data one chooses to emphasize (not all the data have been reviewed here), heritability appears to be somewhere between moderate and very low.

COMPARISON OF IDENTICAL AND FRATERNAL TWINS. Identical twins occur when a single sperm fertilizes a single ovum and, early in the process of development, an extra split occurs. This results in the birth of two individuals who have identical genes. These two individuals are always of the same sex, and almost always they are strikingly similar in physical appearance. The more common type of twins, fraternal twins, occurs when two separate sperm fertilize two separate ova. Thus, fraternal twins are no more alike genetically than ordinary sibling pairs. They are in fact ordinary siblings who happen to be born at the same time. They can be of the same or opposite sex, and their physical resemblance is no greater than that of ordinary siblings. They share on average, like ordinary siblings, 50 percent of their genes.

These facts suggest that a comparison of identical and fraternal twins might help to illuminate the roles of heredity and environment. The two types of twins have in common that each has been born and reared in the same family environment. To the degree that being of the same age is likely to increase the similarity of environmental experience, the two types of twins are again equated. The obvious difference is that identical twins are much more alike genetically—to be precise, twice as much alike—than are fraternal twins. Thus, if IQ is heritable, the correlation between identical twins should be much larger than that between fraternal twins.

There have been literally dozens of studies comparing the IQ correlations of identical and of same-sexed fraternal twins. (The studies typically include only same-sex fraternal pairs, since all identical pairs are necessarily of the same sex.) The studies agree, almost without exception, in reporting a higher IQ correlation for identical twins. The typical correlation found for identical twins is about .87, while that found for fraternal twins is about .53 (Erlenmeyer-Kimling and Jarvik, 1963). This result is consistent with a high heritability of IQ—but it is also open to different interpretations.

There is a large body of evidence indicating that identical twins in fact experience much more similar environments than do fraternal twins. This is presumably a consequence of their striking physical similarity, which evidently encourages their parents, teachers, and peers to regard and treat them very much the same. Further, identical twins appear to be much more closely attached to each other than are same-sex fraternal twins. The result of all this is that identical twins are much more likely to play and spend time together, to have the same friends and teachers, to sleep in the same room, and to wear the same clothes than are fraternal twins (Loehlin and Nichols, 1976). When parents are asked whether or not they have tried to treat their twins "exactly the same," parents of identicals much more often say that they have tried to do just that. We are thus forced to note once more that, in the real world, genes and environment tend to covary—much to the annoyance of investigators of the nature–nurture problem. The difference in IQ correlations between identicals and fraternals must at least in part be caused by the differentially similar environments they have experienced. We have no way of knowing how large a part of the difference to assign to heredity, and how large a part to environment.

The Loehlin and Nichols study contains a further bit of information which indicates that the especially similar treatment given to identical twins does in fact increase the correlation of their IQs. There were 502 pairs of identical twins in the study, and in about half the cases the parents indicated that they had tried to treat the two twins "exactly the same." Those identical twins whose parents did treat them exactly the same resembled each other significantly more in IQ than did those whose parents did not treat them alike. This *must* be an environmental effect, since all identical twin pairs have identical genes.

The twins in the top photo are fraternal twins; the twins in the bottom photo are identical twins. As noted by Loehlin and Nichols (1976), identical twins are much more likely to play and spend time together, to have the same friends and teachers, to sleep in the same room, and to wear the same clothes than are fraternal twins.

The fact that similar treatment affects the IQ correlation of even identical pairs, put together with the fact that identicals are much more likely than fraternals to receive similar treatment, makes clear that some part (perhaps most) of the correlation difference between the two types of twins is environmentally produced.

FAMILY STUDIES OF IQ CORRELATIONS.   There have been many studies designed to show that biological relatives are significantly correlated in IQ, and there is no doubt about this fact. Further, the closer the biological relation, the higher the IQ correlation. This is what one would expect if IQ were highly heritable; but it would also follow from the obvious fact that the more closely related two individuals are biologically, the more similar are their environments. We cannot deduce, from the fact that IQ test scores tend to run in families, the degree to which genetic and environmental factors are involved.

The early family studies, summarized by Erlenmeyer-Kimling and Jarvik (1963), seemed to suggest that the typical parent-child IQ correlation, like that between siblings, was just about .50. That particular value happens to correspond to the proportion of genes shared by parent and child and by pairs of siblings. The correspondence thus seemed to fit a highly oversimplified genetic model, in which IQ was an entirely heritable trait. More recent studies, summarized by Kamin (1979), indicate that the typically reported parent-child IQ correlation is about .33. Two very large-scale, recent parent-child studies reported IQ correlations of .28 (Broman et al., 1975, based on 5,625 pairs) and of .26 (DeFries et al., 1979, based on 2,715 pairs). These relatively modest correlations are not compatible with a very high heritability of IQ.

These and other recently reported family correlations have been summarized by two prominent behavior geneticists (Plomin and DeFries, 1980). They concluded that, although the older data suggested a heritability of about .80, more recent studies suggest a heritability of about .50. Thus, where Jensen (1969) had implied that heredity was about four times as important as environment in determining IQ differences among whites, Plomin and DeFries now imply that heredity and environment are about equally effective. We do not know why more recent heritability estimates are lower than earlier ones. Possibly the more recent studies have been better designed and more carefully carried out. However, it should be understood that the heritability of a trait in a population is *not* a constant; its value can change as changes occur either in the environments to which members of the population are exposed, or in the genetic makeup of the population.

When viewed as a whole, the data on IQ correlations among relatives within the white population suggest, at most, rather moderate heritability, and perhaps very little heritability. There are too many inconsistencies to place any confidence in a numerical estimate as high as .80—or, indeed, in any particular numerical estimate. That at least is the conclusion of the present authors, after reviewing a large and somewhat ambiguous set of research studies.

Group Differences in IQ Scores

From the earliest days of intelligence testing, researchers have spent considerable effort in examining differences among groups of various sorts in average

IQ scores. These studies have, if anything, created more controversy than have studies of individual differences in IQ—and, as we shall see, they have been even less revealing about the nature of IQ, or the ways in which nature and nurture interact in the development of IQ.

SEX DIFFERENCES.   Two large groups of considerable interest to most people are the male and female sexes. The answer to the question of whether the two sexes differ in measured IQ is straightforward: No, they do not. This might be due, however, to the fact that test-makers do not believe that males and females *should* differ in IQ. The tests of general intelligence in common use have all been standardized so as to do away with, or at least to minimize, possible sex differences. The choice of which items to include in an intelligence test is, after all, arbitrary. The test-makers have deliberately eliminated from their tests items that disproportionately favored one sex or the other. Where this has not been done, items favoring one sex have been deliberately balanced by items favoring the other. The equality of the sexes in IQ may thus be more a fact of test construction than a fact of nature. The point is that it would be easy to construct a test with all the surface characteristics of an IQ test to make *either* sex look more "intelligent." For example, Willerman (1979) has reported that among a Texas sample of husbands and wives, one item was successfully passed by 70 percent of males and only 30 percent of females. The item is actually included in the Wechsler test, and it asks what is the temperature at which water boils.

When specialized tests have not been deliberately standardized to remove sex differences, there is some suggestion that males may do a little better on quantitative items, and females a little better on verbal items. These are not large differences, however, and they are not consistently reported in all studies. The most consistently found sex difference—at least after early childhood—is on tasks involving spatial visualization, on which males tend to do better. There has been much effort spent in an attempt to show that this difference is due to a single, sex-linked, recessive gene. The early studies that seemed to show this genetic link have not been successfully repeated, and much disconfirming evidence is now available (Loehlin et al., 1978; DeFries et al., 1979). We do not know to what extent the real sex difference in spatial abilities is genetic, and to what extent it is cultural. The fact that wives are less knowledgeable than their husbands about the temperature at which water boils should not be taken to indicate a genetic intellectual inferiority of females! We might also note from this example that inability to answer an IQ test question does not necessarily imply a handicap in adjusting to the demands of the real world. The Texas wives were probably at least as adept as their husbands in the constructive use of boiling water in the kitchen.

SOCIAL CLASS DIFFERENCES.   There are large and clear differences in the average IQs of members of different social classes and occupations, and they are not surprising in nature. Put most simply, people who work with their heads—and especially professional people—do very well on IQ tests. People who work with their hands do less well, with unskilled laborers having lower scores than skilled laborers. The World War II testing program of the United States Army, using the Army General Classification Test, found distinctively different average IQs across a wide range of civilian occupations.

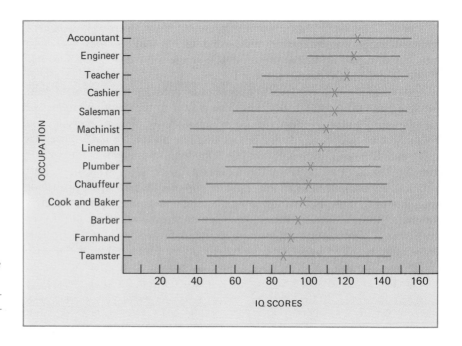

Figure 9-5

The averages and ranges of IQs in a number of different occupations. There are distinctly different average IQs across the range of occupations, and there is also considerable variation within any given occupation. (Harrell and Harrell, 1945)

Table 9–6: Average IQ of Children (Ages 2–18) According to Father's Occupation.

Father's Occupation	Children's Average IQ
Professional	115.9
Semi-professional and managerial	111.9
Clerical, skilled trades, and retail businesses	107.1
Rural owners	94.2
Semi-skilled, minor clerical, minor business	104.4
Slightly skilled	99.1
Day laborers, urban and rural	96.3

From McNemar (1942).

These are illustrated in Figure 9-5; note that there is considerable variation in IQ *within* any given occupation. There is no evidence, by the way, to indicate that within an occupation people with the higher IQs perform their jobs much better.

Perhaps of more interest, children born to parents of different social classes also differ in average IQ—but the differences are not so large as those among their parents. The 1937 restandardization of the Stanford-Binet test found substantial differences among children whose parents had been classified into seven occupational classes. These data are given in Table 9-6.

The existence of IQ differences among adults of different occupations and classes says nothing at all about the genetic and environmental bases of IQ. People with high IQs, no matter how they got them, tend to end up in the more prestigious and economically rewarding occupations. We do not even know whether high IQ is really a *cause* of entering a higher occupation. Possibly, for example, family background, possession of a diploma, or nonintellectual social skills are much more important than IQ in determining occupational level (Jencks, 1972).

The fact that children born into different social classes have different IQs can be—and, as we might by now expect, has been—interpreted in different ways. There is no doubt that the environments of children differ widely across social classes, and it seems reasonable to believe that this produces the observed IQ differences. The data of Table 9-6 make clear, however, that social class differences in IQ appear even before five years of age. That means that environmental differences assumed to affect IQ must be operating before that age, and before the child has been exposed to formal schooling. The other interpretation is to assume that social classes differ genetically, and that genes making for high IQ occur more often in the upper social classes. This idea was argued vigorously by the early American translators of Binet's test (Terman, 1916; Goddard, 1920; Yerkes and Foster, 1923). The same notion has been proposed more recently by Herrnstein (1973), who argued that in a free society people born with "good" genes tend to rise in social class, and to transmit their good genes to their offspring. This must result, according to Herrnstein, in a "meritocracy"—a society in which the upper classes are genetically gifted, and in which the genetically superior children of upper-class parents necessarily (and justifiably) remain in the upper class. This idea and variants of it seem to be as old as civilized man. Plato, for example, argued that slaves were by nature born to be slaves, and that Athenians were born to be free men. The evidence to support the hereditary basis of social class membership has not become much more convincing since Plato's time.

We can note that the 1937 restandardization of the Stanford-Binet test also indicated (Table 9-7) that children born in farm areas had much lower average IQs than children born in cities. This seems an obvious consequence of the greater educational and environmental opportunities available in cities (at least in 1937). The argument has also been made, however, that genetically bright people tended to migrate to the stimulating and rewarding cities, leaving a residue of duller folk, who have genetically dull children, in rural areas. This hypothetical argument is not likely to convince many farmers—no more so than similar arguments about a genetic basis for low black IQ scores have convinced black people, or people sensitive to the effects of racial prejudice and discrimination.

BLACK-WHITE DIFFERENCES. The most inflamed arguments about the heritability of IQ have involved the fact that, in the United States, black people on average tend to score some 10 to 15 points lower in IQ than do white people. This fact has been known for a long time. The Army testing program of World War I indicated such a difference—and it also indicated that black people in some northern states had a higher average IQ than whites in some southern states. To some, the data proclaimed that black people were genetically inferior to white people. To others, the data indicated that IQ was determined by educational and environmental opportunities.

The influential article by Jensen (1969), already cited, not only argued that the heritability of IQ among white people was .80. The difference in average

Table 9–7: Average IQ of Children (Ages 2–18) in Urban, Suburban, and Rural Areas.

Type of Area	Children's Average IQ
Urban	106.2
Suburban	104.9
Rural	96.6

From McNemar (1942).

IQ between black people and white people, Jensen also maintained, was probably of genetic origin. Further, in Jensen's view, attempts at compensatory education of underprivileged children—such programs as Head Start and other interventions aimed at increasing intellectual competence of the children—had failed, and were bound to fail. That was so, said Jensen, because of the high heritability of IQ.

There are few more obvious social facts than the overwhelming discrimination to which black people have been exposed throughout American history. The clear environmental differences between black people and white people seem, to most social scientists, obviously related to the difference in average IQ. The fact is, however, that black people and white people do inherit somewhat different genes, which affect, among other things, skin color, hair texture, etc. Thus, it is difficult to *disprove* the idea that genetic differences between the races *might* be responsible for the IQ difference. (*Why* one would want to prove or disprove such an idea is another question—perhaps better left untouched in this textbook.)

There seems little point in attempting to summarize in detail the multitude of research studies on black–white IQ differences. The topic seems almost to have obsessed many American researchers, which, in view of the importance of race in American society, seems scarcely surprising. There are studies to show that light-skinned black people have higher IQs than dark-skinned black people. This has been interpreted as indicating that degree of black ancestry is a predictor (genetically) of IQ. The same result, however, has also been interpreted as a consequence of the lesser discrimination against light-skinned black people. The fact that northern blacks have higher IQs than southern blacks (and than southern whites in some states) has been interpreted as a result of better educational opportunity—but it has also been interpreted as a consequence of selective migration of genetically bright black people from the South to the North, or as a result of greater black–white intermarriage in the North. The point should be obvious: Until and unless black people have the same environmental experiences as white people, those who wish to argue about the basis of the observed IQ difference will be free to do so. Their arguments may be ingenious, but they will be without convincing evidence. The pity is that in a society which supposedly treats people as individuals, and not as specimens belonging to particular groups, so much time and energy has been wasted on an irrelevant and, strictly speaking, unanswerable question. (See the accompanying box on race and IQ.)

Most present-day psychologists agree that there is *no* evidence that clearly supports a genetic interpretation of black–white IQ differences. Perhaps a smaller proportion, but still a majority, agree that what is known about environmental and cultural differences between the races seems adequate to explain the observed IQ difference. There are still other psychologists, evidently not a majority, who regard the whole field of investigation as an offensive manifestation of white racism.

We conclude our discussion of race and IQ with two final points related to Jensen's controversial 1969 article. Though Jensen asserted that the heritability of IQ among whites is .80, our own review has indicated that this number is unrealistically high. The fact is, though, that even if IQ heritability

HIGHLIGHT
Race and IQ

There are many kinds of studies that make it very implausible to suggest that the black–white difference in average IQ is genetically determined. Lee (1951) studied black children who had arrived in Philadelphia with their migrating parents from the South. When first tested the children had very low IQs, but after enrolling in the Philadelphia schools and living in the city for some time their IQs increased steadily, by an average of about 6 points. There was no such increase in IQ over time observed among a control group of black children who had been born in Philadelphia. This result indicates that superior educational and cultural opportunities in the city (at least at the time of Lee's study) served to elevate the environmentally depressed IQ scores of southern black children.

There is clearly no support for a genetic interpretation in a study by Eyferth (1961), conducted in Germany. The children in this study were all born out of wedlock to white German mothers. The fathers were American servicemen, some black and some white. The race of the father made no overall difference in the average IQs of the children. Other researchers (Willerman et al., 1974) studied 101 white women who had borne children by black fathers, and 28 black women who had borne children by white fathers. There is no genetic reason to suppose that the IQs of these two types of interracial children should be different, and there were no significant differences between the two sets of parents in socioeconomic status. The average IQ of interracial children born to white mothers was 102, compared to 93 for equally interracial children born to black mothers.

This outcome makes no genetic sense, but is open to a number of environmental interpretations—for instance, the mother is the main "teacher" of the child, and white mothers had not experienced racial prejudice while growing up.

The effects of transracial adoption (at least on IQ) have been studied by Scarr and Weinberg (1976). The average IQ of 99 black and interracial children adopted before they were 1 year old by advantaged white families was a very high 110. That average score is considerably higher than would have been observed if the children had not been adopted. The families adopting these children were obviously able to endow them with high IQs by nongenetic means. That is not to say that the adoption of black children by white families is necessarily a good policy; and it is not to say that being reared in a *white* family increased the adopted children's IQs. If the same children had been adopted into advantaged *black* families, the same IQ result would presumably have occurred. We have no information about what would happen if white children were adopted into black families, since such adoptions are very rare in our society.

To sum up, those studies that have most directly examined whether there might be a genetic black–white IQ difference have consistently failed to find supporting evidence. We cannot prove the nonexistence of such a difference, but we cannot prove the nonexistence of unicorns, either. We should be aware that our persistent interest in this question may well have nonscientific roots. A word to the wise is sufficient.

were very high, both within the white and black populations, this would *not* necessarily mean that a difference between the two races in *average* IQ had *any* genetic basis! To see this clearly, imagine two sacks, each containing the same mixture of seeds from many different genetic varieties of corn. The seeds from the white sack are all planted in a patch of very fertile soil, with very uniform environmental conditions. The seeds from the black sack are all planted in uniformly poor soil. Now, *within* each of the two plots of land, the differing heights to which the various corn plants grow will be determined entirely by heredity (the seed). The *average* height of corn plants, however, will be less in the poorer soil—even though exactly the same mixture of seeds has been planted in each plot. The different results *between* the two plots will be determined entirely by environment. This type of example should make clear to you the difficulty—or even absurdity—of asking whether heredity or environment is responsible for differences between human groups. The (highly disputable) existence of high IQ heritability *within* one or both races does not, despite Jensen's assertions, have any implications for understanding the different averages *between* the two groups.

The final point to be made has to do with the concept of heritability itself. The concept is relevant only to *differences* among individuals in some measured trait—not to the average level of that trait. Thus, for example, any environmental treatment that immediately doubled everyone's IQ would have no effect on the heritability of IQ. Those who had average IQs before the new environmental treatment would still have average IQs—but average IQs would now be 200. The fact that the heritability of a trait is high in no way implies that its *average* level cannot be profoundly affected by appropriate environmental intervention.

IQ Testing and Society

The controversy now surrounding the use and interpretation of IQ tests has a long and sometimes unpleasant history. Perhaps hindsight makes ethical judgments easier than they appeared at the time, but the social biases and racism of the early mental testing movement in the United States seem shocking by today's standards. When Lewis Terman first published his Stanford-Binet test in 1916 he wrote confidently that black and Mexican children *would* be found to have lower average IQs than whites, and that such differences could never be eradicated by educational or cultural changes. He argued that such children ". . . should be segregated in special classes. . . . They cannot master abstractions, but they can often be made efficient workers. . . . There is no possibility at present of convincing society that they should not be allowed to reproduce. . . . They constitute a grave problem because of their unusually prolific breeding" (p. 92). Writing later of children in the low IQ ranges, Terman (1917) urged society to "curtail the increasing spawn of degeneracy" (p. 165).

The major social involvement of the early IQ testers, however, was with the long national debate over immigration policy that took place before and after World War I. The United States Public Health Service in 1912 invited Henry Goddard to apply the new mental tests to samples of European immigrants arriving at Ellis Island, New York. The tests, Goddard reported, showed that 83 percent of Jews, 80 percent of Hungarians, 79 percent of Italians, and 87 percent of Russians were "feeble-minded." There was no problem, Goddard believed, posed by the fact that immigrants did not know English. The verbal tests could be translated, and they could be supplemented with "culture-fair" performance tests. The use of mental tests "for the detection of feeble-minded aliens," Goddard proudly reported (1917), had greatly increased the number of would-be immigrants deported from Ellis Island.

Those who opposed immigration from the countries of southeastern Europe were greatly encouraged by IQ data collected by the United States Army during World War I (Yerkes, 1921). The first mass mental testing in history took place during the war, when people drafted into the Army were given one of two specially developed group IQ tests. The Alpha test was a typical paper-and-pencil verbal test, while the Beta test was a performance test specially designed for those who were illiterate or who could not understand English-language instructions. The data from some two million tested draftees, as we have already seen, indicated that black people had a lower average score than white people. The most immediately relevant findings, however, concerned the IQs of immigrants who had been drafted into the Army. The data indicated clearly that the highest IQs were scored by immigrants from England, Scotland, Canada, and the countries of northern and western Europe. The lowest IQs were those of immigrants from southeastern Europe—Italians, Russians, Poles, and Jews. The psychologists who summarized these findings wrote simply: "The Latin and Slavic countries stand low" (Yerkes, 1921).

The Army immigrant data were analyzed in great detail by Carl Brigham in his book *A Study of American Intelligence* (1923). Those immigrants who had lived in America for 20 years or more before being tested in the Army, Brigham reported, had IQs every bit as high as native-born Americans. The immigrants who had lived in the country fewer than five years tended with alarming frequency to be feeble-minded. These facts might have suggested that IQ scores were heavily influenced by familiarity with American culture and language, even when "non-verbal" performance tests were used. That was not Brigham's interpretation. "We must assume," Brigham declared, "that we are measuring native inborn intelligence." The explanation, according to Brigham, was that immigrants who had arrived in the country 20 years ago were mostly from northern and western Europe, with much "Nordic blood." The more recent immigrants, from southwestern Europe, contained inferior "Alpine" and "Mediterranean" blood.

The conclusion of Brigham's book is a profound embarrassment today, but at the time—only some 60 years ago—it was taken as serious and responsible science. The genetically inferior, Brigham wrote, were reproducing their poor stock at an alarming rate. Further, ". . . we are incorporating the negro into our racial stock, while all of Europe is comparatively free from this taint. . . . The steps that should be taken . . . must of course be dictated by science and not by political expediency. . . . The really important steps are those looking toward the prevention of the continued propagation of defective strains in the present population" (p. 210). The "prevention" of reproduction by defective stocks already in the country, Brigham urged, should be coupled with a law designed to reduce the number of inferior Alpine and Mediterranean immigrants.*

The Army data, and Brigham's book, were cited repeatedly as Congress

---

* At a later date (1930), Brigham publicly retracted his earlier analysis of the Army data, confessing that he had been wrong and "pretentious." By that time the new immigration law had already been in effect for six years, and Brigham had become Secretary of the College Entrance Examination Board. There he developed a test with which many students are familiar, the Scholastic Aptitude Test.

debated the new immigration law of 1924. The new law did in fact dramatically reduce the proportion of immigrants coming from southeastern Europe. This was done by assigning each European country an annual quota of allowable immigrants—and by basing the quotas on the United States census of 1890, before the massive influx of southeastern Europeans had begun. The naive genetic interpretation of the Army IQ data, widely accepted among psychologists of the time, helped in some measure to pass a racist immigration law that transformed American society. The overconfident and ethnocentric interpretation of IQ data can have profound consequences. The relevance of this early episode in the history of IQ testing to today's concern over black–white differences seems obvious. Psychologists know more about their own creation, IQ tests, than does anybody else, and their conflicting opinions will be listened to. There is no more reason to allow psychologists to have the final say about IQ tests, however, than there is to allow physicists to have the final word about the uses of atomic bombs, or of nuclear power plants.

Summary

1. Alfred Binet set out to devise a test that would predict a child's performance in school. He used the concept of *mental age* (*MA*) to assess the child's mental ability as compared to his or her *chronological age* (*CA*). Stern developed the concept of the *intelligence quotient* (*IQ*), the ratio of MA to CA multiplied by 100; at any given chronological age the average IQ is 100.

2. The Stanford-Binet test was a revised version of Binet's test, which was introduced in the U.S. by Lewis Terman in 1916. Since then, the test items have been modified and restandardized in 1937, 1960, and 1972.

3. Achievement tests measure how much one has learned before taking the test; aptitude tests are used to predict some future performance. The difference between the two lies more in the purpose to which the test is put than in the types of questions asked.

4. People are considered mentally retarded if they have an IQ below 70 coupled with inadequate social and occupational adjustment. For the great majority of retarded persons no physical cause can be specified; some cases of severe retardation are related to biological accidents or genetic disorders such as Down's syndrome.

5. A 50-year study begun by Terman in 1922 showed that people with very high IQs tend to live productive and successful lives, disproving the notion that such people are somehow "freakish."

6. Both the Stanford-Binet test and the Wechsler Intelligence Scales are individual tests, designed to be administered by a trained examiner to one person at a time. The Wechsler scales were the first to use the concept of a *deviation IQ*, comparing a person's score to the scores of others of the same age in the standardization sample.

7.   The Army Alpha and Beta tests are examples of group tests; they were developed to test draftees in World War I. The Alpha test is a verbal paper-and-pencil test; the Beta test was designed as a performance test for illiterate or foreign-born draftees.

8.   Thurstone argued that there were seven independent or "pure" factors of mental ability – verbal comprehension, word fluency, number, space, memory, perceptual speed, and reasoning.

9.   Guilford proposed 120 factors of intelligence, each representing a different intellectual ability. Guilford and his followers developed radically different mental tests, some of the most interesting of which tested divergent rather than convergent thinking.

10.   Whether intelligence is inherited or whether it is a function of environment is the subject of much controversy. The *heritability ratio* is one effort to answer the question quantitatively.

11.   Various ways of trying to control for one factor or the other include studying identical twins raised apart; comparing adopted children's IQs to those of both their adoptive and biological parents; and studying adopted children in families that also have biological children. There are difficulties in all of these approaches, and we can only say that heritability appears to be somewhere between moderate and low.

12.   Researchers have also examined differences among groups in average IQ scores based on sex, race, and social class. There are such differences, but we cannot say whether they are genetically or environmentally based.

Suggested Readings

BLOCK, N. J., and DWORKIN, G. *The IQ controversy.* New York: Pantheon, 1976. A well-selected and broad set of relevant readings, some old and some new.

BRODY, E. B., and BRODY, N. *Intelligence: Nature, determinants, and consequences.* New York: Academic Press, 1976. An advanced and thorough review, with balanced coverage of the nature–nurture controversy.

EYSENCK, H. J. *The structure and measurement of intelligence.* New York: Springer-Verlag, 1979. A recent review, with a clearly hereditarian emphasis.

JENSEN, A. R. *Genetics and education.* New York: Harper & Row, 1972. Reprints several of the author's articles, including the 1969 *Harvard Educational Review* article that rekindled the nature–nurture debate.

KAMIN, L. J. *The science and politics of I.Q.* Potomac, Md.: Erlbaum, 1974. Reviews much of the same material covered by Eysenck's book, but with a clearly environmental emphasis.

LOEHLIN, J. C., LINDZEY, G., and SPUHLER, J. N. *Race differences in intelligence.* San Francisco: Freeman, 1975. Though focused on data relevant to race differences, this book is also broadly concerned with the heritability of IQ.

SAMUDA, R. J. *Psychological testing of American minorities: Issues and consequences.* New York: Dodd, Mead, 1975. Testing from a minority perspective.

Part Four Motivation and Emotion

10 Biological Bases of Motivation

W hat makes the jogger jog, the canary sing, the dolphin come up for air? Why does the cat stalk the mouse, the stallion seek the mare? When we ask questions like this we are asking questions about *motivation*. In nonscientific terms, motivation is "the reason for a person's or an animal's actions."

The word "motivation" comes from the same Latin root as the words "motion" and "motor." When psychologists study motivation the central problems sound a lot like those for the physics of motion: What starts a person or an animal moving, what keeps it moving, what determines the direction of its movement, and what stops it? Hunger is a motivator; so is thirst, pain, excessive heat or cold, and many other physical and psychological conditions.

In this chapter we will first discuss theories of motivation, and then examine some specific motivators, such as hunger and thirst. The emphasis here will be on the basic motivations shared by animals and people. The kinds of motivation that are considered characteristically human will be covered in Chapter 11.

Theories of Motivation

The concept of motivation is extremely important in psychology. The goal of any science is the ability to make accurate predictions; thus, many psychologists feel that the primary goal of psychology is to predict behavior. But, whereas the planets move around the sun, or hydrogen combines with oxygen, in a perfectly predictable fashion, behavior appears to be a lot more variable. One of the chief sources of this variability is motivation. For example, we can put a rat in a maze through which it has run accurately a hundred times before, and if it is not hungry or thirsty it might wander aimlessly or just go to sleep. We can't always tell how much an animal knows just by observing a small piece of its behavior: If it isn't motivated it may not perform an act that it has previously learned. This is referred to as the *difference between learning and performance*. In order to predict performance, we have to know about motivation.

If behavior weren't variable we wouldn't have to talk about motivation at all. For example, when someone shines a bright light in your eyes your pupils contract. We don't ask what motivates you to contract your pupils, because they *always* contract when there is an increase in illumination. But if you are offered a candy bar you might refuse it on one occasion and on another occasion accept it eagerly. The concept of motivation can help us account for the fact that even though the stimulus (the candy bar) is the same, the response is different.

Historical Theories

FREE WILL VERSUS DETERMINISM.   People have always been interested in the question of what makes us do what we do. Before Darwin presented his evidence that human beings are simply a fancy kind of animal, most people believed that the rules for human behavior are quite different from the rules for animal behavior. The prevalent belief from the time of Plato and Aristotle through the Middle Ages and probably even today is that people's behavior is under the control of their minds and that they are free to choose what they will do. Although their decisions might be influenced by outside stimuli and by internal needs and desires, their actions are controlled by human reason. This view is referred to as the doctrine of *free will.* For someone who believes in free will, a scientific theory of human motivation is useless, because it is impossible to predict what a person will choose to do.

Even in the time of Plato there were people who argued with the idea of free will. The Greek philosopher Democritus believed that all events in nature are the results of inflexible chains of cause and effect. If we knew all the laws of cause and effect we would be able to predict perfectly the behavior of people, as well as the motions of inanimate objects. This doctrine is called *determinism.*

The deterministic viewpoint became increasingly popular after the publication of Charles Darwin's *Origin of Species* (1859) and the eventual acceptance of Darwin's ideas by the scientific community. If humans and animals have the same ancestral origins and are closely related biologically, it is reasonable to assume that human behavior—like animal behavior—is under the control of the laws of cause and effect.

INSTINCTS.   A very important concept that Darwin did not originate but that he did help to bring into prominence was the concept of *instinct.* Darwin believed that instincts were of great importance in determining the behavior of people and animals. Natural selection, he held, operated in the same way on instincts as on any other innate characteristic: Slight variations of a given instinct occur in a population, and the variation that is most successful is preserved (because its possessor is more likely to survive) and is passed on.

To Darwin, an instinct was basically just a complicated reflex: an innate pattern of behavior that is emitted in response to some stimulus. Some later theorists, though, believed that instincts provided not only the behavior itself but the *motivation* behind the behavior. For example, William James (1890) assumed that a hen possesses not only the innate behavior pattern for sitting on eggs, but—more important—an innate tendency to *want* to sit on eggs. In James's own words:

> To the broody hen the notion would probably seem monstrous that there should be a creature in the world to whom a nestful of eggs was not the utterly fascinating and precious and never-to-be-too-much-sat-upon object which it is to her.

James felt that "man has a far greater variety of impulses than any lower animal," so, therefore, man must possess more instincts.

The belief that the motivation behind human behavior is provided chiefly by instincts reached its height in the second decade of the twentieth century. Unconscious instincts, such as repressed sexual desire, played a central role in the theories of Sigmund Freud (see Chapter 14). In the United States, some psychologists drew up lists of "instincts" such as curiosity, pugnacity, and gregariousness. Almost every kind of human behavior could then be attributed to the motivating force of some instinct or other: A man who washed his hands was impelled by the Instinct of Cleanliness; a woman who bought a pencil was responding to the Instinct of Acquisitiveness. The problem was that saying that a behavior was motivated by an instinct didn't help at all in understanding the behavior—saying that people have an instinct of cleanliness doesn't tell us any more than saying that they generally keep themselves clean. To poke fun at the way the concept had outgrown its usefulness, Ayres (1921) published a paper subtitled "The Instinct of Belief-in-Instincts."

Homeostasis and Drive Theory

The idea that replaced the concept of instinct was based on the notion of *homeostasis*. The physiologist Walter Cannon (1939) introduced this term to describe the way the body maintains a balance or equilibrium in its internal environment. For instance, if the temperature of the body drops just a little, the blood vessels in the skin constrict so that less heat escapes into the air (see Figure 10-1). If the temperature goes up, the blood vessels in the skin dilate, and the sweat glands begin to function. Thus, the temperature of a healthy person normally remains within narrow limits, thanks to the body's internal "thermostat." In a similar way, if the amount of water in the tissues is too high the excess is excreted in the urine; if it is too low the person becomes thirsty and will drink the necessary amount of fluids. In general, whenever the body deviates too far in one direction or another from its ideal state, a response is triggered that restores it to equilibrium. The term *homeostasis* is used to mean both the ideal balanced state and the process by which that state is maintained; the bodily functions that accomplish this are called *homeostatic mechanisms*.

What does homeostasis have to do with motivation? The clearest statement of the theory came from Clark Hull (1943). To Hull, any deviation from homeostatic balance produces a *need*. A need, in turn, produces a *drive*. A drive is a motivational force, an inciter of action. For example, an animal deprived of

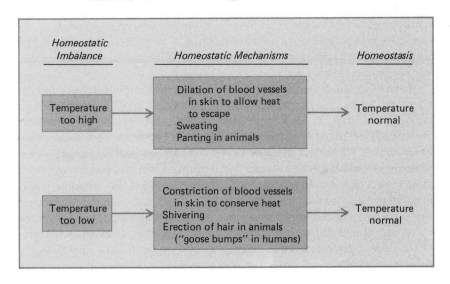

Figure 10-1

This chart shows how homeostasis works in the area of temperature regulation in humans and animals.

nourishment for a day or two has a need for food. The need creates a drive; in this case the drive is called *hunger.* The drive motivates the animal to search for food, and to eat it when it is found. Eating the food soon restores the animal to a state of homeostasis. The result is what Hull called *drive reduction.* Drive reduction, according to this theory, is what gives positive reinforcers (such as food) their power to increase the probability of a response in operant conditioning (see Chapter 6).

Needs do not only result from a *lack* of something. Pain or any strong stimulus is assumed to produce a deviation from homeostasis. The result is a drive to escape the stimulus. The cessation of pain is a highly effective primary reinforcer.

PROBLEMS WITH DRIVE THEORY.   Drive theory is not a "historical theory" of motivation; updated versions of drive theory are still popular. However, not too much of Hull's original formulation has remained intact. As it was quickly realized, all needs do not produce drives. The example usually given was that of carbon monoxide poisoning. A person exposed to this gas might be dying for lack of oxygen, but oxygen deprivation creates no drive. The recent popularity of thermal pools has provided some additional tragic evidence of homeostatic imbalance without a drive. People have died, while immersed to the neck in hot water, because their bodies gave them no signal that they were becoming dangerously overheated. (The usual physiological mechanisms for controlling body temperature don't work under water.)

There can be needs without drives; there also can be drives without needs. Motivation sometimes seems to arise as a result of external stimuli, instead of from some internal physiological imbalance. An external stimulus of this sort, one that has the capacity to motivate behavior even if a drive was apparently not present initially, is called an *incentive.* A good example of an incentive is an attractive member of the opposite sex—to a male rat, for instance, a receptive female rat. The presence of this incentive is likely to arouse a sex drive that was previously quiescent. Another incentive, to most humans and to animals of many species, is anything that tastes sweet, whether it reduces the hunger drive or not. Rats will press a lever to receive a drop of saccharin solution, and will continue to do so over months of testing. Moreover, sweet foods retain their incentive value even in the absence of a need for nutrition. You might have just finished a big meal and not be the least bit hungry, but when offered a tempting dessert you may not be able to resist it.

Even when the drive-inducing qualities of external stimuli are added, there is a great variety of human and animal behavior that cannot be explained in terms of the kinds of drives we have been discussing. The concept of homeostasis originally pertained to physiological changes in body parts such as the blood vessels, heart, lungs, and kidneys. Drive theorists applied the notion to the organism as a whole. Some assumed that if the organism is not suffering from a physiological deprivation or motivated to escape from a strong stimulus, it will do nothing at all. But that is not the case. Animals act as though they *want* to be stimulated, want novelty, want to explore. Monkeys will learn to solve mechanical puzzles even if they are never rewarded for it (Harlow, Harlow, and Meyer, 1950), and will perform work in order to see interesting things—a toy train, for example—through a window (Butler, 1953). Even rats will learn to press a lever just to make the illumination in their cages increase and decrease (Roberts, Marx, and Collier, 1958), as well as to gain access to a running wheel (Collier and Hirsch, 1971). And human beings do all sorts of bizarre things that drive theory can't account for: They scare themselves with ghost stories and roller coaster rides, eat food spicy enough to stimulate the pain receptors in the mouth, and go to movies designed to arouse the sexual drive but not to satisfy it. Many psychologists believe that organisms are born with an "exploratory drive," and that they have an innate need for a certain amount of stimulation. Lack of stimulation is what makes solitary confinement a universally dreaded punishment.

The instinct theorists of the 1920s spoke of an "instinct of curiosity." Are we any further along when we speak of an "exploratory drive"? The concept of drive has one theoretical advantage over the concept of instinct. Instincts are assumed to provide both the energy or motivation behind a given action and, in addition, to specify the action itself. Drives are assumed only to provide the energy for action. Thus, a given sample of behavior can be analyzed into two components: the action itself (say, pressing a lever) and the motivation behind the action (say, the hunger drive produced by a certain period of food deprivation).

The concept of drives has often been useful. It is most useful when we are talking about relatively clearcut states of physiological deprivation such as hunger and thirst. However, even in these cases there are difficulties with the traditional view of drive as a product of homeostatic imbalance. We will discuss some of these difficulties in the next section of this chapter, where specific drives are covered in greater detail.

Hunger

Everyone has felt hunger. It is a universal source of motivation. Because it is easily produced in the laboratory and easily satisfied, and because an organism does not quickly die if its food needs are not met, hunger has been studied more thoroughly than any other motivation. Yet there is still much that we do not understand about this very complicated subject. One problem is that mechanisms that regulate food intake appear to differ in different species. Thus we cannot be sure that experimental results found with dogs will hold true for rats, or that results found with rats will hold true for people. Humans, of course, are the most difficult species to study. Their eating behavior is controlled by social and cognitive factors as well as by physical ones. And many of the experiments that have been most helpful to our understanding of hunger and feeding behavior in animals cannot, for obvious reasons, be performed on humans.

Physiological Mechanisms and Food Intake Regulation

Organisms must regulate their food intake both on a day-to-day basis, to meet their immediate physiological requirements, and on a long-term basis, to maintain a stable (adult) body weight. A large animal, such as a horse or a cow, that eats food low in caloric value (such as grass) must eat almost continuously to get enough nutrition. But humans and most animals that have been studied in the laboratory (mainly dogs, cats, rats, mice, and guinea pigs) eat *meals.* That is, they eat for a while, and then they stop eating. After a lapse of time they eat again. The number of meals taken a day (when allowed free access to food) varies: Humans generally take 2 to 4, cats 9 to 10, rats 12 to 15, guinea pigs 22 to 25. The basic questions here are: What makes an organism start eating? What makes it stop? What determines the size of a meal?

THE STOMACH AND THE MOUTH.   An obvious place to look for the origin of hunger and satiety is the stomach. Surprisingly, though, the stomach does not seem to play an important role in regulating food intake. People whose stomachs have been removed for medical reasons still get hungry and eat normal amounts of food. And rats that have had all the nerves from the stomach to the brain cut also maintain their food intake normally (Morgan and Morgan, 1940).

Additional information about the stomach's role in food-intake regulation comes from experiments with rats in which a plastic tube is surgically inserted into the stomach or the esophagus (the passageway from the mouth to the stomach). It is then possible to place food or liquid directly into a rat's stomach, bypassing its mouth. In one experiment (Miller and Kessen, 1952) milk or a saline solution was injected directly into rats' stomachs. The rats learned to go to the place where they received the milk injections (in preference to the place where they received the saline), even though they were never able to taste or swallow it. Tasting or swallowing does have an effect, though: Rats that received a quantity of milk directly into their stomachs drank more additional milk than ones that had taken the same quantity in the normal way, by mouth (Berkun, Kessen, and Miller, 1952). And hospitalized people being maintained on intravenous feeding still report feeling hungry, although they do not actually eat much if offered food.

MONITORING OF BLOOD SUGAR.   One plausible way for the body to regulate food intake would be through the level of glucose (blood sugar) in the circulatory system. Jean Mayer (1953) proposed that the changing level of glucose is monitored by "glucostats" in the brain. The mechanism has to be a fairly complex one, though—not one that simply equates hunger with low glucose levels and satiety with high levels. Diabetics have elevated glucose levels, yet they tend to eat more, not less, than healthy people. The mechanism postulated by Mayer would keep track of the *rate* at which glucose is being used by the body's cells: A low rate would produce hunger, a high rate satiety. The rate can be measured (in the laboratory and, theoretically, in the body) by comparing the amount of glucose in the outgoing blood in the arteries with that in the incoming blood in the veins. Mayer found that the difference between these two measurements was largest a little while after a big meal, and gradually got less. Subjects' reports of hunger coincided with the times when the difference was minimal. According to this theory, diabetics feel hungry because they have a lot of glucose in *both* arterial and venous blood, so the difference is small. Similarly, injections of insulin, which lower glucose levels in both arterial and venous blood, also produce hunger. Nondiabetic rats given daily injections of insulin overeat and become fat.

There apparently are other substances in the blood, besides glucose, that

APPLICATION
Specific Hungers

Experiments have shown that some kinds of animals are able to regulate their intake of specific nutritional substances, such as fats, carbohydrates, proteins, and various vitamins and minerals. Is this also true of humans?

In a famous experiment with three toddlers performed in a hospital setting, the children proved able to regulate their diets satisfactorily when free to select from a variety of nutritious foods (Davis, 1928). Whether the results would have been the same if cake and candy had been among the alternatives is difficult to say. There have certainly been many reported cases of people who have sickened or died from malnutrition because they have chosen (for one reason or another) to adhere to a diet that did not meet their nutritional needs. And thousands of people died of scurvy before it became commonly accepted in the early 1800s that citrus fruits would prevent this dreaded disease—a fact that had been reported half a century earlier by the Scottish physician James Lind.

Most of the work on specific hungers has been done with rats. Rats are able to balance their intake of fats, carbohydrates, and proteins, and will press levers for hours to supply themselves with one of these nutrients if it is missing from their diet—even if the other substances are freely available (Collier, Hirsch, and Kanarek, 1977). They will consume large quantities of calcium after removal of the parathyroid glands (which regulate calcium balance), and large quantities of salt after removal of the adrenal glands (which regulate the body's salt content). In the case of salt, the preference for salty foods follows immediately after salt depletion—no learning seems to be necessary.

Choosing other necessary substances, however, seems to require experience. Rats fed on a diet deficient in a vitamin such as thiamine will gradually eat less and less of that diet, and their weight will drop. When offered a different type of food they will accept it eagerly, although rats are generally very cautious about eating anything new. The old diet will always be avoided unless there is nothing else to eat. Evidently they have learned to associate it with feeling ill. The same thing happens when a rat is fed some kind of poison: Even if hours elapse between when the rat eats a particular kind of food and when it becomes ill, it is unlikely to try that food again (Garcia and Koelling, 1966; Rozin and Kalat, 1971).

Whether this sort of ability—obviously very important for rat survival—exists in other species remains to be shown. Rats seem to be particularly good at maintaining their diet at an optimal level. For example, when given a diet high in bulk and low in calories, rats eat enough to maintain a constant caloric intake. Cats, on the other hand, will eat a constant amount of bulk and will therefore lose weight.

---

help to regulate intake of food. If blood from a satiated rat is transfused into a hungry one, the hungry rat eats much less than usual. Transfusions in the opposite direction, however, have no effect: The satiated rat does not begin to eat again after receiving blood from a hungry animal (Davis, Gallagher, and Ladlove, 1967). One candidate for this mysterious "satiety factor" is a hormone called cholecystokinin, which is produced by the small intestine soon after a meal. When this hormone is injected into hungry animals it temporarily inhibits eating (Gibbs, Young, and Smith, 1973).

THE ROLE OF THE HYPOTHALAMUS.   The search for mechanisms that control hunger and satiety has led most often to the part of the brain known as the *hypothalamus* (see Chapter 2). The hypothalamus itself is composed of a number of sub-areas that can be distinguished anatomically and on the basis of their functions. One of these sub-areas is the *lateral hypothalamus*. This part of the brain has been identified as an excitatory area for eating and drinking. When a rat's lateral hypothalamus is destroyed, it will at first neither eat nor drink, and

Figure 10-2

This rat's ventromedial nucleus has been damaged, with the result that it has gained so much weight that it weighs three times what a normal rat would weigh.

will die unless it is forcefed (Teitelbaum and Epstein, 1962). If kept alive it will eventually resume eating and drinking, but it will only eat foods that taste good. Electrical stimulation of the lateral hypothalamus causes a previously satiated rat to become hungry and thirsty. If food is not immediately available the rat will press a lever to obtain it (Hoebel, 1971).

If the electrode is located in a different part of the hypothalamus, the *ventromedial nucleus,* stimulation will cause a hungry rat to *stop* eating. The ventromedial hypothalamus (VMH for short) has been called the satiety center; that is where "glucostats" (the blood-sugar monitors) are believed to be located.

If a rat's VMH is damaged or destroyed, the animal will eat more food at each meal and will soon weigh twice or three times as much as a normal rat (Figure 10-2). What's interesting is that the rat won't continue to gain weight indefinitely. At some point its weight will level off and it will eat just enough to maintain itself at that new weight (Teitelbaum, 1961). Moreover, although this rat eats more than a normal rat, in some ways it seems *less* hungry: It is more finicky about what it eats and it won't work as hard to get food (Miller, Bailey, and Stevenson, 1950; Teitelbaum, 1957).

A rat with brain lesions in the VMH will maintain itself at a higher weight than before its surgery; similarly, a rat with lesions in the lateral hypothalamus will eventually maintain itself at a new, lower weight (Keesey and Powley, 1975). In both cases it looks like the homeostatic "thermostat" is still working, but that the setting has simply been changed. This is the *set point theory* of food regulation (Nisbett, 1972). According to this theory the feeding-regulation mechanisms of the obese rat and the obese human are not out of order—they are just set at a higher set point. As long as the weight is below the set point, the person or animal is hungry. Like rats with VMH lesions, many obese people tend to eat more, eat faster, be less active, and be more finicky about what they eat. We will return to the problem of human obesity shortly.

CRITICISM OF HOMEOSTATIC THEORIES OF EATING.   From the homeostatic viewpoint, an animal is assumed to begin a meal whenever some physiological mechanism signals a certain level of depletion or need. Some psychologists have presented strong arguments against this view (Collier, Hirsch, and Hamlin, 1972; Collier, Hirsch, and Kanarek, 1977). For example, when food is readily available, the amount taken in a meal is not related to the length of time since the last meal, and perhaps not even to the amount taken in the last meal (Panksepp, 1973). Mealtimes seem to depend not on the level of depletion but on the time of day (cats and rats do most of their eating at night) and on the availability of alternative activities such as running in wheels. Collier believes that healthy animals in natural environments have developed behavior that assures an adequate intake of food—they *anticipate* their needs rather than respond to them. An example is the behavior of large ruminants such as cows. These animals have a tremendous storage capacity and it takes them a long time to digest their food. They must continually take in food to provide the raw material for the fermentation process. If they waited until their previous meal was digested and assimilated before they began to eat again, they would be in trouble. And animals such as wolves and lions, which must expend large amounts of energy to procure food, could scarcely afford to wait until their supply of energy was depleted before they began to look for more food. Thus, according to Collier, through the course of evolution each species of animal has evolved feeding patterns that are suited to its ecological niche, but are flexible enough to be modified if the environment changes. A good example of this kind of flexibility is the hyena's hunting pack. If the available game is small and a successful hunt results in only the dominant animals eating well and the rest going hungry, the pack splits up into smaller packs. When large game again becomes available, so that a kill will feed many animals, the packs reassemble into larger units (Kruuk, 1972).

Human Obesity

One rarely sees an overweight animal in a natural environment (unless it is getting ready to hibernate). Only humans and a few of the species that humans have domesticated seem to have the capacity to become obese under normal conditions. The study of obesity is important for two reasons. First, obesity is a major health and social problem. Second, understanding obesity is necessary if we are to understand the normal regulation of food intake.

DEFINING OBESITY.   In humans obesity is often defined as being more than about 15 percent over the "ideal" weight, given a person's height and overall body build. However, Mayer (1956) has pointed out that a 6-foot-tall football player weighing 200 pounds is "overweight" according to the charts, yet may have very little body fat. On the other hand, a very inactive person whose weight is at or even below the "ideal" weight may be so lacking in muscle tissue that an abnormally high percentage of that weight consists of fat. Mayer has defined obesity as the condition that is present "when the fat content reaches 30 percent of the body weight." The size of fat deposits can be roughly determined by measuring the thickness of a skin fold, or by measurements of body density. It should be noted that the proportion of body fat increases in normal animals as they age, and at a given age it is higher in females than in males.

CHARACTERISTICS OF OBESE PEOPLE.   As we mentioned earlier, there are some interesting parallels between the behavior of obese humans and that of rats that overeat because of lesions in their ventromedial hypothalamus. Schachter (1971) has spelled out these similarities in detail. First, both obese humans and VMH rats are more sensitive than their normal counterparts to the taste of food. When food or drink is adulterated with quinine, a harmless substance with a bitter taste, obese humans and rats take less of it than normal subjects. When the food tastes good, the obese eat more.

Obese subjects are also less willing to work for food than the nonobese. When rats are rewarded with a pellet of food for each lever press, VMH rats press more than normals. But when they have to press a number of times for each pellet, they press *less* than normal rats (Teitelbaum, 1957). Schachter found a similar result with humans. In a cleverly designed experiment, subjects were invited to help themselves from a bagful of almonds. The almonds were either shelled or unshelled. Nonobese people accepted the offer and ate some nuts about half the time, whether they were shelled or not shelled. Obese subjects almost always accepted the offer of nuts without shells, but almost never accepted when the nuts had to be shelled.

Other reported similarities include general activity level (the obese are less active), emotional responsiveness (the obese react more emotionally), number of

Table 10–1: Some Shared Characteristics of Obese Humans and Rats with VMH Lesions.

1. Eat more when good-tasting food is available.
2. Eat less when the food tastes bad.
3. Are less willing to work for food.
4. Eat faster.
5. Eat fewer meals per day (but more per meal).
6. Tend to be more emotionally reactive.
7. Are generally less active.

From Schacter (1971).

Figure 10-3

When there are a number of food cues, obese subjects will work almost twice as hard as the nonobese subjects to get food. With no food cues, the nonobese subjects worked harder. (Johnson, 1970)

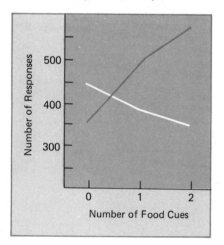

meals eaten per day (the obese eat fewer), and speed of eating (the obese eat faster). Some of Schachter's comparisons are summarized in Table 10-1.

A THEORY OF OBESITY.   Schachter's theory about these VMH rats and obese humans is that they differ from normal-weight organisms not so much in their mechanisms for food-intake regulation as in their general level of responsiveness to all external stimuli. For example, although VMH rats are less active when the room in which they are caged is dark and quiet, they are as active as normal rats when people are in the room tending to the animals. They are *quicker* than normal animals in avoiding an electric shock by jumping into another compartment (Grossman, 1966). Schachter found that human obese subjects also have quicker reaction times when their task is to respond differently to two different stimuli. Moreover, he found that the obese remember more than normal people when slides containing a number of pictures or words are shown to them for 5 seconds.

According to this theory, "When a food-relevant cue is present the obese are more likely to eat and to eat a great deal than are normals. When such a cue is absent, the obese are less likely to try to eat or complain about hunger." The reason they are less willing to work for their food, says Schachter, is simply because food that has to be worked for is more remote and therefore provokes less of a food-acquiring response. There is evidence for this hypothesis from human subjects. Overweight and normal-weight people had to lift weights with their fingers to get food. There were four conditions: They worked for sandwiches wrapped either in clear plastic or in opaque white paper, and they either did or did not get a sample piece of sandwich. Figure 10-3 shows that when there were two food cues (transparent wrapper plus sample sandwich), obese subjects worked almost twice as hard as the nonobese. With no food cues, the nonobese subjects worked harder (Johnson, 1970).

THE SET-POINT THEORY.   Earlier we mentioned Nisbett's theory that overweight people and VMH rats have a higher set-point weight. The assumption is that when they are below this set point, they are in a state of deprivation or homeostatic imbalance, even if their weight is above normal levels. Nisbett believes that this state of deprivation is responsible for the distinctive characteristics of obese people, and not the obesity itself or the mechanisms that caused the obesity.

This theory has been tested in a series of experiments reported by Herman and his colleagues (Herman and Mack, 1975; Herman and Polivy, 1975; Hibscher and Herman, 1977). The experimenters divided their subjects into two categories on the basis of their answers to a series of questions: either "restrained eaters" (dieters) or "nonrestrained eaters" (nondieters). They assumed that restrained eaters, whether they are obese or of normal weight, weigh less than their set-point weight and are therefore in a state of chronic deprivation. Nonrestrained eaters, obese or nonobese, are assumed to be at or near their set-point weights.

The experimental results supported the set-point theory. College men or women who were concerned about their weight and restrained their eating (dieters) showed many of the same traits that Schachter had found in his obese subjects, even if they were at a normal weight at the time of the experiment. Conversely, obese subjects who didn't care about their weight and ate as much as they wanted (nondieters) behaved more like Schachter's nonobese subjects. For example, both obese and nonobese dieters ignored internal cues and ate a lot of ice cream after they had been given two milk shakes to drink as part of a "rating experiment." The milk shakes evidently broke down the dieters' normal restraint, because dieters who hadn't had the milk shakes ate less of the ice cream (as shown in Figure 10-4). This was exactly the opposite of what was found with nondieters (both obese and normal weight).

Another experiment showed that normal-weight subjects who are dieters show the same kind of emotional responsiveness that had previously been linked with obesity. Hibscher and Herman (1977) even showed that both obese dieters and nonobese dieters have elevated blood levels (compared with nondieters) of certain substances known as "free fatty acids." The free-fatty-acid content of the blood has been shown to go up in response to food deprivation (Gordon, 1960).

FAT CELLS. According to Nisbett's theory, the set-point weight determines whether or not a person can maintain a socially acceptable weight without being hungry all the time. But what determines the set-point weight? Nisbett claims that it is the number of fat cells in the body. In one study, fat cells were found to be three times as numerous in obese people as in nonobese (Knittle and Hirsch, 1968). Knittle (1975) believes that the number of fat cells in the body is pretty well fixed by the age of two; it is determined partly by heredity and partly by eating habits in infancy. According to this theory, overeating simply causes the fat cells to increase in size and dieting causes them to shrink, but the number of these cells stays approximately the same. Thus, when an obese person loses weight the fat cells are supposedly "starved," which accounts for the state of chronic deprivation found in habitual dieters.

Not all psychologists believe in the fat-cell theory. Some who *do* believe in it think that it only accounts for a certain kind of obesity—the kind that produces a moderately overweight child who becomes a moderately overweight adult. There are many other types of obesity. Undoubtedly we will eventually find that there are a number of different causes for obesity, some primarily emotional, some primarily physiological, and some primarily due to social or environmental causes. In a society where almost everyone has a car and no one walks, lack of exercise may be an important factor. This idea has led Mayer (1956) to wonder "whether there is not a direct relationship between recent improvements in transportation and increased prevalence of overweight."

The situation for the obese individual is not as hopeless as it would seem from some of the theories we have discussed. Many of these people *do* lose weight, by themselves, under a physician's supervision, or through an organization such as Weight Watchers International. Organizations of this type report considerable success for their programs of weight reduction. Their focus is on learning to eat properly, eating more slowly, and encouraging patience with the weight-loss process. The success of these programs appears to hinge on social reinforcement of a dieting regime. People who have successfully lost weight through these or other programs do not show the symptoms of depression or irritability that might be expected from the set-point theory. On the contrary, weight loss has been associated with favorable changes in emotional and social adjustment (Wilson, 1978).

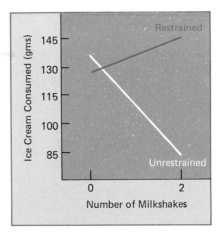

Figure 10-4

In one of a series of experiments done by Herman and his colleagues, the set-point theory was upheld—subjects labeled restrained or nonrestrained, whether obese or nonobese, reacted in different ways to the offer of ice cream after having drunk two milkshakes. (Hibscher and Herman, 1977)

Thirst

People who have suffered from severe water deprivation describe extreme thirst as a much more excruciating sensation than extreme hunger. It is also much more life threatening: We can survive for weeks without food, but only for a few days without water.

We lose water all the time. An average of $2\frac{1}{2}$ liters passes from our bodies each day in urine, feces, and exhaled air. This water must all be replaced by drinking liquid or eating foods with a high moisture content. Under normal conditions organisms do not experience extreme thirst because their patterns of water intake (like their patterns of food intake) *prevent* severe depletion from occurring.

What Starts Drinking?

Most of us would immediately claim that thirst is equivalent to the sensation of a dry mouth and throat. During dehydration there is usually a reduced salivary flow, and that makes the mouth feel dry. But dryness of the mouth does not play an essential role in the regulation of water intake. This has been shown in several ways. People given drugs that cause dryness of the mouth and those who were born without salivary glands drink more frequently, but their total intake is about normal. The same is true of dogs that have had their salivary glands tied off (Montgomery, 1931).

THE HYPOTHALAMUS.   We saw in the previous section that the mechanisms that produce hunger are located primarily in the hypothalamus and not in the stomach. The situation is similar for thirst: The mechanisms are again located primarily in the hypothalamus, rather than in the mouth or throat. Several hypothalamic areas have been implicated; one of these is the lateral hypothalamus, which was previously mentioned in connection with hunger. Lesions in this region interfere with drinking as well as eating—in fact, the effect on drinking seems to be more severe and more persistent. The *preoptic area,* at the very front of the hypothalamus, has also been shown to be involved in thirst. Electrical stimulation of the preoptic area, or the injection of minute quantities of salty water, causes goats to drink excessively (Andersson, 1952; Andersson and McCann, 1955).

In order for the hypothalamus to regulate water intake, it must have some way of obtaining information about the body's need for fluids. This is accomplished by two independent mechanisms, one based on *osmoreceptors,* the other on *volumetric receptors.* These are sometimes called, respectively, the *intracellular mechanism* and the *extracellular mechanism.* The first kind responds to the amount of fluid inside the body's cells, the second to the fluid outside the cells, especially that contained in the circulatory system.

OSMORECEPTORS.   The fluids in the body, both within the cells and outside of them, normally contain about 0.9 percent salt (sodium chloride). When an organism has been deprived of water for a while, the extracellular fluid becomes more concentrated (in other words, saltier). Now there are different concentrations of salt on the two sides of the cell wall, and the result is *osmosis*—the movement of fluids through a semipermeable membrane. In this

case, water moves through the cell wall from inside the cell to outside, decreasing the saltiness of the extracellular fluid but at the same time depleting the cell of water. It is believed that certain cells in the hypothalamus, the osmoreceptors, are sensitive to this depletion. When water moves out of these cells a response is triggered, and signals are sent to other cells in the brain. One result is that the organism becomes thirsty. Another is that the hypothalamus stimulates the pituitary gland to release a hormone (the *antidiuretic* hormone) that causes the kidneys to produce more highly concentrated urine. This means that less water is lost through excretion.

The functioning of the osmoreceptors has been demonstrated experimentally by injecting salty water (more than 0.9 percent salt) into the stomachs or blood vessels of animals. This has the same effect as water deprivation: Because the extracellular fluid becomes saltier than that within the cells, the cells lose water. Such injections cause animals to become thirsty, even if they were previously satiated with water. The same thing happens to people who drink sea water or eat salty foods.

VOLUMETRIC RECEPTORS.　People who do not get *enough* salt also become thirsty. In this case the fluid outside of the cells is less salty than that within, and osmosis causes extracellular water to enter the cells. Now the quantity of extracellular fluid (mainly blood) is depleted. The mechanism that responds to this depletion, called a *volumetric receptor,* is the same one that produces intense thirst in wounded people who have lost a lot of blood. Although, in the case of blood loss, there has been no change in the body's concentration of salts, the total *volume* of extracellular fluid has decreased. The result is a drop in blood pressure. Receptors somewhere in the body—probably in the blood vessels themselves—respond to this drop by signalling the kidneys to release *renin* into the bloodstream. Renin is an enzyme that is responsible for the production of a substance called *angiotensin*. Angiotensin reaches the brain through the bloodstream and stimulates the thirst receptors in the hypothalamus. When angiotensin is injected directly into the hypothalamus of an experimental animal, the animal drinks large quantities of water (Epstein, Fitzsimons, and Rolls, 1970).

It makes sense that there should be more than one way to regulate water intake. Water balance is too essential to life to be dependent on a single mechanism.

What Stops Drinking?

The mechanisms we have described initiate drinking when intracellular or extracellular fluids get low. What stops it? A stomach-load of water is only 25 percent absorbed in 15 minutes; yet dogs (for example) are able to replace their water deficits quite accurately, on one or two short bouts of drinking (Adolph, 1939). What tells them when they have had enough?

A number of experiments have been performed in attempts to answer this question. Many of these experiments have made use of the technique in which a plastic tube is surgically inserted into an animal's esophagus. Water can be put directly into the animal's stomach through the tube, or water that the animal drinks can be prevented from reaching its stomach. The results of such experiments have led to the conclusion that no one factor can account for the cessation of drinking. Three factors seem to be involved: (1) the actual number of licks or swallows of water the animal takes; (2) the volume of water in the animal's stomach; and (3) absorption of water from the stomach and intestines, and the consequent replenishment of intracellular and extracellular fluids.

Temperature Regulation

The temperature of "warm-blooded" or *endothermic* organisms is held within very narrow limits by homeostatic mechanisms that trigger reflexes such as dilation or constriction of the blood vessels in the skin, fluffing of hair or feathers, sweating, and shivering. These mechanisms seem to be regulated by—you guessed it!—the hypothalamic area of the brain, in particular the optic region. Animals with preoptic lesions are unable to maintain a stable body temperature by means of reflexive responses, in either cold or hot environments (Satinoff, 1974).

These lesions do not, however, put an end to temperature regulation by behavioral means. The brain-damaged animals will still press a bar (for example) to provide heat in a cold environment or coolness in a hot environment—just as normal animals do (Lipton, 1968; Carlisle, 1969).

Animals such as fish, frogs, and lizards are referred to as cold-blooded or *ectothermic* because they lack those automatic mechanisms for temperature regulation that warm-blooded animals have. However, it has been shown that such organisms *do* control their internal temperatures, often keeping them within fairly narrow ranges, by behavioral means—just like the warm-blooded animals with preoptic lesions. For example, by shuttling back and forth between sun and shade lizards maintain a body temperature that generally varies by only 3° or 4° C (Heath, 1970). Goldfish can learn to keep the temperature of their aquariums between 33.5° and 36.5° C by pressing levers to warm or cool the water (Rozin and Mayer, 1961).

Newborn mammals, many of which do not have automatic mechanisms capable of maintaining a stable body temperature, also do this sort of thing—normally by huddling more or less closely to their mother and litter mates. When put in an environment that has local variations in temperature, they choose a spot that is warmer than an adult animal would choose (Satinoff and Henderson, 1977).

The homeostatic concept of set point, which we discussed in the section on hunger, applies very nicely to temperature regulation as well. When a warm-blooded organism has a bacterial or viral infection and runs a fever, its set point goes up: Both behavioral and reflexive mechanisms function to maintain the organism at a higher-than-normal body temperature. It is interesting to note that cold-blooded animals such as lizards will also choose to maintain their temperatures at a higher level when they are sick (Bernheim, Vaughn, and Kluger, 1974). Moreover, the higher body temperatures actually increase their chances of surviving an infection. Kluger (1976) injected iguanas with disease-producing bacteria and kept groups of animals at different constant temperatures. Of the lizards that were kept at 38° C (100.4° F—the average body temperature of healthy lizards), two-thirds died. Only 4 percent of the lizards kept at 42° C (107.6° F) died. It is not clear why an elevated body temperature helps a lizard to fight infection. The simplest explanation—that the heat harms the bacteria in some way—has been discarded. Thus, although these findings are very interesting, it would be premature to try to generalize them to mammals.

Sexuality and Mating

The motivations we have studied so far in this chapter have one important thing in common: If the needs that underlie them are not met, the organism dies. The sex drive is different. As far as we know, no one has ever died for lack of sex. In fact, it might be described as a drive without a need, because it involves no deviation from homeostasis and is to a certain extent independent of deprivation and satiation. Deprivation and satiation play *some* role, but not nearly so great as with hunger and thirst.

Although it is not necessary to the survival of the individual, the sex or mating drive is essential to the survival of the species. The strength of the drive is maintained by the process of natural selection—organisms genetically endowed with little or no desire to mate are unlikely to bear young. In the human species the expression of the drive is somewhat fettered by social laws and customs, but it remains a powerful source of motivation. Evidence of this is provided by TV and magazine advertisements, which use sex to sell everything from cars to toothpaste.

Sexual Differentiation

GENETIC SEX.   Nature has happily provided us, in almost every species, with two sexes: male and female. Usually an organism's sex is determined at the time of conception. In humans and other mammals, as we discussed in Chapter 2, an egg carrying an X chromosome unites with a sperm carrying an X chromosome to produce a genetic female, or with a sperm carrying a Y chromosome to produce a genetic male. Thus a cell from a normal female contains two X chromosomes, and a cell from a normal male contains one X chromosome and one Y.

Everyone does not, however, fall into the simple XX or XY classification. For example, there are individuals with an XXY pattern. These people have underdeveloped, but clearly male, genitals. As adults they prove to be sterile and have a somewhat feminine body build. There are also men with an XYY pattern. They are taller than average, and sometimes have genital abnormalities. It was at first thought that this chromosomal pattern is associated with a higher degree of impulsiveness or aggressiveness, because prison populations have a higher incidence of XYY individuals. However, XYY men in the non-prison population do not seem to be any more aggressive than normal XY men (Owen, 1972). Both the XYY and the XXY patterns are associated with an increased risk of mental retardation.

People with only a single X chromosome are identified as female, but they lack ovaries and so do not mature sexually unless hormones are given artificially. They are likely to have other birth defects as well, and tend to be quite short.

HORMONES.   A human embryo is bisexual for the first few weeks of its life. That is, it is capable of growing into either a male or a female. It possesses a pair of primitive sex glands that can become either ovaries or testes. At 7 or 8 weeks after conception these glands begin to develop into ovaries if the sex-chromosome pattern is XX, into testes if it is XY. These sex glands or *gonads* each produce a characteristic type of hormone. The ovaries produce the set of related female hormones called *estrogens,* and the testes produce the male hormones called *androgens,* of which the most important is *testosterone.* The hormones secreted by the embryo's gonads determine what kind of internal and external reproductive organs (the *primary sex characteristics*) will develop. More precisely, if the gonads secrete testosterone, the fetus will develop the characteristics of a male. Otherwise it will develop the characteristics of a female, whether or not its gonads secrete estrogen. In mammals, both male and female embryos are subjected to the influence of the mother's female hormones, so a female is produced unless there is opposition from testosterone. It is interesting that the situation is just the opposite in bird embryos, which are encased in a shell and not exposed to the mother's hormones. A bird embryo will develop into a male unless estrogen is present at the critical stage of development (Wilson and Glick, 1970), whereas a mammal embryo will develop into a female unless testosterone is present at the right time.

The hormones also control the *secondary sex characteristics,* which appear at puberty. In humans these include breasts and hip enlargement in females, beard growth and voice change in males. Puberty is marked by a great increase in the output of sex hormones. The pituitary gland, located in the brain, produces hormones called *gonadotropins,* which stimulate the gonads to produce androgen and estrogen. Oddly enough, both kinds of hormones (which are closely related in biochemical structure) are produced by both sexes, but the testes tend to produce more androgen, the ovaries more estrogen. In males estrogen produced by the testes is normally destroyed by the liver. Breast enlargement in teen-aged boys sometimes results when the liver fails to destroy all the estrogen.

Hormonal sex can override genetic sex more or less completely, depending on how early in development the hormonal influence occurs. There is a condition that occurs in humans called the *androgen-insensitivity* syndrome. People with this condition are genetic males whose embryonic testes secrete testosterone, but for some reason—probably an enzyme deficiency—the testosterone is not used by the body cells and the fetus develops into what appears to be a normal female. The individual is raised as a girl and at puberty the secretion of estrogen is sufficient to cause the development of female secondary sex characteristics. However, menstruation does not occur, because there are no ovaries and the uterus is incompletely formed. Although these people cannot become pregnant, they are in most respects unquestionably female. Some have had successful careers as fashion models; many have married and have adopted children, with very satisfactory results (Money, 1970; Money and Ehrhardt, 1972).

Genetic females may also develop malelike characteristics if subjected to male hormones early in fetal life. When injections of testosterone were given to pregnant female monkeys, their female offspring were born with sex organs that were partly male and partly female, a condition known as *hermaphroditism*. These baby monkeys had a small but otherwise well-developed penis. On the other hand, they also had the internal organs (ovaries, uterus) of a normal female (Goy, 1970).

A synthetic hormone called *progestin*, formerly used to prevent miscarriage in pregnant women, was later discovered to have masculinizing effects on unborn female children. Some of these girls were born with an enlarged clitoris and partially fused labia. The condition was corrected surgically, and they were raised as females. The development of 11 of these girls was studied (Money and Ehrhardt, 1972). They tended to be unusually "tomboyish" in childhood, and preferred toy trucks and cars to dolls.

MALENESS AND FEMALENESS. Of course, girls who *haven't* been exposed to synthetic progestin before they were born sometimes prefer cars to dolls too. The differences in behavior between "normal" boys and "normal" girls are relative rather than absolute: A particular kind of behavior will occur more often, *on the average*, in boys than in girls, or in girls than in boys. That such statistical differences *do* exist in many species is unquestionable. For example, young male rhesus monkeys engage in more "rough and tumble" play than do young females (Rosenblum, 1961). What is not clear is how much these differences depend on genetic and hormonal influences, and how much they depend on the way the individual is treated by parents and others. Even in subhuman species different parental treatment for male and female offspring has been observed. Rhesus monkey mothers with female offspring restrain their infants almost three times as often as mothers of male offspring (Mitchell, 1968). *Restraining* was defined as "active interference with the infant's attempts to leave the mother." The importance of social and parental influences on the develop-

HIGHLIGHT
Mating and Parental Behavior in the Ring Dove

The ring dove is a small relative of the domestic pigeon. It gets its name from the semicircle of black feathers that "rings" the back of its neck. These birds breed freely under laboratory conditions, and have been used extensively for detailed studies of parental behavior (Lehrman, 1964).

When a male and a female ring dove are placed together in a cage, courtship begins almost at once: The male begins to strut about, bowing and cooing. After several hours the birds choose a nesting site; in the laboratory this consists of a shallow glass bowl put in the cage for that purpose. Nest building takes about a week, and is shared by both sexes. During this week the birds also mate. The female lays the first egg about nine days after the begin-

ning of the courtship period, and a second egg two days later. The parent birds take turns incubating the eggs, with the female doing most of the sitting and the male relieving her for about six hours of each day.

The eggs hatch in two weeks, and the newly hatched squabs are fed with a substance called "crop milk," a liquid secreted in the crops of both male and female birds. (The crop is a pouchlike enlargement of a bird's esophagus.) The squabs leave the nest when they are about eleven days old, but the parents continue to feed them—with increasing reluctance—for another ten days. Then courtship begins again, and the cycle repeats itself.

What determines the performance of the actions described above and the physiological

changes that accompany them? Experiments have shown that hormonal factors play an important role, and so do visual and auditory stimuli. (The sense of smell does not seem to be involved; birds are not very sensitive to odors.)

When adult birds are caged separately they never make a nest, no matter how much nesting material is available. If these single birds are offered nests with eggs in them they ignore them. If a male and a female bird are put together and immediately presented with a nest and eggs they will not incubate them. They will do so, however, if the eggs are presented six or seven days later, even though the female has not yet laid her own eggs. Similarly, if the eggs are removed from a nesting pair and baby birds are sub-

ment of "maleness" and "femaleness" is clearly greatest in the human species, as we will discuss further in Chapter 12.

Even when genetic, hormonal, and environmental factors are all (as far as we know) in agreement, there are people who feel that they have been "assigned" to the wrong sex—men who feel that they "should have been" women, and women who feel that they "should have been" men. These people are called transsexuals. A number of such individuals have requested and received surgical and hormonal treatments that produce a change in apparent sexual identity. However, a recent study (Meyer, 1979) has found that these operations do not produce any long-term beneficial effects on the lives of the people who undergo them. On the basis of this study, some hospitals will no longer permit this type of surgery.

Sexual Behavior

Sexual behavior begins, in all species, with some preliminaries called *courtship behavior*. The male sniffs, nuzzles, or otherwise expresses interest in the female; the female either rejects or accepts these advances. If she is receptive to them, she will eventually allow the male to mount. In virtually all mammals except humans, the female always has all four feet firmly on the ground. The male gets on top and *intromission* (entry of the penis into the female's vagina) is from

stituted, the parents will feed the squabs at once, even if their own eggs were not due to hatch for another week. They will have to feed the squabs on regurgitated seeds at first, but very soon (sooner than usual) their crops will start to produce crop milk.

Lehrman and his collaborators showed that a female ring dove that is prevented from mating will lay (infertile) eggs if she can see and hear a male ring dove bowing and cooing in an adjacent cage, behind a glass partition. If the male has been castrated he will not bow and coo, and the female will not lay eggs. The growth of the oviduct and the laying of eggs is dependent on two hormones: estrogen first, then progesterone. Evidently visual and auditory stimuli from the normal male are enough to stimulate the female's ovaries to produce these hormones. The same hormones determine incubation behavior: If a male and a female that have each been injected with proges-

terone are put together in a cage and offered a nest with eggs they will incubate them almost immediately, instead of after six or seven days. Estrogen injections cause them to incubate the eggs after a delay of two or three days.

Growth of the crop and production of crop milk has been shown to depend on the hormone *prolactin,* secreted by the pituitary gland. (Prolactin is also re-

sponsible for milk production in female mammals.) Injections of prolactin will cause either single male or single female ring doves to feed baby birds that are put into their cages. Secretion of this hormone (like that of estrogen and progesterone) is affected by external stimuli: Male birds separated from their mates early in the nesting period will fail to produce prolactin and their crops will not grow. But if they are placed in an adjacent cage and can still see the female sitting on the eggs, their crops will grow just as if they were sharing in the incubation. The presence of squabs also stimulates prolactin production and crop growth.

The conclusion is that the visual and auditory stimuli that appear at different stages of the breeding cycle produce changes in hormonal activity. These hormonal changes produce changes in behavior. The changes in behavior may, in turn, be a source of new visual and auditory stimuli.

behind and above. The female must cooperate by standing still, by arching her back somewhat, and by holding her tail (if she has one) to the side; this response is called *lordosis.*

What follows next differs in its details from species to species, although the outcome is the same. The rat will mount the female a number of times, and achieve 8 to 15 intromissions, each lasting less than a second. During the final intromission the male will *ejaculate* semen (the fluid containing the sperm) into the female's vagina.

The behavior just described evidently has drive-reducing (or incentive) value not only for the male, but for the female as well. It has been shown that receptive female rats will press a lever to gain access to a male rat (Bermant, 1961).

THE INFLUENCE OF HORMONES ON THE FEMALE.   All mammalian females show cyclical variations in hormonal state, called the *menstrual cycle* in primates, the *estrus cycle* in lower mammals. In most species ovulation occurs automatically at some specific point in the cycle, and at that time the female becomes both sexually attractive and sexually receptive to the male. One exception to this rule is the rabbit, which is virtually always receptive and which ovulates only upon mating. The other chief exception is the human female, who ovulates on a cyclical basis but shows little or no (there is still some debate on this question) cyclical change in receptivity or sexual attractiveness.

If the ovaries of a nonhuman female mammal are removed (which is done when female dogs and cats are "spayed"), the animal's hormonal cycle ceases, and so do the periods of sexual receptivity and sexual attractiveness. These functions can be restored by the administration of the ovarian hormones, estrogen and progesterone. Removal of the ovaries in human females sometimes lowers sexual drive, but sometimes it increases it (perhaps because fear of pregnancy is removed), and often it has no effect at all.

THE INFLUENCE OF HORMONES ON THE MALE. In the male cyclical variations in hormonal level occur in such animals as the deer, which confine their sexual activities to a certain season of the year. In most species hormonal production is constant, and the male is able and willing to engage in sexual activity at any time.

The effects of castration (surgical removal of the testes) depend on the age at which the operation is performed. A male that is castrated before puberty will never reach sexual maturity and will never show normal sexual behavior unless the hormones normally secreted by the testes are supplied artificially, by injection. Castration after puberty has a variable effect depending on the species and the amount of previous sexual experience. A male rat will usually cease to attempt to mount a receptive female within 2 or 3 months of castration. An experienced male dog might attempt to mount for a year or more after castration. In humans castration has an unpredictable effect, sometimes resulting in an immediate loss of potency (probably due to psychological factors) and sometimes in a slow decline over a period of years. In both humans and animals sexual desire and ability are restored by the administration of testosterone. By the way, *additional* testosterone administered to a male who already has an adequate supply has little effect on sexual activity (Bermant and Davidson, 1974).

THE ROLE OF EXPERIENCE. In many animals the ability to engage in normal sexual activity depends on their having been reared with others of their kind. Guinea pigs raised in isolation do not show sexual behavior (Valenstein, Riss, and Young, 1955). Isolated male rats do mount receptive females, but it takes them much longer (Zimbardo, 1958). Male beagles raised alone attempt to mount as frequently as normally reared dogs, but they often fail because their attempts are directed toward the female's head or side (Beach, 1968).

In monkeys reared in isolation neither males nor females show normal sexual responses. A group of monkeys was reared in separate cages where they could see and hear—but not touch—other monkeys. In adulthood these animals failed to mate even when a male and a female were caged together for as long as 7 years. When paired with normally reared monkeys none of the isolated males ever achieved a normal mount, and only one female became pregnant. These effects seem to be due not to the infant monkey's lack of a mother, but to its lack of social interactions with other young monkeys. Infant monkeys raised without mothers but allowed to play with one another for only 20 minutes a day later showed perfectly normal sexual behavior (Harlow, 1962).

HOMOSEXUALITY. Homosexual behavior shows up in all human societies and in most animal species. In animals mounting is frequently seen in females as well as males, and males will attempt to mount other males. Often this behavior is associated with dominance rather than with sexuality. However, mounting by female rats and by female monkeys is increased if they are exposed to testosterone early in development. Male rats that are castrated at birth will exhibit the female sexual response as adults if they are given estrogen and progesterone.

In humans, male or female homosexual behavior often shows up as isolated episodes in the lives of otherwise heterosexual individuals. In some societies homosexual behavior is considered normal during adolescence. Later most people in these societies marry and have normal heterosexual relationships (Money and Ehrhardt, 1972). Another type of homosexuality involves people (male or female) who *never* engage in heterosexual behavior.

Many attempts have been made to link homosexuality to physical factors such as chromosomal errors or hormonal abnormalities. It is true that the incidence of homosexual experience is somewhat higher in men with an XXY or XYY chromosomal pattern. However, the number of such cases is so small that these genetic errors account for a negligible proportion of homosexuals. It is the same with hormonal disorders: They are found in some small proportion of homosexuals, but not in most (Money, 1970). Only one bit of data — and a rather weak one, at that — suggests the possibility of an underlying physical cause for homosexuality. A study of identical and fraternal male twins (Kallman, 1952) showed that the identical twin of a homosexual was highly likely to also be homosexual, whereas fewer than half of the fraternal twin brothers of overt male homosexuals had had any homosexual experience after adolescence.

THE HUMAN SEXUAL RESPONSE. In 1966 Masters and Johnson published the results of their pioneering study of human sexuality. In this study volunteer subjects engaged in sexual activity to the point of orgasm, while sophisticated devices monitored a number of their physiological responses. Four different stages of the human sexual pattern were defined:

1. *Excitement.* This stage is characterized by vaginal lubrication, thickening of the vaginal walls, and elevation of the clitoris in females. In the male it involves erection of the penis and elevation of the testes. Nipple erection may also occur, in either sex.
2. *Plateau.* In both sexes heart rate, respiration, and muscle tension increase. The male testes increase in size and are pulled up very high in the scrotum. In the female the outer vaginal wall swells and the clitoris retracts.
3. *Orgasm.* In the male the penis throbs in rhythmic contractions and semen is expelled. Muscles throughout the body contract. The female experiences rhythmic contractions of the muscles of the vagina and uterus. Physiologically, the female's orgasm is quite similar to the male's. No differences were found between orgasms produced through clitoral stimulation and those produced through vaginal stimulation.
4. *Resolution.* A rapid decrease in physiological arousal follows orgasm in males. In females one or several orgasms may occur before resolution.

Since this description is, of course, rather cold and clinical, perhaps we should add that the whole sequence is usually considered highly pleasurable by both of the parties involved.

Parenting

In virtually all species the period immediately following birth is a dangerous time, associated with a high rate of mortality that declines as the organism matures. If the offspring are nurtured and protected by the adult members of a species, more of them are likely to survive. Thus parental care is clearly important to the success of the species as a whole. For this reason, care of the young has evolved in a great variety of species, including those as primitive as insects, spiders, and fish.

As an example, consider the threespine stickleback, a small fish that has successfully colonized almost all the coastal waters of the northern hemisphere (Hartman, 1979). In this animal it is the male that provides the parental care. He carefully builds a nest out of bits of plants and covers it with a mixture of sand and a sticky substance secreted by his kidneys. A receptive female is then enticed into the nest where she lays her eggs. The male fertilizes the eggs by emitting sperm over them, and then guards them until they hatch, meanwhile ventilating the nest by fanning water through it. When the young fish hatch, the father continues to guard them and will even retrieve those that stray from the nest. None of the other things this animal can do—obtaining food, fleeing from enemies—is as complex and demanding as the behavior just described.

In most nonhuman mammals the father plays a relatively minor role; nearly all the parental care comes from the mother. In such animals as the rat and the dog maternal behavior begins before the birth of the young, in the form of nest building. When the young are born, the mother bites off the umbilical cords and cleans off the pups. Almost immediately after the last pup is born the mother begins to nurse, by lying or crouching in such a way that the pups can reach her nipples. She will keep the pups warm, guard them against predators, and retrieve any that wander away or are removed from the nest. During the first day or two a mother dog will leave her litter for only a minute or two at a time, and only for the purpose of relieving bowel and bladder. A female rat that has been separated

Figure 10-5

A female rat will cross an electrified grid to reach her pups more readily than a hungry or thirsty rat seeking food or water. (Warden, 1931)

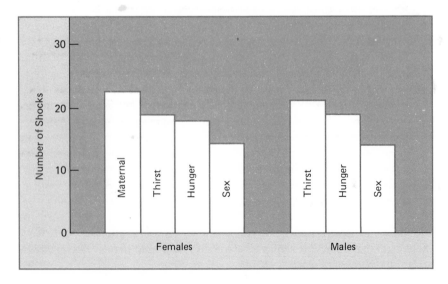

HIGHLIGHT
Sociobiology and Altruistic Behavior

Care of the young is a notable characteristic of the social insects—ants, bees, and wasps. Strictly speaking, this behavior cannot be called "parenting," because the workers that care for the eggs and larva are the sisters of the immature insects. Consideration of the activities of these social insects has given rise to a school of thought called *sociobiology* (Wilson, 1971). The sociobiologists believe that group selection, rather than survival of the fittest individual, is responsible for the evolution of altruistic behavior. (*Altruistic behavior* is defined in this context as any act in which an individual organism endangers its own chances of survival in order to increase the survival chances of other individuals. Parental care and protection of

the nest by "soldier" ants or bees are two examples of altruistic behavior in nonhuman species.)

According to this theory,

Individuals can afford to sacrifice their own personal genetic fitness if they make up for the loss by increasing the fitness of their relatives. Since many of their own genes are shared with the relatives by common descent, helping the relatives actually multiplies part of their own genetic structure (Wilson, 1974, p. 9).

In other words, sociobiologists believe that survival value benefits not the individual or even the species, but the genetic material within the chromosomes. In this view the rest of the organism is just an elaborate device for assuring the survival of its genes! Thus a mammal mother cares for her

young because they each have half their genes in common with her. What about the insects, such as bees, that are cared for by their sisters? Because of the peculiarities of chromosomal inheritance in these insects, a larval bee has three-quarters of its genes in common with each of its sisters, the workers who care for it. It is less closely related to its mother, the "queen" bee, having only half its genes in common with her. Only one-quarter of its genes are shared with each of its do-nothing brothers, the "drones."

The sociobiological viewpoint does a nice job of accounting for the behavior of ants and bees. The theory provides more controversy than enlightenment, however, when attempts are made to apply it to human behavior.

from her pups is so motivated to return to them that, in order to reach them, she will cross an electrified grid more readily than a hungry or thirsty rat seeking food or water (see Figure 10-5).

These innate patterns of behavior are elicited by a complex combination of hormonal states and external stimuli. For example, in many species nesting can be induced by progesterone injections, or by presenting a female with a ready-made litter of pups. Most animals—mammalian and nonmammalian—do not appear to recognize their own young but will respond appropriately to any infant member of their species. (Or even a different species—cowbirds and cuckoos lay their eggs in the nests of other species, where their offspring are fed and cared for by the foster mother and father, often to the detriment of their own less-demanding young!)

MOTHERLESSNESS IN MONKEYS. What exact function does parenting serve? What aspect of parenting is most important to the offspring? In an attempt to answer these questions, newborn monkeys were taken from their mothers and raised with "surrogate mothers" of various kinds (Harlow, 1959). It was found that the most important thing for the monkeys was to have something soft to cling to. Given a choice of a surrogate mother made out of wire and a similar mother covered with several layers of terrycloth, infant monkeys invariably chose the terrycloth mother. They spent much of their time climbing

In an experiment by Harlow (1959), if a monkey was separated from its mother at birth and raised with "surrogate" mothers of different kinds, the monkey would invariably choose the terrycloth mother over the wire mother.

on or clinging to the cloth-covered object, and when frightened, would run to it for reassurance. Monkeys raised without any mother at all, or with only a wire-covered one, withdrew in terror from a strange object, but a monkey with a cloth mother would soon gain enough courage to release the soft cloth and investigate the object.

The results were the same for baby monkeys that were fed from a bottle attached to the wire mother. Even though they got their milk from the wire mother, they spent most of their time clinging to the cloth one. Thus nourishment alone does not seem to form the basis for the emotional attachment between a primate infant and its mother.

Warmth appears to play some role, but not a major one. An infant monkey would readily abandon a warm heating pad in favor of its unheated cloth mother. In a later experiment, though, newborn infant monkeys given a choice between warm wire mothers and cool cloth ones favored the warm mother (Harlow, 1971). However, after the age of 20 days they began to prefer the cloth mother.

In the subprimate mammals warmth may be of greater importance than contact comfort. Puppies given the choice of a fur surrogate mother and a wire one chose the fur mother. But when the fur mother was cooled and the metal one heated, the puppies spent almost all of their time with the metal mother (Jeddi, 1970).

It should be noted, finally, that the infant monkeys "reared by" cloth mothers did not fare so well in the long run. Although they behaved normally, as long as their cloth mother was available, they grew up to be very maladjusted monkeys unable to have normal relationships—either social or sexual. If a female monkey raised on a cloth surrogate became pregnant, she never treated her infant with the tender care shown by a normally reared monkey mother. She refused to nurse the infant and either neglected or abused it.

We conclude that successful parenting of a young monkey or a young human (by mother, father, and/or other adults) must necessarily include cuddling. But cuddling is not enough. Infancy is not only a time of rapid physical growth—it is also a time of rapid learning. One of the most important things that an infant must learn is how to get along with other members of its species. That cannot be taught by a terrycloth mother.

Aggression

The term *aggression* refers to the kinds of behavior that lead to the damage or destruction of something—either another organism or an inanimate object. A coyote killing a lamb, a stallion attacking another stallion, a cornered cat slashing out at a dog, an enraged human destroying an automobile with a sledge-hammer—all these actions fall under the definition of aggression. Clearly, we are not referring to a single type of behavior: There are many different kinds of aggressive responses, and they are elicited by a wide variety of internal and external stimuli (Moyer, 1976). Seven categories of aggressive behavior are described below. It should be noted, however, that it is not always possible to distinguish these types of behavior in practice, because they often overlap. A given aggressive act may be the result of two or three factors acting together.

Kinds of Aggressive Behavior

1. Angry aggression.   This is the classical variety, the type most people think of when they hear the word "aggression." It is generally accompanied by the signs of emotional arousal (see the section on emotion in the next chapter), and is often produced by pain or frustration. For example, two rats put together in a cage and given brief, intermittent electric shocks will attack each other when the shock comes on. Under these circumstances a rat will even attack a doll or a stuffed animal, if another rat is not available. A monkey or a mouse whose tail is pinched will bite its tormenter or (if that is impossible) any other nearby object.

Frustration of goal-directed behavior—for example, preventing a hungry animal from reaching a food reward that it has worked for—generally produces an aggressive response. A pigeon that has been taught to peck a key to obtain grain will attack another pigeon if the grain is withheld (Azrin, Hutchinson, and Hake, 1966). However, frustration does not *invariably* have this kind of effect. The specific theory of frustration and aggression, as well as other theories of the origins of human aggressive behavior, will be discussed in Chapter 18.

2. Predatory behavior.   Quite different from the aroused state associated with angry aggression is the dispassionate stalking of its prey by a carnivorous animal such as a fox, a wolf, or any member of the cat family. One would hesitate to call this behavior "aggressive" and would label it "food-seeking" instead, were it not for the fact that the hunger drive need not be present—the response seems to be elicited simply by the presence of the prey, and may occur even if the predator is totally satiated.

An interesting finding about predatory behavior is that in some animal species it is partly learned through imitation. A kitten learns to kill rats by the age of 4 months if it is normally reared and allowed to see its mother killing rats.

If a kitten is raised in isolation, however, the chances are that it will *not* kill a rat if it is presented with one when it is 4 months old. It can soon learn to do so if it is given the opportunity to watch other cats kill (Kuo, 1930).

3. Fear-induced aggression. This is exemplified by the usually meek animal that, when cornered by a predator, turns on it and attacks it. More generally, any fearful animal is likely to bite when approached too closely by the object of its fear.

4. Operant aggression. An organism may perform an aggressive act simply because it is rewarded for doing it, or punished for not doing it. For example, the tendency of a rat to attack another animal or an object when it is given an electric shock can be strengthened if the shock is turned off whenever the rat attacks. Human adults (Loew, 1967) and children (Lovaas, 1961) who are praised for making hostile remarks tend to become more aggressive. The hired killer, who kills because he is paid to do so, is a good example of this class of aggression.

As in other forms of operant conditioning (discussed in Chapter 6), the reinforcement for aggressive behavior need not follow every response. Once the behavior is learned, an occasional reward (or punishment) is enough to maintain it. This is particularly clear in what is known as *obedient aggression.* A guard dog that attacks on command, or a person who harms someone because he or she is "ordered" to do so, is committing obedient aggression.

5. Territorial aggression. This category of behavior has been studied more thoroughly by ethologists (such as Konrad Lorenz, 1966) than by psychologists. Animals of many different species will stake out a territory, frequently mark it in some way (by spraying the boundaries with urine, for instance), and then threaten to attack any unfamiliar member of its species that intrudes within its borders. Note that this behavior is confined to the territory itself: If the animal is taken out of its own territory, its territorial aggressiveness vanishes.

6. Altruistic aggression. The aggressiveness of a bird or mammal guarding its young, or of a "soldier" bee or ant defending its hive or nest, are examples of altruistic aggression. Moyer (1976) has used the term *maternal aggression* to describe the fierce behavior of a female mammal whose nestful of pups is threatened. In some species, however—notably humans—the same kind of behavior may be shown by the father, or even by unrelated individuals.

7. Intermale aggression. In many species the normal reaction of a full grown male to another, unfamiliar adult male is a hostile one. Frequently the animal will attack without provocation. This behavior is distinguished from territorial aggression because it can occur in any location. Studies of intermale aggression in mice and rats have shown that the stimulus that elicits the attack is the scent of the other male. If the animals' odors are masked by an artificial scent, or if their sense of smell is surgically destroyed, they are unlikely to fight (Ropartz, 1968). Furthermore, in many species such as dogs and wolves (Lorenz, 1966), and even bison (Barash, 1977), the fight will not occur if one animal assumes a stereotyped position of submissiveness.

The male hormone testosterone is of critical importance in intermale aggression. Immature or castrated animals do not show this behavior, but if they are injected with testosterone the aggressiveness appears (Levy and King, 1953). It is also clear that intermale aggression is closely connected with the competition for females. In species that breed only in certain seasons, notably the hoofed mammals, almost all aggressive behavior takes place during the mating season.

Physiological Factors in Aggression

The parts of the brain that seem to play the major role in aggressive behavior are the limbic system and the associated areas of the hypothalamus (see Chapter 2). Damage to one of these brain areas, or stimulation of them through implanted electrodes, is likely to affect one or more of the types of aggressive behavior—especially predatory, angry, and fear-induced aggression. Particularly interesting to psychologists and physiologists are those cases in which only a single kind of aggressive behavior is affected. For example, mild electrical stimulation of one part of a cat's hypothalamus will cause it to attack a rat. Stimulation of another area within the hypothalamus, on the other hand, causes it to ignore the rat and instead launch an enraged attack on the experimenter (Wasman and Flynn, 1962; Egger and Flynn, 1963).

The amygdala, which is part of the limbic system, appears to be of particular importance in aggressiveness. Surgical destruction of all or part of this brain structure generally results in an animal that is docile, unaggressive, and unfearful. In humans there have been reports of abnormal aggressiveness resulting from tumors in the region of the amygdala. In 1966, a young man named Charles Whitman shot and killed 14 people from the observation tower at the University of Texas, before he himself was cut down by police bullets. In autopsy, a walnut-sized tumor was found in his amygdala (Beck, 1978).

Another factor that has been linked to aggressiveness is the level of glucose in the blood. Ralph Bolton, an anthropologist from Pomona College in California, lived for two years among the Qolla, a tribe of Indians that live in the Andes Mountains of Peru (Bolton, 1976). These people have been described as among the most aggressive on earth—their homicide rate is extremely high, and they are constantly embroiled in arguments and brawls. Bolton found, first of all, that the individuals within this group that were rated most aggressive were likely to be suffering from a moderate degree of hypoglycemia (low blood glucose). The people with normal blood glucose levels were less aggressive, and so were those with *severe* hypoglycemia, doubtless because of the weakening effects of this condition.

Secondly, Bolton found that the overall proportion of hypoglycemics in the Qolla population was far greater than in other populations studied: 55 percent had mild or severe hypoglycemia. (In the United States the proportion has been estimated at between 2 percent and 30 percent, but most researchers believe the 30 percent figure to be very exaggerated.) Bolton attributed the remarkable hypoglycemia rate found among the Qolla to three factors: (1) the effects of living at a high altitude; (2) poor nutrition; and (3) the effects of chewing coca leaves, which contain cocaine. Coca (not to be confused with cocoa, which comes from the bean of the cacao tree) deadens hunger pangs and makes its users feel better temporarily, but its long-term effects on the body's metabolism are harmful. Bolton hypothesized that fighting, too, may have temporary beneficial effects: By increasing the secretion of epinephrine by the adrenal glands, it may produce a rise in blood glucose that, though short-lived, results in an increased feeling of well-being while it lasts. Indeed, Qolla individuals sometimes mentioned to Bolton that fighting "makes one feel better."

From as early as two or three years of age, human males behave in a more aggressive fashion than human females (Pederson and Bell, 1970). The same sex difference has been noted in rhesus monkeys (Harlow, 1971) and in a wide variety of mammalian species. This aggressiveness includes not only intermale aggression, but also angry aggression, territorial aggression, and perhaps even operant aggression (male dogs are used as guard dogs more often than females).

In adult male animals, castration greatly reduces all kinds of aggressive behavior. A gelded horse or steer is considerably more tractable and slower to anger than a stallion or bull. The same effect is produced by the administration of estrogens and progesterone to a male animal (Moyer, 1971). Injections of testosterone restore the aggressiveness of castrated animals.

Human motivation is, of course, influenced by many factors other than physiological ones. As we will see in Chapter 11, cognitive, social, and emotional factors are often more important in human behavior than the biological events we have discussed in this chapter.

Summary

1. In motivation theory, James emphasized concepts of impulses and instincts; Cannon put forth the idea of *homeostasis,* or the way the body maintains an equilibrium in its internal environment.

2. The concept of *drives* and *drive reduction* was introduced by Hull. The concept of drives is most useful when talking about relatively clearcut states of psysiological deprivation such as hunger and thirst.

3. Hunger is one of the most universal sources of motivation. Regulation of food intake seems to depend on gastric secretions, a sensation of bulk in the small intestine, blood sugar level, and signals from the hypothalamus.

4. Some experiments support the set-point theory and suggest that obese people have a higher set point than nonobese people. When obese people are below their set point they are in a state of deprivation or homeostatic imbalance, even if their weight is above normal levels.

5. Areas of the hypothalamus are also associated with drinking; *osmoreceptors* in the brain seem to respond to dehydration in the cells by causing the organism to be thirsty and by triggering the release of a hormone, causing the kidneys to excrete less water. *Volumetric receptors* respond to a change in the total volume of extracellular fluid by stimulating the thirst receptors in the hypothalamus.

6. The temperature of warm-blooded organisms is held in balance by homeostatic mechanisms that seem to be regulated by the hypothalamus. The temperature of cold-blooded animals is regulated by behavioral means.

7. Sexual behavior apparently has drive-reducing (or positive incentive) value for both males and females of the species; hormones also play a role in both sexual behavior and the development of secondary sex characteristics.

8. Psychologists have identified at least 10 classes of aggressive behavior; the motivations for aggression are diverse, including pain, fear, predatory behavior, and maternal behavior.

9. The innate patterns of behavior that are part of mothering or parenting in many organisms are elicited by a complex combination of hormonal states and external stimuli.

Suggested Readings

BECK, R. C. *Motivation: Theories and principles.* Englewood Cliffs, N.J.: Prentice-Hall, 1978. Thorough coverage of historical and present-day motivation theories. Also deal with specific motivations such as aggression.

HARLOW, H. *Learning to love.* San Francisco, Cal.: Albion, 1971. The effects of parental care and peer-group interactions on young monkeys. Describes the development of social, sexual, and aggressive behavior in these animals.

KIMBLE, D. P. *Psychology as a biological science.* Santa Monica, Cal.: Goodyear, 1977. A general approach to the biological bases of behavior.

LORENZ, K. *On Aggression* (M. K. Wilson, trans.). New York: Harcourt Brace Jovanovich, 1966. Here Lorenz argues that humans as well as animals have an innate drive to be aggressive.

MONEY, J., and EHRHARDT, A. A. *Man and woman, boy and girl.* Baltimore: Johns Hopkins Press, 1972. Chromosomal and hormonal factors in human sexual identity and behavior.

WONG, R. *Motivation: A biobehavioral analysis of consummatory activities.* New York: Macmillan, 1976. Very detailed discussions of various sorts of motivated behavior, including feeding, drinking, mating, parenting, and stimulus seeking.

11 Human Motivation and Emotion

The previous chapter was concerned with the biological bases of motivation. We discussed motives and drives that are common to a wide variety of species: humans, monkeys, dogs, rats, and even honey bees. In this chapter the focus will be on the human species.

Why do people do what they do? What motivates us to behave at all? And how can we explain why, out of all the things we are capable of doing, we end up doing a certain thing in a certain situation? Answers to these questions are obviously very important, since they concern the core of human nature. The answers are also, as you might expect, very complex.

Human motivation ranges from basic physiological drives (such as hunger), through drives for stimulation that are part of our ability to know and understand our environment (such as curiosity), to socially based drives that we acquire from our culture (such as the desire to achieve).

We will also consider the topic of emotion in this chapter. Motivation and emotion are closely linked—indeed, as we shall see, it is often hard to distinguish between them. Emotions can act as motivators, and motivations can produce emotion. We will begin by distinguishing between primary and secondary motivation.

Sources of Needs and Motives

Primary Motivation: Physiological Needs

We reviewed some of our biological needs in the previous chapter. We need food and water to survive. We also require air and an appropriate temperature range. When we encounter deficiencies in any of these basic needs, we typically take action to correct them.

If you think about your typical daily activities, however, you will quickly see that much of your behavior seems to have little or nothing to do with these basic biological needs. At least at first glance, it is hard to see how reading this book, riding a bicycle, talking with friends, or watching television has anything to do with hunger or thirst. But some of these behaviors may have been motivated by basic physiological needs, through complex conditioning and learning processes.

Secondary Motivation and Conditioning

In Chapter 6 we saw how Pavlov was able to give previously neutral stimuli the ability to elicit behaviors through the process of classical conditioning. A dog will normally salivate when it sees food, but it will not normally salivate when it hears a tone. After repeated pairings of the tone with the sight of food, Pavlov found that the tone alone could elicit salivation. Furthermore, through the process of higher-order conditioning, the tone could be used to create a link between another stimulus, such as a light, and salivation. Seeing a dog salivate when a light flashes would seem very strange unless you knew the dog's conditioning history.

Skinner has also shown us how previously neutral stimuli can become secondary reinforcers, and can then cause learning of new behaviors, through operant conditioning. When a rat learns that pressing a bar leads to food, the bar acquires the properties of a secondary reinforcer and can be used to reinforce other behaviors. A rat will learn to run a maze to get at the bar, will then learn to open a door to get into the maze, and so on until a complex chain of behavior is formed. An uninformed observer looking at several rats who had received such training might mistakenly conclude that rats have a built-in fondness for mazes.

Given the human being's ability to learn extremely complex sequences of behavior, some of our behaviors that seem to have little or nothing to do with basic physiological needs may in fact be the result of such complex chainings of behaviors. One very common secondary motivator is money. Money serves the same function for us as the bar or lever does for the rat—it gets us the food, drink, clothing, and shelter that we need. We are all familiar with the practically limitless list of things that people will do to acquire money.

Functional Autonomy of Motivation

With both classical and operant conditioning, previously neutral stimuli will eventually lose their acquired reinforcing power if they are not, at least some of the time, paired with the original reinforcer (such as food, in the case of hunger). Humans, however, appear to have many "secondary" reinforcers that do not seem to be paired with primary reinforcers. Color preferences or desires for certain kinds of friends, music, and clothing do not seem to need to be associated with primary reinforcers. This observation has led some motivation theorists to believe that acquired motives can have a "life of their own," independent of any association with the satisfaction of basic biological needs.

Perhaps the clearest example of such a learned or acquired motive comes from the work of Neal Miller and others on fear and anxiety. Miller (1948) demonstrated the motivating power of learned fear in rats. The animals were placed in a box that contained a white compartment, a black compartment, and a door between them. First, the rats were given several shocks on the white side of the box through an electrified floor. The animals soon learned to run from the white compartment through the open door into the black compartment. Following this training period, the animals were placed in the white compartment with the door between the compartments closed. Even though the shock was never turned on again, the rats learned to turn a wheel so that they could get out of the white compartment. Later, when the wheel was disconnected so that it no longer opened the door, the rats learned to instead press a bar to open the door. Such bar pressing persisted for hundreds of trials, even though the rats were never shocked again.

Behavior motivated by learned fear, then, can continue indefinitely without the organism ever reexperiencing the pain that created the fear originally. Brown (1961) has argued that much complex behavior in humans is maintained by fear or anxiety. For example, the loss of a valued possession, the esteem of others, or a source of income creates anxiety. A person is motivated to regain the desired object in order to relieve the anxiety, much as the rats were motivated to enter the black compartment in Miller's experiment. In this way, anxiety can maintain behaviors that are not directly tied to biological needs.

Several theorists have taken this kind of analysis one step further and have argued that many acquired motives can become *functionally autonomous* (Woodworth, 1918; Allport, 1937). This means that motives that were originally conditioned to basic biological needs can, through repeated use, become motives in their own right. The behavior of the hoarder who collects money for the sheer pleasure of having larger and larger piles of it, and who does not want to spend it even to provide adequate food and clothing, is an example of functional autonomy.

Some Prominent Human Needs

Affiliation

Wherever people are found, whether in a high-rise office building, along the banks of a tropical river, around a desert oasis, or in a crowded discotheque, one clear fact of human existence is that we spend a great deal of our time with other people. We work together, eat together, and play together. We have developed extremely complex languages for the purpose of communicating with one another. At birth we are completely dependent on other people to satisfy our biological needs, and this dependence lasts longer in humans than in any other species. Stories of hermits who live in isolated caves and shun all human contact capture our interest because such behavior is so unusual. For these and other reasons, the human being is often called the social animal.

In the previous chapter we saw that a monkey that is reared alone (or with a terrycloth "mother" instead of a real one) is likely to be permanently impaired in its ability to form normal relationships with other monkeys. Not surprisingly, the deficits caused by lack of proper parental care and attention are even more serious in humans.

EFFECTS OF LACK OF PARENTING.   Human babies need more than milk and a warm blanket. They need what is usually called "mothering," but which we will call "parenting," since it can equally well be provided by a father—or, for that matter, any caring adult. Case studies of children who have been subjected to early social deprivation show that social isolation can have very serious effects on normal human development. When infants are reared in institutions in which they receive food and medical care but little social stimulation, they show striking deficits in emotional, intellectual, and even physical development (Goldfarb, 1944, 1945; Spitz, 1946). Provence and Lipton (1962) observed institutionalized infants, aged 4 days to 8 months, whose main contact with other humans was limited to the changing of bottles (which were propped in their

APPLICATION
Severe Early Isolation—the Feral Child

From time to time cases have been reported of children who have been living in the wild from a very early age with little or no human contact. Often these *feral children* are living with, and appear to have been reared by, wild animals.

Sargent and Stafford (1965) reviewed a number of these cases. One of the earliest feral children described in some detail was the "Wild Boy of Aveyron." The Wild Boy was discovered by hunters in southern France in 1799. Apparently he had been foraging for himself for some time (he was about 11 years old). Dr. Jean Itard attempted to socialize and teach the boy, but although he did develop some affection for his caretakers and learn a few simple things, he never approached normalcy.

More recently a pair of girls about 2 and 9 years of age were found living with wolves in India in 1920. The younger girl died soon after she was discovered. The older girl, Kamala, had developed wolflife mannerisms: She howled, lapped up liquids, and bared her teeth at anyone who came too close (Gesell, 1940). An even more recent case of a

child being thoroughly socialized by an animal community is that of the Gazelle-boy of the Sahara Desert (Armen, 1974) who was found living with a herd of gazelle. He ran with the herd, had gazelle-like mannerisms, and generally seemed to be an accepted part of the gazelle community.

Attempts to resocialize these feral children have met with varied degrees of success. Itard had very limited success with the Wild Boy of Aveyron. Kamala, the wolf girl, was originally completely hostile toward other humans, but eventually she came to like her playmates and learned to use about 100 words. She did not, however, become a normal or average person. In contrast, Tamasha, the "Wild Boy of Salvador," who was found in the jungle, progressed quite rapidly. He acquired language fairly easily, as well as other habits of human culture, and was able to talk about his experiences in the wild. It is difficult to compare these children because their experiences and situations varied considerably, but it seems that the longer the period of time away from human contact and society, and

the earlier such separation begins, the more difficult it is for the person ever to become integrated into human society.

It is tempting to think that these difficulties of adjustment result from social isolation—that is, to assume that human contact is necessary for normal development and that the absence of such contact is the major source of the feral children's difficulties. There are, however, other possible explanations. For example, how did these feral children get into the wilderness in the first place? One plausible guess is that they were retarded or defective in some other way at birth, and that their parents abandoned them for that reason (Sargent and Stafford, 1965). Another possibility is that the severe malnutrition that most of these children must have experienced caused some central nervous system damage, and that that, rather than their social isolation, was the major problem.

It is because of these ambiguities in the interpretation of isolated cases that the laboratory work on animals by Harlow and others cited in the text is so valuable in trying to understand the effects of extreme social isolation.

cribs) and diapers. By 4 months of age, these infants were acting very differently from children who are raised in normal family settings. They vocalized less, were less interested in manipulating objects, were very passive, and showed delayed onset of language development. Gardner (1972) described a group of infants who required hospitalization and had to be removed temporarily from their parents. These infants became listless and depressed, and failed to gain weight normally. When they went back to their homes they quickly returned to normal. Modern hospitals recognize that young children do not thrive when they are separated from their parents, and make a real effort to keep such separation to a minimum.

It is difficult to pinpoint the specific aspects of social deprivation that led to impaired development in these human infants. It is, however, very clear that a degree of close human contact is necessary for normal development; we need far more than the mere provision of food and shelter. However, while some forms of extreme early social deprivation seem to cause irreversible damage, several investigators have discovered a remarkable resilience even in the face of severe deprivation. Koluchova (1972, 1976) studied the effects of early deprivation on a pair of identical twin boys. The boys lived in a children's home for 11 months, and then lived with their father, stepmother, and four brothers and sisters for the next $5\frac{1}{2}$ years. During this time the boys lived in a closet. They were not allowed out of the house or into the main rooms, and they were completely isolated from the rest of the family. When they were rescued from their plight they had almost no language and appeared to be severely retarded. By age 14, however, their IQs were average, their speech was normal, and they were doing well in school. These examples of rehabilitation give some hope that the negative effects of early social deprivation are at least partially reversible.

NEED FOR AFFILIATION IN ADULTS.   Fortunately, most of us do not encounter such severe early social deprivation. Anyone reading this book is already deeply involved in human society and experiences contact with others as a common, daily fact of life. We all spend time with others and time by ourselves, and we all have some control over our social lives. Sometimes we want to be with others: When Saturday evening approaches, dates, parties, and other social activities are often uppermost in our minds. At other times, we want to be alone: A quiet evening with a book or a solitary stroll is sometimes quite appealing. Given these facts, questions about *when* we will seek out social contact and *why* we do so become important.

In one of the first systematic investigations of changing desires for affiliation, Schachter (1959) did a series of studies of the relationship between fear and the desire to affiliate. On the basis of several case studies of college students' reactions to social isolation, he theorized that an increase in anxiety would lead to an increased desire to be with others. In his initial experiment female college students who volunteered for a psychology experiment were

One clear fact of human existence is that we spent a great deal of our time with other people: working together, eating together, playing together.

divided into two groups. The subjects in the high-fear condition were met by a person who introduced himself as "Dr. Gregor Zilstein of the Medical School's Departments of Neurology and Psychiatry." Following this imposing and ominous introduction, the subjects were told that the experiment involved the use of electric shock. They were told that the shocks would be quite intense and painful, though they were "reassured" that there would be no "permanent damage." This description was, of course, designed to be frightening: No one was ever actually shocked. In the low-fear condition, the subjects were met by a friendly person who told them that the shocks would be extremely mild, and that at most they would feel a tickle. These two situations created different levels of fear in the two groups. Schachter then measured the affiliative desires of his subjects. After explaining that a number of people were waiting to take part in the experiment and that they too would have to wait, each subject was asked to indicate whether she would prefer to wait in a room with other people or by herself. Only 33 percent of the low-fear subjects asked to wait with other people; almost twice as many (63 percent) of the high-fear subjects asked to wait with others. In subsequent experiments Schachter found that fear increased the desire to affiliate even when the subjects knew that they would not be allowed to talk with the people with whom they would be waiting.

Schachter's studies showed that people's desire to be with others increases when they are afraid. There are two reasons for this. First, simply being with others often causes a reduction in fear (Wrightsman, 1960). Second, when people are frightened, they want to find out how others in the same situation are reacting, so they can compare their own reactions with those of similar others (Schachter, 1959; Gerard and Rabbie, 1961). The experiments on fear and affiliation thus uncovered two of the most important aspects of social contact: emotional support from others, and the provision of standards of correctness through social comparison (Festinger, 1954).

AFFILIATION AVOIDANCE. There are, of course, times when we do *not* wish to be around others. When we are embarrassed, the last thing we want is to be around our peers. Our most fervent desire when we have just tripped over a small crack in an otherwise smooth sidewalk, or have just dropped a melting ice cream cone in our lap, is to be alone. For example, when Sarnoff and Zimbardo (1961) told their subjects that they would be participating in a study of oral needs and would be sucking on pacifiers, baby bottles, and breast shields, a clear preference to wait alone was expressed. And just as some people typically desire to be around others, chronically shy individuals often take great pains to avoid social contact (Zimbardo, 1977).

Curiosity and the Need for Stimulation

All animals are "built" to be efficient information gatherers and processors, and this is particularly true of humans. We routinely gather a wide variety of information through our senses. Through sight, hearing, touch, smell, and taste sensors we take in, organize, interpret, and use information about ourselves and our environment. Doing this enables us to understand our world and to take effective action. We not only have the ability to process information, we also have a need to use that ability.

Human information-processing capabilities can be likened to a fine piece of

machinery. An automobile engine, for example, can be efficient, powerful, and smooth, but if it is left unused for 6 months, it will probably be balky, dirty, and unreliable. Similarly, if our information-processing abilities are to work well, they need exercise. Unlike an automobile engine, however, we do not need an outside force to "turn us on." Humans and animals have a built-in need for stimulation that motivates them to seek out sensory stimulation from the environment.

A THEORETICAL ACCOUNT OF CURIOSITY.   The fact that we tend to seek stimulation, and to exhibit preferences for and interest in certain degrees of complexity in that stimulation, is explained by the concept of an *optimal level of stimulation* (Hunt, 1965). According to this theory, we tend to pay attention to stimuli that deviate from our standards of comparison (Miller, Galanter, and Pribram, 1960). Standards of comparison are developed through experience. The first time you see an object, it tends to interest you and hold your attention. However, as you continue to be exposed to that object, you become used to it or adapt to it, and it is less likely to command your attention. For example, if you are used to seeing birds with two legs, another two-legged bird will not be as likely to arouse your interest as a four-legged bird would be. Standards of comparison are also called *adaptation levels* (Helson, 1964). For any given sort of stimulation, the *adaptation level* is the level of stimulation that is perceived as average or normal. Stimuli that fall within the average range are not likely to capture our attention; stimuli that fall outside the average range (such as four-legged birds) are.

Humans and animals have a built-in need for stimulation that motivates them to seek out sensory stimulation from the environment.

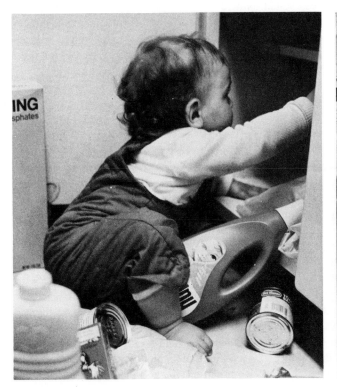

Using these concepts of adaptation level and focusing of attention on incongruous stimuli, Hunt (1965) theorized that there are optimal levels of stimulation. If all incoming stimuli are average, or within our adaptation levels, we become bored. On the other hand, excessive stimulation can be very unpleasant. But stimuli that are a little unusual are interesting. So optimal levels of stimulation are those that contain enough surprises to keep our interest alive and allow us to exercise our information-processing abilities, but are not so different from our experience and expectations that they are frightening or overwhelming. For example, sometimes crowded shopping malls or events with large jostling crowds can be unpleasant because they provide too much stimulation. In contrast, jobs, lectures, or other daily routines that contain no surprises can become unpleasantly boring.

EXPERIMENTS ON SENSORY DEPRIVATION.   If it is true that people need stimulation, and that they prefer such stimulation to be mildly different from their current adaptation levels, then we would expect that a complete absence of stimulation would be very unpleasant and have negative effects on people's efficiency at processing information. Such effects were dramatically illustrated in an early experiment on sensory deprivation reported by Bexton, Heron, and Scott (1954). College student volunteers were paid per day to take part in a study of the effects of reduced sensory input. The subjects spent their time in the study lying on a cot in a sound-deadened room with a constant background noise. They wore translucent goggles, cardboard tubes around their arms, and gloves. This experience was very unpleasant, and most of the subjects refused to continue the experiment after a few days. In this experiment and others like it, the subjects experienced visual hallucinations, rapid changes in mood, and an inordinate interest in normally boring material, such as old stock-market reports. After a period of sensory deprivation such subjects also showed reduced competence on a variety of visual, manual dexterity, and abstract reasoning tasks (Held and White, 1959; Bexton, Heron, and White, 1954; Vernon et al., 1959). Taken together, these studies of sensory deprivation underscore the importance of our need for stimulation.

Competence

Imagine trying the following observational exercise: For one day you pretend that you are a visitor from another world. You know nothing at all about humans, so you watch them to find out what they are like. One of the most basic things that you could say, the most accurate description of the humans you saw, would be that they are almost always *doing* something. Except for periods of sleep, and excluding a few abnormal cases of coma or catatonia, people spend nearly all their time behaving. They ride bicycles, jog around tracks, fly airplanes, ski, scratch their noses, doodle, and tap their feet. What inspires all this activity? Some behaviors clearly serve basic biological needs; hunger, for example, provides the motivation for moving the forkful of spaghetti from the plate to the mouth. But even when all of the basic needs are satisfied, people still talk, work crossword puzzles, and do many other things.

This incessant activity has led a number of psychologists to argue that humans *need* to behave. We saw earlier that people need to exercise their information-processing abilities; we now turn to the related notion that they

Efficacy is the feeling that you have when you do something perfectly, whether it be catching a football, making something with your own hands, or playing a game well. The urge to manipulate the environment and make effective use of your abilities is called effectance motivation.

need to exercise their ability to behave. Woodworth (1958), for example, believed that the great variety of behavior that seems to be completely incidental to any primary needs (such as doodling in a notebook) cannot be adequately explained by the theories of secondary motivation reviewed at the beginning of this chapter. His hypothesis was that the need to deal with the environment is itself a primary drive. Similarly, Goldstein (1939) gave self-actualization the status of a primary drive. His hypothesis, not unlike Woodworth's, was that humans have a basic tendency to actualize or bring into being their inherent abilities, to do things merely because they are capable of doing them.

After reviewing the ideas of Woodworth, Goldstein, and others, White (1959) proposed a theory of motivation based on the idea that people are motivated to develop and exercise *competence* in interacting with their environment. According to this hypothesis, interacting effectively with the environment produces feelings of competence or efficacy. The feeling that you have when you do something perfectly, whether it be making a basketball swish through the net, completing a difficult crossword puzzle, or efficiently knitting an even row of stitches on a sweater, are examples of feelings of efficacy. This urge to manipulate the environment, to make effective use of capabilities, was termed *effectance motivation*. Some of White's most interesting examples concerned the play of children. Although dropping a cookie from a highchair might teach a toddler about gravity, and this knowledge might prove useful later in life, White believed that the child was motivated by the desire to create an effect on the environment. He argued that we need to interact effectively with the environment, and that effective interaction can be its own reward.

Harter (1978) has proposed a revision of White's model that includes a three-stage analysis of the development of effectance motivation. In infancy the effectance motive is thought to be an inherent, biologically based striving to affect the environment. Striking at a rattle, pulling on a string, or biting on a squeaky toy are some examples of this kind of behavior. These sorts of things will happen naturally; they do not require any urging from parents. As children grow older, however, they begin to imitate the behavior of other people, and to choose behaviors that are shaped by the reinforcements that others give for particular kinds of mastery attempts. As children are given chemistry sets or microscopes and are reinforced for using them, or as they see friends and family members spending a lot of time playing sports, the arenas in which they express effectance motivation are shaped. The third stage emerges as people internalize values and begin to give themselves rewards or set goals for themselves based on their own acquired values. As you can see, this theory emphasizes that learning influences effectance motivation and determines how it will be expressed.

Bandura (1977) has proposed a *theory of self-efficacy* that focuses on expectations of efficacy rather than feelings of efficacy. According to this theory, the decision about whether or not to try a particular behavior depends on the person's belief that he or she will be successful. For example, your decision about whether or not to try the crossword puzzle in the Sunday newspaper depends on your belief about your ability to complete the puzzle. Expectations of efficacy will also affect how long a person persists at an activity. For instance, once you begin a crossword puzzle, how long you continue to work on it will depend on your beliefs about your ability to finish it. If you decide that it is too hard for you, you will probably quit after a short time. But if you think you have a good chance of completing it, you might work on it all morning.

There are four sources of efficacy expectations. One is *past performance accomplishments*. If you have solved a number of crossword puzzles in the past, your expectations will be high. If you have not had much success in the past, your expectations will be low. Expectations are also affected by *vicarious experience*. Seeing other people succeed or fail will influence your own expectations of success. If your roommate solves a lot of crossword puzzles, and you think your verbal skills are as good as his, you will be tempted to try one. Another source of expectations comes from *verbal persuasion*. Pep talks from friends or teachers can encourage you to try tasks that you might otherwise avoid. Finally, *emotional arousal* influences efficacy expectations. If thinking about an activity causes nervousness or fear, you will be less likely to think that you can succeed at it.

NEGATIVE EFFECTS OF LOSS OF COMPETENCE.   As you can see, competence is a fundamental aspect of human nature. This becomes dramatically apparent when people are deprived of their feelings of competence. Seligman (1975) has shown in a number of studies what happens when people are put through experiences in which they are unable to control their environment. Such experiences lead them to become depressed at the time and to become passive and unresponsive in later settings in which they do have control (Miller and Seligman, 1975; Roth and Kubal, 1975). The more that people expect to have control, the more adversely they are affected by experiences in which they have no control (Pittman and Pittman, 1979). This kind of evidence underscores the vital importance of feelings of competence and efficacy.

TWO SOURCES OF COMPETENCE MOTIVATION—INTRINSIC AND EX-TRINSIC.   As we have seen, much of an infant's behavior appears to be directed toward producing interesting effects on the environment. We might think of this behavior as a fairly pure example of effectance motivation. But as a person becomes socialized, the issue rapidly becomes more complicated. We might do some things for the pure satisfaction of doing them; many games and other forms of entertainment probably serve this function. But other activities are done with an eye toward gaining something else. We may wash the family car on a Saturday morning motivated more by the thought of next week's allowance than by the sheer joy of seeing a clean automobile. These two kinds of reasons for behaving are called *intrinsic* and *extrinsic motivation*. Things that are done because they are fun, that are ends in themselves, are intrinsically motivated. Things that are done in order to get something else, that are means to an end, are extrinsically motivated (Kruglanski, 1975). For many people, these two kinds of motives represent the basic difference between play and work.

One implication of these definitions of intrinsic and extrinsic motivation is that we will regard activities that lead to other rewards (such as money or candy or other valued possessions) as extrinsically motivated. A clear demonstration of the truth of this idea was provided by Lepper, Greene, and Nisbett (1973). In their study nursery school children who liked to draw for the sheer fun of it were asked to draw some pictures under one of three sets of circumstances. Some of the children were told that they would win an attractive Good Player Award if they drew some pictures. This should have encouraged them to think of drawing as an extrinsically motivated activity ("I did it for the reward"). Other children did not find out about the reward until after they had finished drawing. Those children would not have been thinking of the reward as they drew pictures, so they should have continued to think of drawing as intrinsically motivated ("I did it because I like to draw"). The third group of children simply drew the pictures and were never told about any reward. When all the children were observed during free play periods 2 weeks later, the children who had drawn in order to get the reward were much less interested in drawing as a leisure activity than were the children from the other two groups. This study shows us two things. First, the kinds of activities we are likely to prefer in our free time are those that are intrinsically motivated, those that we think of as ends in themselves. Second, our ideas about what activities are intrinsically motivated can be changed by adding rewards to intrinsically interesting activities. This presents a particular challenge to educators, who must discover how to encourage learning without ruining intrinsic motivation. There are ways to do this—rewards that indicate competence (Boggiano and Ruble, 1979) or that are accompanied by verbal praise (Swann and Pittman, 1977) do not decrease intrinsic interest, but care must be taken by anyone who wants to reward intrinsically motivated activities.

Achievement

The need for achievement includes the desire to excel, to complete difficult tasks, to meet high standards, and to outperform others. People who are high in their need for achievement, called high-need achievers, differ from low-need achievers in a number of ways. For example, they tend to do better on problem-solving tasks (French and Thomas, 1958) and show better performance and more rapid improvement on verbal problems (Lowell, 1952). They also tend to set realistic but challenging goals for themselves. McClelland (1958) showed this with 5-year-old children who were classified as either high- or low-need achievers. The children played a ring toss game in which they tried to toss rings onto a standing peg on the floor. They were allowed to stand as far away from the peg as they liked. McClelland found that the children who had a high need for achievement typically chose to stand at an intermediate distance from the peg, neither so close that the game was very simple, nor so far away that it was almost impossible. Children who had a low need for achievement did just the opposite. Either they stood so close that they were assured of some success, or they stood unrealistically far away. The same findings have been obtained with college students who played the ring-toss game (Atkinson and Litwin, 1960).

McClelland (1961) undertook an extensive historical study of the relationship between achievement themes in literature and the economic productivity of various countries. He found an interesting sequence in a number of different societies: When the use of achievement themes in the society's literature increased, the economic productivity of that society increased a few years later. Similarly, when achievement themes declined, subsequent economic productivity declined. General levels of achievement motivation in a society thus appear to be quite important. Another example of this relationship was given by deCharmes and Moeller (1962), who found that in the United States during the period 1800–1950 the use of achievement themes in children's literature and the number of registered patents rose and fell together.

ATKINSON'S THEORY OF ACHIEVEMENT MOTIVATION.   What determines a person's achievement orientation toward a specific task? Atkinson and Feather (1966) developed a theory that explains orientation as the result of two separate tendencies: the tendency to achieve success and the tendency to avoid failure. The tendency to achieve success is determined by three things: (1) the motive to succeed, or need achievement (nAch); (2) the person's estimate of the likelihood of success in performing the particular task; and (3) the incentive for success, that is, how much the person would like to succeed in that particular task. The tendency to avoid failure is determined by three similar considerations: (1) the motive to avoid failure, which, like the motive to achieve success, varies among individuals; (2) the person's estimate of the likelihood of failure at the particular task; and (3) the incentive value of failure at that task, that is, how unpleasant it would be to fail. The relative strengths of the tendencies to succeed and to avoid failure determine the level of task difficulty people will prefer. When the tendency to succeed is stronger, as it is for people who have a high need to achieve, the preferred tasks are those intermediate in difficulty, in which the likelihood of success is reasonable and the pride in accomplishment fairly high. When the tendency to avoid failure is dominant, however, people either prefer very simple tasks in which the probability of failure is low, or very difficult tasks where the shame in failing is low. As we have already seen, high and low achievers do show this pattern of preferences in risk-taking studies.

With such a wide range of needs, can we predict what people will do in a specific setting at a specific time? Unless we have some way of knowing when particular needs are actively influencing current behavior and when they are not, we will have a difficult time figuring out which of the many possible needs are the important or dominant ones at any moment. In the next section we will look at Maslow's idea that some needs come first and must be satisfied before other needs gain attention.

Maslow's Hierarchy of Needs

A few examples may give you a clue about how Maslow organized needs. First, imagine that you are swimming underwater and you accidentally come up under a large raft where there is no air. As you struggle to reach open water before your lungs burst, are you wondering about what you will have for dinner that evening? Or try this scene: You go on a summer camping trip in a national forest, become separated from your companions, and it is now 5 days since you have eaten. You are tired, cold, and you keep hearing noises at night that sound like bears and wolves. Which of the following concerns do you think would be most pressing: (a) food, (b) safety, (c) need for achievement? Finally, try this more pleasant scene: You have just finished an excellent meal of all your favorite foods and you feel very satisfied, but not stuffed. You are rested, feel somewhat energetic but very relaxed, and have no commitments. You can do whatever you like. What would you do? Your answer may reveal something about yourself; it will also reveal something about the nature of needs. In the first two examples, needs for air, food, and safety became paramount when a deficit was created. The third example illustrates that once a need is satisfied, it is a much less active motive. After a good meal, for example, you would probably not immediately begin searching for more food. Whether a particular need will motivate behavior

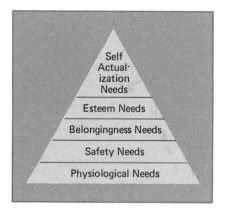

Figure 11-1
Maslow's hierarchy of needs.

seems to depend on two things: (1) whether that need has been satisfied recently, and (2) how strong other, more fundamental needs may be. For example, no matter how hungry we are, the need to breathe will take precedence over the need to eat. This idea, that some needs come first and must be satisfied before other needs gain attention, is basic to Maslow's theory.

THE NEED HIERARCHY.   Maslow (1970) believed that there are five categories of needs and that they are arranged in a *hierarchy* or *sequence* (see Figure 11-1). For a particular need to guide the person, all the more basic needs must be satisfied first. The most basic needs are *physiological;* these must be met if we are to survive, and include oxygen, food, water, and sex (although it is not necessary to the survival of the individual, sex is essential to the survival of the species). Since these primary needs are routinely satisfied for most people in our society, we are free to devote much of our attention to other needs. *Safety* needs form the next category. Again, these needs are often routinely satisfied, but they can become preoccupations if we live in a high-crime neighborhood or near a defective nuclear power plant, or have a hazardous job. Next come needs for *love and belongingness.* Maslow believed that people need to give and receive affection. They also need to feel that they belong to a group or to a society. The need to belong has become increasingly difficult to satisfy as society becomes more mobile. Changing homes, jobs, and schools may frustrate the individual's need to belong. Maslow thought that the growth of encounter groups in the 1960s could be attributed to widespread frustration of the need to belong. Once the needs for love and belongingness are not pressing, then needs for *esteem* arise. These include the desire to think highly of yourself (self-esteem) and to have others think highly of you. Put another way, we need to respect ourselves and to have others respect us. We need this esteem to feel self-confident and self-worthy. Without it we feel inferior and worthless.

You might think that someone who has no worries about food, clothing, or safety, who feels loved and accepted by others, and who commands respect from others and has high self-esteem would be very content. Maslow, however, found such people to be tense and restless, because when all the other needs are satisfied, the need for *self-actualization* becomes dominant. Self-actualization is the realization of our potentials, the exercise of our talents to the fullest. A person with musical talents needs to make music; someone with a logical, inquisitive mind devoted to science needs to be a scientist. Most of us do not reach the self-actualization level because most of us never really satisfy our needs for love and esteem. Those who do become self-actualizers seem to have certain characteristics and talents that set them apart, as we will see in Chapter 14.

Emotion

As we mentioned at the beginning of the chapter, motivation and emotion are very closely linked—in fact, it is often hard to distinguish them. We usually consider hunger, thirst, and sex to be needs or drives; typical emotions are anger, grief, joy, surprise, and embarrassment. But what about pain? A painful stimulus produces both an emotional response and a drive to escape the pain. In the same way, fear is an emotion but also a motivator—for example, the rats that received electric shocks in the white cage (see page 308) presumably became afraid when they were put into that cage again and were motivated to escape. So an unpleasant emotion can serve as a motivator—the organism is motivated to terminate that feeling.

Drives and needs can produce emotions, too. Consider the example we gave of the person swimming underwater who comes up under a raft. The need for air will produce not only a struggle to reach the edge of the raft, but also intense fear. Extreme hunger or thirst is also likely to result in emotional responses such as grief, anger, or fear. Another source of strong emotional responses is the frustration of the sexual or parental drive.

As these examples indicate, there is sometimes no clear-cut dividing line between motivation and emotion. In general, though, we conceive of motivation as arising from some internal source such as deprivation of a biological requirement (food, for instance), and of producing some sort of goal-directed behavior (such as searching for food). On the other hand, we think of emotion as being an internal state usually produced by an *external* stimulus (or stimuli) and *not* necessarily leading to any particular behavior. In fact, a given emotion can result in many different sorts of behavior, even within the same individual.

Emotion is an extremely tricky subject to study. It is especially hard to study under controlled laboratory conditions because it is not always possible to produce a genuine emotion in the laboratory, or even to know for sure when we have succeeded in producing it. There are behavioral and physiological indications that can tell us when a person is fearful or angry, but it is often difficult to tell—except by the person's verbal reports—whether he or she is happy, sad, amused, embarrassed, disgusted, envious, puzzled, worried, relieved, or in love. Thus, there has been relatively little research into these more subtle emotions.

What Produces an Emotional Response?

INNATE VERSUS LEARNED EMOTIONS.   Human beings, as well as animals, have a number of built-in emotional responses. For example, any sudden, intense stimulus is likely to evoke the brief burst of fear known as the *startle* response. Restraint of motion or the sudden withdrawal of a proffered reward generally leads to anger. An infant's smile elicits feelings of love and delight from its parents. The death of a close relative usually results in grief. Human babies just beginning to crawl are afraid to cross a pane of glass 3 or 4 feet above the floor—a device called the "visual cliff," which will be discussed in Chapter 12.

Other stimuli produce emotional reactions that are clearly acquired through experience. If we administer an electric shock to a rat each time we sound a buzzer, the rat begins to act afraid whenever the buzzer goes on. Rats that became ill after eating a certain food reacted with apparent disgust when offered that food at a later time—they would scoop it out of the food dish with their paws and scatter it on the floor of the cage. The delight that some people feel when they listen to a Mozart concerto, or that other people feel when they hear the ding of the ice cream wagon, are other examples of acquired, or secondary, emotional responses.

In one of the most famous—or infamous!—psychological experiments ever

conducted, the behaviorist J. B. Watson taught an 11-month-old baby named Albert to be afraid of white rats (Watson and Rayner, 1920). When Albert was first shown a white rat he was not at all afraid of it. Then the experimenters made a loud noise behind the child each time the rat was presented to him. The noise startled Albert and made him cry. After this happened a few times Albert started to cry whenever he saw the rat. In addition, he became afraid of other, similar things: a white toy rabbit, a Santa Claus beard.

A great deal of time and effort has gone into attempts to answer such questions as: Is the human emotional response to a certain stimulus a primary (innate) or secondary (learned or acquired) response? For example, a common inquiry is: Is the fear of snakes innate or learned? Some psychologists have said "innate," and pointed to the fact that chimpanzees raised in the laboratory are innately afraid of snakes (Hebb, 1946). Others have shown that children under 2 years of age often seem to have no fear of snakes. Neither of these arguments is very persuasive, however: The fact that chimpanzees are innately afraid of snakes doesn't mean that humans are; and the fact that a fear is not present at birth does not mean it is learned. In fact, only two stimuli seem to elicit fear in the newborn baby: a loud noise and a sudden loss of support. Or, rather, they elicit a generalized excitement response, which is all that the newborn seems to be capable of (Bridges, 1932). Over the course of the first 4 or 5 months of life, this generalized excitement becomes differentiated into separate emotions such as anger, fear, and delight. In addition, certain stimuli—such as an unfamiliar human face—that at first elicit neutral or favorable emotional responses produce fearful reactions in older babies.

PREPAREDNESS.   Martin Seligman has proposed a new approach to the old problem of innate versus learned emotional responses. He asks why it was so easy to make little Albert become afraid of furry animals. Other experimenters (English, 1929; Bregman, 1934) tried to repeat Watson's experiment using wooden blocks, wooden ducks, or curtains. They got no conditioned fear at all, even after these objects were paired many times with loud noises. Seligman describes an occasion in his own life when he came down with a violent stomach flu a few hours after eating filet mignon with sauce Béarnaise. After that he couldn't stand sauce Béarnaise, although previously it was one of his favorite foods. But, as he says, "neither the filet mignon, nor the white plates off which I ate the sauce, nor *Tristan und Isolde,* the opera that I listened to [in the time between the meal and the onset of the illness] nor my wife, Kerry, became aversive. Only the sauce Béarnaise did" (Seligman and Hager, 1972, p. 8). Even though Seligman *knew* the sauce was not responsible (because others had eaten it and had not gotten sick, or had gotten sick without eating it), this knowledge did not affect his feelings—what we might call his "gut reaction."

The concept that Seligman developed to account for his acquired disgust is called *preparedness* (Seligman, 1972). The idea is that organisms are more prepared to associate a given emotional response with one stimulus, and less prepared to associate it with another. An experiment by Garcia and Koelling (1966) illustrates this principle. Rats were given water sweetened with saccharin and then made sick by exposure to radiation. Afterward they didn't want to drink saccharin-flavored water. Drinking the water was also paired with a light and a clicking sound, but the rats showed no tendency, later, to avoid either the light or

HIGHLIGHT
Preparedness and Phobias

The idea of preparedness sheds new light on the problem of phobias. People with phobias are terrified of something—cats, or heights, or open spaces. They may be afraid to leave the house because an open area is so frightening to them, or because they are afraid of encountering a cat. Although psychologists have had some success in treating phobias with long-term therapy or behavioral techniques, the notable thing about phobias is how hard they are to get rid of. Sometimes a fear can be traced back to some traumatic incident—a fear of water, for example, can be traced to a near-drowning. But subsequent *non*traumatic contacts with the feared stimulus don't seem to abolish the fear—if anything, they make it worse. This is what makes phobias different from other learned fears: When rats are given electric shock in conjunction with a buzzer, for example,

the fear elicited by the buzzer soon disappears if they experience the buzzer without the accompanying shock. This is not true of phobias.

So the question is: Why are phobias sometimes produced after only a single unpleasant incident, and why is it so difficult to get rid of them? The answer seems to be that we are inherently prepared to be afraid of certain stimuli, so that an association is easily made and is abolished only with difficulty. Most phobias involve certain types of stimuli and not others. For example, phobias to animals (cats, horses, mice, snakes, or spiders) are common. Other phobias involve heights, open or enclosed spaces, fire or water, the dark. It is noteworthy that people very seldom become phobic about bulletin boards or hair ribbons, or even such potentially threatening objects as electric outlets or razor blades.

A child can nearly cut his finger off with a kitchen knife and suffer no permanent psychological scars, but let someone say "boo!" when he is looking at a cat and he may develop a serious problem.

Freud believed that phobias are displaced fear. He described a case in which a 5-year-old child called Little Hans was afraid of horses. According to Freud, Hans was *really* afraid that his father would castrate him for desiring his mother. That fear, being unacceptable, was translated into an *acceptable* fear—fear of horses. But Hans himself described an incident that occurred when he was in a bus: A horse fell down, and it frightened him very much: "It gave me such a fright, really! That was when I got the nonsense" (Freud, 1909, p. 192).

Today, many psychologists feel that Little Hans was, indeed, afraid of horses.

the sound.

On the other hand, when rats were given electric shock after drinking water, they avoided water associated with the light and sound, but didn't object to the saccharin-flavored water. The conclusion is that rats are *prepared* to associate illness with a taste, or electric shock with a visual or auditory stimulus. They are not prepared—or, rather, *less* prepared—to associate illness with light or sound, or shock with a taste.

Preparedness is not a yes-or-no, all-or-none sort of thing; it is a continuum. Each possible association of a stimulus and an emotional response can be given a position on this continuum by asking: How many pairings of this stimulus with this response are necessary in order to condition the association? On the extreme "prepared" end of the continuum the answer may be *none*—some stimuli elicit the emotional response the very first time it is presented. On the "unprepared" end of the continuum the answer is an infinite number—there may be some emotional responses that *never* become linked to a certain stimulus. In between are all the associations that are more or less easy to condition. Clearly, little Albert's fear of furry animals was an easy association to make, and fear of a wooden block is a relatively hard one.

Indications of Emotional Responses

You probably know at any given moment whether you are experiencing an emotion, and if you are, what emotion it is. It is a lot harder to tell the emotions of *other* people. Some people cover their emotions so well that you never know what they are feeling. And some can convincingly feign emotions, or at least pretend to feel them more strongly than they really do.

How do we judge the emotional state of another individual? There are six cues on which we usually base our judgment: situational factors, facial expression, verbal report, voice quality, motor responses, and physiological responses.

SITUATIONAL FACTORS.   You can imagine how someone who has just been told that she won the state lottery feels. Similarly, you can guess the emotions of a person after he has been informed of his mother's death, or after he has slipped on the ice and fallen heavily on his knees. We know how *we* would feel in these situations, and we assume that the other person feels the same way. In addition, we often assume—with less justification—that we know the emotional state of *animals* on the same basis. For example, we might guess that a horse that is being whipped feels anger or fear, even if it shows no outward signs of these emotions.

FACIAL EXPRESSION.   In 1872 Charles Darwin published a book entitled *The Expression of the Emotions in Man and Animals.* In it he described in minute detail the facial expressions of emotion in humans and animals—even naming the particular muscles that come into play in each instance. The principles that Darwin wished to establish were that facial expressions of emotions in humans are innate, not learned; that they are universal in all races of humanity; and that they have their origins in the facial expressions of animals. He pointed out that a human snarl of anger closely resembles the teeth-baring grimace of angry dogs and cats. Young chimpanzees, when tickled under the arms, make a response that looks and sounds very much like human laughter.

Darwin's observations were so thorough and so careful that even today we have little to add to them. We still believe that facial expressions of emotions are not learned. Blind children, who have never seen a smile or a frown on another person's face, are nonetheless able to smile or frown as well as children with normal vision. The universality of facial expressions has also been confirmed. Ekman and Friesen (1969) photographed people portraying various emotions such as grief, happiness, fear, surprise, and disgust. They showed these photographs to subjects in the United States, Brazil, Chile, Japan, and Borneo. All the subjects tended to identify the same faces with the same emotions.

In another experiment Ekman and Friesen (1971) showed their pictures to a group of people who had had little or no contact with Western or Eastern literate cultures: the Fore of New Guinea. With the aid of a translator the experimenters read a simple story to the subjects—for example, "She is just now looking at something which smells bad"—and asked the subject to pick which of three faces best agreed with the story. The Fore subjects picked the "correct" picture almost all the time; the main exception was that fear and surprise proved to be hard to tell apart. Ekman and Friesen also had members of the Fore group feign various emotions. Photos of these portrayed emotions were correctly identified by college students in the United States.

It is important to distinguish between *facial* expressions of emotions—

Darwin stated that facial expressions of emotions in humans are innate, are universal in all races, and have their origins in the facial expressions of animals.

which are unlearned and universal—and *gestures*—which are culturally determined. Morris, Collett, Marsh, and O'Shaughnessy (1979) made an extensive survey of hand and head gestures in many parts of the world. They reported that a given gesture might mean one thing in one place and something quite different somewhere else. For instance, the "thumb up" sign means either "everything's okay" or "hitching a ride" in most countries studied. But in parts of Greece and Sardinia it is unwise to try to hitch a lift with an upraised thumb. There it is an insult, equivalent to the raised third finger in the United States!

VERBAL REPORT. The easiest way to find out what a person is feeling is by asking. When someone says "I'm delighted" or "Ugh, that's disgusting," that person is presumably giving us a description of some internal state that otherwise we might have no way of determining.

How do people learn to make these statements about private aspects of their consciousness? In two ways. A child's parents judge what emotion a child is feeling by the situation (Did she just fall down? Did someone take her toy away?) and by the child's facial expression. The parent then says to the child, "You're sad, aren't you," or "Don't be angry." The child learns to associate the words "sad" and "angry" with a particular internal state. Of course, as you no doubt realize, there is no way of knowing whether that child is *really* sad or angry, or whether her anger or grief feel the same as yours!

The other way we learn to talk about our emotions is by *metaphor.* We often use terms that liken our inner feelings to some objective event in the outside world: "I was crushed," "He suffered a stab of regret," "I'm walking on air."

VOICE QUALITY. It is much harder to feign an emotion (or the lack of emotion) with the voice than with the face. Someone might say "I'm not afraid," but we know by the quaver in his voice that he really is. There is also another kind of quaver, undetectable to the human ear, that occurs in normal speech and that *decreases* when the speaker is nervous or afraid (Holden, 1975). Voice changes of these kinds have been used as the basis of a new kind of "lie detector," called *voice stress analyzers.* The idea behind these devices is that telling a lie produces a state of stress in a person, and that this stress is detectable by the changes it produces in the voice. Since it is still not clear whether the results produced by such devices have any validity, their use has generated considerable controversy.

MOTOR RESPONSES. There are three kinds of changes in motor behavior that result from emotion. The first are postural changes—a happy person stands and walks erect, a sad person slumps, and an angry or fearful one assumes a tense position.

The second kind of change is a rapid, automatic motor response. A sudden loud noise or any intense and unexpected stimulus produces a predictable pattern of involuntary actions called the *startle pattern:* The head moves forward, the eyes blink and the mouth may open, the muscles of the neck stand out, and the arms and legs may jerk (see Figure 11-2).

Third are voluntary behavioral actions. People express their feelings by clapping or "jumping for joy," or by running away from something they are afraid of. The most interesting and complex of these behavioral indications are those that result from anger. These were covered in detail in the section on aggression in Chapter 10.

PHYSIOLOGICAL RESPONSES. Perhaps the most important characteristic of an emotional response is its physiological component. Many—perhaps all—emotions are associated with some change in the body's functions. The most clear-cut and well-known changes are those that accompany the feeling of fear.

Everyone has experienced fear. When you've narrowly escaped an automobile accident, when you think you hear someone breaking into your home, even when you are called upon to answer a difficult question in front of a large audience, you've probably noticed your heart pounding, your knees shaking, your palms sweating, or your mouth feeling dry.

The bodily reactions to a fearful stimulus result from the action of the sympathetic nervous system and from the effects of the hormone *epinephrine*

Figure 11-2

The startle pattern: The head moves forward, the mouth is open, the muscles of the neck stand out, and the arms and legs jerk.

(popularly known as *adrenaline*) secreted by the adrenal glands. These reactions include:

1. The rate and depth of breathing increase.
2. There is an increase in heart rate and in the amount of blood pumped out with each beat.
3. Blood pressure goes up.
4. Less blood goes to the internal organs, more to the muscles.
5. The liver releases extra blood sugar to supply energy.
6. Production of saliva in the mouth, and of mucus in the respiratory passages, decreases.
7. The pupils of the eyes dilate, letting in more light.
8. The galvanic skin response (GSR), changes in the electrical resistance of the skin, goes up. The GSR is related in a complex way to the functioning of the sweat glands in the skin.

The fact that many of these changes are quite easy to measure provides the basis for the ordinary lie detector, or *polygraph*. This device generally measures heart rate, breathing rate, blood pressure, and GSR. The idea behind the polygraph, as with the voice stress analyzer, is that most people cannot tell a lie without feeling at least a little uncomfortable—consciously or subconsciously— and this discomfort is often reflected by a change in one or more of the measured functions. These changes must be compared with the baseline measurements obtained when neutral questions (such as "What's your name?") are asked.

One trouble with the polygraph—and this is a problem with the voice stress analyzer, too—is that some people *don't* get anxious when they tell a lie, and others get anxious even when they're *not* telling one. In addition, it may be somewhat easier to produce a false outcome on the polygraph, simply because it is possible to voluntarily increase some or all of the measurements—by breathing faster, tensing one's body, or thinking about something emotionally arousing. If a person uses these methods when neutral questions are asked, the baseline is raised, and it is often impossible to tell when a lie has actually been told.

Many of the bodily changes that occur with fear also accompany anger, but there are some physiological differences between the two emotions (Ax, 1953). Epinephrine is secreted with anger as well as with fear, but anger involves an additional adrenal hormone, *norepinephrine*. Norepinephrine also increases blood pressure, but it does so not by increasing heart rate but by constricting the blood vessels that supply the muscles. In fact, injections of norepinephrine *slow* the heart.

Attempts to differentiate other emotions on the basis of different physiological responses have been less successful. Averill (1969) had one group of subjects watch a sad movie, while another group watched a funny movie. There were some differences in the bodily responses that were measured, but they were not clear-cut. In fact, it is likely that a given individual produces a characteristic pattern of physiological changes to almost *any* form of emotional arousal. The physiological reactions of a given subject to different sources of stress are quite similar; the reactions of different subjects to the *same* stimulus are quite different (Lacey and Lacey, 1958).

Theories of Emotion

THE JAMES-LANGE THEORY.   If you are walking home in the dark and someone jumps out at you from behind a tree, two things happen. One is that you feel afraid. The other is that your adrenal glands emit epinephrine, your heart starts to pound, and so on. The question is: Which comes first? It may seem obvious to you that first you become afraid and then your body responds to your fear, but it did not seem so obvious to the Harvard psychologist William James or the Danish physiologist Carl Lange. A century ago these two scientists both came to the same conclusion: that the bodily changes come *first*, and then—as a result of these changes—you become afraid. In James's words:

> Common-sense says, we lose our fortune, are sorry and weep; we meet a bear, are frightened and run; we are angry and strike. . . . [T]he more rational statement is that we feel sorry because we cry, angry because we strike, afraid because we tremble. . . . Without the bodily states following on the perception, the latter would be purely cognitive in form, pale, colorless, destitute of emotional warmth. We might then see the bear and judge it best to run, receive the insult and deem it right to strike, but we should not actually *feel* afraid or angry. (1890, p. 449–450)

In 1927 the influential physiologist Walter Cannon published an attack on the James-Lange theory of emotion. He pointed out that, first of all, the bodily changes that are associated with emotional states occur too slowly. When the bear appears, fear is felt immediately, too quickly to be a byproduct of the physiological reactions.

Second, the physiological changes that occur with emotions take place in other situations too, *without* producing the emotions. Many of the same bodily responses that accompany fear—the increases in heart rate, breathing rate, blood pressure, GSR, and so on—can be produced simply by exercising violently. Yet exercise does not have any noteworthy effect on the state of the emotions. These same physiological changes can also be induced artificially, by injections of epinephrine, without resulting in a feeling of fear.

Some recent evidence seems to provide some support for the James-Lange theory. A psychologist (Hohman, 1966) interviewed a group of patients who had suffered serious spinal cord injuries and were unable to feel any sensations in the parts of their bodies below the level of the injury. Some of these people had spinal cord injuries at the neck (cervical) level, and therefore could not feel anything from the neck down; in others the injury was at the lower part of the spine (sacral); the rest were somewhere in between. These patients were asked how the emotions they felt since their accidents differed from the emotions they remembered feeling before they were injured. Were they the same as before, or more intense, or less intense? The people with sacral injuries (who felt no sensations in their legs) reported only minor changes in emotional feelings, but the people with cervical injuries (affecting the entire body) reported a decrease in feelings of fear, anger, grief, and sexual drive (see Figure 11-3). Only the emotion that the experimenter labeled "sentiment" was unaffected. The people with intermediate injuries gave mixed reports—some reported decreases in certain emotions, others did not. The conclusion drawn from these results is that in order to experience strong emotions, it is necessary to have some feedback from the body—some indication of the physiological reactions going on. When the sensations produced by these reactions are absent, the emotions may be felt

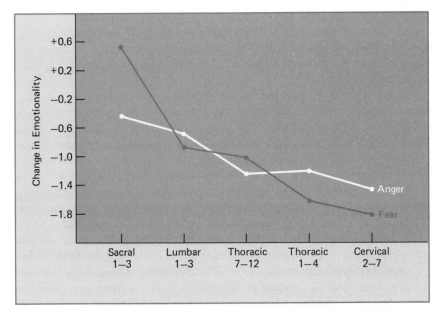

Figure 11-3

According to Hohmann's research, the greater the degree of spinal injury, the greater the decrease in feelings of fear and anger. Those with sacral injuries (who felt no sensation in their legs) reported only minor changes in emotional feelings, but those with cervical injuries (affecting the entire body) reported a significant decrease in feelings of such emotions as fear and anger. (After Hohmann, 1966)

less intensely. If you hear some very sad news and do not cry, you might wonder: Am I really sad, or don't I care very much? Similarly, if you are about to give a speech and you do not feel your heart pounding or "butterflies" in your stomach, you might marvel at how calm you are.

THE CANNON-BARD THEORY.   The theory of emotion that Cannon proposed (1927) and that Bard elaborated (1934) was based on what was known about the brain at that time. Cannon placed the source of emotions in the thalamus, which is located in the center of the brain. According to the Cannon-Bard theory, this is what happens when an emotionally arousing stimulus is perceived: The thalamus sends out impulses to the sympathetic nervous system (producing the physiological reactions) and *at the same time* sends out impulses to the cerebral cortex (producing the conscious feeling of emotion). This means that the bodily changes and the emotional feelings occur simultaneously.

Modern neurophysiology has not substantiated the importance of the thalamus to emotion. The parts of the brain that are now thought to play the major role are the hypothalamus and the *limbic system.* Lesions in certain parts of these areas produce permanent changes in emotional behavior in animals: They become passive and unreactive, or they become overreactive and fly into a rage with little or no provocation, depending on the location of the brain injury. Neurophysiologists have also investigated the limbic system by implanting electrodes in the brains of animals and giving tiny electric shocks to various areas. Depending on where the electrode is placed, the shock may produce fear, rage, passivity, or even pleasure (as we discussed in Chapter 2).

ACTIVATION THEORY.   A number of psychologists have contributed to the development of this theory, which was inspired by physiological findings reported by Moruzzi and Magoun in 1949. Moruzzi and Magoun studied the *reticular activating system* (RAS), which consists of pathways in the brain extending from the brain stem upward to the thalamus and the cerebral cortex. Inputs to the RAS come from all the senses except smell. This system controls *arousal:* When an animal's RAS is damaged, it goes into a coma and is unresponsive to stimulation. Drugs such as amphetamines increase RAS activity, barbiturates depress it.

In a normal individual the reticular system works "something like a fire alarm that gets people into action but does not really say where the fire is" (Beck, 1978, p. 104). At moderate levels of activity it makes a person alert and attentive; but when incoming stimuli are too intense or numerous, the reticular system produces too much arousal or excitement and behavior becomes disorganized. This is presumably what happens to people who "lose their heads" in an emergency, or to soldiers who panic under enemy fire. The notion is that there is some optimal level of emotional arousal—too little produces sleepiness or apathy, too much produces aimless activity and emotional disturbance.

COGNITIVE FACTORS AND THE JUKEBOX THEORY.   This theory is based on an experiment performed by Schachter and Singer (1962); the term *jukebox theory* was coined by Mandler (1962). In Schachter and Singer's experiment subjects were injected with epinephrine (which, as we know, produces the symptoms of fear: increased blood pressure, heart rate, GSR, and so on). They were told that these injections were a new vitamin compound, and that the purpose of the experiment was to study the effects of this compound on visual perception. After the injection each subject was sent into another room to wait, with a second subject, until the compound "took effect." In fact, epinephrine works very quickly, and the 20-minute "waiting period" was really the experiment itself and the "second subject" was really the experimenters' co-worker or stooge.

Soon after the real subject entered the waiting room, the stooge began to behave in a bizarre manner. He used some paper to make paper airplanes (which he flew around the room), or balled the paper up and played basketball (using a wastepaper basket as the goal). He even hula-hooped with a piece of equipment left in the room! During this display of feigned euphoria the stooge invited the real subject to participate in his games.

Whether or not the subjects accepted the stooge's invitation depended on what they had been told about the effects of the injection. Some subjects were told the truth—that the injection would produce a slight hand tremor, increased heart rate, and a flushed feeling in the face. A second group was misinformed—they were told that the drug would cause numbness in the feet, itching sensations, and a slight headache. A third group of subjects were told nothing at all.

What the experimenters found was that the subjects who were *correctly* informed about the effects of the injection did not accept the stooge's invitation to play. They behaved normally. But the subjects who were given the wrong information or no information at all often participated in the games, and sometimes behaved as foolishly as the stooge. In a variation of the experiment the stooge feigned anger and aggression instead of euphoria, and again the subjects who were correctly informed about the effects of the epinephrine behaved normally, whereas those who were not informed were affected by the stooge's put-on emotion. In other words, the same drug given to different groups of subjects made them happy, made them angry, or had no effect at all on their emotions—depending on the subjects' understanding of the situation.

The conclusion drawn from these experiments is that the physiological arousal produced by a drug can set the basis for an emotion, but it is not enough. When subjects *know* what reactions to expect, they correctly interpret their physiological changes as resulting from the injection; when they have no explanation for the effects they are feeling, they interpret these effects in terms of the situation. This is where the name "jukebox" comes in. The injection of the drug—like the coin you drop in a jukebox—starts things going, provides the energy. But the tune played—or the emotion experienced—depends on which button is pushed.

In the years since Schachter and Singer's experiment, a number of similar experiments have been performed. Although some have failed to substantiate the jukebox theory, many have provided support. Some results that are consistent with Schachter and Singer's hypothesis were provided by an experiment in which physiological arousal was induced in some subjects by having them view a sexy movie (Zillman, 1971). When the subjects later had a chance to express anger towards a person who had insulted them, the ones who had seen the sexy movie showed more aggressiveness than those who hadn't. Even physiological arousal produced by fast pedaling on an exercise bicycle has, under some conditions, produced an enhanced emotional response (Cantor, Zillman, and Bryant, 1975).

This brings us back to the data we mentioned earlier, which indicated that people with severed spinal cords are likely to feel emotions less strongly than they did before they were injured (Hohman, 1966). Taken all together, the results of a number of experiments can be summarized in the following way: Emotion-producing stimuli have two effects—a cognitive awareness of the meaning of the stimuli, plus a variety of physiological responses. In order for emotion to be deeply felt, the physiological responses must occur and must be perceived. But these responses are rather vague and generalized, and can be attributed to virtually any emotion. The emotion they *are* attributed to is the emotion that is appropriate to the person's cognitive awareness of the situation.

THE OPPONENT-PROCESS THEORY. The last theory of emotion we will discuss is compatible with any of the previous theories, since it does not attempt to specify where emotion comes from or what it consists of. This theory, instead, is designed to explain the motivation behind such hard-to-understand human behavior as thrill-seeking, masochism, and addiction.

The opponent-process theory, as formulated by Solomon and Corbit (1973, 1974), begins with several assumptions about emotional states:

1. Whenever a stimulus causes an emotional reaction, it also causes another emotional reaction that is opposite to, or the opponent of, the initial reaction. Thus if the sight of a bear causes the emotional reaction of fear (state A), it will also activate the opponent emotional reaction, which in this case might be relief (state B).
2. The opponent process (state B) is aroused more slowly, and decays more slowly, than the initial reaction (state A). In the example, the reaction of relief will lag behind the reaction of fear when the bear is sighted. Similarly,

Opponent-Process Theory and Addiction

One interesting, important, and sometimes puzzling aspect of human motivation is our ability to become addicted to things that we know are not good for us. Such addictions can be extremely debilitating; heroin addiction and alcoholism are all too common examples. Other addictions are not so clearly dangerous, but are definitely bad for our health; cigarette smoking is one of these dangerous but widespread addictions. One interesting approach to understanding why people become addicted, and why "kicking the habit" is so difficult, is provided by Solomon and Corbit's (1973) application of opponent-process theory to addiction.

You read in the text about opponent-process theory. It assumes that every emotional state (state A) has an opponent emotional state (state B). For positive A states, the associated B states are negative or unpleasant. When an addictive substance is taken, a positive A state is created; examples include the "highs" obtained with alcohol or heroin, and the pleasure associated with inhaling cigarette smoke. Once the pleasant A state is aroused, the opponent process also begins to be aroused, taking the edge off the pleasant experience. Initially, the A state is strong and very pleasant, while the B state is weak and slow to occur. With repeated usage, however, the B state is strengthened. Experienced users have mild highs but very intense lows following drug use. Originally, addictive substances are taken because of the pleasant effects they produce. After repeated use, however, they are taken to get rid of or avoid the very unpleasant opponent process.

You can probably see that this is a trap. The more a drug is used, the stronger and more intense the unpleasant B state becomes. How can a person get rid of the B state? The most effective way is to take the drug again, to fight the B state with its associated pleasant A state. But taking the drug again will strengthen the B process in

when the bear goes away, the reaction of relief will go away more slowly than the reaction of fear.

3. With repeated experience, states A and B slowly change character. For example, with repeated sightings of the bear, fear may change to alert tension, while relief may change to joy. To indicate such changes we could relabel the two states A' and B'.

4. As the previous example implies, with repeated experience the B (or B') state gets stronger, but the A (or A') state does not. In the example, moderate relief (B) turns into strong joy (B').

These four assumptions explain a very common sequence of emotional reactions: When the eliciting stimulus is presented (the bear appears from behind a tree), a very strong emotional reaction occurs (stark, petrified fear). As the exposure to the stimulus continues (as the bear continues to stand there), the emotion reduces a bit and remains steady (plain old fear). Solomon and Corbit explain that this reduction from the peak of emotion occurs because the opponent process (relief), as it is slowly activated, subtracts from state A, thereby reducing it. When the stimulus is withdrawn (the bear leaves), an emotion very different from the previous one is experienced. This happens because state A (fear) disappears rapidly when the stimulus is withdrawn, but state B goes away much more slowly. Therefore, when the stimulus is removed, the person experiences state B (relief). This pattern of emotions has repeatedly been found in experiments; it also agrees with many experiences that people report and that we all have had.

As another example, Solomon and Corbit (1974) used Epstein's (1967)

the long run, causing an even more unpleasant aftereffect and thereby increasing motivation to take the drug again. This is the vicious cycle of addiction. The firmly addicted heroin user or cigarette smoker is primarily motivated to avoid the unpleasant state that occurs after the last dose rather than to enjoy the positive highs originally associated with the substance.

The various opponent processes, or B states, can be positive or negative depending upon the nature of the associated A state, but they also differ in other ways. Some opponent processes are relatively weak, others are relatively intense; some are long-lasting and some are short-lived. Addictive substances lead to B states that are intense and long-lasting. Very long-lasting B states, which are sometimes experienced as a "craving" for the addictive substance, make it extremely difficult to give up the addiction. Cigarette smokers, alcoholics, and heroin addicts can experience such cravings for years after their last dose of the substance. These long-lasting B states put great demands on self-control and explain why relapses, even after long periods of abstinence, are common.

One way to break an addiction is to quit all at once, or cold turkey. For a firmly addicted person, this method can be extremely unpleasant. Another way to break an addiction is to reduce gradually the amount of the addictive substance taken. For example, a cigarette smoker who uses two packs a day might gradually reduce the amount to one pack, then switch to a low tar and nicotine brand, then continue to cut down to 15, 10, and then 5 cigarettes a day, finally quitting altogether. Presumably, it is easier to abstain from the one cigarette a day, to which one eventually becomes accustomed, than it is to go immediately from two packs a day to total abstinence. From the opponent-process theory point of view, this makes some sense. As the use of the addictive substance decreases, the B state gradually weakens. There is, however, an insidious catch to this procedure. As the B state weakens, the pleasure of the A state increases—each one of those 5 cigarettes that you allow yourself is wonderful! As the positive side of the addiction becomes stronger during gradual reduction of consumption, the *positive* motivation to smoke reasserts itself. In other words, as anyone who has been addicted to anything knows, it is very hard to quit.

study of parachutists. The first time people jump out of a plane, their initial reaction is terror (state A). When they land, they look stunned (state B). As they become more experienced jumpers, however, both states change. When they jump, they look anxious or tense (A′), and after they land they are exhilarated (B′). This illustrates assumptions 3 and 4 of the opponent-process theory: The states change, and the B′ reaction becomes much stronger with practice. This means that the experience of the A′ state continues to weaken (because a stronger and stronger B′ is subtracted from it), and the after-experience of the B′ state is more intense and lasts longer. This pattern of reactions can explain much thrill-seeking behavior—it is the pleasant aftereffects, together with the weakened aversiveness of the initial reactions, that motivate people to keep taking risks.

Masochistic (self-punishing) behavior can be explained in the same way: The person submits to painful or unpleasant abuse in order to experience the positive opponent process afterward. In sexual masochism, for example, the positive B state associated with the cessation of pain may enhance the pleasure of orgasm for some people.

One other implication of the opponent-process theory should be mentioned. Just as unpleasant initial reactions are followed by a positive opponent process, so will pleasant initial reactions be followed by an unpleasant opponent process. This sequence of reactions appears to be involved in various kinds of addictions, which we discuss in the accompanying box.

The opponent-process theory seems to explain a number of emotional phenomena very well. But why are emotional reactions arranged this way? What is the reason for the existence of opponent processes? According to Solomon and

Corbit, opponent processes allow the organism to damp down emotional reactions, to keep them from becoming too strong or too removed from neutral. Since severe emotional reactions can be debilitating and can interfere with new learning (Spence and Spence, 1966), such an emotional damping system appears to have adaptive survival value.

Summary

1. Human motivation ranges from basic physiological needs, through needs for stimulation (such as curiosity), to socially based needs.

2. Secondary motivations associated with physiological needs may be acquired through conditioning; these acquired motivations, according to some theorists, can become *functionally autonomous.*

3. Some prominent human needs are *affiliation, curiosity, competence,* and *achievement.*

4. Infants reared in institutions in which they receive food and medical care but little social stimulation show striking deficits in emotional, intellectual, and even physical development.

5. The optimal level of stimulation theory attempts to explain curiosity motives; stimuli outside a person's adaptation level allow a person to exercise his or her information-processing abilities and fulfill curiosity needs. Sensory deprivation studies underscore humans' needs for stimulation.

6. Among the theories of competence motives are White's theory of *effectance motivation* and Bandura's theory of *self-efficacy.* Many psychologists believe that loss of competence leads to depression or passivity.

7. Achievement motives are related to the desire to excel, to complete difficult tasks, to meet high standards, and to outperform others.

8. Maslow's hierarchy of needs consists of: physiological, safety, love and belongingness, esteem, and self-actualization needs.

9. The question of whether emotions are innate or learned is still not absolutely resolved. Seligman has proposed the concept of *preparedness*—organisms may be more prepared to associate a given emotional response with one stimulus than with another.

10. There are six cues we usually use to judge the emotional state of others: situational factors, facial expression, verbal report, voice quality, motor responses, and physiological responses.

11. The *James-Lange theory* of emotion asserts that bodily changes are experienced first, then emotion; the *Cannon-Bard theory* maintains that bodily changes and emotions occur simultaneously.

12. Neurological research focuses on the limbic system and the hypothalamus as the parts of the brain that play the major role in emotion.

13. The activation theory emphasizes the *reticular activation system (RAS)* and its effects on arousal, including the idea that there is some optimal level of emotional arousal.

14. The *jukebox theory* states that physiological arousal provides the basis or energy for emotion, but the emotion experienced depends on cognitive factors.

Suggested Readings

ATKINSON, J. W., and RAYNOR, J. O. *Personality, motivation, and achievement.* Washington, D.C.: Hemisphere, 1978. This book contains an interesting, updated series of papers representing the "classic" approach to achievement motivation.

HUNT, J. McV. Intrinsic motivation and its role in psychological development. In D. Levine (Ed.), *Nebraska Symposium on Motivation* (Vol. 13). Lincoln, Neb.: Nebraska University Press, 1965. A number of influential and disparate theoretical approaches are woven into this analysis of intrinsic motivation.

LEPPER, M. R., and GREENE, D. (Eds.). *The hidden costs of reward.* Hillsdale, N.J.: Erlbaum, 1978. Much of the research on rewards and intrinsic motivation is covered in this edited volume.

SCHACHTER, S. *The psychology of affiliation.* Stanford, Cal.: Stanford University Press, 1959. This is a research monograph in which the original studies on affiliation are reported. It is a good example of how a set of studies build upon one another.

SELIGMAN, M. E. P. *Helplessness: On depression, development, and death.* San Francisco: Freeman, 1975. A readable and provocative presentation of the relationship between lack of control and depression.

SOLOMON, R. L. The opponent-process theory of acquired motivation: The costs of pleasure and the benefit of pain. *American Psychologist,* 1980, *35,* 691–712. This is the latest comprehensive statement of the opponent-process theory of acquired motivation.

Part Five Development

12

Childhood

We start life as a fertilized human egg, hardly bigger than a speck of dust. How this single cell becomes a person like you or me is a central question of psychology. This question has intrigued people from the earliest times, and throughout history there have been two contrasting views, each of which emphasized one of the two sources of developmental change: our biological-physical structure or our experiences.

The extreme form of the biological and structural view emphasizes innate characteristics of people and appeals to *rationalism* as the mechanism for gaining knowledge. René Descartes, the seventeenth-century French philosopher, argued that the mind arises through interaction with events in the world, but that it can innately think and reason without any prior experience or learning. *Reason* was the primary source of all knowledge. In contrast, the *empiricism* of John Locke, the seventeenth-century English philosopher, held that *experience* was the source of all knowledge:

> Let us then suppose the mind to be, as we say, white paper void of all characters, without any ideas—How come it to be furnished: . . . . Whence has it all the *materials* of reason and knowledge? To this I answer, in one word, from EXPERI- ENCE. In that all our knowledge is founded; and from that it ultimately derives itself. Our observation, employed either about external sensible objects, or about the operations of our minds . . . supplies our understanding with all the *materials* of thinking. These two [external perception and internal introspection] are the fountains of knowledge whence all the ideas we have, or can naturally have, do spring.

The controversy continues to this day. One contemporary example is the difference of opinion between the followers of B. F. Skinner (1957) on the one hand, and of Noam Chomsky on the other. Skinner argues that all learning, including language learning, is based on experience. Chomsky (1968) argues that we don't actually "learn" language—instead we are born with a "language acquisition device" (an innate knowledge of grammar). We use our experience to learn only the superficial aspects of speech, like the words and sounds of our particular language. The basic structure of language itself, the universal grammar, is wired into the brain (Chomsky, 1975).

Skinner's empiricism and Chomsky's rationalism are extreme and one-sided versions of what must, in fact, be true of all developmental change. Our physical structures and our experiences interact continually to make us what we are. How and when do they do this?

341

Sources of Developmental Change

The Babinski reflex is shown here—the immature form in the top photo, the mature form in the bottom photo.

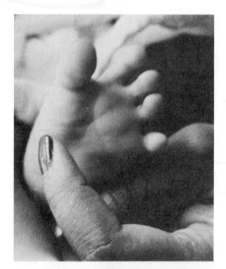

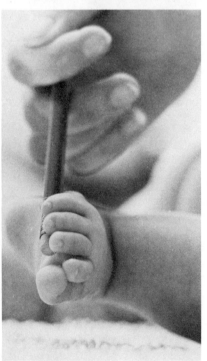

Maturation

One way our behavior changes is through the growth and maturation of our nervous and sensorimotor systems. When an organism can do something it couldn't do before just because of physical growth and development—e.g., when a baby is able to lift its head for the first time—we have a case of pure *maturation*. In its simplest form maturation refers to the development of an ability or skill that was made possible by a structural change in the nervous system and in the associated motor and sensory organs. A classic experimental demonstration of maturation was done by Leonard Carmichael (1927) in his study of the development of swimming in the salamander tadpole. When first hatched, salamander tadpoles do not swim—they just float quietly in pond water and grow as they feed on their yolk sac. In nature these tadpoles begin to swim in about 5 days. During this time they have ample opportunity to profit from experience and practice. Is that opportunity necessary? Carmichael took one group of freshly hatched tadpoles and left them in ordinary pond water. He took another group, hatched the same day, and put them in water that contained chloretone—an anesthetic that effectively prevented movement. When the normally treated tadpoles began to swim, he took the anesthetized tads out of their drugged tank and put them into fresh water. Carmichael reasoned that if practice were necessary for swimming to develop, it would take these practice-deprived tads some time to be able to swim. If practice were unnecessary, then they would swim as soon as the drug wore off. In this particular case, it turned out that practice was unnecessary. The drugged tads began to swim normally as soon as the drug effects wore off.

Examples of maturation in humans are not so easy to find, and are rarely, if ever, so clear cut. One simple case is the Babinsky reflex. When first born, infants flex their toes outward when the sole of the foot is scratched. This form of the reflex changes with the growth of the nervous system so that in older babies of 4–6 months the toes flex inward, as in normal adults. If this reflex change fails to develop, or if an adult regresses to the newborn pattern, it is usually a sign of neurological damage. A change in a reflex is not, of course, totally independent of "experience" in its most general sense. After all, the baby must have proper nourishment, oxygen, and other environmental supports in order to develop neurologically. What maturation means, even in this simple case, is that a specific behavior develops with no specific experiential or environmental events, and that this was made possible by physical development. This development did not happen in the total absence of experience or an environment, but rather within a normal range of both.

Human motor development is, in this sense, primarily maturational. Most normal babies will progress through the same sequence of motor skills and abilities—from crawling to walking—whether they are given special practice or not, and whether they are allowed to move freely, as in our culture, or are

APPLICATION
Rationalist and Empiricist Traditions

People develop as a result of the joint workings of their genetic and biological endowments and their experiences. Developmental theorists sometimes ignore this critical fact and lean heavily toward one or the other philosophical position. Those who emphasize the genetic and biological forces in development tend to believe in rationalism, as did Descartes. Those who emphasize experiential and learning forces in development tend to believe in empiricism, as did Locke. These two contrasting scientific positions have their counterparts in other aspects of psychology, and in theories of education and social policy as well. A rationalist will tend to weigh the role of instinct more heavily than the role of learning in describing animal behavior. An empiricist will have the opposite bias. In discussions of heredity and nature versus nurture and environment, rationalists lean to the nature side, empiricists to the nurture side. Rationalists thus tend to weigh genetic determinants of behavior quite heavily, while empiricists see the causes of behavior in the past and present environments of organisms.

The philosophical orientation of rationalists is generally quite conservative and traditional. If the main source of behavior is innate, then why try to change things by manipulating the environment? For the opposite reason, empiricists tend to believe in social change and social activism. If we are the product of our environments, then we should engineer our environments to improve human nature. We should remember that there are no *necessary* links here. A committed geneticist might quite comfortably believe in socialism and social engineering; a committed learning theorist may well be politically and socially conservative.

In general, though, when political arguments arise over changing or modifying human conditions—as, for example, over the potential efficacy of Head Start or other early enrichment programs—the debate often hinges on basic beliefs about human nature. Is it pliable and susceptible to change (the basic tenet of empiricism), or is it fixed and determined at birth (as an extreme rationalist would argue)? Neither position is useful to a scientist, however much either may enhance a political argument. The scientist is interested in how nature and nurture interact to jointly guide development.

swaddled and bound softly in cloth (Lipton et al., 1965). An experiment by Gesell and Thompson (1929) makes this point rather dramatically. One of a pair of twin boys was given extensive practice climbing stairs. The other was not. When the trained twin acquired skill in this activity, the untrained one was allowed to try it on his own. The advantage of the trained twin over the untrained one lasted no more than a week or two. It seemed that the child who had had early training could not profit from it until his sensorimotor system had developed enough to make him ready for it. Of course, further practice and training can improve these skills enormously. There is a world of difference between an ordinary person who can run easily and swiftly and an Olympic-class runner. Part of the trained athlete's superiority is his or her physical structure and conditioning, and part is technique and style. Physical structure and conditioning is the maturational component of motor development; the technique and style are the learned component. Even in ordinary walking, children seem to acquire the style and gait of their mothers and fathers. This component of walking is not maturational, it is learned. Similarly, the sheer ability to handle a knife and fork depends on maturation, but the style (and the particular table manners involved) are learned. The ability to play a piano must mature; whether one can actually play the piano depends on experience.

Experience

Maturational changes take place normally provided that the experience of the developing organisms is within normal ranges. Other developmental changes reflect more directly the particular life experiences of the growing person. Children growing up in Finland learn Finnish, while children growing up in the United States of America learn American English. And just as maturational changes take place against a backdrop of normal environments and experiences, so must learning take place against a backdrop of normal physical growth and development. This was not always so obvious as it now seems. One of the first recorded experiments in history was reported by the Greek scholar Herodotus. King Psammetchus of Egypt in the 7th century B.C. wanted to demonstrate that Egyptian was the most ancient language in the world. He believed that if children were reared without ever hearing human speech, their first word would be Egyptian! According to Herodutus, he therefore

> contrived the following method of discovery: he took two children of the common sort, and gave them over to a herdsman to bring up at his folds, strictly charging him to let no one utter a word in their presence, but to keep them in a sequestered cottage, and from time to time introduce goats to their apartment, see that they got their fill of milk, and in all other respects look after them. His object herein was to know, after the indistinct babblings of infancy were over, what word they would first articulate. (Herodotus, in Watson, 1968)

We now know that such an experiment is, in fact, impossible. If children do not hear human speech, they will not utter any words at all, and, as we discussed in Chapter 11, if they are deprived of human interaction and stimulation, they show striking deficits in emotional, intellectual, and physical development (Goldfarb, 1944, 1945; Spitz, 1946). Given normal physical growth, specific kinds of experiences and learning are necessary for most normal human activities, from the development of social attachments to the acquisition of language and reasoning skills.

Critical Periods

Some types of learning cannot occur at just any time during development. They must, if they are to occur at all, take place during a specific time in a developing organism's life. The clearest cases can be found in animals other than humans, where experimentation and careful observation are possible. When learning is confined to a specific developmental time, then we say that it depends on a *critical period.* Konrad Lorenz, the Austrian ethologist, first discovered such a period in young goslings. Baby geese, as they grow up in their normal world, follow their mother around everywhere, as do baby ducks and other *precocial* birds (birds that can function immediately after hatching). This behavior was considered natural and innate. The birds were born with an attachment to their mother, and with the tendency to follow her around. Of course, each baby followed its own mother, whom it had learned to recognize, so that even here some experience was necessary. What Lorenz (1937) showed was that during the first 24 hours of its life a young gosling would acquire an attachment to the first moving object it saw, and that thereafter even so ungooselike an object as Dr.

Konrad Lorenz as mother surrogate to young geese.

Lorenz could become a mother surrogate to young geese. These geese, who became *imprinted* on Lorenz, showed no interest whatever in their true mothers.

Since Lorenz's first demonstrations of imprinting, experiments have shown that young ducks or geese will acquire an attachment to the first moving object they see during the critical period, which is from birth to about 36 hours of age (Jaynes, 1958). This attachment is revealed in heartfelt and pitiful distress cries when the imprinted mother surrogate is absent, by contentment upon its return, and by diligent following when it moves about (Hoffman et al., 1974). The word *imprinting* was coined to describe this learning because it occurred so quickly and so completely. This rapid learning grows steadily and reaches its greatest effect within 13 hours for ducks (Hess, 1959; Hoffman, 1978), as can be seen in Figure 12-1.

In humans, such strictly circumscribed periods with such specific effects are not readily apparent. For most human characteristics and skills, long periods of time are needed for nature and nurture to work together. Instead of critical periods, it is more accurate to say that there are loosely defined *sensitive periods* during which circumstances are most favorable for the establishment of various traits and abilities. For example, people seem to be able to learn languages best before the onset of puberty. A foreign language learned after puberty will usually be spoken with an accent; true bilinguals rarely acquire their second language in adolescence or adulthood (Lenneberg, 1967). Why this is so is not well understood. Does knowledge of the first language interfere with acquisition of the second? Are the habits of pronunciation and grammar so strong by adolescence that they cannot be broken? Has the brain lost some of its initial plasticity or capacity for learning? Each of these factors may be partially responsible.

The human infant is born with a foundation of sensory and motor abilities, and with an enormous capacity to learn from experience. What precisely are infants born with, and how do they use their capacities and everyday experiences to become competent human beings?

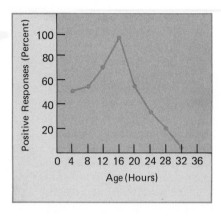

Figure 12-1

As shown here, although the critical period for imprinting for ducks lasts from birth to 36 hours, it is most effective within 13 hours (Hess, 1959)

Developmental Tasks of Infancy

The newborn infant doesn't do very much. Eating, sleeping, and making various noises occupy much of the day and night (Gesell, 1934). Nevertheless, despite the apparent absence of perceptual or cognitive skills, the infant is not a totally disorganized and helpless creature. Newborn babies can discriminate colors, tastes, and smells, and quite early in life can make discriminations between certain speech sounds (Eimas et al., 1971). Their eyes can follow moving objects within a day or two of birth, and can focus within a month. With this rudimentary but important set of early capabilities, the infant must acquire the ability to perceive the world accurately, to move about purposefully, and to develop social relationships with other people. These three areas of competence are the most important tasks of early infancy.

HIGHLIGHT
How Perception Is Studied in Infants

The development of visual perception typifies perceptual development in general. At first the infant has only partial control over eye movements (Ruff and Birch, 1979). Furthermore, it is not clear that the baby has full voluntary control over what he or she looks at; infants' choices regarding what is looked at are very much limited. The main questions about the infant's visual system are how detailed a newborn's analysis of the visual world is, and what properties of objects and people infants notice.

It is difficult to answer these questions because infants are limited in the ways they can respond. One fruitful approach has been to compare how long infants look at various things. This visual preference technique has provided striking evidence that even the youngest infants prefer one pattern to another and thus can discriminate between patterns. Fantz (1963) found that within 48 hours of birth infants preferred faces to uniformly colored disks.

This method, however, cannot be used when two stimuli are equally appealing, so a habituation technique is often used instead. One stimulus is displayed repeatedly, and this suppresses attention to it. Then, the habituated response to this familiar sight is compared with a response to something new. If babies favor this new object, then we can infer that they are able to discriminate between the two stimuli. For example, Friedman (1972) found that newborns familiarized with one checkerboard pattern preferred one with a different number and size of squares.

Although even the youngest infants can tell one form from another, a newborn's perception of a pattern is undoubtedly less detailed than that of an older baby. This may be because the new-

Perceptual Development

The basic machinery for perceiving the world is pretty much ready at birth. Babies' eyes, ears, nose, tongue, and skin act very much like those of adults (Cohen et al., 1979). What the infant must learn is how to use these sensory and perceptual organs, how to control them and interpret the flood of sensations from the world. This integration of the senses does not advance very quickly until 6 to 8 months of age, and it is not complete before 1 year (Gottfried et al., 1977).

Infants also must gradually learn perceptual and object constancies. When an object is moved toward or away from you, its visual size changes, but you perceive it as having the same size. Similarly, when objects rotate in space, their visual shape changes, but you still see the shape as constant. By 2 or 3 months of age babies behave as if they have size and shape constancy (Fagan, 1967; Bower, 1966; Caron, Caron, and Carlson, 1979). However, it is several months before infants display more mature object constancy, looking for the reappearance of an object after it has been hidden from view. For very young infants, disappearance of an object seems total—out of sight, out of mind.

By 6 months it seems that babies experience the physical world pretty much as adults do. The world is no longer, as William James once put it, a "blooming buzzing confusion." Things do not change size or shape as they move; babies look accurately toward sources of sound and aim fairly accurately for things within their pudgy reach.

Motor Development

While the baby is learning to make sense of its perceptual apparatus, it is also becoming more able to do things and act upon the world. The schedule and

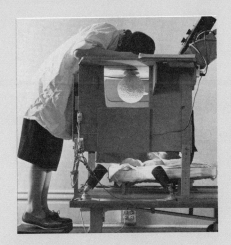

born's vision is somewhat limited by incomplete development of the eye. For example, the lens can focus precisely on an object about 19 cm away (the approximate distance of the face of the parent when holding the baby), but ob-jects farther away appear blurred (Haynes et al., 1965). Using infra-red cameras to record how infants scan visual stimuli, Salapatek (1975) discovered a shift in infants' scanning behaviors that occurs at about 2 months of age. At this time the infant progresses to more thorough scanning of a pattern and concentrates more on the internal areas of a figure than on the edges. This developmental shift applies to faces as well as to geometric shapes: Younger infants concentrate on the edges of faces; older infants attend more to eyes (Haith et al., 1977).

Infants' heart rates have proved to be useful in the study of depth perception. When placed on a *visual cliff*, a platform of clear glass over what looks like a sharp drop, infants' heart rates are faster on the deep side (Campos et al., 1970). Infants as young as 1½ months show depth perception in this situation.

sequence of gross motor abilities is fairly uniform for normal babies. On the average, babies are able to roll over between 2 and 3 months of age, sit without support at about 6 months, and walk alone between 11 and 13 months (Shirley, 1931). While there is some variability in these ages (see Figure 12-2 on the following page), the regularity of the sequence suggests that maturation of muscle, nervous system, and bones is the major pacesetter here. This conclusion is strengthened by the rather small effects of either early deprivation or early experience. In cultures that swaddle infants and provide them with relatively little chance for early exercise and practice, motor development does not seem to be retarded. Studies of the effects of practice on the acquisition of these motor abilities show little if any permanent effects. A practiced baby might be able to do something a little earlier than usual, but such early practice seems to confer no permanent advantage (Stone et al., 1973). The role of special experience in motor development is small. This is not true for other important developmental processes, including early social attachments.

Social Attachments

The first year of life is a critical time in the formation of a person's basic sense of trust in others and faith in the future (Erikson, 1963). A person's feelings in the area of social attachment are rooted largely in the social experiences of this first year of life; among the most important of these experiences are those of the infant with the mother (or other person providing care).

The infant's social attachment usually begins with an intense bond to the mother. Infants may be able to tell their mothers apart from other people as early as their first few weeks (Carpenter, 1975). Between 6 and 9 months a deep social attachment becomes obvious. At that age, and for the next year or more, infants

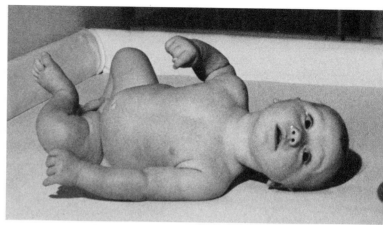

Figure 12-2   *These photos represent some of the stages in the sequence of motor development. Every baby goes through the same sequence, but some go faster than others. Lags of a few weeks in early infancy and a few months in later infancy are normal.*

The stages shown here are: lift head up (1 month), roll over (approximately 4 months), creep (10 months), pull to stand (12 months), climb stair steps (13 months), and, below, getting ready to stand alone (14 months).

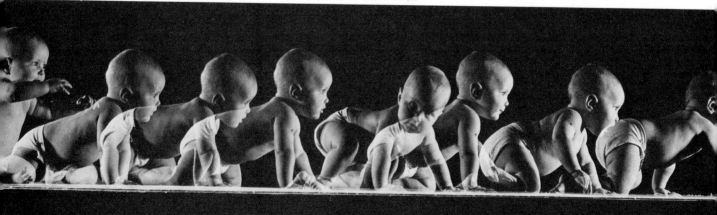

may protest loudly when their mothers disappear from sight (Schaffer and Emerson, 1964). At first infants are disturbed when anyone leaves them, but gradually they become disturbed primarily when their mother leaves. This developmental pattern is quite similar to the growth of the distress reaction in young ducklings as they become attached to their mothers (Hoffman, 1978).

The quality of infants' attachments to their mothers may vary from "securely attached" to "anxiously attached." In studies using the "strange-situation" procedure infants' interactions with their mothers were observed both before and after mothers left the laboratory playroom briefly (Ainsworth and Wittig, 1969). Infants were labeled "securely attached" if they had intermittent pleasant contacts with their mother before the separation, were secure enough to explore the unfamiliar room in her presence, and reacted positively to their mother following the separation. In contrast, "anxiously attached" infants did not explore the room in the pre-separation period, acted very distressed during the separation, and sometimes acted ambivalently toward their mother when she returned. Finally, "weakly attached" infants showed little separation distress and little desire to be near the mother when she returned.

Mothers may contribute to the development of "secure attachment" by prompt and sensitive responses to a child's needs. Mothers classified as sensitive in their interactions with their infants seem to have "secure" infants as measured by the strange-situation tests (Ainsworth and Bell, 1969; Ainsworth, Bell, and Slayton, 1971). The amount of social stimulation that mothers provide for their babies also seems to be related to secure attachment (Clarke-Stewart, 1973).

A question of current importance, given the increasing numbers of working mothers in our society, is whether day care weakens infant-mother attachment, since infants may spend the majority of their waking hours with substitute care givers. The answer seems to be that it does not. For example, Kagan, Kearsley, and Zelazo (1977) found no differences between the responses of home-reared and day-care infants, 3½ to 29 months old, in a strange-situation test.

Mother-infant attachments have traditionally received more attention from researchers than father-infant attachments, therefore more information is available about mother-infant bonds than about father-infant bonds. However, the attachment of infant to father may be just as strong (Lamb, 1977). Of course, infants may have different kinds of relationships with their mothers than with their fathers. Infants may prefer playing with their fathers, as Clarke-Stewart (1978) found for 18-month-olds, but they may tend to seek protection from their mothers rather than their fathers in frightening situations (Lamb, 1976). As family situations change and as fathers participate more in child rearing, it will be interesting to see if patterns of parent-infant attachment change.

Early Childhood

In the first year of life infants gain perceptual and motor control of themselves and of some aspects of their world, and establish strong social attachments to their mother and other constant companions. From then until they start school (in Western culture, usually at 5 to 6 years of age) children acquire fundamental skills and concepts and learn to cope with their physical and social world. According to the most influential theories of personality development, this time period is also crucial to social and sexual growth and to health in adulthood.

Psychosexual and Psychosocial Development

According to psychoanalytic theorists such as Sigmund Freud (1960) and Erik Erikson (1963), people pass through specific psychosexual and psychosocial stages as they develop from infancy through adulthood and old age. Psychosexual development involves the gradual acquisition of identity as a man or woman, as well as basic ways of relating to people and to the world. For Freud, the determinants of adult personality are rooted in early childhood, and the ways that children deal with sexual energy—called *libido*—will determine how they will cope with life as adults. For example, infants' experiences during the first psychosexual stage—*the oral stage*—will affect both their adjustment to later stages and their needs and attitudes toward events, persons, and things in later life that are associated with orality. If oral needs such as suckling are either not met or are overindulged, then the adult may develop an "oral" personality. Oral satisfactions such as food or tobacco will be inordinately craved; other people will not be trusted because of the original betrayal by a mother who perhaps weaned a child from the breast too abruptly. This oversimplified version of oral-stage development does not do full justice to Freud's insights about the importance of early experience in the development of identity and adult personality. We will give here only a bare outline of the theory of psychosexual development, which will be discussed in detail in Chapter 14. The central idea is that a person's energies are focused on various parts of the body during different stages of development. Starting with the mouth at infancy, this focus of libidinal energy shifts to the areas of elimination during the years 2 and 3 (the *anal stage*). The focus shifts to the sexual organs when girls and boys deal with their sexual relationships with and feelings for their parents during the *phallic stage*. Next comes the latency period, which lasts from about age 5 to puberty. The focus here is more on social and intellectual development. The final goal of psychosexual development is the achievement of *genitality*—firm identification with the person's own gender, and the ability to love someone of the opposite sex so the person can marry and have children.

The transition from one psychosexual stage to another is partly maturational. As our bodies mature and grow, we acquire new drives, needs, and satisfactions. This kind of change is most dramatic at puberty. For the young child, the changes from the oral to the anal to the phallic stages are partly maturational. They are also very heavily influenced by the social demands of growing up. Erik Erikson (1963) has enriched Freud's stage theory by adding *psychosocial stages* to the bare-boned psychosexual stages proposed by Freud (see Table 12-1). Erikson views each stage as a time in a person's life when certain basic crises must be resolved. The preschool years provide the child with three such crises. During the first year infants must resolve their feelings of trust versus mistrust in the world and in other people. If during this year they learn to place basic trust in others, then an optimistic and trusting adult life is in store for them. During the second year, when infants continue to learn to cope with and control the world around them, the basic conflict between a sense of autonomy and a doubting, worrisome personality must be resolved. If successful, infants develop a sense of personal competence and confidence in their ability to control

Table 12–1: The Stages of Psychosocial Development Proposed by Erikson.

1. First Year (Trust vs. Mistrust)	Through basic attachment to mother or other caregiver develop basic sense of trust or mistrust, come to respond in that way to the world and other people.
2. Second Year (Autonomy vs. Shame and Doubt)	Conflict between child's need to explore, be independent, and basic dependency on parents. Ideal outcome is sense of competence, self-control; poor outcome is shame and doubt through not feeling in control of oneself.
3. Third through Fifth Years (Initiative vs. Guilt)	Children develop ability to initiate activities, see them through. Parental encouragement or discouragement of such attempts affect children's sense of ability and purpose or direction.
4. Sixth Year through Puberty (Industry vs. Inferiority)	Development of basic competencies in neighborhood and school. Constant testing of child against peers and in school is the basis for feelings of competency (industry) or lack of it (inferiority).
5. Adolescence (Identity vs. Role Confusion)	Need to integrate various roles (as son or daughter, sibling, friend, peer, etc.) into one identity. Inability to do this may lead to role confusion—trying out one role after another, trying to be all things to all people.
6. Early Adulthood (Intimacy vs. Isolation)	Important to develop close relationships with others, to commit self to others and to a career. Avoiding this may lead to a general lack of purpose and isolation from other people.
7. Middle Age (Generativity vs. Stagnation, Self-Absorption)	At this stage people need to feel that they are somehow perpetuating themselves— family and work are basic ways to do this, and they are the focus at this time. Resolution of this crisis can mean the difference between a sense of fulfillment, of life being worthwhile, or a sense of boredom or of having somehow missed the boat.
8. Old Age (Integrity vs. Despair)	Need to develop a sense of what one's life has meant, what life itself is all about, and what death means in context of this.

Adapted from Erikson (1963).

their own fate. The years 3 through 5 are considered critical for acquiring initiative and for minimizing feelings of guilt and dismay. During each of these stages the parents' behavior—whether they encourage or discourage the placing of trust, attempts to control things, and efforts to initiate activities—is crucial for the resolution of basic conflicts. What children learn about themselves during their early years will influence how they cope with later developmental crises.

Learning about oneself involves the central process of *identification*. Children do, of course, imitate their parents, doing things that their mothers and fathers do, and adopting their mannerisms. But they do more than that. They adopt parental values and attitudes, and in many ways *become* symbolic reincarnations of their mother and father. They empathize with them, take joy and pride in their parents' accomplishments, and feel guilt and shame in their parents' failures and shortcomings. Boys' identification with their fathers irreversibly stamps them as males in their society, and girls' identification with their mothers stamps them as females.

Even during the early years of life, sex-role identifications and expectations are apparent. Children as young as 2 or 3 have already absorbed many of society's stereotypes about what behaviors are expected from each sex (Kuhn, Nash, and Brucken, 1978). In one study children were introduced to a male and a female paper doll, "Michael" and "Lisa," and then asked which doll made each of various statements. Both boys and girls believed that Lisa liked to help her mother, talked a lot, said "I need some help," and that she would be a nurse and clean the house when she was grown up. And both believed that Michael liked to help his father, said "I can hit you," and would be a boss when he grew up.

In the tradition of Freudian psychoanalytic thinking, identification theories have described how people acquire sex roles through their relationships with their mothers in childhood, and through the mother's fulfillment of their physical needs.

Although modified versions of identification theory describe different motivations for identification, they agree with Freud that the same-sex parent is the primary source of sex-role behaviors, and that a sex role is acquired as a unit, once and for all, early in life. However, the characteristics of that role change as society's definition of sex roles changes.

Social learning theorists (for example, Bandura, 1969) have proposed an account of sex-role development using learning theory concepts of reinforcement and imitation. If a child is positively reinforced (that is, rewarded) for a behavior, then the probability of repeating the same behavior will increase. For example, suppose that parents give a girl several dolls and pay a lot of attention to her when she mothers the dolls, while giving a boy no opportunities to play with dolls or ignoring his doll play. The girl, but not the boy, will increasingly adopt nurturant behaviors, because they have been reinforced. A girl may learn that, in general, imitation of her mother leads to behaviors that are reinforced, while boys learn to imitate their fathers for the same reason.

Social learning theorists reject the idea that a sex role is adopted as a unit; instead, a child learns, one by one, each of the many behaviors that eventually will constitute a sex role. Also against the view that a sex role is fixed, learning theorists assert, is the belief that any learned behavior can be modified. Finally, learning theorists view the same-sex parent as only one of many sources of sex-role behaviors. Reinforcement by nursery school teachers, for example, may help to shape sex roles. Serbin and O'Leary (1975) found that nursery school teachers unintentionally rewarded different behaviors from boys than from girls, encouraging boys to be aggressive and to tackle different tasks, while encouraging girls to be dependent.

According to social learning theorists, children imitate both parents, as well as other adults, other children, TV characters, and other models. Environmental influences, not internal motivational states, are the key shapers of sex roles. Thus the traditional ways of portraying men and women in our society shape the way children view themselves. Until recently these stereotypes were further reinforced by children's books and stories. Fortunately more enlightened and sophisticated teachers and parents are making changes in the traditional ways that society portrays men and women.

Boys' identification with their fathers irreversibly stamps them as males in their society, and girls' identification with their mothers stamps them as females.

Conceptual Growth

The 1-year-old is in the midst of what the Swiss cognitive psychologist Jean Piaget termed the *sensorimotor stage* of cognitive development (Piaget and Inhelder, 1968). Children of this age know the world predominantly through their physical and perceptual interaction with it (see Table 12-2). There are several ways of "knowing." We know how to ride a bicycle through the largely unconscious motor acts and skills that we use—balance, pedal, brake, and steer. This kind of knowledge is "enactive"—knowing by doing. We know someone's face by perceptual memory of that face. Somehow we have a mental representation of the visual pattern that enables us to recognize the face, or to imagine how it looks.

Babies' knowledge of the world—their mental image of things, events, and people—is inextricably bound up with their own interactions with that world. At first, their knowledge is acquired primarily through touch, and mostly by the mouth. Young infants get to know what objects are like by mouthing them in addition to looking at them and playing with them in their hands. Gradually, the actions performed on objects become more complex, and eye-hand coordination becomes good enough for children to reach accurately for things. Soon the sensorimotor image of objects becomes quite rich and complex. Not only the sight, but the feel, weight, texture, taste, and sounds of an object become an integrated whole.

During this period, as children are learning to differentiate themselves from the larger environment, they also come to appreciate that objects exist even when they are not physically present. They acquire the concept of *object permanence*. Before they have this concept, they believe that anything removed from their sight ceases to exist. For example, if a toy the infant is playing with is removed from view, the infant will not look for it or lift a blanket or cloth to see if the toy is hidden underneath, even if the infant saw the toy being covered with the blanket. To the infant, once the toy is removed from sight, it no longer exists. One of the first signs that a child has obtained object permanence is looking-for or searching behavior. At this point, the child knows the toy is somewhere, but does not know where.

The next stage, beginning at age 2, is the *preoperational* (or *symbolic*) *stage*. Now the child is learning to represent aspects of the world symbolically, in words or in visual images. Children of this age begin to appreciate that some transformations of objects do not matter—the object remains the same. This is the concept of the *conservation of mass*. For example, very young children will often judge that a piece of clay is "more" if it is rolled from a sphere shape to a long cylinder shape. By 6 or 7 years of age, when they have entered the *concrete operational stage,* children know that the mass or amount of clay does not change when its shape is changed. This is one of the many mental operations needed for object constancy—the ability to perceive that objects remain stable despite changes in surface appearance (Gardner, 1978).

How does the child move from one level of cognitive ability to another? Partly through relatively simple learning—learning eye-hand coordination, for example—and partly through the mechanisms of classical or operant conditioning (see Chapter 6). For example, children can learn to associate one event with another so that the sound of someone's voice becomes associated with that person's face. Children learn that doing one thing will result in praise, whereas doing another will bring punishment.

Cognitive growth, however, requires two other kinds of mechanisms, according to Piaget, and these are the fundamental factors in a child's progression from one stage or level of cognitive functioning to the next. These fundamental instruments of cognitive change are *assimilation* and *accommodation*. When a person encounters something new that doesn't quite fit with his or her experience and knowledge, it is *assimilated* to what the person already knows. In other words, the new stimulus is interpreted in terms of what is already known. The "learning" in this case involves interpreting the new stimulus to fit preexisting knowledge. Whenever we interpret new things in terms of their similarity to and differences from the familiar, we are using processes of assimilation.

Sometimes we encounter situations or concepts that are so different from the familiar that they cannot be assimilated. Such events in ordinary adult life are rare. When they do occur, they are either totally ignored or they force us to change our way of thinking—to *accommodate* what we already know to something new and important. In adolescence the facts of sexuality and our new reactions to members of the opposite sex force accommodation—changes in our ways of conceptualizing ourselves and others. In the larger society, great and

Table 12–2: Piagetian Stages of Cognitive Growth.

1. Sensorimotor Stage (Birth to 2 Years)	Children begin to distinguish between themselves and the rest of the world. Begin to organize their experiences, fitting them into schemata—first steps toward intentional behavior. Learn object permanence, and that actions have consequences (cause and effect).
2. Preoperational Stage (2–7 Years)	Children have a growing ability to both remember and anticipate. Begin to use symbols to represent external world internally. Egocentric—cannot put themselves in someone else's place. Tend to focus on one aspect or dimension of an object and ignore all others, cannot mentally retrace steps to reach a conclusion (irreversibility).
3. Concrete Operational (7–11 Years)	Children learn to retrace thoughts, correct themselves; can consider more than one aspect or dimension at a time. Able to look at a problem in different ways and see other people's points of view. Develop concepts of conservation—number, mass, etc.
4. Formal Operational Stage (12 years and up)	Individuals can think in abstract terms; formulate and test hypotheses through logic. Can think through various solutions to a problem or possible consequences of an action. No longer tied to concrete testing of ideas in external world—can test them internally through logic.

Adapted from Piaget and Inhelder (1968).

pervasive new ideas, such as Darwin's theory of evolution, Freud's theory of the unconscious, or Einstein's theory of relativity and the emergence of nuclear power forced people to change their basic conceptions of their biological, social, and physical worlds.

For young children, events and situations that require accommodation are commonplace. Those that cannot be coped with at any given age are ignored. Those that are just beyond the level of the child at any given age, and that cannot be assimilated, force accommodation; they force changes in the way the child represents reality, and changes in the way the child thinks. Learning about language is one example of accommodation. Every child must, at some point in normal development, get the idea that words can represent things—that words "mean" something. This is an important accommodation, usually lost to our memory. But in at least one instance a person could remember that flash of insight, that moment of accommodation. Helen Keller lost her sight and hearing early in childhood, before she learned to speak. When she was about 6 years old, during a session with her tutor, she suddenly understood that a gesture made on one of her hands and the water she felt with her other hand were symbolically related. At that moment she understood the concept of naming, and from then on, Helen Keller thought about the world differently. It was now a place with things that could be named, and which when named were under control—at least to the imagination (Keller, 1903).

The Roots of Language

Realizations of the nature of words, and of language as a medium for communication, are without doubt major accommodations that have enormous consequences for children's learning (Sinclair-de Zwart, 1977). The social ties between child and parents, and between child and other children, are equally important for the growth of language abilities. From early infancy children display perceptual behaviors that aid communication between mother and child. By the age of 3 months children will, when playing with their mother, look at the same things their mother looks at (Bruner, 1974/75). Mother and child usually pay attention to the same things simultaneously. This virtually guarantees that the child will gradually get to know what the mother is talking about—that if the mother names an object, chances are that the child will be looking at and paying attention to that object. The social attachment and shared attention patterns between mother and child set the stage for language learning.

The continual social interaction and communication patterns between mother and child also contribute in important ways. If children are to learn what words mean, they must first know what their mother intends to say. As Macnamara (1972) put it:

> Infants learn their language by first determining, independent of language, the meaning which a speaker intends to convey to them, and by then working out the relationship between the meaning and the language. To put it another way, the infant uses meaning as a clue to language, rather than language as a clue to meaning. (p. 1)

In other words, the infant plays a guessing game. The infant first tries to figure out what the other person is saying. Then the infant gradually maps out the sounds that are heard onto what he or she understands. Mothers help by using "motherese," a form of talking to young children that uses simplified grammar and is carefully tailored to the linguistic and cognitive level of the child. For example, a typical mother might say to her 2-year-old: "That's a lion. And the lion's name is Leo. Leo lives in a *big* house. Leo goes for a walk every morning. And he always takes his cane along" (Snow, 1977). These ideas rarely, if ever, would be expressed to a 2-year-old by saying: "That is a lion named Leo who lives in a large house and goes for a walk every morning invariably taking his cane along." Parents carefully make sure that children attend to them and to what they are talking about, use questions both to test the child and to continue the conversation, and rarely make the mistake of talking about things the child doesn't understand (Gleason and Weintraub, 1978). Children, for their part, give clear signals when they do not understand—they simply turn off. Babies either fuss or go to sleep, young children fidget and look away. The sensitivity of most people to these conversational signals greatly facilitates early language development (Shatz, 1978). When children are deprived of such important and sensitive social interactions, as in some institutions where companionship is limited, language development can be delayed and even permanently impaired.

Moral Development

As children learn to talk and to think about their world, they inevitably encounter problems of interpretation. One area of great importance to people and to society is the attribution of responsibility and concepts of morality. The most direct and simplest way to attribute responsibility for both good and bad actions is to judge them completely by their most obvious characteristics—what people do and the consequences of their actions. This simplistic way of thinking relies entirely on observables, and completely ignores *intentions*. Children in the preoperational stage of cognitive development often judge people this way (Piaget, 1932). If, say, a child breaks a plate while trying to help his or her mother (a bad consequence but a good intention), that child is blamed as much as someone else who broke a plate deliberately (a bad consequence with a bad intention). Several experiments with young children (for example, Piaget, 1932) suggest that they tend to weigh consequences more heavily than intentions in judging whether someone should be rewarded or punished. However, it is not clear whether this tendency is peculiar to young children or whether it is a reflection of common, everyday adult patterns. Consider what adults usually do when a child happens to break a treasured vase or spill ice cream on the damask table linen: They usually get angry, despite the child's plea, "I didn't mean it!" Are young children usually imitating their elders, then, even though they may be basically capable of taking intentions into account?

When children are tested for their ability to use information about someone's intentions, they are usually given a story in which someone's intentions are described first, and then the actions and consequences of that action are told. If children remember only the *last* part of the story, they can't very well take intention into account. When the order of information is reversed—action/consequence first, intention last—children do use intentional information, either because they remember it better or because putting it at the end makes it more salient. Children then say that people should not be punished for doing something bad if their intentions were good and honorable (Austin et al., 1977).

Moral judgment of others is but one aspect of moral development, and perhaps not the most important one at that. Of far greater importance is the development of our own morality and the ways in which we judge ourselves and control our own behavior. Lawrence Kohlberg (1963, 1971) proposed a theory of moral development modelled after Piaget's theory of cognitive development. Children in the sensorimotor and preoperational stages of cognitive develop-

Table 12–3: Kohlberg's Stage Theory of the Development of Moral Reasoning.

I. Preconventional Level

Rules are set down by others.

Stage 1. Punishment and Obedience Orientation
Physical consequences of action determine its goodness or badness.

Stage 2. Instrumental Relativist Orientation
What's right is whatever satisfies one's own needs and occasionally the needs of others. Elements of fairness, reciprocity are present, but they are mostly interpreted in a "you scratch my back, I'll scratch yours" fashion.

II. Conventional Level

Individual adopts rules, and will sometimes subordinate own needs to those of the group. Expectations of family, group, or nation seen as valuable in own right, regardless of immediate and obvious consequences.

Stage 3. "Good Boy-Good Girl" Orientation
Good behavior is whatever pleases or helps others and is approved of by them. One earns approval by being "nice."

Stage 4. "Law and Order" Orientation
Right is doing one's duty, showing respect for authority, and maintaining the given social order for its own sake.

III. Postconventional Level

Individual defines own values in terms of ethical principles he or she has chosen to follow.

Stage 5. Social Contract Orientation
What's right is defined in terms of general individual rights and in terms of standards that have been agreed upon by the whole society. In contrast to Stage 4, laws are not "frozen"—they can be changed for the good of society.

Stage 6. Universal Ethical Principle Orientation
What's right is defined by decision of conscience according to self-chosen ethical principles. These principles are abstract and ethical (such as the Golden Rule), not specific moral prescriptions (such as the Ten Commandments).

Adapted from Kohlberg (1969).

ment are thought to be in a premoral stage (see Table 12-3 for a summary of the stages). Their behavior is governed by rewards and punishments rather than by higher principles. It is bad, for example, to hurt puppy dogs because you will be punished if you do it. This theory seems far too simple. Young children are often guided by compassion and empathy in such matters, and it is a rare child indeed whose actions are as completely governed by rewards and punishments as Kohlberg's theory would have us believe. Nonetheless, Kohlberg's stage theory is interesting and does capture what children often *say* about morality, if not what they do. As with many Piagetian tests with children, what children say and what they can do often lead to very different assessments of their capabilities (Gelman, 1978). Preschool children have not yet learned to describe their thoughts and ideas very well. One of the aims of schooling is to produce articulate children who can talk about their own mental life and social beliefs (Flavell, 1978).

The School Ages

We have forecast the growth of the child during the school years in our discussion of the psychosexual, psychosocial, cognitive, and social development of the preschooler. Children are now faced with a wider social and intellectual world than they knew at home, and they are more open to influences from peers and adults other than their parents. Indeed, the peer group soon becomes a major factor in shaping attitudes, beliefs, and personality (Hartup, 1978).

On the Way to Becoming a Unique Person

The years 6 through 12 are the latency period in Freud's scheme of psychosexual development. On the surface there seems to be no interest in the opposite sex, and little or no interest in sexual matters in general. Boys play with boys and shun little girls; girls play with girls and despise little boys. Friendships are almost exclusively with children of the same sex (Whiting and Whiting, 1975). For Erikson, psychosocial growth centers on the development of basic competencies, and the neighborhood and the school are the central areas of activity. This is a time for steady, unspectacular, but important growth. Children learn to understand death and such political concepts as nations, states, cities, and government, and they begin to appreciate individual points of view (Gardner, 1978).

Children begin to turn more and more to their age mates for information, approval, and models as to what to do when. The school-age child is a conformist through and through. Clothing, taste in music, books, movies, television programs, and even what games are to be played seem to be mysteriously arrived at by consensus, with little or no deviance tolerated. There are inexorable rules of the seasons—one day in spring, baseball is played. Just as suddenly, in fall it's marble time, and woe be to those children who mistakenly carry their baseball mitts during marble season!

Interest in assessing one's own skills and abilities increases during this

During the years from 6 to 12, boys play with boys and shun little girls; girls play with girls and despise little boys. Friendships are almost exclusively with children of the same sex.

Chapter 12: Childhood

360

period, especially in comparison to other children in the same classroom. Younger children show little interest in comparing themselves with others, and tend not to use social comparison information in evaluating their own performances. For example, children of 3 or 4 years who observe that others scored 10 in the same game that they had scored 5 in would still rate their own performance as quite good. Older children use the social-comparison information to lower their estimates of their own performance (Ruble et al., 1976).

This time of surface conformity is also the time when individual differences in important personal characteristics emerge. One such characteristic is the motive to achieve. Achievement motivation varies considerably from person to person, as measured by tests devised by David McClelland (McClelland et al., 1953). At the beginning of the school years children do not differ very much from one another on measures of achievement motivation. By age 12 or 13, however, there are clear differences, at least in boys (unfortunately, girls were not tested in this study.) Not surprisingly, parental styles can influence children's achievement motivations. Children who are high achievers tend to have parents who set high standards and who give them free and warm encouragement. Low achievers' parents tend to be authoritarian and directive, and tend to punish failure rather than reward success (Rosen and D'andrade, 1959). Other factors, including social and school environments, also have a major effect on achievement.

Cognitive Skills

Some of the most obvious changes in children 5 to 13 are in the intellectual domain. Reading and writing skills improve enormously, and children's language becomes more complex, subtle, and rich. In Piaget's theory, children pass from the preoperational to the concrete operations stage just about the time they move into the second grade. The acid test of whether a child is in the concrete operational stage is whether he or she possesses the mental operations that are necessary for *conservation* (Elkind, 1961; Flavell, 1963), the knowledge that quantities and other permanent characteristics of objects remain the same despite such superficial transformations as apparent shape, brightness, or size. When, for example, water is poured from a short wide glass into a tall narrow one, preoperational children will say that there is now more water in the taller glass. Concrete operational children will be able to judge that the amount of water has not changed. They can do this by using three basic mental operations. The first of these is *compensation*. For example, the child says that the water is the same because even though it is higher, it is also narrower—one perceptual quality is *compensated for* by another. A second important operation is *identity*—the material itself, the water, is the same in the two conditions, so that identity must extend to amount. The third operation is *reversibility*—what would happen if the water were to be poured back into the short wide container? Children who can carry out this operation mentally are more likely to judge that the amount of water has not changed.

Is the child in the concrete operational stage qualitatively different from the preoperational child? That is, do the two children think in fundamentally different ways? According to Piagetian theory, yes. The older child is capable of certain mental operations that the younger child simply cannot do. If Piaget's

One test of conservation is to pour water from a short wide glass into a tall narrow one and ask if the amount of water is the same. Preoperational children will say that there is more water in the taller glass; concrete operational children will say that the amount of water has not changed.

theory is absolutely correct, it should be impossible to teach a preoperational child to conserve. Rochel Gelman (1969) tested this notion by taking a group of children who had failed the standard tests of conservation and giving them some specially designed training. Basically, the training consisted of teaching the children to pay attention to the relevant dimensions of situations. For example, for the water problem, children would be taught to look at and compare *both* the *height* and the *width* of containers. This training produced dramatic results: The children performed just like older children on tests of conservation, whereas their matched age mates without training performed like preoperational children. Of course, it could very well be that these children were on the verge of learning to conserve on their own and that the training simply accelerated their normal growth patterns. To some extent, this must be true—we would hardly expect this kind of training to be effective for 2- or even 3-year-old children. On the other hand, in many situations adults would be revealed as nonconservers as well. Consider how successful creative packagers have been in making us believe that the things we buy are actually more than they are.

Perhaps the most reasonable conclusion is that the emergence of operational cognitive skills depends on the availability of certain mental operations, such as compensation, *and* the child's knowledge about which aspects of a situation are important and relevant and which are not. The latter knowledge comes primarily from experience with similar situations; the former undoubtedly comes from a distillation of a variety of experiences and is more general (Weisberg, 1980). Piaget recognizes this distinction between the potential availability of a mental operation—or a problem-solving strategy—and its actual use in a problem situation. Children will often display conservation, for example, in one test and not display it in another. Fully operational children are consistent across all situations; developing children have yet to learn the specific situations that call for the mental and cognitive skills they may have (Flavell, 1978).

The same interplay between possessing a skill and knowing when to use it can be seen in the development of another important cognitive skill, remembering. The difference between having a skill and applying it helps to explain an apparent paradox. Although young children apparently have poor memories, they learn an enormous amount of complex material in a very short time—e.g., they learn a language in about 3 or 4 years! How could a person with a poor memory learn so much vocabulary, to say nothing of the complex grammatical rules that are necessary to produce and understand sentences? How poor can the young child's memory be?

Children in the preschool years perform quite poorly on *tests* of memory compared to school-age children. One such test assesses the ability to remember material immediately after it has been presented, like a telephone number. The number of digits or items that someone can repeat back immediately after hearing them is an estimate of the *memory span*. Most adults have a span of about 7 digits, the usual length of a telephone number (Miller, 1956). Young children have a span of about 5 digits at age 6. This difference between young children and adults is real, but not all that dramatic. Where the real differences appear are in tests that require specific strategies to perform well. For example, most of us know that if we hear a telephone number, we will not remember it beyond a few

seconds if we don't rehearse—repeat it to ourselves several times. This knowledge about memory, or meta-memory (Flavell and Wellman, 1977), is something young children do not yet have, though schoolchildren learn it to a great extent by age 7 or 8. Their memory in itself has not improved, but their ability to remember has improved because they have learned how to sustain the fleeting immediate-memory trace (A. Brown, 1975).

The same thing can be seen in children's abilities to remember lists of words. When adults are given a list of words that belong to discrete categories—four names of countries, four tools, four vegetables, and four names of furniture—they memorize the list in terms of these categories. Even if the list is presented in random order, recall is grouped by categories, so that the four country names will be recalled together, then the vegetables, and so on. This strategy greatly aids recall. Young children do not organize their recall by categories spontaneously, although they can if carefully instructed to (Ornstein and Corsale, 1979). Older children behave like adults, organizing their recall by categories whenever possible. Their memory performance, as a result, is better than that of younger children. Is this improvement in memory strategies simply a function of increased age—possibly of maturation—or is it a by-product of formal schooling?

This kind of question is almost impossible to answer in a society where everyone goes to school. However, we can investigate the problem in parts of the world where formal schooling is not universal. The Kpelle tribe in Africa provided the American psychologist Michael Cole and his colleagues with a rare natural experiment (Cole et al., 1971). Some Kpelle villages had formal European-type schools for their children, and others did not. Here was a perfect opportunity to compare the memory skills of children who went to school with those of children who did not go to school, since all other factors were equal—age, culture, race, language, and virtually all other relevant factors. Somewhat to Cole's surprise, the Kpelle's strategies for remembering lists of words did not change with age alone. High-school-aged Kpelle children who did not have formal schooling did not cluster words in recall, and their recall of word lists did not improve very much with repeated trials. Comparable Kpelle people who went to school remembered pretty much the way American people do: They learned how to rehearse and organize word lists and so could recall them fairly well.

Does this mean that people without schooling have terrible memories? Not necessarily. What it does mean is that people have to learn how to remember different kinds of material. Schooling, in ways that are not yet clear, seems to teach children to memorize essentially meaningless material by rote. This may be because so much educational material demands this kind of skill—for example, multiplication tables, spelling rules, and geographical place names. Not surprisingly, this kind of training helps people in similar kinds of situations, including standard tests of memory.

By the end of the preadolescent years most children have acquired the basic facts of life, including an adequate understanding of numbers and basic arithmetic, reasonable facility in reading and writing, and a fair knowledge of their physical, cultural, and social world. They are ready for the transition from childhood to the world of adults.

Summary

1. The changes that a person undergoes throughout the life cycle are of central importance in the study of psychological development.

2. An important source of developmental change is *maturation,* the ability to do something one couldn't do before, through physical growth and development.

3. Experience is important for development to occur; experience also plays an influential role in the maturation process.

4. Some theorists believe that learning must take place at a specific time during development; this specific development time is called a *critical period.* In humans, it is perhaps more accurate to say that there may be *sensitive periods* for learning; these are periods during which various traits and abilities are most readily acquired.

5. Perceptual development during infancy involves perceptual and object constancies and a shift in the perception of patterns. At the same time, certain motor abilities, such as sitting without support and walking, are acquired. Finally, the first year of life is very important in the social experience of the infant with parents, which affects later attitudes toward social attachments in general.

6. Freud theorized that people pass through various *psychosexual stages*—(oral, anal, phallic, latency, and genital)—as they develop from infancy through adulthood.

7. Erikson modified this to *psychosocial stages,* or periods during which basic crises arise and must be resolved.

8. Learning about oneself involves *identification,* including sex-role identification, which is greatly affected by society's expectations. Social learning theory is an explanation of sex-role development based on concepts of reinforcement and imitation.

9. Jean Piaget identified various stages in a child's awareness of the world, or cognitive development. In childhood one passes through the *sensorimotor, preoperational,* and *concrete operational stages.* Development from one cognitive level or stage to another involves the processes of *assimilation* and *accommodation.*

10. Language development is dependent to a certain extent on the child's early social interactions with parents.

11. Moral development progresses from simple ideas of morality, based almost entirely on consequences of an action, to more complicated ideas that take into account such things as principles and *intentions.*

12. During the school years, children are faced with a wider social and intellectual world, and the peer group becomes a major factor in shaping attitudes, beliefs, and personality. The cognitive abilities of *compensation* and longer memory span develop, and basic skills of reading, writing, numbers, and a fair knowledge of the physical, cultural, and social world are required.

Suggested Readings

American Psychologist, October 1979, S. Scarr, Guest Editor. This issue, prepared to celebrate the International Year of the Child, contains invited essays on important topics, including children's thinking, their socioemotional development, and issues of social policy affecting children and their families.

BORNSTEIN, M. H., and KESSEN, W. *Psychological development from infancy.* Provides a good survey of the major advances in our understanding of infancy.

FLAVELL, J. H. *Cognitive development.* Englewood Cliffs, N.J.: Prentice-Hall, 1977. Piaget's work is somewhat difficult for people just entering the field. This is a clear and concise introduction to his work.

GARDNER, H. *Developmental Psychology: An introduction.* Boston: Little, Brown. 1978. A readable introduction to the major concepts of developmental psychology, providing lucid introductions to the major views in the field, such as those of Piaget, Freud, and Darwin.

STONE, L. J., SMITH, H. T., and MURPHY, L. B. (Eds.) *The competent infant: Research and commentary.* New York: Basic Books, 1973. Presents a variety of articles on the capabilities and characteristics of infants. Their anthology provides excellent source and background material on this topic.

13 Adolescence, Adulthood, and Aging

The term *puberty* derives from the Latin word "pubescere," meaning "to grow hairy." Puberty is defined as the period during which a child attains sexual maturity. In our culture puberty signals the beginning of adolescence; in other cultures it marks the transition to adulthood. In cultures where the change from the status of child to adult is abrupt, this transition may be highlighted with an initiation rite. An initiation rite is a ceremony that specifically signals the child's attainment of adult status. In some cultures, boys' initiation rites involve a display of courage and skill—qualities required by adult men (Benedict, 1934; Brown, 1969; Munroe and Munroe, 1975). Thus boys may be beaten, thrown into icy waters, circumcised, or mutilated. In other societies the initiation rites for boys involve the teaching of ideas considered important for their culture (Whiting, Klucholm, and Anthony, 1958). Consider, for example, the Zuni Indian society in New Mexico. During their initiation rites the boys learn that the sacred Kachina gods used in ceremonies are not real gods but masked adult members of the community, and that "they as mortals, must exercise all the functions which the uninitiated ascribed to the supernaturals themselves" (Benedict, 1934, p. 70).

For girls, initiation rites frequently involve a period of isolation or seclusion from other people. For example, the girl may go to a hut outside the village. During this time other women may teach the girl the skills needed to be a lover, wife, and mother, including information on lovemaking, contraception, and childbirth. The isolated girl may also undergo certain hardships. For example, she may be "deflowered" and subjected to genital mutilation; her skin may be tattooed or scarred; and her teeth may be filed and blackened (Ford and Beach, 1951). When the girl emerges from seclusion, she frequently dons the clothing of an adult woman and is eligible for marriage.

In Western cultures the initiation into adulthood is not marked by dramatic initiation rites. Instead, the change from childhood to adulthood takes place during an extended period of adjustment known as adolescence.

Adolescence

The term *adolescence* derives from the Latin word "adolescere," which means "to grow into maturity." In our culture adolescence is the period between childhood and adulthood during which the individual learns the skills needed to survive as an adult. Unlike puberty, adolescence is a socially rather than

367

biologically determined phase of development. The passage to adulthood is marked by a number of small changes in status during or near the end of adolescence. For example, graduation from high school, the attainment of voting privileges, the right to drink, and the right to drive a vehicle are all events that, to some degree, signify adult status. These events frequently occur at different times, and may or may not coincide with the independence and self-sufficiency usually associated with adulthood. This lack of consistency in the laws and customs signaling the attainment of adult status may be a source of conflict and anxiety for many adolescents in our society (Conger, 1977).

Physical Development

Puberty is marked by dramatic physical changes in both growth rate and sexual characteristics. The initial adolescent growth spurt, a period of rapid growth in height and weight, precedes the onset of secondary sex characteristics (except for the enlargement of the testes and gonads in boys). Thus, for the average boy, active acceleration in growth begins at about 13 years of age, and changes in characteristics such as the growth of coarse pubic hair and facial hair take place later. For girls, rapid growth in height occurs before menarche (the beginning of menstruation), but about $2\frac{1}{2}$ years after the first signs of breast development. The growth spurt generally begins between the ages of $10\frac{1}{2}$ and 16 for boys and between $7\frac{1}{2}$ and $11\frac{1}{2}$ for girls. In both sexes it takes about $4\frac{1}{2}$ years from the first appearance of secondary sex characteristics to the development of the adult configuration of sexual characteristics (Conger, 1977; Marshall and Tanner, 1969, 1970; Tanner, 1970).

The age at which puberty is reached varies across individuals and groups. For example, it is clear that better nourished children reach sexual maturity before children without proper nourishment (Tanner, 1970). Genetic factors are also influential (Tanner, 1962, 1970). And the beginning of puberty sometimes varies across time in the same culture. In the United States, for example, menarche has been occurring at younger ages than in the past. The average girl reached menarche at age 14 in 1910, at 13.4 in 1930, at 13.3 in 1940, and at 12.8 in 1955 (Cagas and Riley, 1970; Malina, 1979). The mean age of menarche decreased by 6 months between 1940 and 1955. However, since the mid-1950s the mean age of menarche has been stable; in a national sample of American girls in the 1960s the median age of menarche was 12.8 (12.5 for black girls, 12.8 for white girls) (MacMahon, 1973). Perhaps nutrition and general health have risen to such a high level among American girls that the average age for menarche will not decrease in the future.

THE EFFECTS OF BEING AN EARLY OR A LATE BLOOMER.   The age at which children go through the dramatic physical changes associated with puberty and later adolescence varies greatly, and these variations appear to have an effect on the adolescent's personality. According to an intensive study of boys aged 14 to 17, early-maturing boys were at an advantage over late-maturing boys. Early maturers were more reserved, self-assured, displayed more socially appropriate behavior, were better able to laugh at themselves, and were more likely to be needed. Boys who were late bloomers were seen as less attractive in physique, less poised, more prone to attention-getting behavior, more tense, more eager and expressive, and less popular with their peers (Jones, 1958; Jones

HIGHLIGHT
Continuity and Discontinuity in Personality

Many psychologists believe that a person's behavior and personality are formed in the early years and resist change in adulthood. This point of view was an outcome, in part, of Sigmund Freud's emphasis on trauma and psychosexual crises during early childhood. However, according to data from a well-known longitudinal study at the University of California in Berkeley, it is incorrect to assume that there is great consistency between childhood behavior and personality in later functioning.

The Berkeley researchers have been following the development of persons born approximately 50 years ago. Thus they have data on development throughout childhood and well into adulthood. One of the more important findings coming out of the study is that there is little continuity in development from childhood to adulthood (MacFarlane, 1963, 1964). Indeed, 50 percent of the children turned out to be more stable and effective adults than any of the researchers would have predicted; 20 percent were less substantial than would have been predicted; and the researchers were correct in their predictions only about 30 percent of the time.

In other words, many dull, unhappy, and unstable children matured into wise, satisfied, and creative adults, and some popular and seemingly stable children had significant problems in adulthood. It appears that many traumatic childhood events can be learning experiences, and that behaviors often change with new experiences and learning. Furthermore, some people seem to be "late bloomers" or "slow jellers" and require time, and perhaps a change of situation, to work through earlier confusions or inhibitions and achieve their potential.

and Bagley, 1950). The late bloomers also reported more feelings of inadequacy and rejection and held more negative self-concepts (Mussen and Jones, 1957). Furthermore, the effects of being an early or late maturer were long-term. When the boys were studied again at age 33, the late maturers were relatively less responsible, dominant, and self-controlled, and more dependent on others. They also made a less favorable impression on others. However, early and late maturers did not differ in marital status, family size, or educational level (Jones, 1957).

The picture for girls is more complicated. According to one study, girls who mature early tended to be at a social disadvantage in late elementary school (Faust, 1960). However, in junior high school and high school the early maturers had more prestige than the late maturers (Faust, 1960). According to another study, early bloomers tended to be more adjusted, self-assured, relaxed, secure, and displayed more adequate thought processes in adolescence (Jones and Mussen, 1958). Thus, while early-maturing females frequently feel different and vulnerable before the age at which most girls reach menarche, they seem to be at a social advantage in later adolescence.

Cognitive Development

At about age 11 or 12 children enter into Piaget's final stage of cognitive development—the stage of formal operations. During this stage they acquire several important cognitive capacities they did not have in childhood (Inhelder and Piaget, 1958; Piaget, 1972).

During the stage of concrete operations, which we discussed in Chapter 12, children can do mental operations in their head, but only if they concern concrete material objects or actions already performed. The most basic change in the formal operational period is adolescents' newfound ability to think about

The ability to test a formula for correctness by using experimental methods (as in this high school chemistry lab) is called hypothetico-deductive reasoning, and is an ability that adolescents gain as part of formal operational thinking.

the possible and the abstract. In contrast to concrete operational children, adolescents can consider that which has not yet occurred, and can imagine all the diverse possible relationships and outcomes in a given situation. For instance, they can reason about contrary-to-fact situations (e.g., if coal were white) and consider all the ramifications of such a situation. Further, formal operational adolescents often display what is called *hypothetico-deductive* reasoning. This is the ability to test systematically a set of possibilities for correctness by using logic and experimental methods. Scientists who test a hypothesis by systematically examining each alternative explanation are using hypothetico-deductive thinking (Flavell, 1963; Inhelder and Piaget, 1958).

Adolescents can also manipulate thoughts and systems of thought mentally. This ability to reason about verbal statements and abstractions is called *propositional* thinking. It enables adolescents to think systematically about the future and about abstract ideology and philosophy.

The development of formal operational thinking makes the adolescent's thought richer and far more flexible than the child's. Adolescents can consider and explore realms of the impossible and improbable, as well as the realm of reality. And they can systematically evaluate the many possibilities in their own lives, as well as the validity of others' assertions and hypotheses (such as political candidates' platforms and ideological claims). This acquisition of the ability to think more abstractly is reflected in the educational system's curriculum. In junior high school and high school students are generally required to apply propositional and hypotheticodeductive thinking in their courses.

Not everyone reaches the formal operations stage. Indeed, according to some studies, only 30 to 40 percent of adolescents and adults in our society display formal operational thinking (Neimark, 1975). Further, this mode of thinking is apparently absent in some nonliterate cultures (Berry and Dasen, 1974; Neimark, 1975).

Given this kind of evidence, Piaget (1972) has modified his original proposal. He now suggests that formal, abstract thought is not necessarily developed without specific schooling and training, particularly in mathematics and science. Furthermore, Piaget now suggests that the content, or subject matter, *is* important—people can apply their knowledge of logic in fields they are familiar with, but may not be able to do so in fields they know little about. Thus, a carpenter may successfully use abstract logical thinking in problems of construction and design, but perhaps not in problems of philosophy and the law. The reverse might well be true for a lawyer.

Social Development

Stanley Hall (1904) was the first social scientist to discuss and study the development of adolescence. In his writings about the period he labeled adolescence as the period of "storm and stress." According to Hall, adolescents typically waver between contradictory and extreme states—for example, between exuberance and lethargy, cruelty and sensitivity, diligence and laziness. He suggested that this storm and stress was a reenactment of an earlier stage of human development during which humans were becoming more civilized.

Hall's theme of storm and stress has been repeated and expanded upon by later theorists (Freud, 1953; Muss, 1975). According to Sigmund Freud (1953), during adolescence the sexual energy of libido repressed during latency re-emerges, and the adult stage of development begins. Thus the young adolescent not only must adapt to dramatic physical changes but also must deal with the rise in level of sexual energy.

According to Freud, the evolution of independence from parents is an important developmental task during adolescence. Adolescents must break childhood ties of emotional dependency and become capable of functioning autonomously from their parents. Freud pointed out that in the course of freeing themselves from emotional dependency, adolescents will necessarily go through a period in which they reject their parents, and a certain amount of parent-child conflict is a result of this.

Another famous theorist, Erik Erikson, also emphasized the importance of developing an autonomous, integrated identity during adolescence. In fact, Erikson's fifth stage of psychosocial development, called "identity versus role confusion," occurs during adolescence.

What does one's sense of identity consist of? Intuitively, it is the gut feeling that one is a unified, consistent person, with non-contradictory beliefs, consistent values and ideas about the important aspects of the world, coupled with a secure sense of one's own worthiness as a human being. The self-concept should be realistic about strengths and weaknesses. For optimal mental health, one's self-concept should be reasonably high—a person should like him or herself. Unfortunately, low self-esteem is one consequence of economic and cultural privation, and can trigger a vicious circle in which the self-concept deteriorates as one grows older. One's sense of identity also includes a system of values, including attitudes toward the importance of education, athletic skills, manual dexterity, artistic sensitivity, and loyalty to friends or family, as well as more general political orientations such as conservative versus liberal. Morality and religious beliefs are central to one's sense of personal identity as well as to one's identification with a larger group.

The quest for an identity is often uneasy and conflict-laden. Indeed, Erikson coined the term *identity conflict* to represent this kind of struggle. According to Erikson, there are a number of negative outcomes that may result from the quest for an identity. The first is identity foreclosure, in which the adolescent consolidates an identity early, before having ample opportunity to experiment with the range of possible identities. Erikson believes that a period of trying out or testing of possible alternatives is healthy. He calls this period of experimenting with different identities—for example, seeing what it would be like to be an actress or a writer—moratorium. If adolescents "foreclose" or decide on an identity without testing a number of alternatives they may not become all they were capable of becoming. On the other hand, if adolescents do not consolidate an identity they may exhibit "identity confusion." These individuals shift from identity to identity without a sense of purpose and may even exhibit delinquent, psychotic, or other negative behaviors (Erikson, 1959, 1963).

Hall, Freud, Erikson, and other theorists (including Freud's daughter Anna) have all viewed adolescence as an especially conflicted period of development. But is this necessarily true? According to research, no.

On the basis of anthropological work in other cultures, notably by Margaret Mead (1928, 1939) in the South Sea community of Samoa, the stereotypic

It appears that for most adolescents the transition from childhood to adulthood need not necessarily be as rocky as many theorists have thought.

picture of the teenager as a troubled, emotionally beset, and confused sexual bungler turns out to be culturally caused. Confusions about sex roles and identities do not exist in the pastoral and relatively uncomplicated life of the Samoans. Who one is, both sexually and in the world of work, is unambiguous and set down clearly and explicitly in the culture.

Other researchers have found that even in our own culture adolescence need not be an especially stressful period (Douvan and Adelson, 1966; King, 1971; Offer, 1969; Offer and Offer, 1974). For example, in one longitudinal study of midwestern adolescent boys, most of the boys showed little evidence of inner turmoil (Offer, 1969; Offer, Marcus, and Offer, 1970). According to the followup study, only a relatively small percentage of the boys (approximately 20 percent) experienced "tumultuous" growth—i.e., showed much turmoil during adolescence (Offer and Offer, 1974).

It appears that for most adolescents the transition from childhood to adulthood is not as rocky as theorists such as Erikson, Hall, and Freud thought. While the changes in adolescence do produce stress for many individuals, the great majority of adolescents appear to be capable of coping with the stresses without a high degree of emotional turmoil (Conger, 1977; King, 1971).

Peer Conformity and the Generation Gap

During early childhood children are more attached to their parents than to their age mates, though they do find age mates quite interesting (Eckerman, Whatley, and Kutz, 1975). However, orientation to peers and conformity increase from the elementary school years until early adolescence, at least in ambiguous situations (Berndt, 1979; Costanzo and Shaw, 1966; Hoving, Hamm, and Galvin, 1969; Shaffer, 1979). For example, when adolescents are asked to make a judgment and the correct response is ambiguous, they rely on their peers' opinions more than younger children do.

This conformity to the peer group frequently results in conflict between parental and peer influences (Berndt, 1979; Bixenstine, DeCorte, and Bixenstine, 1976). In one study children aged 8, 10, 12, 14, and 16 were asked what they would do when their parents and peers had different opinions and gave

conflicting advice about something. The older children were more likely to say they would follow their peers' advice rather than their parents' (Utech and Hoving, 1969).

In reality, however, both parents' and peers' opinions seem to influence adolescents' behavior. Consider, for example, the effects of peer and parental influences on the use of drugs among adolescents. Kandel (1973) examined adolescent drug use in relation to parental and friends' use of psychoactive drugs. Among adolescents whose parents used psychoactive drugs but whose best friends did not, only 17 percent smoked marijuana themselves. However, among adolescents whose best friends used drugs but whose parents did not, 56 percent reported using psychoactive drugs. The greatest use of marijuana (67 percent) occurred among the adolescents whose best friends and parents both used psychoactive drugs, and 92 percent of those whose friends all used drugs were users themselves.

The complexity of peer group influence is illustrated by the work of Michael Siman (1977). He found that he could predict adolescent behavior by considering (1) the standards endorsed by the adolescent's parents; (2) the extent to which the adolescent's parents conformed to this standard; (3) the standards endorsed by the adolescent's peer group; and (4) the extent to which the individual's values conformed or deviated from the peer group's. Both parental and peer norms affected adolescents' behaviors, according to Siman, and the peer group's acceptance of parental norms affected how the adolescent reacted to parental standards. In other words, the peer group acted as a "filter" for parental norms—an adolescent's parents' values were accepted as valid if they conformed to the peer group's perceptions of the average parental norm.

Adolescents' strong orientation to peers has led many people to talk about a "generation gap," meaning that adolescents disagree with their parents about many issues, including basic values. It seems, however, that this gap is illusory. While it is true that adolescents differ greatly from their parents on many relatively unimportant matters such as dress and choice of entertainment, their values concerning important issues are frequently quite similar to those of their parents (Conger, 1977). Even during the height of the counterculture in the

While it is true that adolescents differ greatly from their parents on matters such as dress and choice of entertainment, their values concerning important issues are frequently quite similar to those of their parents, and, indeed, it seems that for many the generation gap is not as wide as it has been portrayed in recent years.

1960s most adolescents and their parents agreed that their differences on ideals and values were not marked (Conger, 1977). According to self-reports, even white civil rights workers (the Freedom Riders) and college radicals and liberals in the 1960s frequently modeled their values and behaviors on those of their parents (Flacks, 1970; Horn and Knott, 1971; Rosenhan, 1970). Further, more recent studies done in the 1970s revealed a surprising degree of agreement among parents and adolescents on the validity of traditional values such as self-reliance, hard work, and the importance of duty before pleasure (Conger, 1977; Thurnher, Spence, and Fiske, 1974). Thus, although the average parent and the average adolescent may differ somewhat on certain issues such as sex, religion, drugs, and social justice, the generation gap is not as wide as it has been portrayed by the media and social critics.

Adolescence and Sexuality

A widespread opinion in American society is that today's adolescents are more sexually active and more oriented toward sexual concerns than were adolescents in the past. The media, including films, music, and television, reinforce this idea by presenting images of highly sexual adolescents. But how much of this image is reality and how much is fact?

Adolescents today are more sexually involved than in the past: Incidents of both petting and sexual intercourse are higher and occur at an earlier age (Conger, 1977; Hopkins, 1977; Sorenson, 1973). However, this is not a recent phenomenon, for the parents of today's adolescents were more sexually active than their parents. According to the famous research done by Kinsey and his colleagues, while only 8 percent of females born before 1900 had premarital intercourse before the age of 20, 21 percent of mothers of today's adolescents had premarital intercourse by the same age (Kinsey, Pomeroy, and Martin, 1953). The figures for intercourse among adolescents in a study published in 1973 were 72 percent for boys and 57 percent for girls by the age 19 (Sorenson, 1973). While this study may overstate the percentages—in another study only 33 percent of males and 55 percent of females in their senior year had had sexual intercourse (Jessor and Jessor, 1975)—there has been a dramatic change in sexual behavior during adolescence during the past century.

In contrast to behavior, adolescents' attitudes regarding sex have not changed as much as many people believe. Most adolescents strongly oppose sex solely for physical enjoyment, exploitation in sexual relationships, and sex among people too young to know what they are getting into (Conger, 1977; Sorenson, 1973). For example, over 80 percent of all adolescents disagreed with the statement that the most important thing in a relationship is sex. And when adolescents rated the relative importance of different goals such as learning about themselves, having fun, and being independent, having sex with different people and "making out" were ranked as among the *least* important goals (Sorenson, 1973). So while contemporary adolescents are relatively sexually active, they have not renounced all traditional values relating to sex.

Moral Development

Moral development continues from childhood into adolescence. As discussed previously, most children reason in what Kohlberg calls a preconventional manner. Young children are concerned with obedience to authority, avoidance of punishment, and hedonistic gains for themselves and the people important to them. Around adolescence most people enter Kohlberg's (1969, 1971) conventional level of moral judgment, which contains two stages—Stages 3 and 4. In contrast to the preconventional moral reasoning of children, which is essentially nonmoral, individuals reasoning at the conventional level have accepted the moral values and standards of their culture.

Stage 3 is frequently called the "interpersonal concordance—good boy, nice girl" orientation. The individual conforms to stereotype conceptions of a "good boy" or a "nice girl." Good behavior is that which helps or pleases others and is approved of by them (Kohlberg, 1969, 1971).

During Stage 4, the "law and order" orientation, norms and values of the society become more internalized. Stage 4 individuals are oriented toward duties, defined responsibility, fixed rules, and maintenance of the social order. Right behavior consists of showing respect to authorities, doing one's duty, and maintaining the social order for its own sake.

Since adults in many nonindustrial societies do not use Stages 3 and 4 (Kohlberg, 1969), Kohlberg's conventional level of moral judgment may be culturally biased (Simpson, 1974). Nevertheless, his description of conventional reasoning captures the flavor of American adolescents' moral judgment.

Early Adulthood

As we have seen, in some societies puberty heralds the beginning of adulthood; in others the child does not become an adult until much later. In the United States it is not clear when an adolescent becomes an adult. Is it at graduation from high school, or when the person becomes self-supporting or moves out of the parental home?

In recent years the question of when an adolescent attains adult status has become even less clear. For example, many college students live away from their

Keniston has proposed a new stage of life, "youth," for those people in their late teens and early 20s caught between adolescence and adult status. It is an ambiguous stage, with many college and graduate students being married and living away from home, and yet still being financially dependent on their parents.

parents, and many marry while still financially dependent on their parents. In other words, many people today spend long periods training for a career or trying to determine what their occupation should be.

Because so many people in their late teens and early 20s are caught in the no-man's-land between adolescence and adult status, Keniston (1970) proposed that a new stage of life has appeared in our culture. This stage, called "youth," is between adolescence and adulthood. According to Keniston, people in this stage are deeply involved in working out their conflicts between maintaining personal integrity and achieving effectiveness in society. Since they realize the potency of societal forces that conflict with their self-identity, youths may refuse to be socialized into the predominant adult society. They may become estranged from the dominant culture and identify with youth cultures instead.

Keniston developed his theory of a "youth" stage to explain the unrest among young people in the 1960s. Regardless of its original use, the theory clearly points out the ambiguous status of young people in our society. An adult is generally seen as responsible, mature, self-supporting, and well integrated into adult society, but people may not develop all these attributes and characteristics simultaneously. Thus there is disagreement among both social scientists and people in general as to when an individual becomes an adult.

Social Development

THEORY. According to a number of theorists, the major task in early adulthood is to establish intimate relationships. Freud believed that successful development during the genital stage meant the ability to "Lieben und arbeiten" (to love and to work) (Erikson, 1963). Therefore he thought that a heterosexual loving relationship was a major component of adult development. Similarly, Erikson's (1963) sixth stage of development, which occurs during early adulthood, is called "intimacy versus isolation." During this stage

> The young adult, emerging from the search for and the insistence on identity, is eager and willing to fuse his identity with that of others. He is ready for intimacy,

that is, the capacity to commit himself to concrete affiliations and partnerships and to develop the ethical strength to abide by such commitments, even though they may call for significant sacrifices and compromises. (Erikson, 1963)

Empirical research has supported Freud's and Erikson's claims that the establishment of intimate relationships is a major developmental task during early adulthood (Gould, 1974; Levinson, Darrow, Klein, Levinson, and McKee, 1978).

According to Erikson (1963), intimacy is not synonymous with sexuality: The mutual respect and caring that create an intimate situation may be expressed in close friendships as well as in sexual relationships. If the young adult does not form some sort of intimate relationship, however, he or she will develop a deep sense of isolation and consequent self-absorption.

THE STATUS OF MARRIAGE.   For many people, the quest for intimate relationships results in marriage. However, the statistics and dynamics relating to marriage have changed greatly over the years.

Consider, first, the age of the individual at the time of his or her first marriage. From about 1900 to the late 1950s, the age at which Americans married for the first time went down. The average bride in 1890 was 22.0 years; in 1956 she was 20.1. Analogous figures for males were 26.1 and 22.5 years. Since the 1950s the trend has reversed, and the average age for marriage has increased gradually. In 1978 the average ages of females and males at marriage were 21.8 and 24.2, respectively. Further, in the 1970s the percentage of people in early adulthood who had never been married increased. In 1960, 53.1 percent of males and 28.4 percent of females aged 20 to 24 had never been married; by 1975 the figures were 59.9 percent and 40.3 percent. In 1978, 47.6 percent of women aged 20 to 24 had never been married. Obviously people are marrying later in life than they did in the recent past (Current Population Reports, 1975, 1979).

Another major demographic trend is the increasing number of marriages that end in divorce. In the 1920s and 1930s, each year only about 1 percent of

The major task in early adulthood seems to be to establish intimate relationships. As Erikson noted, young adults emerge from the adolescent stage of searching for identity eager to join their identity with that of others. If young adults do not form some sort of intimate relationship, it can lead to isolation and a kind of self-absorption.

Chapter 13: Adolescence, Adulthood, and Aging

377

married women aged 14 to 44 were divorced. In the mid-1940s the rate was 2.4 percent; and in the mid-1950s, 1.5 percent (Glick and Norton, 1973). In 1978, 11 percent of women in the United States who had been married were divorced (Current Population Reports, 1978). The rate of divorces is increasing rapidly, and it is estimated that 29 percent of women born between 1940 and 1944 will end their first marriage in divorce (Glick and Norton, 1973). Indeed, for persons under 30 years of age, the rate of divorce rose 296 percent between 1960 and 1978 (Current Population Reports, 1978). While approximately four out of five divorced people remarry, particularly men (Glick and Norton, 1973), the high rate of divorce is a stress for many young adults.

BIRTHRATES AND PARENTHOOD.   Not only are the rates of marriage and divorce changing, but so are the roles within marriage. One of the most important factors affecting the women's role is the declining birthrate. The average number of births for married women decreased steadily in the United States from 7 in 1880 to 2.3 in 1940, but rose during the baby boom from the 1940s until 1957, when the average number of births was 3.8. Since 1957, however, the average has dropped to about 2.11 (Current Population Reports, 1979b). Although the rate of births appears to be rising slightly (Sklar and Berkov, 1975), the rate is lower today than in the past. This change in birthrate has accompanied the entrance of married women into the labor force.

Parenthood influences the quality of life in early adulthood. Young fathers report fewer positive feelings about their lives, perhaps because of the economic burdens and other stresses associated with having to support a family (Campbell, 1975). Indeed, parenthood creates a life crisis for most couples (LeMasters, 1957); married couples with children under age 17 report higher levels of stress than couples with no children or those with adult children.

While parenthood may be very stressful, it provides an opportunity for growth and satisfaction. Erik Erikson concluded that being a caring, directive parent is one way to develop successfully during his sixth stage of development, "generativity versus stagnation." Another way to become a generative adult is to guide young people of the next generation who are not one's own children, for example, by teaching children. According to Erikson, the adult who does not attend to the welfare of the next generation often develops a pervasive sense of stagnation and personal impoverishment (Erikson, 1963).

Moral Development

Moral development may continue into adulthood. While many people attain the highest level of moral judgment during adolescence, others continue to develop their moral reasoning into their 20s and perhaps even later (Kohlberg, 1976; Kohlberg and Kramer, 1969).

During early adulthood a relatively small percentage of adults achieve Kohlberg's third level of moral development, the postconventional level (Kohlberg, 1969, 1971). This consists of Kohlberg's last two stages—Stages 5 and 6. At Stage 5, the "social-contract/legalistic orientation," right behavior is defined in terms of general individual rights and standards that have been critically examined and agreed upon by members of a society. The Stage 5 individual has a clear awareness of the relativism of personal values and opinions, emphasizes procedural rules for reaching consensus in a group, and believes that laws should

be changed in accordance with rational considerations. Aside from what is democratically agreed upon by the group, right is considered a matter of personal value.

In Stage 6, the "universal ethical principle orientation," right is defined by a decision of conscience in accordance with self-chosen ethical principles that are logically comprehensive, universal to all people, and consistent. These principles are abstract, such as ideas of justice, equality of human rights, and respect for the dignity of individual human beings (Kohlberg, 1971).

Kohlberg's postconventional level is the most criticized of his three levels. Many researchers and theorists feel that it is culturally biased—that is, it applies only to Western industrialized societies (Kurtines and Grief, 1974; Simpson, 1974). Furthermore, it is not clear that Stage 6 is developmentally more mature than Stage 5. Indeed, Kohlberg (1978) has recently conceded that Stage 6 may not be separable from Stage 5. However, even though many of Kohlberg's original claims regarding the postconventional level of moral judgment have not been substantiated, it is clear that postconventional reasoning is an adult achievement, and that adults who do attain it differ significantly in their moral perspective from adolescents and other adults.

One of the characteristics of Kohlberg's third level of moral development, the postconventional level, is the belief that laws should be changed according to rational considerations and in an orderly, democratic way. Part of that belief is the willingness to become involved in the voting process, as these people are involved in a voter registration drive.

The Mature Years

During the last decade or so the attitude of both psychologists and people in general toward middle age has undergone a radical transformation. Previously, middle age was regarded as a period in which nothing much happened. Life "ended at forty and there was nothing to do but wait around for retirement and death" (Brim, 1976). Currently, however, it is fashionable to regard middle age as a time of considerable conflict and growth. The term "midlife crisis" has come into vogue. Songs such as "Middle-aged Crazy," movies such as *10,* and magazine articles such as "I Am the Wife of a Man in a Mid-life Crisis" popularize the idea that turmoil is natural at this stage of life. In a humorous essay Gerald Nachman (1979) satirizes the current interest in the topic. Focusing on the plight of those who are afraid they will be "left behind again," he suggests the establishment of a Midlife Crisis Camp for men incapable of devising their own traumas.

> You sign up for a week of intensive anguish, located on 227 acres of choice desolation, reminiscent of the usual barren atmosphere of Middle Crises—drab hotel rooms, murky bars, obscure cafés, empty parks. The camp guarantees to produce a maximum sense of worthlessness and tortured self-doubt in a minimum amount of time. (p. 308)

Researchers interested in midlife development disagree on whether a significant number of individuals experience emotional turmoil disruptive enough to constitute a "crisis." Many believe that the transitions that take place during this time may be accomplished smoothly (Brim, 1976). Nonetheless, there is general agreement that between the ages of 40 and 60 changes do take place in several areas of a person's life, and that each of these changes presents a challenge to the individual, which may or may not be met successfully.

Physical Changes

Although individuals vary in the rate at which these changes occur, virtually all middle-aged people notice signs of deterioration in their physical functioning.

In the 40s, for example, there is usually a decline in near vision, a condition known as presbyopia. The lens of the eye becomes less elastic and loses its ability to accommodate to objects held at close range. Reading glasses or bifocals may be required for the first time. The individual may also notice increased sensitivity to glare—on the windshield of the car, for example, or in brightly lit stores. In their 50s people often find that it takes their eyes longer to adapt to the change in illumination when they enter a darkened theater or when they go outside on a bright, sunny day. Some degree of hearing loss is also found in most people over 40.

Changes in outward appearance also occur. Hair thins or grays noticeably, facial wrinkles become more pronounced, the physique alters (as one individual noted ruefully, "The sand shifts"). Weight gains are common and the ratio of muscle to fat in the body declines. People may also notice a decline in their ability to engage in strenuous activities.

These and other physical changes clearly signal to the individual that he or she is growing older. Both sexes are affected by this realization, but there is some evidence that men are more concerned with health and physical prowess, women with physical appearance. A recent study by Carol Nowak (1977) found that middle-aged women were less able than women of other ages to separate their assessment of their appearance from their assessment of their other qualities. Developing a new wrinkle was often equated with being less interesting or less active. In judging the attractiveness of other women, the middle-aged woman was more likely than women of other ages and all men to equate looking youthful with looking attractive and to minimize the attractiveness of the middle-aged woman she was evaluating. On the other hand, Neugarten (1968) found in her study of 100 people between the ages of 40 and 60 that men were more likely than women to spontaneously make such comments as, "Mentally, I

A common physical change in middle age is a decline in near vision, when reading glasses or bifocals may be worn for the first time.

still feel young, but suddenly one day my son beat me at tennis," or "It was the sudden heart attack in a friend that made the difference. I realized that I could no longer count on my body as I used to" (p. 96).

People adapt to these physical changes on at least two levels. They may pay more attention to diet and exercise and stop smoking in order to slow down the rate of deterioration. At the psychological level, theorists such as Robert Peck (1968) suggest that middle-aged people shift from valuing physical power to valuing wisdom, a term he uses for the mental skills that are derived from life experience.

Menopause

Women typically experience menopause, or the cessation of the menstrual cycle, sometime in their late 40s or early 50s. This change generally marks the end of the reproductive period, although there are reports of women becoming pregnant as much as 18 months after menopause has presumably taken place (Talbert, 1977).

Some women experience physical symptoms during this time, including "hot flashes," headaches, nausea, dizziness, and heart palpitations. There may also be negative psychological effects. A woman may mourn the loss of her ability to bear children or worry about the effect of menopause on her sexuality. Her moods may become less predictable, and she may feel less in control of herself. However, in a study of premenopausal and postmenopausal women Neugarten, Wood, Kraines, and Loomis (1968) found that the anticipation may be worse than the event itself. Although about 50 percent of each group agreed that menopause is an unpleasant experience, postmenopausal women were more likely to say that a woman has some degree of control over the symptoms she experiences. They were also more likely to emphasize positive changes, such as an increased sense of freedom and self-confidence.

In men there is no obvious counterpart to menopause. Most men undergo a decline in and end to fertility sometime during middle and old age, although there are reports of men as old as 94 successfully fathering children (Talbert, 1977).

Middle age and the loss of reproductive capacity need not mean the end of sexual functioning for either sex. Although, for example, a middled-aged man may take longer to attain an erection and a postmenopausal woman may experience some irritation of the vaginal wall during intercourse, the primary barriers to full sexual enjoyment are not physical but psychological. They include tension at home and at work, boredom, and acceptance of the myth that sexual waning is an inevitable part of the aging process (Masters and Johnson, 1966; 1970). In fact, the majority of individuals 40 to 60 continue to engage in regular, satisfying sexual activity (Christenson and Gagnon, 1965; Pfeiffer, Verwoerdt, and Davis, 1974).

The Empty Nest

A major event of the middle years is the departure of children from the home. This period is often called that of the "empty nest," and was once viewed as very trying. In fact, some home-centered mothers do feel a great void when their children leave (Bart, 1971). However, according to recent research, many mothers (and fathers) do not. Women whose children have left home tend to be less suppressed, more satisfied, and less self-pitying (Campbell, 1975; Lowenthal, Thurnher, and Chiriboga, 1975; Radloff, 1975). Indeed, feelings of stress are lower for both the husband and wife when the children are over age 17 (Campbell, 1975). Thus rather than creating a crisis, the "empty nest" may actually relieve parents of drains on their finances and time.

Vocational Changes

The woman whose children have left home sometimes decides to return to work. This decision may carry with it several difficulties. She may find that she no longer has the skills necessary for successful competition in the work world. The jobs that are available to her may be low-paying and monotonous and provide little of the satisfaction for which she is looking. A return to work may also mean a shift in the woman's relationship with her husband, both because she has less time available for household chores and because she is making a greater economic contribution to the family.

Many middle-aged men and women who have been employed throughout their adult life experience increased dissatisfaction with their work. In her book on midlife career changes, Paula Robbins (1978) identifies several sources of this dissatisfaction. Although her research focused primarily on middle- and upper-middle-class men, several of the issues she raises seem equally pertinent to working women and men in blue-collar occupations. Among the most important complaints were:

1. "Being put on the shelf" or "topping out." At some point in their careers most men must face the fact that they have advanced as far as they are likely to. The top jobs within their organization or the positions of greatest recognition within their profession will be held in the future not by them, but by others. Although they may view their current position, in and of itself, as satisfying, they may find the loss of potential mobility hard to accept. The blue-collar equivalent of this dilemma was described by Chinoy (1955, as quoted by Brim, 1976) in his study of automobile workers. He found that many workers dealt with the discrepancy between what they wanted when they were young and what they had accomplished by clinging to dreams of becoming a farmer or small businessman.

2. Lack of challenge. Once the demands of a particular job are thoroughly mastered, boredom may set in and the individual may seek new challenges.

3. Change in values. Middle-aged people may find that they no longer want to pursue the goals that were important to them earlier. The reasons for this shift are varied. It may be the result of exposure to new ideas. For example, many of the men in Robbins's study cited experiences with the antiwar and civil rights movements of the late 1960s and early 1970s as contributing to their changed outlook. It may reflect a shift in orientation. Several authors (Gutmann, 1977; Jung, 1933) have suggested that in middle age men and women reclaim underutilized parts of themselves. Men become more oriented toward nurturance, women toward competitive interaction. Both sexes may seek occupations that allow freer expression of these new interests. Or it may grow out of a resurgence of interest in early dreams that were pushed aside (Levinson, Darrow, Klein, Levinson, and McKee, 1978).

4. Lack of autonomy. People's desire to have more control over their work life is an important motivator during the middle years.

The one factor not mentioned by the men in Robbins's study — although she suggests it may be an important source of dissatisfaction for many workers — is income level. Many middle-aged people realize that they will never have certain possessions or worry that they will be unable to adequately prepare for their retirement.

Despite all these possible difficulties, the middle years can be a time of considerable satisfaction vocationally. People are likely to be at their peak in terms of income, status, and responsibility. In a survey of 100 middle-class and upper-middle-class men and women, Neugarten (1968) found that the majority felt that they had the maximum capacity to handle the demands of their job in middle age. To quote one participant:

> I know now exactly what I can do best, and how to make best use of my time. . . . I know how to delegate authority, but also what decisions to make myself. . . . I know how to buffer myself from troublesome people. . . . (p. 98)

Marriage

As the preceding discussion has made clear, middle-aged men and women experience pressure in several aspects of their lives. It would be surprising if these pressures had no effect on their most intimate relationships.

Several studies (Burr, 1970; Campbell, 1975; Rollins and Feldman, 1970; Thurnher, 1976) show that marital satisfaction, particularly for women, is relatively low at the beginning of this period, until just before the children leave home. Couples report that they are less likely than in the early days of their marriage to confide in each other (Pineo, 1961), to laugh together, or to have a stimulating exchange of ideas (Rollins and Feldman, 1970). A study of midlife marriages by Majda Thurnher (1976) found that couples put greater stress on whether or not the spouse lives up to role expectations (e.g., is a "good mother" or "good provider") and much less stress on personality attributes than do younger or older couples. She suggested that couples may be particularly out of sync during this period of life because each partner is preoccupied with the changes in his or her own life. She quotes one male participant in her study:

> . . . now I go my way and she goes hers and they don't seem to coincide that much. I think one of these days we'll come to a closer understanding. When I stop being so tense about things at work, we should be able to get back on the beam. (p. 132)

This man's optimism about the future is justified, at least for marriages in general. With the departure of the children from the family center, and perhaps also as the couple comes to terms with the issues of the midlife period, marital satisfaction begins to rise (Campbell, 1970; Rollins and Feldman, 1970; Thurnher, 1976). Many, if not most, couples share more activities and strengthen the emotional bond between them in the later years of this period.

Old Age

Just when an individual reaches "old age" is not easily determined. Traditionally, researchers in the field of aging have used age 65 or older as the point at which an individual may be considered "old." However, being old is seen as undesirable in American society, so many people continue to think of themselves as middle-aged until they are well into their 70s. Several studies suggest that it is not until people have experienced many of the changes that we associate with aging (retirement, loss of spouse and friends, poor health) that they are willing to apply the label "old" to themselves.

The relative status of the old in our society, as well as people's willingness to think of themselves as old, may be changing. Organizations such as the Gray Panthers have worked hard to increase the visibility and political power of the elderly. The media also have focused more attention on this age group. In part, these changes reflect changing demographic patterns. Increased life expectancy and a declining birthrate have resulted not only in greater numbers of people over 65 in the United States but also in a greater proportion of people in that age range. As can be seen in Table 13-1, in 1900 there were approximately 3 million persons over 65 in this country; they made up about 4 percent of the population. In the year 2000 there will be more than 30 million people over 65 in the United States. Assuming a continued low birthrate, they will then make up about 12.5 percent of the population—a substantial gain and one likely to lead to increased power and status.

Whether or not they label themselves as "old," individuals in their 60s and

Table 13–1: Population Aged 65 and Over in the United States, 1900–2000.

Year	Number (in Thousands)	Percent of Total Population
1900	3,099	4.1
1910	3,986	4.3
1920	4,929	4.7
1930	6,705	5.4
1940	9,031	6.8
1950	12,397	8.2
1960	16,675	9.2
1970	20,085	9.9
1975	22,400	10.5
Projection:		10.7
2000	30,600	12.5

From Ward (1979), based on U.S. Bureau of the Census, 1973b, p. 2, and 1976, p. 3.

70s encounter new changes in their functioning and in their environment. As in earlier periods of life, these changes require adjustment, and also as in earlier periods, adjustment will sometimes be easy and sometimes difficult.

Physical Changes

Many of the physical changes discussed in the section on middle age become more marked during the later years of life. Visual and auditory capacities generally show further decline. Decreases in muscle strength, reaction time, and stamina continue to occur. Outward appearance continues to alter.

Health becomes an increasingly important issue during this period. Acute (temporary) problems such as injuries and influenza actually tend to decline with age. However, chronic (long-term) problems increase significantly. It's estimated that approximately 80 percent of all older people have one or more chronic conditions, including arthritis and rheumatism, hypertension, heart disease, and cancer (Ward, 1979). According to the U.S. Public Health Service (1975), in 1974 39 percent of people over 65 experienced limitations on major activities (defined as the ability to work, keep house, or engage in school activities) and another 7 percent experienced less serious limitations.

Research suggests that older people learn to live with and accept many of these conditions as an inevitable part of aging. Consequently, self-ratings of health decline less than objective ratings (Riley and Fover, 1968). Nevertheless, perceived and actual health are clearly related to each other—actual health cannot decline too far before perceived health is affected. The importance of this is illustrated in a study by Palmore and Luikart (1972), which found that self-rating of health was the variable most related to life satisfaction among middle-aged and older men and women.

Health is also important because it can limit the degree to which the individual is capable of functioning sexually. It is difficult to obtain reliable estimates of the amount of sexual activity in old age, in part because different studies focus on different aspects of sexuality. Sexual functioning has been variously defined as coitus once a week or more, successful coitus at least once a year, or regular orgasmic release through any means including coitus, masturbation, or nocturnal emission. Further, most research has focused on males. Given the limitations, the bulk of the evidence suggests that even in their 70s the majority of men continue to function sexually (Botwinick, 1973; Kaln and Fisher, 1967). The evidence further suggests that loss of responsiveness is not an inevitable part of aging, but is due instead to factors such as chronic physical problems, lack of an available partner, and the belief that sex after 60 is somehow unusual or immoral (Botwinick, 1973).

Cognitive Changes

One of the most controversial issues in the field of gerontology is the extent to which cognitive capacities decline with advancing age. In part, this conflict reflects the fact that researchers have focused on different aspects of intellectual functioning, including memory, problem-solving abilities, and performance on intelligence tests. In addition, methodological issues make it difficult to interpret the results of many of the studies that have been done. Looking first at methodological problems, three seem to be of particular importance:

1. The research design used. Some studies have used cross-sectional designs, others have used longitudinal designs. Each method has its own biases. Cross-sectional approaches tend to overestimate negative age changes, since people in older age groups have had less education than younger people. Longitudinal approaches tend to underestimate negative age changes because subjects may become "test-wise," and also because less able subjects tend to drop out more often than more competent subjects (Botwinick, 1977).
2. The appropriateness of the tests. Some researchers have suggested that the old perform more poorly than the young on many tests not because they have less ability, but because they are not used to being in a testing situation and see the tasks as irrelevant.
3. The effect of extraneous factors. Overarousal in a laboratory situation and a tendency to tire during extended testing also have been suggested as important factors affecting the performance of older people (Arenberg and Robertson-Tchabo, 1977; Botwinick, 1977).

With these methodological limitations in mind, we will review some of the research findings in the area that has probably received the most attention—performance on IQ tests. Studies using tests such as the Wechsler Adult Intelligence Scale have typically found a "classic pattern of aging." Subtests emphasizing verbal skills (vocabulary, information, comprehension) tend to show little or no decline until well into old age. But subtests that measure memory and perceptual-integrative skills (digit span, digit symbol, picture arrangement) show declining scores from middle age on (Botwinick, 1977). One way of conceptualizing these different types of skills is in terms of "crystallized" versus "fluid" intelligence. *Crystallized intelligence* refers to those abilities that can be "expected to improve by the increased learning, the consolidation of knowledge . . . which accompany aging." Crystallized intelligence is best observed in the verbal subtests, which show relatively little age-related decline. *Fluid intelligence,* on the other hand, refers to those abilities that are most sensitive to "any loss or degeneration of the physiological (principally neurological) substratum supporting intellectual behavior," and is best observed in the more performance-oriented subtests, which do show an earlier decline. Theorists who support this conceptualization suggest that whether or not the older individual is at a relative disadvantage in performing a particular task depends in large part on which type of ability the task demands (Horn and Donaldson, 1976).

It must be emphasized that these tests measure changes in intellectual functioning in *groups.* Decrement is not inevitable in every person. Indeed, numerous individuals continue to function at a high level until they are quite old. Factors such as health, education, and earlier level of performance appear to be far more important than age per se in affecting performance during the later years (Botwinick, 1977).

Retirement

Retirement is one of the most important, and most studied, changes associated with old age. Some people see it as a quite negative change, a separation from an important source of satisfaction and self-esteem. Those who take this point of view have been active in the movement to raise and even abolish mandatory retirement ages. But others view retirement as a positive shift to a life with more free time and more opportunity to pursue non-work-related interests. Some labor unions have demanded "30 and out" plans, allowing workers to retire on full pension after 30 years of service.

How retirement is perceived by the individual worker is crucial because attitude toward retirement is one of the most important predictors of later adjustment and satisfaction (Kimmel, Price, and Walker, 1978; Streib and Schneider, 1971). Other factors that affect adjustment are:

Many view retirement as a positive shift to a life with more free time and more opportunity to pursue outside interests.

1. Health. Several studies have suggested that continued good health is one of the most important predictors of postretirement satisfaction (Kimmel, Price, and Walker, 1978; Streib and Schneider, 1971).
2. Voluntary versus involuntary retirement. It is not easy to define "voluntary"—for example, is retiring before a mandatory time because one is in poor health voluntary? But the more voluntary the retirement, the better the adjustment (Kimmel, Price, and Walker, 1978).
3. Sex. Some evidence indicates that, contrary to stereotypes, women take longer than men to adjust to retirement (Atchley, 1976).
4. Adequate income. Many people face a sharp drop in income upon retirement. Several studies indicate that "the money it brings in" is the most missed aspect of work (Harris poll, 1975), and that the expectation of a reasonable standard of living is a major factor in making a positive adjustment to retirement (Eisdorfer, 1972; Glanser, 1976).
5. Social class. The relationship between social class and adjustment is not clear. On the one hand, upper-status workers generally find more satisfaction in their work roles than blue-collar workers do, and so might be expected to miss working more. But on the other hand, they are more likely to have adequate retirement incomes and to be involved in non-work-related activities that may carry over into retirement (Eisdorfer, 1971).

Overall, most people seem to adjust well to retirement and find it a relatively satisfying experience (Ward, 1979).

Retirement can be conceptualized as a form of withdrawal or "disengagement" from society. People relinquish an important social role, and in the process narrow their life focus. This conception of retirement is one aspect of *disengagement theory*, which was developed in the late 1950s and early 1960s by Elaine Cumming and William Henry (Cumming and Henry, 1961; Cumming, 1963). They postulated that as people age, they and society mutually withdraw from each other. People turn their attention and energy inward; at the same time society takes various roles away from them and, in essence, passes these roles on to others. The purpose of this withdrawal is to prepare for the ultimate withdrawal, which is death. The theory's most controversial aspect is its assumption that withdrawal is mutually satisfying and is, in fact, a necessary part of successful aging.

Several criticisms of disengagement theory have been advanced. For example, Hochschild (1976) argues that it is too vague and that the criteria for counterevidence are unclear. The most sustained attack, however, comes from "activity theorists," who present evidence that the most satisfied older people are not those who withdraw but those who maintain a relatively high level of engagement and activity (Lemon, Bengston, and Peterson, 1972).

Marriage and Widowhood

The upswing in marital happiness that begins in middle age continues into this period of life. Although an increase in tension may occur just before the husband's retirement, the necessary adjustments in the marriage are usually made smoothly and the majority of older couples report high levels of satisfaction (Dressler, 1973; Rollins and Feldman, 1970; Thurnher, 1976).

The death of a spouse, however, is common during this period. One

member of the couple, then, usually the wife, must adjust to widowhood.

In one important study of the process of adjustment, Helen Lopata (1973) focused on 301 widows over the age of 50 living in the Chicago area. She found three general patterns of adaptation. The first pattern involves the "self-initiating woman." This type of woman is both aware that she has to make behavioral and relational adjustments and flexible enough to do so. She selects those aspects of her previous life that can be continued and discards those it would be impossible to maintain. She modifies her relationships with friends and children, builds a life-style suited to her individual needs, and attempts to match available resources and personal goals. The second pattern is generally found with widows living in lower-class ethnic communities. This type of women experiences relatively little change when her husband dies. "Being immersed in kin relations, a very close peer group, or a network of neighbors, such a woman may continue many of her involvements with little modification after becoming a widow." Lopata suggests that a similar pattern may be found with some suburbanites. The third pattern is that of the "social isolate," the woman who was never highly engaged in the broader society and who lacks the resources to develop new roles as her old ones fall away.

Other studies have focused on specific factors that affect the adjustment to widowhood. Among the variables found to affect morale are income level, mobility, health, age (older widows tend to adjust more easily), and availability of alternative roles such as employment or family involvement (Atchley, 1975; Morgan, 1976). In general, the data suggest that most people cope adequately, although there is some evidence that widows and widowers are less happy and satisfied with their lives than those who are still married (Campbell, 1975; Riley and Foner, 1968).

Establishment of Ego Integrity

We have focused so far on specific areas of adjustment in old age. In his classic description of the stages of life Erik Erikson (1963) identified what he felt was the crucial broad task confronting individuals who are approaching closer to death—the establishment of a sense of ego integrity. They must evaluate their lives and affirm to themselves that they were meaningful and "something that had to be." The alternative is despair, a sense that one's life has been wasted and that it is now too late to find fulfillment.

In a similar vein, Robert Butler (1968) suggests that the older individual engages in what he terms the "life review" and that an inability to handle this process may lead to such disorders as depression. And, like Erikson, he argues that a possible, and ideal, outcome is the further evolution of such characteristics as candor, serenity, and wisdom.

Death and Dying

Although death has traditionally been a taboo subject in American culture, interest in this "final stage of development" is currently on the rise. Partly this reflects a recognition that death is "the most mysterious, most threatening, and most tantalizing of all human phenomena" (Shneidman, 1973), and that understanding life and development requires coming to terms with death. It also reflects concern that avoidance of the topic leads to dehumanization of the dying (Kübler-Ross, 1969).

Elizabeth Kübler-Ross has been a pioneer in the study of the dying individual. On the basis of intensive interviews with over 200 terminally ill patients in a Chicago hospital, she outlined five stages that people go through as they approach death (Kübler-Ross, 1969).

The first stage is *denial and isolation.* The initial response by most patients is "No, not me, it cannot be true." They may become convinced that there has been a mixup in laboratory reports, they may turn to faith healers, or they may simply talk cheerfully about their future plans. Kübler-Ross regards this as a healthy reaction, a means of buying time until other, less radical, defenses can be mobilized. The vast majority of patients give up denial and move on to the other stages, although they may temporarily return to this stage later in their illness.

Anger is the next stage and occurs when denial can no longer be maintained. The question becomes "Why me? Why not someone else, who is older or meaner or of less use to society?" These feelings of resentment and envy, as well as concern about being overlooked or treated as of no importance, may result in outbursts of temper. This can be a particularly difficult time for the dying person's family and the hospital staff.

If treated with respect and understanding, the anger usually subsides and people may move on to the third stage, *bargaining.* Now they attempt to reach some sort of agreement, usually with God. "I will be good"—e.g., I will live a life in the service of the church or eventually give my body to science—"if only I am allowed to live." Not all dying patients go through this stage.

The fourth stage is *depression.* Kübler-Ross distinguishes two different types of grief that may be experienced during this time. The first is what she calls *reactive* depression, in which patients respond to current and past losses—the disfigurement caused by the disease, the inability to care for their family because they are ill, the wrongs they committed that cannot be righted. The second is a *preparatory* depression, a reaction to impending losses, the separation from everybody and everything loved.

In recent years, people have begun to pay more attention to the care of the person who is suffering from a terminal illness. Some people believe that the modern hospital, with its emphasis on aggressive therapy and the prolongation of life by any means, does not and cannot provide sufficient support either for the dying person or for the family (Holden, 1976).

One alternative to traditional treatment is the hospice movement, which originated in its modern form in England. The term *hospice* is generally used to describe centers established for the care of patients dying of diseases such as cancer. It can also refer to a community of volunteers and professionals who provide support for patients and their families, both at the centers and in the patients' homes. Although hospices differ, most share certain aims (DuBois, 1980; Holden, 1976):

1. Adequate pain control. The first goal is to make the patient free from pain, and from any fear that pain will return. Movement leaders point out that many hospitals fail to control pain adequately, in part because of the pharmacological ignorance of many doctors, and in part because of concern about addiction and side effects, concerns that are irrelevant to the dying.

2. Psychological support for the patient. "Support" in this sense means doing whatever will give this particular individual the greatest comfort and peace. This may mean getting the house in order and making plans for the children. It may mean providing opportunities for the patient to be with family and friends as much as possible. Or it may mean giving the person an opportunity to see and talk with other dying patients.

3. Support for the bereaved, both before and after the death. Although some family members will need little follow-up, others will need considerable help. The latter may return to the hospice at any time for further care.

It remains to be seen what impact the hospice concept will have in the United States. There may be resistance from traditional health care providers. There is also some concern that hospices will become simply another type of nursing home (Holden, 1976). So far there is little hard evidence that the hospice effectively meets the needs of the dying and their families. However, the hospice concept appears to be a potentially valuable tool in the effort to make the process of dying less frightening and less dehumanizing.

At last, given sufficient time and support, people reach the final stage, *acceptance,* in which they are able to contemplate death with some degree of quiet expectation, without fear or despair. Kübler-Ross emphasizes that this is neither a happy time nor a time of hopelessness and resignation. It is a period of peace.

Several criticisms of this description have been advanced. One of the most frequent is the argument that these reactions do not constitute "stages" in the sense that dying people necessarily advance through them in a predictable sequence. Kübler-Ross herself now acknowledges that the stages do not always occur in the same order and that, indeed, a patient may experience several simultaneously (Kübler-Ross, 1974). Another criticism is that there is no consistent evidence that the "typical" dying patient is characterized by any emotion other than depression (DuBois, 1980). A third criticism is that Kübler-Ross's stages will be taken as a prescription for an "ideal death." To quote Kalish (1977), "Some health caretakers have been observed trying to encourage, or even manipulate, their dying patients through [the] stages; patients occasionally become concerned if they are not progressing adequately, with adequacy also defined in terms of the stages" (p. 494). Finally, it is questionable that acceptance is the only reasonable way to face death. Weisman (1972) points out that "not going gently into that good night but raging" may be an equally appropriate reaction. Despite these criticisms, Kübler-Ross's work has served the useful purpose of drawing attention to an important area of study.

Summary

1. Puberty is marked by dramatic changes in growth rate and the development of primary and secondary sex characteristics.

2. Adolescence is the period between childhood and adulthood during which the individual learns the skills needed to survive as an adult; it is a socially rather than biologically determined phase of development.

3. At about age 12, the child enters Piaget's final stage of cognitive development—formal operations. The most basic change in this stage is the ability to deal with abstract concepts and use both hypothetico-deductive reasoning and propositional thinking.

4. According to Freud, during adolescence the sexual energy of libido, repressed during latency, reemerges, and the adult stage of development begins. Erikson called the search for self-identity the key crisis in need of resolution during adolescent years.

5. Keniston suggested the term "youth" for the stage between adolescence and adulthood, when people spend long periods of training for a career while still dependent on their parents financially.

6. According to a number of theorists, the major task in early adulthood is the establishing of intimate relationships.

7. A major event of the middle years is the departure of children from the home. While some parents do suffer from the "empty nest" syndrome, many welcome their new-found freedom. This is also the time when many women are able to reenter the job market.

8. Physical changes during the midlife years may cause some persons to experience self-doubts or stress; in women, the menopause is characterized by physical changes that may be accompanied by psychological effects as well.

9. Among the major changes occurring in old age are physical change, cognitive change, retirement, and widowhood.

10. Erikson has described the crucial task confronting the person entering old age as the establishment of a sense of ego integrity; Butler suggests that old age is a time in which "life review" is essential.

11. Kübler-Ross has outlined five stages of dealing with death: denial, anger, bargaining, depression, and acceptance.

Suggested Readings

BIRREN, J. E., and SCHAIE, K. W. *Handbook of the psychology of aging.* New York: Van Nostrand Reinhold, 1977. Physiological and cognitive effects of the aging process.

DAVITZ, J., and DAVITZ, L. *Making it from forty to fifty.* New York: Random House, 1976. Interviews with 200 middle-aged adults reveal thoughts, feelings, and actions characteristic of midlife adjustments.

GOETHALS, G. W., and KLOS, D. S. *Experiencing youth: First person accounts,* 2nd ed. Boston: Little, Brown. Autobiographical studies of adolescents with focus on interpersonal problems and personality development.

SARASON, S. B. *Work, aging, and social change.* New York: Free Press, 1977. An examination of our current expectations about professional careers, with suggestions for social policy to facilitate career change.

WOODRUFF, D. S., and BIRREN, J. E. *Aging: Scientific perspectives and social issues.* New York: Van Nostrand, 1975.

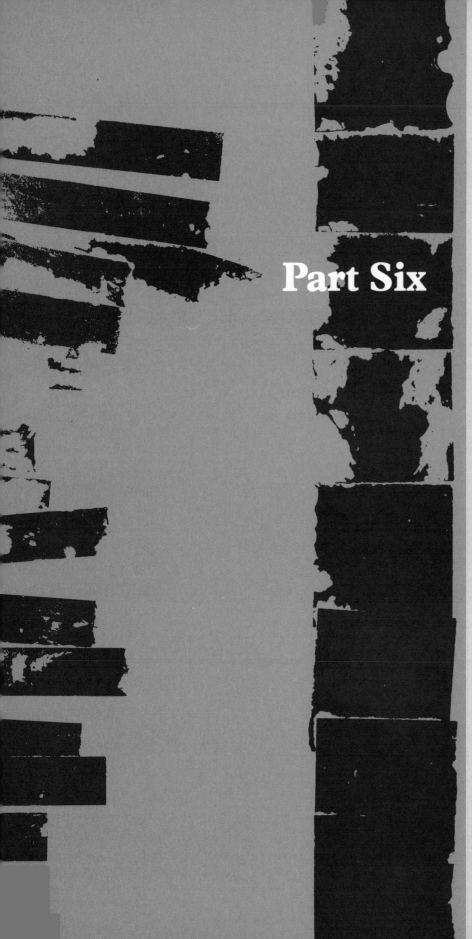

Part Six Personality and Clinical Psychology

14 Personality

There is no one accepted definition of personality; there are many, each resting on different assumptions and stressing different aspects of being. A key theme uniting many definitions, however, is that personality is the organized and distinctive pattern of behavior that characterizes an individual's adaptation to a situation and endures over time. Were it not for this distinctiveness, we would not be able to distinguish one person from another; were it not for the relative permanence of personality, we would not recognize the same individual from one moment to the next.

The study of personality is rich with theories about our inherent nature, about what makes us think, feel, behave, and experience life as we do. Each theory involves a different view of the essence, structure, and functioning of humans and their relationship to the environment. The range of concerns in the study of personality thus includes ideas, motives, attitudes, emotions, life crises, beliefs, values, and the processes by which people try to understand their own behavior, that of others, and the world.

Formal personality theories must specify and answer four major questions:

1. What is the structure of personality? Are there differing levels of structure and are some elements of personality subordinate to others? If there is no overall structure, what is the alternative concept?
2. What motivates us? Why do we act as we do?
3. How does personality grow and change over time? Does it change fundamentally? If so, in what ways?
4. How do we account for human individuality or uniqueness?

The first three questions are concerned with qualities shared by all people, or how we are alike; the last tries to account for uniqueness, or why we are different. Today the focus is on understanding the common qualities, on the characteristics, motives, drives, and behaviors that all people share. Traditionally, however, those studying personality were concerned with what made the individual unique. Let's look first at one of these traditional approaches, the trait theories, which categorized people on the basis of different attributes and traits.

Trait Theories

The earliest approaches to personality accounted for human behavior in terms of people's innate traits or dispositions. Traits were said to be stable, enduring, and consistent. A final important characteristic of traits was that they were continuous rather than discrete. They intertwined with and affected one another, which meant they could be talked about in terms of amount or degree rather than as absolutes. Because of this characteristic, however, it was difficult to find a satisfactory method for fully categorizing traits.

Allport

According to Gordon Allport, no two people are alike, no two individuals respond in the same way to identical stimuli. To study personality, then, is to study single individuals. What are we to look for? Allport says traits. Traits direct action, they motivate us to behave the way we do. However, some traits are more impelling than others.

Allport characterized traits by the degree to which they govern personality. He distinguished three levels:

1. *Cardinal traits.* These are the most powerful and pervasive traits; they dominate a person's whole life. Few people possess cardinal traits. When they do, we often think of them primarily in terms of those traits. If we say someone is Machiavellian, we are referring to the kind of unscrupulous behavior that marks everything this person says, does, and thinks.
2. *Central traits.* These are the few traits that characterize an individual. A study by Allport (1961) showed that people perceive an average of 7.2 central dispositions in those they know well. Central traits are the kind that might be included in a letter of recommendation or a counsellor's report (punctuality, industriousness, honesty, etc.).
3. *Secondary traits.* These are the most limited in frequency and least crucial to an understanding of the dynamics of personality. They include, for example, the kind of music or food one likes.

Although traits must show up regularly in order to be known, Allport's theory allows room for trait inconsistencies, or inconsistencies in an individual's behavior. Inconsistency occurs because there are many traits, many are active at the same time, they overlap, and they are organized in a different way for each individual. This point about differential organization is particularly important. Two people, for instance, may both be accurately described as possessing the trait of "honesty," but for one honesty may extend to a prohibition on even "white lies" (telling people that you like their expensive new clothes even though you actually think they are tasteless), while for the other an apparently harmless deception is acceptable.

Allport's theory has some clear strengths. First, it calls attention to the conscious motives for behavior. Second, it is concerned mainly with current behavior—the way someone reacts now, at this moment. Third, Allport has tried to come to grips with specifying the ways in which people are different, which is one of the key questions that a theory of personality must address.

There are also weaknesses in his approach. For instance, people do behave in apparently inconsistent ways. How is this to be explained within a trait system that emphasizes consistency? Allport dealt with this problem in two ways. First, he pointed out that traits could intertwine with and affect one another, and thus they should be talked about in terms of amount or degree rather than as absolutes. Second, he showed that people have used a vast number of traits—in one analysis, over 5,000—to describe behavior.

Other theorists who used this trait construct tried to reduce the potentially vast number of traits to a more manageable and efficient list. One of the most interesting attempts involved a sophisticated statistical technique called factor analysis, which was used by Raymond Cattell in his study of personality.

Cattell and Factor Analysis

Raymond Cattell, another leading trait theorist, was concerned with the empirical "mapping of the personality": with identifying a reasonable number of traits that can be used to describe all individuals and predict their behaviors. The means he used is called *factor analysis,* a complex statistical process for analyzing a large number of variables simultaneously and grouping these variables in blocks. Two or more factors that correlate highly are assumed to reflect the existence of one underlying trait; for example, think of "warm" and "sociable" as against "aloof" and "cool." Using this procedure, Cattell drew up a 16-factor inventory that he believed gave an adequate representation of personality.

For Cattell, personality is what "permits a prediction of what a person will do in a given situation" (1952, p. 2). So once he could position a person according to the 16 factors, he would attempt to predict many of that person's behaviors. The method involves several steps. Cattell called the 16 factors the *source traits,* the structural influences underlying personality. Source traits interact with one another to produce overt behaviors called *surface traits* (source traits are listed in Table 14-1).

Table 14–1: The Sixteen Factors Used in Cattell's Test.

1. Schizothymia (aloof, cold) vs. Cyclothymia (warm, sociable)
2. Dull (low intellectual capacity) vs. Bright (intelligent)
3. Low Ego Strength (emotional, unstable) vs. High Ego Strength (mature, calm)
4. Submissiveness (mild) vs. Dominance (aggressive)
5. Desurgency (glum, silent) vs. Surgency (enthusiastic, talkative)
6. Low Superego Strength (casual, undependable) vs. High Superego Strength (conscientious, persistent)
7. Threctia (timid, shy) vs. Parmia (adventurous, thick-skinned)
8. Harria (tough, realistic) vs. Premsia (sensitive, effeminate)
9. Inner Relaxation (trustful, adaptable) vs. Protension (suspecting, jealous)
10. Praxernia (conventional, practical) vs. Autia (Bohemian, unconcerned)
11. Naïvete (simple, awkward) vs. Shrewdness (sophisticated, polished)
12. Confidence (unshakable) vs. Timidity (insecure, anxious)
13. Conservatism (accepting) vs. Radicalism (experimenting, critical)
14. Group Dependence (imitative) vs. Self-Sufficiency (resourceful)
15. Low Integration (lax, unsure) vs. Self-Sentiment Control (controlled, exact)
16. Low Ergic Tension (phlegmatic, composed) vs. High Ergic Tension (tense, excitable)

From Cattell (1950) as adapted by Maddi (1968).

Trait models emphasize the structure of adult personality, but they do not tell us how that personality structure develops. To do that, we now turn to the five major approaches to personality and its development.

Five Models of Personality

As mentioned earlier in this chapter, personality theory and research now focus on common themes of personality and personality development. The leading approaches today seek to clarify those processes, dynamics, and factors that guide everyone's behavior. These combine in different ways for each person; thus every individual is unique. However, we can use the same concepts and same notions of human functioning to study every individual.

The approaches to personality may each be thought of as belonging to one of five models of personality: the psychoanalytic, learning, humanist-existential, biological, and cognitive models. Each of these models incorporates a very different notion about people and how they come to be the way they are. Each holds different views on how active or passive people are in the formulation of their personal behaviors, the motivating forces, the role of environment, and the role of internal factors, among other concepts and issues. Each model rests on different assumptions about the best way to understand and explain human behavior. It is important to keep in mind that these are *models,* not reality. And ultimately a particular model's usefulness depends on how well it helps us to organize and predict human behavior.

The Psychoanalytic Model

According to psychoanalytic theory, the most comprehensive and influential of all theories of personality, we are at the mercy of a strict psychic determinism, primarily motivated by "drives" or "instincts" over which we have little control and of which we are only dimly aware.

To Sigmund Freud, human personality is like an iceberg: The tip above the water, a small fraction of the total iceberg, represents our conscious awareness, while the vast mass below represents our unconscious life. Thus the primary motivation for our actions is not always directly accessible to us.

One of the most fundamental conceptual discoveries of psychoanalytic theory is that of the unconscious mind. To Freud, several different things point toward the existence of unconscious thought processes. Slips of the tongue, memory errors, and other apparently trivial phenomena, which are produced without conscious awareness, often can be shown to be connected by some very systematic and very revealing links. Dreams show the same connectedness; though they contain apparently disconnected leaps and illogical gaps, on analysis the psychological connections between elements are clear. From this Freud was led to postulate the existence of the unconscious mind, in which the continuity of the thought process unfolds, blocked from the awareness of the thinker. The unconscious, unknown to consciousness, fundamentally affects the thought, feeling, and behavior of the individual; in it many of the forces that govern people's behavior have their primary representation and their effects.

The Structure of Personality

We can get a clearer picture of Freud's concept of the unconscious and how it exerts its influence by looking more closely at his three-part structure of personality: the id, ego, and superego. Remember, these concepts refer to processes, not actual physical locations in the brain. Also, although they are interrelated, each of the three processes has its own operating principles and functions. Personality and behavior are the products of the interaction, and often conflict, of these three systems.

ID. The id is the most primary of the three personality systems. The other two, the ego and the superego, develop out of the id. However, throughout life they rely on the id as the source of psychic energy for their activities, so in a sense their dependence on the id never ceases. For Freud, the id is the power source that runs the human personality. At the beginning the id is formed of the drives or instincts that the infant possesses at birth. Freud divided the instincts into two broad categories: life instincts (Eros) and death instincts (Thanatos). In terms of drives, these are frequently expressed as sex and aggression. The human organism, Freud believed, simultaneously wants to live and die, create and destroy.

Many psychologists have wished that Freud had not attached the label "sexual" to the first class of instincts, for many of the needs he discussed as belonging to this category—affection, warmth, nourishment—are not what most people would term "sexual." But, as we will see shortly, Freud was attempting to make clear the underlying unity of these needs and their connection with the sexual drive. So we will continue, as most have, to refer to this general class of needs as sexual ones.

The sex instincts are what enable the individual organisms of a species to survive and the species as a whole to perpetuate itself. Freud called the energy that fuels the life instincts *libido*. The death or destructive instincts are less apparent in their operation. Indeed, Freud did not include them in his system until the apparently senseless slaughter of World War I seemed to him to require some such concept. After that, Freud, often a pessimist, expressed the relationship between life and death in a famous dictum: "The goal of all life is death" (1920/1950, p. 38).

The goal of the id is immediate tension reduction. Tension is created by an increase in external or internal stimulation. For instance, when a person experiences a need, such as hunger, this is felt as an uncomfortable state of tension. The id automatically strives to reduce this increase in tension and return to a low energy level. Freud called this the *pleasure principle.*

The id seeks immediate gratification without resort to objective reality. For example, if the organism is hungry, the id will create a mental image of "food" or a mother's breast. Creating an image of the desired object is called *wish fulfillment.* This obviously does not enable an organism to survive—an image of

Jean Cocteau's drawing of Sigmund Freud. The set of eyes peering out from the body is Cocteau's way of symbolizing Freud's emphasis on the effects of the id on human behavior.

food cannot satisfy hunger—so the organism has to evolve a mode of thinking that can relate its needs to the external or objective world, the world where real, material food exists. This mode of thinking, which is based on logic and reason, Freud called *secondary process thinking,* as opposed to the id's *primary process thinking.* This secondary process, which developed out of the id and became differentiated from it, is the *ego.*

EGO.   The ego, in contrast to the id, is concerned with, and aware of, objective reality. The ego seeks actual food, not an image of it. In general, the ego attempts to "match" objects in the external world as closely as possible to the images created by the id. The ego is devoted primarily to protecting the organism and to coping with the real world.

The ego will not allow the organism to release tension until it has located the object in the external world that will satisfy the instinctual need. Because the ego resorts to external reality to satisfy needs, it is said to obey the *reality principle* (as against the id's pleasure principle). If necessary, the ego will delay the organism's attempts at immediate gratification and pleasure, either because these attempts are unlikely to be successful or because greater gratification can be gained by waiting. The ego, therefore, is concerned with what is good and bad for the organism on the basis of external criteria.

The ego is not the "enemy" of the id. In the most fundamental sense it exists to serve the id's needs, to work in its behalf. The two only come into conflict over the best way to do this. The ego seeks to postpone gratification until a real object in the external world has been found to satisfy an instinctual need. The id, on the other hand, demands immediate gratification and has no awareness of or concern about external reality—it is unsocialized and unconscious.

SUPEREGO.   The last personality system to be differentiated from the id is the superego. Often referred to as the "conscience" or "moral arm" of the personality, the superego is concerned with moral ideals. These ideals are originally conveyed to the child by the parents; later other authority figures and the rewards and punishments imposed by society also play a part in shaping the growing child's superego. It is the development of the superego that makes possible the child's development of self-control.

The superego deals in absolute rules—unlike the ego, which seeks compromise, the superego strives for perfection. It does not function merely to postpone id impulses, as the ego does; it seeks to block them permanently. In this effort it is as persistent and unyielding as the id. Many of Freud's patients could be described as being in unbearable conflict between the strong demands of their ids and the absolute prohibitions on fulfilling those demands laid down by their superegos. Their egos were so weakened in the attempt to cope with this psychic conflict that they were no longer able to meet the day-to-day demands of ordinary life.

Psychic Interplay and Conflict

Freud conceived of the psychic system as having a limited amount of energy. The three personality systems compete for this energy, and thus are often in conflict. When one system—the id, for example—dominates the energy supply, the other systems must grow weaker.

The id, which originally had a monopoly on the psychic energy of the organism, uses it in the service of the pleasure principle. The ego and superego, however, postpone and block gratification as well as strive for it. The earlier example of matching real food with an image of food provides a good illustration of this; in this way, the ego diverts the psychic energy of the id and directs it out into the real world. The ego often causes object displacements that form a complex web of preferences, values, interests, and attitudes, which, although they don't directly satisfy the individual's instinctual needs, were originally connected in the history of the individual to objects that did.

Such displacement accounts for the great diversity of human nature and behavior. All our socialized attitudes, interests, and activities, according to Freud, are the result of the displacement of energy from original instinctual desires. It is this process that makes civilization possible, by causing individuals to invest their energies in the activities that make society go rather than in the immediate gratification of their own needs.

Freud was pessimistic about the relationship between the individual and society—he saw it as one of essential conflict. Society requires repression of the most direct expressions of the person's impulses. The price we all pay for this postponement or blocking of direct instinctual gratification is unhappiness. Many pay a higher price in the form of psychosis or neurosis. This issue is explored by Freud in *Civilization and Its Discontents,* a book whose title reveals its general conclusion.

The Development of Personality

Personality theorists differ sharply on the importance of the first years of life in the formation of the personality. Freud is generally regarded as believing that the first 6 years of life determine the basic personality characteristics of the individual. Actually, his assertions are more complicated than that.

As a psychoanalyst, Freud saw mostly neurotic individuals. One of his great discoveries was that the roots of his adult patients' difficulties were in their early childhood experiences. For people in psychological difficulty, the first years of life contain the origins of those difficulties. For more normal individuals, however, who show their normality by responding more directly to events in the present, events that occurred earlier in life play a much less major role. They are capable of growth, change, and development throughout life, under the stimulus of such events as marriage and a career. Still, basic patterns are established at an early age even for normal individuals, and later development is consistent with those patterns.

One major source of these basic patterns is the person's own adaptations to each of the four stages of development through which we all pass. According to Freud, the developmental history of each individual is marked by four distinguishable psychosexual stages, each of which is crucial to personality development. People who do not resolve the developmental challenges and problems of any one of these stages become "fixated" at that stage, fail to properly solve the problems posed by later stages, and as adults have neurotic problems reflecting the stage at which the fixation occurred.

The three early psychosexual stages are characterized by a particular zone or area of the body. The main *erogenous zones*, as these are called, are the mouth, anus, and genitalia. The corresponding psychosexual stages of development are oral, anal, and phallic.

For children to develop into normal adults, they must successfully pass through each stage; the psychic energy of each stage must pass on to the next; and each level must build on the preceding one. Each stage involves a certain amount of frustration and anxiety. If these are not resolved, psychic energy can be left behind. This is the process that causes the child to remain fixated at that stage.

Regression is closely related to fixation. It is the process by which a person "returns" to an earlier stage when experiencing conflict later in life. The stage regressed to is usually the one at which the individual felt comfortable. For example, a child experiencing unresolved conflict may return to an oral stage, with infantile behaviors such as thumb sucking; later, that child, now an adult with other problems, may seek refuge in drink, another type of oral activity.

A person rarely fixates or regresses totally. These are relative conditions. Under a similar set of stresses one individual may regress to an oral stage, a second to a later stage, and a third may not regress at all.

THE ORAL STAGE: MOUTH AS EROGENOUS ZONE.   This stage lasts from birth to about the end of the 1st year of life. In the *oral stage* of psychosexual development, the mouth and oral area are the primary source of pleasure. Feelings of dependency arise during this stage, since the infant is totally helpless. These feelings, which remain with an individual throughout life despite normal ego development, are most likely to arise during periods of anxiety and insecurity. Under duress, the person is likely to regress to such modes of oral gratification as "nervous eating" and cigarette smoking.

At a more general level, a regression to the oral stage would be revealed in the ways a person manages dependency and aggression. Clinging to authority figures and attempting to draw strength from them can be an oral-stage attempt to solve a problem. Similarly, a "biting," aggressive style of wit can represent a return to the biting, aggressive aspects of the later oral stage. It is important to recognize here that the stages represent, for Freud, a very general and even metaphorical way of coping with the world. The oral stage, for instance, involves some very general impulses of dependency.

THE ANAL STAGE: ANUS AS EROGENOUS ZONE.   The *anal stage* coincides with toilet training, which begins about the 2nd year of life. At that time the child confronts the demand that it postpone the execution of an activity that brings pleasure.

The anus, which is made up of sensitive mucous membranes, is a zone from which the child derives pleasure — for example, by defecating. But now he or she must learn to regulate this activity in accordance with sociocultural rules specifying when and where such behavior is appropriate. Thus with toilet training the child is forced to obey the reality principle for the first time, and ego development accelerates during this stage. Because the child cannot immediately gratify his or her anal impulses, frustration unavoidably arises, and behavior becomes much more aggressive; this stands in sharp contrast to the passive and receptive oral phase. For this reason, parent and child often experience conflict at this stage.

Later in life, regression to the oral stage would be signalled by a person's being obstinate, overly concerned with orderliness, or parsimonious. Misers

and, more generally, people who retain things or who are unable to "let go of" control are likely to be at the anal stage.

THE PHALLIC STAGE: THE GENITALS AS EROGENOUS ZONE.   During the *phallic stage* the focus of pleasurable sensation shifts from the anus to the penis in the male and the clitoris in the female. At this time, beginning as early as the 3rd year of life, the child first displays heterosexual behavior, and develops an attachment for the parent of the opposite sex, at the same time becoming jealous of the parent of the same sex. Freud called this the *Oedipus complex* in the case of a boy, and the *Electra complex* in the case of a girl. This complex is resolved by identifying with the parent of the same sex. Freud felt that attitudes toward authority and sexual activity are closely determined by the way in which this resolution is reached.

THE LATENCY PERIOD.   The first three stages of development begin at birth and follow closely on one another. The emergence of the fourth stage is delayed by the intervention of the latency period. The *latency period,* which extends from age 5 through the beginning of adolescence, is brought on by a repression of sexual impulses that resolves the Oedipus and Electra complexes. It is a time during which relatively little personality development takes place from a psychodynamic view. The sexual energy and conflicts that characterize the phallic stage quiet down and the child "forgets" those earlier feelings. Along with this decrease of sexual energy and repression there is a gradual development of the ego and superego. The child comes more under the dictates of the reality principle and moral imperatives, and less under the influence of the id.

THE GENITAL STAGE.   With adolescence and its associated bodily changes, the *genital stage* of personality begins. The previous three stages of development were motivated by energies that were essentially self-gratifying in nature. During the genital stage more altruistic, less self-centered motives become possible. If the child has successfully avoided fixation at an earlier stage of development, then the adolescent has the energies to invest in developing genuine career and academic interests, and genuine caring for peers and members of the opposite sex.

Carl Gustave Jung, 1875–1961.

This has been a short summary of Freud's theory of personality and how it develops. In the chapters to come we will discuss other aspects of his theory, such as defense mechanisms (Chapter 15), the basis of abnormal behavior (Chapter 16), and psychoanalysis as therapy for abnormal behavior (Chapter 17).

Now we will look at some of the variations of Freudian theory that have developed since the time of Freud.

Neo- and Post-Freudian Theorists

The theorists discussed here share a "family" characteristic. They all accepted as valid many of Freud's discoveries, but wished to correct one or two elements that they felt distorted the theoretical structure. Generally they agreed with Freud on the importance of unconscious processes, but sometimes disagreed with him on the origins of the impulses that motivated those unconscious processes.

For instance, Carl Jung, like Freud, retained a picture of personality as a "battlefield" of unconscious urges in conflict with the other systems of the

HIGHLIGHT:
Culture and Personality

Both because of his training in the biological sciences and the intellectual climate of the time, Freud believed that psychological processes are tied to the biological inheritance of the human being. He considered such concepts as the libido, the stages of development, and the Oedipus complex as essentially biological in nature.

There were two important intellectual consequences of this emphasis on biology. First, it means that an individual's development has a fixed, immutable character: The sequence of developmental stages is fixed by the biologically produced shifts in the individual's zones of gratification; and the conflicted nature of the Oedipal situation and its resolution is inevitable because of the developing sexual impulses of the child.

Second, since humans are biologically the same in all cultures, Freud felt that his theory was universal and did not require serious modification for people of another culture. Putting this another way, Freud did not think that the specifics of the culture in which one was reared had an important effect on the psychodynamic unfolding of personality development in the early childhood years.

But other intellectual developments of the early twentieth century challenged this biologically based conceptualization of human nature. About the same time that Freud was formulating and developing psychoanalytical theory, sociology and anthropology were changing people's conception of themselves and the factors that influence behavior.

The vivid descriptions of cultural anthropologists, particularly, were making Westerners aware that other cultures existed with elaborate and stable social systems and cultural arrangements that were impressive in their own right. And in at least some of these cultures such Freudian "universals" as the latency period simply did not occur.

From this cross-cultural perspective, people could be seen as a product of social rather than simply biological forces. Their needs, impulses, and personality patterns were obviously conditioned by institutions such as the family, the educational system, and the social organizations of religion, power, and governance—institutions that differed greatly from culture to culture. Individuals and their personalities did not grow in splendid isolation in which biological patterns dictated a single sequence of development, but in a cultural context that created its own sequences of growth and development.

---

personality. This emphasis on the unconscious is his closest link with Freud. The key difference between them is Jung's replacement of Freud's sexually motivated unconscious with the idea of a *collective unconscious* built of *archetypes.* The collective unconscious is the "memory trace" of our ancestral history, including our animal origins, which exists in each individual and is essentially the same for everyone. It is independent of anything personal in the life of the individual, and at times it can overwhelm both the ego and "the personal unconscious" (our repressed thoughts, forgotten experiences, etc.).

Other neo-Freudians, such as Alfred Adler, Karen Horney, and Erich Fromm, each took issue with Freud and Jung's emphasis on the role of instinct in determining behavior. They emphasized social rather than biological determinants of personality motivation, and believed that anxiety and conflict come from the social conditions in which people find themselves as well as from their inherent personality structure.

The neo-Freudians in general shared with Freud and Jung a belief in the importance of the unconscious, but they gave a more independent role to the ego. Because of this emphasis, they have been called "ego psychologists." In suggesting that the ego had its own powers independent of the id, the ego psychologists were in effect saying that people are capable of a wider sphere of rational activities than orthodox psychoanalytic theory would grant. They saw people as freer, at least potentially, to choose their own fates, as compared to Freud's deterministic outlook.

To critics, neo-Freudians and ego psychologists seem to be "watered-down" Freudians who complicate Freud's theory without moving away from it. We turn now to theories that differ from Freud's in more basic ways.

The Learning Model

The learning and conditioned-response theories of personality are based on research described in Chapter 6. The principles derived from studies of lower-order organisms such as rats and pigeons are applied to analyze the nature of human personality. As you will remember, for learning theorists, animal behavior is externally determined by environmental factors. Their central proposition is that human behavior can likewise be considered as externally determined. Like the rat and the pigeon, the human organism responds to stimuli presented by other people or by the external world. According to learning theorists, the environment controls our behavior, and it does this through the reinforcement contingencies it delivers. Learning theorists hold that the human personality is a set of patterns of learned behaviors. A set of stimulus conditions is presented, the person responds to it, and reinforcement may follow. If it does, the response will be emitted again if the stimulus conditions recur.

A problem that all personality theories must address is the development of uniqueness. Learning theorists believe that people's personalities differ because of childhood differences in stimulus patterns, reinforcement contingencies, and punishment patterns. If we knew someone's reinforcement history, therefore, we would be able to predict that person's present behavior patterns. Even though the human personality is complex, it is based on simple learning principles, such as generalization of previous learning to new situations and the increasing ability to discriminate, through experience, among the stimuli that lead to reinforcement.

Conditioned Anxiety: Dollard and Miller

One of the important contributions of learning theory to personality dynamics is the theory of conditioned anxiety conceived of by John Dollard and Neil Miller (1950).

According to this theory, a tone originally is a neutral stimulus, but if it is frequently followed by an electric shock, it comes to be a cue for fear responses originally produced by the shock (as we discussed in Chapter 11). Animals tested by Dollard and Miller were able to learn new responses to escape from or terminate an anxiety cue. In the same way, a child who is hurt by a fall from a swing may become anxious when near the swing. By stimulus generalization, the child may become afraid of other play equipment and come to avoid playgrounds in order to avoid the anxiety caused by the sight of the equipment.

Two properties of conditioned anxiety make it a particularly important concept in learning theories of personality. First, anxiety may be conditioned to a previously neutral stimulus by just a few pairings, and sometimes by a single pairing. Given the normal hurts and harms of an ordinary childhood, we probably all have many conditioned fears. Second, because people learn responses that get them out of an anxiety situation, they may never discover that the original reason for the anxiety—the physical or emotional pain that once followed the cue—is no longer present. The child who avoids the swing from which he or she once fell may not discover that with a little practice the swing could be easily mastered. The conditioned anxiety theory gives us an insight into why many people continue to engage in patterns of action that seem to be useless or even self-defeating. They do so because these patterns remove them from anxiety cues, and do not allow them to discover that the original source of the fear is gone.

Skinner and Operant Conditioning

Skinner's learning principles proved useful in specifying the ways in which a person's history of reinforcements determines the person's behavior. Skinner's model of learning was discussed at length in Chapter 6, and you may want to reread that section; what follows is a summary in terms of personality theory.

Skinner distinguishes two basic situations in which reinforcement operates. The simplest kind of learning, following Pavlov, is based on classical conditioning, in which an initially neutral stimulus is paired with an unconditioned stimulus that causes an unconditioned response. Pavlov's famous demonstration of the dog being conditioned to salivate at the sound of a tone is an example of this, as is the conditioning of fear to a previously neutral stimulus, which Dollard and Miller used as the basis of conditioned anxiety.

Skinner, however, was most concerned with reinforcement as it occurred in operant conditioning. In this type of conditioning the likelihood of a response being emitted is affected by whether that response was followed by reinforcement in the past. Reinforcement to Skinner is the primary way that people learn responses and control the responses of others.

In the course of personality development a child learns to respond to certain stimuli with certain responses, and to give very different responses to other stimuli. This learning takes place through stimulus generalization and discrimination. A child cuddles a furry toy and is reinforced by its pleasing texture and the parents' smiles. Because of stimulus generalization, the child will at first respond to a real furry cat by cuddling it—it looks like the furry toy and therefore elicits the response given to the toy. The scratches of the squashed cat teach the child stimulus discrimination: The child learns to discriminate between two physically similar stimuli because the environment rewards the response to one and not the other.

One of the classic problems that a personality theorist faces is to account for behavior that is maladaptive or harmful to the individual—in other words, to account for abnormal behavior. Skinner and other learning theorists have proposed several mechanisms to explain this kind of behavior. The first we have already mentioned; conditioned anxiety can cause a person to try to escape from a stimulus situation in which no real reasons for fear remain.

Skinner suggests three other mechanisms that may produce maladaptive behavior. The first is "random" or chance reinforcement. Occasionally the world delivers a reward to people that is quite independent of their actions. Nonetheless, the reinforcement increases the probability that a person will repeat whatever action he or she was emitting when the reward was delivered. This type of reinforcement, where there is no cause-and-effect relation between action and reward, can lead to "superstitious" behavior. For example, a person may wear a particular shirt just before winning a big game, and wear it again because it "brought luck." While this example is fairly harmless, accidental or random reinforcement can also cause maladaptive or self-destructive behavior. For example, depression may accidentally be rewarded by love and attention from a caring friend.

A second reward mechanism for producing unwanted behaviors centers on ambiguities about what exactly is reinforcing, and in what way. Tired parents sometimes do not pay attention to their children until the children get out of hand. The attention may then take the form of scolding, but it may also have rewarding elements. Sadly, some people get so little attention that almost any form of it is rewarding. One patient in a mental hospital, for instance, gradually became too uncoordinated to eat and an attendant had to feed her. It turned out that the few words the harassed but kindly attendant addressed to her while feeding her were one of the few human interactions the patient had all day.

The third mechanism accounting for maladaptive behavior is provided by the Skinnerian discovery of schedules of reinforcement. For any of the reasons we just discussed, undesirable behavior may have been at least occasionally reinforced in the past. The problem is why that behavior does not extinguish in the present. (*Extinction* is Skinner's term for the gradual decrease and final elimination of responses that are not reinforced.) Because they are undesirable, responses such as crying or hostility usually receive reinforcement only inter-mittently. You will recall that responses learned under conditions of intermittent reinforcement are much more resistant to extinction than those that are always reinforced. So the occasional reinforcement of a maladaptive response may be enough to cause it to be emitted at a high rate. In general, then, learning theories of personality can account for the persistence of apparently useless or harmful behaviors.

Social Learning Theory: Bandura

Bandura and other social learning theorists agree that personality consists of patterns of human responses that are learned, and thus they belong to the same class of personality theorists we have just discussed. They acknowledge the validity of the learning mechanisms as defined by Dollard and Miller and Skinner in conditions of direct reinforcement. Their major contribution has been to point out that there is a second kind of learning that is very important for personality development. They show that people can learn by observing the responses of others. In fact, it can be argued that most of our learning is of this indirect, observational kind.

The basic principle of social learning is very simple and accords with common sense: People learn through imitation, based on observation of others.

Children can learn to make a new response just by watching others, without having made that response before themselves, and without being reinforced themselves or even having seen anyone else reinforced for the response. For example, in one study (Bandura, Ross, and Ross, 1961) some nursery school children watched adults behave aggressively toward a doll, while other children watched nonaggressive adults sit quietly, ignoring the doll. The children were later placed in a room with the doll and their behavior toward it was observed. The children who had watched the more aggressive adults were more aggressive toward the doll than the other group.

Whether a person will imitate a model depends on a number of factors:

1. *Whether the model being observed is rewarded or punished.* Although people may imitate a model who is not rewarded, they are much more likely to imitate models who have been rewarded for their behavior than those who have been punished or have not received any reward (Bandura, Ross, and Ross, 1963a).
2. *Characteristics of models.* These characteristics include age, sex, and social status, but the most important is whether or not the model is seen as powerful or weak. Children are much more likely to imitate a model who seems powerful to them than one who seems weak (Jakubczak and Walters, 1959).
3. *The way the model is presented.* Models can be presented symbolically, as in films or on TV, as well as in real-life situations. Models in films and TV are very influential—children watching a model behave aggressively on TV or in a film were just as likely to imitate that behavior as children who observed a model who was physically present (Bandura, Ross, and Ross, 1963b).
4. *Inhibition.* Observing models may help to reduce inhibitions, especially if the model is doing something that is not socially acceptable. In this case the person observing may not so much be learning a new response as gaining the nerve to make a response that before was only imagined (Walters and Llewellyn Thomas, 1963). Again, imitation may depend on the observer's ability to discover the reinforcement structure of the situation. If a model is not punished for an action, this may be particularly effective in removing inhibition of a similar action in the observer.

Bandura and Rosenthal (1966) pointed out another type of learning that is important in social learning theory, and that is the vicarious learning of classically conditioned emotional responses. For example, if a person observes a model reacting with extreme fear and repugnance to a stimulus, the next time that stimulus is presented, the observer may react the same way, even if the model is no longer present. The following is an example (Corsini, 1969):

> Jim, age five, found a dead rat, picked it up by the tail, and brought it over to Rita, also age five, waving it in front of her, and evidently hoping to frighten her. Rita showed interest in the rat and wanted to touch it, much to Jim's apparent disappointment. He then took the rat to Dorothy, age seven, who reacted with apparent disgust and fear and ran away from Jim and toward Rita, screaming. When Jim pursued Dorothy, Rita also ran away from Jim and the rat and began to scream. Later, when Jim showed up with his rat, Rita ran and showed fear even though Dorothy was not around any more.

Fears, particularly, are easily learned this way. Bandura has shown that the conditioned anxiety avoidance sequence described by Dollard and Miller may begin not as the person's *own* anxiety experience, but as a "second-hand" fear acquired from observing another. (This other may be a character in a drama. It is interesting to speculate about how many of our anxieties are acquired from the overcharged excitements of television and movies.)

Social learning theorists have made three important additions to a learning theory of personality: People can learn indirectly by observing the actions of others and the consequences of those actions; people are often sensitive to the social context in which learning takes place; and people interpret experience in the process of learning.

Lately Bandura (1977, 1978) has taken his thinking one step further, by pointing out that people develop self-evaluatory standards that affect their reactions to their own performances. That is, people have standards that they gain self-respect by living up to. They set goals for themselves and derive satisfaction from reaching these goals or disappointment from not reaching them. These self-standards, Bandura points out, are an important part of all of our experience, and "to ignore the influential role of self-evaluation reactions in the self-regulation of behavior is to disavow a uniquely human capacity" (1978, p. 351).

The Biological Model

The biological approach to the study of personality holds that physical constitution, genetic endowment, and other biological features determine at least some of the basic features of personality. Older constitutional theories claimed that almost all the important elements of personality are biological in origin, while the more modern versions state that only some personality characteristics originate in biological factors. Constitutional theories, particularly the older ones, are in sharp opposition to the learning theories just discussed, which emphasize the flexibility of the human personality. But, as we shall see, some of the more modern constitutional theories allow for the effect of learning and view personality as the result of the interaction of constitutional and learned factors.

The Constitutional Approach: Sheldon

The constitutional approach holds that the structure of the body, or body type, determines personality and behavior. Some everyday stereotypes that we all have heard express this view. For instance, all fat people are jolly; thin, frail people are scholarly and ascetic. William Sheldon thought that there was a great deal of truth to these everyday generalizations although they were given short shrift by psychologists. He commented, "It is the old notion that structure must somehow determine function. In the face of this expectation it is rather astonishing that in the past so little relation has been discovered between the shape of man and the way he behaves" (1942, p. 4). After analyzing more than 4,000 photographs Sheldon concluded that there are three basic body types:

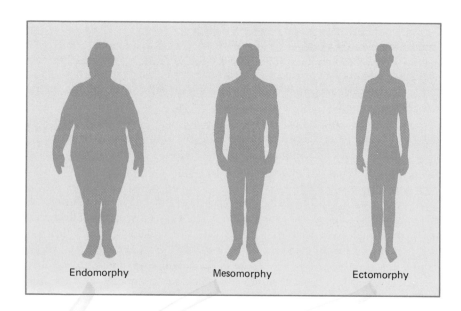

Endomorphy   Mesomorphy   Ectomorphy

Figure 14-1
This diagram shows examples of the three
body types described by Sheldon: endo-
morphy, mesomorphy, and ectomorphy.

endomorphy, mesomorphy, and ectomorphy (see Figure 14-1). *Endomorphs* are usually fat and have underdeveloped musculature. *Mesomorphs* are generally hard, firm, strong, upright, and tough. *Ectomorphs* tend to be slender, fragile, delicate, and have a light muscle structure.

Sheldon also did an extensive analysis of over 500 trait words, using intuitive procedures and correlational methods. The analysis revealed three major groups of traits, and these make up the primary components of "temperament." In relating temperament type to body type Sheldon found that differences in somatotype are strongly associated with differences in temperament. The chubby endomorph was likely to have an easygoing, sociable temperament; the athletic-looking mesomorph would probably be a risk-taking, assertive type; and the physically fragile ectomorph often was withdrawn and restrained.

These findings need to be taken very cautiously. Modern researchers have been particularly critical of the fact that ratings of temperament were made by people (Sheldon and his associates) who were predisposed to find a body type–temperament correlation. In other words, the high degree of correlation found may reflect a bias in the eye of the beholder. When the studies are done in a methodologically more sophisticated way, the connections between body type and temperament are much less strong.

Still, there *is* a relation, and Sheldon must be given credit for forcefully calling our attention to the connection between physique and temperament. Nor did he argue that all of a person's temperamental characteristics mysteriously flowed from that person's physique at birth. He discussed the ways in which a person's physique might cause interactions with other people that could shape temperamental development. For instance, he pointed out that mesomorphs were likely to be recruited for sports because of their physiques and could further develop their competitive temperaments in this setting.

Genetic Theories of Individual Personality Characteristics

In their study of temperament, Thomas, Chess, and Birch (1970) followed the development of 150 children for almost a decade, gathering information from interviews with parents and home observation. They concluded that there are evident temperamental differences in children at birth and that these differences endure in later life. For example, "moody" children are more likely to have behavior problems later in life than even-tempered babies.

Introversion/extroversion is a temperamental pattern that also appears to have a genetic component. Whether as adults people are shy and anxious or friendly and outgoing in their relationships with others and the environment correlates with expressions of these orientations at birth: Friendly infants tend to become friendly teenagers, while cold infants are also somewhat unfriendly as adolescents (Schaeffer and Bayley, 1963). Babies also appear to differ at birth in the way they prefer to be calmed when they are upset: Some like to be held, others want to be left alone. The names "cuddlers" and "noncuddlers" have been applied to these two types (Schaffer and Emerson, 1964). Cuddlers are described by their mothers as snuggling, loving to be held, and cuddling back; mothers of noncuddlers say their children don't like to be held, resist all attempts to do so, and cry or make a noise until they are put down.

As this last example suggests, it is also important to assess environmental influences. A child who at first doesn't seek attachment with the parent may be perceived and treated by the parent as more independent, and thus show a persistence of "noncuddlesomeness" that is the product of interaction with the parent. Similarly, friendly, extroverted babies may draw reinforcing responses from their parents that encourage further development of that pattern. Thomas, Chess, and Birch (1970) observed parental reactions to children's temperamental displays, such as moodiness, and saw how these reactions could support the temperamental patterns that were first used by the child.

As already explained, "genetic" theories of personality are often actually genetic-environmental theories of development. This can be taken one step further: These theories suggest that the influence of genetics will be greatest when the first signs of a predisposition "pull" from the environment some reaction that supports the continuation of that predisposition. The reaction of a parent to a baby, for example, may be greatly influenced by the baby's moody temperament; thus the reaction may lead to the stability or long-term development of that temperament.

A baby who at first doesn't interact with its mother may be treated as more independent, and thus show a persistence of "noncuddlesomeness." In the same way, friendly, extroverted babies may draw reinforcing responses from their mothers that encourage further development of that pattern.

The Humanistic-Existential Model

The common emphasis of humanistic and existential theories is on the total personality as opposed to separate behaviors that make up that personality. In this radically antideterministic view, a view that minimizes not only the effects of environment but also those of biology, the emphasis is on choice and the personal responsibility that being able to make choices implies.

The humanistic-existential model stresses personal experience and what that experience means to the individual as the basis of human personality and behavior. The first thing you must do in seeking to understand the behavior of another person is to understand the way that person constructs his or her world.

We make choices about the actions we perform, and in that sense our actions and personalities are explained by a different system from that used in natural sciences. The ax splits the log because of principles of mass and force; you split the log into firewood because you are planning to build a fire. Humans genuinely do engage in conscious, motivated, goal-directed behavior. But since each choice that we make involves giving up all the other choices available to us at that moment, all choices involve some pain because they mean forgoing other possibilities.

Nonetheless, particularly among the American practitioners of humanistic-existential psychology such as Maslow and Rogers, a more optimistic theme emerges. The basic force motivating human behavior is the need for growth and self-direction. People are seen as continually striving for increased awareness, self-actualization, and the fulfillment of their human potential.

Motives for Growth: Maslow

Abraham Maslow developed his approach to personality from the study of healthy, creative people. In general, he objected to the usual emphasis of personality theories on neurosis and maladaptive behavior, which he argued derived from the fact that most personality theorists were therapists who worked with disturbed individuals. Maslow believed that in every person "there is an active will toward health, an impulse toward growth, or toward the actualization of human potentialities" (1967, p. 153). This view stands in sharp contrast to Freudian and other theories that claim we have impulses, instincts, urges, or traits that stand in opposition to society and that need to be repressively socialized through training and education.

Maslow drew on the work of Kurt Goldstein, a neuropsychiatrist who had developed a theory about positive motives for behavior. In Goldstein's theory any need motivates us to satisfy it. But underlying all these needs is one real drive, one true motive: to self-actualize, to continuously realize our own potential by whatever means we can. The drive for self-actualization is what gives unity and organization to the personality. The tasks we perform to satisfy a need are the way we work toward self-actualization.

We may all share the same drive for self-actualization, but the means and ends we seek vary. This is because, according to Goldstein, we have different inherent preferences and potentialities. These not only help define our means and ends, they also influence our individual development.

According to Goldstein, our drive for self-actualization comes from within, and the healthy individual can overcome "the disturbance arising from the clash with the world, not out of anxiety but out of the joy of conquest" (1939, p. 305). The individual, then, has the possibility of *mastery* or *control* of the environment. However, if the realities of the environment are too inconsistent with the goals of the individual, the individual will break down or redefine his or her goals.

An environment, then, must allow an individual to be in a state that is

Abraham Maslow, 1908–1970.

normal or adequate to his or her nature. If the environment is too unstable, the constancy and identity of the individual are threatened. If in the course of childhood development the environment is too stressful or inconsistent with the needs of the individual, Goldstein says, the child will develop behavior patterns that deter the process of self-actualization. Maslow's need hierarchy, which we discussed in Chapter 11, can be used to clarify the conditions under which this occurs. Maslow divides his need hierarchy into two groups, one based on deficiency, the other on growth. The former (for example, the need for food) Maslow calls *basic needs;* the latter (for example, the desire for beauty, justice, and goodness) are called *meta-needs.* Basic needs, according to Maslow, are basic in the sense that if they are unfulfilled, people give them priority over other needs. A starving person seeks food and has no time or energy for appreciating works of art. For Maslow, self-actualization is the final concern of the person: It can only receive attention after the physiological, safety, belonging and love, and esteem needs of the person have been met.

If the physical and social environments do not provide fulfillment of these basic needs, the person will seek to satisfy these needs by whatever means possible. Thus the environment can either temporarily or permanently block or thwart the natural drive for self-actualization. A person who sees the world as threatening and unpredictable may pursue safety or security needs to the exclusion of self-actualization.

Maslow believed in the possibilities of personal growth and thought it worthwhile to urge people to self-actualize. He took some care to describe in

Table 14–2: The Characteristics of Self-Actualized Individuals.

1. Are able to perceive reality accurately.
2. Are able to accept reality readily.
3. Are natural and spontaneous.
4. Can focus on problems rather than on their self.
5. Have a need for privacy.
6. Are self-sufficient and independent.
7. Are capable of fresh, spontaneous, non-stereotyped appreciation of objects, events and people that they encounter.
8. Have peak experiences, and attain transcendence.
9. Identify with mankind, and experience shared social bonds with other people.
10. May have few or many friends, but will have deep relationships with at least some of these friends.
11. Have a democratic, egalitarian attitude.
12. Have strongly held values and do not confuse means with ends.
13. Have a broad, tolerant sense of humor.
14. Are inventive and creative, and able to see things in new ways.
15. Resist the pressures of conformity to society.
16. Are able to transcend dichotomies, bring together opposites.

From Maslow (1967).

detail the characteristics of the self-actualized person. These characteristics are listed in Table 14-2.

Self Theory: Rogers

Like Goldstein and Maslow, Carl Rogers, in his *person-centered* personality theory, viewed the individual as a whole being composed of complex cognitive, emotional, biological, and other processes and capable of self-actualization. Like Jung and Adler, Rogers also emphasized the role of the *self* and conscious awareness in the life of the individual. Like many other personality theorists, he constantly tried to help people with their problems. Perhaps because many of the people he saw were college students, Rogers came to a more optimistic conclusion about personal growth than did other theorists.

In keeping with the humanistic-existential tradition, Rogers placed great stress on the phenomenal field of the individual, or the individual's total experience at a given moment—experience that is known only to that person and can't directly be known by another. He believed that knowing how people interpret their experiences is the first step in understanding their personality and behavior. But Rogers also pointed out that elements of people's experience may be incorrectly represented by them, or not represented at all. A healthy, mature condition of adjustment exists, he said, when people accurately symbolize to themselves their total experience. Maladjustment arises when there is a gap between people's actual experience and their awareness of it—in other words, when they deny or distort parts of their experience.

The self-image is particularly important in the development of personality. Each of us can be described as having an image of our real self (the self as it is) and of an ideal self (the self we'd like to be). The self-image arises out of interaction with others. Parents, for example, tend to distinguish "worthy" actions and feelings, which are rewarded, from "unworthy" actions and feelings, which are punished. If children are forced to give up or deny the "unworthy" actions or feelings (rather than learn to express them in more acceptable ways), they are compelled to deny a part of their experience. Their self-image then becomes inconsistent with their actual experience. Because their behavior is regulated not just by their own perceptions and feelings, but also by values they have incorporated from their parents and others, their personality is in effect divided.

The condition for self-actualization, therefore, is trusting one's own experience in the evaluation of oneself rather than evaluating oneself on the basis of the needs and interests of others. According to Rogers, a period of positive regard from parents and others in our lives helps us to do this.

It is difficult, on first exposure, for a reader to grasp fully the great difference in emphasis that exists between the humanistic-existential theories and all other theories of personality. In Chapters 16 and 17, where we discuss the humanistic perspective on abnormal psychology and the existential modes of therapy, other aspects of their general perspective will become clear. For now, carry along this theme: People have the freedom to choose the actions they take; because they do so, they have the capacity to grow and develop. But the other side of the coin is that they also have the real possibility of choosing actions that limit or diminish their lives, and it is their own responsibility if they do so.

The Cognitive Model

Cognitive theories of personality draw on what psychologists have learned about the information-processing strategies of human beings. Like humanistic-existential theories, they begin the study of personality by determining the categories and systems people use for organizing their image of the world. Personality, for the cognitive psychologist, is people's particular and unique representations of the interpersonal and physical situations in which they find themselves: Their actions flow from their perspectives.

Personal Construct Theory: Kelly

Kelly's personal construct theory focuses on how people make sense out of, or construe, experience. In Kelly's view, people create personal constructs of reality by actively perceiving, evaluating, and organizing their own experience. Kelly suggests that it is useful to think of ourselves as scientists, going about making sense out of our own world in the same way that scientists make sense out of their field of study. Not only do we construe events and objects, but we also try to find cause-and-effect relationships and use our understanding of these to predict future events. Understanding cause-and-effect relationships also gives us the power to intervene in the world in effective ways, to control events and produce outcomes that we desire.

People constantly try to better predict events in the world, and to Kelly, this is the primary motivating force in personality. Our ability to predict may improve with experience, because experience changes our anticipations (predictions) according to whether or not it fulfills them. Like scientists, we change our hypotheses as new information enters the system, and so learning from experience that one of our anticipations was wrong is a particularly important opportunity for growth.

Kelly stresses the importance of understanding how people view the world and the choices they make on the basis of their world view; to predict what people will do in a given situation, in other words, we must attempt to see the situation through their eyes. It's important to understand the categories into which people put the continuous flux of their experience, and how events and the way they are viewed are connected. The measure of good constructs, then, is how useful they are; they should help people function effectively in their world.

For example, one person, because of his past experiences, perceives examinations as fraught with risk of failure. He is made anxious by being placed in an examination setting. Another perceives examinations as being an interesting intellectual and competitive challenge; she is envigorated by an impending test. The objective circumstances in which these two people find themselves are the same, but this proves to be less important than the fact that they perceive and think about the situation very differently, and their reactions are therefore very different. The general point of the cognitive perspective is that people construct their own pictures of the world. Therefore, as we will see in the chapter on abnormal psychology, they can be led by their past experiences to construe the world as an alien place, in which their efforts count for little, and in which their fate is determined by forces outside their control. In terms of the standard

APPLICATION
The Situation vs. the Person

One of the major controversies in personality psychology (usually debated between personality and social psychologists) is the degree to which people's behavior is a function of their fixed personality characteristics or a relatively free response to the situation in which they find themselves. In classic form the question is, Which is more powerful in the determination of behavior, situational variables or personality variables?

Trait and psychodynamic approaches state that constant, internal, relatively stable forces of personality have a consistent effect on behavior.

Lately, personality researchers—most notably Walter Mischel (1968, 1976)—have put forth a different view. Mischel feels that individual responses in any situation are not reflections of constant traits, but rather depend on and vary according to the situation.

The classic study in this area was conducted by Hartshorne and May (1928) on honesty in chidren. In this study, children were put in a number of situations in which they had a chance to be dishonest and believed they would not be detected. For example, they were given money to play with that they could have kept, they were asked to report about work done at home, or they were observed taking tests to see who would cheat and who would not.

The results showed that children are neither honest or dishonest consistently, but rather that their behavior seems to be specific to the situation, and thus varies with the situation.

Mischel argues that to account for variability in behavior, personality theorists must shift their orientation from a focus on the character structure of the person to a focus on the structure of the situation. The basis for developing theories of personality should not be global traits or states, but the manner in which personality reflects contingencies in the environment.

Mischel uses the stimulus discrimination principle of learning theory as a basis for the argument that people can learn to emit very

vocabulary, such people are depressed. As the therapy chapter will make clear, cognitive therapy concentrates on altering a person's constructions of the world, to make them more accurate, less self-punishing, and more useful in the real world.

All the models we have examined in this chapter—the psychoanalytic, learning, biological, humanistic-existential, and cognitive—require some sort of procedure to identify and locate the various characteristics, traits, and personalities they are studying. There are a number of personality assessment techniques, some suited to and developed by one particular model, some used by all the models. We will look at these assessment techniques in the next section.

The Assessment of Personality

Whatever the theory of personality, it is useful to have methods of describing and assessing it. This is true for two reasons. First, practical decisions may hinge on it. One would not want to put a paranoid schizophrenic in charge of a missile-testing base, nor a psychopathic deviant in a police uniform. And, on the more positive side, it is extremely useful to match people with jobs that suit their personalities. Some people enjoy stress and ought to have jobs in which they will be presented with challenging tasks; others would fall apart in a job in which there was constant stress, challenging or not.

different responses to very similar stimulus situations if their past reinforcement contingencies have led them to do so.

But Mischel does not believe that current responses can be completely accounted for in terms of past environmental reinforcement contingencies and the currently presented external stimuli. He says that besides conditions in the environment, it is necessary to take into account a person's perceptual and cognitive processes—how they uniquely perceive, organize, and interpret their social environments.

First, individuals may differ in their competencies, or ability to generate particular cognitions. These competencies would be related to measures of IQ or social-intellectual capacity. Second, individuals may differ in their encoding strategies, or the way they categorize and label events or other people. Third, individuals may also have different expectations about what will happen if they do this or that in any one situation. Fourth, individuals' subjective values, motives, and incentives are likely to be different in a given situation. Finally, there may be individual differences in self-regulatory systems, or people's unique rules for performance, and their plans.

Mischel argues that it doesn't make sense to ask, Are people or situations more important? He says the more appropriate question is, When are situation variables more important, and when are person variables more important?

He argues that it depends on the strength or weakness of the situations—when they lead everyone to encode the event the same way, induce uniform expectancies, and require skills that everyone can perform, situational variables are more important. A red light is an example of a powerful situation—it will be perceived and processed uniformly by most people and consequently leads to stable, predictable patterns of behavior. However, if you ask how someone will behave at a cocktail party the answer will be much less certain. When situations are ambiguous, person variables will exert a greater influence in determining behavior.

Adopting the approach to personality suggested by Mischel may be difficult for most of us. We are accustomed to describing people in terms of what we "know" of their personality characteristics, and we all have a tendency to perceive more consistency in our own and other's behavior than may actually exist. We will discuss this at greater length in Chapter 18.

A second reason for assessing personality is a scientific one—is is useful in testing personality theories. For instance, according to Maslow's theory, there should be a unique group of people who are self-actualized. These people should share certain qualities or characteristics described by Maslow—a broad and tolerant sense of humor, the tendency to stand by their friends, and so on. But there is no way of proving that there are such people unless we can measure people's sense of humor and tendency to back their values in the face of pressure to conform. Unless we can test for these qualities, we will never know where there is a group of people who have both these qualities as well as the other qualities that Maslow hypothesizes for self-actualized individuals.

Reliability and Validity

As with any testing procedure, with personality assessment we must concern ourselves with two measures of a successful test: reliability and validity. At best, a personality test should give the same result each time it is administered to the same person, assuming there is no reason to believe that his or her personality has changed between tests. This is called *reliability*. In general, there are two ways to check that a test is reliable. The first is used if the test provides a relatively straightforward output such as "true/false" or "agree/disagree" answers. Then reliability is assessed by comparing the correlation between: two halves of the same test (split-half method); two versions of the same test (alternate forms method); or two successive versions of the same test (test-retest method). If the assessment outcome consists of a series of ratings made by a judge, then *interrater reliability* methods are used. These involve having a second observer also rate the person being tested and then calculating the correlation between the two judges' ratings.

Psychologists distinguish between two related but different kinds of validity that a personality assessment instrument may have. *Predictive validity* is of concern when an assessment device is being used largely for practical purposes—when, for instance, the object is to predict how well a person will do in college, as an airplane pilot, or in another job. The performance the assessment instrument is trying to predict is called the *criterion*, and the purpose of the research is to predict it as accurately as possible. Therefore if the maximum correlation ($+1$ or -1) between the assessment instrument and the criterion could be obtained, the research project would be considered wildly successful because the assessment instrument would predict without error whether a person would do well or poorly at the criteria. The predictive validity of an instrument, then, is the degree of correlation between that instrument and the *criterion* performance that is to be predicted.

Construct validity is the second kind of validity that psychologists distinguish. It is generally of interest when personality assessment instruments are being used for theoretical rather than practical purposes. Suppose that a psychologist has developed the construct of "test anxiety," defined as a tendency to become anxious in test situations and thus to perform more poorly than would otherwise be the case. What kind of personality assessment instrument would the psychologist want to develop to measure this construct? What pattern of correlations with other behaviors should the assessment instrument show? To demonstrate construct validity, the assessment instrument should show *moderate* correlations with a number of other behaviors. (Contrast this to the predictive reliability requirement of a high correlation with some single criterion measure.)

Let us explain why we would expect the "test anxiety" measure to correlate only moderately with other measures. Consider the factors that determine how well someone will perform on a math test. Certainly the person's anxiety about taking the test is one such factor, but so is mathematical ability and how much time the person has spent studying for the test. Now imagine six individuals who have the test anxiety acores and math ability scores shown in Table 14-3. Notice that the pattern is about what you would expect; people who are low on test anxiety tend to "work up to" their abilities, while people who are highly "test anxious" do a bit worse than their ability alone would lead us to expect. At the commonsense level, therefore, we have evidence for the construct validity of the test anxiety measure. But what about the correlation between performance on the math test and the test anxiety measure? Table 14-4 presents that information. There the test anxiety scores are listed in ascending order and the math scores are listed in the right-hand column. The correlation is shown beneath the table. The important fact for our purposes is that although the correlation is greater than zero, indicating that there is a link between test anxiety and test performance (recall that a negative correlation is just as useful as a positive one—it simply indicates that scoring at the high end of one scale correlates with scoring at the low end of the other scale), it is by no means a perfect correlation. Instead it is the moderate correlation that we said was good evidence of construct validity. But now we know why. For instance, the last person in the second half of the table is Person 2. He did moderately well on the

Table 14–3: *The Construct Validation of a Test.*

Person	Math Ability 1=low, 10=high	Test Anxiety 1=low, 10=high	Math Test Performance 1=low, 10=high
1	8	1	8
2	8	9	6
3	4	2	4
4	4	8	2
5	7	5	6
6	2	7	1

Table 14–4: *Performance Scores as a Function of Test Anxiety.*

Person	Text Anxiety 1=low, 10=high	Math Test Performance 1=low, 10=high
1	1	8
3	2	4
5	5	6
6	7	1
4	8	2
2	9	6

$r = .41$

math test, even though he was highly test anxious, because he had a high level of mathematical ability. Now you can see why the first requirement for construct validity is a moderate rather than a high correlation between the construct test and some other measure that we expect to be influenced by that test.

The second requirement for validation is that the construct test show not just a single correlation but a pattern of correlations with a number of other behaviors. This is because we expect a construct that will be theoretically useful to have general implications. To see this, consider our example of test anxiety. If a measure of test anxiety correlated only with people's scores on a single other test of math performance, to use an extreme case, then we would doubt that we had a general measure of test anxiety. A general measure ought to correlate with, for instance, performances on English and social studies tests, written and oral tests, and so on through the general domain of testing.

Figure 14-2 presents the different correlational patterns that are desirable in predictive versus construct validation. Predictive validity of a scale is indicated by a single high correlation between that scale and the criterion measure; construct validity by a set of moderate correlations between that scale and multiple behaviors that are thought to be partially influenced by that construct.

To summarize our discussion of personality assessment so far: We have presented the measurement (sometimes called psychometric) characteristics of

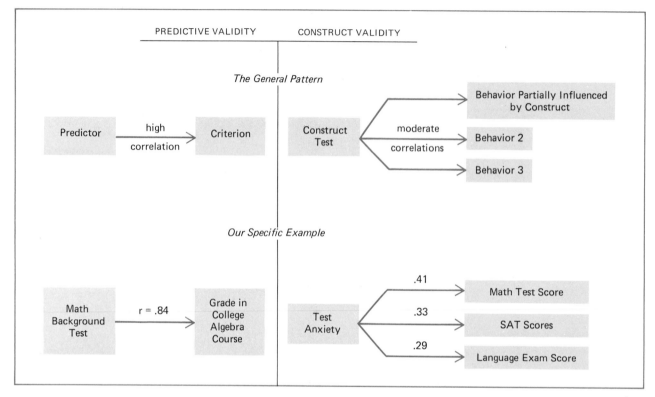

Figure 14-2
These are the different correlational patterns that are desirable in predictive and construct validation.

assessment devices. The first criterion for a successful assessment device is that it be *reliable*—it must give approximately the same result when applied to the same individual. This can be thought of as a precondition of *validity,* which is the second requirement for a successful assessment device. Validity requirements differ according to the purpose of the test. If a test is supposed to predict a person's performance on some practically important task, then predictive validity is sought; if it is designed to measure an individual's disposition or style, then construct validity is investigated. We now turn to four different procedures used to assess personality: observational techniques, scales and self-reports, projective tests, and personality inventories.

Observational Techniques

As we observe other people, we come to certain conclusions about their personalities. If we reduce these observations to writing, a sort of personality assessment emerges. This is perhaps the oldest assessment technique, and one that is still in great use today. But if you think about it for a moment, the difficulties with this procedure will become clear. Different observers may have seen different samples of the person's behavior, and may have different questions in mind when they write their assessments. For these and other reasons, these kinds of assessments have often proved unreliable (and therefore of low validity), so psychologists have come up with ways to make such judgments more precise and systematic. These include structuring the assessment techniques either by structuring the rating system itself, or by structuring the methods of gathering the information on which the assessment is based.

STRUCTURING THE RATINGS.   Instead of making a general summary of someone's personality, observers rate the person on certain specific, defined dimensions. This assures that every observer will rate the same qualities by using a common vocabulary to describe them. The scales can be used during or just after an interview, and can be based on the person's answers to questions, general behavior during the interview, or both.

Sometimes observers are given a set of adjectives and asked to select those that apply to the person they're evaluating. The adjectives can describe various personality characteristics or can refer to the person's moods, skills, physical appearance—depending on the purpose of the assessment.

A variation of this is the *q-sort technique.* Here the observer is given a large set of cards with an adjective or phrase printed on each. The observer then sorts the cards into 9 groups, Group 1 being those statements that best describe the person, and Group 9 those that don't apply to the person at all. Sometimes the judge is told to make the distribution of items conform to a normal distribution, with the fewest cards in Groups 1 and 9, and the most in Groups 3–5. The idea behind this direction is that only a few qualities best describe most of us, a few never apply to us at all, and most are intermediate. Conforming with this direction makes observers more careful about qualities at either end of the scale. It also facilitates comparisons among individuals because exactly the same number of adjectives are reported as most or least typical of each individual.

STRUCTURING THE OBSERVATIONS.   Another way to make observations more reliable and valid is to structure the information on which they are based. In the interview setting this would involve structuring the kinds of questions asked of the person.

An interview in which the judge talks to a person and follows the conversation wherever it leads is called an *open-ended* or *unstructured interview.* A more systematic interview (or more systematic results) can be achieved by asking everyone the same questions in the same order. This kind of interview, the *structured interview,* makes it easier to sort, rate, and analyze the answers. It is also more reliable in that the same results are likely if the interview is repeated. With the open-ended interview, very different results may result the second time (or with a different interviewer).

A compromise format, often called a *semistructured* or *structured/open-ended interview,* sets out a prearranged schedule of questions, but allows the interviewer to explore in depth any of the respondent's answers that seem particularly revealing or important.

STRUCTURING THE SETTINGS OR SITUATIONS.   Judges sometimes form impressions of others by observing their behavior rather than by interviewing them. A clinical or developmental psychologist, for instance, may gain impressions of a child by observing that child interact with parents in the home, teachers in the classroom, and children on the playground.

This kind of observation is more reliable if the situations in which the person performs are structured. In addition, research shows that the predictive validity of observations increases as the test situation more closely resembles the situation in which one is attempting to predict behavior.

One of the most extensive attempts at arriving at personality data from structured settings was made by American Army Intelligence during World War II. At several secret locations in the United States elaborate training centers were built to simulate some of the situations in which undercover agents sent into Nazi-occupied Europe might find themselves. The primary function of these centers was training, but their secondary function was to enable observers to make behavioral assessments of the future agents, focusing on their behavior under stress.

The test situations were structured to be as close as possible to real situations the agents would face. What was supposed to be an after-hours tavern on the base is a good example. Here agents were not on their guard, not expecting any sort of test, so when an acquaintance tried to extract secret information from them, their reactions were revealing of how they would behave in a similar future situation in which their lives might depend on just such an unguarded reaction.

Teams of observers rated the agents at the training centers. Then, overseas, their superior officers and colleagues rated them again in actual situations. Unfortunately, the observers' ratings did not reliably predict success in the field. There were many reasons for this. First and foremost was the fact that most of the war situations were different from the test situations in unpredictable ways.

Two kinds of moderately structured setting assessments reflect the theoretical principle behind the Army Intelligence tests. In the first the test is constructed to make certain elements as similar to those found on the job as possible. Samples of the kinds of work done by people on the job are taken and appear on the test in a simplified version. Second, on the premise that a particularly important component of every job is decision making under stress, stress-producing incidents are included in the test. Both these tests are thought to measure behaviors closely related to on-the-job performances. They put people in job-related situations and observe how they behave.

Scales and Self-Reports

Often people are asked to report on their own personalities. As Allport pointed out, the easiest way to find out about a person is to ask that person. There are many aspects of our own personalities that we are quite aware of and capable of reporting on. The methods used are the same rating scales and adjective cards that we described for observational techniques—the only difference is that people make observations about themselves rather than have other people do it. The reliability of the self-rating is assessed by test-retest correlations, and the predictive and construct validity of the self-report is assessed in the same way that it is with observers' judgments.

The problem with this procedure is that people sometimes do not wish to reveal certain things about themselves because they feel that to do so would be embarrassing or harmful. If asked whether they are "flexible or rigid," or "organized or disorganized," they would probably report that they are flexible and organized because these are seen as the socially desirable answers. So researchers working with self-reports have found it wise to try to balance their scales so that neither end of the scale is the "good" or "bad" end. This is surprisingly hard to do because many words used to describe people carry positive or negative connotations.

One way around this difficulty is to ask people to rate their behavior patterns rather than their personalities. Instead of asking them whether they are "dependable," for instance, the tester would ask questions about missed appointments, forgotten meetings, and tasks left incomplete. Again, though, it is obvious that it is not socially desirable to respond "frequently" to questions about missed meetings, so people may falsely report that they act in socially desirable ways rather than (as in the personality test) that they are socially desirable people.

Another problem with this technique is that people have certain personality characteristics and behavior patterns of which they are unaware. These include, in Freud's terms, defense mechanisms such as repression; or, in behaviorist terms, patterns of behavior such as learned helplessness.

In an effort to reveal underlying problems, conflicts, or qualities that people are unaware of themselves or are unwilling to report, psychologists have devised tests that ask people to report on some seemingly harmless thought or behavior pattern that the testers believe correlates with or reveals the underlying conflict or difficulty. These tests are divided into two groups on the basis of how the correlation between test question and characteristic is established. *Projective tests* generally rely on theoretically asserted correlations; *personality inventories* rely on empirically discovered correlations.

Projective Tests

The typical projective test presents the respondent with a very unstructured task. The key that allows interpretation is the assumption that respondents reveal something about their underlying dynamics by the structure their answers impose on the situation.

    RORSCHACH TEST.   The Rorschach inkblot test is one of the oldest of the projective tests. Figure 14-3 shows a sample inkblot. Each inkblot is a pattern that can look like many things: animals, people, devils, masks, birds.

Rorschach tested thousands of his inkblots for years before choosing the 10 that are still in use today. He tested the blots both on patients who had been classified by disorder in a mental hospital and on normal people. The final 10 were those that best discriminated reactions of patients from those of normal people, and also showed some ability to discriminate among patients according to disorder.

The 10 inkblots are on cards. Most are black, others contain one or more colors. The cards are presented one at a time in a certain order. The person being tested can make one interpretation or many. After showing all the inkblots, the tester goes back over the cards, asking why the person saw what he or she did in the card, what part of the blot looked like that, and so on.

As in some other testing procedures, the tester observes the person's behavior and style of answering, as well as actual answers. The answers are scored in several ways. For example: Did the person see the whole blot or just parts? What is the subject matter or content? What qualities do they seem to respond to (color, shape, etc.)? In all of this the tester is looking for consistencies, for patterns of responding.

From the answers the tester makes inferences about the underlying person-

Figure 14-3
A sample Rorschach inkblot. Some of the inkblots are in one or more colors, but most are black, like this one.

ality structure of the respondent. The inferences are made in accordance with psychoanalytic principles: Recurring themes across pictures are thought to hint at recurring underlying conflicts; sequential responses to the same images reveal material that is causally linked in the unconscious. Stylistic characteristics of the response may also be meaningful: A person who consistently focuses on a part rather than the whole inkblot may be revealing an obsessional concern with detail; someone who persistently sees movement in the figures may be revealing something important about his or her internal functioning.

THE THEMATIC APPERCEPTION TEST. Henry Murray developed the Thematic Apperception Test (TAT) in an attempt to find out more about an individual's functioning with other people. Murray collected a set of photographs and sketches of people, often shown in some ambiguous relationship with other people, and asked the respondent to make up a story based on the picture (see Figure 14-4).

The person is asked to tell what led up to the scene on the card, what's happening in the scene, and what the outcome will be. Basically the tester is interested in several elements of respondents' stories: which character on the card is seen as central to the story, which character respondents identify with, what needs and drives are expressed in the story, and what seems to be helping or hindering the achievement of them. By interpreting the themes of the stories, the detail the respondent uses to illustrate it, and the pattern of consistent themes and images that recur across stories, a skilled interpreter can arrive at surprisingly rich and detailed interpretations of the respondent's character.

But these are still only interpretations. Both the Rorschach and the Thematic Apperception Test result in a complex and free-form mix of descriptive and evaluative statements by the interpreter about the respondent, and, like any other test result, they require validation. If the clinician interprets the fussy, orderly way an individual organizes his TAT answers as revealing an underlying

Figure 14-4

The psychologist shown here is administering the Thematic Apperception Test (TAT). In this test the person being interviewed is asked to tell what's happening in the scene shown, what led up to it, and what the outcome will be.

trait of anal compulsivity, this interpretation requires checking. The respondent may simply have been attempting to live up to what he perceived as the demands of the test situation. Hundreds of studies have attempted to validate elements of projective interpretations, and while they are far too numerous to review in detail here, it is fair to say that many psychologists are not impressed with the validity of the material emerging from projective testing. To develop better test instruments, a new system of test construction was adopted.

Personality Inventories

One of the best known personality tests is the *Minnesota Multiphasic Personality Inventory (MMPI)*. The psychologists who constructed the MMPI started with several hundred statements or test items that were thought to be useful in diagnosing and detecting serious behavior disorders such as depression, paranoia, and hysteria. The test consists of statements to which the person answers "true," "false," or "cannot say." They include statements on the person's past experiences, attitudes, physiological and psychological symptoms, and views of the world. For example:

> I daydream a little.
> People are following me.
> My mother often made me obey even when I thought it was unreasonable.

A test for a specific characteristic is constructed in the following way. The items on the inventory are treated as a source pool. First the test constructor decides what the test will be used for. For instance, it could be used to identify people who perform poorly in highly stressful situations. Then the test constructor identifies a group of people who actually have the characteristic for which the test is being developed. It may, for example, be a group of students who "fall apart" under the pressure of timed tests, or a group of workers who have been identified as poor performers under stress. The test is given to these *criterion groups* and their pattern of answers is compared to the answers given by the normal population. The questions that the criterion and normal groups answer differently (the "discriminating items") are the ones selected to go on the test for poor performance under stress. So research reports developing this kind of test often contain such lists as "25 +" and "37 −." This means that a true (+) answer to Question 25 on the MMPI is characteristic of (for example) a poor performer under stress, and a false (−) answer to Question 37 is also characteristic of that pattern. The set of questions that proves to discriminate the criterion from the normal group, not only on the first application, but through successive sets of trials with different specific criterion groups, becomes the scale for the factor or characteristic in question. For instance, the depression scale of the MMPI has 40–50 items that have been shown to discriminate between depressed people and the rest of the population, and also between depressed people and people with other behavior disorders. Answers are not expressed as raw scores—they are plotted as deviations from the general patterns of answers given by thousands of previous respondents.

The initial use of the MMPI was in psychodiagnostic settings, such as mental hospitals, and this is reflected in the scales that appear on the standard MMPI report form. So, for instance, the "Hy" scale is the "hysteria scale" and was developed with a criterion group of patients in mental hospitals whose observing psychiatrists and psychologists reported them to be high on hysterical symptomatology. Suppose that a person has a high "Pa" scale score. Does this mean that person is a raving paranoid who is or ought to be hospitalized? Certainly not. Many normally functioning individuals have MMPI profiles that are elevated on one or more scales. The MMPI is fruitfully used to characterize the personality profiles of normal individuals (see Figure 14-5). Someone who thinks ahead to anticipate dangers in order to avoid them is a useful person to have around. On the MMPI this tendency might be indicated by an elevated psychasthenia (Pa) scale score, since this scale contains items that reflect a tendency to worry. And the MMPI has been used to identify many characteristics, including some that we do not ordinarily think of as personality traits. For instance, it has been keyed to identify individuals who will be relatively successful salespersons and college teachers (Welsh and Dahlstrom, 1958).

Since the development of the MMPI, other multiphasic inventories have been constructed on the same principles. (*Multiphasic* means that a test measures many aspects of personality, in contrast to a test that measures only one construct—neurotic anxiety, for instance.) These new tests focus less on behavior disorders and more on normal personality characteristics. For instance, the California Psychological Inventory contains scales measuring such "normal" attributes as self-acceptance, sociability, and several kinds of achievement strivings. The content of the items and the labels of the scales of these inventories make them less threatening to respondents, but the developers of the MMPI would point out that research with these new inventories produces dimensions that are quite similar to those included in the MMPI. Apparently the empirical scale construction technique is a powerful one for identifying subgroups of individuals whose personality elements differ from those of the population at large.

VOCATIONAL INTEREST INVENTORIES.   One of the most successful and socially most useful versions of the empirically constructed inventory is one that most people would not consider a personality test at all—the Strong Vocational Interest Inventory. Strong is the name of the psychologist who first developed the test. The current version is named the Strong-Campbell Interest Inventory, and it is concerned with the career choices that people make. It simply asks people to report whether they like, dislike, or are indifferent to a large number of school subjects, activities, amusements, and types of people. Sample items include: geometry or physiology, writing reports or pursuing a bandit in a sheriff's posse, skiing or organizing a play, and ballet dancers or business people. It then compares the interest profile of the person taking the inventory to the profiles of people in various careers. The intuitively appealing theoretical bridge is that people who are happy in their careers have interest patterns that are realized in the practice of that career, and these patterns can be discovered by testing criterion groups of individuals who are happy and successful in their careers. Next the profile of an individual who is seeking a career is compared to these composite profiles so the individual can be given career counseling. There is empirical support for this chain of reasoning. Research evidence indicates that very frequently people find careers consistent with their interest patterns as measured by the vocational inventories. This kind of counseling is one of psychology's success stories.

THOMAS JOHN   MALE   AGE 29   REPORT DATE 7-12-67   NCS CODE 0061   MM 124 0004

MINNESOTA MULTIPHASIC PERSONALITY INVENTORY
By Starke R. Hathaway, Ph. D. and J. Charnley McKinley, M.D.

FILE REFERENCE

T SCORE PROFILE ——— Plotted With K

T SCORE WITH K	RAW SCORE WITH K	T SCORE WITH-OUT K	RAW SCORE WITH-OUT K		
			0	?	?
		56	6	L	L
		48	2	F	F
		57	16	K	K
52	12	49	4	Hs	Hs
		56	19	D	D
		53	18	Hy	Hy
62	24	60	18	Pd	Pd
		65	28	Mf	Mf
		47	7	Pa	Pa
46	21	43	5	Pt	Pt
44	19	41	3	Sc	Sc
45	15	45	12	Ma	Ma
		44	19	Si	Si

	A	R	Es	Lb	Ca	Dy	Do	Re	Pr	St	Cn	WB
RAW SCORE →	6	13	48	10	5	16	14	22	15	19	25	9
T SCORE →	42	45	56	53	41	46	48	54	56	53	50	38
	FIRST FACTOR	SECOND FACTOR	EGO STRENGTH	LOW BACK PAIN	CAUDALITY	DEPENDENCY	DOMINANCE	SOCIAL RESPONSIBILITY	PREJUDICE	SOCIAL STATUS	CONTROL	

-PATIENT VIEWS SELF AS WELL-ADJUSTED AND
SELF RELIANT.
   -TENDS TO GIVE SOCIALLY APPROVED ANSWERS RE-
   GARDING SELF-CONTROL AND MORAL VALUES.
   -INCLINES TOWARD ESTHETIC INTERESTS.
   -INDEPENDENT OR MILDLY NONCONFORMIST.
   -VIEWS LIFE WITH AVERAGE MIXTURE OF OPTIMISM
   AND PESSIMISM.
   -NUMBER OF PHYSICAL SYMPTOMS AND CONCERN
   ABOUT BODILY FUNCTIONS FAIRLY TYPICAL FOR
   MEDICAL OUTPATIENTS.
   -RESPECTS OPINIONS OF OTHERS WITHOUT UNDUE
   SENSITIVITY.
   -HAS SUFFICIENT CAPACITY FOR ORGANIZING WORK
   AND PERSONAL LIFE.
   -LOW ENERGY AND ACTIVITY LEVEL. DIFFICULT TO
   MOTIVATE, APATHETIC.
   -HAS A COMBINATION OF PRACTICAL AND
   THEORETICAL INTERESTS.
   -PROBABLY SOCIALLY OUTGOING AND GREGARIOUS.

THE PSYCHOLOGICAL CORPORATION MMPI REPORTING SERVICE

Scored by NATIONAL COMPUTER SYSTEMS

Figure 14-5

This is a computer printout of a profile and its interpretation for the Minnesota Multiphasic Personality Inventory (MMPI). (Hathaway and McKinley, 1967)

Summary

1. Personality refers to an organized and distinctive pattern of behavior that shows endurance over time and characterizes a person's adaptation to a situation.

2. The earliest ideas about personality attempted to account for a person's behavior in terms of innate traits.

3. The psychoanalytic model assumes that we are primarily motivated by drives and instincts over which we have little control; these motivations exist, for the most part, in our unconscious. Personality is made up of three processes, or systems—the id, the ego, and the superego. A person's behavior is the product of the interaction, and often conflict, of these three systems.

4. According to Freud, personality development takes place during four psychosexual stages: oral, anal, phallic, and genital.

5. According to learning theorists, personality is a set of patterns of behavior that we learn to make in response to specific stimuli, according to how such responses have been reinforced in the past.

6. Social learning theory points out that a second type of learning—imitation based on observation of others—also affects behavior and thus personality.

7. In the biological model, genetic endowment and biological features are assumed to be the determinants of personality. Sheldon's constitutional theory classified personality types according to body type: endomorphy, mesomorphy, and ectomorphy.

8. Humanistic-existential models focus on the total personality as opposed to separate behaviors that make up personality; biology and the environment are minimized as determinants, and personal choice is emphasized.

9. Maslow emphasized the drive for self-actualization, whereas Rogers emphasized the role of self and conscious awareness in the life of the individual.

10. Cognitive models view personality as being the result of a person's unique cognitive organization of the world; in other words, a person's actions flow from his or her perspective. Personal construct theory focuses on how people make sense of their experience.

11. Among the methods used in assessing personality are: q-sort technique, open-ended interviews, structured interviews, projective tests, and personality inventories.

Suggested Readings

BANDURA, A., and WALTERS, K. *Social learning and personality development.* New York: Holt, Rinehart and Winston, 1963. Presents the principles of the social learning approach to personality and reviews modeling, imitation, and identification in the development of personality and the learning of social behaviors.

FREUD, S. *New introductory lectures on psychoanalysis* (W. J. H. Sproutt, trans.). New York: Norton, 1933. An introduction to the psychodynamic approach to personality. Included is Freud's most concise explanation of id, ego, and superego provinces and functioning; anxiety; and the development of the female psyche. In the final lectures the implications of psychoanalysis for religion and social order are presented.

HALL, C. S., LINDZEY, G. (Eds.). *Theories of personality* (3rd ed.). New York: Wiley, 1978. Concise and detailed digest of the major theories of personality. Presents each theorist's conceptualization of man, the structure of personality, mechanisms of development and change, assessment, and (when applicable) therapeutic procedure.

MASLOW, A. H. *Toward a psychology of being* (2nd ed.). New York: Van Nostrand, 1968. Describes the humanistic approach to personality, exploring the fundamental motive of growth and the characteristics of the self-actualized personality. Contrasts the humanistic model with the psychodynamic model and makes comparisons with other humanistic, existential, and neo-Freudian theories.

PERVIN, L. A. *Current controversies and issues in personality.* New York: Wiley, 1978. Personality theories are presented in light of their conflicting positions on a number of current controversies in personality—role of the environment, aggression, altruism, sex differences, and the role of affect. An evaluation of each theoretical viewpoint in terms of social and political implications is provided.

SKINNER, B. F. *Science and human behavior.* New York: Macmillan, 1953. Details an approach to personality based on a functional analysis of cause-and-effect relationships and the application of the principles of operant conditioning to the study of personality and behavior.

VERNON, P. E. *Personality assessment: A critical survey.* New York: Wiley, 1964. Presents the merits and drawbacks of the methods suggested by major personality theorists for the assessment of personality. Includes psychoanalytic and Rogerian interview techniques, the objective approaches of psychometric measurement suggested by the trait theorists Eysenck and Cattell, and techniques that assess major trends in personality, such as the MMPI and self-concept scales.

15

Stress and Coping

Stress is a universal human experience. Unpleasant experiences bring on stress—getting fired, having an illness in the family, or failing an important exam are all stressful. But even generally pleasant events and experiences can have stressful components—a promotion, going away to college, or the purchase of a new house will also cause stress. The common element among these experiences, both pleasant and unpleasant, is that they require some kind of *adjustment* or *adaptation*. Sometimes people are able to adapt to stressful situations fairly easily; at other times they have more difficulty coping with them. Certain people react badly to certain kinds of stresses, but cope well with other kinds; others have different coping patterns. In this chapter we will discuss stress, its causes, people's reactions to it, and the methods people use to cope with it. All of us have at one time or another experienced most of the sources of stress and shown most, if not all, the reactions that we will discuss. Since there are individual preferences for one or another coping style, we will discuss how people can be categorized according to their preferred method of coping.

Stress can be defined as a state that occurs when people are faced with demands from the environment that threaten them in some way. One question this definition raises is whether it is the events themselves that are stressful or rather people's responses to them. It is helpful to think of stress as including both environmental demands, or *stressors,* and the person's reactions to them, the *stress responses.* As we go through the chapter we will refine this definition, make it clearer, and show how it applies to us. We will begin our discussion by examining the sources of stress: physical threats, conflict, frustration, and threats to self-esteem.

Sources of Stress

According to our definition, stress arises from demands placed on the person by the environment. That environmental demand, or *stressor,* can be physical or psychological, intrinsic to a situation or attributed to it by the person involved, universal or unique to one person's experience.

Physical Stressors

Perhaps the most easily understood sources of stress are physical stressors such as extreme heat or cold, noise, and microorganisms. In each case, the stressor

The Three Mile Island nuclear incident, while it did not develop into a disaster, was certainly stressful for all involved. In many cases the threat of a disaster, whether or not it actually occurs, is in itself stressful.

is clear and requires some type of adjustment or coping response from the individual. A person exposed to heat, for example, can adapt physiologically by perspiring or behaviorally by removing clothing or opening a window.

Extreme examples of this category of stressors are disasters such as war, earthquakes, floods, and famines. In these cases, the environmental demands are severe and prolonged, and the individual's adaptation is difficult and often very costly in physical terms. We will talk about the consequences of adapting to prolonged stressors later in the chapter.

Conflict

A second kind of demand that results in stress is conflict. Conflict occurs when a person must choose between incompatible, contradictory, or mutually exclusive goals or courses of action. Two goals are mutually exclusive when the action needed to achieve one automatically prevents the person from reaching the other. Conflict can occur when two inner needs are in opposition, when two external demands pull the person in different directions, or when an inner need is incompatible with an external demand. Psychologists who have described and studied conflict (Lewin, 1931; Miller, 1944) have categorized situations according to the person's tendency to approach or to avoid a goal. We will discuss some of the basic categories of conflict that everyone experiences.

APPROACH-APPROACH CONFLICT.   In this type of conflict people are faced with two equally attractive but mutually exclusive goals—in other words, choosing one automatically means giving up the other. This situation is bound to leave people feeling more discontented than they would be if they had been faced with only one attractive goal. Someone who has two good job offers, for example, may agonize over the decision and feel doubts after making the choice—this stress probably would not have occurred with only one job offer.

APPROACH-AVOIDANCE CONFLICT.   Here the person is confronted with a single goal that has both positive and negative consequences. If you have ever tried to feed a wild animal, you have seen this conflict—the animal wants the food, yet is naturally afraid to come close to a human to get it. People generally experience this sort of stress when they want to do something but know that some of the consequences will be unpleasant. Many people approach marriage with these feelings—love for the other person leads them to approach marriage, but uneasiness about new responsibilities and loss of freedom makes them want to avoid it.

AVOIDANCE-AVOIDANCE CONFLICT.   This type of stressful situation involves an unavoidable choice between two equally unattractive goals or outcomes. A baseball player caught between bases is faced with this sort of conflict: Going forward or going back will result in being tagged out. A middle-aged man may hate the thought of spending the rest of his working years in a field that he finds boring. At the same time he may hate the idea of changing careers at his age, and he probably has family responsibilities that make it hard for him to start over. The response to this type of conflict is often to try to escape—to avoid making any decision at all. This type of conflict often makes people feel out of control—the decision seems forced on them, and this coercion adds to their feelings of stress.

DOUBLE APPROACH-AVOIDANCE CONFLICT.   In this complex situation two possible courses of action each present an approach-avoidance conflict. In other words, you are tempted to both approach and avoid two different goals at the same time. Quite often, the approach-approach conflict is more accurately described as a double approach-avoidance conflict. Think of a college senior attempting to choose between a lucrative job offer and graduate school. Both money and intellectual stimulation are desirable goals to the student and produce the tendency to approach them (approach-approach conflict), while both the lack of money and intellectual stagnation are undesirable goals that produce the tendency to avoid them (avoidance-avoidance conflict). However, the student in this situation is in a double approach-avoidance conflict because taking the lucrative job (approach) offer means intellectual stagnation (avoidance) and going to graduate school (approach) means foregoing a high salary (avoidance).

In all of these conflicts the strength of the goal increases the closer one gets to it. For example, in an approach-avoidance conflict, the tendency to approach will get stronger as one nears the goal, but so will the tendency to avoid. Miller (1944) used the terms *approach* and *avoidance gradient* to describe the strength of the tendency to move toward or away from a goal. Usually, the avoidance gradient, shown in Figure 15-1, is the steeper of the two—that is, the avoidance tendency grows stronger than the approach tendency the nearer one gets to the goal. This doesn't mean that avoidance always wins out, only that the urge to avoid shows a sudden increase in strength as one gets close to the goal.

Brown (1948) devised a way to measure the strength of the tendency in

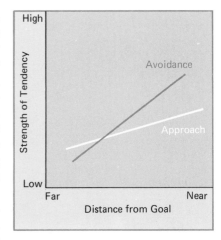

Figure 15-1

The tendency both to approach and to avoid a goal gets stronger as one nears the goal. The avoidance gradient shown here is steeper than the approach gradient, because it increases suddenly as one gets nearer to the goal.

rats to approach or avoid a goal and thus demonstrate approach and avoidance gradients. An approach-avoidance conflict was established by training the rat to run toward a goal box containing food and then shocking it as it reached the goal. The rat was placed in a harness so the pull with which it approached or avoided a goal could be measured. The nearer to the goal the rat got, the less force it applied to the harness—the avoidance tendency had suddenly increased. When the approach and avoidance tendencies became equally strong, the rat sometimes stopped pulling altogether. Whether the rat stopped and where it stopped depended on how hungry the rat was or how strong the shock was. By changing the animal's level of hunger (approach tendency) or fear of shock (avoidance tendency), the experimenter could change the approach-avoidance gradients in predictable ways, thus providing evidence for the validity of the approach-avoidance description of conflict.

Frustration

Frustration is both a result of conflict and a source of stress in itself. We experience frustration when the attainment of some desired goal has been blocked or thwarted.

Coleman and Hammen (1974) have identified five sources of frustration, most of which are a natural outgrowth of our society:

1. *Delays.* In a society in which the value of time (and thus of being on time) is emphasized, any kind of delay is frustrating.
2. *Lack of resources.* We are constantly bombarded by advertising that makes goods seem attractive and necessary to our status and self-worth. When we cannot afford these goods, we feel frustrated.
3. *Loss.* This can be the death of a loved one, or simply the loss of friendships when we move to another part of the country. Loss causes grief, of course, but also frustration, because it makes us feel helpless and reminds us that we have no control over many things that affect our lives.
4. *Failure.* Since our society is a very competitive one, we are bound to experience failure almost all the time. One of the most frustrating aspects of failure is the feeling that we are in some way responsible for it—if only we had done this instead of that, it might never have happened. Whether this feeling is realistic or not, it is frustrating.

In our society the automobile is certainly the source of (or at least the scene of) many stressful occurrences, including traffic jams, accidents, and long lines at the gasoline pump.

5. *Meaninglessness.* It is not easy to live a meaningful life, although this is an ideal in our society. Many people do not have meaningful or fulfilling jobs, for instance, and many are unable to find any work at all. This kind of frustration is made worse by the feeling that society is to blame and there is nothing to be done about it.

Threats to Self-Esteem

The final source of stress discussed here is those events that threaten people's self-esteem. Lynd (1958) has used the term *shame* to characterize the emotional stress response people experience when they behave in a way that unexpectedly results in self-disparagement. This wound to self-esteem requires adjustment to repair a damaged self-image. The conflict is caused by failing to meet expectations or ideals held by oneself or by others, and it is especially stressful when it is unexpected.

Our list of sources of stress, though not exhaustive, does suggest the wide variety of events and situations that call for some kind of coping response. Before we turn to the different ways that people respond to and cope with these stressors, we will consider one general response elicited by most stressors—anxiety.

Stress and Anxiety

Anxiety is a ubiquitous term with many connotations. Is anxiety a symptom of psychopathology or is it a normal reaction experienced by everyone? Is anxiety the same as realistic fear or is it an irrational emotional state? Is anxiety always negative or does it sometimes serve a positive function? It will become clear in our discussion that in different situations and under varying circumstances anxiety can take all of these forms. The fact that "anxiety" has so many meanings in everyday usage may stem, in part, from the different views of anxiety held by the various schools or models of psychology. As we look at how each model explains anxiety, it will become clear that while anxiety is a *reaction* to stressful events, it is also often a *source* of stress to which the individual must adjust. Many of the coping patterns that we will describe are used not to adapt to an environmental demand, but rather to get rid of (or avoid) anxiety.

The Psychoanalytical Model

Sigmund Freud saw anxiety as a consequence of *intrapsychic conflict.* You will recall that Freud divided the mind into three parts: the id, the ego, and the superego. Each part serves a specific function. According to Freud, the id is the source of our primal impulses and drives. The superego is analogous to the conscience or moral sense; it is the product of socialization, the collective voice of parents, church, state, and custom. The superego's demands are often contrary to those of the id. The ego is the mediator between these two opposing forces. Conflict often arises in the course of the ego's attempt to reconcile the demands of the id and the superego, and this conflict produces anxiety. Freudian theorists identify three different types of anxiety. *Reality anxiety* occurs when we are threatened by something in the environment. The threat may be either physical or psychological, but it signifies real danger in the external world. *Moral anxiety* is fear of conscience—we feel guilty when we do, or even think of, something contrary to our moral code. *Neurotic anxiety* is the fear that our instincts will get out of control and make us do something for which we will be punished. It is not so much a fear of the instincts themselves as of punishment for following them.

In Freudian terms, neurotic anxiety occurs when the unconscious forces of the id are in conflict with the superego. The anxiety is a warning signal to the ego that some unacceptable id impulse is about to surface. When this warning is sounded, the ego develops a strategy to reduce the anxiety by reducing the conflict. Thus we may either inhibit or ignore the impulse or obey our conscience; in either case, the conflict is resolved (for the moment). When the ego cannot cope by these direct methods, we turn to defense mechanisms (which will be discussed later in the chapter).

The Learning Model

When experimental psychologists began to study anxiety, they translated Freud's theories into stimulus-response terms and concluded that anxiety is a learned autonomic or internal response. The experimental data produced by Mowrer and Miller are the basis of this learning model of anxiety. However, to describe anxiety in experimental terms, we must include both classical and operant conditioning processes.

An organism can be conditioned to fear a neutral stimulus through classical conditioning techniques. In one experiment (Miller, 1948), for example, rats were shocked repeatedly while a tone was sounded. After many trials of pairing shock and tone the rats showed fear at the sound of the tone alone: The tone had become a conditioned stimulus for the fear response. In other words, the rats had acquired fear through *classical conditioning*.

The rats also learned new responses to avoid the sound of the tone (the conditioned stimulus), and thus they learned new responses to avoid fear (the conditioned response). This part of the learning model uses the principles of *operant conditioning*. The new response was rewarded by the fear reduction brought about by avoiding a previously conditioned stimulus, the tone. The interesting point here is that the rats learned new behavior to avoid a stimulus that in itself was harmless—the tone didn't hurt them, and yet to escape the tone was reinforcing.

Miller and Dollard thus translated Freud's controversial psychoanalytic model of anxiety into stimulus-response terms (Dollard and Miller, 1950). The anxiety that Freud had described as the ego's battle to mediate conflicting id and superego demands was seen by Miller as a learned response; Freud's defense mechanisms were interpreted as learned avoidance responses to alleviate anxiety.

The learning model gave psychologists a new way of studying and analyzing complicated inner feelings such as anxiety. But, like Freud's theory, it should not be accepted uncritically. There is very little evidence that *humans* can be classically conditioned to fear neutral stimuli. Fear is usually extinguished rather quickly when the conditioned stimulus is presented a few times without shock. Some real-life cases do support the idea of learned anxiety—soldiers under fire may develop shell shock, victims of a plane crash may develop a phobia about flying. But not everyone who has these terrible experiences "learns" anxiety from them. When a platoon is under fire some soldiers may develop shell shock and some may not. Some people who have never been on a plane, or have only had perfectly normal experiences on a plane, have a terrible fear of flying.

The Humanistic-Existential Model

Humanistic and existential psychologists see anxiety as resulting from people's failure to achieve their fullest potential and take full responsibility for their lives. Humanists assume that people are motivated to "self-actualize," that is, realize personal fulfillment. Through faulty learning or the diversion of energies to more basic needs, they may fail to achieve self-actualization. This failure to live up to one's potential leads to anxiety-producing self-devaluation that, as in the psychoanalytic model, must be defended against.

What the existentialists add to this theory is the idea that people are responsible for their own self-actualization. According to the existentialists, the individual is constantly aware of "nonbeing" or death, and this concern with nonbeing leads to *existential anxiety,* the fear that one is not leading a meaningful life.

The Biological Model

Psychologists who look at the physiological basis of behavior consider anxiety a biological event. Anxiety, then, is a set of physiological responses to demands placed upon the individual. Indeed, physiological change is one of the most widely used indicators of stress reactions because it is concrete and measurable. Heart rate, respiratory activity, endocrine secretions, sweat gland activity, temperature, and blood pressure are all altered in stressful conditions.

Much of our understanding of the physiology of stress comes from the pioneering work of Hans Selye. As a young medical student, Selye observed physical reactions that were common to most patients, and ascribed them to a general malaise associated with being ill, no matter what the illness. This gave him the idea that there might be a general pattern of reaction to stress that did not differ according to the source of the stress. He called this pattern the General Adaptation Syndrome.

THE GENERAL ADAPTATION SYNDROME. This syndrome is described by Selye (1976) as a three-stage response that begins with an alarm reaction. The *alarm reaction* is characterized by a number of physical changes: increases in heart rate, respiratory activity, endocrine secretions, sweat gland activity, temperature, and blood pressure, as well as muscle tension. You may have observed these reactions in yourself when you are under stress.

In the second stage, the *stage of resistance,* people recover from the initial alarm and try to cope with the stressful situation. The external physical symptoms of stress disappear and the internal responses to stress—hormone activity, heart rate, and blood pressure—become normalized. In this stage everything appears to be under control, but the appearance is deceptive. In

Looking for a job or being trapped in a job we dislike can be a great source of anxiety. Humanistic-existential psychologists would say that the reason this causes anxiety is because we feel unable to achieve our full potential under such circumstances.

fact, the person's emotional and physical resources are being consumed by his or her efforts to control the stress. If the stressful condition continues, the person will enter the third stage—*exhaustion*. If a new stress arises during the stage of resistance, a person will often break down and enter the exhaustion phase immediately.

The adrenal glands play a major role in the General Adaptation Syndrome. The adrenal medulla is controlled by the sympathetic nervous system (see Chapter 2). When it is stimulated in response to some form of excitement, it secretes quantities of epinephrine and norepinephrine into the blood. These hormones increase metabolism and help the body to release energy stores, which causes the physical reactions described as part of the alarm reaction.

The stage of resistance is characterized by increased activity of the adrenal cortex. In order to function, the adrenal cortex must be stimulated by the hormone ACTH, which is produced by the pituitary gland. When an organism is subjected to stress, the pituitary secretions increase. This, in turn, causes the adrenal cortex to produce more hormones. Some of the effects of these hormones on other parts of the body are maintenance of blood pressure, manufacture of red blood cells, blocking of the inflammatory response, and increased blood sugar level.

It is not surprising that with all these physiological responses to stress, people who are exposed to stress over a long period of time often become ill. In the next section we will look at some of these stress-linked disorders.

PSYCHOSOMATIC ILLNESSES. Stress-linked disorders, such as ulcers, migraine, asthma, eczema, and high blood pressure, are called *psychosomatic illnesses*. Scientists who have studied these disorders have been confronted with a number of questions. Why, for example, do some people become ill from stress while others do not? Why does stress cause a physical illness instead of an emotional one? Why does one person get ulcers from stress while another has a heart attack?

Many theories have been developed to answer these questions. One, the *somatic weakness theory,* holds that weakened body systems are vulnerable to stress. People whose lungs have been weakened by smoking are predisposed to asthma when they come under stress. In people whose lungs are healthy, the stress reaction might affect some other area of the body. Genetic factors, diet, and life-style all interact to produce weaknesses in the body's systems.

The *specific-reaction theory,* on the other hand, says that psychosomatic illnesses are the result of the individual's unique reaction to stress. This reaction may be genetically determined. One individual, for example, experiences rapid acceleration of heartbeat under stress. Another produces excess stomach acid. These reactions may determine which system of the body will be prone to a stress-linked disorder.

Finally, the *diathesis-stress theory* holds that it is some combination of environment, stress, and biological predisposition that interacts to produce specific disorders. This view explains, in part, why different people exposed to the same set of stressors develop different symptoms. A person with a predisposition to secrete high levels of pepsinogen is more likely to develop an ulcer when exposed to prolonged environmental stress than one who has a weak respiratory system. The latter person may develop breathing difficulties instead.

One final point before we go on to describe specific disorders. The term *psychosomatic illness* is often misused. Psychosomatic disorders are real physical illnesses that should be treated by a medical doctor. Quite often, because such disorders have a psychological stress component, they are confused with types of neurotic physical symptoms (to be discussed in Chapter 16) that exist primarily in the patient's mind.

Hypertension, or high blood pressure, is one disorder that has been linked to stress. Essential hypertension is chronic high blood pressure that cannot be traced to an organic cause. Acceleration of the heartbeat, often experienced under stress, has something to do with high blood pressure. More important, experts feel, is the constriction of the walls of the arteries, a phenomenon that also occurs under stress. This constriction forces the heart to work harder to drive the blood through the narrowed arteries.

Much research has been done on the link between stress and hypertension. Numerous studies show an association between stress and a short-term rise in blood pressure (Hokanson et al., 1971; Dembroski et al., 1978). These studies consistently demonstrate that people respond to the threat of shock or to challenge with increased blood pressure. However, the blood pressure returns to normal after a short period of time. Long-term or chronic hypertension has been found in people who have lost their jobs (Kasl and Colb, 1970), people who experience daily traffic congestion while commuting (Stokols, Novaco, Stokols, and Campbell, 1978), and even people who are undergoing the stressful experience of hospitalization (Volicer and Volicer, 1977). How these periodic environmental stressors translate into chronic hypertension has not yet been established.

Another set of physiological responses to stress occurs in the *gastrointestinal* system. The body reacts to a stressor by secreting certain hormones that serve to direct energy toward battling the stressor and away from momentarily less important bodily functions such as digestion. Thus in response to stress there is an increase in the flow of the stomach's acidic digestive juices along with an engorgement of the stomach with blood. As a result, the mucous lining of the stomach is stretched out and subjected to excessive amounts of gastric acid. After prolonged exposure to such acids, the mucous layer is eaten through, resulting in ulceration of the stomach wall. Certain individuals seem predisposed to produce high levels of gastric acid. If these people are exposed to prolonged stress, they have an increased likelihood of developing an ulcer.

Stress has been shown also to have effects on the respiratory system that induce asthmatic attacks in some people. Increases in mucus secretion and steroids, increased breathing rates, and constriction of bronchial pathways are all attributable to increased emotionality. Despite the evidence that stress has adverse effects on the respiratory system, there is some debate over the role of stress in the development of asthma, since infections and allergies can also trigger asthmatic reactions. It now seems certain that asthma is a disorder of multiple causation. In an attempt to prove that stress, as well as allergens, could bring on an asthma attack, Dekke (1956) and his associates tested a group of asthmatics. They interviewed them about the kinds of stressful situations that had preceded attacks in the past, then reproduced those situations in the lab. The results of the study show that stress was as capable of causing an attack as any allergen.

Since asthma is quite often a childhood disorder, the role of the family as a source of psychological stress has been examined. For example, a study by Rees (1963) supports the notion that parent-child relationships are a factor in childhood asthma. He found that compared to parents of a control group of children, twice as many parents of asthmatic children were overprotective, rejecting, or perfectionistic. Such parental attitudes could, of course, create an environment sufficiently stressful to aggravate asthmatic symptoms. However, Parker and Lipscombe (1979) recently presented data that show that such parental attitudes are a *result* of having an asthmatic child rather than a cause. Of course, it is still possible that stressful parent-child relationships are an important factor in the *maintenance* of asthmatic conditions.

STRESS AND GENERAL HEALTH.   Recently the focus of research has shifted from how stress leads to a particular psychosomatic illness to how stress affects our health in general.

One set of questions follows from Selye's General Adaptation Syndrome model of reactions to stress. You will recall that one of the physical consequences of adapting to stress is the stage of exhaustion that results in a lowered resistance to infection. Lowered resistance should increase the likelihood of the occurrence of some type of disease. This phenomenon has been studied especially in connection with the kind of stress that accompanies certain life changes. The Social Readjustment Rating Scale has proved to be an invaluable tool in studying this kind of stress. It lists 43 common life events, ranging from the death of a spouse to minor legal problems.

In setting up this scale for the first time, Rahe and Holmes (1967) asked participants to rate each of 43 life events according to the degree of social readjustment called for in response to them. All comparisons were made against marriage, which was assigned an arbitrary value; participants were supposed to judge whether each event listed called for more or less readjustment than marriage. Ratings did not depend on the desirability of the event—it could be positively or negatively viewed—but only on the amount of readjustment required. Consensus was high among participants in the first rating experiment, and it has continued to be high in subsequent experiments, even among adolescents who presumably have not themselves experienced a number of these life changes.

Each of these events was then assigned a value, called a Life Change Unit (LCU). The more stressful an event, the higher its LCU value. But again, the emphasis is on change rather than on the psychological meaning, emotion, or social desirability of the event. The events ranged in stressfulness from death of a spouse down to a vacation or a minor law violation.

The scale has proved to be a useful tool in measuring the relationship between life change and health change. In the typical experiment using the Social Readjustment Rating Scale, people are asked to indicate which of the events listed on the questionnaire happened to them over a fixed time period, 6 months to 1 year ago or 1 year to 2 years ago. The stress value for each event is multiplied by the number of times the event occurred and the values for all events are totaled to produce a score in Life Change Units for the specific time period. Researchers then look at the relationship between Life Change Units, a quantified amount of adaptation, and illness in the individuals.

For example, in one study Rahe and Holmes asked 80 resident physicians to list all the major health changes they had experienced over the preceding 10 years, along with when they had occurred. The physicians also reported on the life changes they had experienced in the same period. Ninety-six diseases or changes in health status were reported. Ninety-three percent of these were associated with a significant life change. The more serious the life change was, the more likely it was to be accompanied by an illness. Most of the health changes occurred about a year after the life change. They included infectious diseases as well as psychophysiological illnesses.

In another study the magnitude of Life Change Units was recorded for victims of coronary heart disease as reported by their kin (Rahe, Romo, Bennett, and Siltanen, 1974). Compared to a 6-month interval 1 year before the coronary, victims had experienced a 50 to 100 percent increase in LCUs in the 6 months *immediately* before the heart attack. An even more dramatic finding was that victims who died from the coronary had experienced an average increase in LCUs of 100 to 200 percent over that 6-month period immediately before the illness.

We should be cautious in interpreting these findings because they are based on retrospective reports that may not be highly accurate. For example, people who are trying to understand their illnesses may recall and interpret past events inaccurately. Also, recent research suggests that negative changes and changes that result from loss are more predictive of future illness than positive changes (Glass, 1977). It seems clear, however, that the cumulative effects of adapting to environmental demands lower the body's resistance to disease.

So far we have been concerned with how individuals respond to stress in terms of *physical* reactions and vulnerabilities. But individuals also differ widely in their perception of what is or is not stressful, and this perception determines their reactions to stress. For this view we will turn to the cognitive model.

The Cognitive Model

The stress experience is more than the sum total of the stressors to which one is exposed. Therefore we should revise our definition of stress to acknowledge the role that the individual plays in the experience of stress. Cox (1978) has described stress as a transaction between people and their environments in which the critical mediating variable is people's *perception* of demand and of their own ability to cope with it. A more useful definition of stress, then, views stress as composed of three elements. First, there is a set of environmental events that may or may not be potentially stressful. Second, there is the individual's cognitive appraisal of the environmental events. And finally, based on the outcome of that appraisal, there is the stress reaction and coping. Of course, there are events that are stressful for everyone. But many events are less well defined and open to the interpretation of the people perceiving them. Let us look now at the role of cognitive appraisal in the experience of stress.

Researchers have provided a number of valuable insights into the roles of predictability and control in coping with stress. They have observed, for

Table 15–1: Life-Change Units Scale.

Life Event	Value
Death of spouse	100
Divorce	73
Marital separation	65
Jail term	63
Death of a close family member	63
Personal injury or illness	53
Marriage	50
Being fired from work	47
Marital reconciliation	45
Retirement	45
Change in health of family member	44
Pregnancy	40
Sex difficulties	39
Change in financial state	38
Death of close friend	37
Change to different line of work	36
Mortgage over $10,000	31
Foreclosure of mortgage or loan	30
Change in responsibilities at work	29
Son or daughter leaving home	29
Trouble with in-laws	29
Outstanding personal achievement	28
Wife beginning or stopping work	26
Beginning or ending school	26
Trouble with boss	23
Change in work hours or conditions	20
Change in residence	20
Change in social activities	18
Mortgage or loan of less than $10,000	17
Change in sleeping habits	16
Change in eating habits	15
Vacation	13
Minor violations of the law	11

From Holmes and Rahe (1967).

example, that when people believe they have some control over a stressor—when they think they can escape it, avoid it, or even just predict it—they will have a milder stress reaction to it. This reduction of stress is based entirely on people's *perception* of their control, not on how much control they actually have.

Geer, Davison, and Gatchel (1970) tested the relationship between perception of control and stress reduction. Their two-part study involved a group of college students. In the first part of the experiment the students were each given 10 trials in which they had to press a reaction-time switch as they felt an electric shock. The shock, which lasted 6 seconds, was always preceded by a 10-second warning signal.

In the second part of the experiment the students were divided into two groups. One group was told that the shock would be reduced to 3 seconds if their reactions became faster. The second group was told only that the shocks would be shorter in duration. In other words, the second group was not told anything that would lead them to believe they would have any control over the duration of the shock.

Stress levels were measured by the galvanic skin response (GSR), a widely accepted gauge of stress. The results showed that in the second part of the experiment the students who felt they had some degree of control over the shocks experienced less stress than those who believed they had none. This difference was observed despite the fact that both groups received exactly the same amount of shock.

Other studies have demonstrated that control over avoidance responses can lead to reduced stress experiences. Hokanson and his colleagues (1971) tested the stress avoidance hypothesis with two groups of college students. Both groups were assigned a learning task. Students who failed to master it received an electrical shock. One group was given the option of asking for "time out" from the stress of learning. The other group received the same number and length of rest periods as the first group, but these students had no control over when the "time outs" occurred.

The students' blood pressure was measured to indicate their stress level. When the researchers analyzed and compared the blood pressure levels of the two groups, they found that the students who could control when they escaped the shock showed less stress (had lower blood pressure) than those who could not. Thus the knowledge that one *could* take a rest as desired was associated with reduced stress (see Figure 15-2).

Langer, Janis, and Wolfer, researchers at Yale, took this hypothesis out of the laboratory and into the field for further testing. Their subjects were patients who were scheduled for surgery in a large hospital.

One group of patients was encouraged to practice a coping exercise to help them avoid stress. They were told they could minimize postoperative psychological and physical discomforts by regulating their own attitudes. In the first part of this coping exercise patients were shown the degree to which attention and cognitions about an aversive event determine the stress one experiences with regard to that event. They were taught to use cognitive control through selective attention, which consisted of concentrating on the favorable aspects of the situation, rather than trying to ignore the event entirely. This served to distract the patients from the negative aspects of surgery.

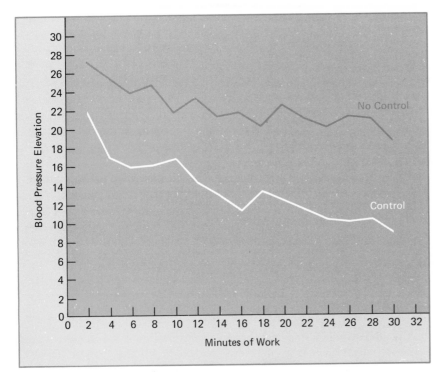

Figure 15-2

The graph shows the results of a study by Hokanson et al. (1971). Students who had control over when they escaped the shock showed less stress (had lower blood pressure) than students who had no control.

A second group of patients was given reassuring information about the surgery and postoperative period. The information was designed to reduce stress by making the upcoming experience understandable. A third group received a combination of these approaches—control exercises and information. A fourth group, the control group, received no special attention.

As might be expected from the data gathered in other experiments, the stress control exercises, which gave the patients some feeling of control and allowed them to avoid stress, were the most effective of all the methods in alleviating pre- and postoperative tension and pain. While the informational approach had some effect on preoperative tension, it had no measurable impact on postoperative stress.

Psychologists have learned that when we attribute stress to our own failings we have a more difficult experience than when we attribute it to some uncontrollable situation. A test conducted by Wortman (1976) and associates at Northwestern University shows the role of attribution at work in a stress situation. In this experiment subjects were given problem-solving exercises. They were told that if they solved the problems correctly, they could prevent a burst of loud, unpleasant noise. The subjects were given false feedback on their performances. They were told that they were getting many problems wrong and thus all received the burst of loud, unpleasant noise, which served as the physical stressor. In addition, some were told that their poor performance showed incompetence and lack of attention, while others were told they had done poorly because the problems themselves were extremely hard.

After the feedback had been given, the subjects were asked to continue

APPLICATION
Anatomy of an Illness, by Norman Cousins

In 1964, Norman Cousins, a writer for the *Saturday Review*, returned home from a trip abroad suffering from what seemed to be the flu. Within a week, however, a mild fever and general feeling of achiness deteriorated into partial paralysis. He was hospitalized, and although there was no agreement on a precise diagnosis, there was general concensus that Cousins was suffering from a serious illness that affected the connective tissue. One fact was agreed upon: He had only one chance in 500 of a full recovery.

Despite this prognosis, by 1975 Cousins had returned to work and assumed his normal activities. His book, *Anatomy of an Illness as Perceived by the Patient,* details his recovery from this "incurable" disease. To what does Cousins attribute his "miraculous" recovery? The answer he gives is surprisingly simple: Since I didn't accept the verdict, I wasn't trapped in the cycle of fear, depression and panic that frequently accompanies a supposedly incurable illness. I must not make it seem, however, that I was unmindful of the seriousness of the problem or that I was in a festive mood throughout. Being unable to move my body was all the evidence I needed that the specialists were dealing with real concerns. But deep down I knew I had a good chance and relished the idea of bucking the odds. (Cousins, 1979, p. 1462)

Cousins reasoned that if negative emotional states could affect the body chemistry negatively, then positive emotions can produce positive changes. Encouraged by his doctor, he prescribed for himself a unique course of treatment based on the "chemistry of the will to live."

Convinced that a hosptial setting, in which routine and regularity take precedence over the patient's needs, would not be conducive to inspiring positive emotions, Cousins relocated to a hotel room, where he began a systematic program of laughter therapy. He watched hours of "Candid Camera" and Marx Brothers and Laurel and Hardy movies. Ten minutes of genuine belly laughter, he said, had an anesthetic effect, and would allow him at least hours of pain-free sleep. For Cousins, at least, laughter was good medicine.

Is it possible, as Cousins asks, that "love, hope, faith, laughter, confidence, and the will to live had therapeutic value?" His case can be considered along with the many experimental studies demonstrating the power of placebos—it has been suggested that Cousins was the beneficiary of a "mammoth venture in self-administered placebos." While it would be unwise to suggest that the mobilization of a patient's hope and faith can substitute for medical treatment, from Cousin's case we see that it would also be unwise to underestimate its value.

---

with the problem solving. As might be expected, those subjects who attributed their failure to their own incompetency had greater stress reactions than those who attributed it to the extreme difficulty of the task.

These studies provide evidence for the wide range of situations in which people's perceptions determine the magnitude of the ensuing stress reaction.

Now let us turn to how people cope with stress.

Coping

Everyone has his or her own characteristic way of handling stress—indeed, people often can be characterized by the way they handle stress. Psychologists have used a number of different approaches to study how we cope with stress, and have even combined several of the models that we looked at earlier (such as biological and cognitive).

Defense Mechanisms: The Psychoanalytical Model

Some of the most common ways of dealing with stress are described in the psychoanalytical model as defense mechanisms. As mentioned earlier, defense mechanisms are automatic and unconscious reactions arising out of the id-superego conflict. A defense mechanism works in one of two ways: (1) It blocks a sexual or aggressive impulse and thus relieves the anxiety and guilt caused by such impulses; or (2) it changes the nature of the impulse itself and both relieves the guilt and anxiety and allows some gratification of the now-transformed impulse.

Freud and his followers identified several strategies that people use to cope with stress or anxiety stemming from intrapsychic conflict.

REPRESSION. People who use this coping method exclude all their drive thoughts and feelings from consciousness. Evidence of repression is underreaction to a relevant situation and indirect indications that the repressed tendencies are actually present. A nasty insult usually elicits some response—a flushed face, a clenched fist, an angry retort—but repression prevents these reactions. One can almost observe the person withdrawing attention from thoughts and sensations in the body—one can sometimes even see the body go limp, especially when a person is repressing anger.

DISPLACEMENT. Repression leads directly to displacement because the most common type of repressive barricade is to focus attention on a substitute—to displace attention. If you have ever been angry at a boss or a professor and were unable to express that anger to that person, you may have found yourself lashing out at your roommate or a stranger in the street. Because you could not show anger at the person who provoked it, you displaced that anger onto a more acceptable target.

PROJECTION. One way to block repressed thoughts and feelings is to attribute them to another person. This is called projection. A man who feels guilty about his aggressive business practices may attribute to his opponents the same practices, and claim their actions made it necessary for him to retaliate. Projection locates the responsibility for one's behavior outside oneself and removes the guilt and conflict that behavior would otherwise cause.

REACTION FORMATION. In reaction formation we reverse our unacceptable feelings. For example, a man may hate his mother because she nags him and makes extraordinary demands on him. The conflict between his angry impulses and his superego's command to honor and love his parents causes him anxiety and guilt. To relieve those feelings, he unconsciously converts his hatred into exaggerated love and devotion and acts like a model son. We sometimes hold a number of deeply felt attitudes that are the direct opposites of our repressed attitudes.

NEGATION. This is another way of refusing to acknowlege unacceptable feelings. The difference between negation and reaction formation is that in negation the feeling is expressed, but with a "negative sign" next to it. Take the example of the man who hates his mother. If his method of coping with the stress this hatred involves is reaction formation, he will say, "I love my mother." If he uses negation to cope, he will state, emphatically, "I don't hate my mother." And often he will make this statement out of the blue, when no one has been questioning or challenging his feelings about his mother.

If he states his love angrily, he will be able to get rid of the anger he is feeling without acknowledging its unacceptable source.

INTELLECTUALIZATION.   This is simply an exaggerated preference for thought over feeling. A person who uses this defense mechanism will talk about sexual or aggressive matters in a very cool, abstract way, without experiencing any of the feelings most of us would have discussing the same things. Teenagers often use this defense mechanism in "bull sessions" in which sexual matters are discussed in the abstract. Intellectualization helps teenagers to get through many of the conflicts that are inevitable in growing up.

UNDOING.   Undoing means following an unacceptable act with one that negates it, thus relieving the guilt and anxiety that resulted from the first act. It is the only defense mechanism that is an "after the fact" response. The other defense mechanisms operate to prevent unacceptable thoughts or feelings from occurring. A husband who habitually argues with his wife in the morning and then brings her flowers when he comes home from work is using the undoing defense. He would be quite surprised if you confronted him with this pattern, though, and would deny that was what he was doing.

REGRESSION.   In this type of defensive behavior a person flees anxiety by retreating into behavior appropriate to an earlier, seemingly safer stage in life. A little girl going through the stress of entering school for the first time may begin to act in a very babyish way: She may suck her thumb, wet her bed, or insist on being carried by her mother or father instead of walking.

SUBLIMATION.   This is the channeling of unacceptable urges and feelings into acceptable activities. Freud interpreted the madonnas painted by the great Leonardo da Vinci as an example of sublimation of the Oedipal feelings—in other words, Leonardo dealt with an unresolved Oedipal conflict by transforming his feelings about his mother into art. Sublimation allows an individual to express repressed, sadistic urges in constructive activities, such as surgery.

Freud believed that the intellectual curiosity of the adult was a sublimation of the child's sexual curiosity. The inhibitions of creativity that he saw in adults seemed to him to derive from the strong repression of childhood sexual curiosity.

Defense mechanisms are very much a part of normal behavior. But, according to Freud, their overuse is a symptom of neurosis. Overuse means either carrying a defense to an extreme, such as marked regression to a childish state, or habitually resorting to the same defense, such as a lifelong repression of sexual feelings.

The Freudian theory of defense mechanisms is but one interpretation of the way people cope with psychological stress. We will now look at coping habits from a combination of approaches.

Patterns of Coping: A Combination of Models

HELPLESSNESS: THE LEARNING AND COGNITIVE MODELS.   Learning theorists suggest that the various methods people use to cope with stress are the result of learning specific response-reinforcement relationships.

An interesting extension of this idea can be found in the work of Martin Seligman and his colleagues. They discovered that dogs exposed to inescapable shock while learning a task later fail to learn a second task in the absence of electric shocks. What is most interesting about these studies is that the animals appear to give up—they stop responding entirely. Seligman has labeled this state "learned helplessness" because what the animals are learning is that there is no connection between their responding and the outcome, or what happens to them.

Learned helplessness has also been demonstrated in humans (Hiroto and Seligman, 1975). It seems that experiences with uncontrollability leads to deficits in learning. People learn that their responses do not affect the outcome of events, and this learned attitude prevents them from acquiring other knowledge or behavior patterns that would help them to gain control over their environment. In particular, learning deficits are characterized by reduced responding.

A person manifesting learned helplessness closely resembles a depressed individual. In fact, some learning theorists have reasoned that learned helplessness explains depression in human beings. However, the issue here is that giving up and doing nothing is one way of coping with stressful situations. It is at times a beneficial strategy, since giving up can be accompanied by reduced stress responses (Gatchel and Proctor, 1976).

While learning theorists see learned helplessness as an entirely learned mode of responding, recent research disputes this. The absence of control over a situation is a key factor in the experience of helplessness, and you will recall that control, in part, depends on a person's perceptions and attributions. Investigations have shown that those who blame themselves for their failure to control a situation have little reason to try to cope with similar situations in the future. On the other hand, people who attribute their failure to control a situation to the situation itself do not become helpless in later situations (Tennen and Eller, 1977). Again, it is the individual's interpretation of the situational demand that determines the stress reaction.

TYPE A BEHAVIOR PATTERNS.   Our discussion so far might have suggested that the perception of control over stress is a good way to combat or reduce stress in our lives. However, one particular kind of coping response calls this idea into question. The coping response is called the Type A or coronary-prone behavior pattern (Friedman, 1969). When confronted by a stressful situation in which they feel they have lost control, Type A individuals struggle to reassert the control they think they have lost. They work faster, strive harder, and become more aggressive. After extended periods of uncontrollable stress, however, Type A people show a dramatic decline in their attempts to gain control of the situation. In contrast, when non-coronary–prone people, called Type B (Glass, 1977), encounter stress, their reactions are calmer and more even. They show neither frantic attempts to gain control in the beginning nor a lack of assertive energy when the stress is prolonged.

You have probably observed many Type A people in your own life. They tend to be impatient, aggressive, competitive individuals who are filled with a sense of urgency. A traffic jam can send a Type A person into a fit of anger—a Type A person cannot stand to be kept waiting even for a few minutes. Type B persons, in contrast, tend to be more relaxed, more accepting of events and occurrences, less rushed.

HIGHLIGHT
Can Stress Be Beneficial?

Can stress *ever* be physiologically beneficial? The positive effects of stress are the provocative subject of a series of studies conducted by Thomas Landauer and his colleague John Whiting (1978).

The impetus for their investigations can be traced to a well-documented though controversial phenomena reported in the late 1950s. It appears that rat pups exposed to a variety of stressors, such as handling, removal from the nest, and painful electric shocks, were tamer, less emotional, and physically larger as adults than rats without stress exposure. However, this happened only if the stressful treatment occurred in the first few weeks of life (within the critical period of growth and development). Taking this lead, Landauer and Whiting sought to determine whether long-term, positive effects of stress could be found for humans as well. Since with rats the most

reliable result of acute stress was an acceleration of physical growth, the researchers focused on finding comparable evidence of stress-related physical growth in adult humans.

One can not subject humans, particularly human infants, to stress-inducing experimental treatments to determine the consequences at adulthood, even if one suspects that those consequences will be positive! Fortunately, an alternative avenue of research was available: Many societies around the world customarily subject infants to a variety of stressful practices, so that a cross-cultural comparison of the effects of "naturally occurring" early stress experiences on later growth and development was possible.

First, researchers categorized societies around the world into those that carefully protected infants during their first few years

and those that subjected them to stress. Societies that were categorized in the stress-inducing group were those that had ritual practices such as circumcision, piercing of the nose, lips, or ears, scarring by cutting or burning, molding of body parts, and physical separation from the mother. One could hardly disagree with the researchers that these events would prove stressful to an infant!

The age criterion for early stress was 2 years, prompted by the fact that this is the average age of weaning in most primitive cultures, and thus could be considered the infant's critical period. The data on growth rates of adults for each of these societies was then independently obtained.

The critical analysis of over 30 societies did indeed yield a correlation between early infant stress and accelerated growth. In societies that had ritual infant

Moreover, attributional processes have also been linked to Type A behavior. Studies have shown that Type A individuals' need to be in control results from their general tendency to see themselves as the causes of all events in their lives (Rhodewalt, 1979). So we see again the importance of cognitive factors not only in our reactions to stressful events but also as contributors to stressful experiences.

HARDINESS.   It might be helpful (as well as encouraging) to look at the positive side of the phenomenon of stress. There are some personality traits that make it *easier* for a person to handle stress. A recent study by Kobasa (1979) at the University of Chicago suggests that our personalities differ in terms of *hardiness*. When "hardy" people are confronted by stress, they are less likely to feel overwhelmed or to become ill. What characteristics make up this trait?

Kobasa studied two groups of executives who had all experienced stressful life events within the past 3 years. Those in one group had become physically ill following the events, while those in the other had not. The hardy executives possessed three characteristics that the others did not: They had a great feeling of control; they had a strong sense of commitment to specific goals in their lives; and they viewed change as a challenge rather than as a threat.

stress practices, adult stature was on the average 2.6 inches greater than in societies where such stress was absent. Further, the growth effect is most pronounced if the stress is present within the first 2 years, confirming assumptions about a critical period for a stress-related effect.

However, one must keep in mind that a correlation between stress and growth is not conclusive evidence of a causal relationship between the two variables. It is possible that a third variable, which is itself correlated with infant stress, may be responsible for greater growth rates. For example, if societies with stressful infant care practices also have diets that include more protein, this would produce a reliable correlation between stress and growth, but would obscure the true cause—diet. In addition to diet, other possible third variable candidates may be genetic differences or factors associated with the culture's geographic region. The researchers' task, then, was to show that the correlation reported was in fact due to the presence or absence of stress and not due to one of these unmeasured variables. To do this, Landauer and Whiting compared cultures that differed only in the presence or absence of infant stress practices. The results of their analysis indicated that when diet, genetic makeup, and geographic region are eliminated, there was no effect on the size of the stress-stature correlation.

Landauer and Whiting also conducted a controlled experiment on the effects of early vaccination. Infantile vaccinations are a fairly benign and ultimately beneficial stress procedure, universal in Western but not African countries. The study was done in a community in Kenya in 1968 and involved giving smallpox vaccinations to a randomly chosen sample of children before the age of 2, and the rest between 2 and 6 years of age. In 1973 followup, measures of the children's growth were made. The results were that children vaccinated before the age of 2 had grown more in the intervening years than those vaccinated later.

Furthermore, working on the assumption that these differences in growth rates may generalize to neurological and intellectual development rates, assessments of each child's cognitive abilities were made. Comparable with the data on acceleration of physical stature, the results indicated an approximately 4-month acceleration in cognitive development. While Landauer and Whiting admit that the results on intellectual acceleration are far from conclusive, these results are intriguing, because they lead to the argument that stress can have beneficial effects on an individual's health, growth, and survival.

Quite at odds with our intuitive notions, it seems that if stress is to have a positive effect on development it must occur within the first 2 years of the infant's life, a period when the child is both vulnerable and helpless. It's possible that acute stress-inducing stimuli occurring at this time may cause changes in the functioning of the pituitary-adrenal system, perhaps mediating the growth effect and later responses to stress. However, this is just speculation. Only additional research will provide us with answers.

Let us give a short example of how such a hardy executive would meet a stressful life event. Say this person is a middle-aged male executive with a wife and children who is being transferred to a new job. This change means he will have to learn to cope with new subordinates and supervisors, find a new home, help his children and wife adjust to new schools and a new neighborhood, learn new job skills, and so on. The hardy executive approaches these readjustments with (1) a clear sense of his values, goals and capabilities, and belief in their importance; and (2) a strong tendency toward active involvement with his environment. He does not passively accept the job transfer; he throws himself into the new situation. He is able to judge the impact of a job transfer on his life and his established priorities. For him, the job transfer can be a step in the right direction. He also—and this very important—feels that although the transfer is a result of orders from above, it is up to him to make a success of it. In other words, he does not experience himself as a victim of threatening change, but rather as an active determinant of the outcome of that change.

Further work in this area may enable social scientists to do more than merely warn people to avoid stressful lives. New studies may show us how to develop the characteristics that can aid in a productive and healthy life.

COPING AND ADAPTATION.   Because we are confronted with psychological stress in some form every day of our lives, we become adept at coping with it. If we are continually confronted with a certain stressor, our coping results in adaptation. The constant noise of a big city, for example, is stressful to a person who has just arrived from the country, but the country-bred visitor who decides to stay in town will gradually adapt to the noise level. The stress response to the noise will diminish and he or she will become less and less sensitive to it.

The ability to adapt to the environment distinguishes living organisms from inanimate matter, and this ability has been one key to survival. Adaptation has made it possible for the human race to thrive in rigorous climates. It has enabled people to endure and emerge from the horrors of war, concentration camps, and natural disasters. On a less dramatic level, it helps us to weather the pressure of deadlines and examinations, the pains of surgery, the trauma of a loved one's death, the overcrowded conditions in our cities. But we pay a price for our adaptability.

When people adapt to stress their responses seem to be minimized. Noise, for example, that might once have disturbed them is hardly noticed. Crowds that might have once made them feel panicky no longer arouse their fears. This adaptation, however, may be only superficial. Continued exposure to a stressor may cause a buildup of stress effects that explode when the stressor is removed. When the period of coping is over, a double dose of reaction sets in, reaction to the stressor *and* to the strain of coping (Glass and Singer, 1972).

One study of men who had just completed a stressful and demanding army training course bears this out. Although the men adapted successfully to the training, they experienced severe anxiety right after graduation. In accord with Selye's General Adaptation Syndrome, Glass and Singer conclude that "adaptive effort may leave people less able to cope with later environmental demands and frustrations, and this reduction in coping ability may be the psychic cost of adaptation to stressful events." In other words, sooner or later you feel the effects of stress—coping makes life easier for the moment, but then you pay the price for having coped.

The constant use of a coping response may in itself produce stress, as was observed in the Type A coronary-prone behavior pattern. Glass and Singer note that the aftereffects of adaptation may take the form of physical and mental disease, psychosomatic disorders, performance and learning deficits, and general social-emotional maladjustments. These aftereffects may not be apparent for a long time. Milgram (1970), studying the effects of urban living, observed that cognitive overload typified city dwellers. Because they have to evaluate and adapt to so many stimuli, they devote less and less attention to each one. This eventually results in the cold attitude often associated with city people: lack of interest in others, unwillingness to aid strangers, rudeness, and lack of social responsibility.

Although stress and our adaptation to it has some negative effects, it also has some benefits. A number of experiments show that laboratory animals who are stressed early in life by handling, electrical shock, or paw pinching function better as adults than do their nonstressed litter mates. They outperform them and are more adaptable to novel or stressful situations.

One way to appreciate the beneficial effects of stress is to observe the effects of a lack of stress. Sensory deprivation studies, in which both animal and human subjects have been deprived of all stimulation, suggest that the total absence of stress is in itself stressful.

Special Issues in Stress and Adjustment

Extreme Situational Stress

We mentioned earlier in this chapter that stress can cause physical illness. Heart disease, high blood pressure, ulcers, and intestinal problems such as colitis are some of the illnesses that have been linked to psychological stress.

Situations of exceptional tension—war, catastrophe, physical assault—often produce characteristic stress reactions. One of the most common of these is combat fatigue. First described by a British pathologist during World War I who named it "shell shock," combat fatigue is characterized by dejection, severe depression, hypersensitivity, sleep disturbance, anxiety, and tremors. It can result from prolonged exposure to battle, or from some traumatic experience in combat such as the death of a comrade. Sometimes combat fatigue strikes after the battle is over. A minor stress may suddenly trigger the anxiety the soldier managed to suppress in the field.

One study conducted during World War II indicated that wounded soldiers were less likely to experience combat fatigue than the unwounded. In fact, according to this study, the more seriously wounded men tended to have the least anxiety of all. The researchers suggested that wounded soldiers had less anxiety because they were removed from the stress of battle, at least temporarily, and seriously wounded men knew they probably would never have to return to the field.

In civilian life catastrophic events can produce a stress reaction not unlike combat fatigue. The victims may show a wide range of symptoms depending on the nature and severity of the catastrophe, its degree of unexpectedness, and their own unique personalities. Still, there is a common behavior pattern following a catastrophic event that psychologists call the "disaster syndrome." (Note that the disaster syndrome differs from Selye's General Adaptation Syndrome in that the stressor is overwhelming.)

The disaster syndrome consists of three stages. In the first, the shock stage, victims appear to be unaware of their injuries or of danger. They are stunned, dazed, and apathetic. In extreme cases, they may be disoriented or show signs of partial amnesia.

In the next stage, the suggestible stage, victims continue to be passive. They will take orders readily, but are often unable to do even the simplest tasks. The recovery stage, which is the final stage, is a time of great stress. Victims are anxious, tense, apprehensive. They may have difficulty sleeping or concentrating and may repeat the story of the catastrophe over and over.

Like combat fatigue, the disaster syndrome may not occur immediately after the catastrophe, but may be brought on by some minor stress several weeks or even months later.

Psychological stress can even result in death. There are numerous documented cases of individuals who died from acute grief, from the shock of losing a loved one, from a threat or a curse, even from a radical loss of self-esteem or status.

R. J. W. Burrell, a South African doctor, reported on six Bantu men who were cursed and told they would die at sunset. Believing strongly in the power of the curse, each one died that very evening. Autopsies could establish no physical cause of death (reported in Seligman, 1975). Walter B. Cannon, a physiologist, was the first to explore voodoo deaths scientifically. He suggested that three factors are involved in the extreme effects of a hex, and that all of them are environmental, not subjective or even mysterious. The first is the physical effects on the body of continuing intense fear. The second factor is the power one attributes to the customs of one's society. People who have heard about voodoo all their lives and seen its effects on others are likely to respond to a hex as they have seen others respond. The third factor is isolation. If people withdraw from the hexed individual and neither talk to nor offer that person support, they reinforce the curse. Without food to eat, without anything to do, with everyone around acting as if the hexed person were already dead, that person loses all emotional and personal support.

The psychological dynamics that precede sudden death in a victim of a voodoo hex are extreme passivity, depression, and submission. The victim is reduced to a stage of helplessness. This effect can be seen in many more cases than South African Bantus. Engel, Schmale, and Greene have been investigating the consequences of psychological loss on physical disease. They have observed that helplessness seems to weaken a person's resistance to physical pathogens that up until then had been warded off. Psychological settings for such sudden deaths involve: collapse or death of a loved one, acute grief, threatened loss of a loved one, mourning or anniversary of mourning, loss of status and self-esteem. Other sudden deaths occurred during danger, on deliverance from danger, and during happy endings.

Aging: Stress and Control

Aging is a life change that brings a good deal of stress. Retirement from work, decline in health, the deaths of loved ones and family members—all inevitable events of old age—cause feelings of loss and anxiety. Another source of stress during this period is loss of control. Illness, decline in income and mobility, and compulsory retirement are a few of the conditions that make old people feel dependent.

We have seen repeatedly throughout this chapter how loss of control heightens stress. In old age this stress accelerates the natural decline in mental and physical abilities. Old people who are institutionalized lose more control over their lives than do those who live in their own homes or with their families.

To demonstrate the effects of institutionalized loss of control, psychologists Ellen Langer and Judith Rodin (1976) studied the residents of a Connecticut nursing home. They divided their subjects into two groups. One group was encouraged by the staff to take more control over their daily lives. They were given choices about where to see their visitors, how their rooms would be arranged, what night they would go to a movie. In addition, they were each offered a plant to care for. If they decided to take a plant, they had to choose one from a selection. The second group was encouraged to let the staff help them and look after them. They were told where they would be allowed to see visitors and what night they were scheduled to attend the movies. They were given plants and were told the nurses would water and care for them.

The attitudes and behaviors of the two groups were studied over a 3-week period. The staff and the residents were interviewed and the activity level of the residents was monitored. The group that was encouraged to be independent showed an improvement in several areas of behavior. They were more active, happier, and more alert than before. The dependent group, in only 3 weeks' time, became generally more debilitated. They were less active and more withdrawn.

Eighteen months later Rodin and Langer (1977) returned to the nursing home to do a follow-up study of their subjects. Using the same methods of interviewing and observation, they discovered that the level of health, happiness, activity, and involvement continued to be higher for the subjects in the responsibility-induced group. Also, their mortality rate was considerably lower than that of the dependency-induced group: 15 percent compared to 30 percent. This study seemed to have great implications for improving the lives of the institutionalized aged.

In another study, however, Richard Schulz and Barbara Hanusa obtained results that suggest the Rodin-Langer findings should be viewed with caution. Like Rodin and Langer, these researchers studied the changes that occurred in the behavior of nursing home residents who were given more control over their daily lives, but they found that the effects of increased control were short-lived. Forty-two months after the study there was no difference between the dependent and responsible groups.

Schulz and Hanusa suggest that attribution played a powerful role in this situation. The aged subjects did not attribute their increased autonomy to themselves, but to the home's administration. Knowing that their increased freedom was something granted by the administration, which could withdraw it if it wished, they continued to feel dependent. Thus any positive reactions were doomed to be temporary.

Summary

1. Stress occurs when a person is faced with environmental demands, whether pleasant or unpleasant, that require some kind of *adjustment* or *adaptation*.

2. *Approach-approach conflict* occurs when a person is faced with two equally attractive but mutually exclusive goals. In *approach-avoidance conflict*, the person faces a single goal that has both positive and negative consequences.

Avoidance-avoidance conflict is the situation in which a person faces an unavoidable choice between two equally unattractive goals. The final category, *double approach-avoidance conflict,* occurs when a person is faced with two goals that each present an approach-avoid conflict of their own.

3.   *Frustration* is both a result of conflict and a source of stress on its own. Five sources of frustration identified by Coleman and Hammen are: delays, lack of resources, loss, failure, and meaninglessness.

4.   In the psychoanalytic model, anxiety is seen as a consequence of *intrapsychic conflict,* or conflict between the id and the superego. Freudians identify three types of anxiety: reality anxiety, moral anxiety, and neurotic anxiety.

5.   In the learning model, anxiety is seen as a learned autonomic or internal response.

6.   The humanistic-existential psychologists view anxiety as a result of an individual's failure to live up to his or her fullest potential.

7.   In the biological model, anxiety is viewed as a set of physiological responses (such as increased heart rate or sweat gland activity) that occur because of demands placed on the individual. Selye observed a general pattern of physiological reactions to stress that occurs no matter what stressor is involved; this is called the *General Adaptation Syndrome.*

8.   Physical disorders linked to stress (such as ulcers or asthma) are known as *psychosomatic illnesses.* Among the theories devised to explain these illnesses are the *somatic weakness theory,* the *specific-reaction theory,* and the *diathesis-stress theory.*

9.   In the cognitive model, the definition of stress includes three elements: the set of environmental events that are potentially stressful; the person's cognitive appraisal of the events; and the stress reaction and coping. Cognitive researchers have conducted studies indicating that stress is based on people's *perception* of their control, not on how much control they actually have.

10.   In the psychoanalytic model, common ways of coping with stress are *defense mechanisms.* They include repression, displacement, projection, reaction formation, negation, intellectualization, undoing, regression, and sublimation.

11.   *Learned helplessness,* according to the learning model, occurs when animals and humans learn that there is no connection between their responses and what happens to them, which leads to a reduced rate of response. Cognitive psychologists add another dimension to this theory, stating that a person's perception and attribution of control determine whether he or she will become helpless in later situations.

12.   Two types of behavior have been identified as being coping patterns based on perceptions of control. *Type A* (coronary-prone) behavior patterns involve responding to a loss of control by more aggressive striving. *Type B* patterns involve responding to a loss of control with calmer, more even reactions.

13. Continually being confronted with and having to cope with a certain stressor results in *adaptation*, the process of becoming less sensitive to a particular stressor. However, researchers note aftereffects of adaptation, including illness, performance and learning deficits, social-emotional maladjustments, and a possible inability to cope with later environmental demands.

14. Severe consequences of psychological stress include a reaction known as the disaster syndrome, which has three stages: the shock stage, the suggestible stage, and the recovery stage.

Suggested Readings

DOHRENWEND, B. S., and DOHRENWEND, B. P. (Eds.). *Stressful life events: Their nature and effects.* New York: Wiley, 1974. Papers by leading researchers in the field discuss how stress can be measured in terms of life events, and the connection between stress and physical illness.

FRASER, M. *Children in conflict.* Garden City, N.Y.: Doubleday, 1973. Deals with the way children in Northern Ireland have learned to cope with an immensely stressful situation in the conflict between Catholics and Protestants.

GLASS, D. C., and SINGER, J. E. *Urban stress: Experiments on noise and social stressors.* New York: Academic Press, 1972. This book presents an interesting series of experiments on human responses to noise as a function of predictability and control.

MAHL, G. F. *Psychological conflict and defense.* New York: Harcourt Brace Jovanovich, 1971. An outline of the psychoanalytical mechanisms involved in coping with stress. Presents an excellent review of psychoanalytic theory.

SELYE, H. (Ed.). *Selye's guide to stress research,* Vol. 1. New York: Van Nostrand Reinhold, 1980. First in an annual series on current topics in stress research, this volume covers such topics as stressful life events research, the effects of learning on physical symptoms, and hormones and stress.

16

Abnormal Psychology

J ohn G. sits alone in his room several hours a day, doing little else but staring at the wall. His family is worried about him. While he is not happy with his situation, he feels there is nothing he can do to improve it. This has been going on for months.

Carla D. derives pleasure from sticking needles into cats and watching their reactions. When her husband objects that it is cruel and inhumane, she tells him that he doesn't understand and that she is "just following orders."

Are these individuals abnormal? From these brief descriptions it is impossible to say. Even with more information, the question would not be easy to answer. Is normal behavior simply behavior that is predictable and socially acceptable? Or is it behavior that is considered acceptable by the individual, however bizarre it may be as viewed by society? In this chapter we will look at some of the answers that have been proposed to this basic problem, discuss models of abnormality, and examine some of the patterns of abnormal behavior.

Abnormal vs. Normal

At first glance it seems easy enough to define abnormal behavior. Since abnormal means "not normal," all we have to do is define normal behavior and conclude that anything other than that is abnormal. Unfortunately, it turns out that normal behavior is difficult to define. Most people have only a vague and circular notion of the distinction between abnormal and normal behavior; if asked, they would probably define abnormal behavior as a deviation from normal behavior, and normal behavior as the absence of abnormal behavior.

Theorists have tried to establish criteria to make this important distinction between the normal and the abnormal. Some have used a statistical model. They argue that normal behavior is simply behavior that is typical of most people. According to such statistical criteria, all people who stray from the statistical average are behaving abnormally. However, others have pointed out that such a definition is too broad and too vague: The abnormal category would include very intelligent people, nearsighted people, and exceptional athletes.

Others have tried to define normal and abnormal behavior in terms of cultural boundaries and expectations. If John G. in our example is serving a prison sentence and staring at his cell wall, this view argues that he is probably behaving normally. If he is a state senator, his behavior is abnormal—it is not what society expects. In the same way, if Carla D. is a research assistant in a psychology lab, her differences with her husband are a matter of attitude toward animal experimentation, not of normal or abnormal behavior.

The view here is that behavior can only be judged in the context of the culture in which it takes place—there are no absolutes. Behavior that is abnormal in some cultures may be acceptable, and thus normal, in others. Heavy drug use or constant intertribal aggression are accepted as normal in some cultures. In ours, they are not.

Yet another approach is to think of normal behavior in absolute or ideal terms. For example, you could define a normal person as one who is happy, effective with other people, sincere, and free of anxiety. However, this type of definition represents an ideal rather than real people. If normal behavior is an ideal, we can't simply define abnormalcy as the absence of the ideal—just about everyone would be abnormal.

Since it has proved difficult to define abnormal behavior in statistical, cultural, or ideal terms, it has been found more helpful to establish a group of criteria that give a picture of abnormal behavior.

1. *Bizarreness and extremeness.* Common examples would be hallucinations, delusions, and uncontrolled violence. Some normal and even ordinary behaviors, such as washing one's hands, could fall into this category as well if done hundreds of times a day.
2. *Disturbance of others.* Unusual behavior that interferes with the well-being of others may be considered abnormal. Drunken driving or molesting a child are examples.
3. *Subjective distress.* People may have inner feelings of distress, panic, or uncontrolled depression and may define themselves as abnormal.
4. *Interference with daily functioning.* If people are unable to meet society's standards of daily functioning and personal relationships, they may be considered abnormal.

Once we agree that a pattern of behavior is abnormal, we are faced with some important questions. What is the specific abnormality? Where did it come from? How common is it in the population at large? What does such behavior typically lead to? What kind of treatment works best? Classification systems for mental disorders have been developed to deal with such questions.

Clinical Classification and Diagnosis

Emil Kraepelin, a German psychiatrist, developed a classification system in 1883 that still serves as the basis of psychiatric categories. Kraepelin tried to distinguish the various mental disorders from one another on the basis of each disorder's symptoms, origin, course, and outcome. The official classification system of the American Psychiatric Association is the *Diagnostic and Statistical Manual of Mental Disorders,* known as the DSM, with the current revision referred to as DSM III.

Criticism of the clinical classification system has grown over the years and the complaints have centered on both specific issues and general implications. First, the diagnostic categories have tended to keep the medical and psycho-

HIGHLIGHT: DSM III

DSM III is the most recent edition of the Diagnostic and Statistical Manual. Prior to its release, it underwent a great deal of field testing to check its appropriateness and adequacy. DSM III includes some major changes from the previous DSM editions.

One of the most central changes in DSM III is the use of five axes in assessing an individual's problem. The first axis is a statement of the specific psychiatric syndrome that the individual displays, such as depression or phobic disorder. The second axis focuses on any long-term personality disorder that the person has shown, such as a compulsive personality disorder. The third axis asks about any medical disorders that the individual may have. A summary of the other two axes is shown in the two tables. Axis IV asks the diagnostician to rate the severity of recent (within the past year) psychosocial stressors; Axis V asks for an evaluation of how well the individual, at his or her best, has functioned over the past year. Obviously, a diagnosis that includes all of this information can be more informative and useful than the simple labels of past classification systems.

An effort to improve on the reliability and validity of classification is found in DSM III's refinements and greater specificity in categories. Relatively vague and all-inclusive categories such as neurosis have been broken into more precise categories such as anxiety disorders, somatoform disorders, and dissociative disorders. Many, however, argue that DSM III now includes many categories that were not previously considered the province of psychiatry or clinical psychology. They are concerned that these new categories (for example, underachievement) simply are not best understood as psychiatric difficulties, and that to include them is unnecessarily alarming and inaccurate.

Obviously, DSM III represents a sincere effort to improve on the weaknesses of previous editions. However, it is also apparent that it raises some new problems and issues that trouble many people in the field. It remains to be seen how useful a tool DSM III will be. Certainly, the effort to test DSM III prior to its recent acceptance were systematic and admirable. Now it faces the test of time and widespread usage.

Axis IV: Scale for Rating Severity of Psychosocial Stressors.

None—No apparent psychosocial stressor.

Minimal—Minor violation of the law, small bank loan.

Mild—Argument with neighbor, change in working hours.

Moderate—New job, death of close friend, pregnancy.

Severe—Major illness in self or family, bankruptcy, marital separation, birth of child.

Extreme—Death of close relative, divorce, jail term.

Catastrophic—Concentration camp experience, devastating natural disaster.

Unspecified—No information or not applicable.

From DSM-III (APA, 1979), as adapted by Coleman (1980).

Axis V: Scale for Rating Level of Functioning.

Levels	Adult Examples
1. SUPERIOR Unusually effective functioning in social relations, occupational functioning, and use of leisure time.	Housewife takes excellent care of children and home, has warm relations with family and many close friends and is effectively involved in several community activities.
2. VERY GOOD Better than average functioning in social relations, occupational functioning, and use of leisure time.	A 65-year-old retired widower does some volunteer work, often sees old friends and pursues many life-long hobbies.
3. GOOD No more than slight impairment in either social or occupational functioning.	A man functions extremely well at a difficult job, but has only one or two good friends.
4. FAIR Moderate impairment in either social relations or occupational functioning, or some impairment in both.	A female lawyer has trouble carrying through assignments, has several acquaintances but hardly any close friends.
5. POOR Marked impairment in either social relations or occupational functioning or moderate impairment in both.	A man with one or two friends has trouble keeping a job for more than a few weeks.
6. GROSSLY IMPAIRED Marked impairment in both social relations and occupational functioning.	A woman is unable to do any of her housework, and has violent outbursts towards family and neighbors.
0 UNSPECIFIED	No information.

From the DSM-III (APA, 1979), as adapted by Coleman (1980).

analytic outlook that at one time characterized the whole field. For example, neurotic behaviors have regularly been defined in terms of anxiety, conflict, and defense mechanisms, which are the hallmark of psychoanalytic theories. But many theorists (those of the learning model, for instance) don't agree with these concepts, and thus find it hard to use this system.

Second, there have been criticisms of the reliability of the DSM system. Reliability of the system means that the results are repeatable—two different psychologists examining the same person should come up with the same diagnosis. However, studies have often failed to show this kind of consistency. Some have even found that the same observer presented with virtually identical descriptions of a patient on two different occasions would often give different diagnoses (Beck, 1962; Wilson and Meyer, 1962).

Models of Abnormal Behavior

In Chapter 14 we discussed models of the normal personality; here we will examine the views these same models take of abnormal behavior and personality. Since each model gives a different picture of human behavior, a particular pattern of abnormal behavior will often be viewed quite differently by each of the models. It is not uncommon to find the same behavior pattern viewed as normal by one model and abnormal by another.

The *psychoanalytic model* generally views abnormal behavior as evidence of unresolved conflicts between the id, ego, and superego. This model sees life as a constant struggle among these three parts of our personality. Somehow we have to harmonize the instinctual and unreasoning desires of the id, the rational and realistic requirements of the ego, and the moral and restrictive demands of the superego. Since conflicts between them can lead to unpleasant and anxious feelings, we normally develop defense mechanisms to help us reduce such conflicts. Abnormal behavior can result from faulty defense mechanisms that allow conflict and anxiety to break through, or from the overuse of defense mechanisms.

According to the *learning model,* abnormal behaviors are learned in the same way that all behaviors are learned. People acquire them through either classical conditioning, operant conditioning, or modeling. Deviant behaviors and extreme reactions can be understood through such concepts as stimulus, response, and reinforcement.

The *biological model* argues that abnormal behaviors can be traced in part to physical disorders. The link between the mind and the body can work in two directions: (1) biological abnormalities can affect mind and behavior; or (2) emotional stress can have a physical effect on us, thus setting the stage for yet a further impact on our behavior. According to the biological model, it makes no sense to separate the mind from the body in explaining abnormal behavior because to do so obscures the critical role played by physical factors.

In the *humanistic-existential model* abnormal behaviors are caused by people's failure to fulfill their personal potential or the potential life holds for them. These failures may occur when people lose sight of or distort their real emotions and thoughts, cut themselves off from those around them, or come to view themselves and their lives as totally meaningless.

The *cognitive model* finds the roots of abnormal behavior in the way we think about and perceive the world. People who distort or misinterpret their experiences, the intentions of those around them, and the kind of world they live in are bound to act abnormally.

Neurotic Patterns and Anxiety

The term *neurosis* is applied to a wide range of behaviors. Sometimes these behaviors differ so much from one another that it is questionable whether they should have the same label. The traditional view is that neurotic behavior patterns share some common themes. One is the central role of anxiety in the problem. Another is the self-defeating aspect of neurotic behaviors. While they may ease or prevent anxiety in the short run, they create yet greater problems for the person in the long run. A third feature is the exaggerated nature of neurotic behaviors. Usually the anxiety, defenses, or other reactions of people who behave neurotically are reasonable to a point; it is the fact that they persist beyond that point that leads to the label of neurosis.

Yet other common themes have been linked to at least some neurotic patterns; for example, feelings of inadequacy, inferiority, guilt, and unhappiness, as well as rigid styles of behavior. While the different models disagree on the causes and treatments of neurotic patterns, all seem to agree that people caught up in such patterns suffer in a very real and ongoing way.

Phobic Neurosis and Anxiety Neurosis

Phobic neurosis involves a persistent fear of a particular object or situation, a fear that is far out of proportion to the actual threat present. For example, it is quite natural to be afraid of a snarling dog that lunges at you in the street; it is not so natural to have exactly the same fear when faced with any dog in any situation. The usual defense against this type of fear is to avoid the source of it. Examples of phobias are *claustrophobia,* fear of closed places (such as elevators or cars); *acrophobia,* fear of heights; *agoraphobia,* fear of leaving the house and of open spaces; and many types of *animal phobias,* such as fear of dogs or mice. Most of us have minor phobias (we may feel uncomfortable in the presence of snakes or at the top of a ladder) that still let us function perfectly normally most of the time—unless we suddenly become the local dog catcher or take up snake dancing, we are fine. People with a fear of crowds or elevators, on the other hand, may be greatly restricted in their daily lives.

Anxiety neurosis involves the same kind of discomfort as phobic neurosis, but the person's anxiety is not clearly linked to a particular object or situation. Since the feeling of anxiety is present in so many situations, it has sometimes been called "free-floating anxiety." Symptoms include tenseness, discouragement, insomnia, irritability, and inability to concentrate. Sufferers feel that their

A study is being made in Houston (Mathew, 1980) of what may be a new phobia—now tentatively referred to as "traffic phobia." This disabling fear is most often associated with freeway driving, and has become a problem in big cities where freeway, throughway, or expressway driving is a major part of everyday life.

CASE HISTORY:
Anxiety Neurosis

Richard Benson, age 38, applied to a psychiatrist for therapy because he was suffering from severe and overwhelming anxiety which sometimes escalated to a panic attack. During the times when he was experiencing intense anxiety, it often seemed as if he were having a heart seizure. He experienced chest pains and heart palpitations, numbness, shortness of breath, and he felt a strong need to breathe in air. He reported that in the midst of the anxiety attack, he developed a feeling of tightness over his eyes and he could only see objects directly in front of him (tunnel vision). He further stated that he feared that he would not be able to swallow.

As the anxiety symptoms became more severe and persistent, the client began to worry about when another acute attack would occur and this apprehension made him more anxious still. He expressed a general concern about his physical well being and he became extremely sensitive to any fluctuations in his breathing or difficulties in swallowing. He began to note the location of doctors' offices and hospitals in whatever vicinity he happened to be, and he became extremely anxious if medical help was not close by.

Mr. Benson stated that he could not fight off his constant feelings of anxiety, and he was unable to control his behavior when the anxiety symptoms occasionally spiralled to a panic attack. He could not sit still when he felt acutely and painfully anxious, and the only way he could find relief from his symptoms was to go home and pace back and forth in his yard. Gradually, he stopped perspiring and the rapid heart rate and other somatic symptoms subsided as well. He went back into the house as soon as he felt calmer, but after a half hour the symptoms often reappeared and the anxiety episode started all over again. At that point, the only way he could bring the anxiety attack under control was to contact his physician for a tranquilizer injection.

From Leon, *Case Histories of Deviant Behavior*, pp. 113–18.

lives are out of control and that disaster is imminent. They are unable to make decisions or form relationships with other people. Physical effects include excessive sweating, nausea, fatigue, and muscular tension.

The *psychoanalytic model* says that both phobic and anxiety neurosis can be traced to an unresolved clash between the id and the ego and superego. If the id's drive for sexual or aggressive expression was harshly punished in childhood, these early punishments have left a mark on the individual. As a result, the individual has come to fear either the person who meted out the punishment or his or her own id impulses.

People who fear their punisher are likely to show a pattern of phobic neurosis. Typically, the fear of the punisher is displaced to a more neutral object or situation, perhaps something that only symbolizes the punisher. In this way people manage to avoid fearing the punisher, who is often very important to them—for instance, their mother or father.

People who fear their own id impulses live in constant fear, since such impulses are always fighting for expression. These people will have anxiety neurosis: free-floating anxiety in all kinds of situations. Their ego constantly struggles to contain their impulses—which is a losing battle. Thus these people experience danger in every kind of situation.

The *learning model* does not make a real distinction between phobic and anxiety neurosis. A phobia is seen as a conditioned fear reaction and avoidance response. For example, as a child you're frightened one night by the loud noises of a thunderstorm. Afterward you may develop an intense fear of the color blue—the color of the bedroom in which you spent that frightening night. The color blue (conditioned stimulus), which just happened to be present at the same time as the loud noises of thunder (unconditioned stimulus), now brings about the same intense fear reaction. According to Mowrer (1947), this classically conditioned fear is reinforced as you avoid the color blue over and over again. Constant avoidance prevents you from realizing that the color blue is really quite harmless. As the fear gets further locked in, so does the pattern of avoidance behavior. In this case you would be displaying a phobic reaction.

The learning model goes on to say that a pattern of anxiety neurosis can be explained in essentially the same way. The only difference is in the number of conditioned stimuli that come to cause the fear reaction. Going back to the thunderstorm example, in addition to fearing the color blue, you may also fear many other stimuli present on the night of the storm (that is, the fear generalizes to other stimuli). The point is that with a thorough enough search, anxiety that appears to be free floating can be broken down into a group of specific fears triggered by specific stimuli. These many fears may come from one situation that yields many conditioned stimuli, or from a series of situations each yielding a variety of conditioned stimuli.

The humanistic-existential model views phobic and anxiety neurosis—indeed, all forms of neurosis—as a failure to fulfill one's potential or life's potential. You may recall from Chapter 14 that Rogers believed that all people have a need for positive regard right from the beginning. However, we do not always receive unconditional regard from others—some people are criticized a great deal as children and in turn become intensely self-critical. These people later find it very hard to accept themselves and their actions because everything they do falls far short of their harsh standards of self-evaluation. They come to perceive their experiences in a selective fashion, denying or distorting any experiences that are contrary to or threaten their self-concept. So much denial and distortion requires a lot of energy. Eventually reality itself is denied and these people no longer know what they feel or think. They experience anxiety and have no energy left for self-actualization, the universal push that Rogers believed is the natural goal of all humans. According to this model, the failure to self-actualize amidst the ongoing denial and distortion is the essence of all forms of neurosis.

The cognitive model explains phobic and anxiety neurosis as problems that can be traced to troublesome thought processes. Albert Ellis (1958, 1973, 1975) argues that such neurotic patterns are due to underlying irrational assumptions that people make. For example, some people believe that if they receive any disapproval at all, they must be totally worthless. Thus they try to avoid disapproval in all their interactions, and they die a thousand deaths whenever they are criticized. Other people assume they must do everything perfectly, thus setting impossible standards for themselves. Since these assumptions lead to expectations that are impossible to fulfill, they assure the very high level of anxiety and dysfunction that characterize phobic and anxiety neurosis, as well as other neurotic patterns. Research has indeed suggested that such irrational assumptions are related to neurotic patterns of behavior. For example, Newmark and his colleagues (1973) found that people classified as neurotic endorse such extreme beliefs or assumptions significantly more often than other people.

Obsessive-Compulsive Neurosis

Obsessive-compulsive behaviors are shown by people who feel forced to repeat unwanted thoughts or ideas over and over, or to repeat certain actions or rituals again and again. Examples are the need to count every step when you walk or to wash your hands every time you touch a doorknob. A minor example that most of us have experienced is having a tune or part of an advertising jingle repeat itself in our heads for no obvious reason and in spite of our attempts to get rid of it. Such an experience is usually no more than mildly annoying; for people with an obsessive-compulsive neurosis, the intrusion may be so severe and constant that they find it almost impossible to function normally.

Obsessions and compulsions represent different aspects of a neurotic pattern. Obsessions are thoughts that repeatedly intrude against one's will and defy one's efforts to ignore them. They may occur in various forms. For example, there are obsessive doubts, such as "Did I turn off the stove before I left the house?" There are also obsessive impulses, which may range from whimsical ideas like winking at passersby to the thought of violent acts such as stabbing one's child. Other people are plagued by obsessive fears, such as "I am going to shout something out in church," even though they have no conscious desire to do so (Akhter et al., 1975).

In the vast majority of cases, such obsessive thoughts never translate into action. However, they are often so dramatic and unpleasant that they cause very high levels of anxiety. Many people who obsess worry most about the possibility that they will someday act out their terrible obsessive thoughts.

Compulsions are acts or rituals that are repeated against a person's will. There are minor compulsions that most people have and that fall well within the realm of normal behavior—for example, repeatedly stepping over cracks in the sidewalk. Also, it is common to have daily rituals—for example, many people go through their morning routines without variation day after day, and are quite upset if something forces them to change the routine.

When compulsive actions become extremely frequent, intense, unyielding, and disruptive to a person's life, they are no longer within the realm of normal behavior. For example, people who feel compelled to take 10 showers a day or to wash their hands 50 times a day are displaying significant compulsive patterns (see Table 16-1).

Sometimes a person shows obsessive thoughts without many compulsive acts, or acts compulsively without experiencing much in the way of obsessive thinking. However, often the two occur together in the same person—in fact, one is frequently a response to the other. A person who compulsively checks the locks on doors and windows is often yielding to an obsessive fear that a burglar will break in. And sometimes compulsive acts are used to control obsessive thoughts. People may occupy themselves with reciting certain words or phrases over and over again to keep an obsessive and frightening image from occupying their minds.

As with other neurotic patterns, the psychoanalytic model begins its explanation of obsessive-compulsive neurosis by pointing to id impulses that were dealt with too harshly during childhood. In this case, the id impulses that were punished too harshly occurred during the toilet-training period of the anal stage. Because these id impulses could not be expressed during that stage, they demand

Table 16–1: Obsessive-Compulsives Rate Aspects of Their Rituals.

Is there resistance to carrying out the rituals?	Definitely Yes 32%	Somewhat 22%	Definitely No 46%
How sensible do you consider the rituals?	Sensible 22%	Rather Silly 13%	Absurd 65%
Does reassurance from others reduce the occurrence of the rituals?	Definitely Yes 27%	Some 15%	Definitely No 68%
Does the presence of others affect the rituals?	Occurs When Alone 20%	Company Irrelevant 76%	Occurs in Company 4%
Amount of family distress caused by the rituals.	Little or None 29%	Moderate 22%	A Great Deal 49%

Adapted from Stern and Cobb (1978).

expression later in life. Frequently, they come to the surface in the form of obsessive thoughts; at other times they are prevented or overcome by counterthoughts or actions. In short, the id and the ego's defense mechanisms are in a seesaw battle. For example, the id impulse to partake in a forbidden sexual encounter (obsessive thought) may be countered by repeatedly thinking other thoughts or by engaging in purifying rituals (compulsive acts) that help deny such obsessive ideas.

The learning model views obsessions and compulsions as learned reactions that are reinforced by their ability to reduce anxiety. For example, compulsively washing one's hands many times a day might be regarded as an escape mechanism from obsessive fears of disease. It is not even necessary that the fear be so specific. As long as a person's general anxiety has regularly been reduced or avoided by such activity, the person will tend to repeat it in the face of danger, real or imagined.

The learning model has not always been clear about how obsessions or compulsions appear in the first place. The compulsive hand-washer may have initially imitated such behavior on the part of a parent, a peer, or a friend. Or washing one's hands as a child may have been followed by such rewards as parental approval or by a parent's repeated clarifications about how such actions ward off germs and disease. It is such a big step from such seemingly innocent early learning opportunities to the unyielding and overwhelming nature of obsessive-compulsive patterns that many theorists have questioned the learning model's explanation of how obsessions and compulsions emerge.

The cognitive model views at least some forms of obsessive-compulsive behaviors as an attempt to assure order and predictability. People who perceive the world as highly threatening may become obsessed with a ritual of meticulous orderliness, arranging their personal environment in exacting ways to maintain their sense of order and control. When the smallest detail becomes disarranged—say, the handle of a cup points the wrong way—their entire sense of order is threatened and they have to repeat the ritual in order to relieve the anxiety once again.

Hysterical Neurosis

Hysterical neurosis refers to a group of neurotic reactions that are quite dramatic. Therefore they are particularly popular in books, movies, and television. It is hard to imagine a season going by without a popular presentation of a multiple personality or amnesiac. Though their popularity in the entertainment media makes it seem that these neurosis are common disorders, they actually represent the smallest percentage of the major neurotic patterns.

There are two types of hysterical neurosis: the dissociative and the conversion. The dissociative type includes disturbances of memory and consciousness, including amnesia, fugue, somnambulism, and multiple personality.

Amnesia is a partial or total loss of memory for a period lasting from several hours to several years. Although people with amnesia usually retain the ability to communicate and reason, they may forget who they are or where they live and will fail to recognize relatives and friends. The forgotten material is not usually irretrievable; it may reappear spontaneously or under hypnosis.

Fugue (from the Latin word meaning "to flee") is amnesia accompanied by actual physical flight—a person in a state of amnesia may simply wander away for several hours, or even move to another area and set up a new life. Years later the amnesia may suddenly reverse—the person then "awakens" in a strange place with a full memory of his or her original identity but with amnesia now about the fugue period.

Somnambulism, or sleepwalking, is also viewed as a dissociative reaction, since the individual's body movements are apparently being controlled without the knowledge or participation of the conscious mind. *Multiple personality* means the presence of two or more separate personalities in the same person. These personalities compete for access to consciousness. Often they alternate, with one personality being in control for a few hours or days and then the other. The most famous accounts of multiple personalities are the books *Three Faces of Eve* and *Sybil.*

Because dissociative hysteria is a relatively rare occurrence, there is a lack of well-documented literature on the subject. It therefore remains one of the least clearly understood neurotic patterns. Nevertheless, the psychoanalytic and learning models have offered some explanations.

The *psychoanalytic model* describes dissociative hysteria as a massive repression, achieved by splitting off part of consciousness. A person has thoughts, commits acts, or raises conflicts so threatening that the only way to resolve them is to separate that part of consciousness completely and become totally unaware that it ever existed.

The *learning model* regards these complete denials, as it does all other neurotic patterns, as avoidance responses. It does not use such concepts as unconsciousness or even split consciousness. Rather, people are seen as ignoring or forgetting significant dimensions of themselves at various times because such reactions enable them to escape or avoid unpleasant events and thus anxiety. While the nature of the pattern in dissociative hysteria is quite severe, it is nevertheless the result of basic learning principles. In the person's past, such

CASE HISTORY:
Conversion Reaction

A young woman of twenty-two was referred to [the clinic] with a six-year history of total incapacity from continuous generalized shaking and trembling movements. Extensive and exhaustive investigations at a number of previous hospitals had effectively excluded structural damage or disease. The history of the complaint was that she had begun to fall helpless to the ground, and to lie there twitching, when she was sixteen, shortly after her parents had refused to allow her to continue for a further year at school, since she was required to earn money for the family. At about the same time their own chronic and severe marital disharmony had become increasingly apparent to her and to the rest of the family. Within a year her attacks of falling had been followed by increasing periods of disability due to the jerking, twitching, and trembling movements, until after 2 years she had become totally helpless and disabled.

On examination the generalized twitching, jerking, and trembling of all her limbs, head, and body effectively prevented her from reading, writing, feeding herself, or indeed looking after herself in any way whatever. She was helpless and bedridden, and her sole recreation was listening to the radio.

From Stafford-Clark and Smith, *Psychiatry for Students,* p. 145.

---

behaviors were reinforced by the immediate reduction of anxiety they brought about. It may be true that other less extreme behaviors would also reduce anxiety, but the individual has not learned such alternative behaviors, or at least has not come to trust or rely on them. The dissociative responses have become the responses used by the individual in certain anxiety-arousing situations.

The other form of hysterical neurosis is the conversion type. People suffering from this neurosis develop physical symptoms, such as blindness or paralysis, for which there is no apparent organic (physical) basis. This neurosis may take many physical forms:

1. *Sensory symptoms:* partial or complete loss of sight or hearing, insensitivity to pain, and unusual tactile sensations such as itchiness or tingling.
2. *Motor symptoms:* paralysis, tremors, rigid joints, and inability to talk above a whisper.
3. *Visceral symptoms:* chronic coughing, headaches, nausea, and shortness of breath.

The *psychoanalytic model* begins its explanation of conversion patterns by pointing to id impulses (for example, sexual desires) that were dealt with too harshly during childhood. For example, during the Oedipal stage, children come to desire the parent of the opposite sex. If this desire is not resolved adequately in the form of identification with the same-sex parent, children may feel threatened and anxious about such sexual impulses. Later in life, when these or similar id impulses emerge in a particularly strong manner, the individual may convert them into a physical channel. Of course, a conversion reaction need not always involve sexual impulses. Abse (1959) described a case in which a man's desire to kill his wife and her lover was so threatening to him that he repressed this desire and instead developed hysterical paralysis of the legs. In this case of conversion reaction, as in others, the conversion to the physical channel helps protect people from expressing or discovering their disturbing impulses. This psychoanalytic notion of conversion is in fact the source of the label "conversion reaction."

The *learning model,* on the other hand, sees no conversion process in the physical problems that are labeled conversion reactions. According to this model, the individual's physical reactions are learned behaviors that are reinforced by their role in helping the individual avoid stressful situations. This does not mean that such individuals are pretending. Rather, their perception and manifestation of such physical difficulties have in the past been reinforced by serving to reduce or avoid the anxiety of key stressful events. Their illness may serve to protect them from social, occupational, or family pressures, and may be further reinforced by the attention and comfort elicited from others. The rather detailed similarities between such patterns and organic-based patterns indicate that the person must have had some experience with the adopted complaint, such as a relative or acquaintance who served as a model.

As in the case of dissociative patterns, the empirical evidence for these explanations of conversion patterns is rather sparse. Thus the hysterical neurotic patterns remain among the more fascinating but least understood forms of neurotic behavior.

Depression

The term *depression* is used to describe a wide range of complaints from a mild feeling of sadness to a highly disabling and severe state. All of us have times when we feel "down" and discouraged, sad and empty. We say we are depressed. Although the experience is by no means pleasant, we know it will go away in a matter of hours, or at most days; it is a temporary mood. While this passing experience gives us some insight into the nature of depression, we need to look a lot deeper to discover its varied characteristics.

There seem to be different kinds of depression. For example, theorists have separated relatively mild patterns from more severe patterns, and depression as a response to an external event (loss of a loved one) from internally caused depression. With the exception of manic-depressive patterns, however, we will discuss depression and its causes as a single phenomenon. This is not to suggest that all patterns of depression are identical or that the distinction among different patterns of depression are valueless, only that there is enough similarity among the various patterns of depression to profitably describe them as one.

Depression is diagnosed from symptoms affecting mood, thought, and activity level. The mood is typified by sadness and general apathy. Depressed persons think of themselves negatively with self-reproaches and blame. Their activity level may shift to either lethargy or agitation. Their hunger and sex drives are low, and they show either insomnia or an increased need for sleep. They avoid social contact. Not all depressed persons have all these symptoms, nor are these symptoms unique to depression. Because the same symptoms are found in many other categories, diagnostic reliability is far from high.

The *psychoanalytic model* generally regards depression as anger turned inward. The reasoning for this conclusion starts with observations of the contrast between normal grief, caused by an event such as the loss of a loved one, and abnormal depression. Freud believed that the tendency toward depression starts, like many other patterns, in early childhood, specifically during the first phase of development, the oral period. If our infantile needs during this time are over- or undergratified, fixation occurs, resulting in overdependence on others. Later in life, after the loss of a loved one through separation or death, our overdependent ego identifies with this lost person. We introject or incorporate the person and essentially make the person part of ourselves. Because, according to Freud, we all have unconscious feelings of hate toward those we love, we now turn those feelings against ourselves. It is, of course, possible to become depressed without actually losing a loved one. A person may experience a "symbolic loss" in which some action or event (perhaps some kind of rejection) is seen as a loss, thus leading to introjection and depression.

The *learning model* argues that depressive reactions begin when the individual's positive reinforcements in life decrease. For example, Lewinsohn (1974) argues that some aspect, subtle or salient, of a person's situation leads to a reduced rate of positive reinforcement, which in turn leads to reduced activities and dejection. This depressed reaction leads to further reductions in positive reinforcement, which in turn further reduce activities and cause greater dejection. A depressive cycle is off and running.

For example, a woman's husband may die, leading to a major reduction in the pleasures and reinforcements she receives. She is less rewarded for being active, initiating conversations, dressing attractively, or acting cheerful. Her range of behaviors becomes more limited and depressive in nature. Such behaviors make it difficult for others to be around her, converse with her, have fun with her, and reward her. This isolation makes her feel more depressed. If such a person lacks the social skills and related abilities that might help her to overcome the lost rewards, she may find it particularly difficult to avoid or break out of this cycle.

The *cognitive model* offers two leading explanations of depression, one by Aaron Beck and the other by Martin Seligman. Beck sees depression primarily as a disorder of thought processes that results in changes in mood and behavior, rather than the other way around. Studies have shown that depressed people continually rate themselves as negative people who lack any ability to achieve happiness and are somehow to blame for most bad events.

Beck argues that such self-devaluations are caused by the illogical thought processes that guide the thinking of depressed persons. For example, depressed people regularly draw conclusions without evidence, attend to only certain aspects of a situation (usually the wrong ones), and overgeneralize from specific occurrences to their whole life or the world. These kinds of repeated cognitive distortions seem quite reasonable and natural to the depressed person and add strength to the person's negative self-view and world view. This negative view flavors all later decisions, behaviors, emotions, and interactions, thus locking in a pattern of depression.

A related viewpoint is that of Seligman's helplessness model. Seligman proposes that depressed people have learned helplessness from earlier experiences and now believe themselves unable to influence and control events. Thus they develop negative symptoms, including hopelessness, passivity, and depressed and negative expectations when faced with stressful situations. An experiment by Miller and Seligman (1973) demonstrated that depressed subjects, unlike nondepressed subjects, did not expect success in performing a skilled task even after they had done it successfully several times. In other words, even success did not give them faith in their ability; helplessness, once learned, apparently does not dissipate easily.

In later studies Seligman found that depressed persons did show improved performance after they were told that their previous failures were due to the fact that the experiment had been rigged against them. He concluded that when depressed persons realize that failure can be attributed to an outside source rather than their own inability, they use their thought processes to diminish their feelings of helplessness.

The *biological model* has offered some important insights about depression. A leading theory is that depression is related to low levels of norepinephrine. You will recall that norepinephrine is a basic neurotransmitter by which a neuron fires another neuron in the central nervous system. One consistent research finding is that depressed persons typically have low supplies of norepinephrine: Their neurons are simply not firing as much as they should be. Consistent with this theory, it has been found that many antidepressant drugs that help to improve feelings of depression also function to raise the levels of norepinephrine in the brain.

Recently, yet another neurotransmitter, *serotonin,* has been linked to depression (Mandels et al., 1972; Van Praag et al., 1973). As with norepinephrine, low levels of serotonin are associated with depression. One of the exciting aspects of these biological findings is that they make it possible for us to develop better medications, such as antidepressants, to alleviate the suffering of depressed persons.

Manic-Depressive Patterns

Manic-depressive patterns involve another dimension beyond the symptoms of depression; namely, manic behavior. A person with a manic-depressive pattern will at times go through periods of intense depression, and at other times go through a manic phase.

Manic behavior may at first appear to be simply a very positive and enthusiastic approach to life. But it soon becomes clear that the behavior and reactions of people at such times are extreme and inappropriate. Often they have extraordinarily energetic feelings of great joy or high agitation, become involved in many different undertakings, and show a heightened pace in behavior and thinking, extreme impatience, poor concentration, and poor judgment. In some cases they will make expensive and extravagant plans that are totally unrealistic in their situation. Most people think of manic behavior as happy behavior, but this is not always so. Sometimes people in a manic pattern are quite irritated and unpleasant in their behaviors. They may be very aggressive, and even become confused, incoherent, disoriented, or even violent.

People who show a history of manic patterns without episodes of depression are said to have a manic disorder, and those who experience periods of depression without any episodes of manic functioning are considered to have a depressive disorder. Those who show a manic-depressive pattern in which periods of

Table 16–2: Changes from Normal to Depressed States.

Items	Normal State	Depressed State
Stimulus	Response	
Loved object	Affection	Loss of feeling, revulsion
Favorite activities	Pleasure	Boredom
New Opportunities	Enthusiasm	Indifference
Humor	Amusement	Mirthlessness
Novel stimuli	Curiosity	Lack of interest
Abuse	Anger	Self-criticism, sadness
Goal or Drive	Direction	
Gratification	Pleasure	Avoidance
Welfare	Self-care	Self-neglect
Self-preservation	Survival	Suicide
Achievement	Success	Withdrawal
Thinking	Appraisal	
About self	Realistic	Self-devaluating
About future	Hopeful	Hopeless
About environment	Realistic	Overwhelming
Biological and Physiological Activities	Symptom	
Appetite	Spontaneous hunger	Loss of appetite
Sexuality	Spontaneous desire	Loss of desire
Sleep	Restful	Disturbed
Energy	Spontaneous	Fatigued

From Beck (1974).

depression alternate with periods of manic behavior have a bipolar affective disorder. The periods are of varying duration—sometimes they go on for months at a time—and seem unrelated to particular situational factors or changes. For this reason, the manic-depressive pattern has often been explained by genetic and/or biological factors. Such explanations have been supported by research into disturbances in the distribution of sodium and potassium levels in the cells (Copper, 1965; Shaw, 1966) and the startling turnabouts in manic-depressive patterns brought about by lithium treatments (see Chapter 17).

Psychoses: Schizophrenia

The main difference between neurotic and psychotic categories is a more extreme or bizarre manifestation of behavior, thought, and emotion. Some believe that there is in fact a qualitative distinction between neuroses and psychoses, which can be seen in the individual's contact with reality. In psychosis the individual loses contact with reality in some central way, and from this loss a variety of severe problem areas emerges. The total personality of the individual typically becomes involved in the disorder and its manifestations. In this section we will discuss the most prevalent, controversial, and puzzling of psychoses—schizophrenia.

The diagnosis of schizophrenia has been applied to such a wide variety of behaviors that many professionals argue that it is a wastebasket category that is not very useful. Still, there are some characteristics that most persons diagnosed as schizophrenic do seem to share: the distortion of reality in some significant way, social withdrawal, and prominent disturbances in thought, perception, motor activity, or emotionality.

Obviously, all of these symptoms can be related. For example, a person who has impaired thought or perceptual processes is also likely to distort reality in many different ways. Or those who see things that are not really there may be distracted in their efforts to express a thought and may seem to be talking incoherently. Thus it is not clear where the central symptom of schizophrenia lies. It could lie in the sphere of thinking, perceiving, emotion, or somewhere else.

Disturbances of Thought, Perception, Emotion, and Motor Abilities

The thought disturbances of schizophrenia are centered on the individual's frequent inability to organize his or her ideas coherently. Often such individuals have trouble sticking to one topic at a time (loose associations). The ends of their statements are only distantly related to the beginnings. For some, the only important consideration is that key words in their statements rhyme (clang associations). And yet others are so affected by the usual rules of thought and communication that they use their own private words that have meaning to no one else (neologisms).

Sometimes it is not the organization of thought but its content that is disturbed. This is best illustrated by the delusions that often form a part of schizophrenic thinking, beliefs that seem totally unfounded and are frequently bizarre. People with delusions of grandeur view themselves as magnificent or powerful persons such as Christ, Einstein, or Joan of Arc. Those who have delusions of influence or control may believe that others are trying to contact them by radar, television, or other means. And those with delusions of persecution imagine that others are trying to hurt or interfere with them.

The perceptual disturbances of schizophrenia center on individuals' inability to selectively filter out the millions of stimuli surrounding them at any given moment and to give order and meaning to their world. The result is that schizophrenic individuals often pay great attention to seemingly irrelevant stimuli and ignore important stimuli. Distraction is a way of life.

Sometimes the perceptual difficulties even extend to hallucinations, which involve perceiving things that are not actually there. People with visual hallucinations may see imaginary persons or objects. Those with auditory hallucinations may hear imaginary voices that command, advise, criticize, or praise them. Other senses may also be involved in hallucinations, as in the case of

CASE HISTORY:
Schizophrenia

Two months before commitment the patient began to talk about how he had failed, had "spoiled" his whole life, that it was now "too late." He spoke of hearing someone say, "You must submit." One night his wife was awakened by his talking. He told her of having several visions but refused to describe them. He stated that someone was after him and trying to blame him for the death of a certain man. He had been poisoned, he said. Whenever he saw a truck or a fire engine, the patient stated that someone in it was looking for him in order to claim his assistance to help save the world. He had periods of laughing and shouting and became so noisy and unmanageable that it was necessary to commit him.

On arrival at the hospital the patient . . . lay down on the floor, pulled at his foot, made undirected, violent striking movements . . . struck attendants, grimaced, assumed rigid, attitudinized postures, refused to speak, and appeared to be having auditory hallucinations. Later in the day, he was found to be in a stuporous state. His face was without expression, he was mute and rigid, and paid no attention to those about him or to their questions. His eyes were closed and the lids could be separated only with effort. . . .

For five days he remained mute, negativistic, and inaccessible, at times staring vacantly into space, at times with his eyes tightly closed. He ate poorly and gave no response to questions but once was heard to mutter to himself in a greatly preoccupied manner, "I'm going to die—I know it—you know it." On the evening of the sixth day he looked about and asked where he was and how he came there. When asked to tell of his life, he related many known events and how he had once worked in an airplane factory, but added that he had invented an appliance pertaining to airplanes, that this had been stolen and patented through fraud and that as a result he had lost his position. He ate ravenously, then fell asleep, and on awaking was in a catatonic stupor, remaining in this state for days. . . .

Kolb, *Modern Clinical Psychiatry*, 1973, pp. 334–35.

people who feel millions of insects crawling on their skin or taste poison in their food.

There can be several sorts of emotional disturbances. Some individuals show extremely inappropriate emotional reaction—for example, laughing at the death of someone dear to them. Others show ambivalent reactions, repeatedly expressing both intensely positive and negative emotions toward the same person or object. And yet others show virtually no reaction at all, no matter what the situation.

The motor activities of a schizophrenic are often quite disturbed. Some people spend hour upon hour gesturing in systematic ways. For example, an individual may bend each finger of each hand in succession, or may raise and lower his or her arms over and over again. Some schizophrenics move about with much excitement, waving, and activity. And yet others who are labeled as catatonic show virtually no movement at all, staying in the same position for long periods of time, whether that be sitting, squatting, or lying. Such people often show a "waxy flexibility"—their hands, arms, and legs can be molded into any position by another person and the position will be maintained.

Different Types of Schizophrenia

Since schizophrenia is characterized by such a wide range of disturbances, it is not surprising that it is categorized into a number of subtypes. If one or two symptoms seem particularly dominant, the schizophrenic individual is labeled accordingly. For example, if the person has many delusions or hallucinations, his or her diagnosis will likely be paranoid schizophrenia. If, on the other hand, the person shows excessive immobility, the diagnosis will be catatonic schizophrenia. The number of subtypes of schizophrenia has both grown and decreased over the years in line with contemporary thinking. Some clinicians have questioned the usefulness of distinguishing so many subtypes.

Research has indicated, however, that it is useful to distinguish schizophrenics according to at least a few dimensions. For example, it has been found that paranoid schizophrenic persons seem distinctly more alert than nonparanoid schizophrenics, and more coherent in their thoughts and statements. One may not agree with their comments, but they are capable of stating them quite coherently. Another useful distinction is between chronic schizophrenics, whose symptoms emerge gradually and last a long time, and acute schizophrenics, whose symptoms emerge rapidly and improve rapidly. The prior social and sexual adjustment (the premorbid adjustment) of schizophrenic persons has also proved to be an important distinction. A schizophrenic person with a "good premorbid adjustment" usually develops symptoms more rapidly and intensely than one with a "poor premorbid adjustment" and tends to improve significantly faster.

Models of Schizophrenia

The explanations of schizophrenia vary greatly. Psychoanalytic theorists are themselves divided in their interpretations. One *psychoanalytic* perspective, that proposed by Freud, views schizophrenia as regression to a pre-ego stage, that very early period in childhood when self-absorption ruled the day. To function without an ego is to function without reality testing (seeing that something exists outside of you), which is certainly consistent with the separation from reality that is so typical of schizophrenia.

An alternative psychoanalytic perspective sees schizophrenia as a total ego defense strategy. According to this interpretation, schizophrenic persons are coping with their early and ongoing traumatic experiences by overrelying on a wide range of ego-defense mechanisms. For example, delusions and hallucinations are said to be exaggerated uses of such defenses as projection, fantasy, and wish fulfillment. Delusions of influence are simply the projections of blame onto others for one's own unacceptable thoughts, behaviors, and failures. Delusions of grandeur represent extreme fantasy and wish fulfillment. And hallucinations enable one to tolerate one's own negative thoughts and ideas by externalizing them as "voices" outside oneself.

Learning theorists also offer more than one explanation for schizophrenia. One learning perspective argues that schizophrenic behaviors, bizarre as they may be, are rewarded by the environment, most notably by the high degree of social attention that such behaviors elicit. Proponents of this explanation point to research and treatment programs that show that schizophrenic talk can often be reduced through systematic efforts to ignore such talk and to reward "normal" talk. A similar learning perspective argues that the central problem is that schizophrenic people are for some reason no longer rewarded by their environment for attending to stimuli that other persons attend to, and thus seem to have lost their ability to attend to objects effectively. Actually, they can attend

This is a picture drawn by a schizophrenic. As the reader can see, it expresses a caged, trapped feeling and a sense of the world surrounding the individual as chaotic and threatening.

quite well; they simply choose to attend to other things (they may attend to inner cues, which other people are not aware of, since attending to external cues has not been reinforced). Yet a third learning perspective believes that schizophenic individuals learn their behaviors by imitating other schizophrenic people in their environment. The theorists who argue this point to studies that suggest that sometimes the parents of schizophrenics are schizophrenic themselves, and thus provide an influential model. However, this perspective does not account for that vast number of schizophrenics who did not have schizophrenic parents or other such models, nor does it explain why so many children of schizophrenic parents are apparently uninfluenced by having such models and remain normal.

The leading *humanistic* viewpoint on schizophrenia is that of R. D. Laing, who argues that schizophrenic symptoms are actually constructive and positive. Laing views schizophrenic individuals as people who are conducting an inward search to discover their inner self and to recapture their wholeness. Because such individuals have been subjected to intolerable pressures and contradictory demands from their environment, particularly from their families, they are less whole and less aware of their inner selves than normal people. Their schizophrenia is simply a withdrawal from others in order to make an inward search, which, if allowed to continue, will result in a strong, well-adjusted person. Laing believes that the efforts of family members, therapists, and others to alleviate schizophrenic symptoms interfere with this constructive process, suspend the person in an endless journey, and prevent the natural positive outcome of the search. In short, Laing believes in allowing schizophrenic people to travel inward, complete their search, and emerge stronger.

Not surprisingly, Laing's theory has raised a great deal of controversy. The main difficulty is his notion that schizophrenic symptoms are constructive. Opponents point to the apparent suffering and limited lives of schizophrenic persons and ask how these can be viewed as positive in any way. Laing counters that the suffering and limitations result from the environment's inappropriate interference with the natural growth process.

The *biological* model is perhaps the most prominent and promising source of explanation for schizophrenia. This is not to say that there is a single biological approach. On the contrary, there have been many theories on the biological germ or dysfunction that is at the root of schizophrenia. For example, Heath and Krupp (1967) believed that the problem was an antibody named *taraxein* found in the blood of schizophrenics. There was a great deal of excitement when Heath and his colleagues first found that normal individuals would sometimes show schizophrenic symptoms when they were injected with taraxein or when they were given rapid blood transfusions from schizophrenic persons. However, later research was not clear-cut or supportive.

For a while there was much interest in a process researched by Hoffer and Osmond (1962, 1967, 1968) called the *transmethylation process.* They argued that in schizophrenics the production of neurotransmitters (biochemicals in the brain that help transmit nerve impulses) such as norepinephrine is somehow sidetracked, and that instead of neurotransmitters, hallucinogens are produced in the brain. These self-made hallucinogens, produced by the transmethylation process, were thought to be at the root of ongoing schizophrenic behavior, just as synthetic hallucinogens such as mescaline and LSD can produce temporary psychotic-like behaviors.

This theory has generated some support over the years. For example, it was found that the body's neurotransmitters and such synthetic hallucinogens as mescaline and LSD-25 have similar biochemical structures. Also, Friedhoff and Van Winkle (1962) found a hallucinogenic compound called *DMPEA* in the urine of 15 out of 19 schizophrenics. However, urinary measures can be affected by a number of factors. Moreover, subsequent findings on the transmethylation process were mixed, and the enthusiasm for this explanation of schizophrenia declined.

A line of biological explanation that has emerged in the last 10 years and that seems to be gaining more and more support is the idea that schizophrenics have too much dopamine (a particular neurotransmitter) at certain centers in the brain. The idea is that dopamine, among its other functions, plays a key role in our effort to attend, perceive, and integrate information. It may help us to link sensations such as a smell or a color with our memories or internal feelings. Imagine a person who has too much dopamine; almost every smell, color, or other perception would trigger a distinct memory or feeling. How upsetting and confusing this would be—and how similar this experience is to schizophrenic symptoms.

The support for this theory is impressive. For example, it has been noted that phenothiazines (antipsychotic medications) not only often remove schizophrenic symptoms, but also bring on the Parkinsonian symptoms of extreme muscle tremors. We know that Parkinsonian symptoms are caused by too little dopamine in the brain. Thus antipsychotic medications apparently reduce schizophrenic symptoms by severely reducing dopamine, perhaps from a level that was much too high in the first place.

It has also been observed that chronic amphetamine abuse often leads to the appearance of schizophrenic symptoms, and amphetamines are now known to stimulate dopamine production. In fact, schizophrenic persons who take even small dosages of an amphetamine show more intense schizophrenic symptoms. Clearly, then, high dopamine levels are involved in schizophrenia. Of course, high dopamine levels are probably only one piece of the complicated and long biological chain involved in schizophrenia, but it is a piece about which we are becoming increasingly sure.

Finally, the *cognitive* model begins its explanation where the biological model leaves off. Maher (1970) argues that there is nothing wrong with the thinking processes of schizophrenics. Rather, such people have a very real biochemical problem that leads them to experience sensory distortions such as odd sensations, visions, or sounds. Their apparent delusions result from their efforts to make sense of these unusual experiences. Since everyone around them denies that they could be experiencing such sensations, they learn to ignore or discount the opinions of others. Thus schizophrenic individuals apply their logical processes to their unique but real experiences, and they apply them in relative isolation.

In trying to come up with an explanation for these experiences, the person may well decide that such odd sounds are coming from another source, a source that other people apparently cannot hear. The individual may further believe that he or she is a special person to be receiving such communications. Or the person may feel that others are lying about not hearing these sounds or are even secretly sending the sounds and voices. Either way, a delusional system emerges, all from trying to logically understand events that cannot be logically explained within the person's framework of knowledge.

Personality Disorders

In a society in which criminal behavior is increasing, many people take advantage of others, and many behave in ways divergent from most ethical and moral standards, people look to psychology for answers. Is antisocial behavior at all levels of our society (including behavior by seemingly respectable persons) a form of abnormality? What accounts for some people's indifference to the moral and legal standards of their society? One answer provided by psychology is the category of *personality disorders,* previously called *antisocial* or *psychopathic personality.*

As the changing labels show, many psychologists have felt uncomfortable about even considering such behaviors as a form of abnormal functioning. Clearly, such patterns are deviant, but deviant does not necessarily equal abnormal. Nevertheless, perhaps because the kinds of behavior involved are so interesting and their impact on society so important (and harmful), the analysis

CASE HISTORY: PERSONALITY DISORDER

"I can't understand the girl, no matter how hard I try," said the father, shaking his head in genuine perplexity. "It's not that she seems bad or that she means to do wrong. She can lie with the straightest face, and after she's found in the most outlandish lies she still seems perfectly easy in her own mind."

He had related . . . how Roberta at the age of 10 stole her aunt's silver hairbrush, how she repeatedly made off with small articles from the dime store, the drug store, and from her own home. . . .

Neither the father nor the mother seemed a severe parent. . . . [However], there was nothing to suggest that this girl had been spoiled. The parents had, so far as could be determined, consistently let her find that lying and stealing and truancy brought censure and punishment.

As she grew into her teens [she] began to buy dresses, cosmetics, candy, perfume, and other articles, charging them to her father. He had no warning that these bills would come. . . . For many of these things she had little or no use; some of them she distributed among her acquaintances. . . . As a matter of fact, the father, previously in comfortable circumstances, had at one time been forced to the verge of bankruptcy.

In school Roberta's work was mediocre. She studied little and her truancy was spectacular and persistent. No one regarded her as dull, and she seemed to learn easily when she made any effort at all. (Her I.Q. was found to be 135.). . .

"I wouldn't exactly say she's like a hypocrite," her father said. "When she's caught and confronted with her lies and other misbehavior she doesn't seem to appreciate the inconsistency of her position. Her conscience seems still untouched. . . ."

Having failed in many classes and her truancy becoming intolerable to the school, Roberta was expelled from the local high school. . . .

Roberta was sent to two other boarding schools from which she had to be expelled. . . . Employed in her father's business as a bookkeeper, she used her skill at figures and a good deal of ingenuity to make off with considerable sums.

Eventually she was hospitalized for psychiatric observation. During her hospitalization she . . . discussed her mistakes with every appearance of insight. She spoke like a person who had been lost and bewildered but now had found her way. . . . (Roberta returned home but her old behavior patterns continued.)

Despite her prompt failures she would, in her letters to us at the hospital, write as if she had been miraculously cured: "This time we have got to the very root of my trouble and I see the whole story in a different light. . . . If, in your whole life you had never succeeded with one other patient, what you have done for me should make your practice worthwhile. . . . I wish I could tell you how different I feel. How different I am! . . ."

From Cleckley (1964), pp. 66–74.

and investigation of antisocial personality patterns has continued, even though psychologists have acknowledged that the category itself may be inaccurate and inappropriate.

Certainly, not everyone who is a criminal has been categorized as having a personality disorder. The label has been applied to those individuals whose personality characteristics pervasively include unsocialized behavior in conflict with society; inability to display loyalty to others; gross selfishness, callousness, irresponsibility, and impulsiveness; inability to feel guilt or learn from experience; and low tolerance of frustration. At the same time such individuals can be quite intelligent. Obviously, these characteristics fit many different actions and people; the level of *personality disorder* has been used for those whose whole life-style is typified by such characteristics.

Theories and research into antisocial personality patterns have centered on two areas: (1) socialization and family background, and (2) biological factors.

The family theories have cut across the psychoanalytic, learning, humanistic, and cognitive models by focusing on such variables as identification, modeling, poor value acquisition, and attitude development. Despite much research, these theories have not produced a clear or coherent picture.

The biological approach has consistently pointed to a few variables. Genetic studies have shown the possibility of a genetic role in antisocial personality patterns. For example, Hutchings and Tednick (1974) found a higher correlation in the rates of criminality between adoptees and their biological parents than between adoptees and their adopted parents. Furthermore, Hare (1970) concluded after a careful examination of the research that people with antisocial patterns may have physiological correlates that make them less inhibited than others. It is important to remember that these indicators are tentative at best and it is difficult to draw conclusions from them. The growing trend in psychology is against considering antisocial personality patterns a homogeneous group or even a legitimate category.

Other Dimensions of Abnormality

Addiction and Alcoholism

Drug addiction is a misuse of drugs that typically involves physiological dependence, increased tolerance, withdrawal symptoms when the user tries to stop taking the drug, and psychological dependence. At first people get pleasurable effects from the drug, but often they come to need greater and greater amounts to achieve the same pleasurable effects (tolerance). In fact, they come to need greater and greater amounts to reach even the basic level of comfort they originally had without any drugs. If they try to stop taking the drug, they experience painful physical symptoms (withdrawal), including hypertension, severe cramps, and restlessness. People who are addicted are on an escalating cycle—they must take more and more of the drug just to break even. If they stay off the drug long enough, they can break this cycle, but withdrawal is a most painful and feared experience that very few addicts can force themselves to undergo.

There are a variety of addictions. Alcoholism is one kind, although many people do not think of alcohol as a drug, mainly because it is legal and accessible. Narcotic addiction (addiction to opium, heroin, and morphine) is a major problem and linked to crime because narcotics are relatively inaccessible and illegal in our society. Yet another very serious addiction is addiction to barbiturates (certain kinds of sedatives and sleeping pills). While there are other drugs that are addictive, these are the most common.

The destruction of their personal and social lives is commonplace among drug addicts. The drug becomes the most important thing in their lives. Their life-styles center on acquiring and taking the drug. Beyond this slavery to the drug, there is the harmful (sometimes toxic) effect that chronic high dosages can have on their bodies, behavior, emotions, and thinking.

In an attempt to answer the question of what makes an addict, Glatt (1974) describes three connected areas of influence: the *host* (mental or physical makeup

of the individual); the *environment;* and the *agent* or nature of the drug involved.

HOST.   Although psychologists have been unable to come up with a personality profile that leads inevitably to dependency, studies suggest that certain characteristics are fairly consistent in addicts. Among these are emotional immaturity, a low tolerance for frustration or tension, and a strong tendency to avoid reality. Because addicts or problem drinkers often seem to run in families, a genetic influence has long been suspected. One study by Goodwin (1973) showed a higher than normal rate of drinking problems among adopted children whose biological parents were alcoholics, even though the children were unaware of their background.

ENVIRONMENT.   As might be expected, both drug and alcohol abuse are more prevalent in sociocultural environments where these substances are readily available. Social acceptability also plays a major role. It is easier for a susceptible individual to become addicted to drugs that are considered "normal," as alcohol is in our culture. Economic factors may also be influential. In times of prosperity money is available to spend on drugs and alcohol. Conversely, during a financial depression these substances provide an eagerly sought escape mechanism.

AGENT.   Obviously, some drugs are more addictive than others. Users of the opiates (heroin in particular) or barbiturates may become addicted in a relatively short time, no matter how psychologically stable they are. Other drugs, including amphetamines, may become addictive through conditioned response to their tension-releasing properties and production of euphoria.

Alcoholism is one of the easier addictions to drift into because alcohol is both easily available and socially acceptable in our society. Alcoholism is a problem that affects a wide range of age groups and cuts across all levels of occupation, wealth, and religion. Male alcoholics have traditionally outnumbered female alcoholics, but the gap seems to be narrowing.

The destructiveness of alcoholism is pervasive and dramatic. Alcoholics can cause themselves grave bodily damage (including liver damage, malnutrition, vitamin deficiency, hypertension, endocrine gland and heart problems), psychological damage (for example, dependence, poor social judgment, and loss of self-respect), and damage to the quality and purposefulness of their lives (loss of job, friends, others' trust, and sense of accomplishment).

The family and friends of alcoholic people suffer greatly as they observe their loved ones destroying their lives. Family and friends are themselves often subjected to abuse, embarrassment, frustration, and financial instability in the course of their relationships with individuals addicted to alcohol. Their lives fluctuate with the alcohol intake of the addicted relative or friend.

Alcoholics also inflict suffering on members of society whom they have never met. The number of crimes and accidents related to alcohol is staggering. Coleman (1980) summarizes this picture: "Alcohol has been associated with over half the deaths and major injuries suffered in automobile accidents each year, and with about 50 percent of all murders, 40 percent of all assaults, 35 percent or more of all rapes, and 30 percent of all suicides. About one out of every three arrests in the United States results from the abuse of alcohol" (p. 314).

Because alcoholism is so prevalent, the efforts to explain it have been many and various. The *psychoanalytic model* provides several viewpoints. One of the more common is that alcoholics are fixated at the oral stage of development—

their needs as infants during the oral stage were either not met or were met excessively. In either case, the frustrated needs, especially dependency and oral needs, may later take the form of alcoholism under a particular set of life events and circumstances.

The *learning model* sees the use of alcohol as a learned method of reducing stress. This theory seems at odds with the obvious punishment and increased stress that ultimately result from long-term usage. One explanation for this seeming contradiction is provided by the concept of a *delay of reward gradient* (Dollard and Miller, 1950). Rewards and punishments decrease in value the further off they seem, and the alcoholic individual chooses the immediate gratification of temporary tension relief.

The *biological model* points to the withdrawal symptoms that occur when a chronic alcohol drinker suddenly stops as evidence that some physiological changes are involved in alcoholism. A group of withdrawal symptoms that occur in many chronic drinkers is called *delirium tremens (DTs)*. A sudden drop in the blood's alcohol level can cause profuse sweating, eye pupil irregularity, delirious experiences, and hallucinations of the most disturbing sort. Of course, such withdrawal reactions do not prove that alcoholism is primarily a physical event that causes psychological dependency, but there is a lot of interest in this possibility. Many people have proposed that alcoholism is indeed a problem "caused" by biological predispositions, metabolic or organic weaknesses, genetic factors, and the like (Williams, 1959; Segovia-Riguelme, Varela, and Mardones, 1971; Goodwin et al., 1973). Others have argued against this perspective, saying that the evidence has yet to clearly establish this point.

Other forms of addiction are unique in certain ways, but basically involve the same dimensions as alcoholism. For example, in narcotic addiction and barbiturate addiction there is significant physiological addiction, bodily and psychological damage, personal damage, family and social impact, and societal implications. And the explanations offered by the various models parallel those offered for alcoholism.

Narcotic addiction has stirred a great deal of attention in recent years because of some critical research findings that may ultimately point to a clear understanding of what addiction is all about, at least in biological terms. A few years ago researchers (Goldstein et al., 1974; Goldstein, 1976; Pert and Snyder, 1973) discovered that the body had certain receptor sites for opiates, including certain sites in the brain, intestines, and other locations. Apparently, opiates operate on a person through their impact on these receptor locations. For example, there is a high number of opiate receptors in that area of the brain that regulates pupil dilation. One effect of opiates is constriction of the pupils. Obviously, they do this by their impact on these particular receptor sites in the brain.

Researchers were able to map the opiate receptor sites throughout the body. They then asked why we have receptor sites in our bodies for foreign substances like opium, morphine, and heroin. A possible answer was that perhaps our bodies have naturally occurring opiates that regularly operate on these receptor sites in all people. The search was on for the body's natural opiates, and indeed, natural opiatelike substances were found in the bodies of human beings and other animals—*enkephalins* and *endorphins*. Enkephalins and endorphins are apparently naturally produced substances that help us cope with pain and stress. Our bodies automatically produce them, use them, and need them to cope effectively with pain and stress.

Putting this startling discovery together with what is known about narcotic addiction, researchers think that addiction may operate in the following way. When first taken, opiates relieve pain or give an extra push to the emotions by filling those receptor sites that have not yet been filled by the body's natural opiates—enkephalins and endorphins. But if a person takes opiates too often, these receptor sites get overloaded and the body's own production of enkephalins and endorphins is decreased or cut off because these substances simply aren't needed as much. At this point, the opiates are needed not just for an extra push but to *make up for* the decreases in normal bodily production of enkephalins and endorphins. Thus the addicted person needs to take more and more opiates to fill those increasingly empty receptor sites. This explanation is certainly consistent with the increasing tolerance we noted earlier. If opiates are withheld from the addicted person, the receptor sites will remain empty for a period of time because enkephalin production has been cut off. With no opiates—foreign or natural—at these sites, the body has no tools to fight pain, stress, and perform certain regulatory functions. The person will feel and react in a most uncomfortable and debilitated manner. This explanation is consistent with the experience of withdrawal. Withdrawal symptoms will continue until the body renews its production of enkephalins and endorphins.

Research in this area is now moving at a rapid pace. As our insights into the biological mechanisms involved in narcotic addiction grow, so should the

Table 16–3: Estimated Incidence of Abnormal Behavior Patterns in the United States.

200,000 reported cases of child abuse.
200,000 or more individuals attempt suicide* (26,000 or more individuals die from suicide).
1,000,000 individuals are actively schizophrenic.
1,000,000 or more students withdraw from college each year as a result of emotional problems.
2,000,000 individuals suffer from profound depression.
6,000,000 or more children and teenagers are considered emotionally disturbed.
7,000,000 individuals are considered mentally retarded.
10,000,000 or more juveniles and adults are arrested in connection with serious crimes* (190,000 or more individuals are sent to prison and 500,000 individuals are in prison).
10,000,000 Americans report alcohol-related problems (1,000,000 individuals are being treated for such).
20,000,000 (at least) individuals suffer from neurotic disturbance.
53,500,000 individuals suffer from mild to moderate depression.

*The incidence of suicide attempts and serious crimes may be much higher due to the large number that are not reported.

After Coleman (1980): Incidence figures based on Berger (1978), the National Institute of Mental Health (1978), the President's Commission on Mental Health (1978), and Uniform Crime Reports (1978).

implications for treating addiction. Possible connections with other forms of addiction may also emerge in the near future. Clearly, this research has provided a dramatic breakthrough in understanding drug addiction.

Since abnormal functioning appears in a wide range of patterns, talking in general terms about "mental illness" or "abnormality" can be uninformative and misleading. Clearly, abnormal functioning in its various forms represents a major problem in our society. People are increasingly seeking the services of mental health personnel and facilities. In part, this rise in the numbers of people seeking help may be due to a lessening of the stigma associated with emotional and behavioral problems, but it probably also reflects an increase in the actual prevalence of such problems. Coleman (1980) summarizes the estimated incidence of major maladaptive behavior patterns in the United States in 1978 in Table 16-3.

There are many different explanations for these numerous and varied problems. Even within each general model of explanation we often find theories that differ greatly. Research has sometimes provided outstanding clarification of a particular type of abnormal functioning, but more often it has simply given us clues that may lead to clarification. At the moment, psychology is in some conflict about the definition of abnormal behavior. This is not an unreasonable state of affairs for a relatively young science; however, it is important that professionals and public alike be aware of the newness and limitations of the field. Only such awareness can assure the openness to new ideas and the support for research that are crucial to an increased understanding of abnormal behavior.

Summary

1. Defining normal and abnormal behavior in statistical, cultural, or ideal terms has proved difficult. Instead, it has been found useful to establish criteria that, taken together, give a picture of abnormal behavior. These criteria are: bizarreness and extremeness; disturbance of others; subjective distress; and interference with daily functioning.

2. The Diagnostic and Statistical Manual of Mental Disorders (DSM III) is the official classification system of the American Psychiatric Association. Critics of the clinical classification system question its reliance on psychoanalytic terms and its reliability.

3. *Neurosis,* a term applied to a wide range of behaviors, generally involves three elements: anxiety, self-defeating behavior, and exaggerated behavior.

4. *Phobic neurosis* involves a persistant, disproportionate fear of a particular object or situation, such as a fear of heights (acrophobia). *Anxiety neurosis* (sometimes called free-floating anxiety) is more generalized; it involves the same fear and discomfort as in phobic neurosis, but is not linked to a specific object.

5. *Obsessive-compulsive* behaviors are those in which a person feels compelled to repeat unwanted thoughts over and over, or to repeat certain actions or rituals.

6.   Hysterical neurosis refers to a group of rather dramatic neurotic reactions that fall into two categories: the *dissociative type* and the *conversion type*. Dissociative disturbances involve problems of memory and consciousness, such as *amnesia, fugue, somnambulism,* and *multiple personality*. In the conversion type of hysterical neurosis, people develop physical symptoms, such as blindness, body aches, or paralysis, with no apparent physical cause.

7.   *Depression* describes a wide range of complaints from mild sadness to a highly disabling state. While the various schools of though differ as to the cause of depression, the biological model has offered some particularly interesting observations. Biological theorists link depression with low levels of certain neurotransmitters.

8.   *Schizophrenia* is another term that is applied to a wide range of disorders; schizophrenia includes disturbances of thought, perception, emotion, and motor abilities. Thoughts may be disorganized or the content of thoughts may be deluded. Disturbances of perception may range from distraction to hallucinations. Emotional disturbances may include inappropriate reactions or ambivalent reactions; motor disturbances may include systematic gesturing or catatonic states.

9.   A biological explanation of schizophrenia that is gaining more and more support is that schizophrenics have an abnormally high amount of the neurotransmitter *dopamine* in certain brain centers. Dopamine affects attention, perception, and integration of information.

10.   Personality disorders should not necessarily be considered abnormal behavior, according to some theorists; they belong more to a legal definition than a psychological one.

11.   Drug addiction (now more commonly known as drug dependence) and alcoholism are other dimensions of abnormal behavior; both of these conditions involve a psychological dependence and a physiological dependence on a specific substance, whether it is heroin, barbiturates, alcohol, or another substance.

12.   The three interconnected areas of influence in drug dependence have been described as: the host, the environment, and the agent. While studies have failed to identify a specific personality profile that inevitably leads to dependence, they have identified certain characteristics that seem to be present in some addicts and alcoholics: emotional immaturity, low tolerance for frustration, and a strong tendency to avoid reality.

Suggested Readings

Agras, W. S., Chapin, H. N., and Oliveau, D. C. The natural history of phobia: Course and prognosis. *Archives of General Psychiatry,* 26 (1972), 315–17. Presents a study following the natural course of phobias over a 5-year period in people whose phobias were not treated by psychotherapy.

BECKER, J. *Affective disorders.* Morristown, N.J.: General Learning Press, 1977. Provides an overview of the problem of depression, citing theories and research from the various models.

FADIMAN, J., and KEWMAN, D. (Eds.). *Exploring madness: Experience, theory, and research.* Monterey, Cal.: Brooks/Cole, 1973. Looks at abnormal functioning through an interesting mixture of personal and literary accounts, research, and theoretical perspectives, including both traditional and radical perspectives.

LEON, G. R. *Case histories of deviant behavior,* 2nd ed. Boston: Holbrook, 1977. Interesting case histories are presented along with interpretations and discussions reflecting the behavioral and cognitive models.

MCNEIL, E. B. *The quiet furies.* Englewood Cliffs, N.J.: Prentice-Hall, 1967. Presents interesting case histories in detail from a psychodynamic perspective.

SELIGMAN, M. E. P. *Helplessness.* San Francisco: Freeman, 1975. Offers the learned helplessness interpretation of depression, a cognitive-behavioral view that has stirred a great deal of research in recent years.

SZASZ, R. The myth of mental illness. *American Psychologists,* 15 (1960), 113–18. Presents a controversial position on the nature and definition of mental illness by one of the field's most interesting figures.

17 Therapy

Maxine G., a patient in a mental hospital, spends an hour each day with a psychologist. She never says a word. At the start of each session, the psychologist says, "This is your time. I'm here to listen if you want to talk." This is followed by an hour of silence.

Arnold Y. scoffs at the idea of psychotherapy. "Whenever I get uptight," he says, "I go to my favorite bar, tie one on, and moan to the bartender for two hours. It's not only cheaper than therapy, it's a lot more fun."

Vivian E. joins a therapy group to help her overcome her painful lack of self-confidence. When she tries to explain her problem during the first meeting, several group members tell her she is talking absolute nonsense. She is extremely upset and never returns to the group.

Which of these individuals is receiving therapy? It is possible to argue that all of them are; it is also possible to argue the opposite. If one purpose of therapy is to provide relief from emotional tension, then conceivably Arnold Y. found therapy in a bar, while Vivian E., we must assume, did not find it at a group session. With Maxine G., it is hard to say without following the future course of her sessions.

Psychotherapy, however, includes more than relief from emotional tension. It must provide a *change* for the better in the person receiving the therapy. Davison and Neale (1978) describe psychotherapy as "a set of procedures by which one person uses language to change the life of another."

Change is the key element in this definition. The change may be cognitive, behavioral, or emotional—that is, therapy may change the way a person thinks, behaves, or feels—or all three. To return to our opening examples, we can see that the bartender's sympathetic ear is unlikely to result in more than a temporary change in Arnold's mood. Maxine G.'s case still raises questions: Is change taking place during her long periods of silence? Is therapy possible without an exchange of words? The result of Vivian E.'s experience also seems less clear. She may well have been changed by her experience (and, we could argue, it is possible that the change will be beneficial in the long run), but is this therapy?

In this chapter we will look at some of the numerous theories and approaches to therapy, their intended purposes, and their demonstrated effectiveness.

489

The History of Therapy

The first attempt at treatment we know of took place roughly half a million years ago, during the Stone Age (Coleman, 1980). There is evidence from the period of a practice known as *trephining,* in which people were treated by chipping a round hole in their skulls with a stone tool, presumably to allow an evil spirit or demon to escape. Some of the unearthed skulls show evidence of healing around the hole, so at least some patients survived this drastic remedy and lived for several years afterward.

From early recorded history there seems to have been agreement among the Chinese, Hebrews, Egyptians, and Greeks that mental abnormalities were the result of possession by *demons.* The accepted method of treatment was *exorcism,* which involved rites of prayer and a variety of techniques designed to make the possessed person's body a most undesirable place for evil spirits. These techniques included drinking vile liquids, which were then regurgitated, presumably along with the offending demon. Other approaches, perhaps designed for more stubborn cases, involved flogging and starvation.

In every age the dominant influence in the choice of therapy has been the particular model of human behavior, both normal and abnormal, used by the therapist.

Hippocrates rejected the prevailing idea of demons and formulated an early medical model. He divided mental illness into three categories: mania, melancholia, and phrenitis, or brain fever. All three were thought to be caused by a disturbance of the body. Treatment, therefore, was aimed at the body and, depending on the category, included vegetarianism, exercise, sexual abstinence, and bleeding.

By the late Middle Ages, however, the demons had returned. Priests took over the treatment of abnormal behavior, first with prayers and sprinkling of holy water, and later with more violent forms of exorcism (driving out the devil). By the fifteenth century abnormal behavior was thought to be due to witchcraft. Treatment consisted of torturing the victims until they confessed, and then burning them to death.

The demon approach was still accepted by both church and state in the early sixteenth century. It was not, however, without opposition. One of the leading attackers was Johann Weyer, who published a book based on a humanitarian model, arguing that witches were mentally ill rather than "possessed." He advocated treatment centered on understanding and help instead of torture and burning at the stake. Although Weyer is regarded as the founder of modern psychopathology, his theories were met at the time with scathing criticism.

Mentally disturbed people who escaped the treatment for witchcraft were usually confined to monasteries or prisons. From the sixteenth century onward, special asylums, or mental hospitals, gradually took over this responsibility. Patients in institutions were usually treated more like animals or prisoners than human beings in need of help. Then, in 1792, a Frenchman, Philippe Pinel, was put in charge of a hospital for the insane near Paris. Pinel made some radical changes. He removed the patients' chains; he moved them from dark dungeons to sunny rooms; and he allowed them to work and exercise outdoors. The results were almost miraculously beneficial.

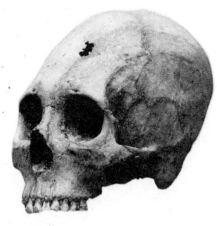

Trephining, or making a hole in the skull to allow an evil demon or spirit to escape, was one of the first attempts at treatment. Notice how in the lower skull the hole has actually begun to grow over—this means that the patient actually survived this drastic treatment and lived for several years afterward.

(Left) This painting by Charles Muller shows Philippe Pinel demanding the removal of the chains from the insane at a hospital in Paris.
(Right) Dorothea Dix was an American who traveled throughout the country speaking for the reform of mental hospitals.

About the same time, reforms were taking place in American mental institutions. One notable advocate of the humanitarian approach was Benjamin Rush, who became known as the father of American psychiatry. Another energetic reformer was a retired schoolteacher from New England, Dorothea Dix. Dix took her humanitarian crusade throughout the country (and several other countries as well) and is credited with the establishment or reform of more than 30 mental hospitals.

Throughout the nineteenth century many state hospitals for mental patients were founded on the optimistic belief that proper treatment in proper surroundings would lead to the discovery of a cure. The result was an increase in admissions, which by the mid-nineteenth century had reached such proportions that the institutions were forced to shift their priority from finding a cure for mental illness to simply providing custodial care. Bars reappeared on windows, doors were locked, and the atmosphere once more became more like that of a prison than a hospital.

Private mental hospitals were usually superior to public ones. Since they had better financing and a lower staff-to-patient ratio, they were often able to provide the quiet therapeutic atmosphere and patient attention that could lead to improvement. However, private hospitals were usually available only to the wealthy. Most people requiring hospitalization went to the inadequate public facilities.

As our knowledge of abnormal functioning improved, it became clear that many people who needed treatment did not have to be in a hospital. Outpatient treatment, usually in the form of hourly sessions, proved helpful to many people. Again, the therapy was available only to those who could afford it. Others in need tended to receive no outpatient treatment or were hospitalized even though they might have done better in private psychotherapy.

Thus effective outpatient and inpatient care was available only to a small number of people with emotional and behavioral problems. The less wealthy were given inadequate custodial care or no care at all. This trend continued until after World War II, when two major developments changed the situation. First, psychoactive drugs were discovered in the 1950s. These drugs had a major effect on the quality of hospital care by providing an easier way to control violent patients and reduce anxiety and depression in others. Such drugs helped to lower the population of public mental hospitals, and this in turn improved the treatment prognosis.

The second major postwar development in psychotherapy came about in the 1960s, partly in response to dissatisfaction with mental institutions. The community mental health movement was formed to deal with the mental health problems on a local level, if possible before they reached the point where hospitalization was needed. Community mental health centers were established to provide help for the many people who could not afford private and sometimes distant treatment. Another objective was to overcome some of the resistance on the part of community members to the idea of psychotherapy.

Services at community mental health centers were tailored to the needs of the community, and included: ongoing psychotherapy; hotline phones so that anyone with a problem could find someone who would listen; public education on problems such as drug abuse; and active participation in controlling factors that may have an effect on the emotional stability of the community, such as poor housing. This tradition of local agencies providing ongoing therapy and other innovative interventions continues today (see Figure 17-1).

In short, inpatient and outpatient treatment has improved considerably in recent years. Yet there is still a lot of room for improvement. For example, treatment in some of our public mental hospitals consists of little more than regular doses of tranquilizing drugs and perhaps a bit of group therapy with other patients. Regular sessions alone with a hospital psychiatrist or clinical psychologist are too often the exception rather than the rule. Many observers believe that treatment in such mental institutions is of little value, especially when the negative effects of being labeled an "ex-mental patient" are considered. Our mental institutions need further reform, and we still have to find a way to make mental health care available at a cost most people can afford.

Figure 17-1

This chart shows the percentage of patients treated in a number of different facilities and by different agencies in 1955 and 1973. Note the increase in patients treated by community mental health agencies and the increase in outpatient treatment in general in 1973. (National Institute of Mental Health, 1975)

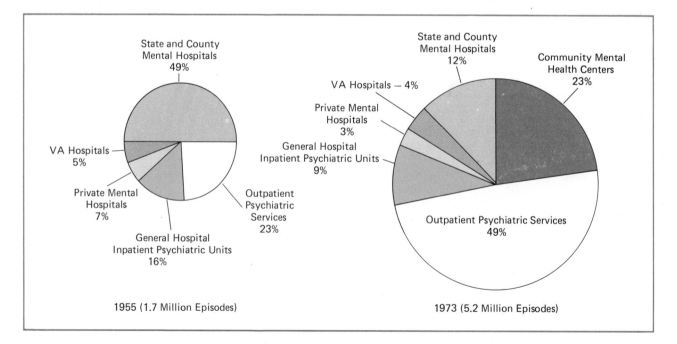

Who Practices Therapy?

Practitioners of psychotherapy are divided into four groups, largely on the basis of the type of training they have undergone: psychiatrists, clinical psychologists, psychiatric social workers, and counselors. The type of training is also likely to have a strong influence on the model used by a particular therapist.

Psychiatrists are the only one of the four groups that start with an M.D. degree. After earning their medical degree, they undertake a residency program in psychiatry for several years. Psychiatrists are the only psychotherapists who are permitted to prescribe psychoactive drugs that affect the way their patients feel and think and, consequently, the way they behave. They are also the only therapists permitted to prescribe electroshock treatment. Because psychiatrists are doctors, they are often thought of as being more extensively trained in psychotherapy than other kinds of therapists. This is not necessarily true, because the 4-year period of medical training involves little psychiatry.

Clinical psychologists do 4 to 5 years of graduate work after graduating from college and obtain a Ph.D. Their training includes laboratory work, research design, and specialized training in abnormal behavior and therapy techniques, usually followed by an internship in which candidates work with clients under professional supervision.

Psychiatric social workers study for 2 years to earn a master's degree, including a year's internship in social work. The number of social workers involved in psychotherapy is growing rapidly in this country. This growth reflects our society's increasing use of psychotherapy services, as well as the heightened degree of training and professionalism now available in the field of social work.

Counseling psychologists and *counselors* earn graduate degrees in psychology or counseling and then do internships in a counseling setting. Often their training and attention is concentrated in specific areas such as student, marriage, or family counseling. Often their practice focuses on problems in adjustment rather than abnormal functioning.

It is not uncommon for these different mental health practitioners to practice similar kinds of therapy or focus on similar problems. For example, marriage and couple counseling is a field of specialization practiced not only by counselors but also by psychiatrists, psychologists, social workers, and other professionals in the field. Another example is family counseling, which is based on the belief that many problems can be traced to faulty relationships among members of the family rather than merely to the personality problems of the individual. Thus practitioners work with all family members rather than focusing on one person.

Many people practice psychotherapy in the course of performing other functions. For example, psychiatric nurses not only carry out the medication orders of staff psychiatrists but also interact with patients in psychotherapeutic ways. Also, while the main function of school psychologists and social workers is the assessment of emotional and behavioral difficulties, they often engage in therapeutic interactions with pupils. These therapeutic functions are recognized by the respective professions and there is an increasing trend to include therapeutic techniques in the training of these professionals.

Thus there are many different types of therapists operating in many different settings. There are also different approaches to therapy, which we shall look at next. The five basic approaches are the same ones that we discussed in relation to abnormal behavior in Chapter 16: the psychoanalytic, learning, biological, humanistic-existential, and cognitive models.

The Psychoanalytic Model of Therapy

The psychoanalytic model, initiated by Freud, locates the origin of abnormal functioning in emotionally painful situations or events experienced in childhood that have resulted in arrested personality development. The patient is thus unable to resolve unconscious conflicts and impulses except by maladaptive defense mechanisms such as excessive repression.

Psychoanalytic therapy—or psychoanalysis, as it is called—is based on verbal techniques. Its basic purpose is to solve psychological problems by bringing the unconscious conflicts into the conscious mind, where they may be confronted and resolved by the person. The focus is on feelings rather than on behavior. Psychoanalysis aims to change the patient's entire life-style and personality rather than just certain behaviors. In Freudian terms, psychoanalysis is designed to strengthen the ego, increase the awareness of the id, and bring the superego under control.

Psychoanalysis is usually an involved process that takes years to complete. The role of the psychoanalyst is largely passive; it is that of a guide and interpreter rather than a teacher. One of the major problems the analyst must deal with is the emotional resistance of the patient to the painful awareness that an emotional problem exists. Therefore, analysis must do more than uncover the emotional origins of problems; if effective therapy is to take place, it must enable the person to acknowledge and confront these problems.

Techniques of Psychoanalysis

Psychoanalysis uses several techniques—most of them originated by Freud— as part of the therapeutic process. One of the best known is *free association,* in which the patient is encouraged to say whatever thoughts come to mind, regardless of how illogical, irrelevant, or embarrassing they seem. Freud said that free association should be like someone viewing scenes from a train window, smoothly flowing by. The theory is that by disregarding intellectual judgment and interpretation, the person will bypass the ego's defenses and produce clues to the unconscious source of the problems. Of course, it rarely happens this easily. What gets in the way is the person's own *resistance,* which occurs in the form of blanks, obviously contrived associations, or disputes with the therapist. The form or source of this resistance is regarded as significant by the psychoanalyst and a possible opportunity for insight and interpretation, because it is a clue that the person is getting close to the source of a problem.

Interpretation is another key technique used by the psychoanalyst to make the unconscious conscious, to bring hidden emotions to the surface. When the person seems ready to face underlying problems, the analyst suggests possible hidden meanings or defense mechanisms revealed by the person's actions or statements. The analyst points out connections and associations the person may not have seen—connections between belief and actions, or between current attitudes and something that happened in the past. The person may deny these connections (this is one form of resistance, and is usually taken by the analyst as a sign that the interpretation is correct) or use them to gain insight into the unconscious source of the problem.

In addition to interpreting a person's resistance, psychoanalysts also interpret the person's dreams. Freud (1933) called dreams the "royal road to the unconscious." By interpreting dreams the psychoanalyst tries to help people recognize unconscious impulses that are threatening to them. By looking at such impulses in the light of day, people can see that they are no longer as scary or as unacceptable as they seemed when they were children. Once people see this, they are able to relax their defenses and bring out more unconscious material.

When we are asleep, the ego and superego are not as much in control as when we are awake, and unconscious impulses surface—but usually in disguise. According to Freud, dreams have two levels of content. One is the *manifest content,* which involves the overt and concrete happenings of the dream. This is the dream as dreamers experience and remember it. The other level is the

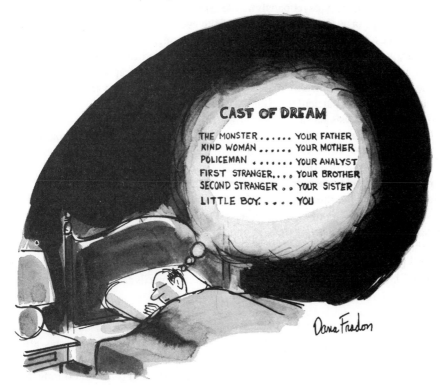

Drawing by Dana Fradon; © 1973 The New Yorker Magazine, Inc.

latent content, the hidden and symbolic meaning of the dream, the disguise that the impulse appears in. It is the latent content that the psychoanalyst helps people to understand and use to gain insight into their hidden motivations.

As psychoanalysis progresses, a special relationship, called *transference,* begins to develop between patient and analyst. Patients begin to form irrational emotional expectations of the analyst. They may feel that the analyst is angry with them, bored by them, disappointed in them, trying to seduce them, or expecting too much of them. Their own reaction may be anger, fear, love, or an effort to dominate the analyst. According to Freud, these unrealistic interpretations are a result of transferring past relationships with important adults (usually parents) onto the analyst, relating to the analyst as if he or she were the parent figure. Although this transference is unconscious, patients expect the analyst to react the way their parents would, so that they can reenact repressed wishes and experiences. A patient with a stern, demanding father, for example, may express the fear that the analyst is displeased with the progress of the therapy. A patient who was emotionally abandoned by an unresponsive mother might feel that the analyst is not really interested in helping with the problem (that is, abandoning the patient again).

Psychoanalysis since Freud

Psychoanalysis as a therapeutic approach has been modified by many people over the years. Just as different psychoanalytic *theorists* have attached greater importance to social drives (as opposed to sexual drives) or to the ego (as opposed to the id), different psychoanalytic *therapists* have emphasized interpersonal relationships or insights into the role of the ego. Thus there may be significant differences among psychoanalytic therapies, though all share the belief that intrapsychic conflict is at the core of the problem and that insight is essential to improvement. However, the precise elements of the intrapsychic conflict and the precise kind of insight that is achieved in therapy may vary significantly depending on the particular psychoanalytic school of thought.

Psychoanalysis has also undergone some significant changes in technique. Sessions five days a week in which the patient lies on a couch, once the hallmark of this approach, still take place, but much less often. More common are sessions once a week in which the patient and the therapist sit face to face. In some psychoanalytic circles there are even efforts to shorten the duration of psychotherapy or to have the therapist play a much more active role. The goals also differ somewhat from Freud's. Today there is more emphasis on present problems and ways to solve them and less on building a psychodynamic history of the person. Techniques are also more flexible—transference may or may not be used, and the therapist may vary techniques to deal with different individuals' problems, or even to deal with one individual's different needs at various points in the therapy.

Criticism of Psychoanalysis

Psychoanalytic approaches have received a great deal of criticism—this after an extended period during which psychoanalysis was almost the only approach to therapy available. Some critics argue that analysis simply takes too long and costs too much money for most people. Others point out that the techniques

APPLICATION
Psychoanalysis

THERAPIST: It sounds as if you would like to let loose with me, but you are afraid of what my response would be (*summarizing and restating*).

PATIENT: I get so excited by what is happening here. I feel I'm being held back by needing to be nice. I'd like to blast loose sometimes, but I don't dare.

THERAPIST: Because you fear my reaction?

PATIENT: The worst thing would be that you wouldn't like me. You wouldn't speak to me friendly; you wouldn't smile; you'd feel you can't treat me and discharge me from treatment. But I know this isn't so, I know it.

THERAPIST: Where do you think these attitudes come from?

PATIENT: When I was nine years old, I read a lot about great men in history. I'd quote them and be dramatic. I'd want a sword at my side; I'd dress like an Indian. Mother would scold me. Don't frown, don't talk so much. Sit on your hands, over and over again. I did all kinds of things. I was a naughty child. She told me I'd be hurt. Then at fourteen I fell off a horse and broke my back. I had to be in bed. Mother then told me on the day I went riding not to, that I'd get hurt because the ground was frozen. I was a stubborn, self-willed child. Then I went against her will and suffered an accident that changed my life, a fractured back. Her attitude was, "I told you so." I was put in a cast and kept in bed for months.

THERAPIST: You were punished, so to speak, by this accident.

PATIENT: But I gained attention and love from mother for the first time. I felt so good. I'm ashamed to tell you this. Before I healed I opened the cast and tried to walk to make myself sick again so I could stay in bed longer.

THERAPIST: How does that connect up with your impulse to be sick now and stay in bed so much? (*The patient has these tendencies, of which she is ashamed.*)

PATIENT: Oh . . . (*pause*)

THERAPIST: What do you think?

PATIENT: Oh, my God, how infantile, how ungrown-up (*pause*). It must be so. I want people to love me and be sorry for me. Oh, my God. How completely childish. It is, *is* that. My mother must have ignored me when I was little, and I wanted so to be loved. (*This sounds like insight.*)

THERAPIST: So that it may have been threatening to go back to being self-willed and unloved after you got out of the cast (*interpretation*).

PATIENT: It did. My life changed. I became meek and controlled. I couldn't get angry or stubborn afterward.

THERAPIST: Perhaps if you go back to being stubborn with *me*, you would be returning to how you were before, that is, active, stubborn but unloved.

PATIENT: (*excitedly*) And, therefore, losing your love. I need you, but after all you aren't going to reject me. But the pattern is so established now that the threat of the loss of love is too overwhelming with everybody, and I've got to keep myself from acting selfish or angry.

(Wolberg, 1977, 560–561)

and complexities of psychoanalysis make it helpful only to people who are in touch with reality and coherent, and possess verbal abilities and verbal interaction skills.

The requirement of coherence is particularly troubling when it comes to treating people whose major symptom is a lack of coherence. It is not surprising, therefore, that psychoanalytic approaches have been regularly applied to problems of anxiety, neurosis, and depression, where the person's intellectual ability is intact, and less often to cases of psychosis, such as schizophrenia. Many psychoanalysts, including Freud, have admitted that psychoanalysis is not an effective therapy for schizophrenia. Beyond the issue of coherence and reality testing, one of the major problems with the psychoanalytic approach is the necessity for establishing a bond of trust between therapist and patient. This can be discouragingly difficult to achieve with schizophrenics, since they often are extremely withdrawn and have strong defenses against the intimacy and trans-ference essential to psychoanalysis.

Finally, there is the criticism that psychoanalysis may be a good way to get at the source of the patient's problem, but not necessarily to treat it. It may be that the quickest and most effective way to solve present problems is to focus on the problems themselves rather than on what caused them. That, at least, is the viewpoint of the learning model.

The Learning Model of Therapy

The learning model sees abnormal functioning as patterns of behavior that are learned by the individual—"bad habits," if you will. Thus the learning approach to psychotherapy involves extinguishing the maladaptive patterns and learning more appropriate ones. The extinction and learning follow the principles of classical conditioning, operant conditioning, and modeling that were discussed in Chapters 6 and 14.

Therapy is centered on the problem behaviors themselves; there is no attempt to work back to their origin in the person's childhood. Thus most learning therapy approaches come under the heading of *behavioral therapy*. The first step in a behavioral approach is to define the problem in terms of measurable behavior. Behavioral therapists are not content with descriptions of feeling or undefined fears. If, for example, a person wants to overcome feelings of help-lessness, the therapist will begin by working with the person to better describe these feelings and to pinpoint what behaviors are affected by these feelings. Helpless to do what? To get to work on time? To complete assignments? To relate to other people? Once the specific behaviors in need of change are de-fined, treatment programs using conditioning techniques are worked out. In this way the therapist adapts the method used to the particular problem, rather than using the same method with all problems.

Systematic Desensitization

Behavioral approaches have been applied quite often to problems of anxiety and neurosis. One of the best-known approaches is *systematic desensitization*. It is based on the principle of reciprocal inhibition, in which the person substitutes for the undesired response a response that is incompatible or competitive with it. For example, anxiety responses may be extinguished by gradually associating the anxiety-producing situation or stimulus with a relaxation response.

First the person is trained in relaxation techniques over a period of several sessions and homework assignments. The next step is to make up a hierarchy in which various aspects of the anxiety-producing situation are ranked from extremely mild to extremely tense and anxiety filled. The client is asked to relax and then to experience or imagine each step in the hierarchy, starting at the lower or mild end. (It is best if the person actually undergoes the experience, but that is not always possible. The alternative to experiencing the anxiety-provoking situation directly is to imagine or visualize it.)

The following hierachy was used with a 40-year-old male who had developed a fear of heights shortly after his discharge from the Air Force during World War II. He was a navigator and had flown a large number of combat missions; he attributed his phobia to his wartime experiences. Items are in order of increasing anxiety.

1. You are beginning to climb the ladder leaning against the side of your house. You plan to work on the roof. Your hands are on the ladder, and your foot is on the first rung.

2. You are halfway up the ladder, and you happen to look down. You see the lawn below you and a walkway.

3. Driving with the family, road begins to climb.

4. Driving with family on California coastal highway, with dropoff to the right.

5. On California seashore cliff, approximately 30 feet from edge.

6. On California seashore cliff, approximately 6 feet from edge.

7. Driving with family, approaching mountain summit.

8. In commercial airliner, at the time of takeoff.

9. In commercial airliner, at an altitude of 30,000 feet.

10. In airliner, at an altitude of 30,000 with considerable turbulence.

11. On a California seaside cliff, approximately 2 feet (judged to be safe distance) from the edge and looking down.

12. Climbing the town water tower to assist in painting, about 10 feet from ground.

13. Same as above, but about 20 feet from ground.

14. On the catwalk around the water tank, painting the tank.

(Rimm and Masters, 1979, p. 48)

Through repeated short exposures while using the relaxation technique, the person learns to imagine each step without feelings of anxiety. As each step in the hierarchy is "conquered," the person moves on until he or she can experience or imagine the highest level, which used to be the most disturbing, without anxiety. The final step is for the person to carry the learned relaxed responses into the actual environment.

In order for systematic desensitization to work, it is obviously necessary that people be able to identify what they are afraid of. For this reason the approach has been most successfully applied to phobias (such as specific fears of animals or heights) and anxieties that can be broken down into basic elements (such as the fear of performing in public).

Systematic desensitization includes two central ingredients: a gradual hierarchy of fears and relaxation training (Wolpe, 1958). Therapists who use this approach argue that the experience of fearful stimuli by themselves—without the relaxation training—will only intensify anxiety. In the next behavioral therapy that we will look at, implosive therapy, therapists argue just the opposite.

Implosive Therapy

In this type of behavioral therapy people are instructed to tackle an undesirable behavior head on by imagining themselves in the worst anxiety-producing situations for long periods of time. A person with a fear of heights, for example, might be told to imagine standing on a narrow ledge on top of a skyscraper or crossing Niagara Falls on a tightrope in a high wind. Rather than ease the anxiety, the therapist attempts to increase it by adding frightening details to the imagined scene. The theory is that prolonged exposure to the

The following is an example of a scene used in implosive therapy with snake phobics.

[Imagine that the snakes are] touching you, biting you, try to get that helpless feeling like you can't win, and just give up and let them crawl all over you. Don't even fight them anymore. Let them crawl as much as they want. And now there is a big giant snake, it is as big as a man and it is staring at you and it is looking at you; it's ugly and it's black and it has got horrible eyes and long fangs, and it is coming towards you. It is standing on its tail and it is looking down at you, looking down on you. I want you to get that feeling, like you are a helpless little rabbit, and it's coming toward you closer and closer; feel it coming towards you. Horrible, evil, ugly, slimy, and it's looking down on you, ready to strike at you. Feel it in your stomach, feel it coming, oooh, it is getting closer and closer and it snaps out at you. Feel it biting at your head now, it is biting at your head; it opens its giant mouth and it has your whole head inside of its mouth. And it is biting your head right off. Feel it; feel it biting, the fangs going right through your neck. Feel it, and now it is starting to swallow you whole. It is pulling you right inside its body, feel yourself being pulled and dragged into its body. Feel yourself inside, helpless, lost, and now you are starting to turn into a snake. Feel yourself turning into a slimy snake. And you are crawling out of its mouth. All the other snakes see you. And they start to attack you. Feel them; they are coming to rip you apart. Do you know how animals attack each other? Look at the snakes attacking you, feel them biting you, ripping you to shreds.

(Hogan, 1968, p. 429)

---

anxiety-producing stimulus in the absence of reinforcement (without the expected or feared consequences) defuses its power.

Proponents of implosive therapy argue that the technique of densensitization successfully reduces anxiety only because it fosters exposure to the feared objects or situations without negative consequences, not because of its gradualism or relaxation training. Thus, they say, why bother with these components? There is evidence, especially in the animal research, that merely preventing escape from a feared stimulus can indeed sometimes extinguish anxiety reactions (Stampfl and Levis, 1967; Baum, 1970). On the other hand, it is not yet clear how to best interpret the human desensitization-implosion therapy research. At this point, there is greater usage of desensitization techniques, probably because many therapists are concerned that implosive techniques may be too fast and harsh for their clients.

Aversive Counterconditioning
With some problems, rather than get rid of a negative response, it is thought to be helpful to develop one. Undesirable habits such as smoking, overeating, or excessive drinking are hard for many persons to break. The behavioral approach of *aversive counterconditioning* seeks to help people to extinguish their excessive attraction to smoking, food, or alcohol by associating a negative reaction, such as nausea or anxiety, with the same stimulus.

The undesirable attraction to the object is extinguished by repeatedly pairing it with an unpleasant consequence such as verbal ridicule, nausea-producing drugs, or electric shock. For example, a chronic overeater is repeatedly offered a large serving of a favorite food, and then given a mild electric shock with each bite. Thus, in conditioning terms, the attractive stimulus, the food, is the conditioned stimulus; it is paired with the unattractive stimulus, the shock, which is the unconditioned stimulus. This pairing produces a fear or revulsion response. When the food comes to elicit fear (or nausea or whatever), its attraction no longer exists—the food is no longer tempting. It is, important, however, to replace the overeating with a more desirable response that is somehow fulfilling or tension-releasing. Otherwise relapse rates in this kind of treatment are high.

Aversive counterconditioning is more exciting in theory than in actuality. Research has shown that its effects are short-lived in many cases. There is also the problem that the learned negative reaction will generalize too much. For example, in addition to feeling nauseated in the presence of chocolate cake, a person may become nauseated at the sight of a wide range of healthful foods. As a result, aversion therapies are usually recommended only after other approaches have failed.

Operant Conditioning Therapies

Operant approaches to therapy borrow from Skinner's (1953) notion that you can shape desired behaviors by rewarding them and by not rewarding undesirable alternative behaviors. One of the best-known operant conditioning therapies is the token economy program. This approach has been used with such problems as schizophrenic disorders, retardation, and school misbehavior and has had some success in problems typically resistant to change.

Token-economy programs are often practiced in controlled environments such as mental hospitals or psychiatric wards. Positive behavior is reinforced by the reward of tokens that can be exchanged later for special privileges. Thus behavior is reinforced right away by the token, but what it's traded in for and when it's traded in are controlled by the therapist. It is a simple system, which is a big advantage—even severely retarded children quickly catch on to the use of tokens.

The therapist (and sometimes the patient as well) controls the choice of specific behaviors that are to be reinforced and the items or privileges for which the tokens may be exchanged. They may, for example, be good for admission to movies, special meals, or other favors that are available only through the program. An advantage of using tokens is that with one item you can reinforce many different people having many different needs or desires.

The target behaviors that are reinforced may range from increased socialization to the completion of assigned chores, depending on each person's problem areas. With the token-economy program the therapist can also shape behavior. This has the advantage that the therapist can start with the behavior the person is already demonstrating. Thus the token-economy approach is good with very apathetic or withdrawn patients, who are not likely to spontaneously show the final, desired behavior (see Table 17-1 on p. 502).

Remarkable results have been claimed for token-economy programs in improving behavior within institutions (Goldfried and Davison, 1976; Hersen, 1976). Since in many institutions no behavior—positive *or* negative—has any effect on subsequent rewards, rewarding positive behavior is bound to increase it to a certain point. There are problems, however. First, a token-economy program requires a lot of staff training, time, and cooperation, and this is a major drawback for many institutions. A second problem is producing behavioral changes that will transfer to the outside world, when patients are discharged and

This boy is receiving reinforcement through a punch card token economy, in which in return for performing certain actions during the day clients receive credits on their punch card, which they can trade in later for candy, special privileges, etc.

Table 17–1: Token Economy: A Sample Treatment Program.

Behavior	Reinforcer	Schedule	Control Stimuli
Smiling	Tokens	Each time detected	As part of greeting
Talking to other patients	Tokens	Each time detected	
Sitting	Tokens	Each time detected	Patients must be with others; not alone
Reading (patient looking at printed material)	Tokens	Each time detected	Appropriate time and place: especially not in group meetings or at medications
Grooming—hair	Tokens or praise	Each time detected	Only when hair is not pulled tightly against head; prefer "feminine" style
Completion of specific assignment	Tokens or free trip out of doors	Each time detected	Prior to reinforcement patient must say something positive about the job she completed

Schaefer and Martin (1969).

their behavior is no longer affected by the direct token-reward relationship. Therapists have begun to work on this problem by trying to shift gradually from tokens to social approval (which *can* be obtained outside the institution).

Of course, an operant approach need not actually use tokens. It may use more direct means of reinforcement, as Lovaas (1977) has in treating autistic children. Lovaas developed an intensive behavior modification program to condition appropriate behaviors in psychotic children. His approach focused on speech training, which was carried out 6 days a week for as long as 7 hours a day. The children were rewarded with food for imitating the sounds produced by the trainer. Lovaas also used punishment in the form of shouting and spanking to suppress undesirable behaviors such as self-destructive acts. Some children took as many as 7,000 trials to learn their first words. As the program progressed, they learned at a faster rate. Treatment lasted 12–14 months, after which the children were transferred to a state hospital. A follow-up study showed that their behavior deteriorated discouragingly over the next 4 years. Better results were achieved with the next group by training the parents to continue the program at home after the child's initial training was finished.

Modeling

Another behavioral approach is *modeling*. In this relatively new technique, a person who fears a certain object repeatedly observes another person—the model—interacting with the object. For example, a person who fears snakes watches a model handling a snake. After the observer sees that the model survives the experience with no bad consequences, he or she comes to believe that there is no basis for an anxiety response (Bandura, 1968). This is a kind of social learning: The person learns something by observing rather than by experiencing it directly.

Modeling is very effective in overcoming neurotic fears because it gives the person a chance to see someone else go through the anxiety-producing situation without getting hurt. Usually neurotic people avoid these situations and therefore never learn that they won't hurt them.

Modeling is also used in programs for people with psychotic patterns of functioning to teach them the social skills they have never had a chance to learn. In this sort of program therapists model appropriate behavior and set up group situations in which patients play different roles with the therapist watching and coaching.

The Biological Model of Therapy

According to the biological model, abnormal behavior is caused by a malfunction of the body. Treatment is therefore designed to make a particular change in the person's biological functioning. This may be done through such means as drugs, electroshock therapy, or psychosurgery.

Chemotherapy

Chemotherapy, the treatment of abnormal behavior with drugs, is the most widespread biological technique. The drugs used in chemotherapy can be classified as antianxiety, antidepressant, or antipsychotic. As their names imply, each type of drug is aimed at treating a specific area of abnormal functioning. Antianxiety drugs are essentially tranquilizers that calm people who are tense or anxious. Antidepressant drugs are designed to lift the mood of a depressed person, and antipsychotic drugs modify the severe manifestations of psychosis.

The treatment of anxiety and neurotic problems with antianxiety drugs is widely practiced not only by therapists, but also by medical doctors who give their patients something to "calm their nerves" and by individuals who swallow a tranquilizer whenever they feel emotionally upset. The popularity of these drugs is due, in large part, to the speed with which they work. (They are also less expensive than psychotherapy.) When they do work, they seem almost to be an instant cure. The "instant cure," however, may be little more than a temporary alleviation of symptoms. There is growing evidence that the so-called minor tranquilizers, such as Librium, Miltown, and Valium, are physically and psychologically addictive when used consistently in high dosages over a long period of time. They are also dangerous (sometimes fatal) and even more addictive when used with alcohol.

Antidepressant drugs are the most common biological treatment for depression. The two main types of antidepressants are *tricyclics* and *monoamine oxidase (MAO) inhibitors,* both of which were discovered by accident. The tricyclics were being tested as a treatment for schizophrenia, and, although they proved to be ineffective, researchers noted that subjects showed an unexpected increase in positive mood. The same result was found when MAO inhibitors were administered as a treatment for tuberculosis.

Tricyclic drugs are usually preferred over MAO inhibitors for depressed persons, first because they have been proven more effective, and second because the MAO inhibitors sometimes have very dangerous side effects, including brain and liver damage, when mixed with certain foods.

The tricyclics, in those cases where they do help, start lifting a person's spirits after a period of approximately 10 days. Further adjustments in dosage are then made until maintenance level is reached.

There are a growing number of antidepressant medications. A given person may be helped significantly by one kind yet be virtually untouched by another. One form of depressed functioning that is relatively unresponsive to these antidepressant medications is the manic-depressive pattern. As you will recall from the chapter on abnormal psychology, this form of depression, with its dramatic manic phase, is distinctly different from other forms. In recent years a different type of drug, not an antidepressant, has been found to significantly reduce the manic-depressive symptoms of people who have experienced them for many years without relief. The drug, *lithium,* must be taken at just the right level to be effective. Below the necessary level, it offers little therapeutic value; above that level, it can be quite toxic and dangerous. For this reason, careful monitoring of people on lithium is critical.

It is not yet clear why lithium works with manic-depressives. One notion is that the problem itself reflects an imbalance of intracellular sodium and potassium and that lithium, which has properties similar to those of sodium, corrects this imbalance (Coppen, 1967). Since the net effect of lithium is to produce a marked reduction in intracellular sodium, it is not surprising that taking too much lithium can be so dangerous.

Chemotherapy has become the most dramatically effective form of treatment for schizophrenia, largely because of the *phenothiazines,* a group of drugs introduced in the 1950s. Because of their success in relieving schizophrenic symptoms, the phenothiazines and related drugs became known as antipsychotic drugs. Before these drugs were discovered, the populations of schizophrenic persons in mental hospitals had been increasing, with no end in sight. With these drugs, however, there has been a reversal in this trend, and in the past few decades the number of schizophrenics in mental hospitals has been reduced dramatically. Indeed, many state hospitals have closed altogether. New philosophies of treatment (for instance, community mental health) and new approaches (for example, token economy) have helped to bring about this trend, but the antipsychotic medications have been the single most important factor (see Figure 17-2).

Research has repeatedly demonstrated the effectiveness of these medications (Casey et al., 1960; Cole, 1964; Freedman, 1977). However, research also points to other issues surrounding the use of these drugs. For example, some people experience uncomfortable and sometimes serious side effects that must be dealt with, such as tremors and problems in motor control. Moreover, those people who have improved on these drugs and have been released from hospitals often show high readmission rates. This has led to what is often called the "revolving door syndrome"—patients improve enough to be released, but they are not really capable of coping with the outside world. Some stop taking their medication and the symptoms recur; others simply do not have the social or vocational skills to cope outside the institution.

Figure 17-2

The use of antipsychotic drugs (phenothiazines and related drugs) since the 1950s has led to a dramatic number of schizophrenics in mental hospitals in this country. (National Institute of Mental Health, 1975)

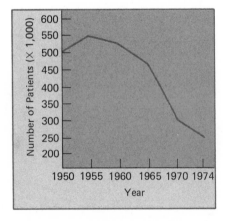

Thus these drugs cannot be said to be a "cure." Some research suggests that the best treatment for schizophrenic functioning is a mixture of psychotherapy and antipsychotic medications. This is where the real value of the drug lies—it brings patients to the point where more traditional forms of psychotherapy are *possible*. Thus, while further clarification and improvement are needed, these medications have already made possible significant progress in the treatment of schizophrenia, where before the prognosis was very poor.

Electroshock Treatment

One of the more controversial biological treatments is electroshock. It is usually used only with people for whom other forms of therapy have not been effective. Therapists have resorted to it less frequently since the antidepressant drugs became available.

Electroshock was first introduced in the 1930s. The basic procedure is to pass a brief electric current of about 100 volts through the brain by means of electrodes placed on either side of the forehead. (In the last few years some therapists have begun placing the electrodes on only one side of the head [Belenky, 1976], the side of the nondominant hemisphere, because this has been found to reduce memory loss.) The result of the shock is a convulsive seizure that lasts for about a minute, following which the person loses consciousness for several minutes. The treatment is often accompanied by a memory loss of unpredictable length, ranging from a few minutes to several hours, along with some more lingering memory difficulties.

Before receiving electroshock today, people are given a sedative and a muscle relaxant, which reduce the risk of injury and seem to minimize the discomfort. Most people receive 6 to 9 treatments at the rate of 3 a week.

Although electroshock apparently reduces symptoms in many cases of depression, no one knows for sure how or why it works. Some experimenters think that it temporarily stimulates the synthesis of norepinephrine in the brain (Kety et al., 1974). Unfortunately, however it works, it is not a final cure—the depression often recurs later in the person's life.

Psychosurgery

The third biological method, psychosurgery, is easily the most controversial. The *prefrontal lobotomy* has been particularly controversial. This brain surgery was based on the notion that the frontal lobes of the brain strengthen or increase emotional responses, which arise in the thalamus and hypothalamus. Thus it was thought that cutting the connections between the frontal lobes and these other brain regions would help in such problems as schizophrenia and depression. In the 1940s and 1950s an enormous number of lobotomies were performed with claims of great success. However, subsequent research found that people who had had lobotomies showed very bad side effects, such as seizures, stupor, and extreme listlessness, to say nothing of impaired mental functioning. This Nobel Prize–winning procedure fell into disfavor as it became evident that its side effects represented a very significant and serious problem. As a result, all forms of psychosurgery are now treated with great caution by both the professional community and the public at large. Ironically, many psychosurgical techniques are now more precise and better controlled than they were in the

1940s and 1950s; however, because of the lobotomy lesson, as well as the success of the relatively less severe medication approaches, psychosurgery today is an experimental and less used approach.

The Humanistic-Existential Model of Therapy

For humanistic and existential psychologists, abnormal functioning results from a failure to reach or strive towards one's full potential. In humanistic theories this is often called a failure to self-actualize; that is, a failure to move toward the fulfillment of one's natural potential as a human being and to be in close touch with who one is, how one feels, and what one actually thinks. In existential theories, too, abnormality represents a failure to reach one's full potential, but this failure is rooted in one's inability to overcome the sources of anxiety built into the existential situation of life, an inability to meet life assertively and give it meaning and take responsibility for one's life. Both theories define abnormal functioning as a failure to be and fulfill oneself, and the humanistic-existential approach to therapy seeks to help people get in touch with their real selves, and then make deliberate choices regarding their lives and behaviors, rather than letting outside events determine their behavior.

Years ago humanistic forms of therapy mainly involved some form of careful and intense self-examination (for instance, Carl Rogers's approach to therapy). In more recent years the search for fulfilling one's potential has also used altered states of consciousness such as meditation or yoga.

Many therapy approaches fall under the humanistic or existential heading. We will examine two that are quite different in everything but their overall humanistic orientation and goals—Carl Rogers's client-centered therapy and Fritz Perls's Gestalt therapy. Each works toward enhanced self-awareness in a different way.

Client-Centered Therapy

You will recall from Chapter 16 on abnormal psychology that client-centered therapists believe that because of the threatening and evaluative environments of their childhood, people find it hard to look at themselves accurately and feel the positive self-regard that everyone needs. Thus they have developed an unending style of self-distortion, selectively perceiving events and behaviors in a way that is consistent with their self-view. Their inaccurate self-view and the energy invested in this constant self-deception make it impossible for them to fulfill their potential.

The idea underlying client-centered therapy is that therapy must create a totally nonthreatening atmosphere in which people can honestly look at and accept themselves and make relevant decisions. More accurate self-awareness and acceptance will in turn lead to the more functional and productive life-style of self-actualization.

Carl Rogers, originator and chief theorist of client-centered therapy.

APPLICATION
Client-Centered Therapy

CLIENT: Well, it happened again yesterday. I got back that exam in American Lit.

THERAPIST: I see.

CLIENT: Just like before. I got an A all right—me and eight others. But on the third question the instructor wrote a comment that I could have been a little clearer or else could have given more detail. The same old crap. I got an A all right, but it's pretty damn clear that I'm like a machine that can generate correct answers without ever understanding. That's it. I memorize, but there's no spark, no creativity. Boy!

THERAPIST: What else can you tell me about the exam?

CLIENT: Well, it was like we talked about before. I'm doing OK, but I just don't feel like I really measure up. I remember my brother bringing home a paper in high school. It was a C, but the instructor said John had real potential. I just don't think I've got it.

THERAPIST: Even though you got an A you are not satisfied.

CLIENT: I know I should be satisfied with an A. Other guys would be. They'd be glad to get an A.

THERAPIST: Mm-hmm.

CLIENT: But I can't. No wonder the folks are so proud of John. He got decent grades, and he was satisfied—not like me. It's a wonder they don't get fed up with my moping around.

THERAPIST: So even with good grades your unhappiness is enough to turn people off.

CLIENT: Sure. But somehow I've got to get rid of this defeatist attitude. I've got to think about the good side.

THERAPIST: Mm-hmm.

CLIENT: A lot of times I've tried to forget my lack of potential. Just go on and plug along.

THERAPIST: Yeah, I guess you really felt people put you down because of this lack of potential?

CLIENT: Boy, did they! Especially my folks. They never really said so, but I could tell from the way they acted.

THERAPIST: Mm-hmm.

CLIENT: They'd say that John really has a head on his shoulder, or (pause) . . . he can think his way out of anything.

THERAPIST: And this made you feel sort of worthless—not hearing things like that about yourself.

CLIENT: That's right!

(Phares, 1979, pp. 360–61)

Thus the humanistic technique created by Rogers (1950, 1961, 1967) allows the client a large role in directing the course of the therapy. For therapy to be effective, the client must perceive the therapist as showing unconditional positive regard, empathy, and genuineness.

Unconditional positive regard is essential to the concept of client-centered therapy. The therapist must consider the client a worthy human being, without qualification. No judgment should be passed, either against or in support of the client's viewpoint or actions. (Rogers referred to this as AT&T, or Attitude of Tentativeness and Tolerance.) The therapist must, however, show a deep faith in the ability of the client to discover the right path to follow. As a result of this unconditional positive regard, when clients reveal bizarre or seemingly terrible thoughts and are still accepted by their therapist, they begin to accept themselves.

Unlike psychoanalysis, in which the therapist attempts to observe and analyze the patient's conception of reality, the client-centered therapist *empathizes* with the client's world by trying to enter it and experience it from the same viewpoint as the client. When listening to their clients, therapists make remarks reflecting the emotional content of what is being said. They do this to make sure they are in touch with it, but also to make sure that clients recognize all that they are saying, or the implications of what they're saying. This has been described as mirroring clients' feelings so that they will see all that is there.

Genuineness means that the therapist must establish a human-to-human relationship with the client, not one that could be interpreted by the client as doctor-patient, expert-amateur, or savior-sinner. For Rogers, the therapist must *feel* a genuine concern and empathy for the client in order for therapy to be effective.

Gestalt Therapy

Another humanistic approach, *Gestalt therapy,* is largely the work of Frederick (Fritz) Perls (1965, 1969). Like Rogers, Perls believed all people are innately good. Abnormal functioning originates in the denial of this goodness and the blocking of its expression. Ordinarily, in whatever we perceive, whether it be ideas, events, or emotions, we concentrate on only part of our whole experience: We focus on the *figure,* or foreground, and largely ignore the *background* against which the figure appears. If we are holding a conversation with a professor who has rejected a term paper, for example, we concentrate our attention on the conversation and our efforts to defend our work (the foreground) and are only partly aware of our anger and frustration against which this conversation takes place (the background). Perls wanted people to perceive the wholeness, or *Gestalt,* of their experiences. (The concept of Gestalt, or whole perception, was discussed in Chapter 4.)

The purpose of Gestalt therapy is to help people become aware of this wholeness by bringing more of the background into the foreground experience. Great importance is placed on the *here and now.* For Perls, nothing else existed. Therapy encourages people to recognize the immediate experience in its entirety, which means knowing what they are feeling as well as thinking, so that their behavior is in harmony with their whole being. To achieve this goal, they must free themselves from trying to live up to the expectations of others. They must be responsible for their own behavior and recognize their capabilities for self-improvement.

Among the techniques practiced by Gestalt therapists, role playing and projection are used to bring out problems caused by expectations or rules of behavior that were originally applied by parents and other authority figures and that people have internalized. The purpose is to show that these problems are really self-imposed, that they do not result from universal rules that everyone must follow.

In the empty-chair technique, for example, clients are asked to imagine that some person with whom they have an emotionally charged relationship (father, mother, spouse) is sitting in the empty chair opposite them. They then talk to this person about the problems in their relationship and their specific feelings toward that person. Then the client switches chairs and talks as if he or she were the other person speaking—this brings out how clients think other persons see them. The empty-chair technique may also be used to encourage clients to talk to different parts of themselves—to their fears, desires, dreams—and to try to confront their feelings and accept them as part of their total makeup.

Another Gestalt technique is to ask clients to act out the opposite of what they feel. People who feel emotionally unresponsive, for example, would be instructed to react as if they were extremely sensitive and emotionally uninhibited. Through this exercise, Perls felt that clients could discover a very real part of their being that had never been allowed open expression.

Throughout Gestalt therapy an effort is made to experience feelings, to acknowledge them, and then work toward changing them if necessary. Gestalt concentrates on the present and how people are now, encouraging them to accept themselves as they are and not as they think they should be.

The Cognitive Model of Therapy

Cognitive therapies start with the assumption that emotional upsets or abnormal patterns of behavior result not from what we feel but from what we think (content) or how we think (process). Even if the problem appears to be one of emotion, behavior, or circumstance, it is our cognitive mediation—our thoughts—that play the most critical role. Thus cognitive theorists are less concerned with the symptoms than with the thinking process that led to them, and they try to change these thoughts or thinking processes in therapy. The cognitive therapies that are best known are those of Albert Ellis and Aaron Beck.

Ellis: Rational-Emotive Therapy

Ellis's Rational-Emotive Therapy (RET) focuses primarily on thought content: that is, on specific irrational thoughts or assumptions that Ellis says lie at the core of abnormal functioning. This approach, which has been most often applied to problems in anxiety and neurotic functioning, argues that therapy should be directed at pointing out the false beliefs that neurotic persons hold and that lead to their feelings of anxiety. Some of the more common false beliefs at the root of abnormal functioning are the following (Ellis, 1962):

1. I must be loved or approved of by virtually every significant other person around me.
2. I must be thoroughly competent, adequate, and achieving in all possible respects or I can't consider myself worthwhile.
3. Certain people are bad, wicked, or villainous . . . they should be severely punished for it.
4. It is awful and catastrophic when things are not the way I want them to be.

Rational-emotive therapy tries to show the client how to separate rational from irrational thoughts and accept reality. Ellis emphasizes tolerance of oneself, of others, and of inevitable frustration in the real world. Instead of irrationally thinking "I ought to succeed" or "I must succeed," the client learns to accept the rational thought, "It would be better to succeed," or "I may fail in this one thing but that doesn't mean I'm a total failure."

This requires, in many cases, big changes in one's basic values and beliefs. In leading clients to this change, RET therapists tend to be more active than therapists of some other approaches. Unlike Rogers's client-centered therapy,

APPLICATION
Rational-Emotive Therapy

CLIENT: I had another anxiety attack yesterday. I was having lunch with some friends in this really nice restaurant in North Dallas. I felt like I couldn't finish my meal. It was just terrible.

THERAPIST: Okay: Now think back to when you were in the restaurant yesterday, and tell me what you experienced. You know, how you felt and what you were thinking.

CLIENT: Okay. . . . Well, the waiter had just served the main course. I noticed I was really tense. I remember thinking . . . What if I have another panic attack, right here? I might not be able to continue eating. I might even faint. That would be terrible.

THERAPIST: Well, you said that you've never actually fainted in situations like this before. And so my guess is you won't . . . but what if you did? How would it be terrible? Do you mean that you would injure yourself physically

or something like that?

CLIENT: No . . . not really. I think I imagine myself, you know, slumped over in my chair. And my friends and everybody else are looking at me, just staring.

THERAPIST: And what are those people thinking?

CLIENT: (*Her eyes begin to tear*) That . . . I can't even have lunch without making an ass of myself . . . that I'm incompetent . . . worthless.

THERAPIST: Okay. Now it looks to me like you think the worst thing that could happen would be that you'd faint. First, that's pretty unlikely, right?

CLIENT: Sure, but what if I *did?*

THERAPIST: Suppose you were in a restaurant and you saw somebody else faint. What would you think about them? Would you judge them to be incompetent and worthless?

CLIENT: I guess I'd think they

were, you know, sick. . . . I'd probably try to help them. No . . . I wouldn't think they were . . . bad . . . or worthless. I see what you mean. Maybe they wouldn't ridicule me.

THERAPIST: I think they wouldn't. But *suppose* they did. There you are, slumped in your chair, and you are just regaining consciousness. And everyone in the restaurant . . . your friends . . . everyone . . . they are jeering at you . . . making fun of you. We just agreed that isn't likely to happen, but suppose everybody in the restaurant just happened to behave like purple meanies?

CLIENT: That would be awful . . . I couldn't stand it. I'd just wither up and die.

THERAPIST: You'd literally, physically wither up and die?

CLIENT: Well, when you put it that way . . . I guess not.

(Rimm and Masters, 1979, pp. 383–84)

---

for example, in RET therapists openly challenge statements that they consider irrational: They don't wait for clients to discover irrationality on their own. They give their own personal opinion when asked by clients, and often when not asked. Instead of occasionally interpreting something, like psychoanalysts, or restating, like Rogerians, they spend a good deal of time telling their clients the way things are and what is wrong with their thinking.

Among the techniques used by RET therapists are role playing and modeling. Both of these techniques may be used in individual sessions or in groups to show clients in what ways their thinking is unrealistic and what the consequences of this irrationality are for their relationships with others and their own self-perceptions.

RET therapists also try to show unconditional acceptance of their clients. Unlike Rogerian therapists, who strive to give unconditional acceptance in a nonjudgmental way, RET therapists will criticize their clients for faulty thinking but still demonstrate that they accept them unconditionally even with their flaws. Furthermore, the therapists point out, clients can learn to accept themselves in the same unconditional way.

At this point, RET is one of the most widely practiced forms of treatment (Garfield and Kurtz, 1976). Some experimental support for this approach has been demonstrated by studies showing that people classified as neurotic hold many more irrational beliefs than control groups of well-adjusted individuals (Newmark et al., 1973). RET therapists claim that their techniques not only work faster than therapies that emphasize insight, but that they are more effective in relieving anxiety as well.

Beck: Cognitive Therapy

Aaron Beck's cognitive therapy (1972, 1973, 1975) has been most often applied to the problems of depression. Beck traces depressed patterns to both problematic thoughts and distorted thinking processes. He argues that depressed persons have basic "rules," not unlike Ellis's irrational thoughts or assumptions, that underlie their depression. For example, "It would be terrible if someone else had a low opinion of me," or "Anything less than total success would be a disaster." While Beck does not describe these rules as irrational, he does see them as very limiting because of their arbitrary, extreme, and unyielding nature. These rules give rise to "automatic thoughts—negative self-verbalizations that pop into a person's head continually throughout the day.

As well as problematic thoughts (such as the rules and automatic thoughts just described), Beck is concerned with distorted thinking processes, which he says characterize depressed functioning. These distortions in thinking include jumping to conclusions without having enough evidence and overgeneralizing from a single event. Usually these distorted thinking processes help to lock in a negative self-view and view of the future.

Beck's cognitive therapy seeks to reveal and change these rules, automatic thoughts, and distorted thinking processes (without trying to find out how or why they arose). Therapy begins with some tasks that lead the person to experience the joy of success—a pleasure that typically escapes very depressed people. People are assigned a series of tasks within their range of ability. This may start with a very simple task, such as buying some items at a nearby supermarket, and move upward to harder ones. As the person's mood becomes somewhat more elevated in the face of undeniable successes, the therapy becomes more cognitive. Clients are helped to recognize and even record their automatic thoughts. They are taught to evaluate and challenge these thoughts rather than accept them automatically. Through a series of cognitive maneuvers, the person comes to further identify and challenge the rules and style of thinking attached to these automatic thoughts.

The treatment program is expected to significantly improve depressed clients in 20 1-hour sessions. Research suggests that Beck's cognitive viewpoint of depression has its merits (for instance, Beck, Weissman, Lester, and Trexler, 1974) and that this cognitive form of psychotherapy significantly reduces depression and even compares well to the treatment effectiveness of antidepressive medications (Rush, Beck, Kovacs, and Hallon, 1977).

Actually, cognitive forms of therapy are relatively new among the treatment models. At first, the few therapies that were cognitive in nature, such as Rational-Emotive Therapy, were seen as part of the behavioral model. However, in recent years there has been a growing appreciation of the unique and subtle role of cognition and mediation in determining human functioning, including abnormal functioning. The cognitive therapists are developing a variety of approaches and techniques for intervening in a wide range of abnormal difficulties. Most of these therapists are research-minded and their influence in the field is growing rapidly.

Other Kinds of Therapy: Mixing the Models

As our discussion of the models of psychotherapy indicates, the field of psychotherapy is indeed varied. The various models of psychotherapy approach abnormal patterns in very different ways. Indeed, even within a given model there is often a diversity of viewpoints and specific approaches. And there are several therapies that do not readily fit into any one model. A case in point is biofeedback.

Biofeedback

Biofeedback training is an approach that has gained notice recently. The idea behind this approach is that anxiety and other discomforts will be lessened if a person can learn to control the bodily responses involved. Experiments have shown that when subjects are given feedback of their present bodily states in the form of audible tones, moving graphs, or dials, they can in turn learn to control such bodily reactions as brain wave pattern, blood pressure, and muscle tension. Since heart rate normally increases as a reaction to fear, for example, people who can be taught to control their heart rate can control their fear.

The biofeedback approach has been most successfully applied as an adjunct to treatment for chronic headaches. Providing people who suffer from headaches with feedback and teaching them to control such things as muscle tension in the forehead region and blood flow in the cranial arteries has proved effective in many cases.

Clearly, the biofeedback approach cuts across the biological, learning, and humanistic models. The biological perspective is represented by the focus on the bodily functions as the center of the problem. The learning approach is at the heart of the training program in which direct control over involuntary processes is learned by observation and feedback. And biofeedback training's function as a technique that enables people to get in touch with hidden dimensions of themselves and their environments has sometimes led to its classification as a humanistic approach.

Group Therapy

Most of the forms of treatment that we have described involve a one-to-one relationship between client and therapist; that is, a client meeting privately with his or her therapist. An alternative format whose popularity has grown in the past few decades is "group therapy," in which several clients simultaneously meet with a therapist. Obviously, such a format is an efficient use of the therapist's time and is usually cheaper for clients. Moreover, group therapy formats seem to have certain therapeutic advantages over individual therapy. For one thing, members of a group may learn from one another's difficulties. It is sometimes easier to observe oneself by looking at and listening to others. For another, people whose problems have a distinct interpersonal dimension often find the group setting the ideal place to develop the interpersonal skills, perspective, and feelings of relaxation they sorely need.

Groups vary in several ways. First, they differ in membership and makeup. For example, many groups consist of strangers whose problems have something in common. In other group formats, such as the increasingly popular *family therapy* or *couple (marital) therapy groups*, the members are hardly strangers.

Family therapy brings all the family members together to work on such issues as communication and interaction. As members become better able to relate to one another, the problems of the family and of individual members should improve significantly. This approach has been particularly helpful in dealing with the problems of children. Working with children alone has often led to only limited success. However, working with them along with their parents and siblings apparently enables a therapist to deal with children's problems in a more comprehensive and successful way. Obviously, working with families, with their many problems and channels of interaction, can be a complex task, and family therapists receive special training in family psychotherapy.

A second way in which groups differ is in their orientation and techniques. There are psychoanalytic, behavioral, and humanistic group therapies. *Encounter groups*, humanistic in orientation, first emerged during the 1960s and have been unique in their emphasis on intensive give-and-take among members and on absolute honesty in group interactions. *Assertiveness training groups*, behavioral in their approach, emerged in the 1970s and have focused on helping individuals to more effectively and appropriately assert themselves, their needs, and their interests in their interactions with others. *Psychodrama* is a form of group therapy that goes back to 1931. It has group members act out their inner feelings and thoughts as if in a play, using at times an actual stage and even a real audience.

Finally, groups vary in terms of their boundaries and goals. Many are strictly for people who are seeking psychotherapy for various emotional or behavioral problems. Many others are not therapy at all, but simply use group processes to help people of all sorts become more in touch with themselves, more effective interpersonally, more skilled at group processes, or more skilled in other designated ways. Such groups exist to make people more effective in life's various roles and relationships. The 1960s and 1970s witnessed a rapid growth of nontherapeutic groups in such forms as sensitivity training groups or management groups.

Problem-Oriented Approaches
Certain problems are particularly resistant to the application of traditional models or forms of therapy. Sometimes a new form of treatment has emerged just for such a resistant problem. Some examples are: (1) self-help approaches

for alcoholism and addiction, (2) treatment for problems in sexual dysfunctioning, and (3) suicide prevention.

SELF-HELP APPROACHES: ALCOHOLISM AND ADDICTION. Traditional therapeutic approaches to alcoholism have had very little success over the years. In 1935 two alcoholic men helped each other recover and began a group known as Alcoholics Anonymous. AA is today a worldwide organization with thousands of groups and more than a million members. It is primarily a nonprofessional program in which alcoholics, past and present, help one another in one-to-one and group formats. The emphasis is on support, insight, self-acceptance, and spiritual development.

At regular meetings problem drinkers and alcoholics are encouraged to give up their drinking habit and to gain insight into their problems and how to deal with them. Alcoholism is regarded by AA as a physiological disease in which the person's body cannot tolerate alcohol, rather than as a sign of psychological weakness or self-indulgence. AA sees alcoholism, therefore, as a lifelong problem, with the only cure being total abstinence. The effectiveness of the AA approach has not been objectively tested. Obviously, it does not work for all alcoholics. The number it does reach and help, however, is considerable.

In 1958 Charles Dederich started a self-help organization for drug addicts called Synanon. Dederich was a former AA member and modeled his therapeutic community after AA. At the same time he gave it a distinct quality by putting greater emphasis on confrontation and making it a full-time residential community. In recent years Synanon has become very controversial. Some say that it has lost its way and developed into an undesirable, cultlike organization. Indeed, there are presently legal cases centering on this very issue. Nevertheless, it did play a pioneering role in the development of self-help organizations for drug addiction. Some of the organizations that are presently active in the treatment and fight against drug addiction are Daytop, Phoenix House, and Odyssey House.

SUICIDE PREVENTION. Suicide is one of our most serious yet least understood problems. One of the greatest difficulties is that there are a great many myths about suicide that tend to lull relatives, friends, and even professionals into a false sense of security about the likelihood of a particular person committing suicide. The recent increase in suicide attempts and actual suicides has led to the establishment of the suicide prevention centers around the country. They provide around-the-clock hotline telephone services for people in distress.

A telephone worker at such a center will seek to (1) establish a relationship with the caller and obtain information, (2) clarify the central problem, (3) assess the potential for suicide, (4) assess the person's strengths and resources, and (5) develop with the person a constructive plan of action, including involvement in an appropriate treatment program.

Suicide prevention centers typically provide in-person treatment services and personnel for longer-term intervention in addition to the hotline, assessment, and referral service. These centers are staffed by psychiatrists, psychologists, social workers, other professionals, and trained nonprofessionals (paraprofessionals).

These programs have in turn led to the development of *crisis intervention* programs for a wide range of difficulties. These take different forms, but all serve to make a trained person available, either over the phone or in personal interviews, to help people faced with a crisis. All sorts of problems may be encountered—from floods, accidents, or illness to crises such as desertion by a spouse, sexual anxieties, or abuse of some sort.

The Effectiveness of Therapy

Over the past few decades, with the emergence of many new approaches to therapy, there has also emerged a debate in which the effectiveness of therapy itself has been questioned. This debate includes questions not only about the effectiveness of therapy in general, but also about how the different forms of therapy compare in terms of effectiveness.

The issue of general therapy effectiveness is a very difficult one for several reasons. First of all, how are we to define success? Is our criterion to be partial change or total change; change in the behavior, emotion, or cognitive spheres; change seen by the person, the therapist, a friend, or a relative? Second, there are so many forms of therapy that we cannot speak of "therapy" as if it represents a general process. Moreover, there are many different kinds of problems in abnormal functioning, so it is impossible to talk about the general effectiveness of psychotherapy. Furthermore, many other life events have an impact on people while they are involved in therapy. How can we sort out these factors in evaluating the role of therapy?

When we seek to compare the effectiveness of particular therapies, we run into these same questions, plus additional difficulties. A major problem is that the various forms of psychotherapy differ in their definitions of psychotherapy success and goals. Then we are faced with the fact that every therapist practices his or her orientation in at least a slightly different manner. For example, there are many differences in technique and interpretation among psychoanalytic psychotherapists. Similarly, there are many variations among behavioral therapists. How, then, can we confidently compare the effectiveness of psychoanalysis to that of behavioral therapy? Are we comparing processes or therapists? Furthermore, there are many different variables and factors that bear on therapy outcome: different settings, formats, personality factors, and so on. Certainly these will complicate our comparison of the effectiveness of various therapies.

It is not surprising, therefore, that despite a great deal of research over the past few decades, our conclusions about the effectiveness of psychotherapy are still tentative. Here are some of the things we do seem to know:

1. Psychothrapy can be a helpful and effective process for certain problems and individuals (Bergin, 1971; Smith and Glass, 1977).
2. Sometimes psychotherapy will provide no help or even have a negative effect (Eysenck, 1952).
3. Often a spontaneous remission will occur after a period of time whether or not the person has been in therapy. Such improvements may be due to factors in the individual's personal life or to some internal factors.
4. In direct comparisons, the major psychotherapy approaches (psychoanaly-

sis, behavioral, humanistic) often demonstrate similar overall rates of effectiveness (Smith and Glass, 1977; Luborsky et al., 1975).

5.   At the same time, some therapy approaches seem superior with specific difficulties (Luborsky and Spence, 1971). For example, the behavioral approach seems most effective with phobias, and the biological approach of antipsychotic medications seems most effective with schizophrenic disorders (May, 1968).

Research efforts in psychotherapy are accelerating, and their results should lead to more effective therapy. We are becoming increasingly aware of the strengths and weaknesses, the similarities and differences, of the various forms of therapy, as well as the key variables of each. One very promising result of this awareness has been a movement to match specific problems and people to specific kinds of therapy and therapists. Of course, if this kind of matching is to become more productive and accurate, we will need much more research.

Summary

1.   Psychotherapy has been defined as "a set of procedures by which one person uses language to change the life of another."

2.   Psychoactive drugs, discovered in the 1950s, had a major effect on the quality of care in public hospitals by making possible outpatient care, reduced inpatient population, and improved treatment prognoses.

3.   In the 1960s, the community health movement introduced practices such as: public education about mental health; crisis hotlines; ongoing psychotherapy services; and community treatment centers offering free or inexpensive care.

4.   Psychoanalysis uses verbal techniques and attempts to solve problems by bringing unconscious conflicts into consciousness where they may be confronted and resolved by the person. Techniques include *free association, interpretation,* and *transference.*

5.   The learning model of therapy involves extinguishing the maladaptive patterns and learning more appropriate ones. Techniques include: *systematic desensitization, implosive therapy, aversive counterconditioning, token economies,* and *modeling.*

6.   In the biological model of therapy, the role of treatment is to change the person's biological functioning. This may be done through chemotherapy (drugs), electroshock treatment, or psychosurgery.

7.   The humanistic-existential approach to therapy involves an attempt to help people become in touch with their selves and subsequently take charge of their lives and behaviors. Among the various kinds of humanistic-existential therapies are Carl Rogers's *client-centered therapy* and Fritz Perls' *Gestalt therapy.*

8. In cognitive therapies, the focus is on thoughts and thinking processes and how they must be changed. Ellis's *Rational-Emotive Therapy (RET)* attempts to show the client how to separate rational from irrational thoughts and to accept reality through role-playing and modeling techniques. Beck's therapy attempts to reveal a person's basic "rules" and distorted thinking processes and subsequently change the "rules."

9. Problem-oriented approaches to therapy include self-help groups, such as Alcoholics Anonymous, and suicide prevention services, which offer crisis telephone lines manned by counselors and therapy services.

Suggested Readings

BELKIN, G. S. *Contemporary psychotherapies.* Chicago: Rand McNally, 1980. Offers an overview of the many forms of psychotherapy practiced in the United States today, and includes a wide range of clinical case studies.

BOOTZIN, R. R. *Behavior modification and therapy.* Boston: Winthrop, 1975. Offers an outstanding introduction to the techniques and research of the behavioral approach, as well as a consideration of the ethical dimensions of the approach.

GARFIELD, S. L., and BERGIN, A. E. (Eds.) *Handbook of psychotherapy and behavior change,* 2nd ed. New York: Wiley, 1978. Good appraisal of the research in the field of psychotherapy, with leading theorists focusing on such issues as methodology, psychotherapeutic processes, outcomes, various approaches, and new developments in the field.

LICHTENSTEIN, E. *Psychotherapy: Approaches and applications.* Monterey, Cal.: Brooks/Cole, 1980. A broad look at psychotherapy, including economic, social, and political influences, with an evaluative framework.

LUBORSKY, L., CHANGLER, M., AUERBACH, A. H., COHEN, J., and BACHRACH, H. M. Factors influencing the outcome of psychotherapy: A review of quantitative research. *Psychological Bulletin,* 75 (1971), 145–85. Raises interesting points about the process of psychotherapy and factors that influence its outcome.

PERLS, F. T. *Gestalt therapy verbatim.* Monterey, Cal.: Real People Press, 1969. Provides a good introduction to Gestalt therapy by the intriguing theorist and therapist who developed this approach.

ROGERS, C. R. *Client-centered therapy.* Boston: Houghton Mifflin, 1951. A comprehensive introduction to the client-centered approach by the originator of this form of therapy.

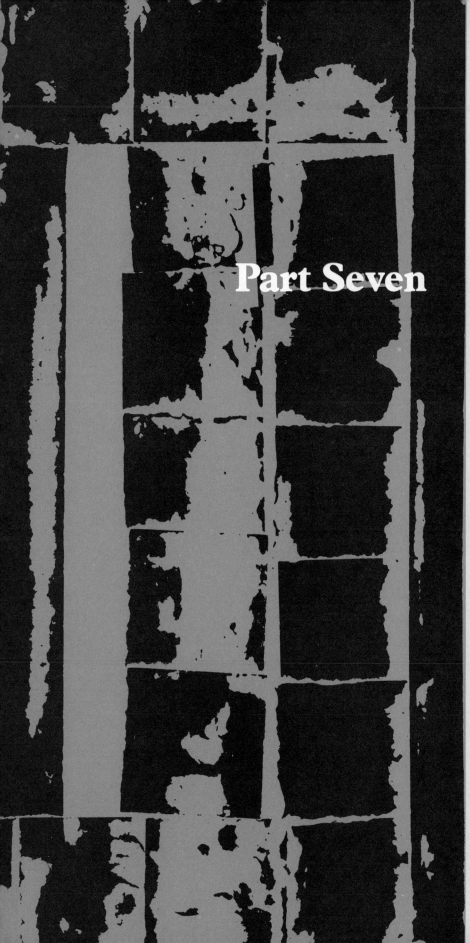

Part Seven

Social Psychology

18 The Individual in Group Settings

In order to carry out our plans, we need to perceive the world around us. Since many of our plans will involve other people, a large part of our perceptual task involves perceiving these other people. The processes of interpersonal perception have similarities to the general processes of perception discussed in Chapter 4. Like object perception, person perception is a categorical process—we do not perceive other people in every detail, we simply perceive enough about them to assign them to a category. For instance, when we drive in to a gas station, you simply see enough about the other people there to figure out who is the gas station attendant. Ordinarily a few details of the uniform are enough to show this.

Person perception, like object perception, is a constructive, interpretive process that works from partial rather than complete information. And, as this suggests, the process can sometimes go wrong. You can be wrong about who the gas station attendant is, and you can be wrong in any of your judgments about other people as well, when you infer too much from partial or incomplete information.

In one way person perception is obviously different from object perception. Unlike rocks, trees, and other physical objects, people have intentions, plans, and personalities. This means that part of the task of perceiving other people is "looking behind" their actions to discover what they are "really like." *Attribution theories* describe the ways in which we go about developing explanations for and interpretations of the actions of others.

Attribution

Think for a minute about how similar we expect other people's judgments of people to be to ours. In spite of the cliche that we're all entitled to our own opinion, we seem to expect that others will see people the way we do and are startled to discover that sometimes they don't. But it is important to stress that there can be great differences in the way an individual may be perceived by other people. The process of attributing characteristics and motives to another person is a complex one, involving interpretation and judgment. Therefore, we can expect that different perceivers will see a certain person in different and even contradictory ways. This may happen for any of the following reasons: different observers have (1) different experiences with the person, (2) different impressions of the person, (3) different beliefs about the nature of personality, (4) different rules for making attributions, (5) different opportunities to observe the person, or (6) different motives and perspectives in the situation in which they encounter the person. In the following sections we will consider each of these factors in turn.

Experience and Attribution

People may have different experiences with another person because they meet that person in different roles or settings. Students who see a professor only in a large lecture class may attribute some of the inevitably formal nature of that situation to the character of the professor. They may, in other words, perceive him as distant, ironic, witty, and pedantic. But the professor's children may see him as close, warm, and relaxed. His colleagues may have yet a third view of him. The point is that these different perspectives are held by people who have had systematically different experiences with a person, and have thereby been led to systematically differing attributions of his personality.

First Impressions and Attribution

It can be expected that the first impressions we form of others will be highly influential in our final impressions of their personalities. An experiment by Luchins (1942) vividly illustrates this. Read the following description and see what impressions you draw about Jim:

> Jim left the house to get some stationery. He walked out into the sun-filled street with two of his friends, basking in the sun as he walked. Jim entered the stationery store, which was full of people. Jim talked with an acquaintance while he waited for the clerk to catch his eye. On his way out, he stopped to chat with a school friend who was just coming into the store. Leaving the store, he walked toward school. On his way out he met the girl to whom he had been introduced the night before. They talked for a short while, and then Jim left for school. After school Jim left the classroom alone. Leaving the school, he started on his long walk home. The street was filled with brilliant sunshine. Jim walked down the street on the shady side. Coming down the street toward him, he saw the pretty girl whom he had met on the previous evening. Jim crossed the street and entered a candy store. The store was crowded with students, and he noticed a few familiar faces. Jim waited quietly until the counterman caught his eye and then gave his order. Taking his drink, he sat down at a side table. When he had finished his drink he went home.

Why do you think Jim crossed the street? Why did he sit by himself? The impression usually formed from this description is that of an extroverted, gregarious person. Therefore, people usually say that Jim crossed the street not to avoid the girl, but to buy something at the store, and that he then sat by himself not because he wanted to be alone, but because he had some work to do. But these interpretations of Jim's actions are caused by people's first impression of Jim as a gregarious person. Look at the paragraph again. The first half of the paragraph describes a series of actions that seem characteristic of an outgoing, extroverted individual. But, beginning with the sentence "After school Jim left the classroom alone," the actions described are those of a withdrawn, introverted person. Indeed, it turns out that if those sentences are read first, the person reading them comes away with an image of a shy person who avoids contact with other people, and thus interprets the actions that others saw as gregarious in a different way.

Sometimes, as in the Luchins example, the first bits of information have more influence than ones that are received later, a phenomenon known as the *primacy effect*. Under other circumstances the opposite can occur; that is, the last few pieces of information carry more weight, a phenomenon known as a *recency effect*. The conditions that determine whether a primacy or recency effect will occur are fairly complex, and have been discussed in more detail in Chapter 7, but the important point is that the order in which we receive information is often a major determinant of our impressions of others.

First impressions of people tend to stay with us. If we at first form the impression that a certain person has high abilities, then we can "explain away" his or her later poor peformance as due to lack of effort or the difficulty of the task. But if we had seen this poor performance first, we might have formed an impression of someone with no talent, and attributed future successes to luck or to an easy task.

Implicit Personality Theories and Social Cognition

Social psychologists have recognized that we all have our own implicit person- ality theories that we apply to people we meet. An implicit personality theory consists of our beliefs about which traits are likely to occur together in people; for example, some people believe that musical ability and a sense of humor go hand in hand, or that someone who does not look you straight in the eyes is bound to be generally untrustworthy.

Because of this, different people can make very different judgments about the same individual, for two reasons: Either their first impressions differ, or their implicit personality theories cause them to come to different conclusions based on the same first impression.

One aspect of implicit personality theory that has long been a source of interest and concern is the pervasive existence of *stereotypes*. Stereotypes are assumptions we make about people based solely or primarily on their member- ship in a group. For example, a stereotyped view of women is that they are emotional, talkative, prone to hysteria, and bad drivers. Negative stereotypes can obviously be quite damaging when they are erroneously attributed to individuals who do not have these characteristics.

One source of stereotypes is the fact that we tend to pay more attention to the *similarities* between ourselves and members of groups to which we belong, but we pay more attention to the *differences* between ourselves and members of groups to which we do *not* belong (Wilder and Allen, 1978). This tendency to focus on the dissimilarity of outgroup members probably encourages the formation of negative stereotypes.

A second source of stereotypes comes from our tendency to form *illusory correlations* (Chapman, 1967). Two things are correlated when they tend to appear together, and most stereotypes are actually assumed correlations. For example, the stereotyped belief that Welshmen are good singers implies that if a man is of Welsh descent, he is probably a good singer. In forming these correlations, we tend to be overinfluenced by distinctive or unusual events. Unusual personal characteristics such as skin color or physical deformity draw our attention (Langer, Taylor, Fiske, and Chanowitz, 1976). Unusual behaviors, particularly negative ones, also draw our attention. Hamilton and Gifford (1976) found that we tend to overestimate the extent to which unusual group membership and unusual behavior go together. Even when such pairings are actually quite infrequent, the combination of unusual personal characteristics and unusual behavior is so memorable that it is difficult to avoid overestimating the extent to which they go together.

Once a person has been assigned to a stereotyped category, our responses to new information are biased by the assumed characteristics of that category. We are likely, for example, to be easily persuaded that the person has other qualities of "that type of person," and may even believe we have actually seen the person behave in ways that are consistent with the stereotype when the person has never in fact behaved in such a way (Cantor and Mischel, 1977). These unfounded beliefs can then influence our behavior toward individuals who are actually "innocent victims" of the tendency to see the world in stereotype (Snyder and Swann, 1978).

Attribution Rules

Sometimes our implicit personality theories don't help us—for instance, in a case in which we are able to observe only one simple action of another person, yet need to make some sort of judgment about what that person is like from this scanty information. When, for example, do we conclude that a kind action means that the person who commits that action is kind? Two rules were suggested by Jones and Davis (1965): First, we learn relatively little from the usual, normal, socially desirable actions of a person. We cannot tell if a person who makes cheerful conversation when we meet him or her for the first time really likes us or is just fulfilling social norms of politeness. On the other hand, if the person behaved rudely or impolitely, we would be likely to infer that that person really did dislike us.

Second, Jones and Davis pointed out the high information value of the "noncommon effects" that are produced by actions or choices made by a person. Suppose that a student has been admitted to two colleges, both of which have good academic reputations, both of which are located in middle-sized towns, but only one of which is coeducational. If the student chooses the coeducational school, then we can infer that a preference for coeducation was the reason for his or her choice, because the colleges were similar in their other characteristics and differed only in this one. The one noncommon effect of the choice is the one we assume dictates the choice, and we infer that the chooser has an intention corresponding to that choice. When there are many noncommon effects, it can be very difficult to decide why the person acted as he or she did. When there are just a few noncommon effects, the task of making attributions for a person's behavior is much easier.

Attributions from Multiple Observations

The attribution rules we have just discussed are the ones we use to infer a person's momentary intentions and enduring personality characteristics from a single action. But we often learn a lot more about other people by observing not one but many of their actions. Kelley (1967) has proposed a set of rules that people use in determining the meaning of a set of observations of another person's actions. Generally we ask, What changes in circumstances cause changes in a person's behavior?

Suppose that you see John laughing at a certain comedian. What sorts of information will help you understand *why* John laughed? Kelley (1967) suggests three dimensions around which we can organize new information: the actor, the entity or stimulus, and time.

Observations of John's behavior over a long period of time give us information about the *consistency* of his response. If John laughs at this comedian every time he sees him, this highly consistent information helps us judge that John really likes the comedian. If John laughs one time but not the next, this inconsistency may lead us to different conclusions.

Distinctiveness information refers to a person's reaction to similar entities or stimuli. Does John laugh at all comedians? If he does, then his behavior shows low distinctiveness, because it does not vary from one comedian to the next. His reaction, then, would not be distinctive to just this comedian.

Consensus information refers to a similar reaction by many actors to one entity. If John laughs at the comedian and everyone else does too (high consensus information), then we conclude that John's reaction is not unique; the comedian is genuinely funny.

Kelley next suggested that certain patterns of these three kinds of information lead naturally to certain kinds of conclusions. For instance, the combination of high consistency, low distinctiveness, and low consensus information leads to an attribution about the actor (see Figure 18-1). If John always (high consistency) laughs at any and all comedians (low distinctiveness), even when other people don't (low consensus), then we know something about John, namely that he is a fool for comedians. On the other hand, high consistency and high consensus information lead to another type of attribution. That is, if everybody (high consensus) always (high consistency) laughs at a particular comedian, particularly if there are some other comedians at whom they don't laugh (high distinctiveness), then we know that the comedian (the entity) is indeed very funny—but this tells us nothing in particular about John.

These principles are thought to be the principles that we all use in drawing conclusions about the motivations, intentions, and dispositions of the people whose behavior we observe. Therefore, the normal way of testing such a theory is by presenting subjects with verbal, written, or videotaped descriptions of people acting in various ways and asking them to make judgments about those people. In 1972, McArthur assessed the validity of Kelley's analysis by presenting subjects with various combinations of consistency, distinctiveness, and consensus information and observing whether the subjects drew conclusions about the person involved, the stimulus, or the specific circumstances—or some complex combination of these possibilities. The results of that study and of others (Karaz and Perlman, 1975; Ruble and Feldman, 1976) generally confirm Kelley's suggestions about the attribution rules used by most of us.

McArthur's observers showed a general tendency to make attributions to the actor even when the evidence did not completely warrant that conclusion. This means that observers were more prone to attribute behavior to internal dispositional states of the actor than to external situational causes, which is as if the ordinary person leans toward being a personality psychologist rather than a social psychologist.

Reviewing the many studies on this topic, Jones (1978) concludes that there

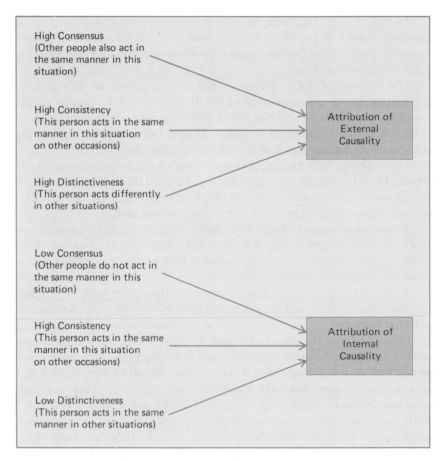

Figure 18-1

The combination of high consistency, low distinctiveness, and low consensus information usually leads to an attribution of internal causality—an attribution about the actor. High consistency, high consensus, and high distinctiveness lead to an attribution of external causality—an attribution about the entity or stimulus. (Kelley, 1967)

is a general tendency to attribute behavior to actors rather than to the situations they are in. Since this tendency has occurred in many experiments in which it is possible to give an independent definition of what an accurate attribution would be, this person-attributing bias is called the *fundamental attribution error* (Ross, 1977).

The social implications of this error are interesting to contemplate. It is as if we oversimplify our complex world by overestimating the role that people play in determining their own actions. A teacher, for instance, may decide that a primary school child's poor performance on an arithmetic quiz indicates a poor arithmetic ability rather than considering the possibility that the child is temporarily discombobulated by the first days of school.

Motivation and Attribution

As well as these informational factors that lead to differences in perceptions of people, there are also the more emotionally colored ones produced by our own motives. As parents, when we hear about our child's poor performance on a test we may be motivated to attribute it to the poor teaching of the teacher, because we are naturally motivated to believe that our child is intelligent.

Another example of motivational bias involves our desire to believe in a just world; we tend, for instance, to want to believe that victims of horrible events must have done something to deserve their fate, because such explanations preserve our ability to believe that people generally receive fair and equitable treatment (Lerner, Miller, and Holmes, 1976). Such tendencies to see the world as we would like it to be may explain why, for example, rape victims are often treated as if they were responsible for their plight.

However, a caution needs to be asserted here. Describing the role of motivation in perception makes it sound as if motivational bias can proceed without limits and lead to exactly opposite conclusions about the same person. Yet in at least one specific instance the evidence does not support this view. It can be predicted from the motivated perception view that teachers should want to take credit for (that is, attribute to themselves) the successes of their pupils, but attribute to the pupils causes of failure. Yet a review of the literature finds surprisingly little tendency to do this (Miller and Ross, 1975).

Attitude Formation and Change

The study of attribution is one part of a broader area that has traditionally been of central concern to social psychologists—the study of attitude formation and change. The previous section focused on our attitudes about the personality characteristics and motivations of others; we can also have attitudes about objects (chocolate eclairs), events (the seizure of hostages in Iran), and abstract ideas (communism and democracy).

Many of our attitudes are formed through communication with other people. We are influenced by our friends' and acquaintances' opinions and by speeches, editorials, and information presented in the media. For example, we are all aware of the ploys used in advertising campaigns to form our attitudes about a particular product. Some advertisements attempt to create a need for a product by convincing us that it is indispensable to daily life. Other ads attempt to alter our already formed attitudes about a product by suggesting that Brand X is better, less expensive, and more effective than Brand Y or Z. Marketing strategies and techniques have also influenced political campaigns in recent years (McGinness, 1969). People have tried to package and sell presidential candidates to American voters just as detergent is sold to them as consumers.

Attempts to form and influence attitudes are widespread in modern life. What factors in a communication affect attitude formation and change? These fall into three categories: aspects of the person doing the communicating, aspects of the communication or message itself, and aspects of the audience.

Aspects of the Communicator
CREDIBILITY AND TRUSTWORTHINESS.   Among the first variables psychologists have examined are the expertise and prestige (the credibility) of the communicator. Hovland and Weiss (1951) gave subjects four communications, each of which were attributed to either a high- or low-credibility source. For

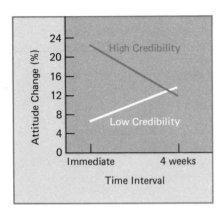

Figure 18-2

Results of an experiment in which subjects were presented with messages from both a high credibility and a low credibility source. When tested immediately following, the messages attributed to high credibility sources were significantly more effective in changing subjects' attitudes. When tested 4 weeks later, however, the advantage of the high credibility source had disappeared—a phenomenon called the sleeper effect. (Hovland and Weiss, 1951)

example, one message about building atomic submarines was attributed either to Robert Oppenheimer, an eminent American physicist (high credibility), or to *Pravda,* a Russian government news agency (low credibility). An opinion questionnaire administered before the communications indicated that the high-credibility sources were judged to be trustworthy by 80 to 95 percent of the subjects, while the low-credibility sources were judged as trustworthy by only 1 to 21 percent of the subjects. Immediately after receiving the communications, subjects answered a questionnaire about their attitudes towards the issues that had been presented. The results indicated that messages attributed to the highly credible sources were significantly more effective in changing subjects' attitudes than those attributed to the low-credibility sources.

These results are compatible with the intuitive belief that a source who is perceived as prestigious, knowledgeable, and an expert in his or her field will have more influence than a source perceived negatively. But is this a lasting effect? Hovland and Weiss measured subjects' opinions one month after the initial experiment. Surprisingly, they found that the relative advantage of the highly credible source over the low-credibility source had disappeared! In other words, the number of subjects influenced by the highly credible source had decreased over time, while the number of subjects influenced by the low-credibility source had increased. Hovland and Weiss termed this increase in the low-credibility source's ability to influence attitudes the *sleeper effect* (see Figure 18-2). They suggested that the effect may be caused by subjects' disassociating the *content* of the communication from the source of the communication. After a certain amount of time the subjects remembered the content of the messages, but they did not seem to associate spontaneously the message with the identity of the communicators. Kelman and Hovland (1953) found that if subjects were reminded of the source of the message several weeks later, and then given a questionnaire to answer, the sleeper effect did not occur.

SIMILARITY.   Another important communicator variable is the speaker's similarity to the audience. An audience that perceives a speaker as similar in appearance, socioeconomic class, or occupation will probably also perceive the speaker as holding similar opinions and attitudes. For example, television commercials sell products by using an actor or actress who is similar in various aspects to the target consumer. Beer commercials are slanted toward the male as consumer, generally portraying a group of male friends, often after an athletic event, drinking the product. Detergent commercials portray the "typical" American housewife (often a "real" person), who attests to the superior qualities of a particular brand. Advertisements that use real people are particularly potent because they combine *similarity* with *trustworthiness.* A housewife from Pough-keepsie who has chosen the correct product in a blind-choice format is not only projecting to viewers that she, like them, has similar detergent-cleaning criteria, she is also honestly endorsing the product.

A study by Brock (1965) examined the effect of communicator similarity in a natural setting with real people as subjects. The subjects were customers who came to a store to purchase paint. The salesman communicated one of two messages to each customer. In one condition he presented himself as knowing very little about paint but added that he had recently bought a similar amount of Brand X paint for the same sort of paint job that the customer needed it for. In this condition the salesman came across not as an expert but as similar to the customer. In the second condition the salesman presented himself as an expert on paint, but his prior purchase of Brand X was for a very different type of paint job from the customer's. The measure of persuasibility or effectiveness was how much of Brand X the customer bought. Which message would influence the customer more, one based on expertise or one based on similarity? Brock found that more of Brand X was purchased by customers who were told about the paint by a "similar" salesman than by an "expert" but dissimilar salesman.

Aspects of the Communication

Another factor that affects attitude formation is the communication or message itself. Some of the possible variables in the message itself are whether to present a one-sided versus a two-sided message, and whether it is possible to "inoculate" listeners against a persuasive message.

ONE- VERSUS TWO-SIDED COMMUNICATIONS.   One issue that confronts a speaker trying to influence an audience is whether to present only *one* side of the issue or whether to include points from the opposite side and then refute them. The classic study examining the effectiveness of one- versus two-sided communications was conducted in response to a serious problem. In early 1945, Germany had lost the Battle of the Bulge and the European war was nearing an end. The Allied command, therefore, began to concentrate more heavily on the war in the Pacific. They realized, however, that there was a morale problem among the soldiers. The troops stationed in Europe were tired of war and wanted to go home, and yet a long, difficult war with Japan lay ahead of them. In order to solve this problem, Army psychologists prepared radio broadcasts designed to persuade soldiers that the war in the Pacific theater would not be over soon, as the soldiers wished to believe, but that victory was attainable within 2 years.

In studying the Army's problem, psychologists (Hovland, Lumsdaine, and Sheffield, 1949) saw the opportunity to examine the one- versus two-sided communication question. Two radio programs were prepared. One program presented only reasons for expecting another two years of war with Japan (one-sided); the other program presented the same reasons plus contradictory reasons for why the U.S. might win the war more quickly (two-sided). The experimental question was whether there would be an advantage in trying to give an impression of fairness through the two-sided communication, or whether it would be a disadvantage to publicize contradictory ideas.

Several hundred soldiers were divided into two groups. Their initial opinions toward the probable duration of the war with Japan were determined in a survey. The soldiers then heard one of the two radio broadcasts, after which their attitudes were remeasured. A control group, who did not hear either broadcast, was included in the experiment—in this way the researchers could determine whether observed changes in attitudes were due to the radio program or due to other events that occurred at the same time.

Before listening to the broadcast, about 37 percent of the men estimated that it would take 18 months or longer to win the war. On the second questionnaire, about the same amount (34 percent) of the control group, who had not heard a persuasive communication, made the same estimate. The experimental group, however, indicated significantly more attitude change than the control group.

Persuasive communications often attempt to alter our attitudes by appealing to our emotions. Charities often use pictures of malnourished orphans to evoke our pity and to open our wallets. Antismoking campaigns attempt to frighten smokers into quitting by tales of lung cancer and death. Good driving habits and the use of seat belts are stressed through pictures of gruesome automobile accidents and mangled victims. In general, triggering people's fears has been a powerful method of persuasive communication. However, what exactly is the relationship between fear level and attitude change?

One of the first studies was conducted by Janis and Feshbach (1953), who presented high school students with persuasive communications about the cause and prevention of tooth decay. Using a slide show-lecture format, they created three versions of the communication which varied in the amount of fear-arousing material. The *high-fear* lecture discussed, in graphic detail, the painful and deleterious effects of poor dental hygiene. The lecture was accompanied by actual slides of diseased gums, rotten teeth, and mouth infections. The *mod-erate-fear* lecture was less vivid in describing the dangers of tooth and gum decay, and the slides showed less extreme cases. The *weak-fear* lecture principally discussed the growth and functions of the teeth and gums, and the slides showed healthy teeth and x-rays of cavities.

Janis and Feshbach found that the strong fear-arousing communication produced the *least* amount of change in toothbrushing habits, and the low fear-arousing communication produced the most change. One explanation for the inefficacy of the strong-fear appeal was that it

Fifty-nine percent of the soldiers in *both* the one-sided and two-sided communication conditions made the 18-month-or-longer estimate. Thus, the persuasive communications significantly altered the soldiers' attitudes towards the war, but presenting one or two sides of the issue did not appear to make a difference in the amount of attitude change.

Intrigued by this finding, Hovland examined the data in terms of the

Figure 18-3

Effects of one- versus two-sided communications on those who initially agreed with the point of view of the communicator and those who initially disagreed. (Hovland et al., 1949)

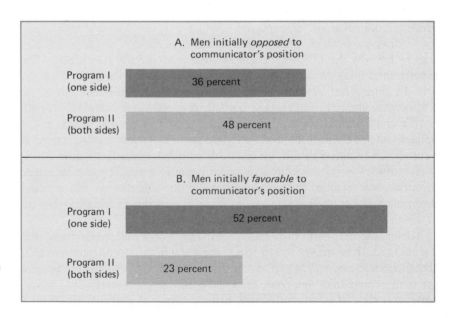

A. Men initially *opposed* to communicator's position

Program I (one side) — 36 percent

Program II (both sides) — 48 percent

B. Men initially *favorable* to communicator's position

Program I (one side) — 52 percent

Program II (both sides) — 23 percent

Chapter 18:
The Individual in Group Settings

may have aroused anxiety in the listener to such an extent that strong counteracting defensive reactions were aroused (Insko, 1967), leading to denial or dismissal of the message.

For some time, it was generally accepted that arousing a high level of fear was an ineffective method of altering attitudes. However, it now appears that, most of the time, fear-producing appeals are very effective. In most of the investigations that have been reported, high-fear messages are more persuasive than low-fear messages, and on a variety of topics such as automobile safety (Leventhal and Niles, 1965; Simonson and Lundy, 1966), capital punishment (Haefher, 1965), eye damage (Kraus et al., 1964), and even dental hygiene (Le-

venthal and Singer, 1966).

The apparent inconsistency of positive and negative results in this area has been discussed by Leventhal (1970), who notes that negative results have generally been interpreted as due to an inability to cope with fear, leading to avoidance reactions and failure to carry out the recommended behavior. In contrast to the "inability to cope" explanation, Leventhal outlines other variables besides fear that can produce negative results. Subjects who feel they are highly vulnerable to the fearful consequences communicated in the message (e.g., heavy smokers who hear a smoking-lung cancer message) feel they are probably going to get cancer anyway whether or not they try to protect themselves,

and so they do nothing. Leventhal also notes that personality variables, such as self-esteem, contribute to the acceptance or lack of acceptance of a message using fear. Subjects who have low self-esteem experience more helplessness and avoidance reactions than do subjects with high self-esteem, at low as well as high levels of reported fear.

Thus, while there have been a few studies in which arousing fear has proven to be ineffective or counterproductive, the bulk of the research shows that fear-producing appeals are very effective. This is particularly true if the messages include recommendations for effective action that will allow the audience to avoid the fear-producing outcomes depicted in the communication.

soldiers' initial opinions on the probable duration of war with Japan. They found that soldiers whose initial attitudes were in *opposition* to the point of view expressed in the broadcast showed more attitude change if they heard the *two-sided* rather than the one-sided communication. These soldiers were obviously very much aware that there were two sides to the issue, and the one-sided communication probably struck them as too blatant an attempt at persuasion. On the other hand, the two-sided communication mentioned those points that the soldiers supported, but stressed the evidence for the other side. For those soldiers who initially *agreed* with the point of view of the broadcast, the *one-sided* communication was more effective in further strengthening their attitudes. These soldiers, already in agreement with the Army's viewpoint, probably began to doubt the correctness of their opinions when they heard the other side of the issue mentioned in the two-sided communication. The one-sided communication, on the other hand, provided them with more reasons to support their already formed attitudes, and presented no discordant ideas (see Figure 18-3).

RESISTANCE TO PERSUASION: INOCULATION. Another way of looking at the whole area of persuasion and attitude change is to ask how to protect or immunize people from persuasive communications. McGuire and his associates have used a biological analogy to explain resistance to attitude change. In order to protect yourself from the flu, for example, you can raise your resistance by getting plenty of rest, eating nutritious meals, and taking vitamins. A second form of protection from the flu is to be inoculated, which involves receiving a weakened or dead form of the disease, stimulating your body's defense system and raising your resistance. Following this biological analogy, McGuire hypothesized that there are two ways to increase resistance to persuasive attempts: One is to make the attitude more resistant or "healthy" by presenting *supporting* arguments; the second is to *inoculate* the attitude-holder with weak versions of counterarguments. This, then, is a variation of the one- versus two-sided communication study.

In order to test inoculation theory, McGuire and Papageorgis (1961) used cultural truisms or widely shared beliefs such as "It's a good idea to brush your teeth after every meal" and "Penicillin has been, almost without exception, of great benefit to mankind." The truisms exist in a "germ-free environment"; people have never heard these attitudes attacked, and therefore they have not developed appropriate defense responses or resistance.

McGuire and Papageorgis divided their study into two sessions—the first was a pretreatment session and the second was a counterargument session. In the pretreatment session half the subjects were given information that supported the cultural truisms and half were given information that presented and then refuted arguments against the truisms. To return to the biological analogy, the supportive information is like taking vitamins and getting plenty of rest to safeguard against a disease, while the refutational defense is like receiving an inoculation of a weakened form of the disease. At the end of the first session subjects were asked to indicate their support of the truisms on a questionnaire.

Two days after the pretreatment session, the subjects returned and were presented with strong counterarguments that attacked the cultural truisms. After receiving the counterarguments, subjects again indicated their support of the truisms. The experimental question was which kind of message, the supportive or the refutational, would provide the most resistance to persuasion.

The first questionnaire, administered after the pretreatment, indicated that the supportive defense produced somewhat more attitude change than did the refutational defense. McGuire calls this a *paper-tiger phenomenon:* Subjects who have not yet been faced with counterarguments are persuaded more by the supportive, or one-sided, information than by the refutational, or two-sided, information. However, the second attitude measure, administered after the strong counterarguments, indicated that the refutational message produced more resistance to attitude change than the supportive message. When subjects finally face adversity in the form of arguments attacking cultural truisms, they are better able to resist persuasion if they have already been exposed to these counterarguments and heard them refuted.

Aspects of the Listener

We can conclude from the section on the communication or message itself that even the most carefully constructed message may not have its intended effect because of particular characteristics of the listener. For example, we have seen in the Hovland et al., (1949) study that the prior opinions of the audience interact very strongly with the one- or two-sided manipulation of the communication. What other aspects of the listener affect attitude formation and change?

INTELLIGENCE AND EDUCATION.   Probably many people believe that a highly intelligent person would be more difficult to persuade than a person of low intelligence. However, several studies conducted by Hovland and his colleagues (Hovland and Janis, 1959; Hovland and Mandell, 1952) failed to find any reliable relationship between intelligence and a resistance to persuasion. Hovland, Lumsdaine, and Sheffield (1949) did find evidence for an interesting relationship between amount of education and attitude change. They examined their data from the World War II one- versus two-sided communication study in terms of the soldiers' educational background and found that the two-sided communication was more effective with better educated soldiers (high school graduates, college graduates, those with advanced degrees), while the one-sided communication was more effective with less educated soldiers (those who had not finished high school). Miller and Buckhout (1973) hypothesize that the educated soldiers acquired habits of thought during their schooling that made them more resistant to the one-sided presentation. The less educated soldiers, on the other hand, were not as critical in their reception of the message and thus were more impressed by the supporting evidence of the one-sided presentation.

SELF-ESTEEM.   A potential factor in people's resistance to persuasion may be their level of self-esteem. An early study (Linton and Graham, 1959) concluded that subjects who are easily persuaded tend to have low self-esteem. However, a distinction must be made between "persistent" self-esteem (the typical, ongoing feelings we have about ourselves) and "transient" self-esteem (feelings about ourselves that are affected by day-to-day events). Gollob and Dittes (1965) and Zellner (1970) experimentally manipulated "transient" self-esteem by giving subjects either success or failure feedback after they had performed a task. After receiving the feedback, subjects answered a questionnaire, read a persuasive communication, and then again answered a questionnaire. The results of both studies indicated that transient self-esteem, induced by failure feedback, was more strongly related to persuasibility than was persistent self-esteem.

MEN VERSUS WOMEN.   An enduring question in this area is whether women are more easily persuaded than men. An early study by Janis and Field (1959) found that women were more persuasible, which the researchers attributed to stereotyped sex differences in female and male roles—men are raised to be relatively independent thinkers, they reasoned, while women are raised to be submissive and yielding to social influence. These early studies helped establish a belief in the greater persuasibility of women.

One researcher (Eagley, 1978) has now completed a careful review of the sex-difference literature on persuasibility and has discovered that the most common finding was *no* sex difference! Of the 62 studies reported in this area, 82 percent found no difference between the sexes and only 16 percent found women to be more persuasible. There are two possible explanations for this. First, Eagley notes that the vast majority of the studies that found women to be more persuasible than men were done before 1970; very few studies conducted in the 1970s found such an effect. She thus suggests that the cultural context in which research is conducted is an important variable. Second, she discusses the importance of the content of the persuasive communication. It has been found that people are more readily influenced by a topic that they personally lack information about or that they find unimportant. In most of the studies, persuasive communications have been based on political or economic topics, which traditionally have been topics in which men are more knowledgeable and interested (Swanson, 1951). Thus, women's greater persuasibility in pre-1970 studies could be a result of the topics used in the persuasive messages. Recent changes in the cultural definitions of sex roles have included politics and economics as topics of interest to women, which may explain the relative absence of the persuasibility effect in post-1970 studies. One study, which found that men were more persuasible than women (Feldman, 1974), used nutrition as the communication topic. Since food preparation is still considered primarily a woman's responsibility, the nutritional topic was one in which women are more knowledgeable and interested. Thus the evidence presented by Eagley in her review of the literature suggests that the sex-difference finding in a small number of early studies was due to social context and communication content factors, not to the inherent persuasibility of women.

Communication Outside the Laboratory

The communication variables we have been discussing have been effective in influencing attitude change in an experimental setting. What variables affect attitude change outside the laboratory? There seem to be at least two—the audience selection effect and the diffusion of communication through a two-step process.

AUDIENCE SELECTION EFFECT.   In a controlled experimental setting, researchers can ensure that the people serving as subjects attend completely to the communication without any distraction. Outside the laboratory, on the other hand, distractions are always present, and speakers can rarely expect that their message will receive the total attention of their audience. More importantly, in the experimental setting each and every subject is fully exposed to the message. In the real world, however, people tend to listen to messages they agree with and to shun persuasive communications that argue for the other side of the issue (Lipset et al., 1954). This is called the *audience selection effect.* For example, a person who advocates capital punishment as an effective deterrent to crime will pass over a newspaper editorial or change the television channel when someone speaking against capital punishment communicates his or her views. Thus, the people who choose not to expose themselves to a communication can be highly biased; unfortunately, this is often the very audience the speaker is trying to reach.

In the audience selection effect, the very people the speaker is trying to reach may choose not to listen—in the case shown here it is very easy to avoid this speaker's message just by walking away.

DIFFUSION OF COMMUNICATION. There is another difference between experimental and real-world settings. In an experimental setting subjects listen to a persuasive communication and then indicate their attitudes without interacting with one another. Obviously, attitude formation and change in the real world does not occur in this sort of vacuum. People discuss and exchange information, and by so doing influence and are influenced by those around them. Katz and Lazarsfeld (1955) have studied attitude formation and change in many real-world issues such as voting in an election. They have found that people tend to vote the same way their family, friends, or fellow employees vote. In particular they found that there were certain people in these formal or informal groups who exerted a great influence on the attitudes of others. These "opinion leaders," however, did not necessarily have the characteristics we usually think of as belonging to a leader, and they occurred in all occupational and socioeconomic levels of society. Furthermore, opinion leadership does not seem to be a personality trait that some people have and others do not; it depends on the topic or issue involved. Thus, there is a two-step process by which information gets spread in a population: Ideas flow from the media and other sources to opinion leaders, and from opinion leaders to the less active sections of the population (Katz and Lazarsfeld, 1955).

Cognitive Dissonance Theory

Some very interesting issues have been raised by asking how our own behavior affects attitude change. Much of the research on this question has focused on how behaving in a way that is inconsistent with an existing attitude can change that attitude, and most of that research has been stimulated by Leon Festinger's theory of *cognitive dissonance*. The basic elements in Festinger's theory are *cognitions*, or bits of knowledge that we have about the world. When two cognitions are inconsistent—that is, when one thought or cognition contradicts the other—a dissonant relationship is said to exist between the two. For example, knowledge that one is a Democrat is dissonant with knowledge that one has just voted for a Republican. According to Festinger, this state of cognitive dissonance produces a psychological tension that a person is motivated to reduce; in other words, having two inconsistent cognitions is unpleasant, and a person will work to get rid of that unpleasant, dissonant feeling.

How might this dissonance be reduced? One way is to change one or more of the cognitions to make them less dissonant. Voters, for instance, might convince themselves that they are not as loyal to the Democrats as they had presumed. This strategy had been proposed by others before Festinger (Heider, 1946; Newcomb, 1953). Festinger's contribution, and the real hallmark of cognitive dissonance theory, was to state more explicitly and in a more testable form *how* these cognitions are made to become less dissonant.

Festinger proposed that certain of our cognitions are more resistant to change than others. For instance, cognitions based on physical reality, such as the knowledge that ice is cold or that you have just eaten spinach, will be particularly difficult to alter. In contrast, cognitions based on opinions and attitudes ("I dislike spinach") are more open to change. Festinger believed that one way dissonance would be reduced would be by altering those cognitions *least* resistant to change. It is in this way that your behaviors may come to

People discuss and exchange information, and by doing so influence and are influenced by those around them. There are certain people even in informal groups who exert great influence on the attitudes of others. These "opinion leaders" occur in all occupations and in all levels of society.

influence your attitudes. Say that your behavior (eating spinach) is dissonant with your attitude ("I dislike spinach"). It is difficult to deny that the behavior has occurred; the easier course of action is to bring the attitude into line with the behavior ("I really do like spinach").

Support for these notions came from a classic experiment by Festinger and Carlsmith (1959). They recruited subjects for what was supposedly an experiment on task performance. When subjects arrived, they were given a series of exceedingly dull, boring tasks to occupy their time. For example, they were required to turn each peg along a number of rows on a pegboard, first a quarter turn to the left, then back a quarter turn to the right. After the tasks were finished the experimenter noted that the actual experiment had to do with mental sets or expectations, which were to be created by a confederate of the experimenter who met subjects before they performed the tasks and convinced them that the tasks were going to be interesting and fun.

Subjects were told that they were in the *control* condition of the experiment—that is, the condition that assessed task performance without the confederate's having raised any expectations. At this point the subjects assumed that they had completed the experiment, but in fact the crucial part was yet to come. Acting somewhat perplexed, the experimenter stated that the confederate had yet to arrive for the next subject, who was to be in the "positive expectation" condition. The experimenter then had what appeared to be a flash of insight: Perhaps the present subject could help by filling in as the confederate. All that was required was to convince the next "subject" (actually a confederate of the experimenter) that the tasks were in fact interesting and fun. For this the subject was offered $1. After complying with the experimenter's request, the subject then indicated his or her own "true" attitudes toward the tasks.

Festinger and Carlsmith had created a situation ripe for dissonance arousal. Subjects' behavior in attempting to influence the confederate was clearly dissonant with their initial attitudes about the tasks. Moreover, the $1 inducement does not seem enough to justify the behavior (that is, to serve as a supportive cognition). It is unlikely that subjects would change their cognitions about the behavior (it would be hard to persuade themselves that they hadn't performed the tasks). Dissonance theory would predict a change in the least resistant cognitions (the attitudes toward the tasks), so that they would no longer be inconsistent with the behavior. In other words, subjects should rate the tasks as having actually been interesting. Compared to a second group of subjects, who were paid $20 for attempting to influence the confederate, and a control group, who simply rated the tasks after completing them, subjects in the $1 condition in fact brought their attitudes into line with their behavior and rated the tasks as more interesting (see Table 18-1). Subjects in the $20 condition should have experienced little dissonance in the first place, since the $20, especially in 1959, provided a ready explanation for their behavior.

This finding of greater attitude change with lower incentive has come to be known as the *induced compliance effect,* and has been repeated in numerous other experiments (Cohen, 1962; Zimbardo et al., 1965). It was not only very large amounts of money that produced differences in attitude change—Cohen (1962) found reliable differences between subjects offered 50 cents and those offered $1. Those offered less money showed greater subsequent attitude change.

*Table 18-1: Attitude Toward the Task.**

Inducement	Attitude
$1	+ 1.35
$20	− 0.5
Control	− .45

*Based on a −5 to +5 scale, where −5 means "extremely boring" and +5 means "extremely interesting."

Festinger and Carlsmith (1959).

A second line of research has also provided support for cognitive dissonance theory. This is in the area of *effort justification,* which is perhaps best captured by the idea that we learn to like what we have suffered to achieve. The basic notion is that when we expend a great deal of effort for little or no reason, dissonance will arise. The cognition that we are doing something effortful is dissonant with the knowledge that we are not gaining anything worthwhile by doing it. As in the induced compliance case, dissonance may be reduced by bringing one's attitude into line with one's behavior. In this case the positive benefits of the activity being undertaken can be elevated as a means of justifying the expenditure of effort. Anyone who has encountered (or been) a zealous jogger will probably have a good intuitive understanding of these notions.

The effort justification hypothesis has received much additional empirical support (Gerard and Mathewson, 1966; Zimbardo, 1965; Wicklund, Cooper, and Linder, 1967). It has been used recently to explain that psychotherapies may be at least partially successful because of the effort they involve for the client (Cooper, 1979; Axsom and Cooper, 1979).

The forgoing discussion only begins to tap the many areas in which cognitive dissonance theory has been brought to bear. However, controversy has often surrounded dissonance theory—as you might expect, since the theory attempts to explain many diverse phenomena. These controversies have led ultimately to refinements of the original theory. Most of these refinements specify in more detail when the tension state of dissonance will arise. Perhaps most importantly, it has been found that the individual must feel that he or she has freely chosen to perform the dissonant behavior (Linder, Cooper, and Jones, 1967); people forced at gunpoint to perform some behavior against their principles should not experience dissonance. The lack of choice makes the behavior irrelevant as an indicator of the person's true attitudes. Also, the outcome of the behavior should be foreseeable to the person before the act is performed (Cooper, 1971). For example, if you make a contribution to a local children's aid group, and only later discover the group to be a front for local religious zealots, little dissonance should be aroused if you realize that you could not have foreseen this. These concepts of choice and foreseeability have recently been combined into the more general concept of personal responsibility (Wicklund and Brehm, 1976), which states that only when we are in some way personally responsible for each of the dissonant cognitions will dissonance be aroused.

Anyone who has ever encountered (or been) a zealous jogger will probably have a good intuitive understanding of effort justification.

Attitudes and Behavior

DO ATTITUDES CAUSE BEHAVIOR? The study of attitudes is interesting in itself, but the main reason that social psychologists have spent so much time and effort studying attitude formation and change is because they have assumed that attitudes guide behavior. Put another way, it was assumed that we could predict how a person would behave if we knew that person's attitudes. This certainly seems like a reasonable assumption, but evidence that attitudes guide behavior has been surprisingly hard to come by. In fact, a number of experiments seem to show that attitudes and behaviors have nothing to do with each other. In the first of these failures to find a consistent relationship between attitudes and behaviors, LaPiere (1934) reported on his experiences in traveling in the United States with a young Oriental couple. In the course of their travels, LaPiere and his companions stopped at a large number of restaurants and hotels. In only one case was the couple not treated hospitably because of their ethnic origin. However, when LaPiere later measured the attitudes of the owners of the establishments that they had visited, over 90 percent of those who responded were negative—they said that as a matter of policy Orientals would not be served in their establishments. The reported attitudes and the actual behavior seemed to be completely unconnected. The LaPiere study contains many procedural flaws—for example, it is quite likely that the people who answered the attitude questionnaire (i.e., owners) were not the same people who had actually provided service (i.e., waiters, hostesses, and desk clerks). But a number of subsequent investigators have found similar discrepancies between attitudes and behavior. Most recently, Nisbett and Wilson (1977) reported a series of experiments that seem to show that even when people think they have acted on their attitudes, they may really have acted in response to outside influences of which they are completely unaware.

All this does not mean that attitudes never guide behaviors, but it does mean that the ways in which attitudes, and other influences, affect behaviors have to be considered very carefully.

STUDYING ATTITUDE-BEHAVIOR RELATIONSHIPS: MEASUREMENT PROBLEMS. Behaviors have different *thresholds* (Campbell, 1963); that is, some behaviors are easier to express than others. For behaviors that are easy to express, even very weak attitudes may cause behavior consistent with those attitudes. For behaviors that are difficult to express, only when the associated attitudes are very strong should behaviors consistent with those attitudes be expressed. The LaPiere study provides a concrete example. It was probably relatively easy for people in that experiment to refuse in a letter to serve an anonymous Oriental couple; it was undoubtedly much more difficult to throw two real, flesh-and-blood people out of the building! This means that moderate or even weak feelings of prejudice could be expressed through the low-threshold behavior (writing the letter), but only extremely strong negative attitudes toward Orientals would be expressed through the high-threshold behavior (throwing people out of a restaurant or hotel). If the thresholds of expression for the attitude measure and the behavior measure are not matched, little consistency between the two can be expected.

Self-Perception and Attitude Change

PERCEIVING OUR OWN BEHAVIOR. Cognitive dissonance theory helps us to understand what happens when we act in ways that are inconsistent with our attitudes. But what about those occasions when our actions are consistent with our attitudes? Or when we don't really have any attitudes in the first place? Darryl Bem (1965, 1972) has suggested that we frequently form our beliefs about ourselves, about what we prefer and what our attitudes are, by acting as observers of our own behavior. This makes sense if you think about how we learn to describe our preferences. For example, a parent noting that for the tenth time in a row little Prunella has eaten only the strawberry portion of her Neapolitan ice cream might say, "You certainly like strawberry ice cream—it's the only kind you ever eat." The general message that is conveyed by such statements is something like this: If you freely choose an activity (or express an opinion), that means you like it (or agree with it). As children we thus learn how to describe our own preferences by observing how we behave. It is not, then, too surprising to find the same processes continuing to occur in adulthood ("I guess I'm a history buff — I keep signing up for these history courses"). When we act as observers of our own behavior, we generally use the same attribution principles that we use when we observe others — that is, the principles of attribution theory described at the beginning of this chapter.

PERCEIVING OUR ABILITIES AND COMPETENCIES.   Most of us are quite concerned with discovering our comparative abilities. How intelligent are we? how good looking? how socially adept? All of these are relative questions; they all ask how we measure up when compared to others. Much of the information we have about ourselves is acquired through making comparisons with others. Festinger (1954) developed a *theory of social comparison* that addresses this important source of self-knowledge. Two of the central points of this theory have to do with social reality and appropriate sources of comparison. In many ways, we depend on others to help us determine what is right and wrong, correct and incorrect, or good and bad. Particularly in new or ambiguous circumstances, the actions of others help us to define what is real. But even in school or employment settings, where our performance is evaluated explicitly and such evaluations are communicated in the unmistakable form of grades and salaries, the meaning of such evaluations is not clear until we have compared ourselves with others. For example, you would probably take a grade of B as a very negative evaluation if everyone else in a class of 50 had received an A. You would, however, have a quite different interpretation of that B if it were the highest grade given in the class. Similarly, a raise of $1000 can be taken as a reward or a punishment, depending on whether your co-workers' raises were generally larger or smaller. Both of these examples also illustrate the second aspect of social comparison: We are most interested in comparing ourselves with others who are similar to us in relevant ways. The meaning of your B grade in a college course in English will not be clarified by finding out how your little brother's friend fared in his seventh grade English quiz. Even within your own class, you will probably be more interested in comparing yourself with other freshmen (if you are a freshman) than with seniors.

Recently social psychologists have turned their attention to the other side of the coin: When do we *not* wish to compare ourselves to others and find out exactly how we measure up?

Jones and Berglas (1978) have coined the term *self-handicapping* to describe some of the ways that individuals strive to protect their self-concepts from negative information. Do you really want to know *for certain* that 40 percent of the people around you are smarter than you are? Would you like to know *exactly* how much other people like you? Jones and Berglas have argued that most of us don't really care to receive unequivocal feedback that might destroy some of our favorite illusions about ourselves. One good way to avoid such unpleasant information is to give ourselves handicaps that can be used as excuses. For example, if you don't study for an examination, then a poor grade does not necessarily imply that you are stupid. Or if you have a hangover or a sore leg when you play tennis, your losses don't have to be taken as an indication of physical inferiority. And if, with such handicaps, you should happen to do well, so much the better; you can take even more pride in your triumph in the face of adversity.

Weiner (1971; 1974) has offered a useful system for classifying the kinds of explanations that people give for their own performances and the performances of others. To illustrate this system, imagine that you have just learned that you received a grade of C on your midterm psychology examination. How might you explain your performance? According to Weiner, you would probably use one or more of the following types of explanations:

1. *Ability:* "I am not too good at this psychology stuff."
2. *Effort:* "I knew I should have studied last night instead of partying."
3. *Task Difficulty:* "That exam was ridiculous—I'll bet most of those psych professors couldn't have done better than a C."
4. *Luck:* "What rotten luck—that professor emphasized all the things I didn't know and didn't ask anything about the stuff I studied."

One of these attributions is avoided by most of us in the face of failure: ability. The self-handicapping strategies described here are designed to allow us to attribute our bad performances to causes that are not damaging to our self-esteem, such as effort, task difficulty, or luck.

Constructive Relationships—Attraction

What causes people to like each other? Why do we like some people very much and dislike others? Whenever two or more people interact, they form attitudes and opinions about each other. These evaluations combine to determine how much attraction people feel for each other. In between the extremes of passionate love and hatred lies a range of positive and negative evaluations that have pervasive consequences for us all. Feelings of attraction influence the groups into which we are accepted (such as fraternities, sororities, and clubs), the kinds of employment we can obtain (as well as salaries and promotions), and even how we fare in a court of law. Where do these attitudes and feelings come from?

Liking and Similarity

It is part of conventional wisdom that birds of a feather flock together. In this case, conventional wisdom is largely correct. A number of experimental studies have borne out this conclusion: As the degree of similarity of attitudes and values held by two people increases, so does attraction (Byrne and Rhamey, 1965). Most of these investigations have been conducted in laboratory settings, in which the degree of apparent similarity can be controlled and manipulated, but there is also evidence of a relationship between similarity and attraction in such varied settings as marriage (Kerckhoff and Davis, 1962) and bomb shelters (Griffith and Veitch, 1974).

While there is a general tendency to like people who are like us, there are

It is part of conventional wisdom that birds of a feather flock together. While there is a general tendency to like people who are like us, there are also a number of exceptions to this rule. One obvious one is implied by another piece of conventional wisdom: Opposites attract. Although we like people who are like us, we also may get along better with people who have complementary characteristics.

also a number of exceptions to this rule. One obvious one is implied by another piece of conventional wisdom: "Opposites attract." Although we like people who are like us, we also may get along better with people who have complementary characteristics. For example, a person who talks a lot is likely to have some friends who are listeners; a dominant person needs someone to dominate and therefore might be disposed to like submissive acquaintances; a sadist is a natural partner for a masochist. Need complementarity is primarily important in long-term relationships. Kerchkoff and Davis (1962), for example, found that couples in the early stages of a relationship were more likely to move toward forming a permanent relationship when they had similar needs; later in the relationship, however, complementary needs became more important.

Another exception to the general similarity-attraction relationship occurs when the "other person" has some very negative characteristic. Novak and Lerner (1965) found that subjects liked a similar partner *less* than a dissimilar partner when the partner appeared to be mentally disturbed. In the same vein, Taylor and Mettee (1971) found that subjects liked an obnoxious partner less when he or she was similar than when the partner was dissimilar. Apparently we don't like being confronted with a person who is very similar to us but who also has an undesirable flaw.

Why do we tend to like similar others? One major explanation employs the principle of cognitive consistency. Cognitive dissonance theory makes it clear that people do not like inconsistency (Festinger, 1957), and a number of other theorists have observed that people prefer consistency (e.g., Heider, 1953). Newcomb (1956; 1971) has applied the principle of cognitive consistency to interpersonal relationships. According to *balance theory,* we tend to like relationships that are balanced or consistent. In the case of similarity, if we are very similar to a person, it "makes sense" (it is consistent or balanced) if we like them. Or, if another person is very dissimilar, it "makes sense" if we dislike them. Since we prefer consistency in our relationships, finding out that a new acquaintance is very similar tends to elicit a consistent or balanced reaction—we like them.

The other reason why we tend to like similar others is because they reinforce and validate our opinions and values. It is reassuring and rewarding to discover that another person agrees with you or holds similar values (Lott and Lott, 1968, 1974; Byrne and Clore, 1965).

The Reciprocation of Liking

A second major determinant of our attraction for another comes from our belief about whether or not that person likes us. Liking tends to be reciprocated. If people obviously like you, then you will probably like them. If people clearly dislike you, you will probably dislike them (Sigall and Aronson, 1969; Byrne and Rhamey, 1965; Tagirui, Blake, and Bruner, 1953). Being liked by others makes you feel good, but being disliked makes you feel bad. It is not surprising that these feelings result in reciprocation of liking and disliking (Byrne and Clore, 1965).

Continuing with this reinforcement analysis, you might expect that, for example, the more good things Tom says about Bill, the more Bill will like Tom. Similarly, the more critical or disparaging remarks Ann makes to Sue, the less Sue should like Ann. However, a study by Aronson and Linder (1965) makes it clear that these predictions must be qualified. In the Aronson and Linder study, subjects overheard another person (actually a confederate of the experimenter) make a number of evaluations of them at different times. For some subjects, the confederate always said nice, positive things. For a second group of subjects, the confederate gave uniformly negative evaluations. As expected, at the end of the experiment subjects liked the confederate who liked them, and disliked the confederate who did not like them. Aronson and Linder also included two other groups. In the gain condition, the confederate began by giving negative evaluations, but over time the evaluations became more and more positive so that by the end of the session the confederate was giving evaluations that were the same as those in the all positive condition. In the loss condition, the same evaluations that were employed for the gain group were given, but their order was reversed: The confederate began with positive comments, but became gradually more negative, so that by the end of the session the evaluations were as negative as those in the all negative condition. The interesting finding was that subjects liked the confederate *more* in the gain than in the all positive condition, and *less* in the loss than in the all negative condition. This finding makes it clear that the *sequence* of liking information can be as important as its positive or negative quality. Gaining liking from a former doubter or losing the liking of an

Table 18–2: Means for Liking the Confederate.

Experimental Condition	Mean
Negative-positive	+ 7.67
Positive-positive	+ 6.42
Negative-negative	+ 2.52
Positive-negative	+ 0.87

Aronson and Linder (1965).

initial admirer has more impact than uniform liking or disliking from another (see Table 18-2).

Physical Attractiveness and Liking

Anyone who has watched television, leafed through a popular magazine, or looked at billboard advertisements knows that our culture values physical attractiveness very highly. Manufacturers spend millions of dollars on advertising for products that are designed to make us look good, and we spend even more millions buying those products. The popularity of diets, exercise clubs, and the latest fashions all attest to our interest in improving our appearance. There are, of course, good reasons for being interested in our appearance, because liking is heavily influenced by physical attractiveness. A large number of investigations all point to the same conclusion: The more physically attractive a person is, the more he or she is liked by others. For example, Walster and his colleagues (1966) measured liking for various partners at a "computer dance" at which each participant was matched with a series of partners of the opposite sex by a computer. They measured a larger number of personal characteristics of the dance participants in an attempt to discover which, if any, of them would influence liking. They found, however, that the only thing that mattered was physical attractiveness. The more physically attractive the partner was, the more he or she was liked. In addition to being liked, physically attractive people are generally assumed to have a number of more positive qualities than their more average-looking counterparts. For example, Dion, Berscheid, and Walster (1972) showed photographs of attractive and average people to their subjects. The subjects attributed more positive personality traits, greater occupational success, and higher marital competence to the physically attractive people.

Jury simulation studies indicate that physically attractive defendants are likely to fare better in court than they would if they were not so attractive. When the appearance of defendants in trials involving offenses ranging from cheating to burglary is varied systematically, the more attractive defendants tend to be found not guilty more often. When they are found guilty, lighter sentences are recommended (Efram, 1974). These studies support the wisdom of a common recommendation that defense attorneys make to their clients: Make yourself look good. The really clever attorney would, however, also take note of the findings of Sigall and Ostrove (1975): When the crime is one that involves taking advantage of one's physical attractiveness, such as confidence games or swindling, then the more attractive the defendant, the harsher the punishment.

Destructive Relationships—Aggression

Unfortunately, one all-too-frequent form of human interpersonal interaction involves the injury (physical and/or psychological) of one participant by another. The term *aggression* (when applied to humans) is used to refer to

HIGHLIGHT
States of Awareness and Aggression

The likelihood that aggression will occur in humans appears to be closely related to the *states of awareness* in which we find ourselves. Some of the evidence for this assertion comes from research inspired by Duval and Wicklund's (1972) *theory of objective self-awareness*. The central idea of the theory is that we can be either *objectively* or *subjectively* self-aware. In the state of subjective self-awareness, attention is focused outward. For example, when a person is driving down a twisting road at high speed, most of his or her attention will be concerned with staying on the road. This state of subjective awareness is probably the most typical state of consciousness. When we are objectively self-aware, however, we turn our full attention onto ourselves. Seeing yourself in a mirror or on closed circuit television would tend to make you consider yourself as an object of attention. When we focus on ourselves, we tend to evaluate ourselves compared to the standards and values which we hold and which are salient or relevant at the time. Duval and Wicklund argue that since most of us frequently fall short of our ideal selves, objective self-awareness is often unpleasant.

One implication of this theory is that when we are objectively self-aware, we will be more likely to try to act in accord with our values. In the case of aggression, this means that if we think aggression is wrong in a particular situation, changing from subjective to objective self-awareness should reduce the likelihood of aggression.

This effect was demonstrated in a study by Sheier, Fenigstein, and Buss (1974). In their study, males were put in a teacher-learning setup, in the role of teacher, and were given the opportunity to give shocks to female learners. Since the general value in our culture is that males should not aggress against females, putting male subjects in a state of objective self-awareness

attempts by one person to inflict pain or injury on another person. A look at the front page of almost any daily newspaper or a television newscast is sufficient to remind us that many relationships among individuals are destructive. Human aggression is a phenomenon that appears in many forms, ranging from verbal insults and individual mayhem and murder to the kind of organized attacks that armies have carried out in numerous wars throughout human history.

Instinct Theories of Aggression

Why is aggression so common? What makes a person want to harm another? The frequency and persistence of violence in human history has led some to believe that we possess an aggressive instinct. Freud, for example, assumed that aggression resulted from a displaced urge that we all have to return to an inert state. This death instinct is usually kept in check by instincts for self-preservation, so it finds expression in hostile actions toward others rather than toward ourselves. Naturalistic observations of a number of animal species has also led Lorenz (1967) to argue that an aggressive instinct is the natural product of evolution, in which the strong and ruthless tend to weed out the weak and passive.

Perhaps the best evidence for some kind of biological influence on aggression has been the finding that males with an extra Y chromosome appear much more frequently in prison populations than would be expected given the frequency of this syndrome in the general population (Jarvik et al., 1973). However, it is still unclear whether the XYY syndrome affects aggression directly, or whether some other characteristics that tend to be associated with this syndrome, such as large size, are really the culprits (Bandura, 1973).

should have reduced their aggression, and that is what happened. This does not, however, mean that objective self-awareness will always reduce aggression. If the situation is one in which the person thinks he or she *should* aggress, then objective self-awareness ought to make aggression *more* likely. Carver (1974), for example, found that when he told his subjects that delivering shocks would be helpful to the confederate, subjects who were objectively self-aware were more aggressive than those who were subjectively self-aware.

The message of these studies is that aggression depends on the person's state of awareness *and* on the value placed on aggression at the time.

There is a third state of awareness, one in which the self is completely submerged as the person is completely caught up in concerns of the moment, with no thought of what others or oneself might think of the behavior being emitted. In the state of *deindividuation* (Zimbardo, 1969), the person loses all concern for him- or herself as an individual, and instead focuses on the present environment with little thought of the past or future. In this state, the normal self-controls (such as values, concerns about the reactions of others, and feelings such as shame and guilt) are disconnected. In this sense, deindividuation is the opposite of objective self-awareness, and is more like an extreme form of subjective self-awareness.

When persons are deindividuated, their behavior tends to be vigorous, repetitive, and difficult to stop. Since the normal self controls are less effective, behaviors that are normally inhibited may occur, and the person may be unresponsive to cues that would usually trigger self-control mechanisms. This means that if the person begins to aggress while deindividuated, such behavior may be of high intensity, difficult to stop, and of an indiscriminate nature. This description fits that of someone who has "gone berserk." It may explain why, from time to time, one reads of violent crimes in which victims are stabbed scores or even hundreds of times.

These findings are of interest because they show how an important personal characteristic that varies from time to time can lead to predictable but complex differences in how much aggression can be expected from the same person in different times, places, and circumstances.

Frustration-Aggression Theory

One explanation of aggression that appears to have some validity was originally formulated by Dollard and his colleagues (1939), who hypothesized that *frustration* (the blocking of the path to a goal) always leads to aggression, and that aggression is always the result of frustration. It has become clear that the initial form of this hypothesis is wrong. Frustration does not *always* lead to aggression; it can, for example, cause depression and lethargy instead (Seligman, 1975). Likewise, aggression is not *always* the result of frustration; soldiers and executioners, for example, engage in aggression when they are ordered to do so. There is, however, considerable support for a more modest form of the hypothesis. Frustration does, under certain circumstances, tend to increase the likelihood of aggression.

One determinant of the frustration-aggression link is the nature of the frustration. *Arbitrary* frustrations do lead to aggression, but nonarbitrary frustrations (those that seem to have an acceptable reason for occurring) do not (Zillman and Cantor, 1976). Capricious or inexplicable sources of frustration thus appear to be most likely to provoke aggressive reactions.

A second major limitation of the frustration-aggression hypothesis is that it is most likely to hold when there are aggressive cues or triggers present. Berkowitz (1969), for example, has argued that frustration produces arousal, but the arousal will only be channeled into aggressive behavior if cues are present that make the possibility of aggression salient. For example, Berkowitz and Le Page (1967) first had a confederate anger their subjects. The subjects were then given the opportunity to aggress against the confederate by giving him electric shocks. When there were no aggressive cues present, subjects engaged in little aggression against the confederate. When aggressive cues were present, in the form of a shotgun and a revolver lying on a table next to the subject, the confederate was much more likely to be given powerful electric shocks.

One implication of the frustration-aggression analysis is that each new frustration will increase the instigation to aggress, until the person finally "blows off steam." After this, the person's arousal level presumably returns to a relatively low level until new frustrations begin to build it up again. This view implies that if aggressive impulses could be drained off in some harmless, socially acceptable way, then the negative effects of uncontrolled aggression could be eliminated. The process of draining off aggressive impulses is called *catharsis*. The most obvious form of catharsis involves aggressing against the source of frustration. Aggression against another person, not related to the original source of frustration, is also presumed to be a way of reducing aggressive arousal. A more controversial notion, *vicarious catharsis,* is that simply observing someone else aggressing serves to reduce the tendency to aggress. A large number of studies have been designed to test the validity of the catharsis hypothesis. The overall message of these studies is that catharsis only occurs when the person actually aggresses against the source of frustration (Doob and Wood, 1972; Konecni and Doob, 1972). Aggressing against some other person, or watching someone else aggress, does not produce a cathartic effect. In fact, as we shall see in the next section, watching someone else aggress *increases* the likelihood of subsequent aggression from the observer.

Social Learning Theory and Aggression

While the frustration-aggression hypothesis has some validity, the best explanation of why aggression occurs is that, like most other human behavior, it is learned. According to *social learning theory* (Bandura and Walters, 1963; Bandura, 1973), we learn to be aggressive in two ways: by being reinforced for aggressing, and by watching other people aggress.

One "good" reason for attacking another person is that such aggression will lead to a reward. In the case of mugging or armed robbery, the potential reward is obvious. The rewards can, of course, be more subtle, involving feelings of power and control or social approval. In street gangs or military organizations, aggressive behavior may be implicitly or explicitly approved by the group members. Geen and Stoner (1971), for example, found that verbal approval is very effective in increasing aggression.

The other major way in which we learn aggressive behavior is through imitating others. An excellent demonstration of learning aggression by imitating the behavior of others was provided by Bandura, Ross, and Ross (1963) in their "Bobo doll" experiment. Young children were shown either a live or filmed adult model, or a cartoon figure, hitting an inflatable punching bag doll. Children who saw any of the three kinds of models displayed more aggression toward the Bobo doll than did children who had not been exposed to a model.

One of the serious questions raised by the Bandura (1963) study and others like it concerns the advisability of exposing children (or adults) to the violence that is typically depicted on television and in motion pictures. At the moment, the available evidence implies that such violence may be contributing to an increase in aggressive behavior. In a study of aggression in institutionalized

The best explanation of why aggression occurs is that, like most other human behavior, it is learned.

juvenile delinquents, psychologists (Parke et al., 1977) showed movies depicting aggression to some subjects, and nonaggressive movies to others. After a week of such movies, those who had been shown the violent films exhibited more aggressive behavior than those who had not. An equally serious effect of viewing filmed aggression appears to be an insensitivity to subsequent acts of real aggression. In one experiment researchers (Thomas et al., 1977) showed children either a violent or a nonviolent film and then measured their physiological reactions when they were confronted with a live example of aggression. The children who had seen the violent film showed less physiological reactivity to the real aggression than children who had seen the nonviolent film. The issue is very complicated, but the bulk of the research on televised and filmed violence indicates that concerns about the effects of television programming on the level of aggression in our society are justified.

Situational Determinants of Aggression

We have seen that such environmental conditions as the presence of weapons and the viewing of violence can increase the likelihood of aggression. A number of other precipitating factors have also been studied. Perhaps the most obvious instigator of aggression is aggression itself. For example, if someone gives you a shove, the likelihood that you will shove back is high (Taylor and Pisano, 1971). The use of aggression as an instigator of aggression is commonly used in laboratory studies.

High levels of arousal, even when the arousal comes from a source that has nothing to do with frustration or aggression, also facilitate aggression. Geen and O'Neal (1969), for example, found that subjects who were aroused by loud noise were more affected by an aggression-laden film than subjects who were not exposed to noise. Zillman (1971) found that increased sexual arousal also made subsequent aggression more likely when subjects were irritated by a confederate. Zillman (1978) believes that heightened, generalized arousal can be attached to aggressive behavior once an inducement to aggress is present.

Perhaps the most common instigator of aggression is aggression itself. If someone gives you a shove, the likelihood that you will shove back is high.

An idea that has some similarity to the arousal-aggression hypothesis is that heat can serve to make aggression more likely. This idea could explain why riots are more likely to happen when the weather is warm (the "long, hot summer" phenomenon). Goranson and King (1970), for example, found that riots were most likely to occur on days when the temperature was significantly above the normal range. Experimental studies of the effects of heat on aggression have, however, been equivocal. Some imply that heat makes aggression more likely (Goranson and King, 1970), but other research seems to show that oppressive heat actually reduces the likelihood of aggressive responses to irritating events (Baron and Bell, 1975), so this question is still open.

Summary

1. *Attribution* is the process by which we perceive people and make judgments about what they are like. It can be influenced by a number of factors, including experience with the person, first impressions, implicit personality theories, attribution rules, and different opportunities to observe the person.

2. There are three dimensions around which we can organize information about a person's behavior: the actor, the entity, and time. The *fundamental attribution error* is a tendency to attribute behavior to actors rather than to the situations they are in.

3. Credibility, trustworthiness, and similarity are important variables in our response to communicators.

4. One aspect of the communication or message itself that can influence us is whether it is a one-sided or two-sided communication. Resistance to persuasion can be created through the process of *inoculation*.

5. There are two variables that seem to affect attitude change in the real world: the *audience selection effect* and the *two-step process of diffusion*.

6. When two cognitions are inconsistent, creating a situation of *cognitive dissonance*, Festinger predicted that people would change the cognition that related to their attitudes, since it is the least resistant.

7. Support for cognitive dissonance theory has been provided by studies involving the *induced compliance effect* and *effort justification*.

8. There is some evidence that attitudes do not have a consistent relationship to behavior. The attitude-behavior problem may be complicated by the possibility that behaviors have different thresholds.

9. When we act as observers of our own behavior, we generally use the same attribution principles that we use when observing others.

10. The most important components of attraction are similarity, reciprocation of liking, and physical attractiveness.

11. There are a number of theories about the cause or source of aggression, including instinct theories, frustration-aggression theory, and social learning theory. The situational determinants of aggression are also important in understanding how and why it occurs.

Suggested Readings

BANDURA, A. Vicarious processes: A case of no-trial learning. In L. Berkowitz (Ed.), *Advances in experimental social psychology*, vol. 2. New York: Academic Press, 1965. Presents the social learning approach to aggression.

BERSHEID, E., and WALSTER, E. H. *Interpersonal attraction* (2nd ed.) Reading, Mass.: Addison-Wesley, 1978. This is a good overall summary of recent research on attraction.

FESTINGER, L. *A theory of cognitive dissonance*. Stanford, Calif.: Stanford University Press, 1957. The original theory of cognitive dissonance is presented here. This should be read prior to Wicklund and Brehm's more recent summary.

KIESLER, C. A., COLLINS, B. E., and MILLER, N. *Attitude change*. New York: Wiley, 1969. This text reviews the major theories of attitude change in a sophisticated, abstract fashion.

NISBETT, R. E., and ROSS, L. *Human inference: Strategies and shortcomings of social judgment*. Englewood Cliffs, N.J.: Prentice-Hall, 1980. The authors present a recent, readable summary of findings on our strengths and weaknesses as intuitive psychologists.

WICKLUND, R. A., and BREHM, J. W. *Perspectives on cognitive dissonance*. Hillsdale, N.J.: Erlbaum, 1976. The huge amount of dissonance research is summarized in this comprehensive review.

19 Social Organizations

The extent to which human beings lead their lives in groups is striking. As children we are dependent on the family group for our care and our survival. Primary school brings with it the peer groups of classmates. By high school we develop sets of friends with whom we spend hours of our time. In college, classes, discussion groups, and extracurricular activities are all done in groups. Next we choose a career, and most careers are located in hierarchical organizations such as business, government, or health delivery services—groups in another guise. Our hobbies and special interests are often pursued in groups, clubs, associations, or volunteer societies. And if we marry and have chidren we rejoin our earliest group of all, the family, and recreate the cycle for another generation.

Much as we might try to resist, these groups shape our perceptions, guide our actions, limit and structure our choices, and affect our lives. Because this is so, it is important that we understand the processes by which groups change our lives. Fortunately, social and organizational psychologists have discovered some common tendencies and processes that function in all groups. An understanding of these general processes can give insight into the particular—and often peculiar and puzzling—happenings that occur in specific groups.

The Individual in the Group

For reasons that will become apparent, groups develop both habitual ways of looking at the world and accepted methods of procedure. In other words, groups have rules that apply to its members. Group members, therefore, are sometimes confronted with the choice of conforming to the group's rules or deviating from them. If they deviate, then they may find themselves under pressure to get back into line or leave the group. However, their choices are not always this bleak—their deviant actions may come to be accepted by the group and regarded as an innovation. They may even become group leaders.

Conformity

Social psychology often deals with value-laden issues. Conformity is one of these, and it is important to recognize this early in the discussion. "Conformity" is a negative word that calls up images of submissive actions by weak-willed people. But consider the following definition of a conforming response: one that agrees with the response of a group, when respondents have insufficient evidence themselves to know that their response is correct. Next consider the following example: You are guiding your sailboat into a harbor in which you have never anchored before. Your charts and the harbor markers show two possible entrances and you are on course for the nearest one. But then you notice that several other boats near you are choosing the other entrance. From the home port markings on those boats, you realize that this harbor is the home harbor for all of them. What's going on? One obvious explanation is that there is some hidden obstruction in the near channel—a recent wreck, perhaps, or a shift in the channel depth—that occurred too recently to get on the charts. You don't know, but to be safe you alter course and follow the other boats to the more distant entrance.

This fits the definition of conformity: You have gone along with the response of the group without having sufficient evidence yourself to judge whether that is the correct response. Yet, because it is so obviously the sensible action to take, it seems wrong to label it "conformity." That is the point: It seems wrong because conformity has negative connotations, but conformity, like other actions, can be good or bad, rational or irrational, depending on the context in which it occurs.

INFORMATIONAL SOCIAL INFLUENCE.   The kind of conformity found in our example, a rational kind of conformity that can be thought of as learning about the world from the actions of others, is called *informational social influence* (Kelley, 1952). It is likely to arise in two cases: when the realities to be learned about are essentially social in nature, and when they have physical components.

In the United States we drive our automobiles on the right-hand side of the road, and in the English language we use the word "chair" to describe a piece of furniture on which a person sits. That these are socially agreed on ways of doing or labeling things rather than physically necessary ways of doing or labeling things is demonstrated by the fact that in England vehicles are driven on the left and the German word for "chair" is Stuhl. In any culture there is an appropriate way to do or describe things, not because it is somehow derived from physical laws, but because people have simply agreed that it is appropriate. People, then, are the best source of information about these social customs. Indeed, they are the only source. Therefore, the only sensible way for a person who is new to a group to learn about its customs is by observing the actions of the group members. This is the normal learning process of socialization, without which no child could become a functioning member of a culture. It continues into adult life, producing what often could be called conformity.

Another word for social realities is *conventions,* those social rules about the "right" clothes to wear, the "right" way to address a faculty member, and so on. Interestingly, though, we sometimes lose track of the social sources of this learning. The right-hand side of the road simply "feels" right to us. Or think about dress styles through the ages. The current style immediately looks right to us, while others look wrong and even absurd, and we forget that styles are not right or wrong because of some internal properties that they have but because people agree on them. In other eras, each style had its period of being entirely acceptable and normal looking.

We learn about social conventions from others. After all, it is others who are responsible for defining what is appropriate in the first place. But when what you need to know are not social but *physical* realities—things that can be measured and monitored—you still may need to look to the opinions of others. In some circumstances direct learning about events or objects might be too time-consuming or costly. Think back, for instance, to the example at the beginning of the chapter, in which the boat owner tried to determine if the channel were clear of obstructions. He could have sailed in and investigated. But he knew that to do this was likely to be hazardous and that he was better off simply going along with the decision of the other sailors.

In one of the earliest studies of conformity, Musafer Sherif made elegant use of an almost totally ambiguous event to demonstrate the ways in which individuals, when making judgments about physical events, are influenced by the judgments of others (Sherif, 1936). To appreciate what he did, you need to know the following: When you look at a stationary, pinpoint source of light in a totally darkened room, the light appears to move, even though it actually doesn't (the *autokinetic effect* discussed in Chapter 4). Furthermore, to each person the "movement" is somewhat different. Sherif realized that this was an excellent experimental context in which to demonstrate how people can be made to conform to a belief about a physical reality.

Next Sherif chose groups to observe the light. Pairs of subjects watched the light, each making an estimation of movement in the presence of the other. At first each member of the pair quite naturally gave a judgment that was different from the other's. One subject might report movement of 12 inches, for instance, while the other might report movement of only 3 inches. As the experiment progressed, however, the estimates of movement came closer and closer together. Each subject was influenced by the judgments of the other, and a joint standard emerged (see Figure 19-1). New people, introduced into the group after the other members had developed a standard, then converged in their judgments toward that standard (Jacobs and Campbell, 1961), thus demonstrating the power of a group in influencing our interpretations and descriptions of physical realities.

Clearly, other people provide information that we use in making judgments about what is going on in the real world. The Sherif experiment proves that, but it does so in a context of lights in a darkened room, which seems rather artificial. There are research examples of the same process taking place in more natural contexts, in the very important area of bystander responses to emergencies.

Some years ago, in a case that attracted national attention, a woman returning to her home late at night was repeatedly attacked and finally stabbed to death while other people watched. The other people neither directly intervened to help nor called the police. This is a shocking but not an isolated case. Many other cases exist in which witnesses have failed to help people in trouble, even when there was relatively little danger to themselves in offering help. It is difficult not to condemn these passive bystanders, and many people have done so. However, Latané and Darley (1970) have discovered different reasons for the failure to help, one of which is the information transmission process we just discussed.

Remember that events that we *later* know are emergencies may not seem so at the beginning. Their meaning may be ambiguous. For instance, suppose that in a big city you see a poorly dressed, unshaven man reeling along the street. He

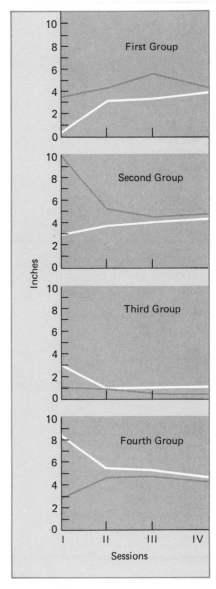

Figure 19-1

In each of the graphs above, you can see that when the two subjects guessed how far a light had "moved," their guesses varied widely. However, as soon as the pairs of subjects began making judgments in each other's presence, their guesses conformed with each other. (Sherif and Sherif, 1956)

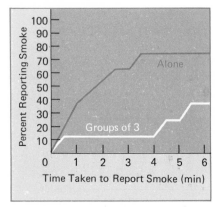

Figure 19-2

As you can see in the graph below, time taken to report smoke and the percent of people reporting smoke were both a function of how many people were in the room when the smoke was observed. If a person was alone, he or she was far more likely to report the smoke, and reported it far more quickly, than if there were three people. (Latané and Darley, 1968)

then sits on a park bench, holding his head in his hands. What is going on? The man could be having a heart attack and need immediate medical attention. Or he could be dazed and drunk. Or he could be tired. What, if anything, should you do? What you decide to do depends very considerably on which of the possible interpretations of the situation you adopt. But suppose other people also witness the incident? From their reactions you will be able to determine their interpretations of the event, and their interpretations may influence your own.

To see if this sort of information-produced conformity takes place in decisions about emergencies, Latané and Darley (1968) set up an experiment in which an ambiguous but potentially dangerous event occurred, in which the person's reactions would be determined by his or her interpretation of it. Students came one at a time to a waiting room to fill out preliminary information before taking part in an interview on "urban settings." While they were filling out the questionnaire, white smoke began to jet through a vent in the wall. The cause of the smoke was not immediately apparent, but one possibility was that it signalled a fire someplace in the building. The people waiting for the interview generally reacted in terms of this possibility. They didn't panic, but they did walk out and find a person to whom they could report. To that person they said something like, "I don't know if there is anything wrong, but smoke is coming into the waiting room, could you please check?"

Other subjects confronted the same ambiguous physical stimulus—smoke—but did so in a different social context. This time, two strangers were also present in the waiting room, also filling out questionnaires, also waiting for interviews. Actually, the two other people were not real subjects, but confederates of the experimenter who went into a pre-prepared act when the smoke began to appear: They noticed the smoke, and then they continued to fill out their questionnaires.

What does that action mean to the subject? It must mean that the others knew that the smoke did not signal a dangerous fire. Perhaps they had had previous experiences in the building, perhaps they had figured out something the subject did not figure out. But whatever it was, they had concluded that it was safe to stay. The results of this experiment are shown in Figure 19-2.

Most of the subjects surrounded by the passive confederates themselves remained passive. They continued to fill out their questionnaires even as the smoke continued to jet into the room. It would be easy to see their behavior as ridiculous and to condemn them as "conformers." But it might be better to think of them as carrying out a generally rational process that in this specific instance led to a less than rational conclusion. The lack of action on the part of the other people conveyed the information that no danger was present in the situation. The subjects integrated this information with the other information available to them, and came to their conclusions. Subjects reported afterward that they thought that the smoke signalled the presence of a chemistry lab somewhere in the building, or was somehow connected with the heating system, or the changeover from the heating to the cooling system. The inaction of the confederates had given them some cues about the meaning of the smoke, and caused them to conclude that whatever it was, it was not a signal of danger.

NORMATIVE SOCIAL INFLUENCE. Up to this point we have been discussing the kind of conformity that results from using information provided by other people about social conventions or physical realities. We called this kind of conformity *informational social influence.* But there is another kind of social influence that occurs when people suppress or downplay their own opinions and "go along with" the group because they want to gain the rewards or avoid the punishments that the group has to give. This kind of conformity can be called compliance to the *normative social influence* of the group. Although it may be rational to give in to social influence for this reason, it is not always admirable, hence the "bad name" conformity has come to have. But certainly this kind of conformity does occur, as was demonstrated in a landmark study by Deutsch and Gerard (1955).

Deutsch and Gerard wanted to demonstrate the existence of both normative and informational social influence. They reasoned that if people were conforming because they were using the judgments of other people to help them form their impressions (informational social influence), it should make no difference whether they gave their judgments publicly or privately. All that should matter is that they hear the judgments of the others. On the other hand, if people felt pressure to conform because they wanted to avoid looking foolish to the others, or did not want to be criticized or rejected by them (normative social influence), then it should make all the difference. Their deviance would become apparent and punishable only if the others knew their identity.

Using a modification of the Asch conformity test, which is described in the accompanying box, in which the subjects communicated with one another over an intercom, the experimenters arranged a social influence test. In a control group, individuals judged the lengths of a series of lines. The right answers were very obvious, and these subjects made virtually no mistakes. Two experimental groups of subjects were asked to make the same judgments, but only after hearing the responses of another group of people to the same task. Although the subjects were unaware of it, the answers of the others were prearranged, and they all gave an identical wrong answer. All experimental subjects faced the same dilemma: Should they trust their own opinion (which was actually correct), or should they conform to the response of the group? One group of subjects knew that their answers would be heard by the other group members. The other group of subjects believed that a temporary flaw in the intercom would prevent the people in the other group from hearing their answers. If subjects were influenced only by the informational content of the others' answers (if they believed that the others were actually correct), then the conformity rate of the two groups would be alike. However, if subjects were also concerned about violating group norms and the possible sanctions the group might inflict on them for doing so, then the group that gave their answers publicly should have a higher conformity rate than the group that gave their answers privately. As Figure 19-3 shows, the data support this hypothesis. Clearly, there is a difference between informational and normative social influence.

In most groups in society, the normal pattern is for everyone to hear everyone else's judgments, which means that both informational and normative social influence pressures operate. This being so, then we would expect that any factors that increase the likelihood of the group's giving rewards for compliance or punishment for deviance, and any factors that increase the value of the reward or the extent of the punishment can be expected to increase conformity to

Figure 19-3

As shown here, the number of socially influenced errors in the experiment was a function of whether subjects reported anonymously or in the presence of others. (Deutsch and Gerard, 1955)

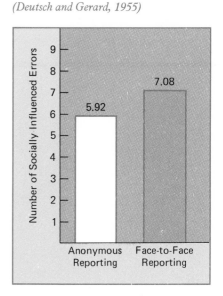

HIGHLIGHT
Conformity Pressures in Groups

Imagine yourself in the following position: You volunteered to be in a psychology study, and you and seven other students are waiting for the session to begin. The experimenter has everyone take a seat, and then explains that the task is to try to guess which of three lines is the same length as a comparison or standard line. When you look at the first set of lines, the correct answer is very obvious. When the experimenter asks the first subject for his answer, he gives the correct one; and so does everyone else in the group. The next few sets of lines are just as easy; everyone is correct, and you settle back anticipating a boring experience. On the next trial, the answer is again obvious, but this time the first subject makes a stupid mistake and picks a line that is clearly *not* the same length as the standard.

You have a hard time keeping yourself from laughing, and you smile as you look around at the other people in the group—but they don't seem to have noticed. You are then shocked when the second person, in his casual tone of voice, makes the same mistake! You take another look at the lines, but it is clear that the first two people are wrong. The third subject agrees with the first two! You look at the lines again, squinting your eyes and moving your head to get a different angle. Everyone else has agreed, and now it is your turn to speak up. You know the other group members are wrong, but if you disagree you will stand out, and may look like an idiot to everyone else. What would you do?

Solomon Asch (1951; 1955) placed a number of students in just such a predicament. In his

line-judging groups, all but one of the participants were actually cooperating with the experimenter. On some of the trials, they gave unanimous but incorrect answers, thereby placing conformity pressure on the one "real" subject. Overall, Asch found that his subjects conformed on about one third of the trials when there was a unanimous incorrect majority. This happened even though they knew that the others were wrong. Conformity in these line-judging experiments provides a good example of public conformity when there is no private acceptance (Kiesler and Kiesler, 1969). Often we use other people's behavior to help us define reality, as you have seen throughout this chapter. Other times, however, we may conform not because we think others are correct, but because we are afraid

normative social influence. In general, the evidence bears this out. For instance, Sakurai (1975) and Dittes and Kelley (1956) found that because people care most about maintaining the positive opinions of people they like or respect, there is more conformity within groups of people who like one another than in groups of people who are indifferent to or don't like one another.

OBEDIENCE: COMPLIANCE TO AUTHORITY.   One of the most striking and disturbing forms of compliance concerns obeying the commands of authority figures. Some of the most hideous crimes in human history have been justified by the claim, "I was just following orders." The systematic extermination of Jews in Nazi concentration camps and the slaughter of women and children in the My Lai incident in the Vietnam War were both explained in this way. Do authority figures really have that much power? Would a normal person be willing to harm another simply because someone in a position of authority told them to do so? Stanley Milgram (1963, 1974, 1977) conducted a series of studies designed to answer these questions.

In the first study, subjects found that they, along with another participant, would be taking part in a study of the teaching-learning process. The learner's job was to answer a series of questions read by the teacher. The teacher's job was

Photographs taken during Asch's line-judging experiment.

of what they will think or do if we disagree with them. This is what happened in the Asch studies. If, for example, subjects were allowed to respond completely anonymously, then they did not conform (Deutsch and Gerard, 1955), making it clear that conformity was motivated by concerns with how the others would react to deviation.

Are such fears about how others will react to deviation justified? Schachter (1951) found that when a person deviated from the group he received harsh treatment, but only when the group was very important to its members. Groups can tolerate deviation as long as they do not intrude upon areas that define the group's nature and reason for existence.

One group characteristic that was studied in Asch's original ex-periments was the size of the group majority. Asch found that conformity increased as the number of opponents increased in size from one to two to three. Beyond three, increasing the size of the incorrect majority had little effect. Other investigators, however, have found that larger size groups tend to elicit more conformity (e.g., Gerard, Wilhelmy, and Conolley, 1968). The importance of the size of the majority probably varies depending on the nature of the task and the setting, but in general substantial conformity is produced by unanimous majorities of three or four.

Another interesting question that Asch (1956) raised concerned the importance of the unanimity of the disagreeing majority. When all of the confederates agreed with one another (and with reality), conformity was highest. However, if one confederate answered accurately, then almost no conformity was observed. Having an ally enabled people to resist the conformity pressures created by the group majority.

to read the questions and to provide feedback. The feedback turned out to be in the form of electric shock. The teacher was told to use a shock machine, to which the learner was wired, which had 30 switches. On the learner's first mistake, the teacher was to flip the first switch, labeled 15 volts. On the next mistake, the second switch, labeled 30 volts, was to be thrown, and so on, all the way up to 450 volts, which was labeled *XXX*, and was beyond the range labeled *Danger: Severe Shock*. In reality, a confederate of the experimenter (a 47-year-old accountant) was always assigned to the role of learner and was never really shocked. The subjects were men from a wide variety of occupations who answered a newspaper advertisement for research participants. After finding themselves "randomly" assigned to the role of teacher, each subject began reading the questions. As the level of shock increased, the learner cried out, gasped, pounded on the wall, and finally fell silent once the 315-volt level was passed. If the teacher expressed reluctance to go on, the experimenter simply told him that he must continue. Milgram was interested in learning if any of these normal, average people would obey the commands of the authority figure (the experimenter). To his amazement, 65 percent of the subjects delivered all 30 shocks, all the way up to 450 volts, even though many of them were obviously very worried and upset about what was happening to the learner.

Perhaps things would have been different if other people would have been present to witness the experiment. To test this idea, Milgram (1964) replicated the study, but this time two peers (again, actually experimental confederates) sat on either side of the subject and helped him to decide how much shock to administer. On each trial the subject's peers suggested increasing the voltage, but the subject always had the option to refuse. Compared to a condition in which the subject was alone, the peers were successful in increasing substantially the amount of shock that subjects gave.

On the other hand, when the subject was paired with two peers who *defied* the experimenter and refused to continue delivering shocks, 90 percent of the subjects refused to obey the experimenter and continue to the 450-volt level.

The Milgram studies demonstrate both the power of authority figures to exact compliance and the important influence that peers can exert in enhancing or minimizing the coercive power of authority. The results again make it clear that group conformity pressures can have both positive and negative effects.

Deviation

What if, due to the strength with which they hold an opinion, or the fact that previously they publicly committed themselves to it, people continue to deviate even in the face of group pressure to conform? Research by Schachter (1951) and Newcomb (1953) shows us the answer. In both cases an actor was planted within a small group of people who otherwise were selected to generally agree about the solution to a problem. The experimenter instructed the actor to oppose the solution held by the rest of the group members, and to speak out for a different solution. Suppose, for instance, the group was asked to make a decision regarding the future of a juvenile delinquent. They were told that the boy had a terrible and rejecting home environment, but was also committing increasingly harmful crimes. Should the boy be given another chance in a foster home, or should he be sent to a relatively severe house of detention? As instructed, the "plant" deviated from the group opinion. If the group favored the foster home, the deviant argued for the house of detention.

An interesting pattern emerged in some of the experimental groups. Once the group's position became clear, other group members directed more than the ordinary amount of attention to those who disagreed, trying to get them to change their position. The experimenters had instructed the deviant in some of the groups to "become convinced" at this point and conform to the group's opinion. This conformity made them acceptable as group members. Other deviants were instructed to stand firm, however, and did not conform to the group's opinion. Communication directed toward them dropped off: Previously they had received more attention than the average group member, but now they received less. It seemed as if the other group members were giving up on the deviants, and further evidence indicates that this was so.

The experimenters wondered whether the group members wished to punish the deviants or even exclude them from the group. Group members were asked to assign several jobs. As the experimenters predicted, deviants were frequently nominated for the relatively boring and menial tasks. The experimenters then explained that it might be necessary to have future meetings with a smaller group. Deviants were frequently "nominated" to be the ones left out—the processes of exclusion were under way.

Consider what this means for those who deviate from the group. Frequently they find themselves excluded from the group when their opinions are discovered. Because their opinions have been contradicted, deviants' values have been threatened and are in need of bolstering. An excellent way of doing this is by finding a group of people who think as they do, thereby receiving social support from them. Thus deviants' future associations are likely to include a disproportionate number of people who agree with them on this one opinion. Naturally, they come to spend more time with these other people and less time with the rejecting majority. They become members of an *outgroup*.

Furthermore, because deviants, more than majority group members, are heavily dependent on the social support they get from their new group, pressures on them to conform within that group are *higher*. Thus their opinions will come to be influenced by this outgroup. Since groups naturally discuss many issues, the group members will be influenced on issues other than the ones that initially led to their joining the group, and there will develop a "group position" on many issues (Darley et al., 1974).

Innovation

At this point the fate of deviants may seem rather bleak: If people don't conform to the opinions of the groups in which they find themselves, they are rejected; if rejected, they seek out a supporting group, only to find themselves subjected to conformity pressures from this new source. But there is another side to this picture: Sometimes a majority will tolerate views that differ. Sometimes they may even come to adopt the very views that they once resisted. Under what conditions will the majority either tolerate or come to adopt deviant opinions?

Two related generalizations can be made. First, those people who have relatively high status within a group are more likely to have their opinions accepted by the group. Second, people whose opinions have been proven valid in the past will be more likely to have their future opinions adopted by the group.

Hollander (1958; 1960) demonstrated that high-status individuals within a group can hold deviant opinions and still stay in favor with the group. He told subjects that a hypothetical person had "been in a group for some while," and had been "an extremely capable performer in the group's activity," or, alternatively, that the person was a new member of the group and had performed in an average or even below average way on the group's task. The subjects were then asked to rate the person about whom they read. As expected, the capable performer who had been in the group for some time was accorded a higher status than the new member. Next, the subjects were asked to rate their degree of approval of certain actions initiated by these people. 72 percent of the subjects reported that they would disapprove a suggestion for a change in group plans if a low-status individual initiated it. Only 18 percent disapproved of the same suggestion when it was initiated by a high-status individual.

It is clear, then, that people's status in a group will affect their ability to make suggestions for change—that is, their ability to have their deviant opinions accepted. High-status individuals whose opinions have been valid in the past are likely to be accepted as innovative by the group.

Leadership

Over half a century's research has been devoted to the study of leadership. Originally these studies took a *trait-centered approach* (Crowley, 1928); that is, they searched for people who possessed the trait of "leadership" or who possessed other traits such as "dominance" or "extroversion." It was assumed that these traits would guarantee their selection as leaders, regardless of the groups in which they found themselves or the tasks faced by these groups. This approach had very limited success, however (Mann, 1959; Stogdill, 1948). Very few traits that were predictive of leadership were found in more than one study. Worse, a trait that was positively related to leadership (for example, sensitivity) in one study was found to be negatively related in another.

Pressed by this evidence to rethink their models of leadership, most psychologists now hold what might be called a *relational theory of leadership* (Gibb, 1969; Zander, 1979). This theory sees leadership as a relationship that arises within a group, a relationship that is influenced by the actions of the person who emerges as leader as well as the actions and perceptions of the other group members. It is also influenced by the purposes for which the group comes together. For example, a group of students, strangers to one another, is brought together and asked to solve problems in set theory. One of the group members, who makes it her hobby to do the problems in the puzzle column of *Scientific American,* notices the similarities between the present problems and the ones in the puzzle column and is the first to suggest the correct solution to the problems. Not unnaturally, she emerges as the group leader. At first it seems that her skill

Leadership styles can vary with the purposes for which the group comes together. Very different styles are called for in conducting an orchestra, performing surgery, and heading a government.

made her the leader. The group chose her as their leader because she demonstrated that she had skills appropriate to the problems that the group faced. But if the group had to solve another kind of problem, a problem for which her skills were less relevant than those of another member, then someone else would have been more likely to emerge as leader. Or if her answer to the first problem had happened to be incorrect, then the group's first impression of her would be unfavorable, and in spite of her skill she might not have been chosen. Her leadership was a direct result of her relationship to the group and her demonstration of her ability to solve the problem at hand.

The *contingency model of leadership effectiveness* (Fiedler, 1967, 1972) has demonstrated important linkages between leadership style, the acceptance of the leader by the group, and the kinds of problems the group is effective at solving. People who are to be assigned a leadership role are asked to think back over other groups in which they had found themselves and picture the person they would most like to work with and the person they would least like to work with in the future. They then rate these two workers negatively or positively on a number of dimensions (for example, intelligence or determination). Typically, there is little difference among people's ratings of their most preferred co-worker, who is generally highly positively rated. On the other hand, there is some divergence in the way people rate their *least preferred co-worker* (*LPC*). Some people give this person relatively positive ratings, while others give him or her sharply negative ratings. Those who give high ratings turn out to be people who are concerned with having good interpersonal relations and with being well regarded by people

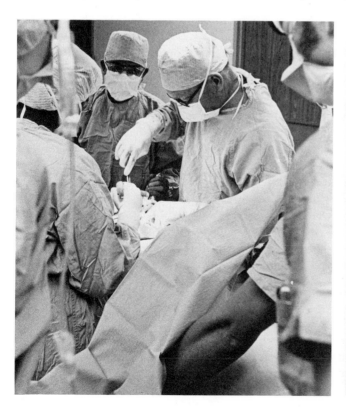

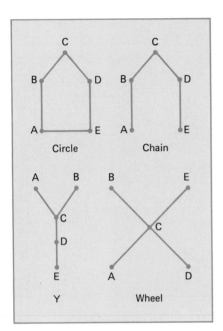

Figure 19-4

These are the communication networks studied by Leavitt. The circle configuration is the most decentralized: Everyone can talk directly to the person on either side. The wheel is the most centralized: All communications must go through the person in the center or hub position. (Leavitt, 1951)

with whom they work (*relation-oriented leaders*). Those who give negative ratings to their least preferred co-worker tend to be people who are concerned with successfully completing tasks, even if they must risk poor interpersonal relations with their co-workers (*task-oriented leaders*).

As might be expected, these two different kinds of orientations lead to two different styles of leadership, each of which can be effective, depending on the setting. For instance, when the group's human relationships are of primary importance, the successful leader is one who is oriented toward developing good interpersonal relations; the task-oriented leader would be ineffective and resented. If, however, the group's relationships are going well and pressure to complete the task successfully is high, then the task-oriented leader would be more successful. Again, successful leadership depends on complex relationships between leaders and group members and is strongly affected by the nature of the task the group faces (Fiedler, 1972).

Sometimes people may become leaders simply by virtue of their position in an organization's communication network. Leavitt (1951), for example, studied the four kinds of communication networks shown in Figure 19-4. The figure indicates in what directions communication can flow (that is, who can talk to whom). In the *circle*, no position conveys an advantage. In the *chain*, those at each end are at a disadvantage since they can each talk to only one other person. In both the *Y* and *wheel* arrangements, however, there is one position on which communications tend to concentrate. Leavitt found that the person occupying such a central position was most likely to become the group leader. This study illustrates how particular roles, no matter who occupies them, tend to produce leaders.

Consistent with Leavitt's findings, a number of other investigators have found that talkativeness leads to leadership. In one study, researchers were able to "create" group leaders simply by getting the least talkative group members to talk a lot (Bavelas et al., 1965). They did this by reinforcing their verbosity. This increase in talking made the group much more likely to view these members as leaders. Apparently, the content or quality of verbalization is not as important as its quantity. Sorrentino and Boutillier (1975) had a confederate talk either a lot or a little, and make either generally high-quality (generally correct) or low-quality (generally incorrect) statements. When the other group members rated the confederate for leadership ability, the quality of his comments made little difference. The major finding was that confederates were rated much more highly as leaders when they talked a lot than when they talked a little. One implication of this research is that if you want to identify the leader of a group, look for someone who talks a lot.

Group Performance

Knowledge about conformity pressures and leadership qualities and styles is clearly important in understanding how groups will perform on various tasks. For example, relation-oriented leaders are generally better for groups that are

either very poorly or very well organized and integrated; task-oriented leaders do better with groups that are intermediate on these dimensions. It has also been found that decentralized communication networks are best for very complex tasks (Shaw, 1954), and centralized networks are best for simple tasks (Leavitt, 1951; Shaw, 1954).

One kind of group performance of special significance is the process of group decision-making. Many of the most important decisions that affect our lives—such as the size and nature of the federal budget, whether or not to go to war, admissions to college and graduate school, and the investment and expansion actions of corporations—are made by groups. Stoner (1961) made a discovery about group decision-making that triggered a great deal of interest. Stoner had his subjects read a series of problems and make choices among several recommendations that varied in the risk of failure they carried. Subjects made private decisions, had a group discussion, and then made the decisions again. After the group discussions, the recommendations tended to become riskier; thus this phenomenon has been termed the *risky shift*. A number of other investigators also found risky shifts following group discussions (Wallach, Kogan, and Bem, 1962). The existence of risky shifts seemed to have obvious importance, since it implied that groups might need to be aware of (and wary of) a tendency to take too many risks. However, it soon became clear that groups often show conservative rather than risky shifts (Zajonc et al., 1968; Pruitt, 1971). It is now clear that both of these effects can be thought of as specific instances of a more general *group extremity shift* (Cartwright, 1971). Group discussion tends to make the average decision of the group members more extreme in one direction or the other than it is when there is no discussion.

Several explanations, each of which has some validity, offer insight into this phenomenon. *Value theory* emphasizes the kinds of social comparisons that tend to occur in groups (Brown, 1965). When alone, individuals try to avoid being either too cautious or too risky; thus they avoid making extreme recommendations. When they find out that others have the same inclination, however, each member may be willing to go with a consistent but more extreme decision because of the emerging group support. Whether a particular decision leads to a risky or conservative shift will be determined by the average group tendency, which presumably will reflect the dominant cultural value for that kind of problem. *Information exchange theories* point out that, given some consensus on a risky or conservative initial tendency, in the course of the group discussion persuasive arguments that some members would not have thought of on their own will be raised and will tend to convince people to be more extreme than they would have been had they not heard those arguments (Vinokur, 1971; Burnstein, Vinokur, and Trope, 1973). Finally, *diffusion of responsibility theory* emphasizes that when decisions are made in a group, the responsibility for a potentially bad decision is diffused among the group members, thus freeing individuals to be more extreme than they might be had they made their decision alone (Wallach, Kogan, and Bem, 1962). Examples of extremity shifts have been found in numerous contexts, including bargaining (Lamm and Sauer, 1974), interpersonal perception (Myers, 1976), and court decisions (Walker and Main, 1973).

What about individual performance in groups? How are performances affected by the presence of audiences or of co-workers? Performance in groups has a long history of study, beginning with Triplett's (1897) investigation of the effects of co-workers on performance. As additional studies accumulated, the findings seemed to be quite contradictory, with some studies showing that individuals performed better alone, and others finding better performance in groups. Robert Zajonc (1965) made sense out of this confusion by proposing a *social facilitation theory*. The central assumption of the theory is very simple: The mere presence of others is a source of arousal. Given this assumption, that people will be in higher states of arousal when in groups than when alone, the performance-in-groups literature makes sense, once the complexity of the tasks involved in the various experiments is taken into account. Increases in arousal are known to enhance performance on easy tasks and to interfere with performance on very difficult tasks (Spence and Spence, 1966; Spence, Farber, and McFann, 1956). Therefore, if the task is easy, performance should be better in a group; if the task is difficult, performance should be worse in a group. In addition to making sense out of the previous work, Zajonc and his colleagues were able to demonstrate the correctness of their analysis in a number of subsequent studies (Zajonc and Sales, 1966; Matlin and Zajonc, 1968).

Although social facilitation theory has been very successful in organizing the performance-in-groups literature, there is still some controversy regarding the cause of the arousal in the presence of others. It is still unclear whether or not the mere presence of other members of the same species is sufficient to cause arousal, but it is quite clear that in general the presence of others does increase arousal and that, at least in humans, concerns about evaluation play a large part in producing these arousal effects (Cottrell, 1972; Good, 1973).

Cooperation

We all seek resources. These resources can be as simple and tangible as food and money or as complex and intangible as status or power. To gain these resources, we must make transactions with other people who have resources to exchange but who also have their own motives. They may complement or conflict with our motives. When people depend on one another for the fulfillment of their needs, they are in a relationship of interdependence. Psychologists have developed their analysis of interdependence in the context of bargaining games (games in which subjects compete for shares of limited resources such as points, money, or prizes), but have then applied it very generally to a wide variety of human interactions.

Social scientists use a *matrix* format to show interdependencies between people (Thibaut and Kelley, 1959). This type of analysis can be applied to real and complex social situations, such as the following: Two men have been arrested. There is clear evidence that they have committed a minor crime for which they could receive a year in jail, and there is circumstantial evidence that they may have committed a major crime, for which they could normally receive a 12-year sentence. The police separate the two and offer each one a deal: If one immediately confesses to the major crime and turns state's evidence on the other, then the prosecutor will recommend a relatively minor sentence (1 year) for that person. Of course, once a confession is obtained from one person, a second confession adds little to the prosecution's case, so only the *first* person to confess will get a light sentence. The other person would receive the major sentence. So the dilemma of each person can be represented in the matrix format, as shown in Figure 19-5.

If you were one of the prisoners, what would you choose? Think about it—it's not an easy decision. If neither confesses, then both get off relatively light. But what if A confesses first, and locks up the state's evidence role for himself, leaving B with a 12-year jail term? Thus both A and B feel a pressure to confess first. Still, if both stand firm and neither confesses, there is the possibility of getting only a light sentence.

Some of the most general properties of interdependent interaction are shown by this example. One of the key properties to notice is the way in which one's fate—one's *outcome* in the matrix format—depends not on one's own choice or action, but on one's choice *in conjunction with* the choice of another. For the prisoner, his choice not to confess may get him off with the light sentence of one year—*if* the other doesn't confess. But if the other does confess, then the late-confessing prisoner will get a 12-year sentence. The fate of each rests in the hands of the other.

A second point made by this example is the wide range of human situations

Prisoner B \ Prisoner A	Confess	Not Confess
Confess	Whoever is first gets 1 year; the other gets 12 years	A = 12 years B = 1 year
Not Confess	A = 1 year B = 12 years	A = 1 year B = 1 year

Figure 19-5

This is a matrix format representing the various choices and outcomes open to the two prisoners in our example above. Note that each people's outcomes in the matrix format depend not on their own choice, but on their choice in conjunction with the choice of another. (Thibaut and Kelley, 1959)

APPLICATION
Marriage as Social Exchange

It is possible to see social exchange processes at work in most interpersonal relationships. In the traditional marriage, for example, the husband was thought to give economic and emotional security to the wife, who because of her dependency valued these commodities. Meanwhile she gave domestic services, children, and sexual favors to the male. This is a nice example of an exchange in which the participants have complementary resources that allow for a satisfactory exchange of rewards. In other words, different people need different things and exchange relationships can become successful long term ones because one person can relatively easily give what another person needs. The example also makes it clear that the traditional image of marriage relies on social diagnoses of the needs of men and women which are certainly arguable, and are currently much argued about.

Changes in the traditional view of marriage can lead to dissatisfaction. For example, if a traditional woman alters her values and begins to be more concerned about intellectual and professional goals, dissatisfaction with a previously acceptable relationship may ensue. Likewise, if a male begins to value family time more and economic considerations less, he may also become less satisfied. In both cases, the previous outcomes are viewed less favorably when the person's set of expectations or *comparison level* changes (Thibaut and Kelley, 1959; Kelley and Thibaut,

1978). If both partners can change, then a new satisfactory relationship may be established. However, if one party cannot or will not change, or if the resources available to either person prevent the kind of change desired by the partner, then the relationship may dissolve.

Dissolution of relationships is much more common now than in the past. One explanation of this fact may be that changes in traditional male and female roles and expectations have created new stresses in marriages that are difficult to resolve. But there is another important consideration. If the outcomes in a relationship fall below a person's minimum requirements, or comparison level, the person will not be satisfied. This by itself does not necessarily

that can be represented in the matrix format. Consider a boy who has gone out with a girl for several months and who now feels he is in love with her. Should he tell her? If he does and she responds that she is beginning to love him too, then we can imagine the increase in his happiness that this will produce. On the other hand, she might say that although she likes going out with him, she doesn't feel that she loves him. And no matter how gently and tactfully this is conveyed, it still would hurt. Again, this is a situation in which the consequences of the boy's choice, to speak or not to speak, depend heavily on the other person's response to his actions.

Psychologists, economists, mathematicians, and sociologists have taken seriously the proposition that much of life can be thought of as a series of *social exchanges* in which people provide each other with mutually satisfying rewards. Using the matrix analysis, they have explored the ramifications of this idea in many areas of life. Many social interactions can be thought of as exchanges between individuals. When a child helps his younger brother he "earns" the brother's gratitude and his father's praise and approval. A worker's successful completion of a task "earns" him the praise of his boss, possible raises, and so on.

Several useful insights arise from this view of social interaction. First, people are unlikely to continue a relationship voluntarily unless both are

mean that the relationship will end. The alternatives must be considered. If the *comparison level for alternatives* is below the outcomes currently being obtained, the relationship will continue even though it is unsatisfactory in an absolute sense. The phrase "the lesser of two evils" contains this idea; if the relationship you are in is better than any of your alternatives, then you will stay in it even though you are dissatisfied. As Kelley and Thibaut (1978) point out, leaving a relationship also has *exit costs*. These exit costs, although still substantial, appear to have been reduced recently. The increased frequency of divorce has coincided with a more lenient public attitude toward such behavior, reducing the "costs" of divorce. In addition, many states have liberalized divorce laws, again reducing exit costs so that unsatisfactory relationships are less likely to persist.

It is clear that viewing marriage as an exchange relationship is a useful analytic approach. It is also clear, however, that participants in such close relationships as marriage, or even friendships, do not like to view their behavior in this way. Indeed, a person would probably feel rejected if a friend or spouse kept a balance sheet of favors rendered and received, and immediately returned every kindness with a similar favor of equal value. Clark and Mills (1979) argue that relationships are thought of in two different categories: *exchange* and *communal*. In exchange relationships, such as business transactions, it is appropriate and fair to keep close track of the benefits that accrue to each participant, and to be concerned with the equity of reward distribution. In *communal* relationships, such as marriage, these concerns are not so appropriate. In these relationships favors are given as affirmations of attraction or on the basis of the needs of the other; they need not and should not be returned "tit-for-tat." In a series of studies, Clark and Mills demonstrated that in exchange relationships, requests for favors and unreturned favors are viewed negatively. In communal relationships, however, requests for favors are viewed favorably, but promptly returned favors are taken as rebuffs. One implication we can draw from these ideas is that the renegotiation of a traditional relationship into some new form, in addition to other difficulties, runs the risk of changing the fundamental character of the interaction from a communal focus to an exchange focus, a change that would have negative connotations for anyone interested in such "nonrational" concepts as love.

receiving reasonable "payoffs" from it. This is a useful thing to remember when you are studying human relationships—if you observe a relationship in which one person seems to be receiving no benefits and much grief, dig deeper. Perhaps that person has hidden needs and is receiving some benefits after all.

Social exchange theory gives us another insight into the way people interact. Our decision as to whether or not we should continue a relationship is based not on the absolute value of the profits we are getting from it but on the relative magnitude in comparison to what we could get elsewhere (Thibaut and Kelley, 1959). This relative magnitude is judged according to the degree of satisfaction or profits we have come to expect from our relationships in general, and the satisfactions that we can expect from the other relationships that are immediately available to us.

This can be seen, for example, in the way workers will cling to even menial and degrading jobs during a depression: They perceive that no other jobs of any sort are available to them. It also helps us to understand those cases in which someone ends a long-term relationship that continues to produce the same level of satisfactions that it always did. The person ends the relationship because the possibility of a new relationship has opened up, and the new relationship holds out the possibility of an even higher level of satisfaction.

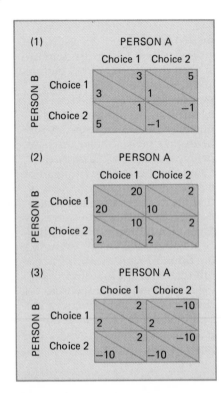

Figure 19-6

Outcomes in three different sets of payoff contingencies. In each case, the number above the diagonal is Person A's outcome, and the number below the diagonal is Person B's outcome. For example, in Matrix 1, if A chooses #1 and B chooses #2, then A's outcome is 1 and B's outcome is 5.

Competition

One discovery of the researchers in this area is that people do govern their behavior according to the contingencies that the environment puts in front of them. That is, the pattern of "payoffs"—gains and losses that are represented in the matrix—does strongly control people's choices. Consider the three matrices in Figure 19-6. All present the same choice to the participant, to make the cooperative or the competitive choice. But matrix two and three both differ from matrix one; matrix two puts a premium on making the cooperative choice and matrix three puts a premium on avoiding the noncooperative choice.

But researchers also discovered an unusual pattern of results. In many bargaining situations an optimal strategy, which means the greatest gains for both players, can be mapped out. But many times people played the games in such a way that their actual payoffs were far below the maximum levels possible. This was most likely to occur when the possibilities of negative outcomes existed. In many situations that can be analyzed from a bargaining and exchange orientation, participants can cause negative outcomes for each other. Lovers can quarrel, labor can strike and management can lock workers out, faculty can give failing grades and students can give low course evaluations. It is in these mixed-motive situations that the behavior of the participants often seems to deteriorate and take on tones of mistrust and suspicion.

A landmark study of the role of threat in bargaining settings was made in 1960 by Deutsch and Krauss. They developed a realistic situation that could contain the possibilities of threat and conflict and that the participants found highly involving. It has come to be known as the *trucking game*. In this game, one player is in charge of the Acme Trucking Company and the other is in charge of Bolt. Each is to deliver goods from their start to their destination; the more quickly they do so, the more profit they make. Each player could take the slow, winding, alternate route, shown in Figure 19-7, but it would take so long that there would be a small loss each time it was taken.

The center route is more direct, so it presented the possibility of profit. But it also contained a one-lane stretch that could be passed by only one truck at a time. Subjects playing this version of the game generally arrived at an alternating strategy, taking turns with the long and short routes, and, over the 20 trials played, earned a reasonable payoff for each player. For other players, however, the game was complicated by the addition of weapons, in the form of gates at the points marked in Figure 19-7. One gate was controlled by Acme and therefore could be used to block the progress of Bolt; the other gate was controlled by Bolt and could block the progress of Acme.

When both players had the use of gates, the situation turned into a payoff disaster; often both trucks would sit at each other's gates while seconds ticked away. The addition of the bilateral threat was actually a hindrance to the players' resolving their potential conflicts and coming to terms with each other.

For a third set of players the trucking game was altered again. This time Acme was given a gate and Bolt was not. This meant that Acme had the unilateral capability to block Bolt's path. Not surprisingly, Acme sometimes used this capacity, and at the end of the game Bolt's payoffs were well below zero, indicating losses rather than profits (although not as bad as those incurred in the bilateral threat condition). Interestingly, Acme, the high-power partici-

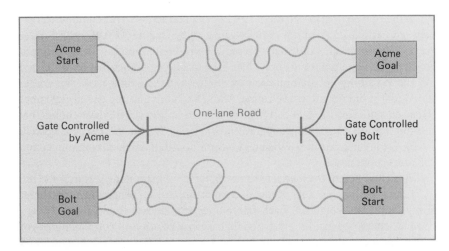

Figure 19-7

This sketch shows the basic layout of the Deutsch and Krauss Trucking Game. Note that both Acme and Bolt controlled gates that could be used to block the progress of the other.

Table 19–1: *Payoffs in the Deutsch and Krauss Trucking Game.*

	Means		
Variable	No Threat	Unilateral Threat (Acme Has Threat)	Bilateral Threat
Summed Payoffs (Acme and Bolt)	203.31	−405.88	−875.12
Acme's payoff	122.44	−118.56	−406.56
Bolt's payoff	80.88	−287.31	−468.56

Deutsch and Krauss (1960).

pant in the interaction, also had a negative payoff over the 20-trial series. Why? Because of the one-lane section of the center highway. This gave Bolt the capacity to block Acme's truck if they met head-on in that section, thereby blocking Acme's chances of a quick and profitable run. So in this situation, the person who has relatively more power suffers from its availability, because it causes others to use whatever negative sanctions are at their disposal. The results of the trucking games are shown in Table 19-1.

Other psychologists, although impressed with the Deutsch and Krauss studies, have cautioned against too widely generalizing the conclusion that the presence of threats or negative sanctions always hinders the resolution of conflict. For instance, Kelley (1965) pointed out that the gate in the trucking game was first an actual block, and only secondarily a threat. That is, the intention to use it in the future (the threat component) had to be communicated by actually using it as a block. Other researchers (Shomer, Davis, and Kelley, 1966) gave subjects both a way of signaling a threat to the other player and a way of actually doing harm. The threat-signaling capability caused an increase in the payoffs earned by the participants.

Other psychologists (Nemeth, 1972) have pointed out that communication between participants had not been possible in the original Deutsch and Krauss games. Communication is usually possible in most of the real-world situations to which psychologists wish to apply their findings. Later studies that have allowed for the possibility of communication between participants have sometimes found that it did not affect the course of the bargaining or the payoff outcomes (Deutsch and Krauss, 1962). Other investigators, however, have found that communication promotes cooperative behavior (Wichman, 1970; Caldwell, 1976). We are not yet sure of the precise conditions under which communication enhances cooperation.

A picture begins to emerge of the complexity of bargaining research and the difficulties of making such general conclusions as, "The presence of threat always increases conflict." Each bargaining situation is found to have very complex characteristics of its own, so that the interrelationship of possibilities of communication, threats, and the balance of alternative causes of action and relative payoffs determines the role of each of those factors in the bargaining outcome. Behind this, there emerges the picture of the bargaining participants, trying to "decode" the complex situation presented to them, each in terms of the underlying motives and dispositions of the other player. As Komaritar, Sheposh, and Braver (1968) found, if one participant in a prisoner's dilemma game is given power over the other, when the high-power person acts cooperatively he or she is more likely to be successful at inducing cooperation from the other player than is a player with less power. The researchers suggest that this is so because it is clear that the powerful ones *could* choose to win more than they do, and therefore they are perceived as intending to act benevolently and as being trustworthy. But of course, as the appearance of the variable of choice reminds us, attribution theory is relevant here. The problem of the participant in the bargaining game is a specific case of the general problem of the interacting individual who attempts to discern the intentional and dispositional characteristics of the other actors in his or her life. Once people come to the conclusion that their opponents are likely to cooperate or compete, they can then shape their own actions accordingly (Kelley and Stahelski, 1970).

Bargaining takes place in many areas of life—shown here are delegates at a national convention, and union leader and company president at the opening of bargaining talks for a new union contract.

The Contexts of Group Activities

Groups conduct their activities in behavior settings, and these settings in turn affect the nature of those activities. Every college student knows this—think of a lecture hall, with rows and rows of chairs, all facing ahead, all bolted to the floor. Now imagine trying to have a group discussion in that room. Nobody could face the person with whom he or she was talking. Students in the first rows would be talking to empty air, those in the back row to the backs of heads. At best the discussion would be awful; more likely it would simply not take place. Clearly the physical and spatial context within which group interactions take place can shape or distort those interactions.

Behavior Settings and Ecological Psychology

Social psychologists who study setting-interaction relationships are generally called *ecological psychologists.* The behavior setting is the basic unit of analysis of ecological psychology. A *behavior setting* is a setting in which a pattern of activities occurs. On a baseball field, pitchers, catchers, batters, and fielders carry out their action patterns. In a bank, tellers, officers, and customers carry out their transactions, watched over by guards. Sometimes the behavior setting is a physical setting such as a baseball field; at other times it is more abstractly defined—for example, editor of the high school newspaper. The key idea is that the setting calls for an occupant who acts to fulfill the requirements of that setting.

Institutions can differ in the number and range of the behavior settings they provide, and this makes a great deal of difference to those people's lives. Roger Barker (1960) and his colleagues painstakingly catalogued all of the behavior settings available to adolescents in a small Kansas town called "Midwest" and in a town about the same size in England called "Yoredale." They found that the two towns differed markedly in that Midwest had a larger number of behavior settings than did Yoredale, and also had a larger number of people taking turns performing in each setting. So, for instance, the American adolescents served in 3.5 times as many behavior settings in which they took positions of responsibility as did their English counterparts.

This is important first of all in what it says about the social learning experiences of the two sets of adolescents. Compared to their English counterparts, the American teenagers have many more possibilities for learning how to play various roles and for practicing the various skills associated with those different roles. The high-school newspaper editor, for instance, learns a whole set of skills concerning clear writing and the technicalities of how a printing press works. But this person also has at least the chance to learn more: skills in working with people, in coordinating their activities, and in being in a position of authority. Many of these skills originally learned in an adolescent behavior setting will create career possibilities later in life, and many of them will enhance a career no matter what it turns out to be.

Second, behavior settings can generate forces that cause people to want to maintain the settings. A high school wouldn't seem complete without a newspaper, and since a newspaper traditionally requires an editor, a person is

HIGHLIGHT
Cognitive Maps

The New York City subway system is complex. With over 200 miles of track, some 500 stations, and 27 different routes, the would-be traveler is faced with a bewildering array of alternatives (Bronzaft, Dobrow, and O'Hanlon, 1976). In 1974 the Metropolitan Transit Authority produced a beautiful subway map. Abstract, with pleasing renditions of subway lines in a rainbow of colors, the maps were designed to simplify the use of the system. There was only one problem: People got lost using the maps. When riders were asked to take trips through unfamiliar parts of the system, 56 percent of the trips were too indi-

rect to be considered "acceptable" uses of the map (Bronzaft et al., 1976).

The town of Goole, England, is not nearly as complicated as New York City, but its residents were also confused by a map created by the town council. The pedestrian map used a standard configuration with reference to the compass, with the north section of town at the top, south at the bottom, east to the right, and west to the left. The problem was that the residents had developed their *cognitive maps* without regard for compass headings. In their cognitive maps, the town entrance was on the right and the

river was on the left (Porteous, 1977). They therefore found the new maps confusing.

These two examples highlight the importance of the mental or cognitive maps that city dwellers have of their environs. Such maps can be used to understand how various residents and groups of residents view their cities. They can be compared with maps from other cities to learn how cities differ. And they can be used by urban planners when changes in city structure are contemplated. Given the differences in cognitive maps between city dwellers and city planners (Applegard, 1976), failure to consider cognitive maps

needed to occupy that setting. So arms are twisted and an editor appears. Generalizing from this, the ecological psychologists realized that the ratio of people needed to people available to fill behavior settings can have very general effects on the social climate of an institution.

Consider a high school, a good example of a single institution that provides a multiple set of behavior settings. In almost all high schools, a standard set of behavior settings exists and needs to be filled. In large high schools, this creates no problems. Indeed, metaphorically, people "wait in line" for each setting. For instance, hundred of students might try out for each athletic team, and most school clubs have more applicants than they can handle. In theoretical terms, that institution is *overmanned*. In a small high school, the situation is often quite different; a small high school is often undermanned. In fact, it was Barker's observation that this condition existed in Midwest. Think of a theatrical play that has twenty roles being given by a group of 12 men and you can imagine what an undermanned institution is like. In this sort of institution, all people must fill multiple settings. The newspaper editor must also be on the girl's basketball team, or it won't have enough people, and the class fat boy is nonetheless going to be fitted into the football team, because his size can be used to advantage in the line and his presence is sorely needed.

It is ecological psychology's central discovery that undermanned and overmanned settings create sharply different institutional climates. On the basis of their observations in over- and undermanned churches, schools, and other institutions, Barker and his associates (1968) concluded that in undermanned institutions, people: (1) expend greater effort to fill the settings, either by

can lead to difficulties more serious than a confusing subway map.

How do people construct their cognitive maps? Lynch (1960) found that individuals use five elements in their mental representations of their environs. *Paths,* the most common element, indicate routes of passage through the environment. *Edges* are boundaries (other than paths) such as rivers, canyons, or walls. *Districts* are large, definable parts of the city such as Chinatown in San Francisco or Greenwich Village in New York. *Nodes* are strategic spots such as crossroads or junctions, and *landmarks* are prominent physical objects such as statues, buildings, or hills. Each person's unique memory for these elements makes up his or her cognitive map of a particular area.

One important determinant of the complexity and richness of cognitive maps is *familiarity*. Initial impressions of a new environment are of course sketchy. With additional experience, aspects of the environment become familiar and stand out in the person's cognitive map. For example, you would expect a freshman and a senior to generate substantially different maps of your campus due to differential familiarity. In one demonstration of this idea, Saarinen (1969) found that people who worked in Chicago's Loop had detailed but firmly bounded cognitive maps of the Loop. Students who were familiar with the Loop but who lived outside had cognitive maps with more amorphous boundaries that included landmarks outside the actual Loop area.

Environments also vary in the ease with which they can be mapped. For example, Milgram (1976) found Paris to be a city high in *imageability*. The existence of well-known paths and landmarks makes Paris a city that creates a high degree of similarity among people's cognitive maps. Other cities are more nondescript and therefore probably leave their residents with more idiosyncratic and ill-defined cognitive maps. It seems likely that cities that are high in imageability are conducive to a feeling of community among their residents. As in Paris, when people can develop similar cognitive maps, they have a common perspective from which to communicate. We would expect more amorphous environs to make a sense of community more difficult.

working harder or putting in longer hours; (2) are involved in more difficult and more important tasks; and (3) participate in a greater diversity of tasks and roles. For instance, members of small churches contributed more money, attended services more regularly, and spent more time in church behavior settings (Wicker, 1969). The underlying realization is that having these behavior settings filled is important to the people in the institution, and therefore the presence of the settings creates forces to have them filled. This is important, but Barker's group discovered more; they discovered that people in undermanned settings came to regard one another differently. Clearly, each individual in an undermanned setting has increased functional importance. So people become less sensitive to differences between people, and when they do discover differences they are less likely to put negative evaluations on those differences. The lowered stress on evaluation is particularly interesting, since in undermanned institutions settings will tend to be performed more poorly. If the newspaper editor only has a few hours to devote to his or her job, then the newspaper will be less professionally polished. But a poor performance is better than no performance at all, and people in undermanned institutions react to that realization by being supportive rather than evaluative of others.

Destructive Environments

Some physical surroundings are destructive, in that they inhibit the development of certain group processes within them. The rigidly row-organized lecture hall that inhibits the possibilities of group discussions within it is an example of this. Robert Sommer has studied interactions in a number of built-form en-

Physical settings can create behavioral settings that encourage or discourage social interaction, as can be seen in this college lecture hall (below), a room in the "new" Army barracks (right, above), and an informal arrangement in a student cooperative (right, below).

vironments, and called attention to a number of examples of settings that have disastrous consequences for the human interactions that take place within them. Given some of the earlier discussions in this text, you will not be surprised to discover that the mental hospital was the source of many of his examples. The common room of a geriatric ward in a Canadian hospital was remodeled, painted a more cheerful color, carpeted, and furnished with new furniture, in the hopes that this would combat some of the apathy and isolation observed among the inmates. But nothing much happened. Patients sometimes sat in their new room, but interactions were minimal. As Sommer and Ron pointed out, the organization of the furniture in the space had a great deal to do with the result. The space was organized with long lines of chairs neatly placed against the walls and in the center of the room, an arrangement that the staff felt was a sensible, tidy one, and one that the custodial staff found easy to keep swept, mopped, and organized. But what are the possibilities for human interaction in such an environment? Picture yourself having a conversation with a person sitting shoulder to shoulder to you. It's awkward, isn't it? Usually people face one another when they talk, so that they can give one another the nonverbal signals that conversation needs to go smoothly. But that's not possible when the chairs are placed side by side.

Imagine yourself and someone else sitting across from each other. On one hand you can look at each other when you talk, and that helps, but the distance between you is too great—normal conversations take place at distances between 2 and 4 feet, and intimacy is lost at greater distances (Hall, 1966). Also, other people, walking through the dayroom, will pass between the two who are conversing, further disrupting their interaction. Clearly, the seating layout was not organized to promote social interaction. In fact it was well organized to inhibit it.

How would you move the furniture around to encourage more positive social interactions? The researchers were able to convince the authorities to add some square tables to the room and to group the chairs in sets of four around these tables (this is the pattern normally seen in dining rooms, work meeting rooms, and other spaces designed to aid communication). The new arrangement worked. Over time the interactions between the patients increased, until within a few weeks the number of interactions had nearly doubled. The change in the physical setting had created behavioral settings that encouraged social contacts.

Density, Crowding, and Privacy

An exciting recent study showing the effects of physical planning of a building on the people living in that building is likely to be of particular interest to college students living in dormitories. To understand it, some background on two related concepts is useful. The *density* of a group of individuals refers to the number of people present in a particular environment. It is often expressed in terms of square-footage—for instance, if 10 people are in a room that is 8 feet wide and 12 feet long (96 square feet), each person can be said to have 9.6 square feet available to him or her.

Intuitively, high-density situations seem to be negative ones, and a great deal of research was attempted to demonstrate that this was so in large-scale urban environments. A number of demographic studies examined the relationship between density indices, such as the number of people who lived in a city

block, and the rate of disease, crime, and mental pathology that occurred in that area. The results of these studies were confusing, sometimes supporting the idea of the existence of a relationship between density and pathology, but sometimes contradicting it. Hong Kong, for instance, has population densities four times as great as even the most crowded American cities, but there are higher frequencies of cases of hospitalization for mental illness and cases of criminal violence in American cities.

These contradictions led researchers to think more carefully about the concept of density and how it related to other elements of human experience. They realized that high density (1) was not always experienced as negative, and (2) had effects that could be sharply altered by the physical arrangements within which it existed. Researchers (Altman, 1975; Stokols, 1972) were led to develop the concept of *crowding,* which they used to describe the psychological state of feeling crowded, surrounded, and intruded on by the people around you. Crowding occurs when there are too many people present or too many activities going on comfortably to attend to. This excessive stimulation can lead to a feeling of stimulus overload (Milgram, 1970). The feeling of being crowded also occurs when one is subjected to a higher degree of social contact than is desired, and so one feels one's privacy or personal space is being violated. Density does not always lead to these conditions and therefore will not always be stressful. And sometimes the potential negative effects of density can be avoided by changing the interaction space to limit overload and create the possibilities of privacy.

With these distinctions in mind, let's look at what researchers found out about college dormitories. In Figure 19-8 you will certainly recognize the upper dormitory plan. It is the familiar "long-corridor dormitory" that must be found on nearly every residential campus in the country. The bottom plan is a new one. In terms of density, the newer dormitory holds as many residents as does the long corridor one. Its important feature is that the lounge space is shared only by

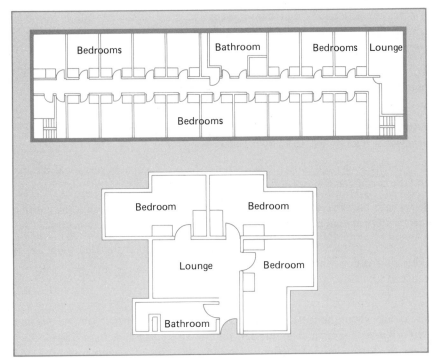

Figure 19-8

The sketch on top is the familiar "long-corridor" dormitory plan that is found in most campuses. The sketch underneath it is a newer plan organized by suites, in which the lounge space is shared only by those who have rooms in that suite, not with all the residents on the corridor, as in the older plan. This difference in arrangement in turn leads to different kinds of social interactions. (Baum and Valins, 1977)

the people who have rooms in the suite. In the long-corridor plan, the lounge is used by all the residents in the hall. Think about using the long-corridor lounge. Private conversations with close friends would be difficult, because other people might wander in at any time. Nor would it be a good place to be alone, because unwanted social interactions might arise. Baum and Valins (1977) reasoned that even though both kinds of dorms had the same population density, the long-corridor dorm residents might feel more crowded. And they, more than the residents of suite-organized dorms, reported that they felt it was useless to try to change things in their dormitory. To see how far the effects of the dormitories generalized, Baum and Valins set up in a psychology laboratory a task in which rather little information was given to the participants. Participants who were residents of the long-corridor dorms were relatively unlikely to seek out information about the experiment. (Compare this result with the discussion of learned helplessness in Chapters 11 and 15.)

Summary

1. Four dimensions of the interaction between individuals and groups are: conformity, deviation, innovation, and leadership.

2. *Conformity* often has a negative connotation, but in some situations it is a sign of rational behavior, not weakness. Examples of rational conformity are conforming actions arising from *informational social influence.* Another type of conformity, *normative social influence,* often involves the suppression of one's own opinions.

3. People who deviate from the group opinion are often ostracized and punished by the group; they then may become members of *outgroups.*

4. Status in a group determines how much influence a person will have in getting his or her opinions adopted by the group; this adoption of an opinion not necessarily held by the majority is called *innovation.*

5. Theories of *leadership* include: trait-centered approach, relational theory, and the contingency model of leadership effectiveness.

6. There are several theories that explain the group extremity shift: value theory, information exchange theories, diffusion of responsibility theory.

7. *Social facilitation theory* is based on the assumption that the presence of others is a source of arousal; depending on the difficulty of the task involved, this can lead to poor or good performance.

8. The *matrix format* is used to show interdependencies between people in situations where competition and cooperation are involved. Another way of exploring such situations is through the *trucking game. Social exchange theory* seeks to explain the interactions of people in terms of a mutual sharing and meeting of needs.

9. Ecological psychologists study setting-interaction relationships; the basic unit of their studies is the *behavior setting.*

10. *Density* refers to the number of people present in a particular environment. High-density situations seem to be negative only when these situations create the psychological state of feeling crowded, surrounded, and intruded on by other people.

11. Ecological psychologists have shown how space can be manipulated to create the possibilities of privacy and to reduce the potential negative effects of density.

Suggested Readings

BAUM, A., and VALINS, S. *Architecture and social behavior: Psychological studies in social density.* Hillsdale, N.J.: Erlbaum, 1977. Contains some good examples of recent developments in ecological research.

DAVIS, J. H. *Group performance.* Reading, Mass.: Addison-Wesley, 1969. Interesting but complex findings on group performance variables are reviewed here.

FIEDLER, F. E., and CHEMERS, M. H. *Leadership and effective management.* Chicago: Scott, Foresman, 1974. An excellent review of leadership research, necessary reading for those who wish to pursue the subject further.

FREEDMAN, J. L. *Crowding and behavior.* San Francisco: Freeman, 1975. This is an award-winning analysis of crowding research that is both readable and entertaining.

KIESLER, C. A., and KIESLER, S. B. *Conformity.* Reading, Mass.: Addison-Wesley, 1969. Well organized and clear, this text reviews the conformity literature in comprehensive but succinct fashion.

LATANÉ, B., and DARLEY, J. M. *The unresponsive bystander: Why doesn't he help?* New York: Appleton-Century-Crofts, 1970. This famous research monograph shows, in an interesting progression of empirical studies, how informational and normative pressures interact when one is faced with the decision to help or not to help in an emergency.

MILGRAM, S. *Obedience to authority.* New York: Harper & Row, 1974. The controversial research on obedience to authority is reported by its author.

SULS, J., and MILLER, R. J. (Eds.). *Social comparison processes: Theoretical and empirical perspectives.* Washington, D.C.: Hemisphere/Halsted, 1977. This edited volume contains a number of recent papers on social comparison.

Appendix Statistics

"You haven't told me yet," said Lady Nuttal, "what it is your fiance does for a living."

"He's a statistician," replied Lamia, with an annoying sense of being on the defensive.

Lady Nuttal was obviously taken aback. It had not occurred to her that statisticians entered into normal relationships. The species, she would have surmised, was perpetuated in some collateral manner, like mules.

"But Aunt Sara, it's a very interesting profession," said Lamia warmly.

"I don't doubt it," said her aunt, who obviously doubted it very much. "To express anything important in mere figures is so plainly impossible that there must be endless scope for well-paid advice on how to do it. But don't you think that life with a statistician would be rather, shall we say, humdrum?"

Lamia was silent. She felt reluctant to discuss the surprising depth of emotional possibility which she had discovered below Edward's numerical veneer.

"It's not the figures themselves," she said finally, "it's what you do with them that matters." (K. A. C. Manderville, *The Undoing of Lamia Gurdleneck*)

Psychologists often use numbers to characterize behavior—for example, how long it takes for a stimulus to evoke a response, the number of correct answers on a test, a subject's rating of preference on a scale from 1 to 10, and so on. These examples of assigning numbers to behavior are *measurement procedures*, as are the more familiar procedures for measuring length and weight, etc. In this appendix we will discuss how some aspects of a group of numbers (for example, test scores) can be characterized by other numbers called *statistics* (for example, the average test score), and how inferences can be drawn from such statistics, a process called *statistical inference*. We will also consider some *experimental design principles* that guide psychologists in collecting their observations of human behavior.

Descriptive Statistics

Frequency Distributions

Descriptive statistics is a set of methods for organizing and summarizing a set of numbers, or data. The *data* may be any set of measurements of a group of objects, people, or events. These measurements or data are usually a sample of the population that is of interest. For example, if we are interested in the

Table 1A: Annual Incomes Sampled from 19 Domestic Workers.

3,000	4,000	6,000
5,000	5,000	4,000
10,000	7,000	10,000
20,000	10,000	9,000
8,000	20,000	4,000
4,000	9,000	4,000
	4,000	

Table 1B: Frequency Distribution of Annual Incomes Grouped in Intervals of $1,000.

Income Interval	Frequency
3,000–3,999	1
4,000–4,999	6
5,000–5,999	2
6,000–6,999	1
7,000–7,999	1
8,000–8,999	1
9,000–9,999	1
10,000–10,999	3
11,000–11,999	0
12,000–12,999	1
13,000–13,999	0
14,000–14,999	0
15,000–15,999	0
16,000–16,999	0
17,000–17,999	0
18,000–18,999	0
19,000–19,999	0
20,000–20,999	2
	19

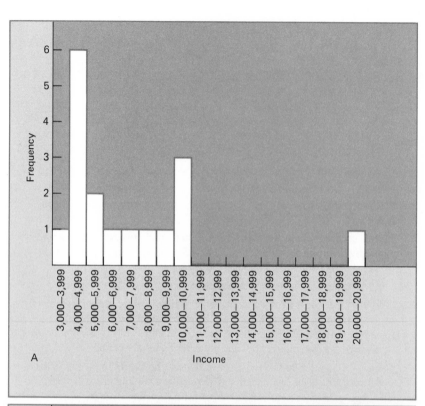

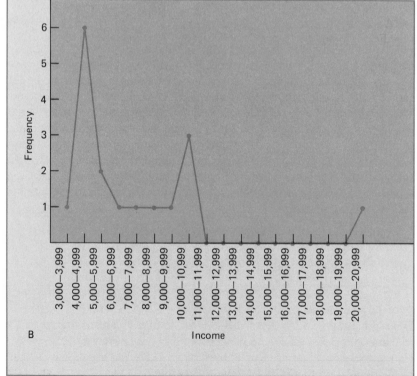

Figure 1

The data in these frequency distributions are from Table 1. A histogram or bar graph is on the top and a polygon is on the bottom.

annual incomes of domestic workers, we might conduct a survey by asking some domestic workers what their annual income is. Here the *population* is incomes of all domestic workers, and the *sample* we take is the actual records of incomes we have at the conclusion of the survey. Table 1A gives some hypothetical incomes reported by each of 19 domestic workers. These data could be described as mostly in the $4,000 range, with some much higher and a few lower. A more precise way of characterizing the incomes in the sample is to specify exactly how many there are in the $3,000 range, $4,000 range, $5,000 range, and so on. This is called a *frequency distribution*. It can be presented as a table (Table 1B) or as a graph (Figure 1). Notice that in Table 1 and Figure 1 we have classified incomes into intervals of $1,000 (called *class intervals*).

Two types of graphs are shown in Figure 1: a histogram (Figure 1A, and a polygon, Figure 1B. A histogram, or bar graph, indicates the frequency of scores in a class interval by the height of a bar above that interval. In contrast, a polygon consists of a series of connected points, one above each interval, with each point's height indicating the frequency of scores in that interval.

Tables and graphs are helpful for showing how numbers are distributed; it is also useful to summarize certain characteristics of distributions in terms of a single number. Figure 2 presents three frequency distributions. The centers of distributions A and B are similar, in that each is above the class interval 50–69. In contrast, the center of distribution C is above the class interval 70–79. In other words, a "typical" score in both distribution A and B is around 45, whereas it is around 75 in distribution C. This central or typical value of a distribution is often described as its *central tendency*.

A second major feature of a distribution is how spread out or variable it is. For example, the scores in distribution A are all closely grouped around the center of the distribution, while they are much more spread out, or variable, in distributions B and C. This feature is often referred to as the spread or *variability* of the distribution. Thus distribution B is similar to distribution A in central tendency, but similar to distribution C in variability.

Central tendency and variation can be more precisely characterized with specific measures or numbers. Such numbers are called *statistics*, since they characterize particular aspects of a group of numbers.

Measures of Central Tendency

Three different statistics are commonly used to characterize the central tendency of a distribution. These are called the mode, the median, and the mean. The *mode* is the number that occurs most frequently in a distribution. For example, suppose your data consist of seven numbers: 11, 7, 7, 10, 11, 8, 11. The mode would be 11, because it occurs more often than any other number. If your data are organized in the form of a frequency distribution, the mode would be the interval having the highest bar above it in a frequency histogram, or the highest point in a polygon (for example, the interval from 4,000 to 4,999 in Fig. 1). (Exactly which number within that interval you use to denote the mode involves issues we need not consider here.) The median characterizes central tendency in a different way. If you order or *rank* the numbers in a distribution, beginning with the largest and ending with the smallest, the

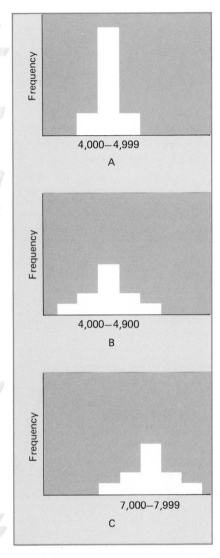

Figure 2

Three frequency distributions. Distribution A has less variability than B but a similar central tendency. Distribution C has a higher central tendency than B, but a similar variability.

median is the number in the very middle. For example, suppose your data consist of seven numbers: 9, 2, 5, 4, 6, 10, 12. You could reorder or rank them as follows: 12, 10, 9, 6, 5, 4, 2. The number 12 would have rank 1, the number 10 rank 2, and so on, until you reached the seventh or lowest ranked number, 2. The number 6 would be the median, because there are as many numbers ranked above it (12, 10, 9) as below it (5, 4, 2). Again, as with the mode, there are some complexities when you use grouped data or when there are ties (two numbers have the same rank). However, it is sufficient here to simply remember that the median is the middle number in a ranked list of data; i.e., there are as many numbers ranked above it as below it.

The third and perhaps most frequently used way of characterizing central tendency is with a statistic called the *arithmetic mean* or *average.* To calculate the mean you add all the entries in the distribution and divide by the number of entries. For example, suppose your data consist of seven numbers: 8, 6, 1, 9, 5, 10, 3. To calculate the mean first add all of the entries:

$$8 + 6 + 1 + 9 + 5 + 10 + 3 = 42$$

Then divide by the number of entries (7):

$$\frac{42}{7} = 6$$

Thus the mean or average of 8, 6, 1, 9, 5, 10, and 3 is 6.

Usually we use different symbols when referring to the mean of a sample versus the mean of a population: $\overline{X}$ stands for the mean of a sample of a population, and the Greek letter μ (mu) stands for the mean of a population. For example, the mean of the sample of incomes in Table 1 is $7,200, therefore $\overline{X}$ = $7,200. We would not, however, know the value of μ, the mean of all incomes, unless we were able to determine the income of every domestic worker in the country.

Often the "average" of a frequency distribution is reported without specifying whether it is the mode, the median, or the arithmetic mean. Which of these it is can make a difference. Consider the hypothetical income data we have been discussing. The modal interval is $4,000; the median is $6,000; and the arithmetic mean is $7,200. How well you think domestic workers are paid will certainly depend on which of these "averages" is reported!

Measures of Variability

Three statistics commonly used to characterize the variability of a distribution are the range, the variance, and the standard deviation. The *range* is simply the difference between the largest and smallest number in the distribution. For example, suppose your data consist of the following five numbers: 20, 15, 5, 30, 10. The range equals the largest number (30) minus the smallest number (5), or 25. Thus the range is based on the largest and smallest numbers in a distribution.

Another more commonly used measure of variability is the variance. The *variance* is basically the average squared difference or *deviation* of each number from the mean of all the numbers. The variance of a sample is called s^2, and the variance of a population is called σ^2, the Greek letter sigma squared. As an example of how to compute a variance, say that the data consist of four numbers: 1, 4, 2, and 1. First the mean, $\overline{X}$, would be calculated:

$$\overline{X} = \frac{1 + 4 + 2 + 1}{4} = \frac{8}{4} = 2$$

Next, the deviation of each of the four numbers from the mean (2) would be squared, as follows:

$(1 - 2)^2 = 1$
$(4 - 2)^2 = 4$
$(2 - 2)^2 = 0$
$(1 - 2)^2 = 1$

To compute the variance you then find the average or mean of these four squared deviations, which is their sum divided by 4:

$$s^2 = \frac{1 + 4 + 0 + 1}{4} = \frac{6}{4} = 1.5$$

The variance is just as important as the mean in interpreting data. For example, look at the hypothetical data in Table 2. An object known to weigh 1.5 grams was weighed on a Truway scale and an Accuway scale on five different occasions. Though the average weight for the two scales is the same, the Truway scale is more variable ($s^2 = 2.5$ grams^2 versus 1.0 grams^2), and so it is less reliable. Thus, Accuway is clearly the preferred scale, but knowing only the average value of the measurements would not tell you this, and thus would not help you make the best choice.

The variance of the measurements in Table 2 is in grams squared, an awkward kind of quantity to think about. If we take the square root of the variance ($s = \sqrt{s^2}$ and $\sigma = \sqrt{\sigma^2}$) we have another measure of variability, the *standard deviation*. For example, the variance of 2.5 grams^2 corresponds to a standard deviation of 1.58 grams. The standard deviation is easier to use because the units are the same as in the original measurements (grams instead of grams squared).

Table 2: The Results of Five Different Measurements on Truway and Accuway Scales.

	Truway	Accuway
1st weighing	1.5 grams	1.7 grams
2nd weighing	1.0 grams	1.4 grams
3rd weighing	2.0 grams	1.5 grams
4th weighing	2.5 grams	1.3 grams
5th weighing	.5 grams	1.6 grams
	$\overline{X} = 1.5$ grams	$\overline{X} = 1.5$ grams
	$s^2 = 2.5$ grams^2	$s^2 = 1.0$ grams^2
	$s = 1.58$ grams	$s = 1.0$ grams

Position in a Distribution

Two commonly used indices of a number's relative position in a distribution are standard deviation and percentiles. The *standard deviation* of a distribution of numbers provides a convenient way of expressing how far away any given measurement is from the average of a set of measurements. Look again at the measurements for the Accuway Scale: 1.3, 1.4, 1.5, 1.6, 1.7. The average, $\overline{X}$, is 1.5 grams; the standard deviation is .1 grams. The measurement of 1.7 grams, then, for instance, is 2 standard deviation units above the mean $(1.7 = \overline{X} + 2s$ or $1.7 = 1.5 + 2(.1) = 1.5 + .2)$. Similarly, the measurement of 1.4 grams is 1 standard deviation unit below the mean $(1.4 = \overline{X} - 1s = 1.5 - .1)$. Thus we can express any measurement in terms of how many standard deviations it is above or below the mean of the set of measurements. Thus, if we let X be any measurement, we may express X as the mean $(\overline{X})$ plus some multiple (z) of the standard deviation (s): $X = \overline{X} + z(s)$.

As an example, look again at the Truway measurements in Table 2. How many standard deviation units above the mean is the measurement of 2.5? In other words, what is z equal to in $2.5 = 1.5 + z(1.58)$? To find out the value of z we first subtract the mean, 1.5, from the measurement, 2.5:

$$2.5 - 1.5 = z(1.58)$$

The last step in finding Z is to divide both sides of the equation by the standard deviation, or 1.58.

$$\frac{1}{1.58} = \frac{z(1.58)}{1.58}$$

$$.633 = z$$

The score of 2.5 is .633 standard deviation units above the mean, 1.5. We can do the same thing for measurements below the mean. In Table 2 the Truway Score of .5 is $-.633$ standard deviation units below the mean, since

$$.5 = 1.5 - (.633)(1.58)$$

or

$$\frac{.5 - 1.5}{1.58} = -.633.$$

Table 3: Truway and Accuway Measurements and Their Standard Scores.

Truway		Accuway	
Raw Score	Standard Score	Raw Score	Standard Score
1.5	0	1.7	+.20
1.0	−.316	1.4	−.10
2.0	.316	1.5	.00
2.5	.633	1.3	−.20
.5	−.633	1.6	+.10

Table 3 gives each Truway and Accuway measurement and its standard score (how many standard deviations above or below the mean it is). When we reexpress a number in terms of standard deviation units, we call that number its *standard score,* or z.

A second way of expressing a number's relative position in a distribution is in terms of the percentage of numbers that are at the same level or below it— that is, give the number's *percentile rank.* For example, by definition of the median, the percentile rank of the median is the 50th percentile. As another example, a score of 80 on a given test is in the 40th percentile if 40 percent of the scores are below it. On another test, however, a score of 80 might be in the 90th percentile, because 90 percent of the scores were at or below 80.

Relative Frequency and Probability

Frequencies can be deceiving! University A reports admitting 20 women to graduate school; University B reports admitting 40. Does this indicate a pattern of discrimination on the part of University A as compared to B? Before reaching any conclusions it would be important at least to determine for each university what proportion or *relative frequency* of admittances were women. Suppose A's total number of admittances is 40 and B's is 80. The picture is now different; it is clear that each university is admitting about 50 percent men and women. Figure 3 shows a relative frequency distribution for the data given in Table 1.

Suppose we took the incomes in Table 1, painted each of the numbers on a marble, and then put them all in an urn, which we then shook up. What are the chances that we would draw a marble with a number between 7,000 and 7,999 on it? Since there are 19 marbles and only one is in the interval 7,000 to 7,999, we can readily see the chances are 1 in 19. What about when we originally sampled the incomes—what were our chances of drawing one income between $7,000 and $7,999? Without knowing the true proportion or *probability* of incomes in this interval in the population, we cannot answer this question. We can, however, say that the true proportion of incomes in the interval $7,000 to $7,999 is the probability that if we *randomly* sample one income from the population, then that income will be between $7,000 and $7,999. By *randomly sample* we mean that every income in the population had an equal opportunity to be selected. In other words, our procedure for sampling incomes has no biases that favor some incomes over others. Such a bias might occur if, for example, we surveyed domestic workers only in one part of the country.

Figure 4 compares a theoretical probability distribution of incomes to the relative frequency distribution of incomes in our sample of 19 incomes. Though we can see that the distribution of incomes in the sample is not exactly the same as the theoretical probability distribution of incomes, it is very similar in shape. When we don't know the true probability distribution for the population we can use the distribution of the sample as our best guess as to the true proportion in the population. Thus, for example, our best guess as to the true proportion of incomes between $7,000 and $7,999 is .053, the proportion

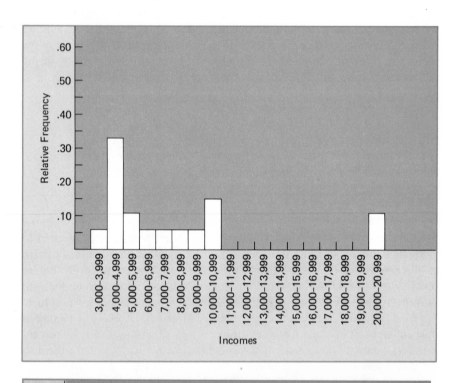

Figure 3

Relative frequency distribution for the scores in Table 1.

Figure 4

Comparison of a theoretical probability distribution of incomes (smooth curve) and the relative frequency distribution of the sampled incomes.

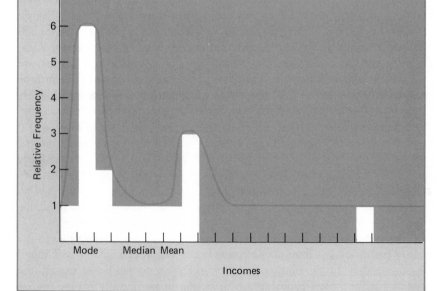

or relative frequency in our sample. When statisticians use quantities or statistics such as relative frequency to guess the true quantity, we say that the sample statistic is used to estimate the population value or *parameter.*

Just as we can use the sample proportion to estimate the true proportion or probability, we can use the mean of the sample, $\overline{X}$, as an estimate of the population mean, μ. In the income example, we would estimate the average income as the sample average: $7,200. Similarly, we can use the variance of the sample to estimate the variance of the population.

Normal Distribution

Many kinds of empirical data are approximately symmetrical, or bell-shaped, as in the sample of IQ data shown in Figure 5. When empirical data are similar to the data in Figure 5 it is often assumed that the true probability distribution is the normal distribution curve shown in Figure 6A. For the normal probability distribution, 68 percent of the numbers are between one standard deviation below the mean and one standard deviation above the mean ($\mu \pm 1\sigma$). Looking at the IQ data in Figure 5, we see that the sample mean is 100 and the sample standard deviation is 15 points. The graph shows us that in this sample of IQ scores 65 percent of the measurements are in the interval from 85 to 115. So for this interval the normal probability distribution is very near the propor- tion of numbers in this interval in the sample. When the sample proportions

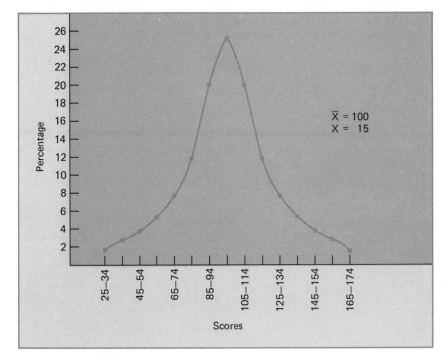

Figure 5
Hypothetical IQ data from a sample of 500 tests.

are so close to the theoretical probabilities of the normal distribution we say the normal curve gives a good approximation of the empirical, sample distribution. The theoretical proportion .68 is arrived at by computing the area under the curve over the interval one standard deviation below and above the mean, as shown in Figure 6A. Similarly, the area under the curve, above the interval from $\mu + 1\sigma$ to $\mu + 2\sigma$, is equal to the proportion .135.

Figure 6

Normal curve: (A) Percent areas from mean to specified distance in deviation units. (B) Standard normal curve.

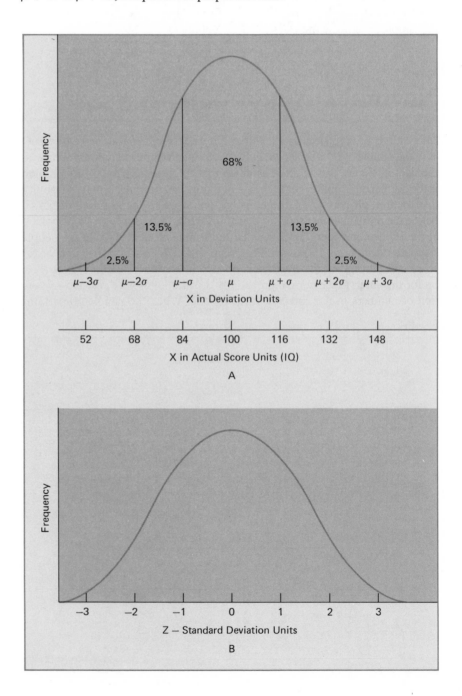

Table 4: Area Under Normal Curve as Proportion of Total Area.

Standard Deviation	(1) Area to the Left of This Value	(2) Area to the Right of This Value	(3) Area Between This Value and the Mean
−3.00	.001	.999	.499
−2.50	.006	.994	.494
−2.00	.025	.975	.475
−1.50	.067	.933	.433
−1.00	.159	.841	.341
− .50	.309	.691	.191
.00	.500	.500	.000
+ .50	.691	.309	.191
+1.00	.841	.159	.341
+1.50	.933	.067	.433
+2.00	.975	.025	.475
+2.50	.994	.006	.494
+3.00	.999	.001	.499

This is very near the sample proportion in the data of Figure 6A. It is very difficult to compute areas under the normal curve, so statisticians have provided tables of different fractions of areas under this curve. Table 4 gives area under the normal curve as a proportion of the total area.

There are many uses for the proportions given in Table 4. One of them is the interpretation of standard scores and the other is in tests of significance.

Standard Scores and the Normal Distribution

It is often useful to express a measurement in terms relative to the rest of the measurements—either as a percentile rank or as a standard score. If the population sampled has a normal probability distribution, then the set of standard scores of that population also have a normal distribution. Figure 6B is the normal distribution of standard scores: the mean of the standard scores is zero ($\mu = 0$), and its standard deviation is equal to one ($\sigma = 1$). Standard scores of a distribution are useful for finding the probability that an observation from a normal population will fall in a given interval. For example, the Graduate Record Exam has a mean of 500 and a standard deviation of 100, as shown in Table 5. The probability that a score picked at random will be below −.5 standard deviations ($-.5\sigma$ below the mean) is given in Table 4, the row containing −.5; that is, .309. The GRE score corresponding to a standard score of −.5 can be computed as follows: we let X denote the unknown GRE score. We know X can be written as

$$X = \overline{X} - (.5)(\sigma)$$

So for the GRE we have

$$X = 500 - (.5)(100) = 450$$

So the chance of sampling a GRE score below 450 is .309.

Table 5: Graduate Record Examination Scores and Their Respective Standard Scores.

GRE Scores	Standard Score
200	−30
300	−20
400	−10
500	00
600	+10
700	+20
800	+30

Mean = 500
Standard Deviation = 100

Table 6: Raw Scores and Statistics from Two Experiments.
The experiments measured the time it takes a rat to traverse a maze.

Time (min)	
Experiment 1	Experiment 2
Rat 1 2.1	Rat 1 2.3
Rat 2 2.4	Rat 2 2.2
Rat 3 1.8	Rat 3 1.9
Rat 4 2.3	Rat 4 1.5
Rat 5 1.9	Rat 5 1.2
$\overline{X} = 2.1$	$\overline{X} = 1.82$
$s^2 = 0.52$	$s^2 = .1736$
$s = .228$	$s = .416$

Statistical Inference and Decision Making

Statistical inference is the process of interpreting variable data. Here we will discuss how to interpret differences among sample means from several groups. Before tackling this question, however, we need to consider just how typical the sample mean really is.

We begin with how well the sample mean predicts the true population mean. Table 6 gives the results of two different experiments on how long it takes rats to complete a maze. The two experiments were conducted under the same procedure, but with different rats. As might be expected, the mean times for the two groups of rats are different. Even if the two groups of rats are from the same population we would still expect the sample means to be different, because random samples drawn from a population do vary. Thus there is a *distribution of sample means,* whose mean, μ, is the same as the mean of the population from which the samples are drawn. The distribution of sample means can be approximated with the normal curve as shown in Figure 7. The standard deviation of the distribution of sample means is called the *standard error of the mean,* $\sigma_{\overline{X}}$, since it reflects the accuracy with which the sample mean estimates the population mean. The formula for the standard error of the mean is

$$\sigma_{\overline{X}} = \frac{\sigma}{\sqrt{N}}$$

where σ is the population standard deviation and N is the number of measurements added together in computing the sample mean.

One characteristic of this formula is that the more samples there are, the smaller the size of the standard error. This is just what we would expect—a

Figure 7
The normal curve distribution of sample means.

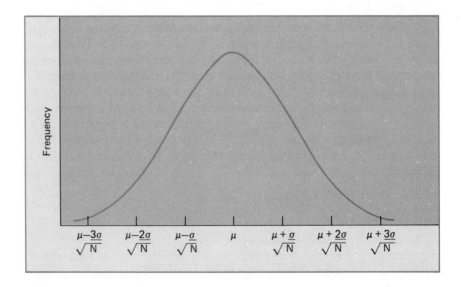

more reliable (i.e., less variable) estimate of the mean *should* be obtained by taking larger samples. A few sample computations will make this observation clear. First, let's consider the theoretical distribution of IQ scores in Figure 5. Here the standard deviation of the population, σ, is assumed to be 16. Now, suppose we administer an IQ test to a group suspected to differ from the norm in their average IQ. Thus, we wish to estimate their average IQ. Suppose we give the IQ test to a sample of 64 people in this group. How much variability will there be in our estimate of the group's average IQ? To answer this we compute the standard error of the mean:

$$\sigma_{\bar{X}} = \frac{\sigma}{\sqrt{N}}$$

For our example,

$$\frac{\sigma}{\sqrt{N}} = \frac{16}{\sqrt{64}} = 2.0$$

Thus, one standard deviation in the distribution of sample means is 2.0. To interpret this, we recall that for the normal probability curve the chances of being between 1 standard deviation above and below the mean is about 68 percent — in other words, the probability that a sample mean based on 64 test scores is between 98 and 102 is .68. Consider, however, taking a sample mean based on only 16 scores. The standard error of the mean in this case is

$$\frac{\sigma}{\sqrt{N}} = \frac{16}{\sqrt{16}} = 4$$

Thus, the standard error in the mean is twice as great as when $N = 64$. Now there is a 68 percent chance that the observed sample mean lies between 96 and 104 — a much wider interval than when the sample size is 64. Thus, the smaller the sample size, the less reliable or accurate is the sample mean as an estimator of the population mean. Furthermore, given the sample size and standard deviation of the population, it is possible to specify the probability that the sample mean will be in a given interval.

Statistical Significance

Many experiments in psychology are concerned with whether the means of two different populations of measurements are the same or different. To answer this kind of question, each population is sampled, and the sample mean for each group is computed. Deciding whether the population means *differ* involves assessing the variability of the sample means to determine if an observed difference between the sample means is reliable, or *statistically significant.* The basic question, then, is whether a difference between two sample means reflects a true difference between population means or is simply the result of the variability inherent in sample means — that is, sampling error.

As an example, let's look at the data from an experiment to test reading comprehension. There are two groups in this experiment. They consist of 5 children in each group, who were randomly selected from elementary schools

Table 7: Hypothetical Comprehension Scores for Two Methods for Teaching Reading.

Teaching Method I	Teaching Method II
80	80
85	85
60	60
75	75
90	30
Mean = 78	Mean = 66

Table 8: A Second Set of Hypothetical Comprehension Scores.

Reading Method I	Reading Method II
70	60
72	58
78	66
84	74
86	72
Mean = 78	Mean = 66

in the area. Each group is exposed to a different reading method. At the end of the learning period a comprehension test is given; the test scores are shown in Table 7. What can be inferred from the data? Is Method I significantly better than Method II? Note that the difference between the means is 12, but the two groups only differ on one score. Thus we would not want to conclude that the groups differ significantly, even though their means differ.

Table 8 shows another set of hypothetical data. Again, the mean difference is the same, but now most of the scores for Method I are higher than most of the scores for Method II. This gives us greater confidence that Method I is better than Method II, but this is just an intuitive judgment—what a test of statistical significance gives us is a precise way to evaluate the reliability of an observed difference between sample means.

The examples comparing reading methods suggest that the reliability of a difference between means depends both on the *size* of the difference in means and on the *variability* of the means. By comparing the magnitude of the difference between the means to the standard error of the difference between the means, we can evaluate precisely the reliability of the difference between the means. This comparison is done by computing a *test statistic*, which is the ratio of the difference between the means, D, and the standard error of the difference between means, σ_D:

$$\text{test statistic} = \frac{D}{\sigma_D}$$

If the difference between the means is a higher number than σ_D, then the difference, D, is classified as statistically significant or reliable. As a rule of thumb, a ratio of 2.0 or more is considered statistically significant. The formula for the standard error of the difference between means is

$$\sigma_D = \sqrt{\frac{\sigma_1^2}{N_1} + \frac{\sigma_2^2}{N_2}}$$

where $\dfrac{\sigma_1^2}{N_1}$ is the variance of the first group mean and $\dfrac{\sigma_2^2}{N_2}$ is the variance of the second group mean.

We will use the data from the reading methods example to illustrate the computation of a test statistic. For the data in Table 7, the difference between the sample means is

$$D = 78 - 66 = 12$$

The standard error of the difference between means is

$$\sigma_D = \sqrt{\frac{106}{5} + \frac{394}{5}} = 10$$

Dividing D by σ_D, we find that

$$\text{test statistic} = \frac{12}{10} = 1.2$$

Since this value is smaller than 2.0, we conclude that the difference between the means is not statistically significant. Using the same procedure, we can compute the test statistic for the data in Table 8. The difference between the sample means is

$$D = 78 - 66 = 12$$

The standard error of the difference between means is

$$\sigma_D = \sqrt{\frac{40}{5} + \frac{40}{5}} = 4$$

Thus, we compute

$$\text{test statistic} = \frac{12}{4} = 3$$

Because the test statistic is well above 2.0, we may conclude that the difference between the sample means is statistically significant. This confirms our intuition about the data in Table 8.

Notice that the sign of the test statistic could be positive or negative, depending on which mean is subtracted from the other ($10 - 12$ or $12 - 10$). In interpreting the test statistic only the number, not the sign, is relevant.

Why is a test statistic of 2.0 the critical value? Just as the normal curve is the distribution of sample means, it is also the distribution of the *differences* between sample means. Since we can treat the test statistic as a standard score when there is no difference between the population means, the chances of a standard score bigger than 2.0 is .025, and the chances of one smaller than -2.0 is .025. Thus, the total probability of a standard score being more than two standard deviations away from the mean is .05, the sum of the two probabilities. This means that, on the average, 5 out of 100 times the test statistic will be more than two standard deviations from the mean by chance, even though there is no difference between the population means. A test statistic greater than 2.0 is often said to be significant at the .05 level.

Correlation

When two measures go together so that it is possible to predict one measure from the other, the two measures are said to be correlated. Height and weight, for example, are correlated, since taller people also tend to be heavier, and vice versa. Similarly, good grades in the freshman year of college tend to go with good grades in the senior year of college. (Of course, there are exceptions. We all know short, heavy people; tall, light people; people who have poor grades as freshmen and good grades as seniors.)

The *correlation coefficient* is a measure of the degree to which two measures are related, or the degree to which one is predictable from the other. For example, weight is a pretty good predictor of height, while parents' IQ is not quite as good a predictor of child's IQ. In other words, weight is more predictable from height than child's IQ is from parents' IQ. When two measures are completely *un*related, they are said to be independent or uncorrelated. For example, hair color and IQ are not correlated, and so the correlation coefficient is zero. Two measures are positively related when high values of

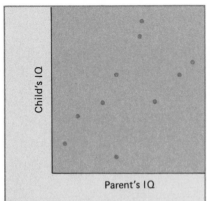
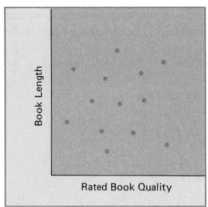
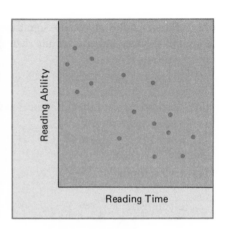

Figure 8

Scatter diagrams for hypothetical data. Each point represents the IQ scores for a given parent-child pair (left); the book length–rated quality for a given book (middle); and the reading ability–reading time scores for a given student (right).

Table 9: IQ Scores from Pairs of Parents and Children.

Observation Number	Parents' IQ	Child's IQ	Product of Deviations from Mean
1	125	110	(125–100.3)(110–100) = 247.0
2	120	105	(120–100.3)(105–100) = 98.5
3	110	95	(110–100.3)(95–100) = −48.5
4	105	125	(105–100.3)(125–100) = 117.5
5	105	120	(105–100.3)(120–100) = 94.0
6	95	105	(95–100.3)(105–100) = −26.5
7	98	75	(98–100.3)(75–100) = 57.5
8	90	95	(90–100.3)(95–100) = 51.5
9	80	90	(80–100.3)(90–100) = 203.0
10	75	80	(75–100.3)(80–100) = 506.0
Mean	100.3	100	SUM DEV = 1300
Variance	232.81	235	
Standard Deviation	15.26	15.33	

one go with high values of the other (e.g., height and weight). Two measures are negatively correlated when high values of one go with low values of the other. For example, there is a negative correlation between the number of cigarettes smoked per day and length of life. A perfect positive correlation is assigned the number $+1$, while a perfect negative correlation is given the number -1. Less than perfect correlations range between -1 and $+1$ with zero (no correlation) being in the middle.

A rough-and-ready estimate of how related two measures are can be obtained by looking at a *scatter diagram* of the two measures. Figure 8 shows three such diagrams. The points in the graph on the left were obtained by testing the IQ of a number of parents and their children, as shown in Table 9. Thus, each point represents a *pair* of measurements. To plot a point in the left graph of Figure 8 we first find the parent IQ on the horizontal axis and the child IQ on the vertical axis and then put a point where the lines intersect.

Notice that in the graph there is a tendency for high parent IQ to go with high child IQ, so the graph indicates a positive correlation. The middle graph illustrates no correlation whatsoever between the rated quality of a book and its length. Here there are just as many high values as low values; the points seem randomly scattered about the graph. The graph on the right illustrates a negative correlation between reading time and reading ability—greater reading ability goes with shorter reading time. Figure 9 gives a number of idealized scatter diagram shapes together with an appropriate numerical value of the correlation coefficient.

Product-Moment Correlation

The product-moment method is the most frequently used method for determining the correlation coefficient (r) of a sample of pairs of measurements. This method provides a way to estimate the true population correlation, which is denoted by the Greek letter ρ (rho).

The formula for computing the sample correlation coefficient is

$$r = \frac{\text{SUM DEV}}{N s_1 s_2}$$

where SUM DEV is the sum of the product of deviation scores, N is the number of pairs of measures, s_1 is the standard deviation of one set of measures, and s_2 is the standard deviation of the other set of measures. To illustrate the computation of r, we will use the data in Table 9. The far right column of this table gives the product of deviation scores for each pair of measurements. The product is obtained by taking the deviation of the parent IQ from the mean parent IQ times the deviation of the child IQ from the mean child IQ. After all these products are computed, we add them up to get *SUM DEV.* In Table 9, *SUM DEV* = 1300. Thus

$$r = \frac{\text{SUM DEV}}{N(s_1 s_2)} = \frac{1300}{10(15.26 \times 15.33)}$$

$$r = \frac{1300}{2339.36}$$

$$r = .56$$

INTERPRETATION OF THE CORRELATION COEFFICIENT. Since the correlation coefficient tells us how predictable the value of one measure is given a value of a second measure, it is often tempting to think that evidence of correlation is evidence of a cause-and-effect relationship. In the case of height and weight there is not much temptation, since it seems silly to say height "causes" weight. We know that both height and weight are the result of a complex of factors—thus they share common causes. In the case of the relation between parent and child IQ it seems more reasonable to infer a cause for the relationship—the child inherits his or her IQ from the parent. However, it is just as reasonable to interpret this correlation the same way we did in the height-weight example: Scores on IQ tests are the result of a complex of factors. Parents and children share a number of environmental as well as

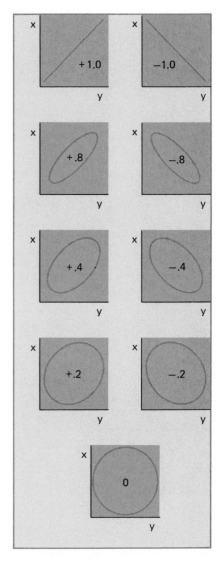

Figure 9

Idealized scatter diagrams and an appropriate correlation coefficient.

heritable factors. As another example, there is a positive correlation between years of education and later income, but this does not mean more education causes higher income. Other factors may cause both: people with money are more likely to send their children to college, more intelligent people attend college, and social pressures that select for college attendance versus nonattendance covary with the kind of job opportunities available.

Just as it can be fallacious to infer causality from correlation, it can be equally fallacious to use the absence of a relationship to argue against a correlation between two variables. As Gregory Kimble notes, Samuel Johnson seems to be responsible for the usual argument against capital punishment (that it is not a deterrent to crime). Johnson had noted that pickpockets operated even at the hangings of other pickpockets. This he took as evidence that punishment is not a deterrent. The problem with this view is that the number of pickpockets might actually be fewer than at other public ceremonies of comparable size. If this were not the case, then the argument would have some validity.

Research Methods and Experimental Design

So far we have looked at methods by which data can be analyzed. Now we consider a variety of ways in which psychological data can be collected. Usually the data collection method depends on constraints imposed by the problem being studied.

NATURALISTIC OBSERVATION. The purpose of this method is to study behavior under natural conditions, without interference from an experimenter. This technique is most popular with ethologists and social psychologists.

CASE STUDIES. Here an intensive study of a single individual is reported. Though a case study allows for an in-depth analysis, it is limited by its anecdotal character. A case study can demonstrate the existence of a phenomenon; it cannot establish general behavioral laws.

SURVEYS. This method involves either interviews or questionnaires given to a large number of individuals. The surveyor makes every effort to insure that the survey sample is representative of the population under study. Perhaps the most famous survey was conducted by Kinsey (published in 1948 and 1953), who studied the sexual attitudes and behavior of American men and women. Surveys are popular with social psychologists, sociologists, and political scientists.

THE EXPERIMENTAL METHOD. This method is usually preferred because it allows the investigator to control the conditions of the study so that factors other than the one of interest do not influence behavior. This goal is accomplished by appropriate selection of the *variable* or *factor* to be manipulated, called the *independent variable*. This variable is chosen carefully so that it varies with the phenomenon of interest. For example, to study how being reared in isolation affects socialization, an experimenter might select two degrees or *levels of the factor* or independent variable of rearing condition. In the *experimental condition* each animal is reared in complete isolation. In the *control condition,* a group of animals is reared under normal conditions, with a mother and siblings. The purpose of the control group is to provide a baseline of normal social behavior against which to compare the animals reared in isolation. Without the control group, it would be impossible to infer whether the effect of isolation made a difference in social behavior. In setting up the control condition the experimenter treats the animals in this group exactly the same as those in the experimental group except with respect to the independent variable. This way one can infer that any differences between the control and experimental groups are due to the manipulation of the independent variable.

Sometimes an experimenter may decide that more than one independent variable is of interest. In this case, the discipline of experimental design provides guidelines to the many ways in which a number of independent variables might be combined. Suppose, for example, the experimenter is interested in the effects of isolation and physical activity on the development of socialization. The independent variable of physical activity might have two levels: normal and deprived (living in a cage in which no activity is possible). This *two-factor* design could be conducted in a number of ways. First, the experimenter might divide in two the groups in the different isolation conditions, one group having normal activity, the other being deprived of activity. Table 10 (top) diagrams this scheme and shows a total of four groups of animals. Table 10 (bottom) shows an alternative. Here the control group is given normal physical activity and the experimental rearing group is deprived of physical activity. This second design is seriously flawed: there will be no way to separate the effects of the rearing variable from the deprived versus nondeprived physical activity variable. In other words, the rearing variable is *confounded* with the physical activity variable. If Group II in the second design shows less socialization than Group I, it will not be known whether the difference is due to being reared in isolation or being deprived of physical activity. In contrast, the design of Table 10 (top) will allow the experimenter to separately analyze the effects of the rearing variable and the physical activity variable.

Besides choice of independent variable to manipulate, there is also a choice of *dependent variables.* In the case of the example concerned with socialization

Table 10: Two Hypothetical Designs for a Two-Factor Experiment.

Rearing Condition		
Normal	GROUP I:	Normal physical activity
	GROUP II:	Deprived physical activity
Isolated	GROUP III:	Normal physical activity
	GROUP IV:	Deprived physical activity
Normal	GROUP I:	Normal physical activity
Isolated	GROUP II:	Deprived physical activity

of animals, it is difficult for the experimenter to decide how to measure degree of socialization. One approach might be to simply count the number of social contacts made by an animal when provided the opportunity; the number of contacts per unit of time would provide a measure of the rate of social contact. Another approach might be to classify a variety of social behaviors and then count the frequency of occurrence per unit of time in each category; this would yield a rate of social behavior for each of the categories. Here there would be a number of dependent measures, one for each category of behavior. Statisticians have developed techniques for analyzing such *multivariate situations*.

REPLICATION. Because psychologists deal with variable, uncertain data, it can happen that the results of an experiment, which seem to support a hypothesis, occur by chance alone. Sometimes there will be a faulty result because of an undetected error in experimental procedure. For these reasons it is necessary to duplicate or replicate results of experiments. Another problem is that in reporting the procedures for an experiment some details may be omitted that are thought to be unimportant but are in fact critical to the outcome of the experiment. When another investigator tries to replicate the experiment on the basis of the reported procedure and fails, it is often likely to be due to such an unreported detail. Sometimes it is possible to trace the differences in procedure—in this case the matter is resolved and may result in an important finding. For this reason it is desirable that replication be done in the laboratory of another psychologist.

Summary

1. Measurement is the assignment of numbers to observations; *statistics* involves descriptions of such sets of numbers or data and the procedures for drawing inferences from the data. These numbers are usually a *sample* drawn from a *population*.

2. *Frequency distributions* specify how many numbers are in each of the class intervals chosen for description of the data.

3. Measures of *central tendency* characterize the 'typical' number in a set of data and include the *arithmetic mean*, the *median*, and the *mode*.

4. Measures of variability characterize how 'spread out' a set of numbers is and include the *range*, the *variance*, and the *standard deviation*.

5. Measures of position in a distribution give a number that specifies a position relative to the rest of the numbers in the set. These include the *percentile rank* and the *standard score*.

6. *Probability* is the true proportion or *relative frequency* of an observation in an interval. *Random sampling* insures that every observation in the population has an equal opportunity to be selected.

7. The *normal probability curve* is often used as the theoretical distribution

of a sample and as the probability distribution of sample means.

8. The *standard error of the mean* indicates the reliability of the sample mean as an estimate of the population mean.

9. *Statistical significance* indicates that a difference between sample means is reliable. The level of significance is the probability that the difference appears reliable when in fact it is not.

10. The *correlation coefficient* expresses the degree to which one measure is predictable from the other. However, a high degree of correlation between two variables does not necessarily mean one causes the other.

11. The *experimental method* of research is useful because it provides some control over the influence of extraneous factors on the behavior of interest. In particular, it allows one to separately analyze the effects of several factors at once.

Suggested Readings

HUFF, D. *How to lie with statistics.* New York: Norton, 1954. An excellent introductory book on the use and misuses of statistics.

KIMBLE, G. A. *How to use (and misuse) statistics.* Englewood Cliffs, N.J.: Prentice-Hall, 1978. A more advanced book on this subject.

MOSTELLER, F., ROURKE, R. E. K., and THOMAS, G. B, JR. *Probability with statistical applications.* Reading, Mass.: Addison-Wesley, 1973. A more advanced introduction to probability and statistics.

MYERS, J. L. *Fundamentals of experimental design,* 3rd ed. Boston: Allyn and Bacon, 1979. An advanced book on experimental design for students who have had some elementary statistics.

WELKOWITZ, J., EWEN, R. B., and COHEN, J. *Introductory statistics for the behavioral sciences.* New York: Academic Press, 1977. A very elementary introduction to statistics.

GLOSSARY

Absolute refractory period. The period just after the firing of a neuron when the neuron cannot be excited, no matter how great the stimulus.

Absolute threshold. The minimum amount of stimulus required to produce sensation at least 50 percent of the time.

Accommodation. (1) The reshaping of the lens that allows the eye to focus on both near and distant objects; (2) according to Piaget, the child's adjustment to new objects or new stimuli by acquiring new responses.

Acetylcholine. A chemical believed to be the major neurotransmitter.

Achievement need. A learned motivation that includes the desire to excel, to complete difficult tasks, to meet high standards, and to outperform others.

Action potential. The rapid change in electrical charge that flows along a neuron and is associated with nerve and muscle activity; this potential is caused by a change in the permeability of the cell membrane.

Activation theory. A theory based on the idea that emotional expressions are not unique but exist on a scale ranging from inactivity to maximum activity.

Addiction. Physical dependency on a drug.

Additive mixture. A color mixture that is produced by focusing light of different wavelengths on the same spot.

Adolescence. In our culture, the period between childhood and adulthood during which a person learns the skills needed to survive as an adult.

Adrenal glands. The two endocrine glands situated above the kidneys; the hormones they secrete affect the body's reaction to stress (epinephrine and norepinephrine) and regulate the functions of metabolism and sexual activity (steroids).

Adrenaline. A commonly used term for **epinephrine.**

Afferent. Neuronal impulses that are directed toward the brain or spinal cord.

Affiliation motive. The need to be with others.

Aggression. Refers to the kinds of behavior that lead to the damage or destruction of something—either another organism or an inanimate object.

Agoraphobia. Fear of open places.

Alcohol. A drug that acts as a depressant on the central nervous system and is found in beer, wine, and distilled spirits.

Alcoholism. A disease in which dependence on alchohol results in impairment of some significant part of the drinker's life and progressively leads to physical damage.

Alleles. Pairs of related genes (such as those determining eye color); one allele is usually dominant and the other recessive.

All-or-none law. The rule that a neuron will always respond with its complete strength (action potential) to a stimulus or will not respond at all, regardless of the stimulus magnitude.

Alpha waves. Brain waves produced when the body is in a state of relaxation.

Altruistic behavior. Behavior that serves or assists others and does not result in any personal gain.

Amnesia. Memory loss caused by head injury or psychological trauma; can be partial or total. See also **anterograde amnesia, retrograde amnesia, organic amnesia,** and repression.

Amphetamines. Stimulants that affect the central nervous system and can cause edginess, anxiety, and increased heart rate; sometimes prescribed for mood or weight control.

Amplitude. The magnitude of a sound or light wave; the main determinants of loudness and brilliance.

Anal stage. According to Freud, the second stage of personality development, when retention and elimination of feces become the focus of a child's erotic feelings.

Analysis-by-synthesis. A theory of perception stating that a person perceives a whole pattern based on his or her analysis of a portion of the available sensory stimuli.

Androgens. Hormones that regulate the growth of secondary sex characteristics, principally in males but also in females.

Androgen-insensitivity syndrome. Occurs in genetic males whose embryonic testes secrete testosterone, but this testosterone is not used by the body cells, and the fetus develops into what appears to be a normal female.

Anesthetic. An agent that blocks the transmittal of nerve impulses so that anesthesia, a loss of sensation and often consciousness, is produced.

Anterorgrade amnesia. Following the onset of amnesia, the inability to learn or retain new information.

Anxiety. A feeling similar to fear or apprehension, but lacking a specific object of threat.

Aphasia. The impairment of the speech and language-comprehension functions because of disease or trauma to certain association areas in the brain.

Approach-approach conflict. Occurs when a person confronts simultaneously two attractive but incompatible goals.

Approach-avoidance conflict. Occurs when a person is simultaneously attracted and repelled by the same goal.

Aptitude. The capability of learning; aptitude tests are designed to measure a person's ability for future learning.

Archetypes. According to Jung, primary ideas shared by all humans; products of the collective unconscious.

Assimilation. The tendency to absorb new information by emphasizing its similarities to old information and fitting it into previously established cognitive structures.

Association. The linking of a stimulus to a response through learning or conditioning.

Association areas. Areas of the cerebral cortex believed to serve in integrating the complex flow of information and responses related to learning, memory, speech, and thinking.

Asymptote. In conditioning, the point at which change in the strength of a response has stopped and learning has levelled off.

Attachment. The behaviors of infants, such as clutching, that promote bonding between infant and parent.

Attention. The process of focusing awareness on a limited set of stimuli.

Attribution theory. A theory concerned with the rules people use in attempting to infer the causes of behavior they observe in others.

Autokinetic effect. The illusion that a stationary spot of light is moving when viewed in a darkened room.

Autonomic nervous system. That portion of the peripheral nervous system which regulates the mostly involuntary functions of internal muscles and glands.

Autonomy. A sense of independence and control over one's own life.

Aversive counterconditioning. By associating an unwanted behavior with negative sensations (pain, discomfort), this kind of therapy attempts to eradicate maladaptive behaviors such as alcoholism and drug abuse.

Avoidance-avoidance conflict. Occurs when a person is faced with opposing, equally undesirable choices from which there is no escape—a choice has to be made.

Axon. The extended portion of nerve fiber that carries impulses away from the nerve cell body to other cells and to muscles and glands.

Axonal transport. In a neuron, all replacement parts are manufactured in the cell body and carried down the axon to their destination in a slow-moving system called axonal transport.

Bait shyness. In animal studies, the tendency of the animal to avoid food it once favored if it has been made sick by it. This avoidance often occurs even if the animal does not get sick until hours after eating the food, and has no reason to suspect that it was the food that caused it to get sick.

Basilar membrane. A membrane within the cochlea containing sense receptors that, when vibrated, produce the neuronal effects of auditory stimulation.

Behavior. All responses or activity of an organism, including thinking, dreaming, and physiological functions; in psychology the emphasis is on behaviors that are observable by others, including conscious processes related verbally.

Behavior modification. Attempts to alter an individual's behavior through operant conditioning techniques.

Bel. Unit of measurement for the intensity of sound. One bel represents a tenfold (10^1) increase in energy, two bels a hundred-fold (10^2), etc. See also **decibel**.

Bel scale. Zero on the bel scale corresponds to the normal threshold energy for a 1,000 Hz tone. Named in honor of Alexander Graham Bell.

Binocular cues. Visual cues from both eyes, combined through **binocular fusion**.

Binocular disparity. The way the same object is seen from two slightly different angles due to the separation of the right and left eyes.

Binocular fusion. The combination of both left and right eye perspectives so that they are experienced as one.

Blocking. A psychological barrier to consciously acknowledging an element of reality one fears.

Blood-brain barrier. A system for protecting the brain from toxic substances: Blood vessels are less permeable in the brain than in other parts of the body. Has prevented the effective use of some new drugs, which will not pass this barrier (for example, use of GABA in the treatment of Huntington's chorea).

Brain stem. Lower part of the brain; consists of the hindbrain (medulla, pons, and cerebellum) and midbrain.

Broca's area. A zone in the left cerebral hemisphere that is believed to control speech.

Cannon-Bard theory of emotion. States that when an emotionally arousing stimulus is perceived, the thalamus sends out impulses both to the sympathetic nervous system and to the cerebral cortex—thus bodily changes and emotional feelings occur at the same time. See **James-Lange theory of emotion; jukebox theory of emotion.**

Case study. A psychological method in which an exhaustive study is made of an individual's history in an attempt to detect environmental influences on the person's behavioral development.

Cataplexy. Immobility following an experience of intense fright or shock; occurs sometimes as a sleep disorder.

Catharsis. Relief from tension associated with repression; obtained by expressing or playing out the experiences that originally led to the repression.

Central fissure. A cleft in each of the cerebral hemispheres that divides the frontal and parietal lobes.

Central nervous system. The brain and the spinal cord.

Cerebellum. The portion of the hindbrain that governs body movement and balance.

Cerebral cortex. The deeply folded gray matter that composes the surrounding layer of the cerebrum.

Cerebral hemispheres. The two large half-sections of the mammalian brain.

Cerebrum. The brain's largest division, consisting of the two cerebral hemispheres and their enveloping layer of cerebral cortex.

Chromosome. Threadlike particle in the cell nucleus that contains genes.

Chronological age. A person's age in years.

Classical conditioning. In this type of learning, a neutral stimulus (CS) is repeatedly paired with an unconditioned stimulus (US), and the subject comes to respond to the neutral stimulus even when it is presented alone.

Claustrophobia. Fear of closed spaces.

Client-centered therapy. An approach of humanistic psychology that assumes the client is the most qualified person to identify and solve his or her own problems; the therapist's role is to create a supportive environment and to facilitate the client's self-discovery.

Clinical psychologist. A psychologist with a Ph. D. who is trained in the diagnosis and treatment of emotional and behavioral problems.

Cocaine. A local anesthetic; produces a state of euphoria, talkativeness, and sometimes muscle tremors.

Cognition. A term that encompasses all the kinds of knowing an individual may have, including thoughts, knowledge, interpretations, and ideas.

Cognitive dissonance. A situation in which a person perceives fundamental discrepancies between two or more beliefs he or she holds or between beliefs and behaviors; when such cognitive dissonance occurs, it often stimulates action to bring opposing beliefs or beliefs and behaviors back into agreement.

Cognitive psychology. A branch of psychology that focuses on mental processes such as thinking, reasoning, and language.

Collective unconscious. According to Jung's theory of personality, the part of an individual's personality that is inherited and shared by all members of the species.

Color blindness. Having some degree of inability to perceive color. See **dichromats** and **monochromats**.

Color constancy. The tendency to perceive a well-known object as being a single color, even if its actual color is modified by changes in illumination.

Compensation. A defense mechanism in which a person substitutes one behavior for another area of personality or ability in which he or she feels inadequate.

Concrete operational stage. The third stage of Piaget's theory of cognitive development (from 7 to 11 years), in which a child learns to think logically and to grasp the concept of conservation.

Conditioned response. The learned response to a conditioned stimulus (CS).

Conditioned stimulus (CS). A neutral stimulus that is repeatedly paired with an unconditioned stimulus (US) in classical conditioning.

Cones. Sensory receptors on the retina, primarily responsible for the ability to see fine detail and color; function best in daylight or bright light.

Conflict. A state of disturbance or tension resulting from opposing motives, drives, needs, or goals.

Conformity. Behavior that goes along with group standards or opinions or that is based on acceptable rules of conduct.

Connotative. The meaning of a word based on its emotional content; the implied meaning of a word. See **denotative.**

Conservation. The understanding that a change in shape of a substance or object does not bring about a change in quantity; according to Piaget, this is an important concept gained during the concrete operations stage of development.

Consolidation theory. Theory suggesting that for a particular memory to be retained permanently, it must have the benefit of an undisturbed period of consolidation (continued neural activity).

Construct validity. A determination of whether or not a test actually measures what it proposes to measure.

Control group. The group of subjects in an experiment who are treated exactly the same as the experimental group(s) except that they are not exposed to the independent variable and thus serve as the basis for comparison.

Convergence. (1) In the nervous system, the process in which nerve impulses from many receptor cells are directed toward the same neuron effector cell. (2) Inward rotation of the eyes to produce fusion of the differing views from each eye.

Convergent thinking. The thought process used to solve a problem with only one logical answer. See **divergent thinking.**

Conversion reaction. A behavior disorder in which the person experiences physical symptoms, such as deafness, blindness, or paralysis, for which there is no organic cause.

Coping. A person's learned behavior for dealing with conflict or stress.

Corpus callosum. The thick band of fibrous white matter that connects the cerebral hemispheres to each other and to other parts of the nervous system.

Corpus striatum. An area of the cerebrum that receives dopamine-containing fibers from the midbrain. A deficiency of dopamine affects the cells of the corpus striatum, producing Parkinson's disease.

Correlation. A relationship or association between two variables.

Cortex. The grayish, thin, unmyelinated covering of the cerebrum; also called **gray matter.**

Covariance. A situation in which a change in one variable is associated with a change in another variable.

Creativity. The ability to make something new or to reach a unique conclusion by putting together concepts in a new way.

Critical period. A specific time in an organism's development during which a certain kind of learning occurs—for example, **imprinting** in ducks and geese, for which the critical period is from birth to 36 hours of age.

Cross-sectional studies. Studies and surveys that involve people representing a variety of age groups, backgrounds, etc.

Culture-fair test. An IQ test designed to be fair to persons of all backgrounds.

Dark adaptation. The process in which visual sensitivity increases after one enters a dark room as pigment in the rods reaches its highest concentration.

Decibel. A unit of measurement for the intensity of sound; 10 decibels equal 1 bel.

Deductive reasoning. Reasoning that begins with general concepts and proceeds to particular concepts.

Deep structure. In language, the underlying organization and intent of sentences.

Defense mechanism. A person's behavior pattern for avoiding anxiety, guilt, or other unpleasant conflcts; examples include repression, reaction formation, rationalization, projection, etc.

Delusion. A false belief that cannot be shaken by presentation of facts or reasoning; examples include delusion of grandeur, delusion of persecution, etc.

Dendrites. Fibers with many branches extending from the receptor end of a neuron.

Denotative. The surface or "dictionary" meaning of a word. See **connotative.**

Dependent variable. In an experiment, the variable that changes or is expected to change when the experimenter manipulates the independent variable.

Depressant. A drug that depresses or lowers the activity of the nervous system.

Depth perception. The ability to perceive three-dimensional space and objects.

Descriptive statistics. Methods of summarizing and describing large amounts of data; for example, the average or mean.

Determinism. The theory that all events in nature (including behaviors) are preceded by specific causes; if the relevant causes are known, an event can be predicted.

Developmental psychologist. The branch of psychology concerned with physiological and behavioral changes throughout the life span.

Deviation IQ. A person's IQ score compared to the average IQ score for the person's age group.

Dichromats. People who are color blind to either yellow-blue or red-green.

Difference threshold. The level of stimulus change necessary in order for a person to perceive a difference; also known as **just noticeable difference (JND).**

Diffusion of responsibility theory. The theory that in groups people are more likely to make extreme choices because the responsibility for the choice will be shared by many, rather than just one person.

Digit span. The number of digits a person can recall immediately after hearing them spoken.

Discrimination. (1) In conditioning, the process of being able to distinguish among stimuli, ignore irrelevant stimuli, and respond to a specific stimulus.

Disjunctive concept. A concept that contains at least one attribute from a class or list of attributes.

Displacement. In psychoanalysis, a defense mechanism in which a person directs an emotional response from its actual object to a safer one.

Dissociative reaction. A behavior disorder in which certain thoughts or experiences are separated from a person's conscious experience; examples include fugue state, amnesia, or (more extreme) multiple personalities.

Distance cues. Cues that assist a person in perceiving distance, such as relative size of similar objects.

Divergent thinking. The type of thinking associated with creativity, in which many new alternative solutions to a problem are found. See **convergent thinking.**

Dizygotic twins. Twins resulting from the fertilization of two separate eggs at the same time; also called fraternal twins. See **monozygotic twins.**

Dominant gene. The member of the gene pair (allele) that takes precedence and determines the particular bodily characteristic.

Dorsal. Referring to the back.

Double blind. Studies or experiments in which *neither* the experimenter *nor* the subject knows which condition or group is the control and which condition or group is the experimental.

Down's syndrome (mongolism). Mental

retardation resulting from extra, 47th chromosome.

Dream. Vivid imagery occurring during sleep.

Drive. The state of arousal or unlearned motivation that occurs when a need is not met.

Drive reduction. The theory that motivated behavior is the response to a drive, and that responses that satisfy drives are reinforced by the subsequent drive reduction.

Drug abuse. The misuse of a drug to the degree that it produces physical or psychological impairment and possibly, but not necessarily, **drug dependence**.

Drug dependence. A physiological and/or psychological need for a drug accompanied by increased tolerance of the drug and withdrawal symptoms if the drug is removed.

Eardrum. The thin, flexible membrane separating the middle ear from the outer ear.

Ectomorph. In Sheldon's constitutional theory, a person with a thin, fragile build and a corresponding introverted, highly sensitive personality.

Effectance motivation. The overall motivation to explore, understand, and manipulate one's environment.

Efferent. Refers to neurons leaving the central nervous system; motor neurons.

Ego. In Freudian terms, the part of the personality that distinguishes between self and the environment and that mediates the demands of the id and the superego.

Eidetic imagery. The ability to retain a mental image of something one has seen for a long period of time; often referred to as **photographic memory**.

Electroencephalogram (EEG). The record of the electrical activity of the brain.

Electroshock therapy. A controversial therapy in which an electric shock is transmitted to the brain to induce convulsions and unconsciousness. Used in cases of severe and prolonged depression.

Elevation. A depth perception cue operating on the principle that the higher an object appears in the visual plane, the farther away it appears.

Emotion. Internal state usually produced by an external stimulus—can result in many different sorts of behavior.

Empiricism. The philosophical idea that all knowledge is based on experience; emphasis is placed on observation and experimentation.

Encoding. The way information is first stored or represented in a memory system.

Encounter group. A type of group therapy emphasizing a number of elements, such as interaction among group members, expression of true feelings, etc.

Endocrine gland. A ductless gland that secretes hormones directly into the bloodstream.

Endomorph. In Sheldon's constitutional theory, a person with a round, heavy build and with a corresponding lethargic, comfort-seeking personality.

Endorphins and enkephalins. Naturally produced, opiate-like substances in the body that help people cope with pain and stress.

Enkephalins. See **endorphins** and **enkephalins**.

Epinephrine. A hormone secreted by the adrenal glands; increases blood pressure and heart rate as a response to an emergency.

Equilibratory sense. The sense of balance. **Semicircular canals** and **vestibular sacs** are the sensory organs responsible for this sense.

Erogenous zones. Areas of the body associated with sexual pleasure.

Eros. According to Freud, the life instinct.

Estrogen. Any of the female hormones that stimulate the development of secondary sex characteristics.

Estrus cycle. Cyclical variations in hormonal state in females of the lower mammal species. Ovulation occurs automatically at some specific point in the cycle, and at that time the female becomes both sexually attractive and sexually receptive to the male.

Ethology. The study of animal behavior, generally in the animal's own environment.

Evaluation. A comparison of a score, object, behavior, or situation with another, and subsequent determination of its relative value.

Excitatory. The capacity of provoking a response.

Existential model. A model of personality theory focusing on the individual and the individual's freedom of choice.

Expectancy. A person's estimate or belief that a specific behavior will lead to a specific reinforcement or outcome.

Experimental group. The group in a scien-

tific observation (experiment) upon whom the dependent variable is tested.

Experimental method. A system of testing an idea or theory in a carefully controlled situation involving independent variables and a dependent variable.

Extinction. The gradual reduction of a conditioned response that occurs because of lack of reinforcement.

Extrovert. A person who is more concerned with the outside world than with self; an outgoing person.

Factor analysis. A process in which various factors representing personality characteristics are evaluated to determine the dimensions of personality.

Fear-induced aggression. Aggressive acts taken by a normally timid or nonaggressive organism to protect itself when cornered or threatened.

Fechner's law. A law concerning the relationship between a stimulus and a sensation. States that the relation between physical stimulus intensity and the strength of sensation is a logarithmic one, in which a constant ratio of stimulus intensity produces a constant difference in sensation.

Figure-ground organization. A basic tendency (which Gestalt psychologists argued is innate) to perceive things (figures) standing out against a background (ground).

Fixation. In Freudian terms, the clinging to childhood emotions or behaviors rather than progressing on to more mature behavior; brought on by frustration during some point in development.

Fixed-interval schedule. A schedule of reinforcement in which the animal or person is reinforced for a response at specific intervals of time—every 3 minutes, or a 9-to-5 working day, for example.

Fixed-ratio schedule. A schedule of reinforcement in which the animal or person is reinforced after a specific number of correct responses (factory "piecework" is an example).

Formal operations stage. According to Piaget, the stage (occurring about age 12) in which the child develops the ability to conceptualize and use abstract thought.

Fovea. A small area on the retina on which the cones are concentrated; thus, the area of greatest visual acuity.

Fraternal twins. Twins resulting from the fertilization of two separate eggs at the same time; also called dizygotic twins. Cf. identical or **monozygotic twins**.

Free association. A process in psychoanalysis in which the patient is encouraged to express whatever thoughts come to mind in a free-floating, nonstructured way.

Frequency. The number of cycles per second of a sound wave; a primary factor in pitch.

Free recall. A type of memory test in which the subject recalls items in a list in any order, rather than in the specific order in which they were presented.

Frequency theory. In hearing, the theory that pitch is determined by the rate of firing of sound receptors. The rate of pulses traveling up the auditory nerve to the brain matches that of a tone over a wide range of frequencies.

Frustration. The psychological state a person experiences when something prevents him or her from reaching a desired goal. Coleman and Hammen (1974) have identified five sources of frustration: delays, lack of resources, loss, failure, and meaninglessness.

Fugue state. Amnesia accompanied by actual physical flight—the person may wander away for several hours, or move to another area and set up a new life.

Functional fixedness. An inability to solve a problem because of a perception of only one function (use) of a particular object.

Fundamental attribution error. The tendency in people to place more value on a person's ability to control a situation than on the intensity of the situational factors themselves.

Galvanic skin response (GSR). A response indicated by electrical changes on the skin; common physiological response to fear is a rise in GSR.

Ganglia. Clusters of nerve cell bodies found outside the spinal cord and brain.

Gene. The basic unit of heredity, located on the chromosomes.

General Adaptation Syndrome. Selye's theory of the way people tend to react to stress, beginning with the alarm reaction and progressing through resistance and exhaustion.

Generalization. Responding in a similar way to a broad category of stimuli.

Generativity versus stagnation. According to Erikson, the crisis that occurs in the middle adult years, in which people need to feel that they are somehow perpetuating themselves through family, career,

etc. The alternative is a sense of meaninglessness.

Genetics. The study of heredity, or how biological traits are passed on from parents to offspring.

Genital stage. In Freudian terms, the period that begins in puberty and lasts throughout life; interest centers on sexuality and the search for intimate relationships.

Gestalt. (1) A whole form or figure; (2) a branch of psychology in which behavior is viewed as an integrated whole, greater than the sum of its parts.

Glial cells. Cells of the nervous system that: (1) are responsible for myelination of axons in the brain; (2) direct the growth of neural pathways or interconnections; and (3) play a general role in nervous system metabolism.

Gonads. Sex glands: ovaries in females produce estrogen, testes in males produce androgens.

Gray matter. See **Cortex**.

Group therapy. Psychotherapy involving a number of people working with one another and with a therapist, rather than each person seeing a therapist alone in private or individual sessions.

Habituation. In conditioning, a decrease in the strength of a response as the stimulus is repeated.

Hallucination. A perception that is not based on reality; a false mental image.

Hallucinogen. A drug, such as LSD, that causes a person to experience hallucinations.

Heredity. The passing on of traits from parents to offspring.

Hering's opponent-process theory. See **Opponent-process theory of color vision**.

Heritability ratio. The ratio depicting the extent to which a trait is inherited rather than produced by environmental causes.

Hermaphrodite. A person with both male and female sexual organs.

Hertz (Hz). A unit of sound wave frequency equal to one cycle per second.

Heterosexuality. The sexual attraction toward members of the opposite sex.

Hierarchy of needs (Maslow). Maslow's system of human needs, consisting of five categories of needs. The most basic are physiological—survival needs for air, food, water; then come safety needs, the need for love and belongingness, esteem needs, and self-actualization needs.

Holophrastic speech. A type of speech used

by infants in which one word or phrase stands for a whole idea. "Milk" in this sort of usage can stand for "I want more milk," "Mommy is pouring the milk," or "I spilled the milk."

Homeostasis. The physiological tendency to maintain an internal, bodily state of balance in terms of food, water, air, sleep, and temperature.

Homosexuality. Sexual attraction toward members of the same sex.

Hormones. Substances secreted by endocrine glands that activate and/or regulate many bodily processes.

Humanistic model. The model of personal abnormality, functioning, and therapy focusing on the worth of the individual and the particular and unique experiences of the individual.

Hypnosis. An artificially induced, sleeplike state in which the subject is extremely open to the hypnotist's suggestions.

Hypothalamus. The lower part of the thalamus in the brain; appears to have a regulatory function in motivation and emotion.

Hypothesis. An assumption that serves as a possible explanation for some response or phenomenon.

Hypothetico-deductive reasoning. A characteristic ability of formal operational thought—the ability to test systematically a set of possibilities for correctness by using logic and experimental methods.

Iconic memory. A kind of short-term memory involving visual images.

Id. In Freudian terms, the part of the personality concerned with the basic needs which place demands on the body.

Identical twins. Twins that develop from the splitting of a single fertilized egg; also called **monozygotic twins**.

Identification. (1) According to Erikson, the process in which an adolescent comes to terms with the adult sex role; (2) a defense mechanism in which an individual unconsciously takes on the characteristics of another.

Identity versus role confusion. According to Erikson, the crisis occurring in adolescence in which the individual must develop a self-concept, adult role, and adult sexuality.

Illusion. A mistaken perception or a distortion of perception.

Illumination. The amount of light falling on a surface.

Imitation. Consciously copying the behaviors of another—an important part of learning in children.

Imprinting. The behavioral responses, such as following, which are learned rapidly and very early in life, and which are not reversible. In ducks and geese the **critical period** for imprinting is from birth to about 36 hours of age.

Incubation. The period of inactivity (or what appears to be inactivity) of thought during which a solution to a problem may occur to a person.

Independent variable. The factor in an experiment that is deliberately varied by the experimenter in order to test its effects on some other factor.

Inductive reasoning. Reasoning that begins with particulars and proceeds to general ideas.

Industry versus inferiority. According to Erikson, the crisis occurring during the school-age years, in which the person must adapt to peers and to the social world outside self and family.

Informational social influence. A positive form of conformity in which social knowledge about a particular event or object provides information about how to respond to it.

Initiative versus guilt. According to Erikson, the crisis occurring around age 4-5, in which the child must work out a relationship between autonomy and aggression or dependence.

Inhibitory. The capacity to stop the firing of a neuron or to reduce or stop a response.

Innate. Unlearned; present at birth.

Insight. (1) Understanding of self and awareness of one's motivations, goals, needs; (2) in learning, a sudden solution to a problem or development of a concept based on understanding and transfer of ideas.

Insight learning. Learning based on a sudden grasp of a problem; frequently involves a novel approach to a situation or problem.

Insomnia. A common sleep disorder in which a person has trouble going to sleep initially or wakes up during the night and has trouble going back to sleep.

Instinct. An innate, unlearned behavior characteristic of a particular species.

Instrumental aggression. Aggression that occurs for another reason other than to just inflict harm; for example, a mercenary soldier's aggression occurs for money.

Intelligence quotient (IQ). The ratio of a person's mental age to his or her chronological age.

Interneurons. Neurons that connect sensory and motor neurons.

Introspection. The process of looking inward to one's feelings and attempting to report on what one observes and experiences. Wilhelm Wundt was a pioneering figure in this approach in Germany in the mid-nineteenth century.

Introvert. A person more involved with self than with the outer world.

IQ. See **Intelligence quotient**.

Iris. The colored portion of the eye; the pigments in the iris determine whether the eye is blue, brown, green, etc.

James-Lange theory. A theory of emotion which states that emotions result from the messages we receive about the way the body is responding. For example, in the case of fear, the James-Lange theory would say that the physiological responses come first, and, reacting to them, we feel afraid.

Just noticeable difference (JND). A difference in a stimulus that is noticed 50 percent of the time. Also called **difference threshold**.

Kinesthetic sense. The sense of movement of the body (and its parts—muscles, tendons, and joints) and body position.

Korsakoff's syndrome. A disorder of memory and orientation resulting from alcoholism.

Language acquisition device (LAD). The innate mechanism (posited by Noam Chomsky) that enables children to learn language and language rules as part of their development.

Latency. According to Freud, the period between the phallic stage and the onset of puberty, in which there is very little interest in sex.

Latent learning. Learning that occurs but is not necessarily manifested in behavior or performance.

Lateral hypothalamus. The portion of the hypothalamus that appears to stimulate eating.

Leadership. The qualities that enable a person to guide and control others or to exercise power over others.

Learned helplessness. Seligman's idea that an organism may learn to be helpless as a result of the repeated demonstration that its responses have no effect on its surroundings.

Learning. A relatively permanent change in behavior as a result of experience or practice.

Learning set. The learning of a particular method or approach that can be applied to the solving of a number of similar problems.

Left hemisphere. In most persons, the dominant hemisphere of the cerebrum, which controls motor activity and speech.

Lens. The transparent part of the eye that focuses light onto the retina.

Libido. Freud's term for instinctive sexual energy that controls our personality.

Light adaptation. The adjustment of the rods and cones in the eye to changes in illumination.

Limbic system. Interrelated structures in the brain that appear to play a role in emotions.

Linear perspective. A depth perception cue based on the apparent converging of two parallel lines at the horizon.

Linguistic relativity. The theory that certain concepts or ways of thinking about things are dependent on the language a person speaks.

Literacy. The ability to read and write.

Longitudinal studies. Studies involving a single group of persons over time (for example, Terman's study of high-IQ children, which has followed them through life for over 50 years). See **cross-sectional studies**.

Long-term memory. The relatively permanent storage of information—storage that continues even when the information is not being used.

Manic-depression. A behavioral disorder characterized by feelings of extreme sadness and lethargy alternating with feelings of ecstasy and frantic activity.

Marijuana. A mild hallucinogen with varying effects on its many users, ranging from mood exaggeration to distorted time sense.

Masochism. Behavior in which a person derives satisfaction from experiencing pain.

Maternal aggression. Aggressive acts by the mother to protect her young.

Maturation. Growth and development

processes attributed to heredity rather than environment.

Mean length of utterance (MLU). A measurement of sentence length used in language studies of children.

Mechanism. A belief that all events in nature (including behaviors) are determined by mechanical causes and that by understanding chemical and physical causes, we can understand the resulting events.

Medulla. Swelling of the brain stem just above the spinal cord; controls important involuntary functions such as breathing, heart beat, and digestion.

Memory. The ability to retain learned information.

Memory span. The number of items that can be recalled after a single presentation.

Menopause. In adult women, the stopping of menstruation and the loss of the ability to reproduce, occurring in the 40s-50s.

Menstrual cycle. The regular cycle of discharge of blood and uterine materials in human females.

Mental age. A measure of a person's intelligence based on the abilities a person is expected to have at that particular age.

Mental retardation. Below-normal intelligence, usually an IQ below 68.

Mesomorph. According to Sheldon's constitutional theory, a person with a muscular, well-developed build and a corresponding outgoing, risk-taking, athletic personality.

Meta-needs. According to Maslow, the "higher" needs, such as beauty, truth, and justice.

Method of loci. A memory-improving technique in which one associates items to be recalled with specific places or locations, such as the various rooms of one's house.

Midbrain. The region of the brain containing the reticular activating system.

Middle ear. The portion of the ear lying between the eardrum and the cochlea.

Mnemonics. Techniques used to improve one's memory.

Modeling. A form of behavior training in which a subject learns to make a response by watching others make a response to a particular stimulus.

Mongolism. See **Down's syndrome.**

Monochromats. People who are missing both color systems and see the world only in shades of gray.

Monocular cues. Visual cues from one eye only.

Monozygotic twins. Twins that develop from the splitting of a single fertilized egg; also called **identical twins.**

Morpheme. The smallest linguistic unit that has meaning.

Motor area. The area of the brain responsible for integrating the responses of the motor neurons, thereby affecting muscular activity.

Motor homunculus. A graphic depiction of a map of the motor cortex, in which each part of the body is shown larger or smaller according to how much motor cortex is devoted to it (see Figure 2-13).

Myelin. The fatty white covering on some axons.

Narcotics. Opium and its derivatives, such as heroin and morphine; drugs with pain-killing powers that produce high drug dependence.

Need. A biological or psychological requirement; a state of deprivation that motivates a person to take action toward a goal.

Negative afterimage. An afterimage that occurs when a person who has been looking at a stimulus looks away; the negative afterimage is perceived in complementary colors to the original stimulus.

Negative reinforcer. An event (such as electric shock) that, if stopped when a response is made, increases the likelihood that the response will be repeated.

Neo-Freudian. A school of psychological thought based on a modification of Freud's theories; includes such theorists as Jung and Adler.

Neuron. The basic unit of the nervous system; consists of a cell body, nucleus, axon, and dendrites.

Neurosis. A broad pattern of psychological disorders characterized by anxiety, fear, and self-defeating behaviors.

Neurotransmitter. One of several chemical substances that play a role at the synapse in transmitting messages from neuron to neuron.

Nodes. Transfer of ions in neurons can only take place at breaks in the myelin sheath, called nodes, that occur every 1 or 2 millimeters along the axon.

Norepinephrine. A hormone secreted by the adrenal glands; promotes the release of sugar into the blood and also acts as a neurotransmitter; also called noradrenaline.

Normal distribution curve. A diagram of scores in which 68 percent of the scores occur between one standard deviation below the mean and one standard deviation above the mean.

NREM sleep. Sleep during which the physiological processes slow down; consists of four stages of sleep through which the person moves in a regular cycle during the night. For the most part, dreaming does not occur in NREM sleep. See **REM sleep.**

Obedient aggression. Aggression that occurs as a response to a command from an authority figure.

Obesity. In humans, defined as being more than 15 percent over the "ideal" weight, given the person's height and overall body build.

Object permanence. The knowledge that an object that is hidden from view does not cease to exist.

Obsessive-compulsive behavior. A behavior pattern in which a person feels compelled to repeat unwanted thoughts or actions over and over again.

Oedipus complex. In Freudian terms, a boy's intimate attachment to the mother and jealousy of the father, occurring during the phallic stage.

Operant conditioning. A type of learning in which specific voluntary behaviors are reinforced.

Opponent-process theory of color vision. One of two leading theories of color vision. States that there are three separate color systems: red-green, blue-yellow, and black-white. The effect of the two components in each system is opposite, so that each system's signal to the brain indicates how much of each component is in the stimulus.

Opponent-process theory of emotion. Theory that the stimulus that causes an emotion also causes another emotional reaction that is opposite to it (for example, fear and relief). Has been used to explain such human behavior as thrill-seeking, masochism, and addiction.

Optic chiasm. The point at which the optic nerves cross to go to opposite sides of the brain.

Oral stage. In Freudian terms, the time in which a child's sexual energy is focused on the mouth (from birth to the age of 2).

Organic amnesia. Amnesia caused by physiological problems such as stroke or disease or by injury.

Orgasm. The third phase of sexual intercourse characterized by ejaculation in the man and vaginal discharge in the woman.

Otoliths. Small calcium deposits in the inner ear which appear to have a function in maintaining equilibrium.

Oval window. The membrane across the opening between the inner ear and the middle ear.

Overextension. In language development, overgeneralization of meaning of words; for example, a child's mistaken notion that all four-legged creatures are dogs.

Paranoid schizophrenia. A severe psychological disorder in which delusions of persecution play a major role.

Parasympathetic system. The branch of the autonomic nervous system that maintains the routine "vegetative" functions such as digestion; tends to conserve energy.

Peer group. A group of social and chronological equals.

Perception. Interpretation of the information provided by one's sensory receptors.

Perceptual constancy. The ability, in perception, to draw similar inferences about the world from different patterns of sensory activity (for example, a person seen from many different angles is still perceived as the same person).

Performance. The act of displaying what has been learned or using learned skills.

Peripheral nervous system. The entire nervous system outside the brain and spinal cord.

Personality. An individual's complex and unique patterns of behavior, motives, emotions.

Phallic stage. According to Freud, the developmental stage in which sex urges are directed toward a parent and in which one establishes a sexual identity (usually between ages 3-5).

Phenylketonuria (PKU). An inherited form of mental retardation caused by a disorder of amino acid metabolism.

Phi illusion. An illusion of movement caused by flashing lights off and on one after another, which makes them appear to move.

Phobic neurosis. Persistent fear of a particular object or situation, a fear far out of proportion to the actual threat present. Examples are claustrophobia (fear of closed places), acrophobia (fear of heights), and numerous animal phobias (such as fear of dogs, mice, snakes, etc.).

Phonemes. The smallest units of speech sounds.

Phrase structure rules. Rules that govern the organization of the various parts of a sentence (such as nouns, verbs, adjectives, etc.).

Pitch. The sensory experience of highness or lowness of a tone corresponding to the frequency of sound waves.

Pituitary gland. An endocrine gland located at the base of the brain and attached to the hypothalamus. Secretes tropic hormones, which affect other endocrine glands, causing them to secrete other hormones. Often called the "master gland" for this reason.

Placebo. A substance (usually sugar) in pill form that is used as a control in drug experiments.

Plateau. According to Masters and Johnson, the second phase of sexual intercourse.

Pleasure principle. According to Freud, the id's process of seeking gratification and pleasure.

Polygenic trait. A trait determined by more than one gene pair.

Polygraph. A lie-detector device that records physiological changes (such as GSR) believed to be associated with lying.

Pons. Part of the hindbrain, just above the spinal cord; acts mainly as a way station for neural pathways going to other brain areas.

Positive reinforcer. An event (such as food) that, if presented just after a response, increases the likelihood that the response will be repeated.

Posthypnotic suggestion. A suggestion to take some action, change a way of thinking, or alter behavior. Given to a subject under hypnosis, but is supposed to take effect after the subject has come out of hypnosis.

Predatory aggression. Aggression that occurs for hunting purposes—the action of a predator on its prey.

Predictive validity. The determination of whether or not a test can accurately predict future results.

Preoperational stage. According to Piaget, the second stage of development (ages 2-7) in which the child learns language and how to use symbols.

Preparation stage. The first stage of creative thinking, in which an individual absorbs the data and ideas needed to solve a problem creatively.

Preparedness. Seligman's theory that organisms are more prepared to associate a given emotional response with one stimulus than another. Has been used to explain why it is more common to develop phobias connected to some stimuli than others.

Primacy effect. Under certain conditions the first few items in a series will be remembered better than those that follow.

Primary drive. A universal drive based on biological needs.

Primary process thinking. According to Freud, the idea that the id seeks immediate gratification through **wish fulfillment.**

Proactive interference. Forgetting or memory difficulties caused by interference of information learned earlier.

Progestin. A female sex hormone that has a role in pregnancy and nursing.

Projection. A defense mechanism in which a person transfers his or her unacceptable thoughts to another person.

Projective tests. Personality tests in which a person's responses to ambiguous stimuli are analyzed.

Propositional thinking. The ability to reason about verbal statements and abstractions.

Psychiatry. The branch of medicine that deals with mental illness.

Psychoactive drugs. Drugs that affect mental processes.

Psychoanalytic model. Model of personality, abnormal functioning, and therapy based on Freud's theories of personality and unconscious mental processes.

Psychodrama. A role-playing technique frequently used as part of group therapy.

Psychogenic. Something that can be attributed to psychological causes rather than organic.

Psychosensory. Pertaining to sensations not originating in the sense organs.

Psychosexual development. Freud's theory of development, in which a person's sexual energies are focused on various parts of the body during different stages of development.

Psychosis. The main difference between neurosis and psychosis is a more extreme or bizarre manifestation of behavior, thought, and emotion with psychosis. In psychosis the individual loses contact with reality in some central way, and from this loss a variety of severe problem areas emerges.

Psychosocial stages. Erikson's stages of development in which a person passes through particular social crises at particular ages.

Puberty. The time of development characterized by the appearance of secondary sex characteristics.

Punishment. An aversive (negative) stimulus that follows a response for the purpose of eliminating that response.

Rationalization. A defense mechanism in which one deceives oneself by giving an acceptable reason to explain an unacceptable outcome or motive.

Reaction formation. A defense mechanism in which the way one feels about something is the opposite of the way one behaves toward it.

Reality principle. According to Freud, the process of the ego mediating the demands of the id and the environment.

Reasoning. The process of logical thinking or problem solving.

Recall. A measure of retention of memory in which a person reproduces or reconstructs the information learned earlier with a minimum of cues.

Recall cues. Cues that assist in retaining and retrieving items of memory.

Recency effect. Under certain conditions, the last few items in a series will be remembered better than the ones preceding them.

Receptor organ. A body part that receives sensory information; eyes, for example, are the receptor organs of vision.

Recessive gene. The member of the gene pair (allele) that carries a weaker characteristic and can determine a trait only when paired with another recessive gene.

Recoding. Coding information that was encoded previously in either the same form or a related form.

Recognition. A measurement of memory retention in which a person is asked to pick out from a list items that were learned previously.

Reconstruction or **redintegration.** In memory, the process of reconstructing or filling in missing information through educated guessing based on information still available and stimulus redundancy.

Redundancy. The idea that activity in one's various sensory receptors is highly correlated, or redundant. For example, when people speak to you, the movement of their lips is highly correlated with the sound of their voice.

Reduplicated babbling. A type of baby talk used by infants beginning at around the sixth month, when for the first time they can control consonants. Consists of a front consonant and a vowel, such as "da da da da da."

Relative refractory period. The period just after the firing of a neuron when the neuron can be excited if the stimulus is great enough.

Regression. A defense mechanism in which a person returns to a childlike state rather than confront a situation as an adult.

Rehearsal. Repeating learned information in one's mind to enhance memory.

Relearning. Even when people seem to have forgotten something they learned earlier, relearning will take place faster than the original learning did. This reduction in time to learn, or **savings**, means they actually did retain some of the information from the first time.

Reliability. The determination of whether a test will produce consistent results on repeated measurements of the same group.

REM Sleep. One of the two types of sleep, characterized by rapid movements of the eyes; is the period during which dreaming is most likely to occur.

Reorganization. A process in which a person orders items of memory and classifies the items into categories to assist in memory.

Repression. A defense mechanism in which a person avoids unpleasant thoughts by blocking these thoughts out of consciousness.

Resistance. In psychoanalysis, the unwillingness or the inability to discuss certain painful areas of experience, by preventing these experiences and ideas from becoming part of consciousness.

Resistance to extinction. A measure of the ability of a conditioned response to resist being eliminated by later trials with no reinforcement.

Resolution. According to Masters and Johnson, the final phase of sexual intercourse; resolution follows orgasm and is the phase in which physiological activity returns to normal.

Response. The measurable behavior of an organism, particularly as a reaction to a stimulus.

Retention. The storage of memory; the maintaining of information.

Reticular activating system (RAS). A network of fibers beginning in the spinal cord and extending up through the midbrain into the higher centers; has a role in attention and arousal.

Reticular formation. See **reticular activating system (RAS)**.

Retina. The inside layer of the eye containing the light-sensitive **rods** and **cones**.

Retrieval. The process of obtaining memory from storage in the brain.

Retroactive interference. The interference of new information with the memory of something learned earlier.

Retrograde amnesia. The inability to remember events and information that were immediately followed by a brain injury or shock.

Right hemisphere. The non-dominant cerebral hemisphere believed to have a role in spatial perception and artistic interpretation.

Rods. Light-sensitive receptor cells found on the retina; sensitive to black and white stimuli but not color.

Rorschach test. A projective personality test in which a person is asked to describe what images come to mind upon viewing various inkblots.

Savings. In relearning, the amount of time saved when seemingly forgotten information or responses are learned again.

Schedule of reinforcement. The schedule determining whether a correct response will be reinforced according to a time interval or after a number of correct responses; the schedule can be fixed or variable.

Schema. The framework a person uses to organize higher-order mental processes.

Schizophrenia. A severe behavioral disorder characterized by retreat from reality, inappropriate emotional responses, distortion, delusions, and jumbled thought processes; the individual generally loses the ability to function in the real world.

Secondary process thinking. In Freudian terms, the ego's attempts to meet the id's demands through rational thought and conscious activity directed toward satisfying specific drives.

Secondary reinforcement. Reinforcement that does not directly satisfy a need but that is directly associated with a primary reinforcing stimulus and comes to take on reward value.

Secondary sex characteristics. Characteristics such as breasts, pubic hair, and voice quality that are unique to each sex but do not play a vital role in reproduction.

Sedatives. Drugs that help people sleep and are highly addictive; barbiturates are a class of sedatives.

Selective breeding. The breeding of laboratory animals for heredity studies; the animals are selected for specific characteristics and are bred with animals with similar characteristics in an attempt to get as pure a genetic strain as possible.

Self. The individual as a unique and conscious being.

Self-actualization. According to Maslow, the ultimate goal of the hierarchy of needs; self-actualized persons have reached the fullest potential of their talents and their feelings of love and self-esteem.

Self-esteem. A person's own judgment of his or her worth and abilities.

Self-perception theory. A theory proposing that people make judgments about themselves based on qualities they view in other people.

Self-report. An observation and rating of an individual made by that individual.

Self theories. Humanistic theories of personality that suggest that people are basically good and have an inborn desire to change for the better and reach self-fulfillment.

Semantic differential. A technique for rating the **connotative meanings** of words along three dimensions: evaluation (good-bad), activity (active-passive), and potency (strong-weak).

Semantic memory. A long-term type of memory for general knowledge.

Semicircular canals. Three canals in the inner ear that function in the perception of body movement.

Sensation. Psychological experience of a stimulus.

Sensitive period. In humans, a period during which circumstances are most favorable for establishment of various traits and abilities (for example, people seem able to learn languages best before the onset of puberty).

Sensorimotor stage. According to Piaget, the first stage of cognitive development (age 1 to 2 years), in which children know the world mostly through their physical and perceptual interaction with it. Acquisition of the concept of **object permanence** or **constancy** occurs during this stage.

Sensory areas. Areas of the cerebral cortex that function in the integration of sensory information from each of the various receptor organs.

Sensory memory. A type of short-term memory in which information lasts for only a few seconds.

Separation anxiety. An infant's fear of losing the mother whenever she disappears for even a few moments.

Serial position effect. In memory, the tendency for the position of items in a list to affect one's ability to recall them—the first and last items are more easily remembered than the rest of the list.

Sex-linked trait. An inherited trait linked specifically to a sex chromosome.

Sex-related aggression. Aggression directly related to sexual potency or sexual rivalry.

Shape constancy. The knowledge that even when an object is viewed from a different angle its shape remains the same.

Shaping. An operant conditioning technique in which behavior is gradually molded into a desired form through reinforcement of successive approximations of the target behavior.

Short-term memory. A type of memory with a somewhat limited capacity; items must be consciously rehearsed to be retained in short-term memory.

Signal detection theory. A theory that attempts to explain perceptual judgments through analysis of a person's sensitivity to sensory stimuli in addition to the criteria a person uses in decision-making.

Sine wave. A simple pressure wave representing one frequency of sound at one amplitude.

Size constancy. A tendency to perceive familiar objects as being the same size even when they cast a different-sized image on the retina because of one's distance from them.

Skinner box. A box devised by Skinner. It contains a lever that an animal can depress to obtain a food reinforcer during operant conditioning trials.

Skin senses. The senses of pressure, pain, hot, and cold.

Socialization. The process in which a person acquires attitudes and values of his or her culture.

Social facilitation theory. A theory suggesting that a person's behavior becomes stronger or more extreme when others are present.

Social learning theory. The theory that people learn through imitation, based on observing others. They can learn without having made the response before themselves, and without being reinforced for making it or seeing others reinforced for making it.

Social psychology. A branch of psychology that studies individual's interactions in groups.

Somatic nervous system. The part of the peripheral nervous system that controls voluntary muscles.

Somatosensory areas. Areas of the cerebral cortex that function in the integration of stimuli from the kinesthetic sense and the skin senses.

Somatosensory homunculus. Graphic depiction of a map of the somatosensory cortex, in which each part of the body is shown larger or smaller, according to how much somatosensory cortex is devoted to it (see Figure 2-13).

Source trait. According to Cattell, one of the basic traits that accounts for a person's behavior and personality.

Split-brain subjects. Subjects who, for medical or for experimental reasons, have had their cerebral hemispheres surgically separated at the corpus callosum and who subsequently have unconnected cerebral hemispheres which appear to function somewhat separately and differently.

Spontaneous recovery. The return of a conditioned response after extinction and without further training trials.

Standardization. Establishing norms through the administration of a test or survey to a group of people representing various backgrounds.

Stanford-Binet test. A modified version of Binet's original IQ test used to assess intelligence in children.

State-dependent learning. The idea that learning a response in a particular environment or emotional or physical state will enable the person to remember the response much better in a similar environment or state.

Statistics. Mathematical relationships and representations that describe events and other data.

Stereopsis. Visual perception of three-dimensional objects.

Stereotype. A preconceived notion of how a group or individual will behave.

Stimulants. Drugs, such as amphetamines,

which accelerate brain and nervous system functioning.

Stimulus-response psychology. The branch of psychology concerned with behavior as seen through stimulus-response relationships and principles of conditioning and simple learning.

Storage. In memory, the persistence of information over time.

Stress. A state of physiological and psychological tension resulting from threatening demands from the environment.

Stroboscopic motion. See **phi illusion**.

Structured interview. A personality assessment technique in which an interviewer asks a subject specific questions designed to provide information about particular areas of personality.

Subtractive mixture. A form of color mixing in which pigments absorb part of the spectrum and the result is color produced by a subtraction of a particular color wavelength.

Successive approximations. In shaping, the process of gradually coming closer and closer to the desired behavior.

Superego. In Freudian terms, the part of the personality that is the conscience and reflects parental and societal codes of morality.

Suppression. A defense mechanism in which incompatible ideas are unconsciously inhibited or eliminated.

Surface structure. In language studies, the parts of a sentence and their superficial relationship.

Surface trait. According to Cattell, one of the behavioral patterns through which source traits are expressed.

Survey method. A method of research involving the collection of data from a large number of individuals.

Sympathetic nervous system. The branch of the autonomic nervous system that functions as the arousal center during emergencies or stress situations.

Synapse. The point between neurons where nerve impulses are transmitted from neuron to neuron.

Syntax. Grammar; rules for organizing and combining words into phrases and sentences.

Systematic desensitization. A type of behavior therapy in which the person substitutes for an undesired response a response that is incompatible or competitive with it.

Tachistoscope. An instrument used in learning and memory studies; exposes cards or slides for very brief periods of time.

Telegraphic speech. Speech that is not complete sentences but can convey meaning. Called telegraphic because the child uses only those words needed to convey meanings, much as we do in writing a telegram.

Territorial aggression. Aggression that occurs to protect a territory or to let an enemy know which boundaries cannot be crossed.

Testosterone. One of the androgens (male hormones) that promotes secondary sex characteristics.

Texture gradient. Distance cues based on the fact that objects lose definition and detail the farther away they are.

Thalamus. A fairly large, bilobed area at the midline of the brain; an important way station for receiving information from the various sense organs and relaying it to the cortex.

Thanatos. According to Freud, the death instinct.

Thematic Apperception Test (TAT). A projective personality test in which a person is shown pictures and must make up stories about what he or she feels is going on in the various pictures, what has led up to this situation, and what will come of it afterwards.

Theory. A formalized statement of particular principles and concepts designed to explain a particular phenomenon or behavior.

Therapy. A set of procedures by which one person uses language to change the life of another (Davidson and Neale, 1978).

Threshold. The minimum stimulus necessary to elicit a response.

Timbre. The characteristic quality of a tone produced by the combination of overtones heard along with the pure tone.

Tip-of-the-tongue (TOT) phenomenon. When trying to remember something, the feeling that one is just about to recall it, that it is on the "tip of the tongue."

Token economy. A behavior therapy technique in which tokens are given to reward desired behavior; the tokens can later be exchanged for a specific reward that the patient desires, such as specific privileges, candy, etc.

Tolerance. The phenomenon in which increasing amounts of a drug are required to produce the same physiological effects.

Traces. A hypothetical impression of memory in the nervous system.

Trait. A characteristic of a person's behavior/personality that can be measured.

Tranquilizer. Drugs that depress nervous system activity and reduce anxiety and tension.

Transference. In psychoanalysis, the process in which a patient transfers love or other emotional attachment from another person in his or her past to the therapist.

Transformational rules. Rules that specify how one sentence can be "transformed" into another; grammatical rules that spell out the relationships between sentences.

Unconditioned response. A response that is elicited by a stimulus without learning (for example, a dog's salivation when presented with meat powder is an unconditioned response).

Unconditioned stimulus. A stimulus that provokes a response in the absence of learning or conditioning.

Unconscious. That part of one's mental life of which one is unaware and over which one has little or no control.

Unstructured interview. A personality assessment technique in which the interviewer and the subject engage in free-flowing conversation.

Validity. The extent to which a test measures what it purports to measure.

Variable-interval schedule. A reinforcement schedule in which the first correct response after varying periods of time is reinforced.

Variable-ratio schedule. A schedule of reinforcement in which a varying number of correct responses must occur before reinforcement occurs (an example would be gambling).

Variance. The mean-square deviation; in other words, the square of the standard deviation.

Ventral. Pertaining to the abdominal side of the body.

Ventromedial hypothalamus. A portion of the hypothalamus believed to have a role in satiation or inhibition of eating.

Verification. The part of the creative process in which the person evaluates the results of the illumination (sudden solution to the problem).

Vestibular sacs. Bony structures of the head that send sensory stimuli about head movement to the brain.

Visual acuity. Ability to discern fine details in spatial patterns of light.

Visual angle. Used to describe the size of an object in terms of how much of your visual field it occupies—that is, how many degrees of the imaginary surrounding circle's circumference it would cover. This is referred to as an object's size in degrees of visual angle.

Visual cliff. The depth illusion device developed to determine whether human infants and other species have depth perception.

Visual field. The three-dimensional space in which all objects are perceived by the eyes at a given time.

Volley principle. The hearing theory based on the idea that hearing receptors respond one after another in rapid succession, signaling pitch of higher frequencies in this way.

WAIS. The Wechsler Adult Intelligence Scale, a battery of tests devised to assess intelligence and cognitive abilities in adults.

Weber's law. The principle that the just noticeable difference (JND) of a stimulus is a constant fraction of the intensity of the original stimulus.

Wernicke's area. An association area located on the lower side of the lateral fissure, near the auditory cortex. Damage to this area produces Wernicke's aphasia, in which people speak fluently, but with bizarre and nonsensical content.

White matter. The fibrous portion of the nervous system; the white appearance is due to the myelin sheath covering the axons.

Wish fulfillment. According to Freud, the id's need for immediate gratification causes it to create an image of the desired object. It is up to the ego to actually acquire the object.

Withdrawal. A pattern of severe physiological symptoms, such as nausea, intense sweating, muscular cramps, possible coma, as well as psychological effects that occur when one stops taking a drug one has become dependent on (addicted to).

X Chromosome. The female sex chromosome.

Y Chromosome. The male sex chromosome.

Young-Helmholtz theory of color vision. States that there are three types of cones, each sensitive to a different part of the visual spectrum.

REFERENCES

Abse, D. W. Hysteria. In S Arieti (Ed.), *American Handbook of Psychiatry* (Vol. 1). New York: Basic Books, 1959, 272–292.

Adolph, E. F. Measurements of water drinking in dogs. *American Journal of Physiology*, 1939, *125*, 75–86.

Agras, W. S. Chapin, H. N., and **Oliveau, D. C.** The natural history of phobia: Course and prognosis. *Archives of General Psychiatry*, *26*, 1972, 315–317.

Aiken, L. R. *Psychological testing and assessment* (3rd ed.). Boston: Allyn and Bacon, 1979.

Ainsworth, M. D. S. *Infancy in Uganda: Infant care and the growth of love*. Baltimore, Md.: Johns Hopkins Press, 1967.

Ainsworth, M. D. S., and **Bell, S. M.** Some contemporary patterns of mother–infant interaction in the feeding situation. In A. Ambrose (Ed.), *Stimulation in early infancy*. New York: Academic Press, 1969.

Ainsworth, M. D. S., Bell, S. M., and **Stayton, D. J.** Individual differences in strange-situation behavior of one-year-olds. In H. R. Schaffer (Ed.), *The origins of human social relations*. New York: Academic Press, 1971.

Ainsworth, M. D. S., Blehar, M. C., Waters, E., and **Wall, S.** *Patterns of attachment: A psychological study of the strange situation*. Hillsdale, N.J.: Erlbaum, 1978.

Ainsworth, M. D. S., and **Wittig, B. A.** Attachment and exploratory behavior of one-year-olds in a strange situation. In B. M. Foss (Ed.) *Determinants of infant behavior* (Vol. 4). London: Methuen, 1969.

Akhter, S., Wig, N. N., Varma, V. K., Pershad, D. and **Verma, S.K.** A phenomenological analysis of symptoms in obsessive-compulsive neurosis. *British Journal of Psychiatry*, 1975, *127*, 342–348.

Alexander, F. *Psychosomatic medicine*. New York: Norton, 1950.

Allport, G. W. *Personality: A psychological interpretation*. New York: Holt, Rinehart and Winston, 1937.

Allport, G. W. *Pattern and growth in personality*. New York: Holt, Rinehart and Winston, 1961.

Altman, I. *The environment and social behavior*. Monterey, Calif.: Brooks-Cole, 1975.

American Psychiatric Association. *Diagnostic and statistical manual of mental disorders* (3rd ed.). Washington, D.C.: American Psychiatric Association, 1979.

Amoore, J. E. Current status of stereochemical theories of odor. *Annals of the New York Academy of Sciences*, 1964, *116*, 457–476.

Amsel, A. Partial reinforcement effects on vigor and persistence: Advances in frustration theory derived from a variety of within-subjects experiments. In K. W. Spence and J. T. Spence (Eds.), *The psychology of learning and motivation*, Vol. 1. New York: Academic Press, 1967.

Andersson, B. Polydipsia caused by intrahypothalamic injections of hypertonic NaCl solutions. *Experientia*, 1952, *8*, 157.

Andersson, B., and **McCann, S. M.** A further study of polydipsia evoked by hypothalamic stimulation in the goat. *Acta Physiologica Scandinavica*, 1955, *33*, 333–346.

Annett, M. The distribution of manual asymmetry. *British Journal of Psychology*, 1972, *63*, 343–358.

Appleyard, D. *Planning a pluralistic city.* Cambridge, Mass.: M.I.T. Press, 1976.

Arenberg, D., and **Robertson-Tchabo, E. A.** Learning and aging. In J. E. Birren and K. W. Schaie (Eds.), *Handbook of the psychology of aging*. New York: Van Nostrand Reinhold, 1977.

Arkin, A. M., Antrobus, J. S., and **Ellman, S.J.** (Eds.) *The mind in sleep: Psychology and psychophysiology*. New York: Halsted, 1978.

Arkin, A. M., Hastey, J. M., and **Reiser, M. F.** Post-hypnotically simulated sleep talking. *Journal of Nervous and Mental Disease*, 1966, *142*, 293–309.

Armen, J. C. *Gazelle-boy: A child brought up by gazelles in the Sahara Desert*. London: Bodley Head, 1974.

Aronson, E., and **Linder, D.** Gain and loss of esteem as determinants of interpersonal attractiveness. *Journal of Experimental Social Psychology*, 1965, *1*, 156–171.

Aronson, E., and **Mills, J.** The effect of severity of initiation on liking for a group. *Journal of Abnormal and Social Psychology*, 1959, *59*, 177–181.

Asch, S. E. Forming impressions of personality. *Journal of Abnormal and Social Psychology*, 1946, *41*, 258–290.

Asch, S. E. Effects of group pressure upon the modification and distortion of judgment. In H. Guetzkow (Ed.), *Groups, leadership and men*. Pittsburgh: Carnegie, 1951.

Asch, S. Opinions and social pressure. *Scientific American*, 1955, *11*, 32.

Asch, S. E. Studies of independence and conformity: I. A minority of one against a unanimous majority. *Psychological Monographs*, 1956, *70*, 9 (Whole No. 416).

Atchley, R. C. Dimensions of widowhood in later life. *The Gerontologist*, 1975, *15*, 176–178.

Atchley, R. C. Selected social and psychological differences between men and women in later life. *Journal of Gerontology*, 1976, *31*(2), 204–211.

Atkinson, J. (Ed.), *Motives in fantasy, action and society*. Princeton, N.J.: Van Nostrand, 1958.

Atkinson, J. W., and **Feather, N. T.** (Eds.). *A theory of achievement motivation*. New York: Wiley, 1966.

Atkinson, J. W. and **Litwin, G. H.** Achievement motive and test anxiety conceived as motive to approach success and motive to avoid failure. *Journal of Abnormal and Social Psychology*, 1960, *60*, 27–36.

Atkinson, R. C., and **Raugh, M. R.** An application of the mnemonic keyword method to the acquisition of a Russian vocabulary. *Journal of Experimental Psychology: Human Learning and Memory*, 1975, *104*, 126–133.

Atkinson, R. C., and **Shiffrin, R. M.** The control of short-term memory. *Scientific American*, 1971, *224*, 82–90.

Atkinson, R. C. and **Shiffrin, R. M.** Human memory: a proposed system and its control processes. In G. H. Bower (Ed.), *Human memory: Basic processes*. New York: Academic Press, 1977.

Austin, V. D., Ruble, D. N., and **Trabasso, T.** Recall and order effects as factors in children's moral judgments. *Child Development*, 1977, *48*, 470–474.

Averill, J. R. Autonomic response patterns during sadness and mirth. *Psychophysiology*, 1969, *5*, 399–414.

Ax, A. F. The physiological differentiation between fear and anger in humans. *Psychosomatic Medicine*, 1953, *14*, 433–442.

Ayllon, T. Intensive treatment of psychotic behavior by stimulus satiation and food reinforcement. *Behavior Research and Therapy*. 1963, *1*, 53–61.

Ayllon, T., and **Azrin, N. H.** *The token economy: A motivational system for therapy and rehabilitation*. New York: Appleton-Century-Crofts, 1968.

Ayres, C. E. Instinct and capacity: I. The instinct of belief-in-instincts. *Journal of Philosophy*, 1921, *18*, 561–566.

Azrin, N. H., Hutchinson, R. R., and **Hake, D. F.** Extinction induced aggression. *American Psychologist*, 1965, *20*, 583.

Bandura, A. A. Social learning interpretation of psychological dysfunctions. In P. London and D. Rosenhan (Eds.), *Foundations of abnormal psychology*. New York: Holt, Rinehart and Winston, 1968.

Bandura, A. Social-learning theory of identificatory processes. In D. A. Goslin (Ed.), *Handbook of socialization theory and research*. Chicago: Rand McNally, 1969.

Bandura, A. *Aggression: A social learning analysis*. Englewood Cliffs, N.J.: Prentice-Hall, 1973.

Bandura, A. Self-efficacy: Toward a unifying theory of behavior change. *Psychological Review*, 1977, *84*, 191–215.

Bandura, A. The self system in reciprocal determinism. *American Psychologist*, 1978, *33*, 344–358.

Bandura, A., Adams, N. E., and **Beyer, J.** Cognitive processes mediating behavioral

Bandura, A., and **Rosenthal, T. L.** Vicarious change. *Journal of Personality and Social Psychology,* 1976, *35,* 125–139.
classical conditioning as a function of arousal level. *Journal of Personality and Social Psychology,* 1966, *3,* 54–62.

Bandura, A., Ross, D., and **Ross, S. A.** Transmission of aggression through imitation of aggressive models. *Journal of Abnormal and Social Psychology,* 1961, *63,* 575–582.

Bandura, R., Ross, D., and **Ross, S.** Imitation of film-mediated aggressive models. *Journal of Abnormal and Social Psychology,* 1963, *66,* 3–11. (a)

Bandura, A., Ross, D., and **Ross, S. A.** Vicarious reinforcement and imitative learning. *Journal of Abnormal and Social Psychology,* 1963, *67,* 601–607. (b)

Bandura, A., and **Walters, R. H.** *Social learning and personality development.* New York: Holt, Rinehart and Winston, 1963.

Barash, D. P. *Sociobiology and behavior.* New York: Elsevier, 1977.

Barber, T. X., Spanos, H. P., and **Chaves, J. F.** *Hypnosis, imagination, and human potentialities.* New York: Pergamon, 1974.

Barber, T. X., and **Wilson, S. C.** Hypnosis, suggestions, and altered states of consciousness: Experimental evaluation of the new cognitive behavioral theory and the traditional trance-state theory of hypnosis. In Edmonston, W. D., Jr. (Ed.), *Conceptual and investigative approaches to hypnosis and hypnotic phenomena. Annals of The New York Academy of Sciences* (Vol. 296), 1977, 34–47.

Bard, P. On emotional expression after decortication with some remarks on certain theoretical views. Parts I and II. *Psychological Review,* 1934, *41,* 309–329 and 424–449.

Barker, R. G. Ecology and motivation. In M. R. Jones (Ed.), *Nebraska Symposium on Motivation* (Vol. 8) Lincoln: University of Nebraska Press, 1960.

Barker, R. G. *Ecological psychology: Concepts and methods for studying the environment of human behavior.* Stanford, Cal.: Stanford University Press, 1968.

Barmark, S. M. and **Caunitz, S. C. B.** Transcendental meditation and heterohypnosis as altered states of consciousness. *International Journal of Clinical and Experimental Hypnosis,* 1979, *27,* 227–239.

Baron, R. A., and **Bell, P. A.** Aggression and heat: Mediating effects of prior provocation and exposure to an aggressive model. *Journal of Personality and Social Psychology,* 1975, *31,* 825–832.

Barron, F., Jarvik, M. and **Bunnell, S., Jr.** The hallucinogenic drugs. *Scientific American,* April 1964.

Bart, P. Depression in middle-aged women. In V. Gormick and B. K. Moran (Eds.), *Woman in sexist society: Studies in power and powerlessness.* New York: Basic Books, 1971.

Bavelas, A., Hastorf, A. H., Gross, A. E., and **Kite, W. R.** Experiments on the alteration of group structure. *Journal of Experimental Social Psychology,* 1965, *1,* 55–71.

Baum, A., and **Valins, S.** *Architecture and social behavior: Psychological studies in social density.* Hillsdale, N.J.: Erlbaum, 1977.

Baum, M. Extinction of avoidance responding through response prevention (flooding). *Psychological Bulletin,* 1970, *74,* 276–284.

Bayley, N., and **Oden, M. H.** The maintenance of intellectual ability in gifted adults. *Journal of Gerontology,* 1955, *10,* 91–107.

Beach, F. A. Coital behavior in dogs: III. Effects of early isolation on mating in males. *Behavior,* 1968, *30,* 218–238.

Beck, A. T. Reliability of psychiatric diagnosis: A critique of systematic studies. *American Journal of Psychiatry,* 1962, *119,* 210–216.

Beck, A. T. *Depression: Clinical, experimental and theoretical aspects.* New York: Harper & Row, 1967.

Beck, A. T. *Depression: Causes and treatment.* Philadelphia: University of Pennsylvania Press, 1972.

Beck, A. T. *Diagnosis and management of depression.* Philadelphia: University of Pennsylvania Press, 1973.

Beck, A. T. *Cognitive therapy and emotional disorders.* New York: International Universities Press, 1975.

Beck, A. T., Weissman, A., Lester, D., and **Trexler, L.** The measurement of pessimism. *Journal of Consulting and Clinical Psychology,* 1974, *42,* 861–865.

Beck, R. C. *Motivation: Theories and principles.* Englewood Cliffs, N.J.: Prentice-Hall, 1978.

Becker, J. *Affective disorders.* Morristown, N.J.: General Learning Press, 1977.

Békésy, G. von. Taste theories and the chemical stimulation of single papillae. *Journal of Applied Physiology,* 1966, *21,* 1–9.

Békésy, G. von. Human skin perception of traveling waves similar to those on the cochlea. *Journal of the Acoustical Society of America,* 1955, *27,* 830–841.

Belkin, G. S. *Contemporary psychotherapies.* Chicago: Rand McNally, 1980.

Bellack, A. S., and **Hersen, M.** *Introduction to clinical psychology.* New York: Oxford University Press, 1980.

Belsky, J., and **Steinberg, L. D.** The effects of day care: A critical review. *Child Development,* 1978, *49,* 929–949.

Bem, D. An experimental analysis of self-persuasion. *Journal of Experimental Social Psychology,* 1965, *1,* 199–218.

Benedict, R. *Patterns of culture.* Boston: Houghton Mifflin, 1934.

Benson, H. *The relaxation response.* New York: Morrow, 1975.

Berger, R. J. Experimental modification of dream content by meaningful verbal stimuli. *British Journal of Psychiatry,* 1963, *109,* 722–740.

Berger, R. J., and **Oswald, I.** Eye movements during active and passive dreams. *Science,* 1962, *137,* 601.

Bergin, A. E. The evaluation of therapeutic outcomes. In A. E. Bergin and S. L. Garfield (Eds.), *Handbook of psychotherapy and behavior change: An empirical analysis.* New York: Wiley, 1971.

Berglas, S., and **Jones, E. E.** Drug choice as a self-handicapping strategy in response to noncontingent success. *Journal of Personality and Social Psychology,* 1978, *36,* 405–417.

Berko, J. The child's learning of English morphology. *Word,* 1958, *14,* 150–177.

Berkowitz, L. *Aggression.* New York: McGraw-Hill, 1962.

Berkowitz, L. The frustration-aggression hypothesis revisited. In L. Berkowitz (Ed.), *Roots of aggression.* New York: Atherton, 1969.

Berkowitz, L., and **LePage, A.** Weapons as aggression-eliciting stimuli. *Journal of Personality and Social Psychology,* 1967, *1,* 202–207.

Berkun, M. M., Kessen, M. L., and **Miller, N. E.** Hunger-reducing effects of food by stomach fistula versus food by mouth measured by a consummatory response. *Journal of Comparative and Physiological Psychology,* 1952, *45,* 550–554.

Berlyne, D. E. Conflict and information-theory variables as determinants of human perceptual curiosity. *Journal of Experimental Psychology,* 1957, *53,* 399–404.

Bermant, G. Response latencies of female rats during sexual intercourse. *Science,* 1961, *133,* 1771–1773.

Bermant, G., and **Davidson, J. M.** *Biological bases of sexual behavior.* New York: Harper & Row, 1974.

Berndt, T. J. Developmental changes in conformity to peers and parents. *Developmental Psychology,* 1979, *15,* 608–616.

Bernheim, H. A., Vaughn, L. K., and **Kluger, M. J.** Induction of fever in lizards in response to gram-negative bacteria. *Federation Proceedings,* 1974, *33,* 457.

Berry, J. W., and **Dason, P.** (Eds.). *Culture and cognition: Readings in cross-cultural psychology.* London: Methuen, 1974.

Bettelheim, B. *The empty fortress.* New York: Free Press, 1967.

Bexton, W. H., Herm, W., and **Scott, T. H.** Effects of decreased variation in the sensory environment. *Canadian Journal of Psychology,* 1954, *8,* 70–76.

Bixenstine, V. E., Decorte, M. S., and **Bixenstine, B. A.** Conformity to peer-sponsored misconduct at four grade levels. *Developmental Psychology,* 1976, *12,* 226–236.

Blizard, D. A., Cowing, P., and **Miller, N. E.** Visceral responses to opposite types of autogenic training imagery. *Biological Psychology,* 1975, *3,* 49–55.

Block, N. J., and **Dworkin, G.** *The IQ controversy*. New York: Pantheon, 1976.

Bloom, L. *Language development: Form and function in emerging grammars*. Cambridge, Mass.: MIT Press, 1970.

Bloom, L. *One word at a time*. The Hague: Mouton, 1973.

Boggiano, A. K. and **Ruhle, D. N.** Competence and the overjustification effect: A developmental study. *Journal of Personality and Social Psychology,* 1979, *37,* 1462–1468.

Bolton, R. Aggression and hypoglycemia among the Qolla: A study in psychobiological anthropology. In K. E. Moyer (Ed.), *Physiology of aggression and implications for control*. New York: Raven Press, 1976.

Bootzin, R.R. *Behavior modification and therapy*. Boston: Winthrop, 1975.

Boring, E. G. *A history of experimental psychology* (2nd ed.). New York: Appleton-Century-Crofts, 1950.

Botwinick, J. *Aging and behavior*. New York: Springer, 1973.

Botwinick, J. Intellectual abilities. In J. E. Birren and K. W. Schaie (Eds.), *Handbook of the psychology of aging*. New York: Van Nostrand Reinhold, 1977.

Bourne, L. E., Jr., Ekstrand, B. R., and **Dominowski, R. L.** *The psychology of thinking*. Englewood Cliffs, N.J.: Prentice-Hall, 1971.

Bower, T. G. R. Slant perception and shape constancy in infants. *Science,* 1966, *151,* 832–834.

Bowers, K. S. The effects of demands for honesty on reports of visual and auditory hallucinations. *International Journal of Clinical and Experimental Hypnosis,* 1967, *15,* 31–36.

Bowers, K. S. Hypnosis: An informational approach. In Edmonston, W. E., Jr. (Ed.), *Conceptual and investigative approaches to hypnosis and hypnotic phenomena. Annals of the New York Academy of Sciences* (Vol. 296), 1977, 222–237.

Bowlby, J. *Attachment and loss (Vol. 1): Attachment*. New York: Basic Books, 1969.

Bowlby, J. *Attachment and loss (Vol. 2): Separation*. New York: Basic Books, 1973.

Bowman, C. H., and **Fishbein, M.** Understanding public reaction to energy proposals: An application of the Fishbein model. *Journal of Applied Social Psychology,* 1978, *8,* 319–340.

Bransford, J. D., and **Franks, J. J.** The abstraction of linguistic ideas. *Cognitive Psychology,* 1971, *2,* 331–350.

Bransford, J. D., and **Johnson, M. K.** Contextual prerequisites for understanding: Some investigations of comprehension and recall. *Journal of Verbal Learning and Verbal Behavior* 1972, *11,* 717–726.

Bregman, E. An attempt to modify the emotional attitude of infants by the conditioned response technique. *Journal of Genetic Psychology,* 1934, *45,* 169–198.

Brennan, W. M., Ames, E. W., and **Moore, R. W.** Age differences in infants' attention to patterns of different complexities. *Science,* 166, *151,*354–356.

Bridges, K. M. B. Emotional development in early infancy. *Child Development,* 1932, *3,* 324–354.

Brigham, C. C. *A study of American intelligence*. Princeton, N.J.: Princeton University Press, 1923.

Brigham, C. C. Intelligence tests of immigrant groups. *Psychological Review,* 1930, *37,* 158–165.

Brim, O. J. Theories of the male mid-life crisis. *The Counseling Psychologist,* 1976, *6*(1), 2–9.

Broadbent, D. E. *Perception and communication*. London: Pergamon, 1958.

Broadbent, D. E. The hidden preattentive processes. *American Psychologist,* 1977, *32,* 109–118.

Brock, T. C. Communicator-recipient similarity and decision change. *Journal of Personality and Social Psychology,* 1965, *1,* 650–654.

Brody, E. B., and **Brody, N.** *Intelligence: Nature, determinants, and consequences*. New York: Academic Press, 1976.

Broman, S. H., Nichols, P. L., and **Kennedy, W. A.** *Preschool IQ: Prenatal and early developmental correlates*. Hillsdale, N.J.: Erlbaum, 1975.

Bronzaft, A. L., Dobrow, S. B., and **O'Hanlon, T. J.** Spatial orientation in a subway system. *Environment and Behavior.* 1976, *8,* 575–594.

Brooks, L. R. Spatial and verbal components of the act of recall. *Canadian Journal of Psychology* 1968, *22,* 349–368.

Brown, A. L. The development of memory: Knowing, knowing about knowing, and knowing how to know. In H. W. Reese (Ed.), *Advances in child development and behavior* (Vol. 10). New York: Academic Press, 1975.

Brown, J. K. Adolescent initiation rites among preliterate people. In R. E. Grinder (Ed.), *Studies in adolescence* (2nd ed.). New York: Macmillan, 1969.

Brown, J. S. Gradients of approach and avoidance responses and their relation to level of motivation. *Journal of Comparative and Physiological Psychology,* 1948, *41,* 450–465.

Brown, J. S. *The motivation of behavior*. New York: McGraw-Hill, 1961.

Brown, R. *Social psychology*. New York: Free Press, 1965.

Brown, R. *A first language: The early stages*. Cambridge, Mass: Harvard University Press, 1973.

Brown, R. In memorial tribute to Eric Lenneberg. *Cognition,* 1976, *4,* 125–153.

Bruner, J. S. From communication to language. *Cognition,* 1974/75, *3,* 255–287.

Bruner, J. S. and **Goodnow, J. J.** *A study of thinking*. New York: Wiley, 1956.

Burks, B. S. The relative influence of nature and nurture upon mental development: A comparative study of foster parent–foster child resemblance and true parent–true child resemblance. *Yearbook of the National Society for the Study of Education,* 1928, *27,* (Part 1) 219–316.

Burnstein, E., Vinokur, A., and **Trope, Y.** Interpersonal comparison versus persuasive argumentation: A more direct test of alternative explanations for group-induced shifts in individual choice. *Journal of Experimental Social Psychology,* 1973, *9,* 236–245.

Burr, W. Satisfaction with various aspects of marriage over the life cycle: A random middle class sample. *Journal of Marriage and the Family,* 1970, *32*(1), 29–37.

Burt, C. L. Ability and income. *British Journal of Educational Psychology,* 1943, *13,* 83–98.

Burt, C. The genetic determination of differences in intelligence: A study of monozygotic twins reared together and apart. *British Journal of Psychology,* 1966, *57,* 137–153.

Buswell, G. T. Fundamental reading habits: A study of their development. *Supplementary Educational Monographs, No. 21,* 1922.

Butler, R. A. Discrimination learning by rhesus monkeys to visual-exploration motivation. *Journal of Comparative and Physiological Psychology,* 1957, *50,* 239–241.

Butler, R. N. The life review: An interpretation of reminiscence in old age. In B. L. Neugarten (Ed.), *Middle age and aging*. Chicago: University of Chicago Press, 1968.

Byrne, B. Item concreteness vs. spatial organization as predictors of visual imagery. *Memory and Cognition,* 1974, *2,* 53–59.

Bryne, D., and **Clore, G. L.** A reinforcement model of evaluative responses. *Personality: An International Journal,* 1970, *1,* 103–128.

Byrne, D., and **Rhamey, R.** Magnitude of positive and negative reinforcements as a determinant of attraction. *Journal of Personality and Social Psychology,* 1965, *2,* 884–889.

Cagas, C. R. and **Riley, H. D., Jr.** Age of menarche in girls in a west-south-central community. *American Journal of Diseases of Children,* 1970, *120,* 303–308.

Caldwell, M. D. Communication and sex effects in a five-person Prisoner's Dilemma game. *Journal of Personality and Social Psychology,* 1976, *33,* 273–280.

Campbell, A. The American way of mating. Marriage si, children only maybe. *Psychology Today,* 1975, *8,* 37–41.

Campbell, D. T. Social attitudes and other acquired behavioral dispositions. In S. Koch (Ed.), *Psychology: A study of a science (Vol. 6)*. New York: McGraw-Hill, 1963.

Campos, J. J., Langer, A., and **Krowitz, A.** Cardiac responses on the visual cliff in prelocomotor human infants. *Science,* 1970, *170,* 196–197.

Cannon, W. B. The James-Lange theory of emotions: A critical examination and an alternative theory. *American Journal of Psychology,* 1927, *39,* 106–124.

Cannon, W. B. *The wisdom of the body.* New York: Norton, 1939.

Cantor, J. R., Zillmann, D., and **Bryant, J.** Enhancement of experienced sexual arousal in response to erotic stimuli through misattribution of unrelated residual excitation. *Journal of Personality and Social Psychology,* 1975, *32,* 69–75.

Cantor, N., and **Mischel, W.** Traits as prototypes: Effects on recognition memory. *Journal of Personality and Social Psychology,* 1977, *35,* 38–48.

Carlisle, H. J. The effects of preoptic and anterior hypothalamic lesions on behavioral thermoregulation in the cold. *Journal of Comparative and Physiological Psychology,* 1969, *69,* 391–402.

Carlson, N. R. *Physiology of behavior.* Boston: Allyn & Bacon, 1977.

Carmichael, L. The development of behavior in vertebrates experimentally removed from the influence of external stimulation. *Psychological Review,* 1926, *33,* 51–58.

Carmichael, L. A further study of the development of vertebrates experimentally removed from the influence of external stimulation. *Psychological Review,* 1927, *34,* 34–47.

Carmichael, L., Hogan, H. P., and **Walter, A. A.** An experimental study of the effect of language on the representation of visually perceived form. *Journal of Experimental Psychology,* 1932, *15,* 73–86.

Caron, A. H., Caron, R. F., and **Carlson, V. R.** Infant perception of the invariant shape of objects varying in slant. *Child Development,* 1979, *50,* 716–721.

Carpenter, G. Mother's face and the newborn. In R. Lewin (Ed.), *Child alive.* London: Temple Smith, 1975.

Cartwright, D. Risk taking by individuals and groups: An assessment of research involving choice dilemmas. *Journal of Personality and Social Psychology,* 1971, *20,* 361–378.

Cartwright, D. S. *Theories and models of personality.* Dubuque, Iowa: William C. Brown, 1979.

Cartwright, R. D. Happy ending for our dreams. *Psychology Today,* December 1978.

Carver, C. S. Facilitation of physical aggression through objective self-awareness. *Journal of Experimental Social Psychology,* 1974, *10,* 365–370.

Carver, R. P. Speed readers don't read: They skim. *Psychology Today,* August 1972.

Casey, J. F., Bennett, I. F. and **Lindley, C. J.** Drug therapy in schizophrenia: A controlled study of the relative effectiveness of chlorpromazine, promazine, phenobarbital and placebo. *Archives of General Psychiatry,* 1960, *2,* 210–220.

Cattell, R. B. *The culture free intelligence test.* Champaign, Ill.: Institute for Personality and Ability Testing, 1949.

Cattell, R. B. *Personality: A systematic, theoretical, and factual study.* New York: McGraw-Hill, 1950.

Chapman, L. J. Illusory correlation in observational report. *Journal of Verbal Learning and Verbal Behavior,* 1967, *6,* 151–155.

Chomsky, N. *Syntactic structures.* The Hague: Mouton, 1957.

Chomsky, N. *Language and mind.* New York: Harcourt, Brace and World, 1968.

Chomsky, N. *Reflections on language.* New York: Pantheon, 1975.

Christensen, C. V., and **Gagnon, J. H.** Sexual behavior in a group of older women. *Journal of Gerontology,* 1965, *20,* 351–356.

Clark, H. H., and **Clark, E. V.** *Psychology and language: An introduction to psycholinguistics.* New York: Harcourt Brace Jovanovich, 1977.

Clark, M. S., and **Mills, J.** Interpersonal attraction in exchange and communal relationships. *Journal of Personality and Social Psychology,* 1979, *37,* 12–24.

Clarke-Stewart, K. A. Interactions between mothers and their young children: Characteristics and consequences. *Monographs of the Society for Research in Child Development,* 1973, *38* (6–7, Serial No. 153).

Clarke-Stewart, K. A. And daddy makes three. *Child Development,* 1978, *49,* 466–478.

Clarke-Stewart, K. A., and **Apfel, N.** Evaluating parental effects on child development. In L. S. Shulman (Ed.), *Review of research in education* (Vol. 6). Itasca, Ill.: Peacock, 1979.

Cleary, T. A., Humphreys, L. G., Kendrick, S. A., and **Wesman, A.** Educational uses of tests with disadvantaged students. *American Psychologist,* 1975, *30,* 15–41.

Cleckley, H. *The mask of sanity* (4th ed.). St. Louis, Mo.: Mosby, 1964.

Cohen, A. R. An experiment on small rewards for discrepant compliance and attitude change. In J. W. Brehm and A. R. Cohen, *Explorations in cognitive dissonance.* New York: Wiley, 1962.

Cohen, L. B., DeLoache, J. S., and **Strauss, M. S.** Infant perceptual development. In J. D. Osofsky (Ed.), *Handbook of infant development.* New York: Wiley, 1979.

Cohen, L. B., and **Gelber, E. R.** Infant visual memory. In L. B. Cohen and P. Salapatek (Eds.), *Infant perception: From sensation to cognition (Vol. 1): Basic visual processes.* New York: Academic Press, 1975.

Cole, J. O. Phenothiazine treatment in acute schizophrenia: Effectiveness. *Archives of General Psychiatry,* 1964, *10,* 246–261.

Cole, M., Gay, J., Glick, J. A., and **Sharp, D. W.** The cultural context of learning and thinking. New York: Basic Books, 1971.

Coleman, J. C., Butcher, J. N., and **Carson,** **R. C.** *Abnormal psychology and modern life* (6th ed.). Glenview, Ill.: Scott, Foresman, 1980.

Collier, G., and **Hirsch, E.** Reinforcing properties of spontaneous activity in the rat. *Journal of comparative and physiological psychology,* 1971, *7,* 155–160.

Collier, G., Hirsch, E., and **Hamlin, P.** The ecological determinants of reinforcement. *Physiology and Behavior,* 1972, *9,* 705–716.

Collier, G., Hirsch, E., and **Kanarek, R.** The operant revisited. In W. K. Honig and J. E. R. Staddor (Eds.), *Handbook of operant behavior,* Englewood Cliffs, N.J.: Prentice-Hall, 1977.

Coltheart, M., and **Glick, M. J.** Visual imagery: A case study. *Quarterly Journal of Experimental Psychology,* 1974, *26,* 438–453.

Conger, J. J. *Adolescence and youth: Psychological development in a changing world* (2nd ed.). New York: Harper & Row, 1977.

Cooper, J. Personal responsibility and dissonance; the role of foreseen consequences. *Journal of Personality and Social Psychology,* 1971, *18,* 354–363.

Cooper, J. Dissonance and psychotherapy: The use of effort justification in the reduction of snake phobia. Unpublished manuscript. Princeton University, 1979.

Cooper, L. A., and **Shepard, R.N.** Chronometric studies of the notation of mental images. In W. G. Chase (Ed.), *Visual information processing.* New York: Academic Press, 1973.

Coppen, A. The biochemistry of affective disorders. *British Journal of Psychiatry,* 1967, *113,* 1237–1264.

Corballis, M. C. Laterality and myth. *American Psychologist,* 1980, *35,* 284–295.

Corballis, M. C. and **Beale, I. L.** *The psychology of left and right.* Hillsdale, N.J.: Erlbaum, 1976.

Coren, S., and **Porac, C.** Fifty centuries of right-handedness: The historical record. *Science,* 1977, *198,* 631–632.

Corsini, R. J. A medley of current personality theories. In R. J. Corsini (Ed.), *Current personality theories.* Itasca, Ill.: Peacock, 1977.

Costanzo, P. R., and **Shaw, M. E.** Conformity as a function of age level. *Child Development,* 1966, *37,* 967–975.

Cottrell, N. B. Social facilitation. In C. G. McClintock (Ed.), *Experimental social psychology.* New York: Holt, Rinehart and Winston, 1972.

Cowan, W. M. The development of the brain. *Scientific American,* 1979, *241*(3), 112–133.

Cox, T. *Stress.* Baltimore, Md.: University Park Press, 1978.

Craik, F. I. M., and **Lockhart, R. S.** Levels of processing: A framework for memory research. *Journal of Verbal Learning and Verbal Behavior,* 1972, *11,* 671–684.

Craik, F. I. M., and **Tulving, E.** Depth of processing and the retention of words in episodic memory. *Journal of Experimental Psychology*, 1975, *104*, 268–294.

Cumming, E. Further thoughts on the theory of disengagement. *International Social Science Journal*, 1963, *15*, 377–393.

Cumming, E., and **Henry, W. E.** *Growing old.* New York: Basic Books, 1961.

Current Population Reports, Population Characteristics Series p–20, No. 287: Marital status and living arrangements: March 1975. Washington, D.C.: U.S. Government Printing Office, 1975.

Current Population Reports, Population Characteristics Series p–20, No. 338: Marital status and living arrangements: March, 1978. Washington, D.C.: U.S. Government Printing Office, 1979.

Current Population Reports, Population Characteristics Series p-20, No. 341: Fertility of American women: June 1978. Washington, D.C.: U.S. Government Printing Office, 1979.

Darley, J. M., Moriarty, T., Darley, S., and **Berscheid, E.** Increased conformity to a fellow deviant as a function of prior deviation. *Journal of Experimental Social Psychology*, 1974, *10*, 211–223.

Dart, R. A. The predatory implemental technique of *Australopithecus, American Journal of Physical Anthropology*, 1949, *7*, 1–38.

Darwin, C. *The expression of the emotions in men and animals.* London: Murray, 1872.

Darwin, C. R. *On the origin of species by means of natural selection, or the preservation of favoured races in the struggle for life.* London: Murray, 1859.

Davis, C. M. Self-selection of diet by newly weaned infants. *American Journal of Diseases of Children*, 1928, *36*, 651–679.

Davis, J. D., Gallagher, R. J. and **Ladlove, R. F.** Food intake controlled by a blood factor. *Science*, 1967, *156*, 1247–1248.

Davison, G. C., and **Neale, J. M.** Abnormal psychology: An experimental clinical approach (2nd ed.). New York: Wiley, 1978.

deCharms, R., and **Moeller, G. H.** Value expressed in children's readers: 1800–1950. *Journal of Abnormal and Social Psychology, 1962, 64*, 136–142.

DeFries, J. C., Johnson, R. C., Kuse, A. R., McClearn, G. E., Polovina, J., Vandenberg, S. G., and **Wilson, J. R.** Familial resemblance for specific cognitive abilities. *Behavior Genetics*, 1979, *9*, 23–43.

Dekker, E., and **Groen, J.** Reproducible psychogenic attacks of asthma. *Journal of Psychosomatic Research*, 1956, *1*, 58–67.

Dember, W. N. Birth order and need affiliation.

Journal of Abnormal and Social Psychology, 1964, *68*, 555–557.

Dembroski, T. M., MacDougall, J. M., Heid, J. A. and **Shields, J. M.** Effects of level of challenge on pressor and heart rate responses in type A and B subjects. *Journal of Applied Social Psychology*, 1979, *3*, 209–228.

Dement, W. C. *Some must watch while some must sleep.* San Francisco: Freeman, 1974.

Dement, W. C., and **Kleitman, M.** The relation of eye movements during sleep to dream activity: An objective method for the study of dreaming. *Journal of Experimental Psychology*, 1957, *53*, 339–346.

Deutsch, J. A. *The structural basis of behavior.* Chicago: University of Chicago Press, 1960.

Deutsch, M., and **Gerard, H. B.** A study of normative and informational social influences upon individual judgment. *Journal of Abnormal and Social Psychology*, 1955, *51*, 629–636.

Deutsch, M., and **Krauss, R. M.** The effect of threat upon interpersonal bargaining. *Journal of Abnormal and Social Psychology*, 1960, *61*, 181–189.

Deutsch, M., and **Krauss, R. M.** Studies of interpersonal bargaining. *Journal of Conflict Resolution*, 1962, *6*, 52–76.

Dion, K. K., Berscheid, E., and **Walster, E.** What is beautiful is good. *Journal of Personality and Social Psychology*, 1972, *24*, 285–290.

Ditter, J., and **Kelley, H. H.** Effects of different conditions of acceptance upon conformity to group norms. *Journal of Abnormal and Social Psychology*, 1956, *53*, 100–107.

Diven, K. Certain determinants in the conditioning of anxiety reactions. *Journal of Psychology*, 1936, *3*, 291–308.

Dohrenwend, B. S., and **Dohrenwend, B. P.** (Eds.). *Stressful life events: Their nature and effects.* New York: Wiley, 1974.

Dollard, J., and **Miller, N. E.** *Personality and psychotherapy.* New York: McGraw-Hill, 1950.

Dollard, J., Doob, L., Miller, N. E., Mower, O., and **Sears, R.** *Frustration and aggression.* New Haven, Conn.: Yale University Press, 1939.

Doob, A. N., and **Wood, L.** Catharsis and aggression: The effects of annoyance and retaliation on aggressive behavior. *Journal of Personality and Social Psychology*, 1972, *22*, 156–162.

Douvan, E. A. and **Adelson, J.** *The adolescent experience.* New York: Wiley, 1966.

Dressler, D. M. Life adjustment of retired couples. *International Journal of Aging and Human Development*, 1973, *4*(4), 335–349.

DuBois, P. M. *The hospice way of death.* New York: Human Sciences Press, 1980.

Duncker, K. On problem-solving. *Psychological Monographs*, 1945, *58*, 5 (Whole No. 270).

Duval, S., and **Wicklund, R. A.** *A theory of*

objective self-awareness. New York: Academic Press, 1972.

Eagly, A. Sex differences in influenceability. *Psychological Bulletin*, 1978, *85*, 86–116.

Ebbinghaus, H. *Memory: A contribution to experimental psychology* (H. A. Ruger and C. E. Bussenius, trans.) New York: Teachers College, 1885.

Eckerman, C. O., Whatley, J. L., and **Kutz, S. L.** Growth of social play during the second year of life. *Developmental Psychology*, 1975, *11*, 42–49.

Edmonston, W. E., Jr. (Ed.) Conceptual and investigative approaches to hypnosis and hypnotic phenomena. *Annals of The New York Academy of Sciences* (Vol. 296), 1977.

Efran, M. G. The effect of physical appearance on the judgment of guilt, interpersonal attraction, and severity of recommended punishment in a simulated jury task. *Journal of Research in Personality*, 1974, *8*, 45–54.

Egger, M. D., and **Flynn, J. P.** Effect of electrical stimulation of the amygdala on hypothalamically elicited attack behavior in cats. *J. Neurophysiol.*, 1963, *26*, 705–720.

Eimas, P., Siqueland, E. R., Jusczyk, P., and **Vigorito, J.** Speech perception in infants. *Science*, 1971, *171*, 303–306.

Eisdorfer, C. Adaptation to loss of work. In Frances M. Carp (Ed.), *Retirement.* New York: Behavioral Publications, 1972.

Ekman, P., and **Friesen, W. V.** The repertoire of nonverbal behavior—categories, origins, usage and coding. *Semiotica*, 1968, *1*, 49–98.

Ekman, P., and **Friesen, W. V.** Constants across cultures in the face and emotion. *Journal of Personality and Social Psychology*, 1971, *17*, 124–129.

Elkind, D. Children's discovery of the conservation of mass, weight, and volume: Piaget's replication study II. *Journal of Genetic Psychology*, 1961, *98*, 219–227.

Ellis, A. *Reason and emotion in psychotherapy.* New York: Lyle Stuart, 1962.

Ellis, A. *Humanistic psychotherapy: the rational-emotive approach.* New York: Julian, 1973.

Ellis, A. *A new quide to rational living.* Englewood Cliffs; N.J.: Prentice-Hall, 1975.

English, H. B. Three cases of the "conditioned fear response." *Journal of Abnormal and Social Psychology*, 1929, *34*, 221–225.

Epstein, A. N., Fitzsimons, J. T., and **Rolls, B. J.** Drinking induced by injections of angiotensin into the brain of the rat. *Journal of Physiology* (London), 1970, *210*, 457–474.

Epstein, S. M. Toward a unified theory of anxiety. In B. A. Maher (Ed.), *Progress in experimental personality research* (Vol. 4). New York: Academic Press, 1967.

Erikson, E. H. Identity and the life cycle. *Psychological Issues*, 1959, *1*.

Erikson, E. H. *Childhood & society.* New York: Norton, 1963.

Erlenmeyer-Kimling, L., and **Jarvik, L. F.** Genetics and intelligence: A review. *Science,* 1963, *142,* 1477–1479.

Estes, W. K. A study of motivating conditions necessary for secondary reinforcement. *Journal of Experimental Psychology,* 1949, *39,* 306–310.

Evans, F. J. Hypnosis and sleep: The control of altered states of awareness. In Edmonston, W. E., Jr. (Ed.), Conceptual and investigative approaches to hypnosis and hypnotic phenomena. *Annals of The New York Academy of Sciences* (Vol. 296), 1977, 162–174.

Eyferth, K. Leistungen verschiedner Gruppen von Besatzungskindern in Hamburg—Wechsler Intelligenztest für Kinder (HAWIK). *Archiv für die gesamte Psychologie,* 1961, *113,* 222–241.

Eysenk, H. J. The effects of psychotherapy: An evaluation. *Journal of Consulting Psychology* 1952, *16,* 319–324.

Eysenck, H. J. The case of Sir Cyril Burt. *Encounter,* 1977, *48,* 19–24.

Eysenck, H. J. *The structure and measurement of intelligence.* New York: Springer-Verlag, 1979.

Fadiman, J., and **Kewman, D.** (Eds.). *Exploring madness: Experience, theory, and research.* Monterey, Calif.: Brooks/Cole, 1973.

Fagan, J. F. Infants' recognition of invariant features of faces. *Child Development,* 1976, *47,* 627–638.

Fantz, R. L. Pattern vision in newborn infants. *Science,* 1963, *140,* 296–297.

Faust, M. S. Developmental maturity as a determinant in prestige of adolescent girls. *Child Development,* 1960, *31,* 173–184.

Fazio, R. H., Zanna, M. P., and **Cooper, J.** On the relationship of data to theory: A reply to Ronis and Greenwald. *Journal of Experimental Social Psychology,* 1979, in press.

Feather, N. T., and **Simon, J. G.** Reactions to male and female success and failure in sex-linked occupations: Impressions of personality, causal attributions, and perceived likelihood of different consequences. *Journal of Personality and Social Psychology,* 1975, *31,* 20–31.

Fechner, G. *Elements of psychophysics* (H. E. Adler, trans.). New York: Holt, Rinehart and Winston, 1966 (originally published in 1860).

Feldman, M. W., and **Lewontin, R. C.** The heritability hang-up. *Science,* 1975, *190,* 1163–1168.

Ferster, C. B., and **Skinner, B. F.** *Schedules of reinforcement.* New York: Appleton-Century-Crofts, 1957.

Ferster, C. B. Positive reinforcement and behavioral deficits of autistic children. *Child Development,* 1961, *32,* 437–456.

Festinger, L. A. A theory of social comparison processes. *Human Relations,* 1954, *7,* 117–140.

Festingen, L. A theory of cognitive dissonance. Evanston, Ill.: Row, Peterson, 1957.

Festinger, L., and **Carlsmith, J. M.** Cognitive consequences of forced compliance. *Journal of Abnormal and Social Psychology,* 1959, *58,* 203–210.

Fiedler, F. E. A theory of leadership effectiveness. New York: McGraw-Hill, 1967.

Fiedler, F. E. Personality, motivational systems, and behavior of high and low LPC persons. *Human Relations,* 1972, *25,* 391–412.

Fishbein, M. Attitude and the prediction of behavior. In M. Fishbein (Ed.), *Readings in attitude theory and measurement.* New York: Wiley, 1967.

Fisher, S., and **Greenberg, R. P.** *The scientific credibility of Freud's theories and therapy.* New York: Basic Books, 1977.

Flacks, R. The revolt of the advantaged. In R. Sigel (Ed.), *Learning about politics.* New York: Random House, 1970.

Flaherty, C. F., Hamilton, L. W., Gandleman, R. J., and **Spear, N. E.** *Learning and memory.* Chicago: Rand McNally, 1977.

Flavell, J. *The developmental psychology of Jean Piaget.* Princeton, N.J.: Van Nostrand, 1963.

Flavell, J. H. Metacognitive development. In J. M. Scandura and C. J. Brainerd (Eds.), *Structural/process theories of complex human behavior.* Alphen a.d. Rijn, The Netherlands: Sijthoff & Noordhoff, 1978.

Flavell, J. H. and **Wellman, H. M.** Metamemory. In R. V. Kail, Jr., and J. W. Hagen (Eds.), *Perspectives on the development of memory and cognition.* Hillsdale, N.J.: Erlbaum, 1977.

Ford, C. W., and **Beach, F. A.** *Patterns of sexual behavior.* New York: Harper & Row, 1951.

Foss, D. J., and **Hakes, D. T.** *Psycholinguistics: An introduction to the psychology of language.* Englewood Cliffs, N.J.: Prentice-Hall, 1978.

Foulkes, D., Larson, J. D., Swanson, E. M., and **Rardin, M.** Two studies of childhood dreaming. *American Journal of Orthopsychiatry,* 1969, *39,* 627–643.

Fraser, M. *Children in conflict.* Garden City, N.Y.: Doubleday, 1973.

Freedman, D. X. Pharmacotherapy. In F. J. Braceland et al. (Eds.), *Year book of psychiatry and applied mental health.* Chicago: Year Book Medical Publishers, 1977.

French, E. G., and **Thomas, F. H.** The relation of achievement to problem-solving effectiveness. *Journal of Abnormal and Social Psychology,* 1958, *56,* 45–48.

Freud, S. *New introductory lectures on psychoanalysis* (W. J. H. Sproutt, trans.). New York: Norton, 1933.

Freud, S. The interpretation of dreams. In J. Strachey (Ed. and trans.), *The standard edition of the complete psychological works.* London: Hogarth, 1950. (Originally published in 1900.)

Freud, S. The analysis of a phobia in a five-year-old boy. In *Collected Papers,* Vol. 3. London: Hogarth, 1950. (Originally published in 1909.)

Freud, S. Beyond the pleasure principle. In J. Strachey (Ed. and trans.), *The standard edition of the complete psychological works.* London: Hogarth, 1955. (Originally published in 1920.)

Freud, S. *A general introduction to psychoanalysis.* New York: Washington Square Press, 1960. (Originally published by Boni & Liveright, 1924.)

Freud, S. Civilization and its discontents. In J. Strachey (Ed. and trans.), *The standard edition of the complete psychological works* (Vol. 21). London: Hogarth, 1961. (Originally published in 1930.)

Friedhoff, A. J., and **Van Winkle, E.** Isolation and characterization of a compund from the urine of schizophrenics. *Nature,* 1962, *194,* 897–898.

Friedman, M. *Pathogenesis of coronary artery disease.* New York: McGraw-Hill, 1969.

Friedman, S. Habituation and recovery of visual response in the alert human newborn. *Journal of Experimental Child Psychology,* 1972, *13,* 339–349.

Fromkin, V. A. Personal communication, 1976.

Garcia, J., and **Koelling, R. A.** Relation of cues to consequence in avoidance learning. *Psychonomic Science,* 1966, *4,* 123–124.

Garcia, J., McGowan, B. K., and **Green, K. F.** Biological constraints on conditioning. In A. H. Black and W. F. Prokasy (Eds.), *Classical conditioning II: Current theory and research.* New York: Appleton-Century-Crofts, 1972.

Gardner, H. *Developmental psychology.* Boston: Little, Brown, 1978.

Gardner, R. A., and **Gardner, B. T.** Teaching sign language to a chimpanzee. *Science,* 1969, *165,* 664–672.

Gardner, R.A., and **Gardner, B. T.** Reply to Terrace. Personal communication, 1980.

Garfield, S. L., and **Bergin, A. E.** (Eds.) *Handbook of psychotherapy and behavior change* (2nd ed.). New York: Wiley, 1978.

Gatchel, R., and **Proctor, J. D.** Physiological correlates of learned helplessness in man. *Journal of Abnormal Psychology,* 1976, *85,* 27–34.

Gauron, E., and **Dickinson, J. K.** Diagnostic decision making in psychiatry. *Archives of General Psychiatry,* 1966, *14,* 233–237.

Gazzaniga, M. S. The split brain in man. *Scientific American,* 1967, *217,* (2), 24–29.

Geen, R. G., and **O'Neal, E. C.** Activation of cue-elicited aggression by general arousal. *Journal of Personality and Social Psychology,* 1969, *11,* 287–292.

Geen, R. G., and **Stonner, D.** Effects of aggressiveness habit strength on behavior in the presence of aggression-related stimuli. *Journal of Personality and Social Psychology,* 1971, *17,* 149–153.

Geer, J. H., Davison, G. C., and **Gatchel, R. I.** Reduction of stress in humans through nonveridical perceived control of aversive stimulation. *Journal of Personality and Social Psychology,* 1970, *16,* 731–738.

Gelman, R. Cognitive development. In L. W. Porter and M. R. Rosenzweig (Eds.), *Annual Review of Psychology* (Vol. 29). Palo Alto, Calif.: Annual Reviews, 1978.

Gelman, R. Conservation acquisition: A problem of learning to attend to relevant attributes. *Journal of Experimental Child Psychology,* 1969, *7,* 176–187.

Gerard, H. B., and **Mathewson, G. C.** The effects of severity of initiation on liking for a group: a replication. *Journal of Experimental Social Psychology,* 1966, *2,* 278–287.

Gerard, H. B. and **Rabbie, J. M.** Fear and social comparison. *Journal of Abnormal and Social Psychology,* 1961, *62,* 586–592.

Gerard, H. B., Wilhelmy, R. A., and **Conolley, E. S.** Conformity and group size. *Journal of Personality and Social Psychology,* 1968, *8,*8 2.

Gesell, A. L. *Infant behavior.* New Haven, Conn.: Yale University Press, 1934.

Gesell, A. L. *Wolf child and human child, being a narrative interpretation of the life history of Kamala, the wolf girl; based on the diary account of a child who was reared by a wolf and who then lived for nine years in the orphanage of Midnapore, in the province of Bengal, India.* New York: Harper & Brothers, 1941.

Gesell, A. L. and **Thompson, H.** Learning and growth in identical twins: An experimental study by the method of co-twin control. *Genetic Psychology Monographs, Vol. 6* (1), 1929.

Geshwind, N. Specializations of the human brain. *Scientific American,* 1979, *241* (3), 180–199.

Gewirtz, J. L. Mechanisms of social learning: Some roles of stimulation and behavior in early human development. In D. A. Goslin (Ed.), *Handbook of socialization theory and research.* Chicago: Rand-McNally, 1969.

Gibb, C. A. Leadership. In G. Lindzey and E. Aronson (Eds.), *Handbook of social psychology* (2nd ed.) (Vol. 4). Reading, Mass.: Addison-Wesley, 1969.

Gibbs, J., Young, R. C., and **Smith, G. P.** Cholecystokinin decreases food intake in rats. *Journal of Comparative & Physiological Psychology,* 1973, *84,* 488–495.

Gibson, J. J. *The senses considered as perceptual systems.* Boston: Houghton Mifflin, 1966.

Glamzer, F. D. Determinants of a positive attitude toward retirement. *Journal of Gerontology,* 1976, *31,* (1), 104–107.

Glass, D. *Behavior patterns, stress and coronary disease.* Hillsdale, N.J.: Erlbaum, 1977.

Glass, D. and **Singer, J.** *Urban stress.* New York: Academic Press, 1972.

Gleason, J. B., and **Weintraub, S.** Input language and the acquisition of communicative competence. In K. Nelson (Ed.), *Children's language* (Vol. 1). New York: Gardner Press, 1978.

Glick, P. C., and **Norton, A. J.** Perspectives on the recent upturn in divorce and remarriage. *Demography,* 1973, *10,* 301–314.

Glucksberg, S., and **Danks, J. H.** *Experimental psycholinguistics.* Hillsdale, N. J.: Erlbaum, 1975.

Glucksberg, S., and **King, L. J.** Motivated forgetting mediated by implicit verbal chaining. *Science,* 1967, *158,* 517–519.

Glucksberg, S., Krauss, R. M., and **Weisberg, R.** Referential communication in nursery school children. Method and some preliminary findings. *Journal of Experimental Child Psychology,* 1966, *3,* 333–342.

Glucksber, S., and **Weisberg, R. W.** Verbal behavior and problem solving: some effects of labelling in a functional fixedness problem. *Journal of Experimental Psychology,* 1966, *71,* 659–64.

Goddard, H. H. Mental tests and the immigrant. *Journal of Delinquency,* 1917, *2,* 243–277.

Goddard, H. H. *Human efficiency and levels of intelligence.* Princeton, N.J.: Princeton University Press, 1920.

Goldfarb, W. Infant-rearing as a factor in foster home placement. *American Journal of Orthopsychiatry.* 1944, *14,* 162–167.

Goldfried, M. R. and **Davison, G. C.** *Clinical behavior therapy.* New York: Holt, Rinehart and Winston, 1976.

Goldfarb, W. Effects of psychological deprivation in infancy and subsequent stimulation. *American Journal of Psychiatry,* 1945, *102,*18–33.

Goldstein, K. *The organism, a holistic approach to biology derived from pathological data in man.* New York: American Book, 1939.

Gollob, H., and **Dittes, J.** Different effects of manipulated self-esteem on persuasibility depending on the threat and complexity of the communication. *Journal of Personality and Social Psychology* 1965, *2,* 195–201.

Good, K. J. Social facilitation: Effects of performance anticipation, evaluation, and response competition on free associations. *Journal of Personality and Social Psychology,* 1973, *28,* 270–275.

Goodenough, D. R. Dream recall: History and

current status of the field. In A. M. Arkin, J.S. Antrobus, and S. J. Ellman, *The mind in sleep: Psychology and psychophysiology.* New York: Halsted, 1978.

Goodwin, D.W., Powell, B., Bremer, D., Hoine, H., and **Stern, J.** Alcohol and recall: State-dependent effects in man. *Science,* 1969, *163,* 1358–1360.

Goodwin, D. W., Schulsinger, F., Hermansen, L., Guze, S. B. and **Winokur, G.** Alcohol problems in adoptees raised apart from alcoholic biological parents. *Archives of General Psychiatry,* 1973, 28, 238–243.

Goranson, R. E., and **King, D.** Rioting and daily temperature: Analysis of the U.S. riots in 1967. Unpublished manuscript, York University, Toronto, 1970.

Gordon, E. S. Nonesterified fatty acids in the blood of obese and lean subjects. *American Journal of Clinical Nutrition,* 1960, *8,* 704–747.

Gould, R. Adult life stages: Growth toward self-tolerance. *Psychology Today,* March 1974, 74–78.

Green, D. M., and **Swets, J. A.** *Signal detection theory and psychophysics.* New York: Wiley, 1966.

Greenman, G. W. Visual behavior of newborn infants. In A. J. Solnit and S. A. Provence (Eds.), *Modern perspectives in child development.* New York: Hallmark, 1963.

Gregory, R. L. *The intelligent eye.* New York: McGraw-Hill, 1970.

Gregory, R. L. *Eye and brain* (2nd ed.). New York: World University Library, 1973.

Grice, G. R. The relation of secondary reinforcement to delayed reward in visual discrimination learning. *Journal of Experimental Psychology,* 1948, *38,* 1–16.

Griffitt, W., and **Veitch, R.** Preacquaintance attitude similarity and attraction revisited: Ten days in a fall-out shelter. *Sociometry,* 1974, *37,* 163–173.

Grinspoon, L. Marijuana. *Scientific American,* December 1969.

Grossman, S. P. The VMH: A center for affective reactions, satiety, or both? *International Journal of Physiology and Behavior,* 1966, *1,* 1–10.

Guilford, J. P. *The nature of human intelligence.* New York: McGraw-Hill, 1967.

Guilford, J. P., and **Hoepfner, R.** *The analysis of intelligence.* New York: McGraw-Hill, 1971.

Gutmann, D. The cross-cultural perspective: Notes toward a comparative psychology of aging. In J. E. Birren and K. W. Schaie (Eds.), *Handbook of the psychology of aging.* New York: Van Nostrand Reinhold, 1977.

Guttman, N., and **Kalish, H. I.** Discriminability and stimulus generalization. *Journal of Experimental Psychology,* 1956, *51,* 79–88.

Haith, M. M. The response of the human newborn to visual movement. *Journal of Experimental Child Psychology*, 1966, *3*, 235–243.

Haith, M. M., Bergman, T., and Moore, M. J. Eye contact and face scanning in early infancy. Unpublished manuscript, University of Denver, 1977.

Hall, E. T. *The hidden dimension.* New York: Doubleday, 1966.

Hall, G. S. *Adolescence.* New York: Appleton, 1904.

Halverson, H. M. An experimental study of prehension in infants by means of systematic cinema records. *Genetic Psychology Monographs*, 1931, *10*, 107–286.

Hamilton, D. L., and Gifford, R. K. Illusory correlation in interpersonal perception: A cognitive basis of stereotypic judgments. *Journal of Experimental Social Psychology*, 1976, *12*, 392–407.

Hanson, H. M. Stimulus generalization following three-stimulus discrimination training. *Journal of Comparative and Physiological Psychology*, 1961, *54*, 181–185.

Hardyk, C., and Petrinovich, L. F. Left-handedness. *Psychological Bulletin*, 1977, *84*, 385–404.

Hare, R. D. *Psychopathy: Theory and research.* New York: Wiley, 1970.

Harlow, H. F. The formation of learning sets. *Psychological Review*, 1949, *56*, 51–65.

Harlow, H. F. The nature of love. *American Psychologist*, 1958, *13*, 673–685.

Harlow, H. F. Love in infant monkeys. *Scientific American*, July 1959, *201* (1).

Harlow, H. F. The heterosexual affectional system in monkeys. *American Psychologist*, 1962, *17*, 1–9.

Harlow, H. F. *Learning to love.* San Francisco: Albion, 1971.

Harlow, H., and Harlow, M. K. Effects of various mother–infant relationships on rhesus monkey behaviors. In B. M. Foss (Ed.), *Determinants of infant behavior* (Vol. 4). New York: Barnes & Noble, 1969.

Harlow, H. F., and Harlow, M. The affectional system. In A. M. Schrier, H. F. Harlow, and F. Stollnitz (Eds.), *Behavior of nonhuman primates* (Vol. 2). New York: Academic Press, 1966.

Harlow, H. F., Harlow, M. K., and Meyer, D. R. Learning motivated by a manipulation drive. *Journal of Experimental Psychology*, 1950, *49*, 228–234.

Harlow, H. F., and Suomi, S. J. Nature of love—simplified. *American Psychologist*, 1970, *25*, 161–168.

Harlow, H. F., and Zimmermann, R. R. Affectional responses in the infant monkey. *Science*, 1959, *130*, 421–432.

Harrell, T. W., and Harrell, M. S. Army General Classification Test scores for civilian occupations. *Educational and Psychological Measurement*, 1945, *5*, 229–239.

Harter, S. Developmental differences in the manifestation of mastery motivation on problem-solving tasks. *Child Development*, 1975, *46*, 370–378.

Harter, S. Effectance motivation reconsidered. *Human Development*, 1978, *21*, 34–64.

Hartmann, F. Three spines on a stickleback, *Natural History*, 1979, *88*(10), 32–35.

Hartup, W. W. Children and their friends. In H. McGurk (Ed.), *Issues in childhood social development.* London: Methuen, 1978.

Hayes, C. *The ape in our house.* New York: Harper & Row, 1951.

Haynes, H., White, B. L., and Held, R. Visual accommodation in human infants, *Science*, 1965, *148*, 528–530.

Hearnshaw, L. S. *Cyril Burt: Psychologist.* Ithaca, N.Y.: Cornell University Press, 1979.

Heath, J. E. Behavioral regulation of body temperature in poikilotherms. *Physiologist*, 1970, *13*, 399–410.

Heath, R. G., and Krupp, I. M. Schizophrenia as an immunologic disorder. *Archives of General Psychiatry*, 1967, *16*, 1–33.

Hebb, D. O. On the nature of fear. *Psychological Review*, 1946, *53*, 259–276.

Heidbreder, E. The attainment of concepts: III. The problem. *Journal of Psychology*, 1947, *24*, 93–138.

Heider, E. R., and Olivier, D. C. The structure of the color space in naming and memory for two languages. *Cognitive Psychology*, 1972, *3*, 337–354.

Heider, F. Attitudes and cognitive organization. *Journal of Psychology*, 1946, *21*, 107–112.

Held, R., and White, B. Sensory deprivation and visual speed: An analysis. *Science*, 1959, *130*, 860–861.

Helmholtz, H. *Treatise on physiological optics* (J. P. C. Southall, trans.). New York: Dover, 1962. (This translation originally published in 1925.)

Helson, H. *Adaptation-level theory.* New York: Harper & Row, 1964.

Herman, C. P., and Mack, D. Restrained and unrestrained eating. *Journal of Personality*, 1975, *43*, 647–483660.

Herman, C. P., and Polivy, J. Anxiety, restraint, and eating behavior. *Journal of Abnormal Psychology*, 1975, *84*, 666–672.

Heron, W., Doane, B. D., and Scott, T. H. Visual disturbances after prolonged perceptual isolation. *Canadian Journal of Psychology*, 1956, *10*, 13–16.

Herrnstein, R. J. *IQ in the meritocracy.* Boston: Atlantic Monthly Press, 1973.

Herrnstein, R. J., and Hineline, P. N. Negative reinforcement as shock frequency reduction. *Journal of the Experimental Analysis of Behavior*, 1966, *9*, 421–430.

Hersen, M. Token economies in institutional settings: Historical, political, deprivation, ethical and generalization issues. *Journal of Nervous and Mental Disease*, 1976, *162*, 206–214.

Hess, E. W. Two conditions limiting critical age for imprinting. *Journal of Comparative and Physiological Psychology*, 1959, *52*, 515–518.

Hibscher, J. A., and Herman, C. P. Obesity, dieting, and the expression of "obese" characteristics. *Journal of Comparative and Physiological Psychology*, 1977, *91*, 374–380.

Hilgard, E. R. Hypnosis. *Annual Review of Psychology*, 1975, *26*, 19–44.

Hilgard, E. R. The problem of divided consciousness: A neodissociation interpretation. In Edmonston, W. E., Jr. (Ed.), *Conceptual and Investigative approaches to hypnosis and hypnotic phenomena. Annals of the New York Academy of Sciences* (Vol. 296), 1977, 48–59.

Hilgard, E. R., and Bower, G. H. *Theories of learning* (4th ed.). Englewood Cliffs, N.J.: Prentice-Hall, 1975.

Hilton, I. Differences in the behavior of mothers toward first- and later-born children. *Journal of Personality and Social Psychology*, 1967, *7*, 282–290.

Hiroto, D. S., and Seligman, M. E. P. Generality of learned helplessness in man. *Journal of Personality and Social Psychology*, 1975, *31*, 311–327.

Hochberg, J. *Perception* (2nd ed.). Englewood Cliffs, N.J.: Prentice-Hall, 1978.

Hochschild, A. R. Disengagement theory: A logical, empirical, and phenomenological critique. In J. F. Gurbrium (Ed.), *Time, roles, and self in old age.* New York: Behavioral Publications, 1976.

Hoebel, B. G. Feeding: Neural control of intake. In V. E. Hall, A. C. Giese, and R. Sonnenschein (Eds.), *Annual Review of Physiology*, 1971, *33*.

Hoffer, A., and Osmond, H. Some schizophrenic recoveries, *Diseases of the Nervous System.* 1962, *23*, 204–210.

Hoffer, A., and Osmond, H. Nicotinamide adenine dinucleotide (NAD) as a treatment for schizophrenia. *Journal of Psychopharmacology*, 1966, *1*, 79–95.

Hoffer, A., and Osmond, H. Nicotinamide adenine dinucleotide in the treatment of chronic schizophrenic patients. *British Journal of Psychiatry*, 1968, *114*, 915–917.

Hoffman, H. S. Experimental analysis of imprinting and its behavioral effects. In G. Bower (Ed.), *The psychology of learning and motivation* (Vol. 12). New York: Academic Press, 1978.

Hoffman, H. S., Eisever, L. A., Ratner, A. M., and Pickering V. Development of distress vocalization during withdrawal of an imprinting stimulus. *Journal of Comparative and Physiological Psychology*, 1974, *86*, 563–568.

Hoffman, M. L. Moral development, In P. H.

Mussen (Ed.), *Carmichael's manual of child psychology* (Vol. 2). New York: Wiley, 1970.

Hogan, R. A. The implosive technique. *Behavior Research and Therapy*, 1968, *6*, 423–431.

Hogarty, G. E., and **Goldberg, S. C.** Drug and sociotherapy in the aftercare of schizophrenic patients. *Archives of General Psychiatry*, 1973, *28*, 54–64.

Hohmann, G. W. Some effects of spinal cord lesions on experienced emotional feelings. *Psychophysiology*, 1966, *3*, 143–156.

Hokanson, J., DeGood, D.E., Forrest, M., and **Britton, T.** Availability of avoidance behaviors in modulating vascular stress responses. *Journal of Personality and Social Psychology*, 1971, *19*, 60–68.

Holden, C. Lie detectors: PSE gains audience despite critics' doubt. *Science*, 1975, *190*, 359–362.

Holden, C. Hospices: For the dying, relief from pain and fear. *Science*, 1976, *193*, 389–391.

Hollander, E. P. Conformity, status and idiosyncrasy credit. *Psychological Review*, 1958, *65*, 117–127.

Hollander, E. P. Competence and conformity in the acceptance of influence. *Journal of Abnormal and Social Psychology*, 1960, *61*, 361–365.

Holmes, T. H., and **Rahe, R. H.** The social readjustment rating scale. *Journal of Psychosomatic Research*, 1967, *11*, 213–218.

Honig, W. K., and **Staddon, J. E. R.** (Eds.), *The handbook of operant behavior*. Englewood Cliffs, N. J.: Prentice-Hall, 1977.

Honzik, M. P., Macfarlane, J. W., and **Allen, L.** The stability of mental test performance between two and eighteen years. *Journal of Experimental Education*, 1948, *17*, 309–334.

Hopkins, J. R. Sexual behavior in adolescence. *Journal of Social Issues*, 1977, *33*, 67–85.

Horn, J. L., and **Donaldson, G.** On the myth of intellectual decline in adulthood. *American Psychologist*, 1976, *31*, 701–719.

Horn, J. L., and **Knott, P. D.** Activist youth of the 1960's: Summary and prognosis. *Science*, 1971, 3975, 977–985.

Horn, J.M., Loehlin, J. C. and **Willerman, L.** Intellectual resemblance among adoptive and biological relatives: The Texas Adoption Project. *Behavior Genetics*, 1979, *9*, 177–208.

Horner, M. Toward an understanding of achievement-related conflicts in women. In J. Stacey, S. Béreaud, and J. Daniels (Eds.), *And Jill came tumbling after: Sexism in American education*. New York: Dell, 1974.

Horner, M. S. The measurement and behavioral implications of fear of success in women. In J. W. Atkinson and J. O. Raynor (Eds.), *Personality, motivation, and achievement*. New York: Halsted Press, 1978.

Hoving, K. L., Hamm, N., and **Galvin, P.** Social influences as a function of a stimulus ambiguity at three age levels. *Developmental Psychology*, 1969, *6*, 631–636.

Hovland, C. I., Lumsdaine, A. A., and **Shef-**ditioned responses. I. The sensory generalization of conditioned responses with varying frequencies of tone. *Journal of General Psychology*, 1937, *17*, 125–148.

Hovland, C. I., and **Janis, I. H.** *Personality and persuasibility*. New Haven, Conn.: Yale University Press, 1959.

Hovland, C. I., Lumsdaine, A.A., and **Sheffield, F. D.** *Experiments on mass communication*. Princeton, N.J.: Princeton University Press, 1949.

Howe, K. G., and **Zanna, M. P.** Sex-appropriateness of the task and achievement behavior. *Eastern Psychological Association*, New York, 1975.

Hubel, D. The brain. *Scientific American*, 1979, *241*(4), 44–53.

Hubel, D. H., and **Wiesel, T. N.** Receptive fields of single neurons in the cat's striate cortex. *Journal of Physiology*, 1959, *148*, 574–591.

Hubel, D. H. and **Wiesel, T. N.** Brain mechanisms of vision. *Scientific American*, 1979, *241*(3), 150–162.

Huff, D. *How to lie with statistics*. New York: Norton, 1954.

Hull, C. L. *Principles of behavior*. New York: Appleton-Century-Crofts, 1943.

Hunt, E., and **Love, T.** How good can memory be? In A. N. Melton and E. Martin (Eds.), *Coding processes in human memory*. Washington, D.C.: Winston Wiley, 1972.

Hunt, J. McV. Intrinsic motivation and its role in psychological development. In D. Levine (Ed.), *Nebraska Symposium on Motivation, 1965*. Lincoln, Neb.: University of Nebraska Press, 1965.

Hurvich, L.M. Two decades of opponent processes. In F. W. Billmeyer, Jr., and G. Wyszecki (Eds.), *Color 77*. Bristol, England: Adam Hilger, 1978.

Hutchings, B., and **Mednick, S. A.** Registered criminality in the adoptive and biological parents of registered male adoptees. In S. A. Mednick, F. Schulsinger, J. Higgins, and B. Bell (Eds.), *Genetics, environment and psychopathology*. New York: Elsevier, 1974.

Hutt, C. Exploration and play in children. In P.A. Jewell and C. Lorzos (Eds.), *Play, exploration and territory in mammals. Symposium of the Zoological Society of London*. (No. 18), New York: Academic Press, 1966.

Inhelder, B., and **Piaget, J.** *The growth of logical thinking from childhood to adolescence*. New York: Basic Books, 1958.

Insko, C. A. *Theories of attitude change*. New York: Appleton-Century-Crofts, 1967.

Iverson, L. I. The chemistry of the brain. *Scientific American*, 1979, 241 (3), 134–149.

Jacobs, R. C., and **Campbell, D. T.** The perpetuation of an arbitrary tradition through several generations of a laboratory microculture. *Jour-*nal of Abnormal and Social Psychology, 1961, *62*, 649–658.

Jakubczak, L. F., and **Walters, R. H.** Suggestibility as dependency behavior. *Journal of Abnormal and Social Psychology*, 1959, *59*, 102–107.

James, W. *Principles of psychology*. New York: Holt, 1890.

Janda, L., O'Grady, K., and **Capps, C.** Fear of success in males and females in sex-linked occupations. *Sex Roles*, 1978, *4*, 43–50.

Janis, I. L., and **Feshback, S.** Effects of fear-arousing communications. *Journal of Abnormal and Social Psychology*, 1953, *48*, 78–92.

Janis, I. L., and **Field, P. B.** Sex differences and personality factors related to persuasibility. In I. L. Janis et al. (Eds.), *Personality and persuasibility*. New Haven, Conn.: Yale University Press, 1959.

Jarvik, L. F., Klodin, V., and **Matsuyama, S. S.** Human aggression and the extra Y chromosome: Fact or fantasy? *American Psychologist*, 1973, *28*, 674–682.

Jaynes, J. Imprinting: The interaction of learned and innate behavior: III. Generalization and emergent discrimination. *Journal of Comparative and Physiological Psychology*, 1958, *51*, 234–237.

Jeddi, E. Confort du contact et thermoregulation comportementale. *Physiology and Behavior*, 1970, *5*, 1487–1493.

Jencks, C. *Inequality*. New York: Basic Books, 1972.

Jensen, A. R. How much can we boost IQ and scholastic achievement? *Harvard Educational Review*, 1969, *39*, 1–123.

Jensen, A. R. *Genetics and education*. New York: Harper & Row, 1972.

Jensen, A. R. Sir Cyril Burt (obituary). *Psychometrika*, 1972, *37*, 115–117.

Jensen, A. R. Kinship correlations reported by Sir Cyril Burt. *Behavior Genetics*, 1974, *4*, 1–28.

Jensen, A. R. Heredity and intelligence: Sir Cyril Burt's findings. Letter to the *London Times*, December 9, 1976, p. 11.

Jensen, A. R. *Bias in mental testing*. New York: Free Press, 1980.

Jessor, R., and **Jessor, S. L.** The transition from virginity to non-virginity among youth: A social-psychological study over time. *Developmental Psychology*, 1975, *11*, 473–484.

Johnson, W. G. The effect of prior-taste and food visibility on the food-directed instrumental performance of obese individuals. Unpublished doctoral dissertation, Catholic University of America, 1970. Cited in S. Schachter, Some extraordinary facts about obese humans and rats. *American Psychologist*, 1971, *26*, 129–144.

Johnson-Laird, P. N., and **Wason, P. C.** *Thinking: Readings in cognitive science*. Cambridge: The University Press, 1977.

Jones, E. E., and **Berglas, S.** Control of attributions about the self through self-handicapping strategies: The appeal of alcohol and the role of underachievement. *Personality and Social Psychology Bulletin,* 1978, *4(2),* 200–206.

Jones, E. E., and **Davis, K. E.** From acts to dispositions: The attribution process in person perception. In L. Berkowitz (Ed.), *Advances in experimental social psychology* (Vol. 2). New York: Academic Press, 1965.

Jones, H. E., and **Conrad, H. S.** The growth and decline of intelligence: A study of a homogeneous group between the ages of ten and sixty. *Genetic Psychology Monographs,* 1933, *13,* 223–298.

Jones, H. E., and **Jones, M. C.** A study of fear. *Childhood Education,* 1928, *5,* 136–143.

Jones, M. C. The later careers of boys who were early or late maturing. *Child Development,* 1957, *28,* 113–128.

Jones, M. C. A study of socialization patterns at the high school level. *Journal of Genetic Psychology,* 1958, *92,* 87–111.

Jones, M. C., and **Bayley, N.** Physical maturing among boys as related to behavior. *Journal of Educational Psychology,* 41, 129–148.

Jones, M. C., and **Mussen, P. H.** Self-conceptions, motivations and interpersonal attitudes of early and late maturing girls. *Child Development,* 1958, *29,* 491–501.

Jouvet, M. The states of sleep. *Scientific American,* February 1967.

Juel-Nielsen, N. Individual and environment: A psychiatric-psychological investigation of monozygous twins reared apart. *Acta psychiatrica et neurologica Scandinavica,* (Monograph Supplement, 183), 1965.

Julesz, B. *Foundations of cyclopian vision.* Chicago: University of Chicago Press, 1971.

Jung, C. G. The stages of life. In J. Campbell (Ed.), *The Portable Jung.* New York: Viking, 1971.

Just, M. A., and **Carpenter, P. A.** A theory of reading: From eye fixations to comprehension. *Psychological Review,* 1980, *87* (4), 329–354.

Kagan, J. New views on cognitive development. *Journal of Youth and Adolescence,* 1976, *5,* 113–129.

Kagan, J., Kearsley, R. B., and **Zelazo, P. R.** The effects of infant day care on psychological development. *Educational Quarterly,* 1977, *1,* 109–142.

Kahn, E. and **Fisher, C.** REM sleep and sexuality in the aged. Presented at the Seventh Annual Scientific Meeting of the Boston Society for Gerontologic Psychiatry, September, 1967.

Kalish, R. A. Death and dying in a social context. In R. H. Binstock and E. Shanas (Eds.), *Handbook of aging and the social sciences.* New York: Van Nostrand Reinhold, 1976.

Kallman, F. J. Comparative twin study on the genetic aspects of male homosexuality. *Journal of Nervous and Mental Disease,* 1952, *115,* 283–298.

Kamin, L. J. The effects of termination of the CS and avoidance of the US on avoidance learning. *Journal of Comparative and Physiological Psychology,* 1956, *49,* 420–424.

Kamin, L. J. Temporal and intensity characteristics of the conditioned stimulus. In W. F. Prokasy (Ed.), *Classical conditioning: A symposium.* New York: Appleton-Century-Crofts, 1965.

Kamin, L. J. Predictability, surprise, attention, and conditioning. In B. A. Campbell and R. M. Church (Eds.), *Punishment: A symposium.* New York: Appleton-Century-Crofts, 1968.

Kamin, L. J. Heredity, intelligence, politics and society. Invited address, Eastern Psychological Association, Washington, 1973.

Kamin, L. J. *The science and politics of IQ.* Hillsdale, N.J.: Erlbaum, 1974.

Kamin, L. J. Psychology as social science: The Jensen affair, ten years after. Presidential address, Eastern Psychological Association, Philadelphia, 1979.

Kandel, D. Adolescent marijuana use: Role of parents and peers. *Science,* 1973, *181,* 1067–1070.

Kangas, J., and **Bradway, K.** Intelligence at middle age: A thirty-eight year follow-up. *Developmental Psychology,* 1971, *5(2),* 333–337.

Karaz, V., and **Perlman, D.** Attribution at the wire: Consistency and outcome finish strong. *Journal of Experimental Social Psychology.* 1975, *11,* 470–477.

Kase, S. V., and **Cobb, S.** Blood pressure changes in men undergoing job loss: A preliminary report. *Psychosomatic Medicine,* 1970, *6,* 95–106.

Kassin, S. M., and **Wrightsman, L. S.** Prior confessions and mock juror verdicts. *Journal of Applied Social Psychology,* 1980, *10,* 133–146.

Katz, E., and **Lazarsfeld, P. F.** *Personal influence.* Glencoe, Ill.: Free Press, 1955.

Keesey, R. E., and **Porvley, T. L.** Hypothalamic regulation of body weight. *American Scientist,* 1975, *63,* 558–565.

Keller, H. *The story of my life.* New York: Doubleday, Page, 1903.

Kelley, H. H. Two functions of reference groups. In G. E. Sovanson, T. M. Newcomb, and E. L. Hartley (Eds.), *Readings in social psychology* (2nd ed.). New York: Holt, Rinehart and Winston, 1952.

Kelley, H. H. Experimental studies of threats in interpersonal negotiations. *Journal of Conflict Resolution,* 1965, *9,* 79–105.

Kelley, H. H. Attribution theory in social psychology. In D. Levine (Ed.), *Nebraska Symposium on Motivation,* 1967, *15,* 192–238.

Kelley, H. H., and **Stahelski, A. J.** Errors in perceptional intentions in a mixed-motive game. *Journal of Experimental Social Psychology* 1970, *6,* 379–400.

Kellogg, W. N. and **Kellogg, L. A.** *The ape and the child.* New York: McGraw-Hill, 1933.

Kelman, H. C., and **Hovland, C. I.** "Reinstatement" of the communicator in delayed measurement of opinion change. *Journal of Abnormal and Social Psychology,* 1953, *48,* 326–335.

Keniston, K. Moral development, youthful activism and modern society. *Youth and Society,* 1969, *1,* 110–127.

Kerckhoff, A., and **Davis, K. E.** Value consensus and need complementarity in mate selection. *American Sociological Review,* 1962, *27,* 295–303.

Kety, S. Biochemical and neurochemical effects of electroconvulsive shock. In M. Fink, S. Kety, and J. McGraugh (Eds.), *Psychobiology of convulsive therapy.* Washington, D.C.: Winston, 1974, 285–294.

Kiesler, C. A., and **Pallak, M. S.** Arousal properties of dissonance manipulations. *Psychological Bulletin,* 1976, *83,* 1014–1025.

Kiesler, C. A., and **Kiesler, S. B.** *Conformity.* Reading, Mass.: Addison-Wesley, 1969.

Kimble, G. A. *How to use (and misuse) statistics.* Englewood Cliffs, N.J.: Prentice-Hall, 1978.

Kimmel, D. C., Price, K. F., and **Walker, J. W.** Retirement choice and retirement satisfaction. *Journal of Gerontology,* 1978, 33(4), 575–585.

Kinchla, R. A. The measurement of attention. In R. Nickerson (Ed.), *Attention and performance: VIII.* Hillsdale, N.J.: Erlbaum, 1980.

Kinchla, R. A., and **Allan, L. G.** A theory of visual movement perception. *Psychological Review,* 1969, *76,* 537–558.

Kinchla, R. A., and **Wolfe, J. M.** The order of visual processing: "Top-down," "bottom-up," or "middle-out." *Perception and Psychophysics,* 1979, *25(3),* 225–231.

King, S. H. Coping mechanisms in adolescents. *Psychiatric Annals,* 1971, *1,* 10–46.

Kinsey, A. C., Pomeroy, W. B., and **Martin, C. E.** *Sexual behavior in the human male.* Philadelphia: Saunders, 1948.

Kinsey, A. C., Pomeroy, W. B., Martin, C. E., and **Gebhard, P. H.** *Sexual behavior in the human female.* Philadelphia: Saunders, 1953.

Kleinhauz, M., Dreyfuss, D. A., Beran, B., Goldberg, T., and **Azikri, D.** Some after-effects of stage hypnosis: A case study of psychopathological manifestations. *International Journal of Clinical and Experimental Hypnosis,* 1979, *27,* 219–226.

Kluger, M. J. The importance of being feverish. *Natural History,* 1976, *85(1),* 70–75.

Knittle, J. L., and **Hirsch, J.** Effect of early nutrition on the development of rat epididymal fat pads: Cellularity and metabolism. *Journal of Clinical Investigation,* 1968, *47,* 2091.

Knittle, J. L. Early influences on development of adipose tissue. In G. A. Bray (Ed.), *Obesity* *in perspective*. Washington, D.C.: U.S. Government Printing Office, 1975.

Kobasa, S. Stressful life events, personality and health: An inquiry into hardiness. *Journal of Personality and Social Psychology, 1970, 37,* 1–11.

Koestler, A. *The act of creation.* New York: Macmillan, 1964.

Koffka, K. *The principles of Gestalt psychology.* New York: Harcourt, Brace, 1935.

Kohlberg, L. Stage and sequence: The cognitive-developmental approach to socialization. In D. A. Goslin (Ed.), *Handbook of socialization theory and research.* New York: Rand-McNally, 1961.

Kohlberg, L. Development of children's orientation towards a moral order. 1. Sequence in the development of moral thoughts. *Vita Humana,* 1963, *6,* 11–36.

Kohlberg, L. From is to ought: How to commit the naturalistic fallacy and get away with it in the study of moral development. In T. Mischel (Ed.), *Cognitive development and genetic epistemology.* New York: Acadehic Press, 1971.

Kohlberg, L. Moral stage and moralization: The cognitive-developmental approach. In T. Lickona (Ed.), *Moral development and behavior: Theory, research, and social issues.* New York: Holt, Rinehart and Winston, 1976.

Kohlberg, L. Revisions in the theory and practice of moral development. *New Directions for Child Development,* 1978, *2,* 83–88.

Kohlberg, L. and **Kramer, R. B.** Continuities and discontinuities in childhood and adult moral development. *Human Development,* 1969, *12,* 93–120.

Köhler, W. H. *The mentality of apes.* New York: Harcourt Brace Jovanovich, 1925.

Köhler, W. *Dynamics in psychology.* New York: Liveright, 1940.

Koluchova, J. Severe deprivation in twins: A case study. *Journal of Child Psychology and Psychiatry,* 1972, *13,* 107–114.

Konečni, V. J., and **Doob, A. N.** Catharsis through displacement of aggression. *Journal of Personality and Social Psychology,* 1972, *23,* 379–387.

Kosslyn, S. M., Ball, T. M., and **Reiser, B. J.** Visual images preserve metric spatial information: Evidence from studies of image scanning. *Journal of Experimental Psychology: Human Perception and Performance,* 1978, *4,* 47–60.

Krauss, R. M., and **Glucksberg, S.** Social and nonsocial speech. *Scientific American,* 1977, *236,* 100–105.

Kremer, E. F., Morgan, C. D., Saunders, R., and **Gaylor, M. S.** Treatment of chronic hyperpathic pain with temperature biofeedback. Unpublished mimeographed manuscript.

Kruglanski, A. W. The endogenous–exogenous partition in attribution theory. *Psychological Review,* 1975, *82,* 387–406.

Kruuk, H. *The spotted hyena: A study of predation and social behavior.* Chicago: University of Chicago Press, 1972.

Kübler-Ross, E. *On death and dying.* New York: Macmillan, 1969.

Kübler-Ross, E. *Questions and answers on death and dying.* New York: Macmillan, 1974.

Kuenne, M. R. Experimental investigation of the relation of language to transposition behavior in young children. *Journal of Experimental Psychology,* 1946, *36,* 471–490.

Kuhn, D., Nash, S. C., and **Brucken, L.** Sex role concepts of two- and three-year-olds. *Child Development,* 1978, *49,* 445–451.

Kuo, Z. Y. The genesis of the cat's response to the rat. *J. Comp. Psych.,* 1930, *11,* 1–30.

Kurtines, W., and **Grief, E. B.** The development of moral thought: Review and evaluation of Kohlberg's approach. *Psychological Bulletin,* 1974, *81,* 453–470.

Lacey, J. I., and **Lacey, B. C.** Verification and extension of the principle of autonomic response-stereotypy. *American Journal of Psychology,* 1958, *71,* 50–73.

Lachman, R., Lachman, J. L., and **Butterfield, E. C.** *Cognitive psychology and information processing.* Hillsdale, N.J.: Erlbaum, 1979.

Laing, R. D. Is schizophrenia a disease? *International Journal of Social Psychiatry,* 1964, *10,* 184–193.

Laing, R. D. *The divided self.* Middlesex, England: Penguin, 1965.

Lamb, M. E. The effects of maternal deprivation on the development of the concepts of object and person. *Journal of Behavioral Science,* 1973, *1,* 355–364.

Lamb, M. E. Twelve-month-olds and their parents: Interaction in a laboratory playroom. *Developmental Psychology,* 1976, *12,* 237–244.

Lamb, M. E. Father–infant and mother–infant interaction in the first year of life. *Child Development,* 1977, *48,* 167–181.

Lamm, H., and **Saver, C.** Discussion-induced shift toward higher demands in negotiation. *European Journal of Social Psychology,* 1974, *4,* 85–88.

Lang, P. J., Rice, D. G., and **Sternbach, R. A.** The psychophysiology of emotion. In N. S. Greenfield and R. A. Sternbach (Eds.), *Handbook of Psychophysiology.* New York: Holt, Rinehart and Winston, 1972, 623–643.

Langer, E., and **Rodin, J.** The effects of choice and enhanced personal responsibility for the aged: A field experiment in an institutional setting. *Journal of Personality and Social Psychology,* 1976, *34,* 191–198.

Langer, E., Janis, I. L., and **Wolfer, J.** Reduction of psychological stress in surgical patients. *Journal of Experimental Social Psychology,* 1975, *11,* 155–165.

Langer, E. J., Taylor, S. E., Fiske, S., and

Chanowitz, B. Stigma, staring, and discomfort: A novel stimulus hypothesis. *Journal of Experimental Social Psychology,* 1976, *12,* 451–463.

LaPiere, R. T. Attitudes and actions. *Social Forces,* 1934, *13,* 230–237.

Latané, B., and **Darley, J. M.** Group inhibition of bystander intervention in emergencies. *Journal of Personality and Social Psychology,* 1968, *10,* 215–221.

Latané, B., and **Darley, J. M.** *The unresponsive bystander: Why doesn't he help?* New York: Appleton-Century-Crofts, 1970.

Layzer, D. Heritability analyses of IQ: Science or numerology? *Science,* 1974, *183,* 1259–1266.

Leahy, A. Nature–nurture and intelligence. *Genetic Psychology Monographs,* 1935, *17,* 241–306.

Leask, J., Haber, R. N., and **Haber, R. B.** *Eidetic imagery in children, II: Longitudinal and experimental results. Psychonomic Monograph Supplements,* 1969, *3,* 25–48.

Leavitt, H. J. Some effects of certain communication patterns on group performance. *Journal of Abnormal and Social Psychology,* 1951, *46,* 38–50.

Lee, E. S. Negro intelligence and selective migration: A Philadelphia test of the Klineberg hypothesis. *American Sociological Review,* 1951, *16,* 227–233.

Lehrman, D. S. Interaction of hormonal and experiential influences on development of behavior. In E. L. Bliss (Ed.), *Roots of behavior.* New York: Harper & Row, 1962.

Lehrman, D. S. The reproductive behavior of ring doves. *Scientific American,* November 1964, *211*(5), 48–54.

LeMasters, E. E. Parenthood as crisis. *Marriage and Family Living,* 1957, *19,* 352–355.

Lemon, B. W., Bengtson, V. L., and **Peterson, J. A.** An exploration of the activity theory of aging: Activity types and life satisfaction among in-movers to a retirement community. *Journal of Gerontology,* 1972, *27*(4), 511–523.

Lenneberg, E. *Biological foundations of language.* New York: Wiley, 1967.

Leon, G. R. *Case histories of deviant behavior, an interactional perspective* (2nd ed.). Boston: Allyn & Bacon, 1977.

Lepper, M. R., Greene, D., and **Nisbett, R. E.** Undermining children's intrinsic interest with extrinsic rewards: A test of the "overjustification hypothesis." *Journal of Personality and Social Psychology,* 1973, *28,* 129–137.

Lerner, M. J., Miller, D. T., and **Holmes, J. G.** Deserving versus justice: A contemporary dilemma. In L. Berkowitz and E. Walster (Eds.), *Advances of experimental social psychology* (Vol. 12). New York: Academic Press, 1975.

Leventhal, H. Findings and theory in the study of fear communications. In L. Berkowitz

(Ed.), *Advances in experimental social psychology* (Vol. 5). New York: Academic Press, 1970.

Leventhal, H., and **Niles, P.** Persistence of influence for varying duration of exposure to threat stimuli. *Psychological Reports,* 1965, *16,* 223–233.

Leventhal, H., and **Singer, R.** Affect arousal and positioning of recommendation in persuasive communications. *Journal of Personality and Social Psychology,* 1966, *4,* 137–146.

Levinthal, C. F. *The physiological approach in psychology.* Englewood Cliffs. N.J.: Prentice-Hall, 1979.

Levinson, D. J., Darrow, C. N., Klein, E. B., Levinson, M. H. and **McKee, B.** *The seasons of a man's life.* New York: Knopf, 1978.

Levy, J. V. and **King, J. A.** The effects of testosterone proprionate on fighting behavior in young male C57 BL/10 mice. *Anat. Record,* 1953, *117,* 562–563.

Lewin, K. Environmental forces in child behavior and development. In C. Murchison (Ed.), *A handbook of child psychology,* Worcester, Mass.: Clark University Press, 1931.

Lewin, K. *Field theory in the social sciences.* New York: Harper and Brothers, 1951.

Lewinsohn, P. H. A behavioral approach to depression. In R. J. Friedman and M. M. Katz (Eds.), *The psychology of depression: Contemporary theory and research.* Washington, D.C.: Winston-Wiley, 1974.

Lichtenstein, E. *Psychotherapy: Approaches and applications.* Monterey, Calif.: Brooks/Cole, 1980.

Linder, D. E., Cooper, J., and Jones, E. E. Decision freedom as a determinant of the role of incentive magnitude in attitude change. *Journal of Personality and Social Psychology,* 1967, *6,* 245–254.

Linn, R. *You can drink and stay healthy.* New York: Watts, 1979.

Lipton, E. L., Steinschneider, A., and **Richmond, J. B.** Swaddling, a child care practice: Historical, cultural, and experimental observations. *Pediatrics,* 1965, *35,* 521–567.

Lipton, J. M. Effects of preoptic lesions on heat-escape responding and colonic temperature in the rat. *Physiology and Behavior,* 1968, *3,* 165–169.

Locke, J. An essay concerning human understanding. London: Basset, 1690.

Loehlin, J. C., and **Nichols, R. C.** *Heredity, environment and personality.* Austin, Tex.: University of Texas Press, 1976.

Loehlin, J. C., Lindzey, G., and **Spuhler, J. N.** *Race differences in intelligence.* San Francisco: Freeman, 1975.

Loehlin, J. C., Sharon, S., and **Jacoby, R.** In pursuit of the "spatial gene": A family study. *Behavior Genetics,* 1978, *8,* 27–41.

Loew, C. A. Acquisition of hostile attitude and its relationsip to aggressive behavior. *Journal of Personality and Social Psychology,* 1967, *5,* 335–341.

Lopata, H. Z. *Widowhood in an American city,* Cambridge, Mass.: Schenkman, 1973.

Lorenz, K. The companion in the bird's world. *Auk,* 1937, *54,* 245–273.

Lorenz, K. Z. *On aggression.* New York: Harcourt, Brace and World, 1966.

Lott, A. J., and **Lott, B. E.** A learning theory approach to interpersonal attitudes. In A. G. Greenwald, T. C. Brock, and T. Ostrom (Eds.), *Psychological foundations of attitudes.* New York: Academic Press, 1968.

Lott, A. J., and **Lott, B. E.** The role of reward in the formation of positive interpersonal attitudes. In T. L. Huston (Ed.), *Foundations of interpersonal attraction.* New York: Academic Press, 1974.

Lovaas, O. I. Effect of exposure to symbolic aggression on aggressive behavior, *Child Development,* 1961, *32,* 37–44.

Lovaas, O. I., Schreibman, L., Koegel, R., and **Rehm, R.** Selective responding by autistic children to multiple sensory input. *Journal of Abnormal Psychology,* 1971, *77,* 211–222.

Lovaas, O. I. The autistic child. New York: Halsted, 1977.

Lowell, E. L. The effect of need for achievement on learning and speed of performance. *Journal of Psychology,* 1952, *33,*31–40.

Lowenthal, M. F., Thürnher, M., and **Chiriboga, D.** *Four states of life: A comparative study of women and men facing transitions.* San Francisco: Jossey-Bass, 1975.

Luborsky, L., Singer, B., and **Luborsky, L.** Comparative studies of psychotherapies: Is it true that "Everyone has won and all must have prizes?" *Archives of General Psychiatry,* 1975, *32,* 995–1008.

Luborsky, L., and **Spence, D. P.** Quantitative research on psychoanalytic therapy. In A. E. Bergin and S. L. Garfield, (Eds.), *Handbook of psychotherapy and behavior change: An empirical analysis.* New York: Wiley, 1971.

Luchins, A. J. Mechanization in problem solving: The effect of *Einstellung. Psychological Monographs,* 1942, *54,* 6 (Whole No. 248).

Luria, A. R. *The mind of a mnemonist.* New York: Basic Books, 1968.

Lynch, K. *The image of the city.* Cambridge, Mass.: MIT Press, 1960.

Lynch, W. C., Hama, H., Kohn, S., and **Miller, N. E.** Instrumental control of peripheral vasomotor responses in children. *Psychophysiology,* 1976, *13,* 219–221.

Lynd, H. *On shame and the search for identity.* New York: Harcourt Brace Jovanovich, 1971.

MacFarlane, J. W. From infancy to adulthood. *Childhood Education,* 1963, *39,* 336–342.

MacFarlane, J. W. Perspectives on personality consistency and change from the guidance study. *Vita Humana,* 1964, *7,* 115–126.

Mackintosh, N. J. *The psychology of animal learning.* New York: Academic Press, 1974.

Mackintosh, N. J. A theory of attention. *Psychological Review,* 1975, *82,* 276–298.

MacLean, P. D. Contrasting functions of limbic and neocortical systems of the brain and their relevance to psychophysiological aspects of medicine. *American Journal of Medicine,* 1958, *25,* 611–626.

MacMahon, B. *Age at menarche, United States* (Vital and Health Statistics, Series 11, No. 133, DHEW Publication No. [HRA] 74–1615). Washington D.C.: Government Printing Office, 1973.

MacNamara, J. Cognitive basis of language learing in infants. *Psychological Review,* 1972, *79,* 1–13.

Maher, B. A. Delusional thinking and cognitive disorder. Paper presented at annual meeting of the American Psychological Association, 1970.

Mahl, G. F. *Psychological conflict and defense.* New York: Harcourt Brace Jovanovich, 1971.

Main, M. Exploration, play and level of cognitive functioning as related to child–mother attachment. Unpublished dissertation, Johns Hopkins University, 1973.

Malina, R. M. Secular changes in size and maturity: Causes and effects. *Monographs of the Society of Research in Child Development,* 1979, *44*(3–4, Serial No. 179), 59–120.

Mandler, G. Emotions. In T. M. Newcomb (Ed.), *New directions in psychology.* New York: Holt, Rinehart and Winston, 1962.

Maniscalco, C. I., Doherty, N. E., and **Ullman, D. G.** Assessing discrimination: An application of social judgment technology. *Journal of Applied Psychology,* 1980, *65,* 284–288.

Mann, R. D. A review of the relationships between personality and performance in small groups. *Psychological Bulletin,* 1959, *56,* 241–270.

Marshall, W. A., and **Tanner, J. M.** Variations in pattern of pubertal changes in girls. *Archives of Disease in Childhood,* 1969, *44,* 291–303.

Marshall, W. A., and **Tanner, J. M.** Variations in the pattern of pubertal changes in boys. *Archives of Diseases in Childhood,* 1970, *45,* 13–23.

Maslow, A. H. *Toward a psychology of being.* Princeton, N.J.: Van Nostrand, 1962, pp. 23–24.

Maslow, A. H. Neurosis as a failure of personal growth. *Humanitas,* 1967, *3,* 153–170.

Maslow, A. H. *Motivation and personality* (2nd ed.). New York: Harper & Row, 1970.

Mason, W. A. Early social deprivation in the nonhuman primates: Implications for human behavior. In D. C. Glass (Ed.), *Environmental influences*. New York: Rockefeller University Press and Russell Sage Foundation, 1968.

Massaro, A. J. Retroactive interference in short-term recognition memory for pitch. *Journal of Experimental Psychology*. 1970, *83*, 32–39.

Masters, W. H., and **Johnson, V. E.** *Human sexual response*. Boston: Little, Brown, 1966.

Masters, W. H., and **Johnson, V. E.** *Human sexual inadequacy*. Boston: Little, Brown, 1970.

Matas, L., Arend, R. A., and **Sroufe, L. A.** Continuity of adaptation in the second year: The relationship between quality of attachment and later competence. *Child Development* 1978, *49*, 547–556.

Matlin, M. W., and **Zajonc, R. B.** Social facilitation of word associations. *Journal of Personality and Social Psychology*, 1968, *10*, 455–460.

May, P. R. A. *Treatments of schizophrenia: A comparative study of five treatment methods*. New York: Science House, 1968.

Mayer, J. Genetic, traumatic and environmental factors in the etiology of obesity. *Physiological Reviews*, 1953, *33*, 472–508.

Mayer, J. Regulation of energy intake and the body weight: The glucostatic theory and the lipostatic hypothesis. *Annals of the New York Academy of Science*, 1955, *63*, 15–43.

McArthur, L. A. The how and what of why: Some determinants and consequences of causal attribution. *Journal of Personality and Social Psychology*, 1972, *22*, 171–193.

McCarley, R. W. Where dreams come from: A new theory. *Psychology Today*, December 1978.

McClelland, D. C. Risk-taking in children with high and low need for achievement. In J. W. Atkinson (Ed.), *Motives in fantasy, action, and society*. Princeton, N. J.: Van Nostrand, 1958.

McClelland, D. C. *The achieving society*. Princeton, N. J.: Van Nostrand, 1961.

McClelland, D. C. *Power: The inner experience*. New York: Irvington, 1975.

McClelland, D. C., Atkinson, J. W., Clark, R. A., and **Lowell, E. L.** *The achievement motive*. New York: Appleton-Century-Crofts, 1953.

McClelland, D. C., and **Watson, R. I.** Power motivation and risk-taking behavior. *Journal of Personality*, 1973, *41*, 121–139.

McClelland, L., and **Cook, S. W.** Promoting energy conservation in master-metered apartments through group financial incentives. *Journal of Applied Social Psychology*, 1980, *10*, 20–31.

McGinniss, J. *The selling of the presidency*. New York: Simon & Schuster, 1969.

McGlothlin, W. H. Drug use and abuse. *Annual Review of Psychology*, 1975, *26*.

McGuire, W. J., and **Papageorgis, D.** The relative efficacy of various types of prior belief-defense and producing immunity against persuasion. *Journal of Abnormal and Social Psychology*, 1961, *62*, 327–337.

McNemar, Q. *The revision of the Stanford-Binet scale: An analysis of the standardization data*. Boston: Houghton Mifflin, 1942.

Mead, M. *Coming of age in Samoa*. Chicago: University of Chicago Press, 1928.

Mead, M. *From the South Seas: Studies of adolescence and sex in primitive societies*. New York: Morrow, 1939.

Mednick, S. A. The associative basis of the creative process. *Psychological Review*, 1962, *69*, 220–232.

Mendels, J., Fieve, A., Fitzgerand, R. G., Ramsey, T. A., and **Stokes, J. W.** Biogenic amine metabolites in cerebrospinal fluid of depressed and manic patients. *Science*, 1972, *175*, 1380–1382.

Merriam-Webster: *Webster's New Collegiate Dictionary*. Springfield, Mass: Merriam, 1973.

Messe, L. A., Arnoff, J., and **Wilson, J. P.** Motivation as a mediator of the mechanisms underlying role assignments in small groups. *Journal of Personality and Social Psychology*, 1972 *24*, 84–90.

Milgram, S. Behavioral study of obedience. *Journal of Abnormal and Social Psychology* 1963, *67*, 371–378.

Milgram, S. Group pressure and action against a person. *Journal of Abnormal and Social Psychology*, 1964, *69*, 137–143.

Milgram, S. The experience of living in cities. *Science*, 1979, *167*, 1461–1468.

Milgram, S. *Obedience to authority*. New York: Harper & Row, 1974.

Milgram, S. Psychological maps of Paris. In H. Proshansky, W. Ittelson, and L. Rivlin (Eds.), *Environmental psychology* (2nd ed.). New York: Holt, Rinehart and Winston, 1976.

Milgram, S. *The individual in a social world*. Reading, Mass.: Addison-Wesley, 1977.

Miller, D. T. and **Ross, M.** Self-serving biases in the attribution of causality: Fact or fiction? *Psychological Bulletin*, 1975, *82*, 213–225.

Miller, G. A. The magical number seven plus or minus two: Some limits on our capacity for processing information. *Psychological Review*, 1956, *63*, 81–97.

Miller, G. A., and **Buckhout, R.** *Psychology: The science of mental life*. New York: Harper & Row, 1973.

Miller, G. A., Galanter, E., and **Pribram, K. H.** *Plans and the structure of behavior*. New York: Holt, Rinehart and Winston, 1960.

Miller, G. A., and **Isard, S.** Some perceptual consequences of linguistic rules. *Journal of Verbal Learning and Verbal Behavior*, 1963, *2*, 217–228.

Miller, N. E. The influence of past experience upon the transfer of subsequent training. Unpublished doctoral dissertation, Yale University, 1935.

Miller, N. E. Experimental studies of conflict. In J. McV. Hunt (Ed.), *Personality and the behavior disorders*. New York: Ronald Press, 1944.

Miller, N. E. Studies of fear as an acquirable drive: I. Fear as motivation and fear-reduction as reinforcement in the learning of new responses. *Journal of Experimental Psychology*, 1948, *38*, 89–101.

Miller, N. E. Learnable drives and rewards. In S. S. Stevens (Ed.), *Handbook of experimental psychology*. New York: Wiley, 1951.

Miller, N. E. Learning of visceral and glandular responses. *Science*, 1969, *163*, 434–445.

Miller, N. E., Bailey, C. J., and **Stevenson, J. A. F.** Decreased "hunger" but increased food intake resulting from hypothalamic lesions. *Science*, 1950, *112*, 256–259.

Miller, N. E. and **DiCara, L.** Instrumental learning of heart-rate changes in curarized rats: Shaping, and specificity to discriminative stimulus. *Journal of Comparative and Physiological Psychology*, 1967, *63*, 12–19.

Miller, N. E., and **Dworkin, B. R.** Visceral learning: Recent difficulties with curarized rats and significant problems for human research. In P. A. Obrist, A. H. Black, J. Brener, and L. V. DiCara (Eds.), *Cardiovascular psychophysiology: Current issues in response mechanisms, biofeedback, and methodology*. Chicago: Aldine, 1974.

Miller, N.E. and **Kessen, M. L.** Reward effects of food via stomach fistula compared with those of food via mouth. *Journal of Comparative and Physiological Psychology*, 1952, *45*, 555–564.

Miller, W. R., and **Seligman, M. E. P.** Depression and learned helplessness in man. *Journal of Abnormal Psychology*, 1975, *84*, 228–238.

Milner, B. Memory and the medial temporal regions of the brain. In K. H. Pribram and D. E. Broadbent (Eds.), *Biology of memory*. New York: Academic Press, 1970, pp. 29–50.

Milner, B., Branch, C., and **Rasmussen, T.** Evidence for bilateral representation in non-right-handers. *Transactions of the American Neurological Association*, 1966, *91*, 306–308.

Milton, G. A., and **Lipetz, M.E.** The factor structure of needs as measured by the EPPS. *Multivariate Behavioral Research*, 1968, *3*, 37–46.

Mitchell, G. D. Attachment differences in male and female infant monkeys. *Child Development*, 1968, *39*, 611–620.

Money, J. Sexual dimorphism and homosexual gender identity. *Psychological Bulletin*, 1970, *74*, 425–440.

Money, J., and **Ehrhardt, A. A.** *Man and woman, boy and girl*. Baltimore: Johns Hopkins University Press, 1972.

Montgomery, M. F. The role of the salivary

glands in the thirst mechanism. *American Journal of Physiology*, 1931, *96*, 221–227.

Moore, C., and Shiek, D. Toward a theory of early infantile autism. *Psychological Review*, 1971, *78*, 451–456.

Morgan, C. D., and Murray, H. A. Method for investigating fantasies—the Thematic Apperception Test. *Archives of Neurology and Psychiatry*, 1935, 34, 289–306.

Morgan, C. T., and Morgan, J. D. Studies in hunger: II. The relation of gastric denervation and dietary sugar to the effect of insulin upon food-intake in the rat. *Journal of Genetic Psychology*, 1940, *57*, 153–163.

Morgan, L. A. A re-examination of widowhood and morale. *Journal of Gerontology*, 1976, *31*(6), 687–695.

Morris, D., Collett, P., Marsh, P., and O'Shaughnessy, M. *Gestures*. New York: Stein & Day, 1979.

Moruzzi, G., and Magoun, H. W. Brain stem and reticular formation and activation of the EEG. *Electroencephalography and Clinical Neurophysiology*, 1949, *1*, 455–473.

Mosteller, F., Rourke, R. E. K., and Thomas, G. B., Jr. *Probability with statistical applications*. Reading, Mass.: Addison-Wesley, 1973.

Mowrer, O. A stimulus-response analysis of anxiety and its role as a reinforcing agent. *Psychological Review*, 1939, *46*, 553–565.

Mowrer, O. H. On the dual nature of learning—a reinterpretation of "conditioning" and "problem solving." *Harvard Educational Review*, 1974, *17*, 102–148.

Mowrer, O. H., and Mowrer, W. M. Enuresis—a method for its study and treatment. *American Journal of Orthopsychiatry*, 1938, *8*, 436–459.

Moyer, K. E. The physiology of aggression and the implications for aggression control. In J. L. Singer (Ed.), *The control of aggression and violence: Cognitive and physiological factors*. New York: Academic Press, 1971.

Moyer, K. E. Kinds of aggression and their physiological basis, In K. E. Moyer (Ed.), *Physiology of aggression and implications for control*. New York: Raven Press, 1976.

Müller, G. E., and Pilzecker, A. Experimentelle Beiträge zur Lehre von Gedächtnis. *Zeitschrift für Psychologie (Supplement no. 1)*, 1900.

Munroe, R. L., and Munroe, R. H. *Cross-cultural human development*. Monterey, Cal. Brooks/Cole, 1975.

Munsinger, H., and Kessen, W. Uncertainty, structure, and preference. *Psychological Monographs*, 1964, *78*, (Whole No. 586), 1–24.

Munsinger, H., Kessen, W., and Kessen, M. L. Age and uncertainty: Developmental variation in preference for variability. *Journal of Experimental Child Psychology*, 1964, *1*, 1–15.

Murray, H. A. *Exploration in personality*. New York: Oxford University Press, 1938.

Murray, H. A. *Thematic Apperception Test manual*. Cambridge, Mass.: Harvard University Press, 1943.

Muss, R. *Theories of adolescence* (3rd ed.). New York: Random House, 1975.

Mussen, P. H., and Jones, M. C. Self-conceptions, motivations and interpersonal attitudes of late and early maturing boys. *Child Development*, 1957, *28*, 243–256.

Myers, J. L. *Fundamentals of experimental design* (3rd ed.). Boston: Allyn and Bacon, 1979.

Nachman, G. The menopause that refreshes. In P. I. Rose, (Ed.), *Socialization and the life cycle*. New York: St. Martin's Press, 1979.

Nauta, W. J. H., and Feirtag, M. The organization of the brain. *Scientific American*, 1979, *241*(3), 88–111.

Navon, D. Forest before trees: The precedence of global features in visual perception. *Cognitive Psychology*, 1977, *9*, 353–383.

Neimark, E. D. Intellectual development during adolescence. In F. D. Horowitz (Ed.), *Review of child development research* (Vol. 1). Chicago: University of Chicago Press, 1975.

Neisser, U. *Cognition and reality: Principles and implications of cognitive psychology*. San Francisco: Freeman, 1976.

Neisser, U. *Cognitive psychology*. Englewood Cliffs, N.J.: Prentice-Hall, 1967.

Nelson, K. Structure and strategy in learning to talk. *Monographs of the Society for Research in Child Development*, 1973, *38* (1–2, Serial No. 149).

Nemeth, C. A critical analysis of research utilizing the prisoner's dilemma paradigm for the study of bargaining. In L. Berkowitz (Ed.), *Advances in experimental social psychology* (Vol. 6). New York: Academic Press, 1972.

Neugarten, B. L., Wood, V., Kraines, R. J., and Loomis, B. Women's attitudes toward the menopause. *Vita Humana*, 1963, *6*, 140–151.

Neugarten, B. L. The awareness of middle age. In B. L. Neugarten (Ed.), *Middle age and aging*. Chicago: The University of Chicago Press, 1968.

Newcomb, T. An approach to the study of communicative acts. *Psychological Review*, 1953, *60*, 393–404.

Newcomb, T. The prediction of interpersonal attraction. *American Psychologist*, 1956, *11*, 575–586.

Newcomb, T. M. Dyadic balance as a source of clues about interpersonal attraction. In B. I. Murstein (Ed.), *Theories of attraction and love*. New York: Springer, 1971.

Newman, H. H., Freeman, F. N., and Holzinger, K. J. *Twins: A study of heredity and environment*. Chicago: University of Chicago Press, 1937.

Newmark, C. S., Frerking, R. A., Cook, L.,

and Newmark, L. Endorsement of Ellis' irrational beliefs as a function of psychopathology. *Journal of Clinical Psychology*, 1973, *29*, 300–302.

Nisbett, R. E. Hunger, obesity, and the ventromedial hypothalamus. *Psychological Review*, 1972, *79*, 433–453.

Nisbett, R. E., and Wilson, T. D. Telling more than we can know: Verbal reports on mental processes. *Psychological Review*, 1977, *84*, 231–259.

Norman, D. A. *Memory and attention* (3rd ed.). New York: Wiley, 1979.

Novak, D., and Lerner, M. Rejection as a consequence of perceived similarity. *Journal of Personality and Social Psychology*, 1968, *9*, 147–152.

Novak, M. A., and Harlow, H. F. Social recovery of monkeys isolated for the first year of life: I. Rehabilitation and therapy. *Developmental Psychology*, 1975, *11*, 564–565.

Nowak, C. A. Does youthfulness equal attractiveness? In L. E. Troll, J. Israel, and K. Israel (Eds.), *Looking ahead: A woman's guide to the problems and joys of growing older*. Englewood Cliffs, N.J.: Prentice-Hall, 1977.

Offer, D. *The psychological world of the teenager: A study of normal adolescent boys*. New York: Basic Books, 1969.

Offer, D., Marcus, D., and Offer, J. L. A longitudinal study of normal adolescent boys. *American Journal of Psychiatry*, 1970, *126*, 917–924.

Offer, D., and Offer, J. Normal adolescent males: The high school and college years. *Journal of the American College Health Association*, 1974, *22*, 209–215.

Olds, J. Pleasure centers in the brain. *Scientific American*, 1956, *195*, 105–116.

Olds, J., and Milner, P. Positive reinforcement produced by electrical stimulation of septal area and other regions of rat brain. *Journal of Comparative and Physiological Psychology*, 1954, *47*, 419–427.

O'Leary, V., and Hammock, B. Sex-role orientation and achievement context as determinants of the motive to avoid success. *Sex Roles*, 1975, *1*, 225–234.

Oller, D. K., and Warren, I. On the nature of phonological capacity. *Lingua*, 1976, *39*, 183–199.

Orne, M. T. The construct of hypnosis: Implications of definition for research and practice. In Edmonston, W. E., Jr. (Ed.), *Conceptual and investigative approaches to hypnosis and hypnotic phenomena. Annals of the New York Academy of Sciences* (Vol. 296). 1977, 14–33.

Orne, M. T., Sheehan, P. W., and Evans, F. J. Occurrence of posthypnotic behavior outside the experimental setting. *Journal of Personality and Social Psychology*, 1968, *9*, 189–196.

Osgood, C. E., Suci, G. J., and Tannenbaum,

P. H. *The measurement of meaning.* Urbana, Ill.: University of Illinois Press, 1957.

Owen, D. R. The 47, XYY male: A review. *Psychological Bulletin,* 1972, *78,* 209–233.

Pallak, M. S., and Pittman, T. S. General motivational effects of dissonance arousal. *Journal of Personality and Social Psychology,* 1972, *21,* 349–358.

Palmore, E. and Luikart, C. Health and social factors related to life satisfaction. *Journal of Health and Social Behavior,* 1972, *13,* 68–80.

Palombo, S. R. *Dreaming and memory: A new information-processing model.* New York: Basic Books, 1978.

Panksepp, J. Reanalysis of feeding patterns in the rat. *Journal of Comparative and Physiological Psychology,* 1973, *82,* 78–94.

Parke, R. D., Berkowitz, L., Leyens, J. R., and Sebastian, R. The effects of repeated exosure to movie violence on aggressive behavior in juvenile delinquent boys: Field experimental studies. In L. Berkowitz (Ed.), *Advances in experimental social psychology* (Vol. 8). New York: Academic Press, 1975.

Parker, G., and Lipscombe, P. Parental overprotection and asthma. *Journal of Psychosomatic Research,* 1979, *23,* 295–300.

Pavio, A. Comparisons of mental clocks. *Journal of Experimental Psychology: Human Perception and Performance.* 1978, *4,* 61–71.

Pavlov, I. P. *Conditioned reflexes* (G. V. Anrep, Trans.) London: Oxford University Press, 1927.

Peck, R. C. Psychological developments in the second half of life. In B. L. Neugarten (Ed.), *Middle age and aging.* Chicago: The University of Chicago Press, 1968.

Pedersen, F. A. and Bell, R. Q. Sex differences in preschool children without histories of complications of pregnancy and delivery. *Developmental Psychology,* 1970, *3,* 10–15.

Pederson, L. L., Scrimgeour, W. G., and Lefcoe, N. M. Variables of hypnosis which are related to success in a smoking withdrawal program. *International Journal of Clinical and Experimental Hypnosis,* 1979, *27,* 14–20.

Perls, F. S. *Gestalt therapy verbatim.* Lafayette, Calif.: Real People Press, 1969.

Perry, C. Variables influencing the posthypnotic persistence of an uncancelled hypnotic suggestion. In Edmonston, W. E., Jr. (Ed.), *Conceptual and investigative approaches to hypnosis and hypnotic phenomena. Annals of The New York Academy of Science* (Vol. 296), 1977, 264–273.

Pert, C. B., and Snyder, S. H. Opiate receptors: Demonstration in nervous tissue. Science, 1979, *179,* 1011–1014.

Peterson, L. R., and Peterson, M. J. Short-term retention of individual items. *Journal of Experimental Psychology,* 1959, *58,* 193–198.

Pfeiffer, E., Verwoordt, A., and Davis, G. C.

Sexual behavior in middle life. In E. Palmore (Ed.), *Normal aging II: Reports from the Duke longitudinal studies, 1970–1973.* Durham, N.C.: Duke University Press, 1974.

Phares, E. J. *Clinical psychology: Concepts, methods, and profession.* Chicago: Dorsey, 1979.

Piaget, J. *The moral judgment of the child.* New York: Harcourt, Brace, 1932.

Piaget, J. Intellectual evolution from adolescence to adulthood. *Human Development,* 1972, *15,* 1–12.

Piaget, J., and Inhelder, B. *The psychology of the child.* New York: Basic Books, 1968.

Pineo, P. C. Disenchantment in the later years of marriage. *Marriage and Family Living,* 1961, *23,* 3–11.

Pittman, T. S. Attribution of arousal as a mediator in dissonance reduction. *Journal of Experimental Social Psychology,* 1975, *11,* 53–63.

Pittman, N. L., and Pittman, T. S. Effects of amount of helplessness training and internal–external locus of control on mood and performance. *Journal of Personality and Social Psychology,* 1979, *37,* 39–47.

Plomin, R., and DeFries, J. C. Genetics and intelligence: Recent data. *Intelligence,* 1980, *4,* 15–24.

Pollack, I., Rubenstein, H., and Decker, L. Intelligibility of known and unknown message sets. *Journal of the Acoustical Society of America,* 1959, *31,* 273–279.

Pollard-Gott, L., McCluskey, M., and Todres, A. Subjective story structure. *Discourse Processes,* 1979, *2,* 251–281.

Porteous, J. D. *Environment and behavior.* Reading, Mass.: Addison-Wesley, 1977.

Posner, M. I. Abstraction and the process of recognition. In G. H. Bower and J. T. Spence (Eds.), *The Psychology of Learning and Motivation: Advances in Research and Theory* (Vol. 3). New York: McGraw-Hill, 1969.

Premack, D. *Intelligence in ape and man.* Hillsdale, N.J.: Erlbaum, 1976.

Provence, S., and Lipton, R. C. *Infants in institutions.* New York: International Universities Press, 1962.

Pruitt, D. G. Conclusions: Toward an understanding of choice shifts in group discussion. *Journal of Personality and Social Psychology,* 1971b, *20,* 495–510.

Rachlin, H. *Introduction to modern behaviorism* (2nd ed.). San Francisco: Freeman, 1976.

Rachman, S. Sexual fetishism: An experimental analogue. *Psychological Record,* 1966, *16,* 293–296.

Radloff, L. Sex differences in depression: The effects of occupation and marital status. *Sex Roles,* 1975, *1,* 249–281.

Rahe, R., Romo, M., Bennett, L., and Siltanen, P. Recent life changes, myocardial in-

farction, and abrupt coronary death: Studies in Helsinki. *Archives of Internal Medicine,* 1974, *133,* 221–228.

Raines, H. Marijuana from many sources softening cancer chemotherapy. *New York Times,* December 23, 1979.

Raphael, B. *The thinking computer: Mind inside matter.* San Francisco: Freeman, 1976.

Raven, J. C. *Progressive matrices.* London: Lewis, 1947.

Rees, L. The significance of parental attitudes in childhood asthma. *Journal of Psychosomatic Research,* 1963, *7,* 181–190.

Rescorla, R. A., and Wagner, A. R. A theory of Pavlovian conditioning: Variations in the effectiveness of reinforcement and nonreinforcement. In A. H. Black and W. F. Prokasy (Eds.), *Classical conditioning II: Current theory and research.* New York: Appleton-Century-Crofts, 1972.

Reynolds, G. S. *A primer of operant conditioning* (rev. ed.). Glenview, Ill.: Scott, Foresman, 1975.

Rhodewalt, F. The coronary-prone behavior pattern, psychological reactance, and the self-attributor. Unpublished doctoral dissertation. Princeton University. 1979.

Rife, D. C. Handedness, with special reference to twins. *Genetics,* 1940, *25,* 178–186.

Riley, M., and Foner, A. *Aging and society, Vol. I: An inventory of research findings.* New York: Russell Sage, 1968.

Rimm, D. C., and Masters, J. C. *Behavior therapy: Techniques and empirical findings* (2nd ed.). New York: Academic Press, 1979.

Robbins, P. *Successful midlife career change.* New York: AMACON, 1978.

Rimland, B. *Infantile autism.* New York: Appleton-Century-Crofts, 1964.

Roberts, C. L., Marx, M. H., and Collier, G. Light onset and light offset as reinforcers for the albino rat. *Journal of Comparative and Physiological Psychology,* 1958, *51,* 575–579.

Rock, I. *An introduction to perception.* New York: Macmillan, 1975.

Robin, J., and Langer, E. Long-term effects of control-relevant intervention with the institutionalized aged. *Journal of Personality and Social Psychology,* 1977, *35,* 897–902.

Roffwarg, H. P., Herman, J. H., Bowe-Anders, C., and Tauber, E. S. The effects of sustained alterations of waking visual input on dream content. In A. M. Arkin, J. S. Antrobus, and S. J. Ellman (Eds.), *The mind in sleep: Psychology and psychobiology.* New York: Erlbaum, 1978.

Rogers, C. R. *Client-centered therapy.* Boston: Houghton Mifflin, 1951.

Rokeach, M. *Beliefs, attitudes, and values.* San Francisco: Jossey-Bass, 1968.

Rokeach, M., and Kliejunas, P. Behavior as a function of attitude-toward-object and attitude-toward-situation. *Journal of Personality and Social Psychology* 1972, *22*, 194–201.

Rollins, B. C. and **Feldman, H.** Marital satisfaction over the family life cycle. *Journal of Marriage and the Family,* 1970, *32*(1), 20–28.

Ropartz, P. The relation between olfactory stimulation and aggressive behavior in mice. *Animal Behavior,* 1968, *16*, 97–100.

Rosch, E. Human categorization. In N. Warren (Ed.), *Advances in cross-cultural psychology,* Vol. 1. London: Academic Press, 1977.

Rosch, E., and **Lloyd, B. B.** (Eds.). *Cognition and categorization.* Hillsdale, N.J.: Erlbaum, 1978.

Rose, A. M. A current theoretical issue in social gerontology. In B. L. Neugarten (Ed.), *Middle age and aging.* Chicago: The University of Chicago Press, 1968.

Rose, S. *The conscious brain.* New York: Knopf, 1975.

Rosen, B. C. and **D'Andrade, R.** The psychological origins of achievement motivation. *Sociometry,* 1959, *22*, 185–218.

Rosenblum, L. A. The development of social behavior in the rhesus monkey. Unpublished Ph.D. dissertation, U. of Wisconsin, 1961. Cited in D. P. Kimble, *Psychology as a Biological Science.* Santa Monica, Cal.: Goodyear, 1977.

Rosenhan, D. L. The natural socialization of altruistic autonomy. In J. Macaulay and L. Berkowitz (Eds.), *Altruism and helping behavior.* New York: Academic Press, 1970.

Rosenzweig, M. R. Environmental complexity, cerebral change and behavior. *American Psychologist,* 1966, *21*, 321–332.

Ross, L. The intuitive psychologist and his shortcomings: Distortions in the attribution process. In L. Berkowitz (Ed.), *Advances in experimental social psychology* (Vol. 10). New York: Academic Press, 1977.

Roth, S., and **Kubal, L.** The effects of noncontingent reinforcement on tasks of differing importance: Facilitation and learned helplessness. *Journal of Personality and Social Psychology,* 1975, *32*, 680–691.

Rozin, P., and **Kalat, J.** Specific hungers and poison avoidance as adoptive specializations of learning. *Psychological Review,* 1971, *78*, 459–486.

Rozin, P., and **Mayer, J.** Thermal reinforcement and thermoregulatory behavior in the goldfish, *Carassius auratus. Science,* 1961, *134*, 942–943.

Ruble, D. N. and **Feldman, N. S.** Order of consensus, distinctiveness, and consistency information and causal attributions. *Journal of Personality and Social Psychology,* 1976, *34*, 930–937.

Ruble, D. N., Parsons, J. E., and **Ross, J.** Self-evaluative responses of children in an achievement setting. *Child Development,* 1976, *47*, 990–997.

Ruff, H. A., and **Birch, H. G.** Infant visual fixation: The effects of concentricity, curvilinearity, and number of directions. *Journal of Experimental Child Psychology,* 1974, *17*, 460–473.

Rumbaugh, D. M. *Language learning by a chimpanzee: The LANA project.* New York: Academic Press, 1977.

Rumbaugh, D. M., Savage-Rumbaugh, E. S., and **Gill, T. V.** The chimpanzee as an animal model in language research. In R. L. Schiefelbusch and J. H. Hollis (Eds.), *Language intervention from ape to child.* Baltimore, Md.: University Park Press, 1979.

Rundus, D. Analysis of rehearsal processes in free recall. *Journal of Experimental Psychology,* 1971, *89*, 63–77.

Rush, A. J., Beck, A. T., Kovacs, M., and **Hollon, S.** Comparative efficacy of cognitive therapy and pharmacotherapy in the treatment of depressed outpatients. *Cognitive Therapy and Research,* 1977, *1*, 17–37.

Saarinen, T. F. *Perception of the environment.* Resource Paper no. 5. Association of American Geographers, 1969.

Sakurai, M. M. Small group cohesiveness and detrimental conformity. *Sociometry,* 1975, *38*, 340–357.

Salapatek, P. Pattern perception in early infancy. In L. B. Cohen and P. Salapetek (Eds.), *Infant perception: From sensation to cognition* (Vol. 1): *Basic visual processes.* New York: Academic Press, 1975.

Salapatek, P., Bechtold, A. G., and **Bushnell, E. W.** Infant visual acuity as a function of viewing distance. *Child Development,* 1976, *47*, 860–863.

Salapatek, P., and **Kessen, W.** Visual scanning of triangles by the human newborn. *Journal of Experimental Child Psychology,* 1966, *3*, 155–167.

Samuda, R. J. *Psychological testing of American minorities: Issues and consequences.* New York: Dodd, Mead, 1975.

Sarbin, T. R. Attempts to understand hypnotic phenomena. In L. Postman, *Psychology in the making.* New York: Knopf, 1962, 745–784.

Sarbin, T. R., and **Coe, W. C.** *Hypnosis: A social psychological analysis of influence communication.* New York: Holt, Rinehart and Winston, 1962.

Sargent, S. S., and **Stafford, K. R.** *Basic teachings of the great psychologists.* Garden City, N.Y.: Doubleday, 1965.

Sarnoff, I., and **Zimbardo, P. G.** Anxiety, fear and social affiliation. *Journal of Abnormal and Social Psychology,* 1961, *62*, 356–363.

Satinoff, E. Neural integration of thermoregulatory responses. In L. V. DiCara (Ed.), *Limbic and autonomic nervous system: Advances in research.* New York: Plenum, 1974.

Satinoff, E., and **Henderson, R.** Thermoregulatory behavior. In W. K. Honig and

J. E. R. Staddon (Eds.), *Handbood of operant behavior.* Englewood Cliffs, N.J.: Prentice-Hall, 1977.

Scarr, S., and **Weinberg, R. A.** IQ test performance of black children adopted by white females. *American Psychologist,* 1976, *31,* 726–739.

Scarr, S., and **Weinberg, R. A.** Intellectual similarities within families of both adopted and biological children. *Intelligence,* 1977, *1,* 170–191.

Schachter, S. Deviation, rejection, and communication. *Journal of Abnormal and Social Psychology,* 1951, *46*, 190–207.

Schachter, S. *The psychology of affiliation: Experimental studies of the sources of gregariousness.* Stanford, Cal.: Stanford University Press, 1959.

Schacter, S. Some extraordinary facts about obese humans and rats. *American Psychologist,* 1971, *26*, 129–144.

Schacter, S., and **Singer, J. E.** Cognitive, social, and physiological determinants of emotional state. *Psychological Review,* 1962, *69*, 379–399.

Schaefer, E. S., and **Bayley, N.** Maternal behavior, child behavior, and their intercorrelations from infancy through adolescence. *Monographs of the Society for Research in Child Development,* 1963, *28* (3, Serial No. 87).

Schaffer, H. R., and **Emerson, P. E.** The development of social attachments in infancy. *Monographs of the Society for Research in Child Development,* 1964, *29* (3, Serial No. 94).

Schaffer, H. R., and **Emerson, P. E.** Patterns of response to physical contact in early human development. *Journal of Child Psychology and Psychiatry,* 1964, *5*, 1–13.

Schaie, K. W., Labouvie, G., and **Buech, B. V.** Generational and cohort-specific differences in adult cognitive functioning: A fourteen-year study of independent samples. *Developmental Psychology,* 1973, *9*, 151–166.

Scheier, M. F., Fenigstein, A., and **Buss, A.** Self-awareness and physical aggression. *Journal of Experimental Social Psychology,* 1974, *10*, 264–273.

Schmidt, H. O., and **Fonda, C.** The reliability of psychiatric diagnosis. *Journal of Abnormal and Social Psychology,* 1956, *52*, 262–267.

Schneider, W., and **Shiffrin, R. M.** Controlled and automatic human information processing. I. Detection, search, and attention. *Psychological Review,* 1977, *84*, 1–66.

Schreiber, F. R. *Sybil.* Chicago: Regnery, 1973.

Schutz, R., and **Hanusa, B.** Long-term effects of control and predictability-enhancing interventions: Findings and ethical issues. *Journal of Personality and Social Psychology,* 1978, *36*, 1194–1201.

Schwartz, B. *Psychology of learning and behavior.* New York: Norton, 1978.

Schwartz, M. *Physiological Psychology.* Englewood Cliffs, N.J.: Prentice-Hall, 1978.

Schwartz, M. D., and **Errera, P.** Psychiatric care in a general hospital emergency room. *Archives of General Psychiatry,* 1963, *9,* 113–121.

Sears, R. R., Maccoby, E. E., and **Levin, H.** *Patterns of child rearing.* New York: Harper & Row, 1957.

Segal, S. J., and **Fusella, V.** Influence of imaged pictures and sounds in detection of visual and auditory signals. *Journal of Experimental Psychology,* 1970, *83,* 458–474.

Segovia-Riguelma, N., Varela, A., and **Mardones, J.** Appetite for alcohol. In Y. Israel and J. Mardones (Eds.), *Biological basis of alcoholism.* New York: Wiley, 1971.

Selfridge, O. G. Pandemonium: A paradigm for learning. In D. V. Blake and A. M. Uttley (Eds.), *Proceedings of the Symposium on the Mechanisation of Thought Processes.* London: Her Majesty's Stationery Office, 1959.

Seligman, M. E. P. Phobias and preparedness. In M. E. P. Seligman and J. L. Hager (Eds.), *Biological Boundaries of Learning.* New York: Appleton-Century-Crofts, 1972.

Seligman, M. E. P. Depression and learned helplessness. In R. J. Friedman and M. M. Katz (Eds.), *The psychology of depression: Contemporary theory and research.* Washington, D.C.: Winston-Wiley, 1974.

Seligman, M. E. P. *Helplessness: On depression, development, and death.* San Francisco: Freeman, 1975.

Seligman, M. E. P., and **Hager, J. L.** *Biological boundaries of learning.* New York: Appleton-Century-Crofts, 1972.

Selye, H. *The stress of life* (2nd ed.). New York: McGraw-Hill, 1976.

Selye, H. (Ed.). *Selye's guide to stress research* (Vol. 1). New York: Van Nostrand Reinhold, 1980.

Sem-Jacobsen, C. W., and **Torkildsen, A.** Depth recording and electrical stimulation in the human brain. In E. R. Ramey and D. S. O'Doherty (Eds.), *Electrical studies on the anesthetized brain.* New York: Hoeber, 1960, 275–290.

Serbin, L. A., and **O'Leary, K. E.** How nursery schools teach girls to shut up. *Psychology Today,* 1975, *9,* 57–58, 102–103.

Shaffer, D. R. *Social and personality development.* Monterey, Cal.: Brooks/Cole, 1979.

Shatz, M. The relationship between cognitive processes and the development of communication skill. In C. B. Keasey (Ed.), *Nebraska Symposium on Motivation* (Vol. 26). Lincoln, Neb.: University of Nebraska Press, 1978.

Shatz, M., and **Gelman, R.** The development of communication skills: Modification in the speech of young children as a function of listener. *Monographs of the Society for Research in Child Development,* 1973, *38*(5) (Whole No. 152).

Shaw, D. M. Mineral metabolism, mania, and melancholia. *British Medical Journal,* 1966, *2,* 262–267.

Shaw, M. E. Some effects of unequal distribution of information upon group performance in various communication nets. *Journal of Abnormal and Social Psychology,* 1954, *49,* 547–553.

Shaw, R., and **Bransford, J.** Approaches to the problem of knowledge. In R. Shaw and J. Bransford (Eds.), *Perceiving, acting, and knowing.* Hillsdale, N.J.: Erlbaum, 1977.

Sheldon, W. H. *The varieties of temperament: A psychology of constitutional differences.* New York: Harper, 1942.

Shepard, R. N., and **Metzler, J.** Mental rotation of three-dimensional objects. *Science,* 1971, *171,* 701–703.

Sheppard, H. L. Work and retirement. In R. H. Binstock and E. Shanas (Eds.), *Handbook of aging and the social sciences.* New York: Van Nostrand Reinhold, 1976.

Sherif, M. *The psychology of group norms.* New York: Harper & Row, 1936.

Shields, J. *Monozygotic twins brought up apart and brought up together.* London: Oxford University Press, 1962.

Shirley, M. M. *The first two years: A study of twenty-five babies: I. Postural and locomotor development.* Minneapolis, Minn.: University of Minnesota Press, 1931.

Shneidman, E. S. *Deaths of man.* New York: New York Times Book Co., 1973.

Shomer, R. W., Davis, A., and **Kelley, H. H.** Threats and the development of coordination: Further studies of the Deutsch and Krauss trucking game. *Journal of Personality and Social Psychology,* 1966, *4,* 119–126.

Sigall, H., and **Aronson, E.** Liking for an evaluator as a function of her physical attractiveness and nature of the evaluations. *Journal of Experimental Social Psychology,* 1969, *5,* 93–100.

Sigall, H., and **Ostrove, N.** Beautiful but dangerous: Effects of offender attractiveness and nature of the crime on juridic judgment. *Journal of Personality and Social Psychology,* 1975, *31,* 410–414.

Siegel, S. Morphine analgesic tolerance: Its situation specificity supports a Pavlovian conditioning model. *Science,* 1976, *193,* 323–325.

Simon, M. L. Application of a new model of peer group influence to naturally existing adolescent friendship groups. *Child Development,* 1977, *48,* 270–274.

Simpson, E. L. Moral development research: A case of scientific bias. *Human Development,* 1974, *17,* 81–106.

Sinclair-de Zwart, H. Language acquisition and cognitive development. In T. E. Moore (Ed.), *Cognitive development and the acquisition of language.* New York: Academic Press, 1973.

Skinner, B. F. *Science and human behavior.* New York: Macmillan, 1953.

Skinner, B. F. *Verbal behavior.* New York: Appleton-Century-Crofts, 1957.

Skinner, B. F. *Beyond freedom and dignity.* New York: Knopf, 1971.

Sklar, J., and **Berkov, B.** The American birth rate: Evidences of coming rise. *Science,* 1975, *189,* 693–700.

Skodak, M., and **Skeels, H.** A final follow-up study of one hundred adopted children. *Journal of Genetic Psychology,* 1949, *75,* 85–125.

Slobin, D. I. *Psycholinguistics.* Glenview, Ill.: Scott, Foresman, 1971.

Smith, F. *Understanding reading.* New York: Holt, Rinehart and Winston, 1970.

Smith, M. E. An investigation of the development of the sentence and the extent of vocabulary in young children. *University of Iowa Studies in Child Welfare,* 1926, *3,* No. 5.

Smith, M. L. and **Glass, B. V.** Meta-analysis of psychotherapy outcome studies. *American Psychologist,* 1977, *32,* 752–760.

Snow, C. E. Mother's speech to children learning language. *Child Development,* 1972, *43,* 549–565.

Snyder, M., and **Swann, W. B., Jr.** Behavioral confirmation in social interaction: From social perception to social reality. *Journal of Experimental Social Psychology,* 1978, *14,* 148–162.

Solomon, R. L. and **Corbit, J. D.** An opponent-process theory of motivation: I. Temporal dynamics of affect. *Psychological Review,* 1974, *81,* 119–145.

Solomon, R. L., and **Corbit, J. D.** An opponent-process theory of motivation: II. Cigarette addiction. *Journal of Abnormal Psychology,* 1973, *81,* 158–171.

Solomon, R. L., Kamin, L. J., and **Wynne, L. C.** Traumatic avoidance learning: The outcomes of several extinction procedures with dogs. *Journal of Abnormal and Social Psychology,* 1953, *48,* 291–302.

Sorenson, R. C. *Adolescent sexuality in contemporary America: Personal values and sexual behavior ages 13–14.* New York: Abrams, 1973.

Sorrentino, R. M., and **Boutillier, R. G.** The effect of quantity and quality of verbal interaction on ratings of leadership ability. *Journal of Experimental Social Psychology,* 1975, *11,* 403–411.

Spence, J. T., and **Spence, K. W.** The motivational components of manifest anxiety: Drive and drive stimuli. In C. D. Spielberger (Ed.), *Anxiety and behavior.* New York: Academic Press, 1966.

Spence, K. W., Farber, I. E., and **McFann, H. H.** The relation of anxiety (drive) level to performance in competitional paired-associates learning. *Journal of Experimental Social Psychology,* 1956, *52,* 296–305.

Sperling, G. The information available in brief visual presentations. *Psychological Mono-*

graphs, 1960, *74* (11, Whole No. 498).

Sperry, R. W. The great cerebral commissure. *Scientific American,* 1964, *210*(1), 42–52.

Sperry, R. W., and **Hibberd, E.** In G. E. W. Wolstenholme and M. O'Connor (Eds.), *Growth of the nervous system.* London: Churchill, 1968.

Spiegel, H. A single-treatment method to stop smoking using ancillary self-hypnosis. *International Journal of Clinical Hypnosis,* 1970, *18,* 235–250.

Spitz, R. A. Hospitalism: An inquiry into the genesis of psychiatric conditions in early childhood. In R. S. Eissler et al. (Eds.), *The psychoanalytic study of the child* (Vol. 1). New York: International Universities Press, 1945.

Spitz, R. A. Hospitalism: A follow-up report. In R. S. Eissler et al. (Eds.), *Psychoanalytic study of the child* (Vol. 2). New York: International Universities Press, 1946.

Spooner, A., and **Kellogg, W. N.** The backward conditioning curve. *American Journal of Psychology,* 1947, *60,* 321–334.

Staats, C. K., and **Staats, W.W.** Meaning established by classical conditioning. *Journal of Experimental Psychology,* 1957, *54,* 74–80.

Stafford-Clark, D., and **Smith, A. C.** *Psychiatry for students* (5th ed.). London: Allen & Unwin, 1978.

Stampfl, T. G., and **Levis, D. J.** Phobic patients: Treatment with the learning theory approach of implosive therapy. *Voices: The art and Science of Psychotherapy,* 1967, *3,* 23–27.

Stern, G. G. *People in context.* New York: Wiley, 1970.

Stern, J. A., Brown, M., Ulett, G. A., and **Sletten, I.** A comparison of hypnosis, acupuncture, morphine, valium, aspirin, and placebo in the management of experimentally induced pain. In Edmonston, W. E., Jr. (Ed.), *Conceptual and investigative approaches to hypnosis and hypnotic phenomena. Annals of The New York Academy of Sciences* (Vol. 296), 1977, 175–193.

Sternberg, S. High-speed scanning in human memory. *Science,* 1966, *53,* 421–457.

Stevens, K. N. and **House, A. S.** Speech perception. In J. V. Tobias (Ed.), *Foundations of modern auditory theory,* Vol. 2. New York: Academic Press, 1972.

Stevens, S. S. The direct estimate of sensory magnitudes—loudness. *American Journal of Psychology,* 1956, *69,* 1–25.

Stinett, N., Carter, L. M., and **Montgomery, J. E.** Older persons' perceptions of their marriages. *Journal of Marriage and the Family,* 1972, *34,* 665–670.

Stokols, D. On the distinction between density and crowding: Some implications for future research. *Psychological Review,* 1972, *79,* 275–278.

Stokols, D., Novaco, R. W., Stokols, J., and Campbell, J. Traffic congestion, type

A behavior and stress. *Journal of Applied Psychology,* 1978, *63,* 467–480.

Stone, L. J., Smith, H. T., and **Murphy, L. B.,** (Eds.). *The competent infant: Research and commentary.* New York: Basic books, 1973.

Stoner, J. A comparison of individual and group decisions, including risk. Unpublished master's thesis, MIT, 1961.

Streib, G. F., and **Schneider, C. J.** *Retirement in American society.* Ithaca, N.Y.: Cornell University Press, 1971.

Stromeyer, C. F., and **Psotka, J.** The detailed texture of eidetic images. *Nature,* 1973, *225,* 346–349.

Stroop, J. R. Studies of interference in serial verbal reactions. *Journal of Experimental Psychology,* 1935, *18,* 643–662.

Suls, J., and **Miller, R. J.** (Eds.). *Social comparison processes: Theoretical and empirical perspectives.* Washington, D.C.: Hemisphere/Halsted, 1977.

Suomi, S. J. Development of attachment and other behaviors in rhesus monkeys. In T. Alloway, P. Pliner, and L. Krames (Eds.), *Advances in the study of communication and affect (Vol. 3): Attachment behavior.* New York: Plenum, 1977.

Suomi, S. J., and **Harlow, H. F.** Social rehabilitation of isolate-reared monkeys. *Developmental Psychology,* 1972, *6,* 487–496.

Swann, W. B., and **Pittman, T. S.** Imitating play activity of children: The moderating influence of verbal cues on intrinsic motivation. *Child Development,* 1977, *48,* 1128–1132.

Szasz, T. The myth of mental illness. *American Psychologist,* 1960, *15,* 113–118.

Tagiuri, R., Blake, R., and **Bruner, J.** Some determinants of the perception of positive and negative feelings in others. *Journal of Abnormal and Social Psychology,* 1953, *48,* 585–592.

Talbert, G. B. Aging of the reproductive system. In C. E. Finch and L. Hayflick (Eds.), *Handbook of the biology of aging.* New York: Van Nostrand Reinhold, 1977.

Tanner, J. M. *Growth at adolescence.* Philadelphia: Davis, 1962.

Tanner, J. M. Physical growth. In P. H. Mussen (Ed.), *Carmichael's manual of child psychology* (Vol. 2) (3rd ed.). New York: Wiley, 1970.

Tarshis, B. *The ''average American'' book.* New York: Atheneum/SMI, 1979.

Taylor, S., and **Metlee, D.** When similarity breeds contempt. *Journal of Personality and Social Psychology,* 1971, *20,* 75–81.

Taylor, S. P., and **Piano, R.** Physical aggression as a function of frustration and physical attack. *Journal of Social Psychology,* 1971, *84,* 261–267.

Teghtsoonian, R. On the exponent in Stevens' Law and the constant in Ekman's Law. *Psychological Review,* 1971, *78,* 71–80.

Teitelbaum, P. Random and food-directed activity in hyperphagic and normal rats. *Journal of Comparative and Physiological Psychology,* 1957, *50,* 486–490.

Teitelbaum, P. Disturbances in feeding and drinking behavior after hypothalamic lesions. In M. R. Jones (Ed.), *Nebraska Symposium on Motivation.* Lincoln, Neb.: University of Nebraska Press, 1961.

Teitelbaum, P., and **Epstein, A. N.** The lateral hypothalamic syndrome: Recovery of feeding and drinking after lateral hypothalamic lesions. *Psychological Review,* 1962, *69,* 74–90.

Tennen, H., and **Ellir, S.** Attributional components of learned helplessness and facilitation. *Journal of Personality and Social Psychology,* 1977, *35,* 265–271.

Terman, L. M. *The measurement of intelligence.* Boston: Houghton Mifflin, 1916.

Terman, L. M. Feeble-minded children in the public schools of California. *School and Society,* 1917, *5,* 161–165.

Terman, L. M. *Mental and physical traits of a thousand gifted children. Genetic studies of genius, Vol. 1.* Stanford, Cal.: Stanford University Press, 1925.

Terrace, H. S., Petitto, L.A., Sanders, R. J., and **Bever, T. G.** Can an ape create a sentence? *Science,* 1979, *206,* 891–901.

Thibant, J. W., and **Kelley, H. H.** *The social psychology of groups.* New York: Wiley, 1959.

Thigpen, C. H. and **Cleckley, H.** *The three faces of Eve.* Kingsport, Tenn.: Kingsport Press, 1954.

Thomas, A., Chess, S., and **Birch, H. G.** The origin of personality. *Scientific American,* 1970, *223,* 102–109.

Thomas, M., Horton, R., Lippincott, E., and **Drabman, R.** Desensitization to portrayals of real-life aggression as a function of exposure to television violence. *Journal of Personality and Social Psychology,* 1977, *35,* 450–458.

Thompson, W. R., and **Heron, W.** The effects of restricting early experience on the problem-solving capacity of dogs. *Canadian Journal of Psychology,* 1954, *8,* 17–31.

Thorson, G., Hochhaus, L., and **Stanners, R. F.** Temporal changes in visual and acoustic codes in a letter-watching task. *Perception and Psychophysics,* 1976, *19*(4), 346–348.

Thurnher, M. Midlife marriage: Sex differences in evaluation and perspectives. *International Journal of Aging and Human Development,* 1976, *7*(2), 129–135.

Thurnher, M., Spence, D., and **Fiske, M.** Value confluence and behavioral conflict in intergenerational relations. *Journal of Marriage and the Family,* 1974, *36,* 308–319.

Thurstone, L. L. Primary mental abilities. *Psychometrika Monographs,* 1938, No: 1.

Tizard, B., and **Hodges, J.** The effect of early institutional rearing on the development of eight-year-old children. *Journal of Child Psychology and Psychiatry*, 1978, *19*, 99–118.

Tolman, E. C., and **Honzik, C. H.** Introduction and removal of reward, and maze performance in rats. *University of California Publications in Psychology*, 1930, *4*, 257–275.

Tolman, J. and **King, J. A.** The effects of testosterone propionate on aggression in male and female C57BL/10 mice. *British Journal of Animal Behaviour*, 1956, *4*, 147–149.

Triplett, N. The dynamogenic factors in pacemaking and competition. *American Journal of Psychology*, 1897, *9*, 507–533.

Tryon, R. C. Individual differences. In F. A. Moss (Ed.), *Comparative psychology.* Englewood Cliffs, N. J.: Prentice-Hall, 1942, 330–365.

Tuddenham, R. D., Blumenkrantz, J., and **Wiklin, W. R.** Age changes on AGCT: A longitudinal study of average adults. *Journal of Consulting and Clinical Psychology*, 1968, *32*, 659–663.

Tulving, E. Relation between encoding specificity and levels of processing. In L. S. Cermak and F. I. M. Craik (Eds.), *Levels of processing and human memory.* Hillsdale, N.J.: Erlbaum, 1978.

Tulving, E. and **Watkins, M. J.** Continuity between recall and recognition. *American Journal of Psychology*, 1973, *86*, 739–748.

Turvey, M. T., and **Shaw, R. E.** Memory (or, knowing) as a matter of specification not representation: Notes towards a different class of machines. In L.S. Cermak and F. I. M. Craik (Eds.), *Levels of processing and human memory.* Hillsdale, N.J.: Erlbaum, 1978.

U.S. Census Bureau. Demographic aspects of aging and the older population in the United States. Current Population Reports, Series P-23, No. 59. Washington, D.C.: U.S. Government Printing Office.

U.S. Public Health Service. Current estimates from the health interview survey: United States—1974. Vital and Health Statistics, Series 10, No. 100, National Center for Health Statistics. Washington, D.C.: U.S. Government Printing Office.

Utech, D. A., and **Horing, K. L.** Parents and peers as competing influences in the decisions of children of differing ages. *Journal of Social Psychology*, 1969, *78*, 267–274.

Valenstein, E. S. *Brain control: A critical examination of brain stimulation and psychosurgery.* New York: Wiley, 1973.

Valenstein, E., Riss, W., and **Young W. C.** Experiential and genetic factors in the organization of sexual behavior in male guinea pigs. *Journal of Comparative and Physiological Psychology*, 1955, *48*, 397–403.

Van Praag, H., Korf, J., and **Schut, D.** Cerebral monoamines and depression: An in-

vestigation with the probenecid technique. *Archives of General Psychiatry*, 1973, *28*, 827–831.

Vernon, J. A., McGill, T. E., Gulick, W. L., and **Candland, D. R.** Effect of sensory deprivation on some perceptual and motor skills. *Perceptual and Motor Skills*, 1959, *9*, 91–97.

Veroff, J., Wilcox, S., and **Atkinson, J. W.** The achievement motive in high school and college-age women. *Journal of Abnormal and Social Psychology*, 1953, *48*, 102–119.

Verplanck, W. S. The control of the content of conversation: Reinforcement of statements of opinion. *Journal of Abnormal and Social Psychology*, 1955, *51*, 668–676.

Vinokur, A. Effects of group processes upon individual and group decisions involving risk. *Dissertation Abstracts International*, 1971 (Vol. 31) (12-A), 6721–6722.

Vogel, G. W. Sleep-onset mentation. In A. M. Arkin, J. S. Antrobus, and S. J. Ellman (Eds.), *The mind in sleep psychology and psychobiology.* Hillsdale, N.J.: Erlbaum, 1978, 97–112.

Volicer, B. J., and **Volicer, L.** Cardiovascular changes associated with stress during hospitalization. *Journal of Psychosomatic Research*, 1978, *22*, 159–168.

von Frisch, K. Honeybees: Do they use direction and distance information provided by their dances? *Science*, 1967, *158*, 1072–1076.

Walker, T. G., and **Main, E. C.** Choice-shifts in political decision making: Federal judges and civil liberties cases. *Journal of Applied Social Psychology*, 1973, *2*, 39–48.

Wallach, M., Kogan, N., and **Bern, D.** Group influence on individual risk taking. *Journal of Abnormal and Social Psychology*, 1962, *65*, 75–86.

Walster, E., Aronson, V., Abrahams, D., and **Rottman, L.** Importance of physical attractiveness in dating behavior. *Journal of Personality and Social Psychology*, 1966, *4*, 508–516.

Walters, R. H., and **Llewellyn Thomas, E.** Enhancement of punitiveness by visual and audiovisual displays. *Canadian Journal of Psychology*, 1963, *16*, 244–255.

Ward, R. A. *The aging experience.* New York: Lippincott, 1979.

Wasman, M., and **Flynn, J. P.** Directed attack elicited   s om hypothalamus. *Arch. Neurol.*, 1962, *6*, 220–227.

Wason, P. C., and **Johnson-Laird, P. N.** *Psychology of reasoning: Structure and content.* London: Batsford, 1972.

Waters, E., Wippman, J., and **Sroufe, L. A.** Attachment, positive affect, and competence in the peer group: Two studies in construct validation. *Child Development*, 1979, *50*, 821–829.

Watson, J. B., and **Rayner, R.** Conditioned emotional reactions. *Journal of Experimental Psychology*, 1920, *3*, 1–14.

Webb, W. B., and **Cartwright, R. D.** Sleep and dreams. *Annual Review of Psychology*, 1978, *29*.

Weigman, A. D. *On dying and denying.* New York: Behavioral Publications, 1972.

Weiner, B. *Achievement motivation and attribution theory.* Morristown, N.J.: General Learning Press, 1971.

Weiner, B., Frieze, I., Kukla, A., Reed, L., Rest, S., and **Rosenbaum, R. M.** Perceiving the causes of success and failure. In E. E. Jones et al. (Eds.), *Attribution: Perceiving the causes of behavior.* Morristown, N.J.: General Learning Press, 1971.

Weisberg, R. *Memory, thought and behavior.* New York: Oxford University Press, 1980.

Welkowitz, J., Ewen, R. B., and **Cohen, J.** *Introductory statistics for the behavioral sciences.* New York: Academic Press, 1977.

Welsh, G. S., and **Dahlstrom, W. G.** (Eds.). *Basic readings on the MMPI in psychology and medicine.* Minneapolis: University of Minnesota Press, 1965.

Wertheimer, M. *Productive thinking.* New York: Harper, 1945, 1959.

Wever, E. G., and **Bray, C. W.** The perception of low tones and the resonance-volley theory. *Journal of Psychology*, 1937, *3*, 101–114.

White, R. W. Motivation reconsidered: The concept of competence. *Psychological Review*, 1959, *66*, 297–333.

Whiting, B. B., and **Whiting, J. W. M.** *Children of six cultures.* Cambridge, Mass.: Harvard University Press, 1975.

Whiting, J. W. M., Klucholm, R. C., and **Anthony, A.** The function of male initiation ceremonies at puberty. In E. Maccoby, T. M. Newcomb, and E. L. Hartley (Eds.), *Readings in social psychology.* New York: Holt, Rinehart and Winston, 1958.

Whorf, B. L. Languages and logic. In J. B. Carroll (Ed.), *Language, thought and reality: Selected writings of Benjamin Lee Whorf.* Cambridge, Mass.: MIT Press, 1956.

Wichman, H. Effects of isolation and communication on cooperation in a two-person game. *Journal of Personality and Social Psychology*, 1970, *16*, 114–120.

Wickens, D. D. Characteristics of word encoding. In A. W. Melton and E. Martin (Eds.), *Coding processes in human memory.* Washington, D.C.: Winston, 1972.

Wicker, A. Attitudes versus actions: The relationship of verbal and overt behavioral responses to attitude objects. *The Journal of Social Issues*, 1969, *25*, 1–78.

Wicklund, R. A., and **Brehm, J. W.** *Perspectives on cognitive dissonance.* Hillsdale, N.J.: Erlbaum, 1976.

Wicklund, R. A., Cooper, J., and **Linden,**

D. E. Effects of expected effort on attitude change prior to exposure. *Journal of Experimental Social Psychology*, 1967, *3*, 416–428.

Wiesel, T. N., and **Hubel, D. H.** Single-cell responses in striate cortex of kittens deprived of vision in one eye. *Journal of Neurophysiology*, 1963, *26*, 1003–1017.

Wilder, D. A., and **Allen, V. L.** Group membership and preference for information about others. *Personality and Social Psychology Bulletin*, 1978, *4*, 106–110.

Willerman, L. *The psychology of individual and group differences.* San Francisco: Freeman, 1979.

Willerman, L., Naylor, A. F., and **Myrianthopoulos, N. C.** Intellectual development of children from interracial matings: Performance in infancy and at four years. *Behavior Genetics*, 1974, *4*, 83–90.

Williams, R. J. Biochemical individuality and cellular nutrition: Prime factors in alcoholism. *Quarterly Journal of Studies on Alcohol*, 1959, 20, 452–463.

Wilson, E. O. *The insect societies.* Cambridge, Mass.: The Belknap Press of Harvard University Press, 1971.

Wilson, E. O. Introduction to *Ecology, Evolution and Population Biology* (Readings from Scientific American). San Francisco: Freeman, 1974.

Wilson, G. T. Methodological considerations in treatment outcome research on obesity. *Journal of Consulting and Clinical Psychology*, 1978, *46*, 687–702.

Wilson, J. A., and **Glick, B.** Ontogeny of mating behavior in the chicken. *American Journal of Physiology*, 1970, *218*, 951–955.

Wilson, M. S., and **Meyer, E.** Diagnostic consistency in a psychiatric liaison service. *American Journal of Psychiatry*, 1962, *119*, 207–209.

Winston, P. H. *The psychology of computer vision.* New York: McGraw-Hill, 1975.

Wolberg, L. R. *The technique of psychotherapy* (3rd ed.). New York: Grune & Stratton, 1977.

Wolff, E. *Practical hypnotism.* New York: Louis Tannen (no date).

Wolpe, J. *Psychotherapy by reciprocal inhibition.* Stanford, Calif.: Stanford University Press, 1958.

Woodworth, R. S. *Dynamic psychology.* New York: Columbia University Press, 1918.

Woodworth, R. S. *Dynamics of behavior.* New York: Holt, Rinehart and Winston, 1958.

Wortman, C., Panciera, L., Shusterman, L., and **Hibscher, J.** Attributions of causality and reactions to uncontrollable outcomes. *Journal of Experimental Social Psychology*, 1976, *12*, 301–306.

Wrightsman, L. S. Effects of waiting with others on changes in level of felt anxiety. *Journal of Abnormal and Social Psychology*, 1960, *61*, 216–222.

Wyld, H. C. The superiority of received standard English. *Society for Pure English, Tract XXXVII*, 1931, 603–617.

Yarrow, L. J., Rubenstein, J. L., and **Pedersen, F. A.** *Infant and environment: Early cognitive and motivational development.* New York: Wiley, 1975.

Yerkes, R. M. (Ed.) Psychological examining in the United States Army. Washington, D.C.: *Memoirs of the National Academy of Sciences* (No. 15), 1921.

Yerkes, R. M., and **Foster, J. C.** *A point scale for measuring mental ability.* Baltimore, Md.: Warwick and York, 1923.

Young, W. C., Goy, R. W., and **Phoenix, C. H.** Hormones and sexual behavior. *Science*, 1964, *143*, 212–218.

Zajonc, R. B. Social facilitation. *Science*, 1965, *149*, 269–274.

Zajonc, R. B., and **Sales, S. M.** Social facilitation of dominant and subordinate responses. *Journal of Experimental Social Psychology*, 1966, *2*, 160–168.

Zajonc, R. B., Wolosin, R. J., Wolosin, M., and **Sherman, S. J.** Individual and group risk taking in a two-choice situation. *Journal of Experimental Social Psychology*, 1968, *4*, 89–106.

Zanna, M. P., and **Cooper, J.** Dissonance and the pill: An attribution approach to studying the arousal properties of dissonance. *Journal of Personality and Social Psychology*, 1974, *29*, 703–709.

Zellner, M. Self-esteem, reception, and influenceability. *Journal of Personality and Social Psychology*, 1970, *15*, 87–93.

Zelnik, M., and **Kanter, J. F.** The probability of premarital intercourse. *Social Science Research*, 1972, *1*, 335–341.

Zielman, D. *Hostility and aggression.* Hillsdale, N.J.: Erlbaum, 1978.

Zillman, D. Excitation transfer in communication-mediated aggressive behavior. *Journal of Experimental Social Psychology*, 1971, *7*, 419–434.

Zillman, D., and **Cantor, J. R.** Effects of timing of information about mitigating circumstances on emotional responses to provocation and retaliatory behavior. *Journal of Experimental Social Psychology*, 1976, *12*, 38–55.

Zimbardo, P. G. The efforts of early avoidance training and rearing conditions upon the sexual behavior of the male rat. *Journal of Comparative and Physiological Psychology*, 1958, *51*, 764–769.

Zimbardo, P. The effect of effort and improvisation on self-persuasion produced by role playing. *Journal of Experimental Social Psychology*, 1965, *1*, 103–120.

Zimbardo, P. G. The human choice: Individuation, reason, and order versus deindividuation, impulse, and chaos. In W. Arnold and D. Levine (Eds.), *Nebraska Symposium on Motivation.* Lincoln, Neb.: University of Nebraska Press, 1970.

Zimbardo, P. G. *Shyness: What it is, what to do about it.* Reading, Mass.: Addison-Wesley, 1977.

Zimbardo, P., Weisenberg, M., Firestone, I., and **Levy, B.** Communicator effectiveness in producing public conformity and private attitude change. *Journal of Personality*, 1965, *33*, 233–255.

Zimmerman, D. W. Durable secondary reinforcement: Method and theory. *Psychological Review*, 1957, *64*, 373–383.

Zuckerman, M., and **Wheeler, L.** To dispel fantasies about the fantasy-based measure of fear of success. *Psychological Bulletin*, 1975, *82*, 932–946.

and Walter, A. A. An experimental study of the effect of language on the presentation of visually perceived form. *Journal of Experimental Psychology*, 1932, *15*, 73–86. **Table 8-2** Luchins, A. J. Mechanization in problem solving: The effect of *Einstellung. Psychological Monographs*, 1942, *54*, 6 (Whole No. 248). **Fig. 8-14** After Figure 4, 5A, 5B, and 6 in *Productive Thinking*, enlarged edition by Max Wertheimer, edited by Michael Wertheimer. Copyright© 1945, 1959 by Valentin Wertheimer. Reprinted by permission of Harper & Row, Publishers, Inc. **Fig. 8-15** Glucksberg, S., and Weisberg, R. W. Verbal behavior and problem solving: Some effects of labeling in a functional fixedness problem. *Journal of Experimental Psychology*, 1966, *71*, 659–664. Copyright 1966 by the American Psychological Association. Reprinted by permission. **Table 8-3** Mednick, S. A. The associative basis of the creative process. *Psychological Review*, 1962, *69*, 220–232.

Table 9-1 Terman, L. M., and Merrill, M. A. *Measuring intelligence.* Boston: Houghton Mifflin, 1937. **Table 9-2, Fig. 9-2** Honzik, M. P., Macfarlane, J. W., and Allen, L. The stability of mental test performance between two and eighteen years. *Journal of Experimental Education*, 1948, *17*, 309–334. **Fig. 9-3** Schaie, K. W., Labouvie, G., and Buech, B. V. Generational and cohort specific differences in adult cognitive functioning: A fourteen-year study of independent samples. *Developmental Psychology*, 1973, 9, 151–160. **Tables 9-4, 9-5** Horn, J. M., Loehlin, J. O., and Willerman, L. Intellectual resemblance among adoptive and biological relatives: The Texas Adoption Project. *Behavior Genetics*, 1979, *9*, 177–208. Scarr, S., and Weinberg, R. A. Intellectual similarities within families of both adopted and biological children. *Intelligence*, 1977, *1*, 170–191. Courtesy of Mensa, 1791 West 3rd St., Brooklyn, NY 11223. **Fig. 9-5** Harrell, T. W., and Harrell, M. S. Army General Classification Test scores for civilian occupations. *Educational and Psychological Measurement*, 1945, *5*, 229–239. **Table 9-6, 9-7** McNemar, Q. *The revision of the Stanford-Binet scale: An analysis of the standardization data.* Boston: Houghton Mifflin, 1942.

Fig. 10-2 Photo courtesy Dr. Neal E. Miller. **Table 10-1** Schacter, S. Some extraordinary facts about obese humans and rats. *American Psychologist*, 1971, *26*, 129–144. Copyright 1971 by the American Psychological Association. Reprinted by permission. **Fig. 10-3** From Johnson, unpublished doctoral dissertation, Catholic University of America, 1970; cited in Schacter, S. Some extraordinary facts about obese humans and rats. *American Psychologist*, 1971, *26*, 129–144. Copyright 1971 by the American Psychological Association. Reprinted by permission. **Fig. 10-4** Hibscher, J. A., and Herman, C. P. Obesity, dieting, and the expression of "obese" characteristics. *Journal of Comparative and Physiological Psychology*, 1977, *91*, 374–380. Copy-

right 1977 by the American Psychological Association. Reprinted by permission. **Fig. 10-5** Warden, C. J. Animal motivation: Experimental studies on the albino rat. New York: Columbia University Press, 1931.

Fig. 11-3 Hohmann, G. W. Some effects of spinal cord lesions on experienced emotional feelings. *Psychophysiology*, 1966, *3*, 143–156. **Fig. 11-2** Photo by Smolam, Stock, Boston.

Fig. 12-1 Hess, E. H. "Imprinting" in animals. *Scientific American*, March 1958. Copyright © 1958 by Scientific American, Inc. All rights reserved. **Table 12-1** Erikson, E. *Childhood and society.* New York: Norton, 1963. **Table 12-2** Piaget, J., and Inhelder, B. *The psychology of the child.* New York: Basic Books, 1968. **Table 12-3** Kohlberg, L., and Kramer, R. B. Continuities and discontinuities in childhood and adult moral development. *Human Development*, 1969, *12*, 93–120.

Table 13-1 Ward, R. A. *The aging experience.* New York: Lippincott, 1979. Based on data from U. S. Bureau of the Census 1973b, 1976.

Table 14-1 Cattell, R. B. *Personality: A systematic, theoretical, and factual study.* New York: McGraw-Hill, 1950. **Table 14-2** Maslow, A. H. Self-actualization and beyond. In J. F. T. Bugental (Ed.), *Challenges of humanistic psychology.* New York: McGraw-Hill, 1967. Used with permission of the McGraw-Hill Book Company. **Fig. 14-5** Hathaway, S. R., and McKinley, J. C. *Minnesota Multiphasic Personality Inventory Revised 1967.* New York: The Psychological Corporation, 1970. Copyright 1970 by the Psychological Corporation and reproduced with permission.

List on p. 436 Adapted from Coleman, J. C., and Hammen, C. L. *Contemporary psychology and effective behavior.* Copyright © 1974 by Scott, Foresman and Company. Reprinted by permission. **Table 15-1** Holmes, T. H., The social readjustment rating scale. *Journal of Psychosomatic Research*, 1967, *11*, 213–218. Copyright 1967, Pergamon Press, Ltd. Reprinted with permission. **Fig. 15-2** Hokanson, J., De Good, D. E., Forrest, M., and Britton, T. Availability of avoidance behaviors in modulating vascular stress responses. *Journal of Personality and Social Psychology*, 1971, *19*, 60–68. Reprinted by permission of Academic Press and the authors.

Tables in box on p. 461 Coleman, J. E., Butcher, J. N., and Carson, R. C. *Abnormal Psychology and modern life* (6th ed.). Glenview, Ill.: Scott, Foresman, 1980; from DSM III, American Psychological Association. Copyright 1977 by the American Psychological Association. Reprinted by permission. **Case History, p. 464** Abridged from Leon, G. R., *Case histories of deviant behavior* (2nd ed.). Boston: Allyn and Bacon, 1977,

pp. 113–118. **Table 16-1** Adapted from Stern, R. S., and Cobb, J. P. (1978) Phenomenology of obsessive-compulsive neurosis. *The British Journal of Psychiatry*, *182*, 233–239. **Case History on p. 469** Abridged from Stafford-Clark, D., and Smith, A. C. *Psychiatry for students* (5th ed.). London: George Allen & Unwin, 1978, p. 145. **Table 16-2** Beck, A. T. The development of depression: A cognitive model. In R. J. Friedman and M. M. Katz (Eds.), *The psychology of depression: Contemporary theory and research.* Copyright © 1974 by Hemisphere Publishing Corporation, Washington, D. C. Reprinted by permission. **Case History on p. 475** Abridged from Kolb, D. *Modern clinical psychiatry* (8th ed.). Philadelphia: Saunders, 1973, 334–335. **Case History on p. 480** Abridged from Cleckley, H. *The mask of sanity* (4th ed.). St. Louis, Mo.: C. V. Mosby, 1964, pp. 66–74. **Table 16-3** From *Abnormal Psychology and Modern Life*, 6th Edition, by James C. Coleman. Copyright © 1980, 1976 by Scott, Foresman and Company. Reprinted by permission.

Fig. 17-1 National Institute of Mental Health, DHHS. **Application on p. 497** Abridged from Wolberg, L. The technique of psychotherapy (3rd ed.). New York: Grune & Stratton, 1977, pp. 560–561. Copyright © 1977 by Lewis R. Wolberg, M. D. Reprinted by permission of the author. **Application on p. 499** Rimm, D. C., and Masters, J. C. *Behavior therapy: Techniques and empirical findings* (2nd ed.). New York: Academic Press, 1979, p. 48. Copyright©1979 by Academic Press. Reprinted by permission. **Application on p. 500** Hogan, R. A. The implosive technique. *Behavior Research and Therapy*, 1968, *6*, 423–431. Copyright 1968 by Pergamon Press, Ld. Reprinted with permission. **Table 17-1** Schaefer, H. H., and Martin, P. L. *Behavior therapy.* New York: McGraw-Hill, 1969. Used with permission of McGraw-Hill Book Company. **Fig. 17-2** Courtesy National Institute of Mental Health, DHHS. **Application on p. 507** Abridged from Phares, E. J. *Clinical psychology: Concepts, methods, and profession.* Copyright 1979 by The Dorsey Press. Reprinted by permission. **Application on p. 510** Abridged from Rimm, D. C., and Masters, J. C. *Behavior Therapy: Techniques and empirical findings* (2nd ed.), pp. 383–384. Copyright © 1979 by Academic Press.

Fig. 18-1 Kelley, H. H. The processes of causal attribution. *American Psychologist*, February 1973, 107–128. Copyright 1974 by the American Psychological Association. Reprinted by permission. **Fig. 18-2** Hovland, C. I., and Weiss, W. The influence of source credibility on communication effectiveness. *The Public Opinion Quarterly*, 1952, 15, 635–650. **Fig. 18-3** Hovland, C. I., Lumsdaine, A., and Sheffield, F. *Experiments on mass communications.* Princeton, N.J.: Princeton University Press, 1949. **Table 18-1** Festinger, L., and Carlsmith, J. M. Cognitive consequences of forced compliance. *Journal of Abnormal and Social Psychology*, 1959, *58*, 203–210. Copyright 1959 by the American Psychological Association. Reprinted by permission. **Table 18-2** Aronson, E., and Linder, D. Gain and loss of esteem as determinants of interpersonal attractiveness. *Journal of Experimental Social Psychology*, 1965, *1*, 156–171. Copyright © 1965 by Academic Press.

Fig. 19-1 Sherif, M., and Sherif, C. W. *An outline of social psychology* (rev. ed.). Copyright © 1948, 1956 by Harper & Row, Publishers, Inc. Reprinted by permission of the publisher. **Fig. 19-2** Latané, B., and Darley, J. M. Group inhibition of bystander intervention in emergencies. *Journal of Personality and Social Psychology*, 1968, *10*, 215–221. Copyright 1968 by the American Psychological Association. Reprinted by permission. **Fig. 19-3** Deutsch, M., and Gerard, H. B. A study of normative and informational social influences upon individual judgment. *Journal of Abnormal and Social Psychology*, 1955, *51*, 629–636. Copyright 1955 by the American Psychological Association. Reprinted by permission. **Fig. 19-4** Leavitt, H. J. Some effects of certain communication patterns on group performance. *Journal of Abnormal and Social Psychology*, 1951, *46*, Fig. 4, p. 42. Copyright 1951 by the American Psychological Association. Reprinted by permission. **Fig. 19-7 Table 19-1** Deutsch, M., and Krauss, R. M. The effect of threat upon interpersonal bargaining. *Journal of Abnormal and Social Psychology*, 1960, *61*, 181–189. Copyright 1960 by the American Psychological Association. Reprinted by permission. **Fig. 19-8** Baum, S., and Valins, S. *Architecture and social behavior: Psychological studies in social density.* Hillsdale, N.J.: Erlbaum, 1977.

Photographs

4 The Bettmann Archive **5** The Bettmann Archive **6** The Bettmann Archive **7** (left) Hugh Rogers, Monkmeyer Press Photo Service (right) Stock, Boston **10** Owen Franken, Stock, Boston **11** Sybil Shackman, Monkmeyer Press Photo Service **21** Sybil Shelton, Monkmeyer Press Photo Service **32** United Press International **39** Mimi Forsyth, Monkmeyer Press Photo Service **83** United Press International **85** Sybil Shackman, Monkmeyer Press Photo Service **86** Gisele Freund, Monkmeyer Press Photo Service **87** Georg Gerster, Photo Researchers, Inc. **93** (left) Jeff Albertson, Stock, Boston (right) Paolo Koch, Photo Researchers, Inc. (bottom) Russ Kinne, Photo Researchers, Inc. **96** (top) NASA/Photo Researchers, Inc. **103** (left) Tom McHugh, Photo Researchers, Inc. (right) Richard Frieman, Photo Researchers, Inc. **108** Bernard Pierre Wolff, Photo Researchers, Inc. **125** The Bettmann Archive **128** (left and right) The Bettmann Archive **134** Ray Ellis, Rapho/Photo Researchers, Inc. **136** Charles Gatewood **139** Les Mahon, Monkmeyer Press Photo Service **156** Eliot Elisofon © 1958 Time Inc. **157** Monkmeyer Press Photo Service **158** Jeff Albertson, Stock, Boston **159** I. Springer **160** Peter Southwick, Stock, Boston **164** United Press International **169** Sybil Shelton, Monkmeyer Press Photo Service **173** Photo courtesy of Harry F. Harlow, University of Wisconsin Primate Laboratory **174** Mimi Forsyth, Monkmeyer Press Photo Service **180** Ray Ellis, Photo Researchers, Inc. **182** (left) Richard Frieman, Photo Researchers, Inc. (right) Bell Laboratories, Inc. **183** Paolo Koch, Photo Researchers, Inc. **190** Abram G. Schoenfeld, Photo Researchers, Inc. **202** Mimi Forsyth, Monkmeyer Press Photo Service **203** Robert Goldstein **221** (left) Erika Stone, Photo Researchers, Inc. (right) Stan Goldblatt, Photo Researchers, Inc. (bottom) George Malave, Stock, Boston **227** United Press International **250** Bruce Roberts, Photo Researchers, Inc. **252** Photos courtesy The Psychological Corporation **265** Photos by David Stickler, Monkmeyer Press Photo Service **267** Mimi Forsyth, Monkmeyer Press Photo Service **281** Jack Prelutsky, Stock, Boston **285** Jan Halaska, Photo Researchers, Inc. **289** Katrina Thomas, Photo Researchers, Inc. **295** Photo Researchers, Inc. **300** Photo Courtesy of Harry F. Harlow, University of Wisconsin Primate Laboratory **311** (left) Jeff Albertson, Stock, Boston (right) Patricia Hollander Gross, Stock, Boston **312** Clif Garboden, Stock, Boston **313** (left) Alice Kandell, Photo Researchers, Inc. (right) Peter Menzel, Stock, Boston **315** (top, left) United Press International (top, right) United Press International (middle, left) Vivienne, Photo Researchers, Inc. (middle, right) Marc Anderson (bottom, left) Marc Anderson (bottom, right) Keith Gunnar, Photo Researchers, Inc. **317** Sybil Shelton, Monkmeyer Press Photo Service **322** David A. Krathwohl, Stock, Boston **325** (top, left) Tim Carlson, Stock, Boston (top, right) Paul Conklin, Monkmeyer Press Photo Service (bottom, left) David S. Strickler, Monkmeyer Press Photo Service (bottom, middle) Jon Rawle, Stock, Boston (bottom, right) Richard Frear, Photo Researchers, Inc. **326** Smolam, Stock, Boston **333** David R. Frazier, Photo Researchers, Inc. **342** (top) Ray Ellis, Kay Reese & Associates (bottom) Ed Lettau, Photo Researchers, Inc. **344** Thomas McAvoy, Life Magazine © 1955 Time Inc. **347** (left) David Linton, Scientific American (right) William Vandivert **348** (top, left) Jan Lukas, Photo Researchers, Inc. (top, right) Martine Franck/VIVA 1978 Woodfin Camp & Associates (middle, left) W. W. Wilson, Monkmeyer Press Photo Service (middle, center) Raimondo Borea, Editorial Photocolor Archives (middle, right) Erika Stone, Photo Researchers, Inc. (bottom) Richard Checani, Kay Reese & Associates **353** (left) Laimute E. Druskis, Editorial Photocolor Archives (right) David S. Strickler, Monkmeyer Press Photo Service **360** Sybil Shelton, Monkmeyer Press Photo Service (middle) Ann Chwatsky, Editorial Photocolor Archives (bottom) Carl Weese, Rapho/Photo Researchers, Inc. **361** Sam Falk, The New York Times **362** Paul Conklin, Monkmeyer Press Photo Service **363** Perry Ruben, Monkmeyer Press Photo Service **368** Jean B. Hollynan, Photo Researchers, Inc. **370** Mimi Forsyth, Monkmeyer Press Photo Service **372** Strix Pix, Monkmeyer Press Photo Service **373** (left) Strix Pix, Monkmeyer Press Photo Service (right) Ray Ellis, Photo Researchers, Inc. **374** (left) F. B. Grunzweig, Photo Researchers, Inc. (right) Marc Anderson **376** (left) Robert Kingman, Photo Researchers, Inc. (right) Myron Wood, Photo Researchers, Inc. **377** (left) Paul S. Conklin, Monkmeyer Press Photo Service (right) Nancy Hays, Monkmeyer Press Photo Service **379** Jan Lucas, Photo Researchers, Inc. **380** Sybil Shelton, Monkmeyer Press Photo Service **382** Irene Springer **383** Marc Anderson **387** (left) Bill Anderson, Monkmeyer Press Photo Service (right) Paul Segueira, Rapho/Photo Researchers, Inc. **389** (left) Michael Uffer, Photo Researchers, Inc. (right) Ray Ellis, Rapho/Photo Researchers, Inc. **390** Jack Prelutsky, Stock, Boston **401** The Bettmann Archive **405** The Bettmann Archive **413** (top) Marion Bernstein (bottom) Sybil Shelton, Monkmeyer Press Photo Service **414** United Press International **425** Photo Researchers, Inc. **426** Van Bucher, Photo Researchers Inc. **434** United Press International **436** (top) Arthur Grace, Stock, Boston (left) Arthur Grace, Stock, Boston (right) Photo Researchers, Inc. **439** Ed Lettau, Photo Researchers, Inc. **452** Dick Hanley, Photo Researchers, Inc. **463** Georg Gerster, Photo Researchers, Inc. **467** Owen Franklin, Stock, Boston **471** Hella Hammid, Rapho/Photo Researchers, Inc. **477** United Press International **481** Charles Gatewood, Stock, Boston **490** The American Museum of Natural History **491** (left and right) The Bettmann Archive **501** Photo by Shirley Miller Higgins, courtesy of New Castle State Hospital, New Castle, Indiana **506** Courtesy of Carl R. Rogers **534** Tyrone Hall, Stock, Boston **535** Ken Karp **537** Bettye Lane, Photo Researchers, Inc. **541** (left) Anestis Diakopoulos (right) Christopher Brown, Stock, Boston (bottom) Catherine Howell, Photo Researchers, Inc. **542** Nina Howell Starr, Photo Researchers, Inc. **543** Stock, Boston **547** (left) United Press International (right) Robert A. Isaacs, Photo Researchers, Inc. **548** (left) Bill Young, United Press International (right) Daniel S. Brody, Stock, Boston **554** Harry Wilks, Stock, Boston **557** William Vandivert and Scientific American, Inc. **560** Marianne Barcellona, The New York Philharmonic Orchestra **561** (left) Robert De Gast, Rapho/Photo Researchers, Inc. (right) United Press International **563** Ken Karp **570** (left) Peter Southwick, Stock, Boston (right) United Press International **574** (top, right) United Press International (middle) Frank Siteman, Stock, Boston (left and bottom) Joseph Schuyler, Stock, Boston **576** Jim Anderson, Woodfin Camp and Associates, Inc.

NAME INDEX

SUBJECT INDEX

Location constancy, 109–10
Loci, method of, 203, 204
Longitudinal studies, 249, 381
Long-term memory, 192, 197–200
Lordosis, 295
Love, need for, 320
LSD (lysergic acid diethylamide), 34, 138
Luchins's water jar problem, 235–36

Magnitude estimation, 65
Maladaptive behavior. *See* Abnormal behavior
Maleness, 293–94
Manic-depressive patterns, 472–73; lithium therapy for, 504
MAO inhibitors, 503–4
Marijuana, 82, 138–39
Marriage: demographic trends in, 377; middle age and, 383–84; in old age, 388; as social exchange, 566–67. *See also* Divorce
Maslow's hierarchy of needs, 319–20, 415
Maslow's theory of personality, 414–16
Maternal aggression, 302
Mating, in the ring dove, 294–95
Matrix analysis of interdependence, 565–66
Maturation, 342–43
Maze studies, latent learning and, 173–75
Meals, 282
Mean, 584; distribution of sample means, 592–93; standard error of the, 592–93
Meanings of words, 211–14; denotative and connotative, 212–14; overextension of, 221
Mean length of utterance (MLU), 224
Median, 583–84
Meditation, 132–34; stress-related diseases and, 133
Medulla, 41
Memory: of children, 362–63; consolidation theory of, 191, 196; constructive, 200–2, depth-of-processing theory of, 198–200; early ideas on, 191; echoic, 193; iconic, 193; improving, 202–6; long-term, 192, 197–200; multiprocess theories of, 191–92; photographic (eidetic imagery), 205; sensory, 192–93; short-term, 192–97; tasks used to test, 183–85; visual, 200–1
Memory-scanning procedure, Sternberg's, 196–97
Memory span, 362
Memory systems: of computers, 181–82; definition of, 179; developing theories about, 182; human, 191–202; terminology for describing, 179–82
Menopause, 381–82
Menstrual cycle, 295
Mental age, 242–44
Mental hospitals, 490–92
Mental retardation, 250
Mesomorphs, 412
Metaphor, 326
Microelectrode, 38

Midbrain, 41–42
Middle age, 379–84; "empty nest" period of, 382; marriage and, 383–84; physical changes in, 380–81; vocational changes in, 382–83
Minnesota Multiphasic Personality Inventory (MMPI), 427–29
MLU (mean length of utterance), 224
Mnemonics, 202–6
Mnemonists, 205
Mode, 583
Modeling, 502–3. *See also* Imitation
Money, as secondary motivator, 308
Monkeys, motherlessness and, 299–301
Monoamine oxidase (MAO) inhibitors, 503–4
Monochromats, 84
Monocular cues for depth, 101
Moon illusion, 103
Moral anxiety, 438
Moral development: during adolescence, 375; in early adulthood, 378–79; in childhood, 357–59
Moratorium, 371
Morphemes, 211
Morphine, 137
Motherlessness in monkeys, 299–301
Motion: induced, 111; stroboscopic, 111
Motivation, 277–334; achievement, 361; attribution and, 526–27; definition of, 277; determinism and, 278; drive theory of, 279–81; effectance, 316; free will and, 278; functional autonomy of, 308–9; homeostasis and, 279; hunger as, 281–87; instincts and, 278; intrinsic and extrinsic, 317–18; in Maslow's theory of personality, 414–15; parenting, 298–301; secondary, 307–8; sexuality and mating, 291–97; temperature regulation, 290–91; theories of, 277–81; thirst as, 288–90. *See also* Needs
Motor cortex, 46
Motor development, 342–43, 346–47
Motor homunculus, 46
Motor neurons, 31, 36–37
Mouth, food intake regulation and, 282
Movement, perception of, 109–11
Müller-Lyer illusion, 109
Multiple personality, 468
Myelin, 32, 34
Myelination, 32
Myopia (nearsightedness), 82

Narcotic addiction, 481, 483–84. *See also* Drug addiction
Narcotics, 136–37
Naturalistic observation, 598
Nearsightedness (myopia), 82
Need(s), 279; for achievement, 318–19; for affiliation, 309–12; basic, 415; for competence, 314–18; for stimulation, 312–14; Maslow's hierarchy of, 319–20, 415; physiological, 307, 320; for self-actualization, 316, 320, 414–16; sources of, 307–9

Negation, 447–48
Negative afterimage, 77
Negative reinforcers, 156. *See also* Punishment
Negative set, 235–37
Neocortex (cerebral cortex), 45–51; association areas of, 47–48; right and left sides of, 48–51; sensory and motor areas of, 46–47
Neo-Freudians, 405–7
Nerves, 37
Nervous system, 30–39; development of, 31–32; study of, 38–39. *See also* Central nervous system; Peripheral nervous system
Neuromuscular junctions, 36
Neuron doctrine, 38
Neurons, 30–34; connections among, 32; electrochemical effects and, 33–34; interneurons, 31, 39; mechanisms of, 32–34; motor, 31, 36–37; sensory, 31; study of, 38–39; vision and, 78–79
Neurosis: hysterical, 468–69; obsessive-compulsive, 466–68; phobic and anxiety, 463–65
Neurotic anxiety, 438
Neurotransmitters, 34–36; schizophrenia and, 478–79
Nodes, 34
Norepinephrine, 34, 35, 55, 327, 440; stimulants and, 135
Normal distribution, 589–91
Normative social influence, 554–56
NREM sleep, 121–23

Obedience, 556–57
Obedient aggression, 302
Obesity, 284–87
Objective self-awareness, theory of, 544
Object permanence, concept of, 354
Observation, 20; naturalistic, 598
Observational techniques for personality assessment, 422–24
Obsessive-compulsive neurosis, 466–68
Oedipus complex, 405
Old age, 384–90; cognitive changes in, 386–87; ego integrity in, 389–90; marriage and widowhood in, 388–89; retirement in, 387–88; stress and loss of control in, 454–55
Olfaction, 85–86
Olfactory epithelium, 86
Operant aggression, 302, 304
Operant conditioning, 154–70; applications of, 166–69; avoidance learning, 165–67; behavioral medicine and, 168–69; blocking phenomenon and, 171; delay of reinforcement in, 163; language acquisition and, 218; partial reinforcement in, 158–59; Pavlovian conditioning compared to, 167–70; personality theory and, 408; punishment in, 163–64; reinforcement schedules in, 160–62; secondary reinforcement in, 164–65; shaping procedures in, 157,